'If Howard Marks was the king of the cannabis smuggle, Luis Navia is the Howard Marks of the cocaine trade. Both men were well-educated individuals who found they had a forte for the organisation and shipment of drugs.

'I was on the other side of the fence in law enforcement, fighting the global fight against these smugglers, but *Pure Narco* demonstrates the "war on drugs" is not always black and white. Luis comes across as a guy you could have a beer with and actually like and respect. This is in no small part due to author Jesse Fink, who you can tell got totally along with his central character. Fink gives a balanced portrayal of his subject and allows you to see the warts.

'What *Pure Narco* brought back to me was the sheer violence of the era. I was based in Miami in the late 1980s/early '90s as a drugs liaison officer for the British Government and was working with cops who were veterans of the "Wild West" of South Florida. Pablo Escobar was on the rampage. After a bomb went off or there was a shooting in Colombia, our guys down in Bogotá would get calls from London to check they were alive. How Luis survived to tell this story is beyond belief.

'Operation Journey was my life for over two years and it was a truly world-class international case. So I was glad to be part of Luis's downfall and give him his personal road to Damascus. But until this book I really never fully realised how much our lives were intertwined. Luis's story proves fact is stranger than fiction. *Pure Narco* is a great read.'
Graham Honey, HMCE Senior Investigation Officer (Retired)

'USCS Commissioner Raymond Kelly described Operation Journey, the global law-enforcement action taken against Luis Navia and the Colombian cocaine organisation Los Mellizos, as a "powerful new blueprint for fighting the international drug trade".

'The cartel trafficked eye-watering quantities of cocaine and were well organised with a worldwide reach. Law enforcement had to be better (and luckier) than them to take them down.

'*Pure Narco* offers a rare insight into the drug traffickers' world and law enforcement's efforts to arrest them and seize the drugs.'
Graham Titmuss, HMCE Investigation Officer (Retired)

'I first met Luis Navia in Miami in 2002. He was cooperating with authorities and had some significant information to share with the United Kingdom. I remember leaving the prison after two days of visits and thinking what an amazing character he was. The discussions with

Luis changed my perspective on top-level drug trafficking and traffickers; it was a moment of enlightenment.

'Much is written and appears on screen about the drugs business but so often it misses the mark. That's not the case with this insightful book: *Pure Narco* hits the spot and tells it as it was. Law-enforcement officers have a saying that all top traffickers end up dead or in prison. Very few survive to tell the tale. Typical of the man, Luis is a survivor and tells his own tale in great depth and clarity. This is how it was. But Luis also needed a sympathetic ear to get the best out of his unique story and Jesse Fink has done that by writing the very best account of a remarkable life in cocaine trafficking.

'Contrary to what we read in news reports and see on TV, trafficking is a highly complex business. It's not just based on violence, corruption, greed and all the other stereotypes. Every big cocaine shipment happens because of the fixer, the broker, the emissary. Luis Navia was all of these. The reality is the biggest deals or shipments happen because of key individuals with the people and business skills to make things happen. Luis is one of those people. He brought people together, he solved problems, he found a way to get things done.

'What makes Luis's story so unique was his ability to transcend the politics between rival groups (cartels). His strength of personality, charm and business brain made him a valued business associate on so many major shipments. Typically, Luis made and lost a fortune: which is so often the case at the top level of international cocaine trafficking. *Pure Narco* explains how that's possible and why the business is both richly rewarding while being a precarious and perilous existence. It also explains how the big deals were conceived, planned and delivered. The mechanics of the deals are set out here, as Luis explains the key stages required for a successful shipment and deal. No other book on drug trafficking provides this level of detail.

'I knew back in the 1990s that the work we were doing was groundbreaking, and that it was an era that would be looked back upon by historians. *Pure Narco* is a great book and an important part of social history. I loved every page. Having this account from Luis Navia will be part of his legacy. If you have an interest in and want to understand how international drug trafficking really works, you must read *Pure Narco*.'
Barry Clarke, HMCE Investigation Officer (Retired)

'As a former police officer and homicide investigator in the Houston Police Department, I saw another side of drug trafficking, as I investigated murders that resulted from drug-trafficking deals gone bad to kidnappings for ransom on drug debts. I subsequently made the jump to federal law enforcement as a Special Agent with USCS, now United States Homeland Security Investigations (HSI).

'In Houston, as part of a large-scale drug smuggling investigation, I was assigned as the case agent for the prosecution of the captain and crew of the M/V *Cannes* and brought them to trial and sentencing for a shipment of cocaine that totalled four tons. We knew then that the criminal organisation behind it was large in terms of the amount of cocaine shipped worldwide – we just didn't know how large. The *Cannes* would in turn lead us to Luis Navia, one of the biggest drug traffickers ever known – but never heard of.

'Jesse Fink's in-depth, entertaining and informative account of Luis's life during the height of the cocaine trade in the United States in the 1980s and '90s is like a speck in the eyes of a race-car driver moving at 200 miles an hour, albeit a large speck. *Pure Narco* reveals how a seemingly regular "businessman" can in reality be a successful drug trafficker.'

Vicente Garcia, HSI Assistant Special Agent in Charge (Retired)

'As a former detective who investigated a number of Colombian *narcos*, I can say that Jesse Fink has done a fantastic job of bringing the violent world of the drug cartels to light through Luis Navia. Luis is one hell of a character. For all the stuff he has lived through, he should be at least 200 years old. Luis is like the proverbial cat who has nine lives. What a life!'

Roberto Diaz (pseudonym), Metro-Dade Police Department Detective (Retired)

BOOKS BY JESSE FINK

15 Days in June (2007)
Laid Bare (2012)
The Youngs (2013)
Bon (2017)
Pure Narco (2020)

PURE NARCO

ONE MAN'S TRUE STORY OF 25 YEARS INSIDE THE COLOMBIAN AND MEXICAN CARTELS

JESSE FINK AND LUIS NAVIA

JOHN BLAKE

First published in the UK by Blink Publishing
An imprint of Bonnier Books UK
80-81 Wimpole Street, London, W1G 9RE
Owned by Bonnier Books
Sveavägen 56, Stockholm, Sweden

www.facebook.com/johnblakebooks
twitter.com/jblakebooks

First published in paperback in 2020

Paperback ISBN: 978 1 78946 336 1
eBook ISBN: 978 1 78946 351 4
Audio Digital Download ISBN: 978 1 78946 322 4

British Library Cataloguing-in-Publication Data:

A catalogue record for this book is available from the British Library.

Design by www.envydesign.co.uk

Printed and bound in Great Britain by Clays Ltd, Elcograf S.p.A

1 3 5 7 9 10 8 6 4 2

John Blake Publishing is an imprint of Bonnier Books UK
www.bonnierbooks.co.uk

narco

(nɑːkəʊ)

noun

Word forms: plural -cos

informal

a drug smuggler

Collins English Dictionary

'You North Americans are very lucky. You are fighting the most important fight of all – you live in the belly of the beast'

Ernesto 'Che' Guevara

Luis Navia

To my family, for their unconditional love and support; to all those people who didn't shoot me; and to Bob and Eric: I was fortunate enough to fall into their hands

Jesse Fink

To all the victims of cocaine, the cartels and the 'war on drugs'; to my family, for tolerating my book-writing adventures; and to Greg Stock: I'll get you the $500 I owe you ASAP

For security, privacy and legal reasons, the names, nicknames and identifying characteristics of certain individuals, places and businesses in this book have been changed. Everything else remains factually true to the best of the authors' knowledge and has been independently verified wherever possible. As international drug traffickers generally don't make a habit of keeping diaries and photo albums, this book is largely based on Luis Navia's personal recollections and is an account of his life, criminal career and capture as related by him.

Mr Navia maintains what follows is true but it is not to be taken as definitive. Scenes depicted herein, including dialogue, have been rendered to the best of his memory and from other available resources. Every effort has been made to verify the accuracy of these accounts, including correct spellings of names and other details. Any errors will be corrected in future editions.

Any individual or organisation that has not been prosecuted for alleged crimes is presumed innocent until found guilty.

SATURDAY, AUGUST 26, 2000

'OPERATION JOURNEY' DISMANTLES COLOMBIAN ORGANIZATION THAT SHIPPED COCAINE TO 12 NATIONS NEARLY 25 TONS OF COCAINE SEIZED

WASHINGTON, D.C. -- The Drug Enforcement Administration, the U.S. Customs Service, and the Joint Interagency Task Force-East (JIATF-East) today announced the conclusion of 'Operation Journey', a two-year, multi-national initiative against a Colombian drug transportation organization that used commercial vessels to haul multi-ton loads of cocaine to 12 countries, most of them in Europe and North America.

The investigation, which involved authorities from 12 nations and three continents, has resulted in the arrest of 43 individuals, including the alleged leader of the maritime drug transportation organization, Ivan De La Vega, and several of his subordinates. A Colombian citizen, De La Vega was arrested in Maracaibo, Venezuela, on Aug. 16, and turned over to U.S. custody. He faces federal drug charges in Ft. Lauderdale, Fla.

Since its inception, Operation Journey has resulted in the seizure of 22,489 kilograms of cocaine or nearly 25 tons of cocaine. On the streets of Europe, this cocaine could generate roughly $1 billion at the retail level. The location of these seizures ranged from the Netherlands to Venezuela. The operation has also resulted in the seizure of commercial shipping vessels, go-fast boats, and communications equipment.

The operation began as separate investigations by the DEA Country Office in Athens, Greece, the Customs Special Agent-in-Charge office in Houston, together with major input from European law enforcement agencies and JIATF-East. Over time, numerous domestic and international agencies joined the operation. Eventually, all merged their cases into a single probe. Prosecutors from the Narcotic and Dangerous Drug Section of the U.S. Justice Department's Criminal Division were brought in to provide key legal guidance. The Justice Department coordinated with Customs, the DEA, and officials from other nations to develop the prosecution strategy to dismantle this organization.

Foreign authorities played critical roles in Operation Journey, making numerous arrests and several large seizures. The operation would not have been possible without the efforts of law enforcement agencies from Albania, Belgium, Colombia, France, Greece, Italy, the Netherlands, Panama, Spain, Great Britain, and Venezuela.

The organization targeted by Operation Journey served as a one-stop shipping service for Colombian cartels interested in moving cocaine via maritime vessels to U.S. and European markets. Based in Colombia and Venezuela, the organization used a fleet of 8-to-10 commercial freighters capable of hauling huge loads of cocaine anywhere in the world. Some of these ships were owned by shipping firms in Greece and other nations, while others were owned by this Colombian organization.

U.S. agents were able to document the movement of at least 68 tons of cocaine by this organization over a three-year period. At the retail level, this amount of cocaine could generate roughly $3 billion in Europe. Several of these cocaine shipments were intercepted. Most had occurred before agents learned about them. Operation Journey culminated during the past two weeks with enforcement actions in Venezuela and Europe. As a result of a collaborative international effort, Venezuelan authorities raided the command-and-control structure of the organization, using roughly 200 anti-drug officers, as well as an array of helicopters, airplanes, and boats.

During the initial raid, Venezuelan authorities arrested Ivan De La Vega and Luis Antonio Navia. De La Vega was arrested pursuant to a provisional arrest warrant prepared by U.S. federal agents in Houston. Navia is a Cuban national with U.S. residence status. He is a U.S. Customs fugitive wanted on prior federal drug charges. Both were turned over to U.S. authorities. On August 19, U.S. agents flew the pair to the Southern District of Florida, where they face federal drug charges.

Source (abridged from the original): DEA

Contents

PART 5

WILD WEST

PART 6

WAR ZONE

PART 7

SCARFACE

PART 8

BLAME IT ON CANCÚN

PART 9

MAGOO IN MEXICO

PART 10

CATCH ME IF YOU CAN

Northern South America and the Caribbean Sea

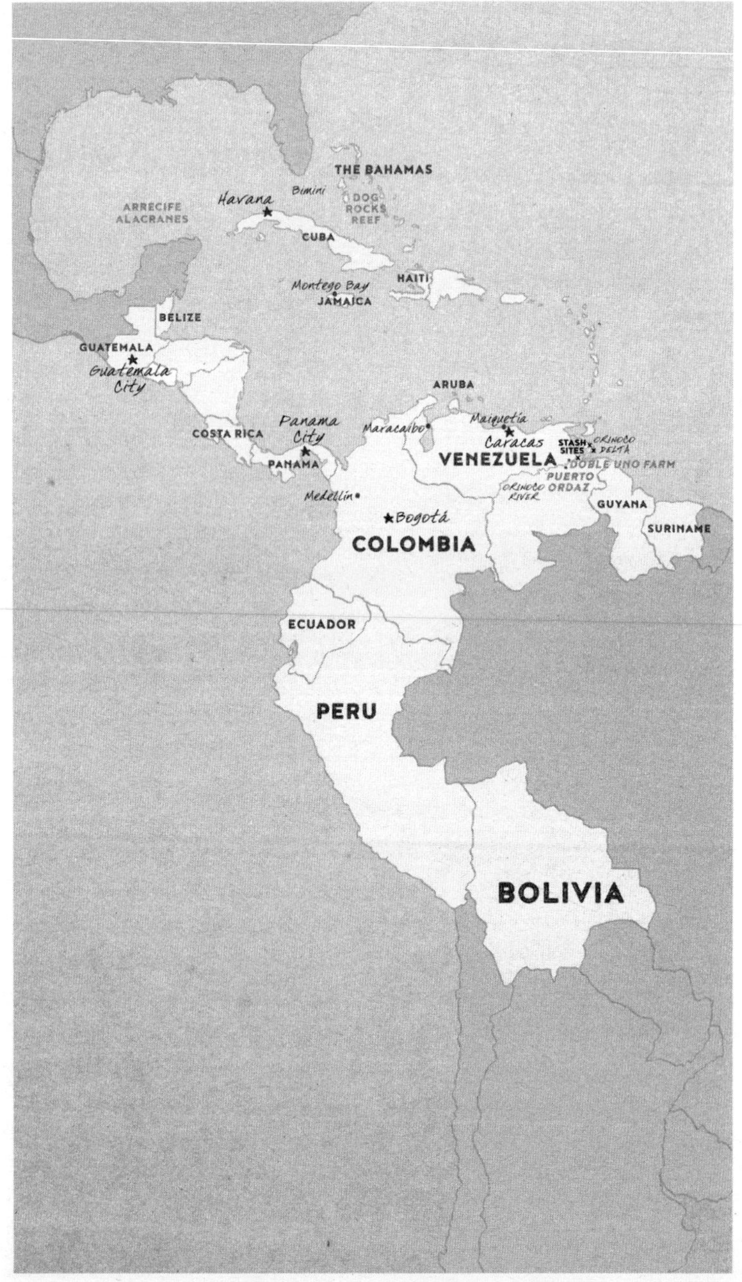

Colombia

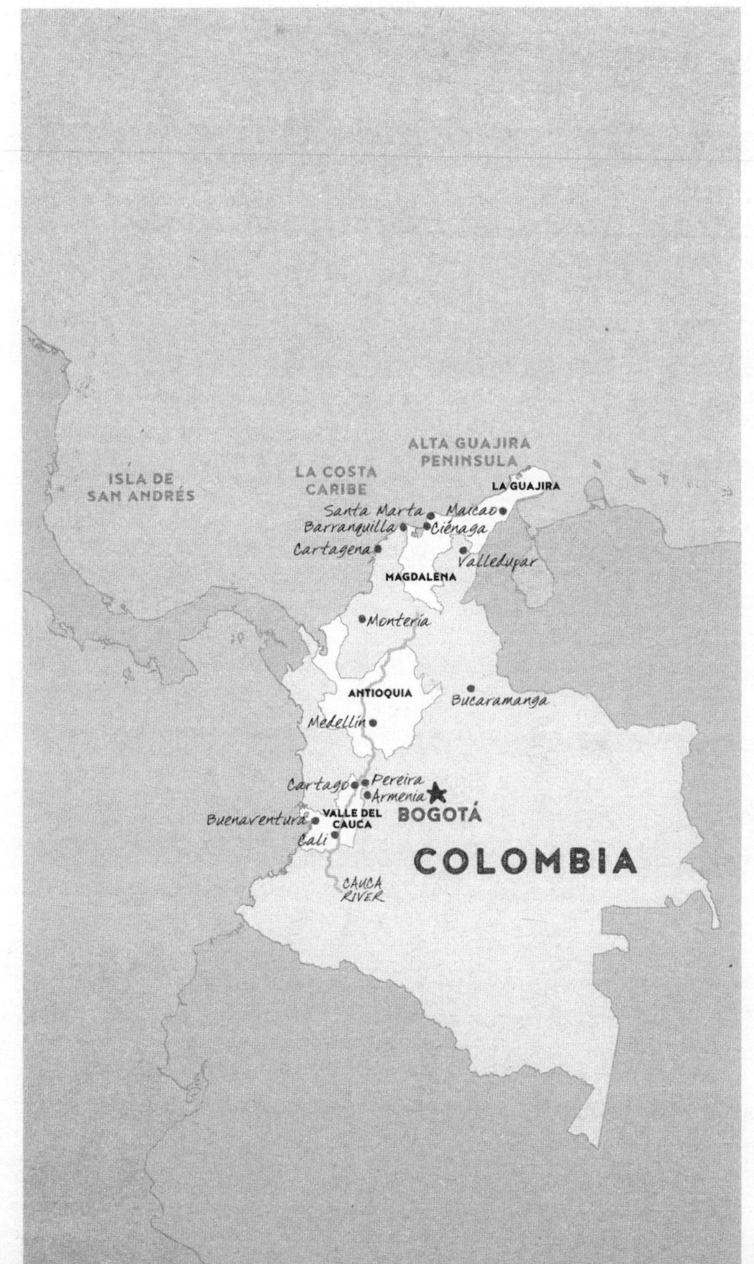

ALTA GUAJIRA PENINSULA
LA COSTA CARIBE
ISLA DE SAN ANDRÉS
LA GUAJIRA
Santa Marta
Maicao
Barranquilla
Ciénaga
Cartagena
Valledupar
MAGDALENA
Montería
ANTIOQUIA
Bucaramanga
Medellín
Cartago
Pereira
Armenia
BOGOTÁ
VALLE DEL CAUCA
Buenaventura
Cali
COLOMBIA
CAUCA RIVER

Mexico

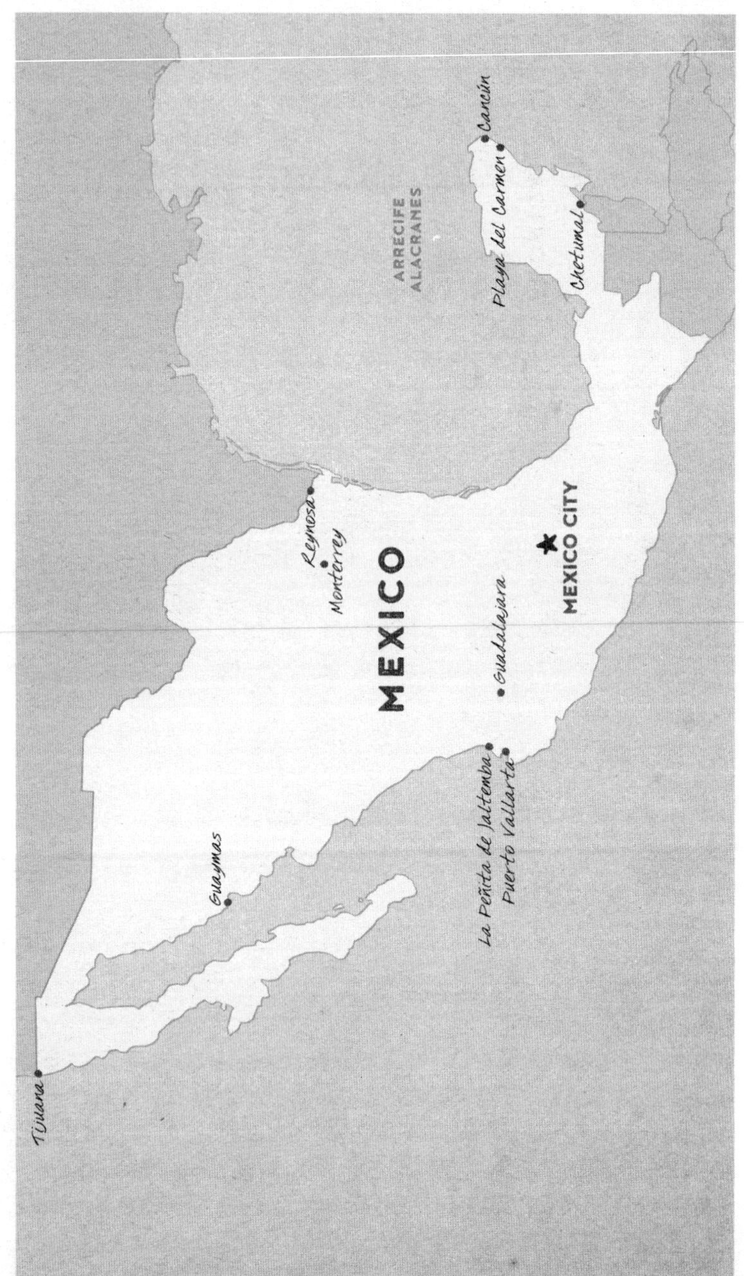
MEXICO
MEXICO CITY
Tijuana
Guaymas
La Peñita de Jaltemba
Puerto Vallarta
Guadalajara
Monterrey
Reynosa
ARRECIFE ALACRANES
Playa del Carmen
Cancún
Chetumal

Florida (with Miami inset)

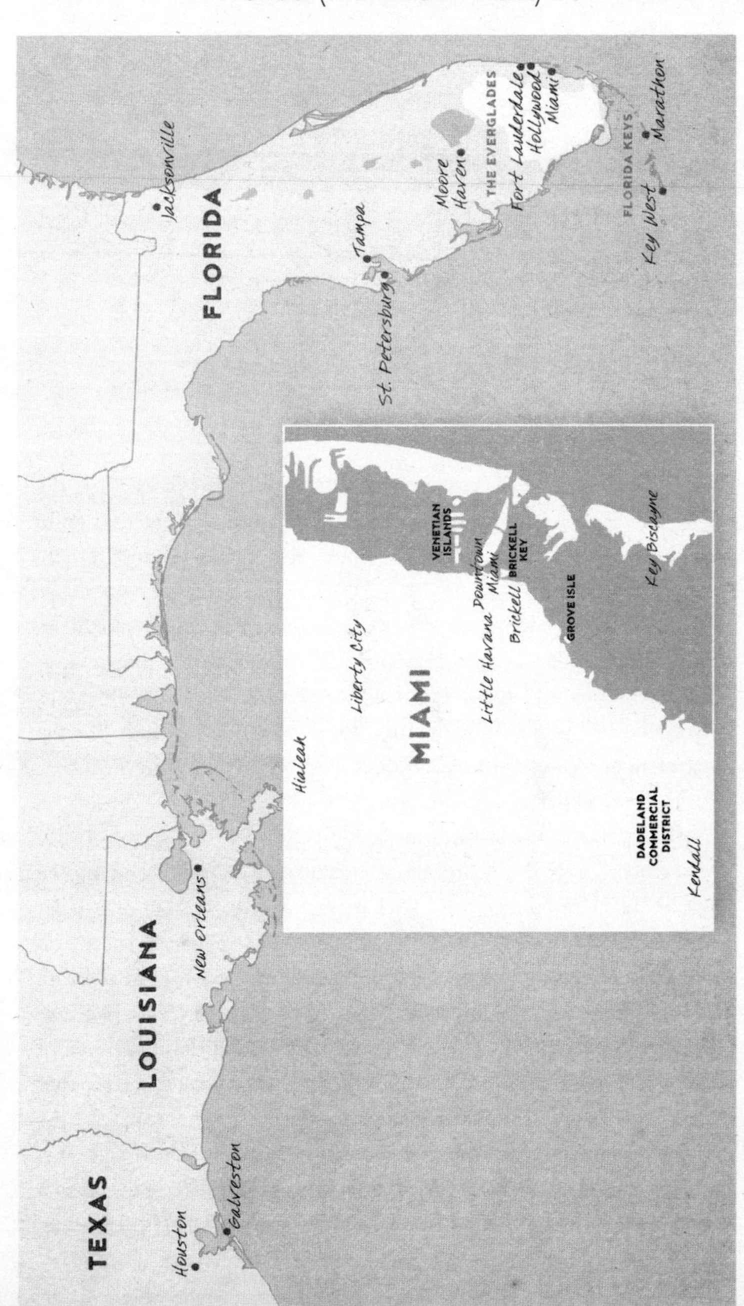

FOREWORD
The Trip

WHAT A *LONG STRANGE TRIP IT'S BEEN*, released in 1977, is the title of Grateful Dead's second compilation album. It's a good description of Luis Navia's life and could also have been an alternate title to this book.

Jesse Fink's account of Luis's life – his trip – as a major drug trafficker provides an entertaining and informative glimpse into the treacherous and too-often deadly realm of a cocaine smuggler during the 1980s and '90s. In parts, for good reason, it reads like the debriefing of a cooperating defendant, backed up with references that reflect Jesse's skills as a researcher.[1]

As a narcotics investigator in the early '80s for the Durham Police Department in North Carolina, I was at the opposite end of the distribution chain: undercover, buying grams and eight balls of powder cocaine. Towards the end of the '80s, Luis's and others' successful smuggling efforts were evidenced on the streets of America with an increase in the quantity and quality of cocaine, along with a decrease in its price. Near the end of my tenure with the Durham PD, one of our investigations resulted in the seizure of three kilos of cocaine that entered the United States through the Florida Keys. I now wonder if the unidentified fingerprints found on the wrappers might have been Luis's.

Anyway, my personal 'trip' continued with a four-year tour as a special agent with the United States Customs Service (USCS), beginning in 1987 on the Texas–Mexico border. At that time marijuana and small quantities of black tar heroin were the primary drugs seized at the border. Having perfected the art of smuggling, it came to no one's surprise that the Colombians utilised the Mexicans to introduce their contraband into the US. It all started with a few kilos added to loads of marijuana. After reading *Pure Narco*, I now wonder if some of the cocaine we seized in Laredo also had Luis's fingerprints on it.

Like a motivated drug trafficker, a good narcotics agent is always looking to get closer to the source. So I jumped over to the Drug Enforcement Administration (DEA) in 1991 and subsequently transferred down to Colombia. Stationed on the coast in Barranquilla, the majority of the office's investigations involved maritime smuggling. The names of the Colombians Luis worked with were part of our daily vocabulary. They were our targets.

In August 2000, I was asked to go to Venezuela and assist with an investigation run by one of the other agents in the office. Heading to Caracas from Colombia, I had limited knowledge of the case and when I arrived felt I was placed on a 'need to know' status. Again, after reading this book I have a better understanding as to why: only the traffickers benefit from interagency squabbles and infighting.

This time, however, we were able to identify the fingerprint. In doing so, it led to the arrest of USCS Special Agent Robert Harley's fugitive, Luis Antonio Navia, and the intersection of my life with Luis's own. There is no need for me to comment on my initial meeting in Maracaibo with Luis; Jesse illustrates it quite well with Luis's own words. But, as Jesse points out, Luis's story is not over.

A contemporary of Luis's, who came over to 'Team America' – what we call it when a drug trafficker turns government informant – once told me no one retires from this business. They either end up in federal prison for the rest of their life or dead.

Luis is one of the lucky ones. My wish for him is that he finishes his trip well and finds true redemption.

DEA Special Agent (Retired) Eric Kolbinsky, St. Petersburg (FL)

INTRODUCTION
Life on a Coin Toss

ADJECTIVES SUCH AS 'SINGULAR' and 'extraordinary' tend to be overused by biographers to describe the lives of the people they're writing about, not to mention the publicists who are paid to promote their books. Actors, musicians, politicians, sportspeople, reality-TV stars: so many public figures are relentlessly hyped in the press or on social media when beyond their fleeting celebrity there's nothing really singular or extraordinary about these people's lives at all.

This, however, cannot be said for Luis Antonio Navia. For a man who is neither a public figure, nor a celebrity, nor an influencer, indeed someone you've never heard of (and I had never heard of him until I started writing what would become *Pure Narco*), he truly has led a singular and extraordinary life. If the old truism holds that everyone has a book in them, Luis has at least two or three, if not more.

Not only was this privileged son of Cuban high society one of America's most successful cocaine traffickers for nearly 25 years, but he was also a hunted international fugitive before his 16 August 2000 arrest in Maracaibo, Venezuela, in one of the biggest multinational law-enforcement takedowns of all time, Operation Journey. At its conclusion it was hailed as the biggest-ever coke bust in Venezuelan history.

Luis was convicted of serious narcotics offences, went to federal prison, got out early after cooperating with authorities, loaned his knowledge and the insights he gained from a quarter century of smuggling for the world's deadliest cartels to help the United States Government fight the so-called 'war on drugs', and today, as a reformed civilian, runs a construction business in Miami, Florida.

This is a man who knows just about everything there is to know about cocaine and just about everyone who has ever worked making it, transporting it and selling it. It's why to this day American feds and law-enforcement agencies from Great Britain and mainland Europe still come to Luis for leads or background when working important cases. It's also why Colombian cartel figures currently in jail come to him for help: as a paid private consultant, he can help build the weight of their testimonies when they cooperate in return for reduced sentences.

When a man survives so long at the top in such a bloody but lucrative business without resorting to violence or intimidation yet can still find the time to pack school lunches for his kids, a degree of *braggadocio* or egotism is perhaps to be expected. Especially when murderous drug lords such as the late Pablo Escobar and the incarcerated Joaquín Guzmán aka 'El Chapo' have become wildly popular anti-heroes to millions of people around the world. (We truly live in strange times when such amoral killers become idols. Tom Wainwright, author of the book *Narconomics*, coined a term for this phenomenon: 'reputational laundering'. It's true and damning.)

This, however, was not my experience of Luis in the two-and-a-half years I spent working on this book. I got to know him very well and cannot recall a moment when he was anything other than modest about his exploits and self-effacing. He never attempted to talk up his past when he so easily could have. Nor did he try to convince me he was anything other than a former criminal with an abiding love for making money who got busted in just about the most spectacular way possible. For those two reasons alone he is commendable.

Most remarkably, though, few *narcotraficantes* (*narcos* for short) can say they've managed to successfully juggle a normal family life while transporting billions of dollars of blow and are not only alive but walking the streets today to tell their story.[2] Even fewer go from selling grams to college students at Georgetown University in Washington, DC to operating a fleet of container ships to deliver tons to the mafia in Europe. It's the stuff of criminal fantasy but for Luis every bit of it was true.

In 2020, Luis turned 65. He referred to himself many times as 'Mr Magoo' or 'Inspector Clouseau', a comic innocent in a world of true bad guys and the polar opposite to Jon Roberts, the alleged 'cocaine cowboy' who made out in the Evan Wright book *American Desperado* and the Billy Corben documentary *Cocaine Cowboys* that he was so evil, so violent, he was two steps removed from Genghis Khan.

While preparing to write this book I began reading *American Desperado* but gave up on it a third of the way through; after the part about skinning the Việt Cộng soldier alive, it just didn't strike me as truthful.[3] The late Roberts, who died in 2011, came across as a sociopath, highly unlikeable, lacking insight and, worst of all, a shameless liar. It didn't ring true to Luis, either, who knew and worked with many of the same people Roberts did.

'Jon Roberts was a fucking psycho. He was just an asshole with a gun. I've been around a lot of killers, people who were real killers, *assassins.* If you owed them money, they assassinated you. No torturing, no bullshit, they assassinated you. Don't think what they do is the act of a coward. It's the act of a person that's determined and will carry out his determination. Nobody enjoyed skinning nobody alive. Believe me, it's a bunch of bullshit.'

At least as I saw it, Luis came across as neither criminal nor violent – rather, confoundingly normal and, for the majority of the time, even-tempered. He wasn't what I had expected for a man who had been a big-time narco. But I wasn't totally naïve: he was flawed too. There was more to his story than he let on. There was darkness behind the comedy. His affability and charm, however, made it very easy to miss.

*

In late 2017 we met through a mutual friend in Miami who doesn't want to be identified for fear of harm coming to her or her family. For months this woman urged the two of us to connect. She told me Luis had been approached by a writer for *Harper's Magazine* in the US for a profile piece but, rather than agree to tell his whole story to the press, he preferred doing his own book. He needed someone to write it. So we began emailing each other, with our anonymous female friend CCed in each conversation.

In those first few emails, Luis was cagey and seemed reluctant to share anything useful, which was perhaps understandable given that we came from different backgrounds, had opposing ideas about the importance of money, didn't know each other and were living on opposite sides of the world. I'd just spent four years writing a biography of AC/DC singer Bon Scott. Cocaine trafficking really was not in my wheelhouse, as an American might say, though I'd spent a lot of time talking to recovered drug addicts for my book on Bon. I was ready to walk away and turn my attention to something else. But soon Luis and I were speaking on the phone almost every day. Our conversations would go for hours. After that, our anonymous female friend left us to our own devices.

It's worth pointing this out right from the start: Luis is a funny man. I immediately felt engaged by his sense of humour, street lingo and crazy stories that were worthy of a Quentin Tarantino film. Had he not been a narco he would have been a great stand-up comedian and probably died of a cocaine overdose a long time ago, such is the intensity with which he has led his life. How much he padded out his stories only he can really know, though he assured me everything happened the way he told it.

For such a larger-than-life personality, though, he maintains a very private existence. He doesn't have a landline where he lives, doesn't get mail at home and doesn't have his real address on any form of official identification. His driver's licence has an address for a massage parlour in Miami.

'I cannot put my head on a pillow at night and know that my address is on a driver's licence or I get mail; I *can't*. That will never leave my body or my spirit, that lifestyle of incognito. I still keep to my old ways. I don't bring anybody home. *Nobody*.'

When one time he got an AT&T bill with his real name on it, he 'fucking freaked out' and phoned the telecommunications company to tell them, 'I've just been kidnapped in Colombia!' He requested they change it to a 'nice Jewish name' as he was still getting kidnapping threats and wanted to keep as low a profile as possible. AT&T complied 'right away'.[4]

Luis was also a complex character because while he could be genuinely endearing and lovable, a sort of diminutive, cuddly Cuban-American version of John Travolta's Chili Palmer from *Get Shorty*, some of his behaviour was not always so heartwarming, which he would justify through a well-practised line in moral relativism or equivalence. Whatever the cartels did was no worse than the US Government. Alcohol is a greater killer than cocaine but you never hear about that. And so on. Sometimes I readily bought his excuses and could see the logic of his thinking; but many more times I did not.

I never forgot he was someone who willingly consorted with (and by extension arguably abetted) some of the most violent criminals, some effectively serial killers, ever to walk the face of the earth. He liked to joke that being shot or decapitated were natural deaths 'because it's natural to the business you're in'. He's also the only person I know who can count as close personal friends half a dozen people who have appeared on the Specially Designated Nationals and Blocked Persons List, the register of terrorists and drug traffickers whose assets are frozen, among other punitive measures, by the Office of Foreign Assets Control of the United States Department of the Treasury (USDT). He even gets a mention in the Paradise Papers, second only to the Panama Papers as the biggest leak of offshore investment documents in history.[5]

So he was no angel. He'd run with some bad people. His cognitive dissonance was strong. Our anonymous female friend joked, 'Luis is like Tony Montana if he hadn't died and got caught and had started a construction business in Miami. *Scarface* as senior citizen.'

The comparison was funny but not entirely accurate: Luis was educated and had never so much as purchased a gun let alone massacred a group of Colombian assassins with Montana's 'little friend': a Colt AR-15 machine gun with attached M203 grenade launcher. But I saw her point. Any man who's spent most of his adult life in and around the cartels and its 24/7 adrenalin rush is going to have a tough time readapting to the torpor of normal society.

I hate to admit it, perhaps it was a reflection on my comparatively uneventful life, but this mix of good and evil, lightness and depravity is the very thing that made Luis an inordinately charismatic interviewee. He could be wholly unsympathetic at times because he remained so steadfastly unapologetic about his 25 years of crime, but he was the coolest person I'd ever met. He'd *lived*.

As he memorably described it, 'Gangsters want to live a great three years than just a mediocre 30. If I die, I *die*. Go out with a bang. What's life? We go on to the next one.'

Luis's life was like the adventure I'd never had: a tale of pure escapism that could sit comfortably alongside an old shopworn VHS cassette of *Romancing the Stone*. The fact of the matter is I got completely sucked in.

*

So, you might be thinking, who the hell is this guy, why is he of any consequence and why should you care about him enough to pick up this book? Like *The Wolf of Wall Street* by Jordan Belfort, when you strip it down to its core, *Pure Narco* is a story of one man's unrepentant, unapologetic greed.

Money was a driving obsession for Luis in an industry – cocaine – where it was so easy to come by that the value of it almost became meaningless. This is perhaps the reason why when he had money he dealt with it so wastefully. As long as there was another load of coke to transport, he could always make more money in 24 hours than most people would make in ten years.

Yet I believe Luis for all his ex-gangster bluster does wrestle with genuine regret and remorse for his criminal past, even if he might pretend otherwise behind the almost impenetrable shield of what I see as innate Miami *cubano* machismo, but what he regards as street-learned Colombian toughness. He is not one to make such personal admissions. Belfort, on the other hand, who ripped off so many innocent people, has never struck me as particularly guilt ridden – just an opportunistic narcissist who got lucky when Leonardo DiCaprio and Martin Scorsese decided to make a movie of his book.

As a drug-trafficking story Luis's is certainly unique: his is a tale so wild you simply couldn't make it up. As he puts it poetically in his distinctive wiseguy patois, it was like 'a fucking tornado around a fucking drain'. But it's more than that. Luis's life was also one of wasted opportunities, and there's a human message running through all of the pages that follow: appreciate what you have, right now, take advantage of the opportunities you are given and don't fuck it up.

Pure Narco is not your typical true-crime story.

*

With his receding silver hair, ample middle-aged girth, button-down shirts, neat chinos and clean sneakers, Luis looks just like any unremarkable, inoffensive Latino middle manager you might see in a South Korean SUV on an American highway going about his daily commute to his boring office job in a technology park or industrial estate. He is not the machine gun–wielding narco cliché as depicted in films or television. The only thing that gives away his freewheeling past is a penchant for elegant eyewear (a beautiful pair of clear-framed Oliver Peoples sunglasses with neck strap rarely leaves his face; he won't pose for photos without them) and an abiding love of 1970s rock.

He did have an opportunity to go straight in the early 1980s when he briefly owned/leased 22,000 acres of sugarcane and a rice mill in Florida, later a macadamia farm in Costa Rica, and again in the late 1990s when he dreamed of 'cornering the market' in Central American and Mexican coffee, but he left cash crops and all vestiges of respectability behind. Instead he fell under the spell of cocaine and became the unlikeliest of drug traffickers.

Luis was born into considerable wealth and privilege in 1950s Cuba, not the other way around like most narcos who are born into a hardscrabble life of crushing poverty in Colombia or Mexico. He arrived in 1960s Miami as a pampered kid and went to the best schools and universities in Florida and Washington, DC, where he began his drug career selling grams to fellow students. He never *had* to become a criminal; he chose his path. His introduction to the cartels in the late 1970s came not through family ties or ethnic background but by not-so-innocently meeting Bia Gálvez, a beautiful but mysterious red-haired Aruban woman at his 23rd birthday party. Then, like something out of *Body Heat*, he ran off with Bia into the hot Florida night.

The next 22 years contained enough adventures for 22 lifetimes and he got through most of it with almost complete anonymity.

Luis could have got out early, gone straight and stayed that way, but the cartels came to like him and he came to like them – and when you do a job so well, the mob eventually wants a piece of the action too.

'I always worked for the Colombian and Mexican cartels doing transport; but the Lucchese group [the mafia] in Florida was one of my clients. I worked with so many groups and nobody else did that. When I look back on how many groups I worked with, it's incredible.'

He also claims to have worked with, known intimately or had memorable encounters with some of the heavyweight players in the cocaine business of the 1970s, '80s and '90s: the aforementioned Pablo 'El Patrón' Escobar, Luis 'Miki' Ramírez, Fernando 'El Negro' Galeano, Iván 'El Enano' Urdinola, Luis Hernando 'Rasguño' Gómez, Fernando 'Marulo' Marulanda, Hernán 'Papito' Prada Cortés, the Mejía Múnera brothers, Alcides 'El Metro' Ramón Magaña of the Juárez Cartel, Cuban crime overlord Alberto Sicilia Falcón, Jamaican kingpin Leebert 'The Indian' Ramcharan, and many more.

Outside of Escobar, Galeano and Sicilia Falcón, names straight out of the Netflix series *Narcos* and *Narcos: Mexico*, most of these people and other narcos mentioned in this book are probably unfamiliar to readers. But to law-enforcement agents working in the frontline of the war on drugs and those brave journalists in Colombia and Mexico reporting on that never-ending war, they represent the crème de la crème of international drug-trafficking royalty. Luis was the Zelig of cocaine. He was independent, adaptable and non-violent. Simply put, some of the world's baddest people felt *safe* working with him.

'I didn't pose a threat to anybody and I never, *ever* failed them on a trip. I also had the common intelligence not to steal, be faithful, say the truth and do my best. Saying that, the truth and doing your best isn't going to cut it, either. "Hey, I did my best but we didn't make it" possibly goes by once, and it depends who you're working for.

'Definitely I survived because I was non-violent. Non-violence is a very powerful weapon. It's like that Gandhi shit. Non-violence can beat violence. It just takes a long time. But the main thing is good business. The people I worked with were all great personalities: rare, powerful people with fascinating trajectories. They didn't get to where they got to by being dumb. They were very smart and very different to me yet they found me interesting and they all told me I was crazier than they were.

'When I look back, I cannot classify myself as normal. The morality part and all the touching moments, I don't know. I'm not too much of a moral . . . you know, *spiritual* kind of guy. People get so carried away with "good" and "bad". Some people are just wired differently. People will do anything for money and they'll do more to make more, and they'll do whatever they need to do to protect their money. It's that easy. It doesn't take a genius to figure that one out.'

If I have any personal criticism of Luis maybe it's that he's just not remorseful enough, having done what he did and having seen what he saw. As a high-level transporter for the Colombian and Mexican cartels, he cannot completely divorce himself morally from the crimes those groups were involved in, both direct through selling a product that has addicted millions and indirect through their violence. Any which way he cuts it (and he does try and likely forever will), his time as a drug trafficker wasn't victimless; he was still complicit in the drug industry's heavy toll. For him to pretend otherwise would be utterly tone deaf to its casualties and victims. This book is not an endorsement of drug trafficking or the narco lifestyle.

But this is a point that needs to be rammed home: none of us had Luis's life. His values were shaped by his own experiences and he is a product of his family upbringing, personal circumstances and the times. He wasn't born *into* crime, though a life in it spent much of the time on the run has irrevocably altered the way he sees the world and directed his passage through it as an adult male.

Having spent the better part of three years talking to him daily, I also believe that for a former criminal he has a surprising degree of insight to recognise his character shortcomings. (I certainly witnessed him develop a deeper self-awareness as we worked on the book.) He makes up for these shortcomings with a winning personality and his strong loyalty to old friends who are incarcerated or have fallen on hard times. This same personality – humorous, reckless, impulsive and completely unconventional – is what helped him survive in such a volatile and dangerous profession for so long, allowed him to work with so many different cartels, and is ultimately what makes his story redemptive.

*

During his 25 years as a narco, Luis Antonio Navia was never a 'Colombian shipping magnate', a 'major investor', or a 'member' of Pablo Escobar's notorious Medellín Cartel, among other things that have been printed in newspaper stories or broadcast on television about his life in the drug trade. But he was responsible for the trafficking of '200 tons, easy' of cocaine,[6] worth about $10 billion on today's market prices in Europe. Some inside American law enforcement have put the number much higher – 300 tons – and that doesn't include the 25 tons in the Venezuelan jungle he was planning to shift to Europe when he got busted by the authorities for the first and last time.

Incredibly and perhaps unjustly for a crime that carried the maximum penalty of life imprisonment, he only served five years in jail of a 108-month or nine-year sentence (already reduced from an original 11 years) and was not named as an 'organiser, manager or leader in the offence', in the words of his sentencing documents, which would have got him a stiffer sentence; only for 'management responsibility over the ship which represented the property belonging to the organisation'. He was held accountable in a court of law for 9375.5 kilos, just over ten tons.

Luis never went into the United States Federal Witness Protection Program (Witness Security Program or WITSEC) and wasn't offered it. He claims anything he did say to the US Government was done with the knowledge, if not the blessing, of his criminal associates in Colombia. He accepted responsibility for his errant ways, avoided trial by pleading guilty, and did his time.[7]

He did not reoffend when he left jail, apart from a minor traffic violation in 2013. He was ordered to pay a monetary penalty of $100 for crimes that would have normally required him to pay anywhere from $17,500 to $8 million in restitution.

'One of the figures they came back with figured that I owed

$56 million in taxes, undeclared income, restitution and all that shit. It was ridiculous. My attorney, Ruben Oliva, did a great job. You don't want to do restitution. Even if you get $500,000, *man*, that's a pain in the ass to deal with. That's a big weight on you going forward. Every pay cheque they take something. So Ruben got me no restitution, a $100 fine and that was it.'

No longer a drug trafficker, fugitive or prisoner, he's free to tell his story.

*

Typically during those early months of 2018 in Sydney, Australia, I'd wake up to birdsong, a cup of coffee and a WhatsApp call from Luis, who had a habit of changing his profile photo regularly – usually a gleaming white Miami high-rise building, but other times Kim Jong-un (during the first USA–North Korea summit in Singapore) or John Belushi's character Jake Blues from *The Blues Brothers* (somewhat macabre, given Belushi was killed by a 'speedball', a mixture of cocaine and heroin).

On occasion, though, we'd get to speak on the phone only when he had a few spare minutes at his construction job. He'd been doing it full-time ever since he got out of jail and in recent times had been combining it with consulting work for the US Government. His days were full, sometimes having to drive 160 kilometres a day. Frequently we'd text, Luis usually doing so from his car between schlepping on worksites around Miami.

'Fifty per cent of my text messages to you, Jesse, are made while I'm driving. Which is a lot more dangerous than the activity I was involved in for 25 years.' Wisely, he ended up recording messages instead: 'My risk of dying while dictating is less than texting.'

There were times when he was too tired to remember much at all. He was, by his own admission, not very good with recalling exact dates from the late 1970s and early '80s, when he was off his face so much of the time on cocaine. Because of this and his tangential, non-linear way of thinking – often he'd say whatever came into his head, go on an extended riff about something inconsequential then forget what he'd originally been talking about – I had some trouble constructing timelines for parts of the book.

He flirted with pulling out altogether when he got worried the content would adversely affect his construction business or he was getting grief from 'the love of my life', Isabelle Meneses, an Ecuadorian-born, naturalised American.[8] They'd been dating since his release from prison but she would not meet me or even speak to me, such was her unbending opposition to bringing up Luis's past for this book.

Luis and I would quite often get heated with each other and frequently disagreed on various matters, not least the title (he was worried that any association with the word narco in such a prominent way would forever stain his reputation; my view was he should have thought about that much earlier, like 1979), but in all the time we worked on the book we never had a blow-up that wasn't reconcilable. That, to his credit, was a mark of the man: even if he went too far and lost his cool he'd be quick to apologise.

At the time we started work on this project, *Narcos* and its follow-up, *Narcos: Mexico*, were flavour of the month and to me Luis's story seemed like another TV series waiting to happen. He loved to talk of his dealings in Hollywood. There were a couple of aborted scripts lying about, a 'treatment'. Some industry movers and shakers – agents, directors, studio heads, investors – were apparently interested in Luis, but we needed something substantial to tie all his anecdotes together. When I initially proposed meeting him in Colombia, he was reluctant. I could sense a line had been crossed for him because of his cooperation with the US Government. There was no going back.

'It's not too good as far as safety is concerned. I do go back to Colombia but I keep a certain low profile. I don't announce my arrivals [*laughs*].'

In the end, it took a year and a half to get contracts signed and to book my plane ticket to Miami via Dallas–Fort Worth to meet Luis in person. He greeted me at the airport luggage carousel, we hugged, and within minutes of getting in his car he told me he was resigned to the fact his life could be snuffed out at any minute from an assassin's bullet. He didn't fear death but accepted what was coming to him. As someone who'd never so much as copped a speeding ticket, it was an unsettling feeling being in the car with Luis, knowing I too could be collateral damage in any prospective freeway machine-gun ambush, *Scarface* style.

Before arriving in Miami I told Luis about my daily jogs in Sydney and he complained he never got to do anything for his body, because he was too busy dealing with city compliance inspectors and construction workers. (There maybe was some truth in that, but I'd often call Luis when he was out to dinner and having a royal time with friends, or opening a bottle of whisky or vodka at home in Miami. The tinkle of ice cubes has a very distinct sound down a phone line.) He expressed a desire to start yoga and said he was in great fettle but needed to lose a few pounds around the middle. The last time he had worked out was when he was in prison, where he did it 'every day, religiously. I did a lot of pull-ups, a lot of dips. I'm very wide-shouldered. I've got a lot of muscle up here. I gotta start at least walking.'[9]

For all its mafia entanglements, though, the construction business is still a walk in the park compared to the drug trade.

'I think I did it backwards. I retired at 25, now I started to work at 50. It's crazy, man. Back in the day if you would've told me that I would be spending most of my time in metal-fabrication shops or in Hialeah [a working-class city of Miami-Dade County with a high concentration of Hispanics], I would've told you you were nuts. I deal with people on a "Fuck you, you sonofabitch, you piece of shit, you motherfucker, you dumbass" basis every day. I do not go to an office and deal with nice professional people at all. You know, I'm happy I got out of the [cocaine] business, but if you're well hooked up, it's a *hell* of a business. The thing is to know when to get out. Get out in time. Deal with it with a level head and have an exit plan. Make $10 million, invest in real estate and get the fuck out.'

*

Luis was very proud of his daughter, Juliana, 26, who was in law school and working in a law firm, and his son, Santi, 23, a budding artist and architecture student who helped his father out on job sites. They'd grown up while he was on the run in Colombia, Mexico, Panama, Jamaica and Greece and didn't know of their father's double life until he was out of jail and they were in their teens. Both are completely removed from the narco world but fully support Luis in writing his life story.

'I was a normal father and a very loving dad. We had family dinners, went to restaurants, celebrated Thanksgiving and Christmas. We were a normal family. The only difference was that I was in the drug business. My daughter used to see me walk out of the house every day in a coat and tie. It wasn't that wild shit you see on TV when they rush the kids out of the apartment because people are coming to kill them. It's a very different reality than you see all the time on TV. I watch these TV shows and think, "What fucking *world* do they live in?" You can move thousands of kilos of cocaine for the major cartels and still be a normal human being.'

That said, the body count of friends and others he'd known while moving cocaine was very high and they died in horrible ways – beheadings, torture, clubbings, shootings, plane crashes. Luis's time as a drug trafficker was far from drama free. Yet through all of the chaos around him, amid all the dangers and threats to his life, just like Mr Magoo, he had managed to stay alive.[10] Somewhat surprisingly, he wasn't sentimental about his fallen comrades.

'They all did something to deserve that. They knew what they were doing; it was their destiny. For me to survive with all the different wild and crazy shit that happened, my planets were aligned 24/7 for 25 years.'

*

I grew to like Luis very much and now consider him less the subject of this book and more a close friend. We shared many private stories and came to confide in one another over simple life matters: relationships, money, families, our purpose being on this earth. What started out as a simple writing exercise ended up affecting the way I thought about my own life, as well as the choices I'd made. Was I right to have stuck to such a straight path when I had so little financially to show for it? Why hadn't I made $100 million by my mid-40s when Luis had? It elicited many moments of introspection and reflection.

Sometimes, for a laugh, Luis would send me unsolicited videos of twerking Brazilian women or, disturbingly, bloody aftermath scenes from narco shootouts in Colombia and Mexico: heads blown off, bodies torn apart by bullets. ('I get these random videos from people, even law enforcement, that are not too nice.') Other times he would send me hilarious, philosophical voice recordings in the middle of the night while he was drunk or stoned, covering topics from the Incas to Powerball to our shared love of early '70s Elton John to The Holy Bible to the Fifth Amendment.

'You don't come through with what you promise, then you *die*. It's like the mafia story; it's biblical! It *is* the Bible! Death's the first thing about the Bible: that people will kill people. The other thing about the Bible is betrayal. People will betray people. The Bible's kinda cruel. The Bible's pretty much what the real world is about. You read the Bible, you read about everything. *Goddamit*, Adam and Eve. There's Adam, there's Eve, the apple and the snake. Thank God fucking Adam and Eve weren't Chinese, 'cause if they had have been Chinese they would have eaten the fucking snake.'[11]

Often when on the phone with Luis I'd hear Bob Marley & the Wailers, Al Green or salsa music playing in the background. Other times he'd send me videos of him drumming (he'd played since his teens and got in a lot of practice in prison), the Australian band INXS or clips from Oliver Stone's *Natural Born Killers*. The Javier Bardem scenes in the Coen Brothers' *No Country for Old Men* elicited some lengthy commentary.

Scene #1: 'This is so much bullshit. This guy's an idiot. An assassin would never want to leave another body behind. It's just more evidence and more huntdown material.'

Scene #2: 'That's another bullshit scene that breaks every rule of Smuggling 101. You get to a place, you find some dope, if there's somebody alive, you gotta kill 'em. Either you don't kill 'em and you don't steal the dope. Or you steal the dope and you kill 'em. You *never* go back to a crime scene. This sonofabitch comes *back* to a crime scene!'

I was getting one-on-one lessons in narco life. After one depressing discussion about the violence of Colombian paramilitaries, Luis joked I should 'do some mushrooms, man, go out and smoke some weed, hug a tree and then think about what I told you. Australians come from the best blood there is: outlaw blood. Twenty-five years, brother. It's got to have some side effects. I don't have that many wrinkles, so the side effects are all inside; it's all mental [*laughs*].'

I opened up old atlases to find places Luis told me about that I'd never heard of. He'd lived a fast, glamorous life in some exotic locations: Miami, Bogotá, San Andrés, Cancún, Montego Bay, Panama City, Athens. I read all the books and articles there were to read and watched all the films and documentaries there were to watch: countless Spanish names, mind-numbing statistics, endless arguments for and against the war on drugs.

In many ways the interpersonal dynamic I enjoyed with Luis was like being a detective in an interview room grilling a criminal mastermind: clues and leads would keep coming the harder I pressed. Often it felt like I was getting a debriefing of a conspiracy; but at other times I was a priest hearing confession; or a shrink diagnosing a patient. Mostly, though, I was just Luis's confidant; albeit one part of a very odd couple. For that reason I feel qualified in the pages that follow to make occasional judgements of Luis's harebrained actions, selective evasiveness or self-suiting revisionism. He is not above reproach and I think he'd be the first to admit it.

But rarely would 24 hours go by when Luis didn't give me a huge belly laugh. His humour is what helped him survive in the drug business and it was this same humour that was critical to us getting the job done and keeping our sanity during the research and interviews. Even when I hated him for the way he kept sabotaging himself with his drinking and unhealthy habits, I came to care about the man. That's what we do with our friends.

*

Pure Narco is an inside look at the drug trade from an American who talks like a smuggler, who knows the lingo, all the inner workings, all the personalities involved. A friend of Luis's, a Colombian drug trafficker who was captured in 1999's Operation Millennium (*Operación Milenio*), a DEA takedown in Colombia and Mexico that netted one of the heads of the Medellín Cartel, Fabio Ochoa Vásquez, remarked during the writing of this book that 'it's a miracle Luis is alive.

He was one of the few guys that worked with everybody, every fucking cartel in the book, was not even Colombian, and is *alive*. All it would have taken for him to be killed is one guy thinking he was a DEA agent or who didn't like him. Just out of spite or revenge they could spread a rumour he was a DEA agent. Back then they'd kill you on rumours.'[12]

Another friend of his, a high-powered Miami lawyer who represents some of the most powerful narcos in the world today, says Luis is unusual among ex–cocaine traffickers for the strength of his simultaneous relationships with law enforcement and with veterans of the drug world. He jokes Luis is a moving target: 'Whenever I'm with him I wear an extra heavy coat.'

Beyond being a biography, this book should be a deterrent for anyone considering a career in drug trafficking. It brought up some bad memories for Luis and at times it shocked me. But whenever I wavered at the risks involved, I reminded myself that *Pure Narco* was a tale worth telling. There were the mob connections (American, British, Albanian, Spanish, Italian, Russian), the stories of the glamorous women (invariably 'knockouts' or 'headturners'), the drugs, the money, the violent deaths, the ever-present spectre of Pablo Escobar during his rise as a narco – all-important action and 'colour' in a business that for the majority of the time can be utterly tedious.

'There's not a lot of action in moving dope,' says Luis, playing down the glamorisation of the drug trade. 'The plane picks up and drops off and you don't even *see* the dope.'

Yet there were difficulties for me as a writer. The benchmark for any true-crime tale is undoubtedly Nicholas Pileggi's superb 1985 book *Wiseguy*, later turned into the Martin Scorsese film *GoodFellas* with a script by Pileggi and Scorsese. The reality is it's almost a thankless task to follow.

Not that I would ever compare this book to *Wiseguy*, but Pileggi had somewhat of an authorial advantage in having grown up in an Italian-American Brooklyn neighbourhood like his subject, the late Lucchese family mobster Henry Hill, and then worked for decades as a crime reporter of the American mafia. He could infuse a lifetime's personal perspective, authority and firsthand colour to the stories Hill was telling him as a federally protected witness.

I grew up on the other side of the world to Luis, in a different era, and the South American cocaine milieu was totally foreign to me, so I was never there to experience what he had seen with his own eyes. We could only meet in Miami, owing to safety reasons, work and family commitments, and travel restrictions. It thus became a time-intensive research job. Much of the background work for *Pure Narco* involved poring over documents in Spanish and Greek, languages I don't speak. What secondary sources were available more often than not contained contradictory or inaccurate information, so verification was time consuming and not everything could be verified.

Who exactly was involved in Operation Journey was difficult to determine, even to some of the agents who were there on the ground on a 'need to know' basis in Europe and South America. A Freedom of Information request to obtain Luis's case file by one of the agents involved proved fruitless after months of haggling, most of it heavily redacted with black strikethrough lines like a classified FBI memo – a complete waste of time. In the end, reconstructing the week of Luis's attempted escape and capture took two years' work on its own. There were also things I had to leave out or obscure for the sake of his and his family's personal security.

Other times I was totally perplexed by whom exactly Luis was talking about: seemingly every second drug thug in Colombia is called 'El Mono' (Blondie), 'El Gordo' (The Fat One) or 'El Negro' (Blackie).[13] There were people he mentioned of which no photograph or documentary record seemed to exist at all, but he and others assured me that they were very real and had lived or were still living to this day. It was an elaborate jigsaw puzzle with some very dark pieces. So I have described people and events as best I can, despite working within those limitations.

But even when I thought Luis was winding me up on something or stretching the truth, things would check out if there was information at hand. There is simply no possible way a man could make all of this up, provide such a wealth of names, numbers and details that can be corroborated, and then fool the world's leading law-enforcement agencies for over a decade. If he is ever proven to be a fantasist, he is the greatest fantasist who ever lived.

At times I must admit I had my concerns Luis could well be an unreliable narrator, because the stories were simply so *out there*. So where there are any disputes over what took place, I have faithfully recorded both sides or voiced my own suspicions and Luis's reaction. Ultimately, though, this is his story; it wasn't incumbent upon me or necessary to get every available account of what happened from the people Luis knew over the course of his life. I'd need over 2000 pages to do that and, in any case, for very good reasons not everyone from his past wants to talk to a writer. Here, the most important accounts are told faithfully: those of Luis, his family, his former wife, and the agents who worked to bring him down.

Drawing out Luis's inner demons, the real meat of the story, was going to test me as an interviewer too. His was a sad tale as much as it was 'colourful'. He was much more than a mugshot – all narcos are – yet we rarely, if ever, get to see the human behind the criminal. I'd had what I considered a reasonable moral compass all my life. Luis had really only found his after 25 years of getting away with what he could. He knows that and will readily admit to it. But getting him to face up to hard truths about what he was involved in (as well as his personal complicity) was not always easy.

As his nephew Andrés Blanco puts it thoughtfully: 'Luis tends to romanticise this period of his life. It's like a defence mechanism; like at this point in your life how can you look back and feel it was all for nothing? So he looks back on it in a very romantic sense and doesn't always see the ugly side of things and what other people had to suffer and endure as a result of his decisions that, at the end of the day, caused quite a bit of suffering to people close to him. This book is his way of processing it all; it's ultimately positive.'

*

The men and women of the British and American agencies who brought Luis to justice, chief among them active USCS (later United States Immigration and Customs Enforcement or ICE) Special Agent Robert Harley and retired DEA Special Agent Eric Kolbinsky, are the real heroes of this story.[14] They'd not only saved his life by putting him in jail but they made him confront some parts of his character he'd spent the better part of his life ignoring.

Even Luis acknowledges that Harley, who lives in St. Petersburg, on Florida's Gulf Coast, 'gave me my freedom. A lot of people get out of the business and they can never adjust; very few adjust comfortably without regrets or being sour about it all. I've been able to find happiness and adjust; let's just leave it at that.'

Responds Harley: 'I gave him his freedom? Ah, not true [*laughs*]. Luis and I have had a nearly 30-year-long, odd "relationship". He's a real character; has been since high school. I think his life is a great story about choices, their consequences, and a chance at redemption not squandered. It will read like fiction.'

Luis's ex-wife Patricia Manterola, who endured so much while her husband was on the run yet kept their young family together and alive, also deserves the highest praise. When Luis says Patricia 'went through hell and back', he's really not exaggerating. After rebuilding her life following Luis's imprisonment and becoming a mortgage broker, her de facto partner Ignacio Bargueño died at the age of 50.[15] She has subsequently remarried.

Patricia met Luis when she was still a teenager and spent her 20s travelling between Colombia, Mexico and Central America with a lover who was a fugitive from the United States Marshals Service (USMS). She was only 30 when Luis was locked away in an American federal prison.

Strikingly youthful for a woman in her early 50s, with a vivacious personality, great figure, straight blonde-highlighted hair to her shoulders, a megawatt smile and the eyes of a Russian Blue cat, Patricia is a beautiful woman. A Colombian national and permanent resident of the United States, she speaks elegantly accented English, much like the Spanish actress Penélope Cruz. Her home is in Brickell, a waterside neighbourhood in Miami that has become an elite playground for Latin American and European multimillionaires, its streets clogged with Maseratis and Mercedes-AMGs. Hearing English spoken in her neighbourhood these days is rare.

'When I remember that part of my life it's like someone else lived through that, not me,' she says. 'But the good thing is it always leaves me with a smile on my face. *Everybody* liked Luis. They always found him funny. He speaks very bad Spanish [*laughs*]. Well, *now* he speaks better. Back then he would make some kind of mistake and everybody would laugh. He was fun. Everything looked like an adventure in the beginning. I was a kid. *Imagine*. I had braces. I didn't realise what I was getting into.'

*

In 2000, not long after the DEA had dismantled the Medellín and Cali cartels (operations dramatised in the first three seasons of *Narcos*), the United States Department of Justice (DOJ), the DEA (part of the DOJ), the USCS, the Joint Interagency Task Force-East (JIATF-East) and law-enforcement agencies in Great Britain, Venezuela, Colombia, the Netherlands, Greece, Italy, Albania, Panama, Belgium, Spain and France combined forces for the conclusion of Operation Journey, an elaborate two-year takedown that targeted the narco empire of Los Mellizos ('The Twins'), a Colombian cartel named after identical twin brothers Víctor Manuel Mejía Múnera and Miguel Ángel Mejía Múnera.

The Mejía Múneras were big-time traffickers and identified as such by the DEA as early as 1995. They were so powerful DEA administrator Thomas A. Constantine stated in congressional testimony that the brothers had 'links to both the North Valley and Cali syndicates' and 'will attempt to fill the void created by the arrest of the [Cali Cartel's] Rodríguez Orejuela brothers'. Madrid newspaper *La Razón* even went so far as to name them as the biggest drug trafficking 'clan' since the bloody reign of the Medellín Cartel, a state-sized drug syndicate that under the guile and tyranny of Pablo Escobar would go on to control 80 per cent of the global cocaine trade.

The mission to destroy The Twins' cartel involved 12 nations, 14 agencies, over 200 agents, boats, helicopters and sophisticated surveillance equipment, and resulted in 43 arrests. The publication of this book marks the 20th anniversary of this momentous event. So in the DEA's storied history of takedowns, Operation Journey is one of the most significant.

It had its origins in British and Spanish maritime law-enforcement operations in 1996, started out being called Operation Jezebel by Brits stationed in Colombia; *Operación Transatlántico* by the Colombians themselves; overlapped the DEA's earlier Operation Millennium, Her Majesty's Customs and Excise's (HMCE's) 11-year mega-dragnet Operation Extend, the Greeks' Operation Odessa and the US Coast Guard's (USCG's) Operation New Frontier; and in Venezuela, the location of Luis's ultimate capture, was christened *Operación Orinoco* or Orinoco 2000 after the famous river, brown like a milky coffee, that runs for 2000 kilometres from the Sierra Parima in the state of Amazonas, close to the border with Brazil, to Delta Amacuro on the Atlantic Ocean.[16]

But, as former DEA agent Eric Kolbinsky wrote in the foreword, even after its various offshoots coalesced under a single name, 'inter-agency squabbles and infighting' nearly put paid to its successful resolution. One thing I learned from writing *Pure Narco* is just how difficult it must be to mount an international antinarcotics operation when factoring in not just the serious potential for leaks but the dysfunctional politics and rivalries involved.

Operation Journey, however, proved a gamebreaker for all sorts of reasons and received saturation press coverage around the world. *The Washington Post* said it had a 'Hollywood-like conclusion' while Britain's *Sunday Telegraph* also thought it fit for the big screen, ending 'in a speedboat chase complete with volleys of bullets similar to the opening sequence of the latest Bond film'.[17]

Senior investigation officer (Gold Command) Graham Honey, who led the British effort for HMCE, says 'the half-dozen of us who were really close to that case, we look back on it as the pinnacle of a career; you will never get a case like that now. I don't think any law-enforcement organisation since that time has ever, *ever* worked a case like that where you've had the number of agencies involved, the amount of drugs being moved and *how* they were being moved. The amounts of cocaine [the cartel] was moving on those jobs was unbelievable. I don't think there's anything of that scale happening now. That was unprecedented.'

*

To give some perspective on the significance of the cocaine seizure of which Luis was involved in 2000, the following year, 2001, it was announced that 13 tons of cocaine had been intercepted on a fishing boat 1500 miles south of San Diego in the 'largest cocaine seizure in US maritime history'. The cocaine impounded in Operation Journey was *double.* The cocaine moved by ships that were being monitored by Operation Journey was *five* times that amount, and much more again was transported without ever being detected.

Luis, the man who initiated and arranged an important part of Los Mellizos' smuggling operations to Europe on a fleet of oceangoing bulk carriers, what USCS Commissioner Raymond Kelly called a 'drug armada', was the point man for the Colombian and Mexican cartels if they wanted to shift a serious amount of coke.

And no wonder it was being moved to Europe. At the time a kilo of cocaine that would cost $1700 in Colombia would fetch $50,000 in Europe, double the price it would get in the US. Do the math: 68 tons at $50,000 a 'key'.[18] That's $45 million a ton or over $3 billion for the lot. A $48,300 profit margin on a single key. The Mellizos' share of that European market was 'massive', says Luis. 'They were the top suppliers of the European market, without a fucking doubt.'

The famous 1984 raids on the huge cocaine-processing complex Tranquilandia ('Quiet Village') in the jungles of Caquetá, southern Colombia, only recovered 15 tons, which were destroyed.[19] In 2007 the United States Coast Guard (USCG) impounded 20 tons from a Panamanian cargo ship. The same year, a jointly conducted Mexican federal police and marines operation in Manzanillo claimed to have confiscated a then world-record 26 tons. Twenty-one tons were seized in California in 1989, 26.5 tons in South Florida in 2016, and almost 20 tons in Philadelphia in 2019. The largest single cocaine bust in recent Colombian history was 12 tons in 2017, but in 2019 the Colombian Government announced 94.2 metric tons (103.8 tons) had been seized in various operations over a 105-day period, mostly on the open sea.[20]

But these are just numbers; there will *always* be bigger busts. And in any case whatever is caught is only a small fraction of what actually gets through. So-called 'narco subs', crudely built semi-submersible submarines or 'low-profile vessels', now account for up to 40 per cent of drugs arriving in the United States, but only five per cent of those drugs are being intercepted.

However, when Commissioner Kelly stood before the cameras in a Washington, DC press conference to announce Luis had been arrested along with Los Mellizos' 'communications chief' Iván de la Vega Cabás in Maracaibo, Venezuela, and flown to the United States in handcuffs, he made very plain it was an enormous triumph for the authorities.[21] The timing was also deliberate, the press conference held just days before President Bill Clinton made a state visit to Cartagena to meet Colombia's president, Andrés Pastrana Arango, to cement the two countries' alliance in the war on drugs with $1.3 billion as seed money for Pastrana's anti-drug 'Plan Colombia'.

'This investigation was unique for the incredible volume of cocaine it kept off the streets of America and Europe,' said Kelly. 'This case also demonstrates what can be achieved when nations of the world work together against a common enemy. Operation Journey should serve as a model for international law-enforcement cooperation.'

When Luis describes it, though, he plays it down: 'It was like three minutes of the four-hour story. But it's what brought me down.'

*

In *Wiseguy*, Nicholas Pileggi described Henry Hill as a 'mechanic' in the American mafia and in effect that's also what Luis was in the cocaine business. He was an expert in the machinery of the drug trade and knew what went where and who did what. The difference is Hill effectively started at the bottom. Luis, by his own admission, got a Wonka Golden Ticket to the highest levels of the Colombian cartels.

Pressed on what exactly he did for these criminal groups, he says 'logistics' but the bottom line was he made them money; he was an 'earner'. However, in the structure of those same cartels for which he earned that money, he was a transporter, a delivery expert: traditionally an important position outsourced to non-Colombian nationals. Transporters were prized for their connections to lucrative markets, especially Europe, because from the early 1980s onwards US law authorities were well and truly on to the cartels and smuggling coke to North America was becoming much more difficult, dangerous and violent. Europe remains where the big money is because of the high prices people are prepared to pay for a kilo of cocaine.

'From the day I set foot in Colombia to the day I was arrested in Venezuela, I was working *all the time.* I don't have one per cent of the money I should have with the amount of "merchandise" I moved. Billions went through my hands.'

Luis believes had he not wasted so much of his life drinking and drugging, he'd have $100 million stashed away. He could have made much more if he'd actually owned the cocaine but only ever took a percentage for the transport.

'It's crazy. I don't even know where all the fucking money went, compared to what we moved. What I made with my right hand I spent with my left. I had a lot of good connections. It's *all* about connections. I was totally consumed by what I was doing and constantly thinking of the mission at hand, making sure the load will make it and have no problems and then, after that, immediately concentrating on the next load: a never-ending saga of load after load. If I lost a load, I was good for seven good ones. Because of my averages I was a very prized "batter", let's say. If we played seven times, seven times I'd hit home runs. But every once in a while I'd strike out. I had a great record as a transporter.

'I've always thought smugglers were the true essence of the cocaine business, not pushers or distributors. Smuggling is the most important part of the business because it's the part that brings in the revenue. If your loads don't make it and there is no product for the distributors to sell, then the business goes bankrupt. I always did my homework. People like me were of great value because we were the ones that put the product where the money was. The smuggle is also the toughest part of the business. There's no cutting corners.'

*

Luis worked for 'huge' cartel figures in Colombia and Mexico and 'never for a middleman', which offered him a degree of immunity and protection. No would-be kidnapper would dare try to shake down Luis when they knew the fearsome reputations of the bosses or *capos* (drug lords) behind him.

'The reason I survived was everybody knew I was not my own boss; I was always working for someone who was very feared *behind* me, and that's why people never stole merchandise from me.'

In a global drug market increasingly controlled by Mexican cartels, Europe somehow remains the domain of Colombians.

'The US had a proactive government that would fucking go chase people all over the world. I was an independent guy who had my own routes and I went to different sources of supply and I made money for them and for myself. Was I part of the Medellín Cartel? No. I worked *with* the Medellín Cartel, I worked *with* the Northern Valley Cartel, I worked *for* people from the Coast Cartel.[22] That protection saved me big time. I was a drug smuggler. I had connections to Belize, The Bahamas, Jamaica, Guatemala, Mexico, Europe, so that was all very valuable.'

And with each load Luis was involved in delivering, the thrill just ratcheted up with every 'first'. The first grams he sold at Georgetown University. The first 100 keys sent to Los Angeles.[23] The first airdrops aboard his own plane in The Bahamas. The first landings in Mexico. The first fastboats to Belize. The first freighter job. As the numbers kept getting higher – 100, 500, 1000, 2000, 3000, 4000, 5000 keys – so did the endorphin hit.

It was also harder for him to get out.

*

Luis frequently refers to himself as the 'last independent smuggler' but the sheer scale of his drug trafficking (cocaine in the *hundreds* of tons) arguably makes him the biggest homegrown cocaine smuggler in American history: more than 'The Man Who Made It Snow', the late Max Mermelstein, who went into witness protection after testifying against the Medellín Cartel; more than George Jung, played by Johnny Depp in *Blow*, who went to jail for 20 years; and more than Barry Seal, the murdered pilot and confidential informant (CI) made famous by the Tom Cruise film *American Made*. Pablo Escobar made sure Seal was killed in 1986 for betraying him.

'I lasted 25 years. I took up residence in Colombia. I was one of *them*. I married a Colombian. I stayed there. Those other guys would go down to Colombia and couldn't wait to get out.[24] I enjoyed the country. I *loved* Colombia. By far I am more Colombian than Cuban. In my heart of hearts I am Colombian. The guys from Medellín were really fucking cool. Very cultured. It was amazing to be around these people.

'But the other thing about people from Medellín is they are tough, astute and calculating. That's one thing I saw in Colombians that I never saw in Cubans. Their word was their bond but they'd kill you and they'd think nothing of it. I grew up thinking killing was the worst; then you realise humans are all a bunch of cockroaches and half of them deserve to be whacked anyway for all the shit they do.

'Either you're gonna do things right or you're not, but if you don't do things right then don't come crying to anybody if they fucking whacked you. You deserved it. You had no business going into somebody else's business and stealing from 'em. I'm not a big proponent of humans. They're not in my highest category. I'll cry more over the death of a fucking polar bear or a Bengal tiger than I will a fucking crooked human.

'Just because you're a human doesn't give you a right to life or anything, you know. What makes you special? Because you can *talk*? Some people it's better that they don't even talk. I realise how fucked up humans are and that's why I don't have the highest regard for human life. If you get whacked, you get whacked. You should definitely not go into this business and be deceitful to anybody. Especially when you know this motherfucker will whack you. Then you're just psycho, suicidal and stupid. Then it's an insult to this person's intelligence and, worse, an insult to his position as a cartel boss.'

When I asked Luis how he morally dealt with violence knowing it was part of his line of work, he was refreshingly upfront even if the import of what he was saying was slightly disturbing. Describing the brutal murder of a friend, a broker called Juan Diego, he simply says, 'He got tortured – *bad* – by Mexicans. He got killed in an unfriendly way.'

Luis's world is a netherworld where the execution of a human being is judged by degrees of kindness or friendliness, as if any murder could ever be justified.

'I'm *against* torture, Jesse. I'm *against* psychopaths. But if someone needs to get whacked, whack his ass. That was his doing. In his heart of hearts he knows what he did to suffer that fate. He must have done something wrong. I have no moral problems with that. To this day, you tell me you're a hitman, I'm like, "Hey, that's your job. That's *perfect*, man. Be good at it. This world needs everything." I had no control of yea or nay. I was never a jury or a judge. Violence wasn't my thing. I always knew I didn't stand a chance in that world as a bad guy. I never owned a gun. Killing was beyond my pay grade. I would never be an assassin. I don't like that being my business model.

'Some people think it's easy: you kill somebody, you make $100,000. But you've got to *love* what you do. I would never love killing. Killing was not born in my *soul*. What was born in my soul was making money. Maybe that's where I'm fucked up. Making money. Maybe I should have been more like a Buddhist and meditated, so my soul unites with my brain and soothes it a bit and teaches my brain a little bit of knowledge about living. Living is not only about money.'

Was he ever affected emotionally by the cartels' violence?

'I never was. In that sense, Isabelle tells me I'm amoral. I've got to be truthful with you, right?'

*

What you're about to read is a true-crime tale of a period that was largely bypassed in *Narcos* and occupies a zone relatively unexplored in drug-related non-fiction: the time between the demise of the Colombian cartels and the rise of the Mexican cartels. The utterly ruthless Mexicans operate sophisticated distribution networks through gangs in the United States and can move more cocaine through tunnels under the US–Mexico border than the Colombians could ever manage by airdropping in The Bahamas. They also move cash back into Mexico the same way. As Luis says, 'Nobody knows it came in, nobody knows it came out.'

The Colombian era seems almost romantic in comparison.

'The Colombians are always seen as foreigners and they're always getting fucked. They always want to fuck the third-world guy. There's a lot of big-money people in the United States who have made billions off the Colombian mafia and they've retired in time and they've cleaned their money and they're here in the US and they've built buildings and everything. But they gotta blame *somebody*. So they're always blaming the third-world countries; they're the source of the problem. They're the producers.

'The root of the problem is *here*, not there. The corruption is *here*. There's such a culture of non-education in America. There have been a lot of anti-drug educational programs but they haven't worked. The country uses all its money on its military budget and is so cheap, so cruel and so unjust to its own citizens that it doesn't even give them universal health care. Let alone all the money that is spent on the DEA budget on a war that has proven to be totally dysfunctional.'

Remnants of the mighty Medellín and Cali cartels still exist, along with the smaller cartels and gangs the Colombians call BACRIM (*bandas criminales* or criminal bands), but they are more likely to cooperate with each other than fight. Those cartels that remain are working with the few guerrillas still holding out in the jungle, and Mexicans and Venezuelans are shifting most of the product.[25] At time of writing, before COVID-19 or coronavirus completely shut down international travel, the United States Department of State (DOS) was advising travellers not to go to Venezuela at all, due to 'crime, civil unrest, poor health infrastructure, kidnapping, and arbitrary arrest and detention of US citizens'. In Mexico law and order has completely broken down in some areas due to the power of the cartels.

'Some cartel guys are still in Medellín. Some of them are living in Europe. Some of them are dead or in jail. Everything has *evolved*. Now you just don't have Medellín–Cali. It's all over the place. Everybody works with everybody.'

*

Today 30 per cent of the cocaine traffic to Europe, a continent that accounts for 30 per cent of the global cocaine market, goes through West Africa. The story of cocaine smuggling in the 2020s is less about Colombians in Miami than Nigerians in São Paulo. It's a global industry.

International criminal syndicates have learned from the mistakes of decades past. As part of multifarious money-laundering schemes, drug barons in Latin America are no longer putting profits into the vaults of Miami banks, exchange houses or trading companies, but into gold mines deep in the Amazon rainforest, laundering money by using front companies to sell 'dirty' gold to refineries and pocketing 'clean' cash in return.

Or they pack hundreds of millions of dollars on ships to China, where money-laundering laws are lax ('they don't believe in money laundering – money is money') and, according to Luis, 'The Chinese with the Mexican money buy like a billion of whatever – dishwashers, sewing machines, lamps, picture frames, bedsheets, kitchenware, everything you see at Walmart – and, that's it, it goes into the world market and it gets laundered.'

Illegal drugs are a $320 billion a year industry and there are 18 million users of cocaine worldwide. Over 300 million people have tried cocaine at least once in their lives. The United States, Spain, Australia and the United Kingdom are the world's biggest cocaine buyers, while tiny Albania is the biggest user of coke per capita.[26] Colombia, the land of Pablo Escobar, still produces 70 per cent of the world's cocaine, where it fetches $2200 a kilo. That same kilo sells for $53,000 to $55,000 in Europe.

The United States continues to spend $40 billion each year on the war on drugs, while its citizens spend $150 billion buying them. Mexicans have taken over the methamphetamine racket from bikers, state-based legalisation and high-quality hydroponics have effectively killed off marijuana smuggling, and opioids such as fentanyl and heroin wreak havoc in small-town America.[27] Cocaine, legally a narcotic but medically a stimulant, remains defiantly popular and accounts for the most spending on any single drug in the United States, even if overall consumption is falling in favour of marijuana and meth. In South America, coca-leaf production is at historically high levels. The biggest users of cocaine are still young people. The allure of cocaine remains as strong as ever.

*

Pure Narco is the first book I have written in official collaboration with someone else. I wanted Luis's unique, engaging voice to come through but with the right amount of background where necessary. Endnoting was essential. I have given ample space for that voice and the quotes you will read are delivered just as he said them.

Over the three weeks I spent with him in Miami in November 2019, Luis and I met almost every day for a Cuban sandwich and coffee at Latin Café 2000 on the corner of NE 25th and Biscayne Boulevard. We got to know each other extremely well, I met all his friends, workmates and family, and we found some commonality despite our disparate backgrounds, criminal histories and core beliefs.

This is above all Luis's story but it is also a chronicle of an era as well as an honest insight into Latin American narco culture. It is a tale about money, what it means to be 'rich', and knowing when enough is enough. My role was not only to record, research and write that story but shepherd into print and give historical context to what hitherto had been a collection of hazy memories and funny anecdotes told by Luis to fellow inmates in the prison yard or over long dinners with friends in Miami, Key West and Tampa.

By necessity it required some compression and rearranging of people and events into a more straightforward narrative, especially in the mid-1980s and late '90s, because there were simply so many side stories and so much to tell. In the end, pulling all these strands together was a process I was to enjoy immensely, even though Luis made it very plain to me throughout that we were both potentially putting ourselves at risk by writing this book. Dredging up 'old battle scars', as he put it, is a dangerous game.

'I got into this fucking nasty business and it didn't change me totally but it left a scar. My collateral damage is heavy. There's no life-insurance coverage in book contracts. Don't think I don't worry. Publicity sometimes can be a double-edged sword. The book could do me more harm than good. Nobody knows jack shit about me and my business. Nobody's done due diligence on me. They believe I'm just Luis Navia, the construction guy.

'I'm putting everything on the line for this. "*This fucking asshole.* I mean, this guy must have been the biggest jerk-off in history. He was in the drug business for 25 years, moved 200 tons, and now he has to dig holes." Man, that's fucked up. I'll probably leave Miami; I don't want to stay living here anyway. I'll probably change my name, move to Mexico. Become "Luis Navarro". *Boom.* Why not? I already got my kids grown up. Why do I need to be Luis Navia?'

The same night we did our first interview, he called me very late. He'd been talking to another drug trafficker friend about the journey he was about to take as an author. Coming from an unrepentant narco, what he was about to say was quite an admission.

'Smugglers are adrenalin junkies that love the rush and the thrill and they go to exotic lands to do it; to get the true thrill of this whole thing, the thrill of the *smuggle*. Getting a high off logistical feats that you put together if you use your brain. That's what it is. Pushers and distributors are just people who receive what the smugglers bring in and switch suitcases full of cash. They're just waiting to get busted. We didn't kill nobody. We were building up an enterprise; a business enterprise. We thought we were outlaws. I could walk into a restaurant and there could be ten people there with more money than I had, but I was an outlaw, like a walking deity. That was a bigger trip.

'Yet we were so mistaken because the government doesn't consider you an outlaw. Outlaws are when there are no laws. The government considers what you are doing as a continuing criminal enterprise. We were just goddamn criminals. And if we didn't kill nobody, we were associated with people that did. So when a DEA agent comes along and snaps some handcuffs on you, there you go: the big outlaw with $60 million in the bank just got arrested by the guy who makes $45,000 a year.[28]

'I was a drug trafficker in the true sense of the word: a pure narco. I stayed true to the drug business, not the killing business, not the paramilitary business, not the kidnapping business. I wasn't a part-time killer or part-time kidnapper or part-time sonofabitch. I always kept a family. Your family is so important. Even if it's just the three of you and you've got to share a hot dog, you're tight. In general, I've been a good person and cared for others, but the truth is I was involved with some nasty people. My focus was on the smuggling, although in the end it's all got a blemish of nastiness no matter what part of the overall business you're involved in.

'I had already made five, six million dollars when I owned sugar land in Florida and should have got the fuck out of the dope business, but I never got out. And that was my mistake. We were so mistaken, we thought, "Yeah, we're cool," this *adrenalin*, but you can get just the same rush by doing other things. Those people in Silicon Valley with their computers and shit, tell me they're not on a fucking high. Really, in the end it messed up my life. I mean, I'm alive, and that's great and I have some great stories but really, where's it all at? It's a miracle my family didn't get hurt more. But you can't just live life on a coin toss. And I was flipping a coin every day of my life.'

Jesse Fink, Sydney, Australia

PURE NARCO

PROLOGUE

Do the Right Thing

9pm, Caracas, Venezuela
Saturday, 12 August 2000

THE UNRAVELLING OF LUIS ANTONIO NAVIA'S 25-year career as a narco, 12 years on the run from the law and five years as an international fugitive started when he walked out of the front doors of the Tamanaco InterContinental to his waiting taxi.

The eight-floor, 528-room concrete hotel, built in the 1950s, hadn't aged well but offered guests some respite from the sprawling *barrios* of the Venezuelan capital, nestled among an oasis of trees, tennis courts and manicured lawns just off the Autopista Prados del Este, a main highway, and right in the shadow of the green hills of the Cordillera de la Costa.

It was a quiet, tropical night in the 'City of Eternal Spring', wet but still hot, and as Luis took a moment to drag on a short Belmont cigarette, the most popular brand in the Bolivarian Republic, there was no sign of what was about to hit him.[29] For the moment, his ride – and his impending fate – could wait.

Within less than a week the 45-year-old Cuban-American would be captured by the Bolivarian National Guard of Venezuela, threatened with being cut up with a scalpel, detained at a military base, dispatched in a convoy of seven black Chevrolet Suburbans to the airport where Luis had once kept a Cessna 441 Conquest II for his bicontinental drug-smuggling operations, and sent to Florida on a USCS Lockheed P-3 Orion to face the full force of stateside justice.

The plane had been configured like the cargo hold of a C-130 Hercules, with jump seats on the sides. It had been a quick 'in and out' for the US authorities with full permission from the Venezuelan Government. Luis, handcuffed, took his seat near a window for the three-hour ride. The DEA and USCS agents on board offered him water, coffee, Oreos, chocolate-chip cookies and potato chips.

As the aircraft hummed at 30,000 feet on its flight path over the Caribbean Sea, a feeling of calm came over him; a sort of tranquillity, like the weight of the world had finally been taken off his shoulders. The Carlos the Jackal of the drug world had been caught. His days as an international drug smuggler were over.

An agent seated next to Luis, sensing his uncharacteristic quietness, turned to him at one point and tapped him on the shoulder: 'Luis, you'll be alright. Just do the right thing and you will be alright.'

He was filmed when he arrived after midnight at Fort Lauderdale–Hollywood International Airport, accompanied by four agents and greeted on the tarmac by two others in navy raid jackets, one emblazoned with 'US Customs Police', the other 'DEA'. The footage would later be used in a combined DEA/USCS/JIATF-East press conference in Washington, DC in front of the world's assembled media to announce the takedown of 'one of the largest drug transportation groups ever targeted by law enforcement'.

Handcuffed but neat as always, Luis returned home to the United States dressed in a white shirt, khaki slacks and brown Sperry Top-Sider shoes. His 48-year-old, dark-skinned Colombian accomplice, Iván de la Vega Cabás, was more casual: he wore a white and navy striped polo shirt, a navy cap, navy shorts and leather sandals. His hands were tied with PlastiCuffs. Both men were nonchalantly chewing gum, like they were in the pro shop signing their scorecards after 18 holes of golf, not about to spend years in prison. The two drug traffickers seemed awfully relaxed about what awaited them, including a 90-day stretch in solitary confinement – for good reason.

The Americans had saved their lives.

PART 1
TAKEDOWN

1

El Senador

WHEN LUIS FIRST ARRIVED IN Venezuela from Italy that June, he'd entered on a fake Mexican passport under a fake name, 'Luis Antonio Novoa Alfandari', with a fake birthdate. He was pretending to be a Mexican businessman with interests in latex rubber gloves and coffee, and it was the perfect cover.[30] It was just one of many alter egos he used in his line of work. On the street, he was sometimes called 'Julio Novoa'. In South American cocaine circles, he was variously called 'El Senador' (The Senator), for his sharp dress sense, and 'The Greek', for the shipping company he now worked for in the port of Piraeus, Athens: Callisti Maritime.[31]

Located a few blocks from the water in an attractive three-storey building at 61–65 Filonos Street, Callisti was the European front for what was then the deadliest drug cartel in Colombia, Los Mellizos, named after Miguel and Víctor Mejía Múnera. Born in 1959, The Twins were Cali brothers who had worked their way up from humble beginnings as *cuida cargas* (men who control or guard loads of cocaine for the owners) on fastboats in the Pacific Coast port of Buenaventura to becoming the biggest cocaine kingpins in Colombia, with complete control of the cocaine trade in the departments of Sucre and Bolívar, and the Venezuelan state of Delta Amacuro.[32]

Only a few high-ranking people in the cartel knew Luis's real name, one of them a Mellizo himself, Víctor Mejía Múnera, another Los Mellizos *contador* or accountant Félix Antonio Chitiva Carrasquilla aka 'La Mica', who'd once moved merchandise for Pablo Escobar.[33] However, the Mejía Múnera brothers and Chitiva didn't know Luis was actually *working* for the organisation – the news of his involvement on this latest smuggling operation never got to them. He much preferred it that way and 'always kept someone in the middle' and 'was not directly involved', avoiding wherever possible face-to-face meetings with the leadership of the cartels for whom he rendered his services. In effect, he was a shadow, a ghost.[34]

In South America, Luis always had at least $20,000 in cash at his hotel and made a point of walking around with $3000 to $5000 in his pocket, 'enough to make a run'. He spent many hours at the pool getting a deep brown tan, hanging out in the bar and restaurant, and making love back in his suite to his 21-year-old, red-haired Panamanian girlfriend, Michelle Arias.[35] If ever he were in mortal danger, Luis would get on the phone to Michelle and say the codeword 'Antonio', his middle name.

They'd met drinking whisky in the upstairs lounge of the Davidoff cigar store in the World Trade Center office building in Panama City, Panama, where Michelle worked as a manager. Together the two lovers had travelled to Santo Domingo in the Dominican Republic, Madrid, Athens, Milan, and finally Venezuela. Luis, then a resident of Panama, was separated at the time from his wife and the mother of his children, Patricia Manterola, and an attempt at reconciliation hadn't panned out the way he'd hoped. Luis hadn't been the most faithful husband during his short marriage. Patricia had simply had enough of his shameless philandering, heavy drinking and 'gypsy' ways and rightly walked out.

Luis was no Antonio Banderas or Jordi Mollà. He didn't look like your stereotypical ponytailed Hispanic cocaine trafficker from Hollywood movies. He was short, just 168 centimetres tall, somewhat jowly, with salt-and-pepper-coloured hair and beard, a slightly bulbous nose, and an ample stomach courtesy of his taste for booze, good food and disdain for exercise.[36] He was constantly on edge and uncomfortable, completely stressed out from his separation from Patricia, and had developed a growing dependency on anti-anxiety medication and antidepressants.

Though Luis tried to think about his unusual predicament at the most 'three times a year', life on the run was tough on his nerves. He'd left the United States in a hurry in 1988 to preempt an indictment – a formal charging document approved by a grand jury – he thought was about to come out of Arizona. Luis had been smuggling coke on his own plane, a Panamanian-registered Merlin twin-engine turboprop, from Colombia to the resort town of Puerto Vallarta outside Guadalajara, Mexico, and then to Tucson. A white American narco in Tucson, known only to Luis as 'The Doc', his point man to the Mexican cartels, had been caught and Luis feared The Doc was about to rat him out. So he immediately fled to the coffee city of Pereira, Colombia, and continued his flourishing drug business in South America.

On 3 March 1995, he was formally indicted in the Southern District of Florida, again for drug trafficking ('conspiracy to possess cocaine with intent to distribute'), this time for a string of smuggles in the Florida Keys that Luis claims, with some justification, he did not lead. But it didn't change the fact he'd been named and outed as a cocaine smuggler. The jig was up.

Five months later, it was official: Luis was a US Government fugitive.

*

In truth, though, being forced into exile had been more than tolerable; in fact, it had been a breeze. Luis was a Latin American living in Latin America who had easily transitioned to the nuances and rhythms of life south of the border. He spoke Spanish, had enough money to buy whatever he wanted whenever he felt like it, and had a Colombian wife, Colombian daughter and Mexican son.

His only real misfortune was a 35-year-old USCS special agent, Robert Harley, who'd brought the original indictment against him out of Key West, Florida, and was doggedly working to hunt him down while clearing out hundreds of other cases in his day job.

Harley had long been burning the candle at both ends, working in a long-term undercover operation with the Miami field division of a Federal Bureau of Investigation (FBI) organised crime unit, while going to the University of Miami law school at night. Earnest, hardworking, aspirational and dedicated to the job and his long-term girlfriend, Mary, he was a handsome man: like a blonder, shorter, stockier version of Mark Hamill from *Star Wars*. Always armed, when suited up he made a point of carrying a SIG Sauer P229 9mm; in polarised sunglasses and Bermuda shorts, a Ruger SP101 five-shot stainless .38 Special. He'd narrowly missed catching Luis in Mexico and had gathered more than enough intelligence to bring him in.

'I had a lot of crap going on in those years,' says Harley. 'They were the busiest years of my life, between 1993 and 1999. That's when I really worked the most.'

He wasn't about to give up now.

2

The Venezuelan Job

So Luis instinctively knew Robert Harley and USCS, the DEA or US Marshals could break down his door any minute. This awareness didn't help his stress levels. He rarely got enough sleep. He was also deeply unnerved by the paper trail being left behind by the Venezuelan job, the biggest smuggle of his career; an elaborate criminal enterprise he'd been working on for nearly a year.

Luis's assignment in South America that August was to oversee the departure of the Maltese-flagged bulk freighter *Suerte I* from Puerto Ordaz to Rotterdam, the Netherlands, and then Antwerp, Belgium. Puerto Ordaz is a big port on the Orinoco River and part of the city of Ciudad Guayana, where ships load up with cargo then navigate through 180 kilometres of winding, jungle-choked waterways and mangrove swamps to the Atlantic Ocean.

From The Plains (Los Llanos) region in Colombia, bales of cocaine would be airdropped over the border to pre-arranged locations in the remote Orinoco Delta, a vast wilderness in eastern Venezuela. For landing planes, Los Mellizos also had a mile-long runway on a 5000-acre farm called Doble Uno, less than 100 kilometres from Puerto Ordaz.

Once the *Suerte* was out on the open sea, 30 miles off the coast, it would rendezvous in the dead of night with a fleet of *pangas*, or fastboats, commanded by Jorge García aka 'Cuñado' (Brother-in-Law), a fit, lean Colombian in his late 20s who wore dental braces and since March 2000 had headed up the cartel's operations in the jungle. He had been directly responsible for supplying the cocaine to the *Suerte.*

From these boats Jorge and his men would onload over five tons of coke, conceal it in hidden compartments on the so-called customised 'mothership', and the *Suerte,* with *cuida cargas* aboard to guard the load, would set off for Europe.

When the ships reached Spanish territorial waters, local criminal clans with direct links to the Eastern European mob would intercept a consignment of the cocaine off the Galician coast on fishing boats.[37] From there it would sail for the English Channel, where another consignment would be offloaded to another fishing boat for eventual sale and distribution in Great Britain.

If everything went smoothly, five tons of coke would be successfully delivered to the cartel's mafia customers in Albania, Spain, Russia and England and the boat would dock at its final destination, Antwerp, completely 'clean'. There would be nothing for any cop or narc to find.

*

It was a brilliant, watertight plan. But something was skewiff in Caracas. Luis could feel it in his bones. There'd been whispers among cartel members something might be going down, but the order hadn't been given by the leadership of Los Mellizos to abort.

'It was getting screwy. I was very nervous. I kinda felt there was a little heat on us; that we were being watched. Caracas was already turning a little sour with [Venezuelan president] Hugo Chávez coming in the previous year. I had been planning to meet my family and my sister and her kids in Barcelona in July, but I couldn't go because my Mexican passport was missing.'

Patricia had turned up in Spain with Juliana, six, and Santi, three, as her husband had requested, but without a passport to travel on from Venezuela, Luis hadn't shown. It was going to take some arranging for his counterfeiter, a woman called Natalia Hoyos, to travel 2600 kilometres from Guatemala City to Caracas with a replacement.[38] Luis had many fake passports to choose from – over seven – but hadn't thought to bring a spare to Venezuela. The one he wanted Natalia to bring was another Mexican passport, this one under the name 'Louis Anton Naviansky'.[39]

'I always tried to keep the same initials because that way I didn't have to change my shirts, because all my shirts were monogrammed. I had them made at Mario Pelizza, the tailor for the Mexican president. It's more expensive to change your wardrobe than get a new passport. The *Suerte* was supposed to have arrived a lot earlier, it was delayed, so I just couldn't leave Venezuela without a passport and without the *Suerte* having arrived. I figured once the *Suerte* docked, we'd loaded the shit and it was gone, I'd have Natalia come in from Guatemala with my Naviansky passport.'

So, instead, it was simply easier to have the whole family fly to Venezuela. Not the most normal thing to do in the middle of a major international drug conspiracy, but Luis couldn't see any other way around it and he was desperate to see his kids.

*

Patricia, who'd been furious at Luis's no-show in Barcelona, had already left for a pre-arranged holiday with her Italian boyfriend. So it was left to Luis's sister, Laura, to drag her two teenage sons, Andrés and Martin, as well as Juliana and Santi all the way from Europe to Caracas.[40]

'I was upset with Luis because all my pre-arranged travel plans got messed up,' says Laura. 'I was also upset because it wasn't till the absolute last minute that we found out he wasn't coming at all. I had to cancel a trip to Paris with my children. Patricia had dropped off my niece and nephew on my second day in Barcelona, and Luis never showed up to pick them up. I had to travel to Venezuela to take the kids to him.'

It wasn't, however, a straightforward procedure getting them through immigration. Juliana arrived without the right visa, leaving the already harried Laura to plead with officials to let them into the country.[41]

'It was incredibly aggravating and stressful. Juliana had a Colombian passport with no Venezuelan visa. It could have ended badly, but having lived in Latin America for many years, I knew a few hundred dollars would go a long way in solving the problem.'

Luis had to wait outside the terminal with his driver while all this was going on, wisely refusing to come inside because of the police presence. (He knew Juliana would say *Papá* if she so much as saw him, and they had different passports.) In the end, once the bribe had been paid, they were allowed to stay on a 30-day visa and Patricia cut short her trip in Italy and travelled to the Venezuelan embassy in Colombia to sort out the paperwork.

Naturally, when Laura met her brother outside the airport and offloaded Luis's kids to his and Michelle's care for a few days, she was livid. But not as angry as Patricia was when she eventually turned up from Colombia to take them back home to Mexico City. As far as she remembers it, there would be no introductions to Luis's buxom blonde lover. Michelle was keeping her distance, perhaps wisely. All the same, Patricia had a sense she was close by.[42]

'I knew Luis had a new girlfriend with him in Caracas because she did something to Juliana's hair. She put in highlights [*laughs*]. *Imagine*. My daughter was six years old.'

As for the kids, they were blissfully unaware anything was going down and had no idea their father was even involved in crime. Laura's 16-year-old son Andrés, however, was starting to have suspicions about the man he called 'Uncle Lou', who'd booked rooms 1116 and 1117 at the Gran Meliá.

'I'd never seen him in worse shape,' he says. 'He was fat, stressed, smoking cigarettes. He looked like hell. He was always secretive. We'd order room service and I'd go to sign the cheque, and he'd say, "*Don't* sign your name!" But he'd always been a bit eccentric, so I didn't question it. There were always stacks of cash and bags of money around. He never had a cell phone. My uncle was always in a payphone booth or standing by a payphone, making phone calls. He'd be like, "Come with me, I've got to run a few errands." But running a few errands with Luis was to watch him stay on a payphone. I was like, "I'm bored. I'm not coming with you anymore." That was his office.'

3

Midnight Run

THE *SUERTE* HAD LEFT Greece with a Ukrainian crew and captain in April, gone to the Black Sea to pick up a legitimate cargo and then sailed to Lagos, Nigeria. From there it was supposed to travel on to Brazil to pick up sugar but instead went straight to Venezuela and reached the mouth of the Orinoco on 4 August 2000. It arrived in Puerto Ordaz the next day, where it loaded up with iron ore.

Now a week later, the boat's Ukrainian captain and crew were being sent home. They'd left Puerto Ordaz and were staying at the Tamanaco, where they settled their 'back pay' or bonuses in cash – tens of thousands of dollars in US currency – with Callisti chairman and fellow hotel guest Angelos Kanakis.[43] Luis, with a room nearby at the Gran Meliá Caracas on Avenida Casanova, had been visiting Kanakis over two nights.

An entire replacement crew of nine Filipinos and six Bangladeshis, along with a Filipino captain, Néstor Suerte, had been recruited in Chittagong, Bangladesh, by Luis's diminutive, 40-year-old Bangladeshi-Colombian colleague Jamil Nomani aka 'Indurain'.[44]After flying into Caracas from Dhaka via Amsterdam on Dutch airline KLM, the new crew was getting ready to leave that night from Puerto Ordaz for the *Suerte*'s midnight run to Rotterdam.

From the mid-1990s Los Mellizos had been moving massive loads of cocaine, hundreds of tons, on freighters from Central and South

America to Cuba, North America and Europe in one of the biggest narco conspiracies of all time. They even sold 'a lot' of coke to the Hells Angels in Canada, who were 'a big client'.[45] Some ships were intercepted but others made it. In fact, Luis estimates the cartel had successfully smuggled ten times the amount that was ultimately seized by authorities: 'About 200,000 kilos, definitely, in a short period of time. Probably ten, 12 freighters got through, *easily*. There was a lot of merchandise that made it.'[46] Jorge García had even bought an Antonov cargo plane to courier dope to Albania, from where it would be distributed by the Albanian and Russian mob for sale on the street in Eastern Europe.

But this drug run was different because the *Suerte* was coming *from* Greece, then going *back* to Europe on a route the cartel called 'Los Quesos' – The Cheese. It was so named because it ended up in the Netherlands, the home of edam, maasdam and gouda.

*

The cartel had 25 tons stored at its base in the jungle, ready to be sent out to sea. But with a single vessel only able to successfully conceal five to six tons, it was going to take the better part of a year to get it all to Europe. Which was why Luis had thought to bring the structural, architectural and engineering plans of two new ships he was proposing to buy with his Greek smuggling partner, Callisti Maritime owner Elias Lemos.

Callisti Maritime had, according to Luis, a 'very ambitious plan to buy a lot of ships' with the end goal being for four vessels to operate at any one time. The going price for a freighter was '$2 mil, $2.3, $3 mil, some $3.5'. Luis was deep in discussions with the Colombians about where they were going to build the stashes on the vessels to hide the dope and wanted there to be no disagreements or misunderstandings.

'I was in South America so the Mellizos could see what they were buying. "Are these plans good for you? Can you see that you can put in a nice stash unit in these ships? Are they adequate? *Yeah?* Everything cool? *Okay.*" And they hand over seven, ten, 12 million dollars in Europe for us to buy these two ships. We were actually looking at three ships but I took the plans for two.'

Iván de la Vega Cabás, a gopher for Los Mellizos, was his contact when he got to Venezuela from Milan that June. What Luis had expected would be a two-week trip to South America instead turned into two months. Iván, in turn, would pass the proposal on to the Mellizos' *oficina* in Bogotá, which would then send their men to board the ships and weld the tailor-made compartments to hide the cocaine.[47] But the decision to hire a whole new replacement crew for the *Suerte* in Bangladesh had irritated Luis.

'I was always against it. I said, "Fuck this shipping bullshit. We're all going to go down the drain because of the paper trail." That's the thing I always told Jorge García, who was Iván's boss: "This is going to come back and bite us in the ass." Jorge was head of operations, head of logistics, head of shipping, coordinating the shipping of merchandise to Europe. Jorge reported directly to Los Mellizos. He was the one who brought me into the Mellizos organisation.

'I said to Jorge, "Listen, this is bullshit. We'll do this freighter thing and we'll buy a couple of freighters but we've gotta buy fastboats. We should be transporting 5000 kilos on 80- or 90-foot open fishermen [boats] with three inboard diesel Caterpillars with four islanders from San Andrés that nobody knows from Adam, and if they do get busted they don't know jack shit. There's no paper trail. All they have is 5000 kilos, a big boat and four crewmembers with nothing to say.

'I knew exactly what I wanted to do: build offshore fishing boats in Brazil, bring them up the coast, park 'em up in Fortaleza, park a couple in Trinidad, and use those. If we have to, we fucking sink the boat after we give the Spanish people the dope and fly the islanders back through Cape Verde and there's no paper trail. We cannot have *crews*. We cannot have 15 fucking Ukrainians and 20 fucking Filipinos. You can't be big in an evil business and have offices like we had in Greece, in Mayfair in London, in Milan. I say to them, "Here we are dealing major amounts of cocaine and we've got *shipping offices*? We're all going to get busted." I realised later that all of this was going to fuck us up and get us into a heap of trouble. We got away from our basic roots.'

In an ideal world, Luis and Jorge wouldn't have been shipping coke out of South America at all.

'Our plan was to start plantations in Africa and avoid having to cross the Atlantic by boat and having to pay that freight.[48] Looking back now, it had all the ingredients of a clusterfuck with the Africans; too many volatile characters, too much power, money, ego. It would have been been crazier than humans could handle efficiently.'

*

The Orinoco Delta, all 43,646 square kilometres of it, full of Warao Indians, jaguars, anacondas and crocodiles, was a cocaine smuggler's paradise. The cartel had picked just about the remotest part of it: the Mariusa National Park (*Parque Nacional Delta del Orinoco*) in the centre of the delta.

'The eastern part of Venezuela was actually not even Venezuela, it was Guyana. But the Venezuelan Government claims Guyana or a big part of Guyana [the vast Guayana Esequiba or Essequibo region west of the Essequibo River, roughly 40 per cent of the former British Guiana]. The Orinoco Delta, that is *huge*. It makes the Everglades look like a little fucking backyard. There are tribes in there that are so remote maybe they haven't even seen white men. We had a "fishing station" with dugouts and fastboats; not fastboats like cigarettes, big *pangas* – 34-foot, centre console, two Yamaha outboard engines – so the merchandise would be airdropped to that area where we had that fishing station. We called it a fishing station or fishing camp because supposedly that's what they were. People there at a fishing camp, *fishing*.'

The cocaine, in hundreds of bales of 30 to 35 kilos each, would be hidden in rectangular, waterproof plastic barrels shaped like phone booths, wrapped in fishing nets and anchored under the surface of the water. To any surveillance aircraft overhead, nothing appeared out of the ordinary. The fishing camps would await their instructions to move the merchandise out to sea once boats had left the delta.

'The ships used to come into Puerto Ordaz and drop off sugar or whatever they picked up in Brazil or brought from Africa, and they would pick up aluminium, iron ore, whatever, and if you look at the mouth of the Orinoco, once you're out of there you're already into the Atlantic. It avoids that whole hot spot, which is from Panama all the way to Venezuela. That's why that area was so good.'

The operation had an apartment with a radio in Puerto Ordaz to communicate with Jorge García and his men at the fishing camps in the delta. Calls would be made in the early evening or early morning.

'The merchandise would be airdropped into the fishing camps and when you airdrop merchandise you put a little neon glow stick on the bales. So we were on the radio one day and they get on the radio from the fishing camp. We're like, "How did everything go, did you receive the airdrop? Was everything good?" And they go, "Yeah, the only problem is some of the locals, the [South American] Indians, were startled when they saw lights coming from the sky." These are Indian tribes that are very far removed from civilisation – simple Indians. They see lights falling from the sky.

'And the answer to the people in the fishing camp from the apartment, from their boss in Venezuela who worked with us, was, you know, "Give 'em aspirins, give 'em aspirins for their headache." That means *shoot them all*. So they went and killed them. It was not my decision and completely out of my hands. It's one thing to kill someone in the business – you *choose* to be involved in it – but killing totally innocent people? *No*. That bothered me. It hurt my soul.'

4

The Cab Ride

LUIS PUT OUT HIS cigarette and nodded to the bellhop that he was ready to get inside the taxi, a yellow Mazda sedan. The bellhop opened the door and Luis got in. He asked to be taken to the Gran Meliá, ten minutes away. The driver turned on the meter and pulled away from the Tamanaco. They'd gone only three or four blocks through bumpy, rain-slicked streets when he decided to speak to Luis. He was of Portuguese descent, not a *mestizo*, in his late 40s, early 50s. He'd been watching his well-dressed passenger in the rearview mirror the whole time.

'Hey, didn't I pick you up last night?'

'Yes, I think you did.' Luis had noticed when he'd got in but hadn't said anything.

'Listen, my friend. Something really weird happened to me last night after I picked you up. They stopped me, the *Guardia Nacional*, and interrogated me for three hours about who the fuck you were. They said they think you're involved in some kind of *narcotráfico*."'

Drug traffic. The *Guardia Nacional Bolivariana* (GNB) is the Venezuelan National Guard, well known for its torture of prisoners.

'*Whoaah*. I freaked out. Seeing that taxi driver twice in two nights was a thing of fate. It was unbelievable.'

In his line of work, Luis never used a regular driver for one good reason: 'Whenever you have a designated driver he knows there's some designated bullshit going on.'

He had to think fast.

'"*Man*," I said with my Mexican accent as I was Mexican at the time, "no, that's a mistake. I'm a Mexican entrepreneur here doing business in Caracas, that's an insult, that's crazy." But by now I was really scared. I could feel my blood pressure was going up. "Please stop the cab. I'm going to get off. I need to walk and get some air." I gave the guy 50 bucks, *boom*, and got out of the cab. I then called Michelle at the hotel and all the time I'm thinking to myself, 'We're being watched. We are *fucked*.'

*

It was a Code Red Antonio. How had he been clocked? *Who* had clocked him? Was the DEA in Caracas? Had someone in the cartel ratted on him? Right now, in a state of high panic in a phone booth somewhere in the teeming Sabana Grande shopping district, was not the time or place to work it all out. There was no time to even go collect his things. He just needed to fucking run.

'Call the front desk, call downstairs, tell them you're having a bunch of people coming in from out of town,' Luis told Michelle from the payphone. He was frantic but still trying to work all the angles.

'What the hell's going on, what are we . . .'

'Listen, Michelle, listen carefully: you're having some Mexicans coming in and you want to reserve a table for 12 at the restaurant. Tell them you want to make sure you have all the best champagne on ice. You might want to hire some *mariachis*. Do they know any *mariachis* in town?'

A *mariachi* band is not the first thing that comes to mind when trying to evade police but that's Luis Navia: he was thinking ahead. They were doing a classic runner.

'I knew the hotel would parlay that information to the DEA right away and then they'd be thinking, "Oh shit, the Mexicans are coming, the big guys from Mexico, this and that," so they wouldn't make a move on us right away. They'd be so caught up on this whole thing about this party that they'd be like, "Wow, this idiot's gonna bring the fucking Mexicans over, this is gonna be great, now everybody's gonna get nailed."'

Luis continued directing Michelle: 'And you come out, you give the bellhop 50 bucks. You tell him to go get roses, go get whatever. And then you say you're going to do some last-minute errands. Do *whatever.* You walk out of the hotel and walk towards the avenue and I'll pass by in a taxi and pick you up.'

'I can't believe this.'

'Shut up, Michelle. Just go with the flow. You don't understand the seriousness of this. Do as I say or we're *fucked.*'

'What the fuck, Luis? I'm leaving all my stuff back at the room, my ring, my . . .'

'You can put the ring on your finger or in the bag. Bring nothing else. *Period.* Okay, maybe your clothing. That's it.'

It was a wise decision.

'Sure enough, *boom*, I pass by in the taxi and Michelle gets in, *boom bam*, we switch taxis three times, I knew that we were being followed, and from a couple of payphones while we were switching taxis I called Iván.'

It was now approaching midnight.

'We're fucked, Iván. We are *fucked.* You have to get out of your hotel. We need to meet up and you need to get the fuck out of here. They're onto us. This is *exactly* what happened, Iván. The taxi driver told me this. You gotta understand this is *real.* A taxi driver doesn't come up with this shit just off the top of his head.'

'*Wha . . .*' Iván was still half asleep and hadn't processed the full enormity of what was going on. He just sort of groaned back at Luis, like he was crazy.

'Listen to me. The taxi driver told me. That's *it.* You can do whatever the fuck you want but I'm out of here. You can either come with me or not but I'm outta here. I'm gone.'

'Okay, okay.'

Soon enough, Iván too began panicking. There was barely enough time to get his things together. He arranged to meet Luis on the street.

'So Michelle and I picked him up and switched taxis again, *boom*, then the three of us headed down to Maiquetía.'

5

Flight to Maracaibo

CARACAS LIES AT AN ELEVATION of 900 metres. Simón Bolívar International Airport at Maiquetía is situated 30 kilometres north on the Caribbean Sea at 72 metres. Container ships are visible off the coast not a far distance from the runway. Normally it's only a short descent to the airport via four-lane highway, 45 minutes, but the trip ended up taking hours because of mudslides. Venezuela had declared a national emergency.

'At the time there had been torrential rains and unbelievable boulders, *huge* boulders, six foot, eight foot, had come down from the mountain into the port town of Maiquetía. There were boulders in the middle of the fucking town. It was a natural disaster–type situation. So we had to take some side roads to Maiquetía.'

There were no planes to catch as it was now 2 or 3am, and in any case Luis had no passport because it was missing. Not the best situation for fleeing the country.

'The way it all happened was very fucking strange. I just don't lose passports. *Never in my life*. I'd realised it was missing a few days earlier but didn't really give it much thought, although I was worried. It wasn't like me to lose my passport like that. Something was wrong. It was in the back of my head but at that point I hadn't made a decision as to what to do there yet. I was already too far into the smuggle; there was too much pressure in getting that boat loaded and out of there, so that overrode everything else. So I put it behind me but I realised they – not the DEA, the *Guardia Nacional* – must have come into my room at the hotel in Puerto Ordaz and stolen my passport. They didn't take my wallet. That's where I was before coming to Caracas.'

He'd have to wing it without his passport and try using his Mexican driver's licence. Iván knew there was a flight at 6am. Luis was already nervous enough about airports.

'An airport is a shopping centre with a runway and a police station. *Period.* I avoided airports like the plague. We found out there was a domestic flight to Maracaibo, which is closer to the border with Colombia. My plan was to go to Bogotá and go talk to the Mellizos, the owners of the merchandise. Go back to Colombia. Try to get away from these guys. There was nowhere open at four o'clock in the morning so Michelle and I check into this sex motel and open the door and the first thing I see is like this wooden horse, with stirrups and the whole nine yards. A wooden horse, for you know, getting, you know, *weird*. And I don't know what happened but Michelle and I were so, I don't know if it was the adrenalin or the fear, I don't know what got into her, but we began fucking like crazy. Three, four, five times a day when we were on the run.'

*

The trio arrived at the ticketing counter and said their names without showing identification. Maracaibo was a one-hour flight west from Caracas, just over 500 kilometres. Maicao, a few clicks past the border in Colombia, was another 130 kilometres, a two-and-a-half-hour drive in a taxi.

While they'd been fleeing Caracas, the *Suerte* had left Puerto Ordaz for its rendezvous with Jorge's *pangas* 30 miles out to sea from the Orinoco Delta. Luis had no way to get in touch with Jorge García in the jungle or Indurain, his recruiter in Caracas.

'All the time Iván and I were heading towards Maracaibo, and for those days that we were in Maracaibo, nobody [in Los Mellizos] knew what was going on with us. They didn't know what we knew. Nobody knew.'

It turned out Jorge and Indurain, on 12 August, the same day Luis had caught the taxi at the Tamanaco in Caracas, had already given the order to load the *Suerte*, which had sailed to its offshore location. However, the next day, a patrol boat of the Coast Guard Command of the Bolivarian Navy of Venezuela, thinking Jorge was smuggling contraband sugar, attempted to stop his *panga*, the *Orca*, with 3000 kilos of coke packed tightly inside along with an accomplice called 'El Negro', and another *panga* carrying 2200 kilos, Jorge's brother 'Kike' or 'Kique' and a man called Paul Perez.

The Coast Guard vessel had no idea the *Suerte* was already being monitored by the GNB, which had been patiently waiting for the cocaine to be taken aboard the ship before arrests could be made. A gun battle ensued between the Coast Guard and the *Orca*, Jorge began throwing bales overboard and with his small band of men he escaped into the mangroves, paying off indigenous people to find their way out of the Orinoco Delta. The 3000 kilos in Jorge's boat was never recovered but the second *panga* and its 2200 kilos was seized, along with six more boats, plus the cartel's communications equipment.

A five-day chase followed, with over 40 GNB soldiers pursuing the five escapees in the most difficult conditions, with tidal changes, endless mud and rising swamp water. Two cartel members left behind by the group were arrested at the fishing camps, and 16 altogether were arrested on the ground in connection to the Orinoco smuggle. If anyone could find his way out of the wilderness it was Jorge, who could fly a helicopter and was a skilled navigator. But the GNB's operation was blown. After waiting 14 hours for the drop-off that never came, the *Suerte* set course for Trinidad and Tobago with nothing aboard but iron ore.

'That's why Jorge went out [from the fishing camp] to deliver the merchandise. If he had known the extent of the fuck-up, obviously he wouldn't have been going out on a boat to deliver the merchandise to a ship that he knew was compromised. Those two days that everybody lost touch, nobody knew what the fuck was going on. Iván and I knew what was going on but we didn't want to call it in yet. We didn't want to fucking drop that pill on the Mellizos.'

Which was understandable. The GNB, led by Brigadier General

Antonio Alizo Castillo, Colonel José Antonio Paez, Division General Gerardo Daniel Briceño García and Captain Nelson Aguilar, ended up officially recovering 8800 kilos (just shy of ten tons) of cocaine in hundreds of bales from the Mellizos' fishing camps.[49] In dollar terms, about $440 million worth of blow, and that's a conservative valuation. What happened to the remaining 15-and-a-bit tons stashed in the delta is anyone's guess. The Twins were going to be mightily pissed – and Jorge, as the load's organiser, would be held personally responsible.

Either he made up the shortfall or he was a dead man.

6

Into the Black

AN OIL TOWN OF two million people with a heavily polluted lake from hundreds of oil wells, Maracaibo, in Zulia state, didn't have a lot to recommend it, but for 260 nights a year electrical storms roll in at the mouth of the Catatumbo River that empties into the 5000 square-mile Lake Maracaibo and put on the world's greatest lightning show.

Luis and Michelle weren't doing any sightseeing. They checked into another sex motel and didn't do a whole lot but eat *cazuela de mariscos* (seafood stew) at a local Peruvian restaurant while Luis waited for the Naviansky passport to be hand-delivered by his counterfeit passport lady, Natalia Hoyos. She had to fly from Guatemala City to Caracas to Maracaibo, a trip that involved a lot of connections and delays. Natalia duly arrived, Luis paid her, and she went back to Guatemala. It was disgustingly hot, August, the middle of summer, ten degrees north of the equator.

'Maracaibo's a fucking ugly city, the worst taxis with no air conditioners; it's as hot as a motherfucker. It's always hot in Maracaibo.'

Luis thought he'd successfully given the GNB the runaround and everything was still salvageable now that he had his passport, which is why he'd held off trying to contact Jorge or Indurain to abort the loading of the coke. He had no idea Jorge had been involved in a gun battle or Indurain had let the *Suerte* leave for the Caribbean.

'I knew we were hot but I thought we were going to pull it off. I was just concerned with getting my ass to safety. I was ready to cross the border.'

Back in Colombia, The Twins knew nothing, either. Or so at least Luis thought.

On their second day in Maracaibo, Iván told Luis he had run into Heiner Arias Gómez aka 'Julián', a hitman for the cartel.[50] Iván called Luis to meet him on a park bench down by the lake. He'd already organised a taxi to the border for the next day. He was scared.

'I think they're going to kill us here.'

'Listen, nobody knows what the fuck's going on,' Luis replied. 'If Heiner was going to kill you, you wouldn't be here telling me that right now. You'd be dead. And I'd be dead. We'd all be dead. We wouldn't be having this conversation.'

But if Heiner wasn't going to kill them, there was every chance the GNB would. And who else was coming for them? Luis also suspected Iván knew more than he was letting on.

'Iván was shitting in his pants because I think he knew more than he wanted to say. He didn't want to scare me that much. He knew we were fucked. He didn't want to be the one to call it in and tell the Mellizos that the whole thing got blown to pieces.'

Rattled, Luis then made his fatal mistake: calling Elias Lemos. What he didn't know was that the two calls he made from a phone booth at Galerías Mall on Avenida La Limpia were not going to Elias's mobile phone in Athens but to Paris, France. Their conversations, under three minutes, were being tapped by the authorities. Elias, already under arrest, was being told what to say on the phone.

'I had to say *something* to Elias. I had to say, "This is going to be aborted. We're fucked." I didn't know how big this thing [Operation Journey] was. The phone was on roaming. So every time I called, [the DEA] grabbed the phone call and they realised I was in Maracaibo. That first time I called, they mobilised a bunch of people to Maracaibo. They traced it from Europe. They didn't know where Iván and I were. We could have gone anywhere, we could have gone towards Guyana, we could have gone south towards Manaus on the Amazon, we could have gone towards Valencia, Venezuela. They had no idea.

'The second phone call was to tell Elias, "You're not going to hear from me for a few months, I'm crossing, and I'm going under the radar; I'm going into the black." That was my last phone call. But that one they were ready for. They really triangulated that one; they triangulated it to the phone booth at Galerías Mall.'[51]

*

It was 16 August. Luis had been on the lam, running from arrest, in Venezuela for all of four days. From the phone booth he and Michelle had gone to kill some time at the cinema.

'We were at a movie theatre and I saw some really weird activity. I saw some people at the exit doors.'

Unsettled, he went out into the lobby to get some popcorn, to see what else was going on. There was another guy who seemed to be watching him. After the movie was over, Luis went to a currency shop and bought a Bank of Scotland note because it had a whisky distillery printed on it, and Luis liked whisky. Michelle went off to do some shopping. They tried to act as normal as possible.

'I then went to the barbershop and sent Michelle to change some dollars. It was at the barbershop that these people came up to me. I was shaving my beard but keeping my moustache for a change of look for the crossing to Colombia. I was relaxing, I had my eyes closed and suddenly this guy says, 'Hey, *queda quieto. Guardia Nacional. Está detenido por sospecha de narcotráfico*.'

Translation: Hey, stay still. National Guard. You are being detained on suspicion of drug trafficking. It was the chief of security of the mall, a retired *Guardia Nacional* officer, who advised him he was about to be handed over to the six GNB officers standing behind him in khaki commando gear and armed to the teeth with machine guns.

The barber was frozen with fear. Luis had to grab his hand to stop the tremors.

'He was literally *shaking*. I thought, "This guy's going to cut my jugular." And I go, "*Narcotráfico?*"'

Luis surrendered without being handcuffed. He didn't want to make a scene. But before he was escorted from the building, he motioned to the GNB officers to come with him to a laundry room out the back of the shop where there were two washing machines.

'Listen, this is a mistake,' he said, walking backwards into the room and raising his hands in protest. 'Let's not make a scene here and let's talk. I'm a Mexican entrepreneur. I'm here on business. I don't know where you got your information but I'm sure we can clear this up. I'd like to talk to the attorney at the Mexican embassy.'

It was all a stalling tactic, of course. One of the washing machines had its door open and in his back pocket Luis had the smugglers' codewords scrawled on a piece of paper. As he was talking away, somehow he managed to slip it in unnoticed.

'If they found the piece of paper I'm no fucking Mexican businessman.'[52]

7

The Gringo

THE GNB WAS VERY interested to know more about the missing Jorge García. Iván had already been arrested and Michelle, who had wandered off in the mall when Luis was apprehended, had gone back to the sex hotel. The GNB suggested Luis call her and they picked her up. All three were being detained at the police station but were kept separated.

The *Suerte* had by now been stopped by a US Navy (USN) vessel off the coast of Grenada while refuelling en route to the Netherlands, and handed over to the USCG. It was later escorted to Galveston, Texas, where it arrived early that September.[53] No cocaine was found on board. Another ship in the Mellizos' conspiracy, the *Privilege*, again with an all-Filipino crew, had left the Orinoco for the Adriatic with a load of asphalt on 16 August and, as the target of a smaller Spanish operation called *Operación Ostra*, would be raided 650 kilometres southwest of the Canary Islands in Spain. As it was in international waters and flying the flag of the Democratic Republic of São Tomé and Príncipe, the Spanish first had to get permission from the Africans to raid the vessel.

The *Privilege* was found not to contain any cocaine, even though it was pulled apart for three weeks by the *Armada Española* (AE or Spanish Navy), *Servicio de Vigilancia Aduanera* (SVA or Customs Surveillance Service) and *Cuerpo Nacional de Policía* (CNP or

National Police Corps) on the orders of a Spanish National Audience Court judge, Baltasar Garzón, on 31 August. Over 100 people were involved in the search but could not locate the five tons they believed was on board, even though some reports suggested the cocaine had been found.

The police interview began. Luis was handcuffed to a metal chair that was bolted to a cement floor in a bare white room with blood stains on the walls. His interrogators threatened to cut him up with a scalpel, a *bisturí*.[54]

'You could *see* the blood on the wall. It didn't faze me. I mean, I was *concerned*. You know, something comes over you that just nullifies [sic] you. You're in fucking limbo. You realise your life just went down the complete drain but you're in limbo. Because if you really swallowed the whole pill of what was happening, I think you'd fucking overdose and die. But sometimes I think your body has defence mechanisms that won't let that happen. Someone with chronic high blood pressure, now that could be a situation where his pressure could go to 230 over 130 and he'd fucking croak. That didn't happen. I took it pretty good.

'The Venezuelan police were saying, "We're going to cut you up into little pieces if you don't tell us where the money is." I didn't really care. I didn't believe they were going to cut me up into little pieces and all this shit. They were playing good cop, bad cop. There was a Colombian cop who was the nice cop. The Venezuelan cop was the bad cop.'

With Luis refusing to play ball, he was removed again and put in the back of a black Suburban outside the police station. The air-conditioning was on full bore. The Colombian cop was in the front to his right, the Venezuelan to his left in the driver's seat, saying nothing, completely nonchalant. It was late afternoon and still hot as fuck, but the car wasn't moving.

'Then suddenly I looked to my right and I see this pair of fucking white skinny legs, long legs. The guy's knees were up to almost the window. And he was in shorts. And then I saw like a Hawaiian shirt, and I said, "This is it. I'm fucked. This is it. We're dead. We're *fucked*. The Americans are here. It's over. The *gringos* are here.'

For Luis Antonio Navia, 'El Senador', 'The Greek', the man with seven passports who'd been on the run for over a decade, it really was over.

He just had no idea how.

PART 2
ROCK 'N' ROLL DRUMMER

8

Silver Platter

'I'M THE LAST GUY in the world that should have gotten involved in this business, because I had no reason to. I had a great family background, a great, *great* education. I went to Georgetown University. *Jesus Christ*, you can't get better than that. I had great business opportunities. El Chapo had no other option. It was either this or he would never get rich in his life. But what happened is I got involved with cocaine in such a highfalutin, can't-say-no way that it was put to me on a silver platter. I didn't have to go out and deal with gangs, selling shit. From day one it was just put on a silver platter for me on a very big level. Such a big level we used to ship 2000, 3000 keys. You think I ever saw a key? I *never* saw a key. It was just a phone call. It was like trading on Wall Street.'

*

Luis Navia came into the world at the private clinic El Centro Médico Quirúrgico (The Surgical Medical Centre) in the leafy upmarket neighbourhood of Vedado in Havana, Cuba, on 27 August 1955. Vedado was the most exclusive part of town and his parents, Luis Navia y Cuscó and María S. Bonavia, had a huge apartment, a whole floor, to welcome their first child. But three years later, with the addition of a sister, Laura, the Navia family had an even bigger spread, upgrading to a 5000 square-foot two-storey house at

Calle 194 entre 15 y 17 in Biltmore, a new residential area north of the city.

The sale price of $280,000 was a lot of money at the time but still less than his father, Luis Sr, would earn each year in bonuses. María was charming, vivacious, good-looking, doting and much younger than her husband – 14 years younger. They were a beautiful and well-to-do Cuban family and hardly had to lift a finger with eight full-time employees, including three maids, two chauffeurs and a butler. The two kids even had their own individual nannies.

It was a charmed existence for Luis Sr, befitting someone who was the right-hand man to legendary sugar magnate Julio Lobo y Olavarria, very likely at the time the richest man in Latin America with an estimated fortune of $200 million.[55] Lobo's flagship company, Galbán Lobo Trading Company, was the largest sugar-trading concern in the world in a country whose backward, agrarian economy depended on the price of its sugar exports.

The 'sugar-wolf of Cuba', as newspaper *The Panama American* called Lobo in 1956, owned over a dozen sugar mills; had offices on Wall Street; a huge portfolio of assets in land, telecommunications, insurance and shipping; an enormous art collection; as well as arguably the world's best private collection of Napoleon-related items; and even boasted his own bank, El Banco Financiero SA.

Luis Sr was less flamboyant in his spending than Lobo but equally cultured, with an appreciation for good tailoring and the finer things in life, a trait that would be deeply ingrained in his only son from an early age. Born in 1908, Luis Sr had risen to his lofty position as Lobo's confidant from a lower-middle-class background, starting at Galbán Lobo at 13, qualifying as an accountant, and becoming vice-president by 1957. He also served on the boards of the Bank of Nova Scotia and the Royal Bank of Canada. He had impeccable English because he was often sent to New York for work.

'My dad was the real person behind the everyday business that Julio Lobo trusted with making intelligent decisions; not his relatives by blood who didn't have brains that were caught up in their high-society shit. My earliest memory is in the kitchen in the house at Biltmore with the employees. I've got pictures from the day I was born. The photographer that was in charge of taking pictures of me and my sister built a house on what my mother paid him just to take pictures of us.'

It was an idyllic childhood in mobbed-up, swinging, pre-revolutionary Havana, and Luis spent many days playing and swimming at Playa Varadero, east of the capital, or dancing around the living room to standards 'El Manisero' and 'El Bodeguero'. But he was too young to be aware of the political and criminal dimensions of doing business in Cuba.

*

In 1956, notorious East Coast mobster Meyer Lansky, friend of Charles 'Lucky' Luciano and Benjamin 'Bugsy' Siegel, famously known as the 'mob's accountant', sent his emissary, Boston lawyer Julius E. Rosengard, to Cuba to get part-financing for the 21-floor, 378-room, $14 million seaside Havana Riviera on Malecón and Paseo, complete with casino.

Cuban dictator and Lansky's friend Fulgencio Batista through the country's national development bank, *Banco de Desarrollo Económico y Social* or Bank for Economic and Social Development (BANDES), was underwriting most of the construction costs. Batista had made Lansky an advisor on gambling reform in 1952 and, like the true crook he was, was getting paid off in millions of dollars in bribes a week. The hotel and casino opened on 10 December 1957.[56]

Rosengard, one of Lansky's inner circle, an accountant and Lansky's 'gambling representative' according to the FBI, was also treasurer and a board director of the Compañía de Hoteles La Riviera de Cuba SA, the front company for the project. Bugsy Siegel posthumously sat on the board. So Julius was duly referred to Luis Sr and the financing he sought was arranged, including an injection from Lobo's bank, Banco Financiero. The American and the Cuban went on to become good friends. So good that Luis Sr loaned Julius $120,000 of his own money over two instalments in 1957 and 1958, an enormous sum, to which Julius stumped up his wife Emma's jewels as surety.[57]

'Julius and my dad developed a strong friendship aside from their business dealings. My mother and Emma also became very close. My dad was never involved in any illegal activity or had any association whatsoever with Meyer Lansky and he didn't need to. He never mentioned any funky business. Julius and my dad bonded because of the type of people they were: extremely discreet right-hand men behind the scenes. This is my thinking. You know, you gotta keep somebody clean. If not, it's a clusterfuck.

'Julio was the outgoing speculator; my dad was the conservative administrator making sure things didn't go out of whack. My dad was a very conservative man. He was always well cashed. He didn't go out with hookers. He didn't have gambling problems. He was a clean-cut, hardworking guy. He was totally dedicated to Julio Lobo and Galbán Lobo. He was of impeccable moral structure.'

Either way, the timing of Luis Sr's business dealings with Rosengard was unfortunate. By New Year's Day 1959 Cuba was a communist state in the hands of revolutionary leader Fidel Castro. Batista had fled with his cronies to the Dominican Republic and then Portugal, along with planeloads of loot. The party for the mafia in Cuba was over – as was Julio Lobo's sugar empire.

'The last sugar mill Galbán Lobo bought was the Hershey Corporation mill outside Havana. I have letters written by my dad of him telling Julio Lobo not to buy the Hershey mill because of the trouble with Fidel.'

Lobo wasn't having it. He had even sent money to the left-wing rebels in their early days, not knowing how much he was accelerating his own demise.

'Navia,' said Lobo, as he referred to his friend by the patronym, 'that kid Fidel we will manipulate like a puppet.'

'No, Julio, you are wrong. The situation is worse than you think, and it's too late to handle that puppet.'

Luis Sr was right. Castro, Che Guevara and the guerrillas rolled into Havana on 8 January 1959 on their US Army–surplus military jeeps. Casinos were trashed. The writing was on the wall for Galbán Lobo. Soon, the hotels and casinos that had sprung up all over the capital in the 1950s were nationalised by the state and Lansky's prize jewel, the Havana Riviera, was wrenched from him. Gambling became illegal. By early 1960, Luis Sr had made up his mind and booked a flight to Boston.

'My dad left to have a doctor's check-up for a heart ailment and never came back. He claimed he'd had a stroke. He conjured the whole trip as a ruse to leave Cuba without raising suspicion – he wanted to start setting things up in the States for the eventual exile he knew was coming. Julio stayed in Havana a little longer. My dad knew at that point they were fucked.'

That October, Lobo rejected an offer from Cuban Central Bank president Guevara to become Minister of Sugar in exchange for all but one of his mills and his residence. The Hershey Corporation mill Luis Sr warned him not to buy would be appropriated by the state, like practically everything else privately owned in Cuba.

'Fidel Castro was never a communist. He was just out for himself. Julio knew that he was going to be offered the position by Che Guevara and discussed it with my dad and whomever was giving him the backing he needed at the time. And they both had decided to refuse. They knew that a meeting was scheduled but no date and time was given. Suddenly Julio gets a call at two in the morning and goes to the meeting and refuses Guevara's offer.

'Guevara had received him in his office with his boots on the table, wearing the green military pants and a "wife beater" T-shirt, which Cubans call a *camiseta*. Julio was shocked because he had no regard or respect for the stature of the man he was receiving. Julio took a heavy hit – from [a fortune of] $200 million down to maybe $20 to 30 million he had offshore. That's what I've heard. Batista was the big one; since he knew what was coming, they say he took $300 million out of the country.'

Two days after his meeting with Guevara, Lobo left Cuba for good, leaving most of his possessions, including his Napoleonic collection, behind. He would end up dying in 1983 with comparatively very little in an apartment in Madrid.

9

Tom Sawyer Land

AFTER A FEW MONTHS of being settled in Miami along with 100,000 other Cuban émigrés, Luis Sr called for his family to follow him. Luis estimates his father managed to get out with about $600,000 to $750,000 in cash, plus various accounts held in his name in foreign banks.

On 22 May 1960, María, Luis and his lookalike 15-month-old sister Laura flew to Florida on Pan-American Airways accompanied by two maids, and booked into Cabana 41 at the Key Biscayne Hotel and Villas. At the time Key Biscayne, a paradisiacal island connected by a causeway to Miami, was an area largely made up of World War II veterans and dotted with retirement villages, but is now one of the most expensive residential areas in the United States, with some homes worth tens of millions of dollars. What used to be a favoured destination for senators and presidents is now a hub for rich South Americans.

It was quite the introduction to American life. In Cabana 40, right next door, then Vice President and Republican candidate Richard Nixon would recuperate from his close 1960 electoral loss to Democratic candidate John F. Kennedy. On 14 November that year, less than a week after the poll, President-elect Kennedy visited Nixon at the hotel. Luis Sr and Nixon had come to be formally introduced by Cuban-American Bebe Rebozo, Nixon's best friend and the owner of the Key Biscayne Bank. The three became friends, Nixon later bought two homes next to Rebozo, and the Navias attended the 1968 presidential inauguration of Nixon, the same year Luis's parents became American citizens, conferring those rights on their two children.[58]

When not in Miami, the Navias holidayed with the Rosengards in Hyannis Port, Massachussetts, not far from the Kennedy family compound. María was afraid of flying so they would catch a train from Miami to Boston, where they were picked up by the Rosengards' uniformed chauffeur in a black Cadillac Fleetwood limousine. Luis's memory of those days vacationing with the mob lawyer is a fond one.

'Julius and Emma had a house on the shore of Nantucket Sound in Cape Cod. Julius's pastime in Cape Cod was painting and he had his studio he called "Camp David", after his son, in the back on the house. They gave me one of those little red wagons called a Radio Flyer and we built it with one of the nannies that they had at the home.'

But throughout Luis's childhood his father remained a distant parent. Luis Sr was busy all the time, travelled a lot for work, was not quite present when he was at home, and put an emphasis on education and study rather than play. Of course, this meant that Luis both idolised and feared his father, who enjoyed fine Scotch whisky but was never drunk. He carried himself as a total gentleman at all times and always wore impeccable attire. Galbán Lobo's New York trading office, Olavarria and Company, kept an apartment year round at the five-star Sherry-Netherland on Fifth Avenue until 1962.[59]

'Always the best suits in New York. Tailor made. Ties from A. Sulka or Countess Mara. Shirts all monogrammed. Handcuffs. Not handcuffs, cufflinks [*laughs*]. With me, they had to handcuff me. My dad always stressed an education. Never did he mention money. My dad never spoke about money. *Never.* It was my mother who always put a lot of value on money. That I got from her. Greed was instilled in me by my mother. My dad was a very serious man. He had a great sense of humour but I am very much like my mother. Probably a little bit too much.

'If I would have had my dad's seriousness I would have been better off in life. My sister's totally like my dad. She demands respect. I'm like my mother. My mother used to joke around all the time. I was a fucking pain in the ass. If she said be home by six I'd be home by eight, because I was out swinging from trees into Pines Canal, spearfish hunting in the flats, riding my bike with my friends. I was always out there. I never did homework. My mother used to come after me, hit me, throw something at me. Are you kidding? My dad, all he had to do was *look* at me.'

*

In 1962, Luis Sr and a group of exiled Cubans partnered with local American sugar growers to form the Glades County Sugar Growers Cooperative in Moore Haven, Florida. The coop had 50 members, 280,000 acres of land under ownership and 150,000 cultivated with sugarcane. Luis Sr was comptroller (chief financial officer), vice-president and head of marketing for the refinery, Moore Haven Sugar House.[60] Its success earned the attention of the local mafia, but old connections made in Havana put paid to any extortion.

'They were going to market refined sugar all over Florida, which they did under the name Sunshine Sweets. Green Brothers was the exclusive broker to distribute the sugar. [Florida mobster] Santo Trafficante Jr wanted some kind of "in" because obviously this was a big deal. My dad really didn't want that whole situation, didn't want that weight on his shoulders, so he asked Julius for advice and Julius went to Meyer Lansky, obviously, and went to bat for my dad so that there was no involvement from the mob in Tampa.'

Back under the swaying palms of Key Biscayne, Luis was enrolled at Key Biscayne Elementary School and Laura at Little Island Playhouse Pre-School. The Navias had bought a house at Harbor Court near the yacht club. Luis was spending a lot of time in the pool learning how to swim from Dick Cutrera, a local swimming instructor.

'The first thing Cutrera tells me is, "Never go off the high board. Don't even go off the *low* board." Sure enough, first thing I did was I went off the high board. You tell me not to do something and I would find a way to do it.'

At school he was no less rebellious. One incident saw him sent to the principal's office.

'One guy was picking on me in third grade. Lynn Morris. We were eight years old. I was always a little guy. I never had problems with anybody, because I was a little guy but I got along with everybody. My personality was my sword; it has always been my sword. I could use it to gain and I could use it to defend. But one day Lynn Morris was bothering me, *really* bothering me, so, you know, back then you had to ask permission to go to the teacher's desk to sharpen your pencil. So I asked permission, I got up, went, sharpened my pencil, Lynn Morris was sitting in front of me, and as I was walking back from the teacher's desk I went *whaaaack* with my pencil and stabbed him in his left leg, in the shin. The pencil went inside his leg. *Boom*. That was like, shocking. He never bothered me again.'

Luis wasn't expelled. Along with his friends he took out his frustrations on the local wildlife.

'We would have been reported to the Humane Society. We used to take like lighter fuel and throw it on frogs and light them on fire. We used to take lizards and hang 'em and light them on fire. We used to go hunting rabbits, snakes, racoons. They call it animal abuse. It was just normal back then. We were living on Key Biscayne. It was wilderness. We always had BB guns and slingshots. We'd ride around on bikes with BB guns and shoot somebody's window. It was like growing up in Tom Sawyer Land.'

10

Grams in Georgetown

LUIS EARNED HIS FIRST dollar putting up chairs for $5 at the local church, but in the ninth grade at the all-boys Belen Jesuit Preparatory School, age 14, he first learned the economics of supply and demand.[61] His parents thought he was being 'an entrepreneurial young man'. The priests didn't agree.

'I would take a couple of dozen sandwiches from home and make seven, eight dollars. Back then that was a lot of money. Every day. Ham and cheese, and some were more expensive, so I put in a *croqueta*, which is a Cuban croquette. I used to sell those things for like 50 cents. Between 35 and 50 cents, you'd come home with eight bucks. Then the priests busted me and they didn't let me sell any sandwiches anymore. So then instead of taking ten sandwiches I'd take five and charge more for those five.

'Belen was a great school. My dad had the money to pay for any university I wanted to go to. But I never liked studying, I was never turned on by studying, I never thought study would get me anywhere. I didn't see myself as an accountant, attorney, doctor. I just saw myself as a businessman. I was a disciplinarian's nightmare. Without studying, without doing any homework, without doing jack shit, I got Bs, Cs, a couple of Ds, like in math, because I really hated math. Algebra, I never understood that shit. If I'd done an hour a night, I would have been Bs and As, without a doubt.'

Around the tenth and 11th grade Luis began growing out his hair, playing drums, and smoking high-grade marijuana from dealers who had smuggled it in from The Bahamas. For summer-vacation money, he worked at AAA, the emergency road service, taking calls. He and his friends would spend weekends getting stoned and watch the sunsets over Biscayne Bay. Music was a big part of his life. The first record he ever played on a phonograph was 'I Want to Hold Your Hand' by The Beatles.

'What impressed me about The Beatles wasn't really their music or anything; it was just the fact they were young and they were millionaires. The thought that 20-year-olds were *millionaires*? That really got me into it. "Playing drums should be a good thing." So I started to play drums. I was always into hard rock. Santana. Pink Floyd. Jethro Tull. The Who. Kinks. Led Zeppelin. The Beatles. Rolling Stones. Cream. Blind Faith. Jeff Beck. Rod Stewart. That was my thing. I never went for Barry Manilow.'

He wasn't much of a reader, but Mario Puzo's *The Godfather* left an impression.

'Man, that really grabbed my attention. I said, "This is where it's at. This kind of fucking life, this kind of *power*, this kind of money." It thrilled me.'

His first official girlfriend was Claudia Betancourt aka 'Clau', a 'hot item' with 'a great body and dynamite ass' from one of Key Biscayne's Cuban families who he'd met at the yacht club, around the age of 12. They spent their afternoons and weekends in paradise, waterskiing on Biscayne Bay or boating with Clau's father, Omar, to The Bahamas.[62] But a girl called Liz Francis claimed his virginity at 15.[63] She had green eyes, looked 'like a little Liz Taylor' and they went together to the senior prom.

'The Cuban girls didn't put out. Liz lived five blocks from me. She was more liberal about having sex and I was getting more action from Liz. I always worked my personality big time. I wasn't a super-good-looking guy. I wasn't tall. But I always had a girlfriend. I never had problems in that department.'

By the end of high school, he was back with Clau. When she turned 20, it happened: she finally put out.

*

Luis graduated as a senior from Belen in 1973 and was accepted into the University of Miami to study business and accounting. His proud father celebrated the achievement by buying him a 1973 Chevrolet Malibu. Luis Sr, still sensing there was some hope for his son, promptly took his only boy to New York to meet the law firm Milbank, Tweed, Hadley & McCloy, 'the top lawyers in the nation, the lawyers for the Rockefellers'. They stayed at the St. Regis on 55th Street and Luis Sr would take Luis for veal scaloppine alla marsala at his favourite restaurant, L'Aiglon.

'No matter who I've ever dealt with in the drug business, none of these guys measure up to the people my dad dealt with. He dealt with ambassadors, Wall Street, big people in the sugar trade. He was in a whole different ball game. Even though I was in an evil industry, cocaine, I dealt with the most powerful people in *that* industry. That's a power trip. Let's say you're in the computer business and you deal with Bill Gates or Steve Jobs. Or you're in finance and you deal with Warren Buffett. In my world every day when I woke up the people that I dealt with were the leaders of that industry.'

The following year, 1974, Luis enrolled in his first classes at UM and took to collegiate life, even running for senator, a student government position nominally representing 1000 undergraduate students. He lost by two votes. But any studiousness was shortlived.

'I took a snort with my older cousin. We were at his house for Thanksgiving and we went to the back where the pool was and he said, "Try this." It was definitely a picker-upper but the reason I mostly enjoyed cocaine was the euphoric-type feeling I got when you drink and snort. The cocaine counteracts the drinking, you wake up and you can drink more. When I started snorting I stopped doing the pot.

'Your mind is a lot more complicated than your body. That's why coke is so amazing. Forget your body. It's your *mind*; that's what it really takes over. People don't understand that because they don't ever get enough good coke. Coke really hits your mind; that's why Edgar Allan Poe snorted. When you snort the real shit you actually get to a state of euphoria or as close as you can to euphoria.'

Luis's parents hadn't lost hope. A Cuban historian friend of theirs got Luis into prestigious Georgetown University in Washington, DC in the summer of 1974, through the proverbial back door.

'There was an opening in the Portuguese department. It hadn't filled its quota. So I sneaked in through the Portuguese department and ended up mostly taking business courses, which is what I liked. So I was a Portuguese major but taking mostly accounting and business courses.'

Luis never went to Portuguese class and to this day doesn't speak Portuguese. But speaking Spanish at home each day in Key Biscayne had made him bilingual. At Georgetown, he made his first coke deal.

'I had a connection in Miami and I knew a guy that sold in Georgetown. I had a friend of mine bring up nine ounces [255 grams] and I sold them. Back then that was an *amount*; not everybody had nine ounces. I made $700, $800 an ounce. I didn't cut 'em or anything. It was just a straight handover.'

He also dropped out. He was 20 years old. The Malibu had been totalled in an accident. He'd stayed in Washington all of a year and a half. It was 1976.

'It was such a fucked-up major that classes were at 7.30 in the morning. Back then I was smoking pot with my roommates from Ecuador and shit. Who the hell was going to wake up at 7.30 in the morning? Like an idiot I partied and hung out with my friends. Everybody around me was becoming a professional. All my friends were very grounded; they knew what they wanted to do and the direction they were going in. I didn't have a solid compass pointing to where I wanted to go.

'I was never convinced that schooling was the answer to my success. My grades weren't that great so my dad called me back to Miami: "No more Georgetown for you. Come back because you're not taking full advantage of what you should and you're just out there on your own. Time's up."'

11

The FM Scam

His dad was right. Options were fast running out for Luis and so were his chances. He took some accounting courses at Florida International University (FIU) but failed to graduate. He did, however, show some aptitude for selling drugs, both at FIU and his first adult job, assistant bookkeeper, at Top-40 radio station WMJX Stereo FM or 96X. It serviced the Miami–Fort Lauderdale area. His business card read, 'Luis Navia, Jr, Accounting.'

'I would buy the ounces in Miami for $1200, cut 'em, and send 'em up to Boston to my friend who used to pay me $1800 for 'em. At 96X, I would log in the commercials, and the [air] times, and then the bookkeeper would price it and invoice it. As assistant bookkeeper, they would give me the log sheets for when a commercial ran [on air] and I had to log it in to another sheet. But I was never at my desk for the bookkeeping and I was always inside the music-production part of the radio station with the DJs and the station program manager, because that was the fun part. I always fulfilled what I had to do but I spent a lot of time with the DJs.

'I'd buy a pound of pot for $300 and then ounce it out and make $600, and then sell those ounces to the radio station employees, DJs mostly. I went to see Led Zeppelin with one of the managers and when Robert Plant came out on stage we had like a fuckin' ounce of cocaine with us and we were right there, and *boom*, that was unbelievable.

We were the only people with fuckin' cocaine like that. We had a dozen girls with us.'

On weekends he was partying out. Luis and a group of friends had taken a six-month lease on a house on Key Biscayne in front of the Sonesta Beach Resort. A young Andy Garcia, who'd go on to be a Hollywood star, would drop by.[64]

'We had a big 96X party at the house with the 96X band and we bought these large garbage cans and we filled them with all kinds of liquor and Kool-Aid and we put acid in there and fuckin' next day there were fuckin' people spread out, passed out in the neighbour's yard, people passed out all over the fuckin' neighbourhood. I found a chick in my closet a day later. She was still passed out. It was crazy.'

*

At the time, 96X, '100,000 Watts', was trailing behind competitor Y100 (WHYI) in the ratings and the pressure was on to lift listener share in order to be able to charge more per minute for commercials, which was how radio stations delivered profits to their owners. Then Luis got involved.

'96X lost their licence because of me. The station ran some contests that weren't actually living up to what they claimed to live up to. At the time, radio stations were rated in their market according to the Nielsen Audio [Arbitron Radio] survey books.'

Over 2700 such books were mailed out to random addresses in Miami–Fort Lauderdale each ratings period by Nielsen, asking households to fill in their radio-listening habits and then mail the books back. One afternoon, Luis's very good friend and former Belen classmate Jorge Lopez called him at the station.

'I received four Nielsen books. What the fuck is this? You must know: you work in a radio station.'

Jorge's whole family lived with him and they'd received not one but four April–May survey books at the one address. His mother listened to classical music, his dad to Cuban music, his brother to hard rock.

'I said, "What? From *Nielsen*? Oh, my God, Jorge, this is fucking *gold*." So I went to the station and I said, "Hey, my friend has four Nielsen books. He's willing to put down that the whole fucking family listens to 96X from morning to midnight." What I wanted out of the deal was I asked for $5000 and I think I got $3500 in cash; quite a bit of money. Jorge got a rug and furniture for his house; we got a bunch of [free] Marantz amplifiers. We sold some of the Marantz amplifiers so I walked out of there with $6000. When people asked, Jorge said that he won a "contest".'

The four adulterated survey books actually made a difference. The Lopezes wrote down that they listened to 96X around the clock and 96X went from a 3.2 listener share to 5.7 in the survey and #1 in the Top-40 category. From charging $40 a minute for commercials, 96X FM's owners Bartell Broadcasting could now ask for $120. It was a perfect scam.

'Then suddenly the rumour started to spread that Nielsen had jigged up the books, and sure enough it came back to the station. Bartell owned six stations and Bartell was owned by Charter Broadcasting, a public company. The general manager that ran 96X was Mort Hodgson; his father was one of the founders of Charter, a really rich family from Atlanta. So he never got fired but he had to call it in that there was funky shit going on with the books.'

Hodgson, who was general manager, blew the whistle on his own station on 14 August 1978 to the Federal Communications Commission (FCC), the national body that regulated American radio broadcasting and which had already been investigating 96X for ethical breaches since 1975. On 18 January 1978 a preliminary decision had been made not to renew 96X's licence for 'repeated misconduct in nine contests over a two-year period'. An FCC administrative law judge had labelled 96X's contests and giveaways misleading and deceptive. This was the last straw. Luis was fired, along with two senior executives. In September, industry magazine *Record World* reported a 'part-time bookkeeper' was the culprit. Nielsen reissued the surveys and ordered they be taken again.

'I thought they were going to come down on me with some kind of FCC charge because they found out it was me. I was the one who rigged the whole thing, so that's when I left to fucking Ecuador for a month with my friends from Georgetown. I went to Guayaquil and, *fuck*, what a great place to go. On Holy Week we went to

Lima, spent a week there, partied our brains out and came back to Ecuador.'

An unforgiving FCC finally revoked 96X's licence on 14 February 1981. The last song it played on air, amid the DJ's tears, was The Beatles' 'The Long and Winding Road'.

12

Deathtrap

After the 96x fiasco and his Sundance Kid getaway in Ecuador, Luis had landed a job as a salesman for New England Mutual Life Insurance of Boston and things were looking up. So on 25 August 1978, two days before his birthday, Clau decided to throw her boyfriend a welcome-home party.

'I was just sitting on the sofa, had a drink in my hand, and in through the door comes this girl. White. *Stunning.* Red curly hair. You know, *whoaah.* Bra-less. Fuckin' great tits just looking atcha. Gold chains, gold Rolex, beautiful green Thai silk dress . . .'

The whirlwind's name was Bia Gálvez: 28, a mother of two with an exotic accent, a head of tight ginger curls, arched eyebrows, a perfect nose, a strong bust and a wide smile: like a young Susan Sarandon.

'I mean, *wooow.* Just *sexual.* She was off the fucking wall. Bia was about six years older than me and we started talking and before you know it, we said to each other, "What are we doing here? Let's get out of here." And she left behind her date, Carlos, and I left behind Clau, and we went straight to her apartment on Brickell Key.'

Just walked right out. They didn't emerge for two days.

'The first thing I fell for was his sex appeal,' Bia remembers. 'Luis was a very smart man, fun to be with, a gentleman, a great lover.'

'We woke up the whole fucking neighbourhood,' laughs Luis.

'Went into the shower, broke the showerhead, broke the soap tray. She was too much for me to handle; too much at the same time. It was a pretty fucked-up thing to do [to Clau]. The next day Carlos was like, "I'm going to get that son of a bitch." But when he found out who Bia was and who protected her, he definitely calmed down real quick. We never heard from him again. I don't really know what I told Clau. It is what it is. Shit happens, man. It was instant fucking lust with Bia. It's a big wound for Clau. I feel real bad about her. I don't know how to ever make it right to her.

'I grew up a bit of a spoiled child. I was a rich kid from Key Biscayne. I was always frivolous about what I was going to do. I wasn't set in my ways, like, "I want to be a lawyer or a doctor." I wasn't the happiest camper. I was selling *insurance*. Not taking advantage of Georgetown was a complete fiasco. My life was a trainwreck. But then I met Bia and it was instant love and lust. Later it was money. The lifestyle, the coke, the exoticness. I was the perfect candidate to be swept off my feet and derailed. She was a deathtrap and a lovetrap at the same time, and I don't regret any of it.

'Back then, my mother thought Porfirio Rubirosa was the ultimate playboy. He was a Dominican who married Ava Gardner. He lived off rich women. So here I am, living the young man's dream to meet an older woman with a lot of money that's gonna teach him sex and you're gonna learn life through the eyes and in the arms of an older woman that's *experienced*. That's a dream come true. Three years after I met her I already had $5 million.'

*

'I need to go to San Francisco,' Bia told him in bed. 'Will you join me there?'

'I've got work but I figure I can skip a few days. So sure, yeah.'

'You don't need to pack anything, Luis. We'll buy whatever we need there.'

Bia hailed a cab to the executive airport at Palm Beach International, 120 kilometres north of Miami, and Luis went along for the ride, promising to meet her out west in a few days' time. A Learjet was waiting when they arrived.

'I saw some big, round, football-type things wrapped up inside the plane. Bia said it was "raw emeralds" from Colombia, still embedded in the rock. I had never seen a kilo before. I only dealt in ounces.'[65]

It wasn't the time to ask any questions.

When Luis flew to San Francisco on a later commercial flight, Bia, as she had promised, dressed him on arrival, buying suits and ties from expensive boutiques. They got a room together at the St. Francis, a five-star hotel in Union Square. In the city, Luis met a man called Brian Livingston, a wealthy *bon vivant* in his early 30s who liked to get stoned on weed and buy properties up and down the northern Californian coast. Brian, who Luis describes as 'a gentle soul, like a big teddy bear, a very good man', gave them a Dodge Magnum to drive at their leisure.

After a couple of days, Bia took Luis out to Sausalito, where they parked in front of the Golden Gate Bridge at dusk. Eddie Money's 'Wanna Be a Rock 'N' Roll Star' was playing on the radio. They had a bottle of Dom Pérignon and a couple of champagne flutes. By now he'd twigged as to what was really going on.

'Listen it's not emeralds. It's cocaine,' Bia told him. 'This is my business. Are you willing to stay with me?'

Luis looked out at the lights on the bay before turning to face her. His life was about to take a critical turn.

'Bia, I always wanted to be a rock 'n' roll drummer and, fuck, this is a lot better than rock 'n' roll.'

And that was when Luis, just 23 years old, a failed career in radio behind him, a fledgling salesman for New England Mutual Life Insurance, fell in with the Medellín Cartel, the most violent criminal organisation in the history of the world.[66]

PART 3
BISCAYNE BANDIDO

13

La Mona

BIA AND LUIS ENDED up staying a month in San Francisco, flitting between their hotel in Union Square and Brian Livingston's apartment in Sausalito, with its collection of museum-grade Persian rugs. Their host had a background in Thai stick and hash, but after the mid-1970s like a lot of marijuana dealers he realised there was far more money to be made in cocaine.

By the end of 1978, he was not just one of the Bay Area's biggest cocaine dealers – he was a pipeline to the insatiable coke market on the West Coast, where profits were even better than Florida. Brian was also about the best contact it was possible to have: he had a solid reputation for being an honest operator, he wasn't violent, he paid on time and he paid well.

'If Brian would have been a typical coke dealer,' says Luis, 'this thing could have gone sour real quick.'

Everyone was making money. Luis's new girlfriend was making so much money that when he suggested to Bia that it might be time to go back to his day job at New England Mutual – as he explained, technically he hadn't taken leave or given notice and they'd be wondering where he was and what he'd been up to – she bought a $1 million life-insurance policy right on the spot so that he wouldn't have to go back empty-handed to Miami after being out west for a month. The premium was $30,000 a year and she took two years on a monthly payment plan.

'This should tide you over for a while with these idiots,' she said.

When eventually Luis returned east, he duly got a trophy and was named Salesman of the Month – ironic for a man who was selling life-insurance policies to the Medellín Cartel. New England Mutual sent him to its headquarters in Boston to do a special course. He even managed to sell another million-dollar policy to a Jewish businessman from Panama. He was on a roll in his personal and professional life and it had all started with the most fatal of attractions.

*

Bia Gálvez was born in 1949, grew up in the islands of the Netherlands Antilles, was of Dutch-French background mixed in with Venezuelan, and descended from a long line of liquor and cigarette *contrabandistas*: smugglers. To this day there's a boulevard in the capital of Aruba, Oranjestad, named after her grandfather who made the family fortune.

Her father, Roland, according to Luis, 'owned a bar in some whore town called San Nicolas in Aruba' and Bia admits: 'Our relationship was not so good. He was very conservative and old-fashioned; though a very good man with a good heart.'

But her formative teenage years, the 1960s, had been spent in Colombia's second biggest city, Medellín, with her mother, three sisters and brother. According to Luis, Bia was a wild child, totally 'off the charts', who'd gone to school with nuns but now she was in league with the devil: the Medellín Cartel.

'When I was 13 I went with my twin sister, Andreina, to a boarding school in Medellín,' she says.[67] 'My mother and the rest of the family moved there later on when my father bought a house. I stayed four years in that boarding school and after I finished school we lived at my father's house. It was there I began meeting people [from the drug world]. We were the generation that tried to change society: Jimi Hendrix, Janis Joplin. We used to escape from our home in Aruba to go to parties.'

After graduating from school Bia moved back to Aruba for a period, then returned to Medellín, marrying a Colombian called Manolo Varoni when she was 19. She bore him two children within two years. The relationship didn't last but in Medellín Bia met an American marijuana dealer, Peter Sharwood, who was dating her sister.

Sharwood and his business partner, Marcos Geithner aka 'Sy', later became customers when Bia moved to San Francisco in the mid-1970s and 'began working with Fabio Ochoa Vásquez and some other guys' selling cocaine. All she will say about her introduction to Ochoa, one of the most powerful narcos of all time, is that they met through a 'friend'. Her two kids stayed behind in Aruba with her family. At the time the going rate for a kilo of cocaine was roughly $65,000 in California and from Bia the pair 'bought a lot'. On each kilo she was making $5000 profit clear, so half a million dollars on each consignment of 100 keys.

The man she worked for, 'Fabito', wasn't just anybody. Not only was he one of the five most powerful figures in the Medellín Cartel (alongside his two older brothers Jorge and Juan David, Pablo Escobar and José Gonzalo Rodríguez Gacha aka 'The Mexican') but Luis says Fabio and Bia were close.[68] They became even closer when Brian Livingston joined her client list out west, along with his business partner David Patten.[69]

At 28, Bia moved to Miami. Fabio Ochoa was living in Coral Gables in southern Miami and Bia began dating one of Ochoa's first cousins. When they broke up, she was introduced through another 'friend' to a fresh source of supply or 'SOS': Oscar Peláez Monsalve aka 'El Poli' (The Cop).

*

About 173 centimetres tall, light skinned, handsome, solid and muscular, with a broad nose, straight brown hair and deep-set, dark-green eyes like a clean-shaven Waylon Jennings, Poli was a mysterious cartel figure from Medellín who'd got his nickname in that city for a number of reasons: he'd actually been a policeman, killed a lot of people as a policeman, and, after retiring and joining the cartel in the mid-1970s, he killed even more people, including policemen. He and Bia began working together immediately.

'He called me "La Mona". I was Poli's distributor, not his friend. But with the Ochoas there was some friendship.'

Poli, like Pablo Escobar, wasn't a pure narco: he was a rarer breed of criminal: a *bandido*, a bandit or outlaw.

Says Luis: 'Pablo Escobar never said he was a *narcotraficante*: that's what TV said he was. Pablo always said, "*Soy un bandido.*" And he *was* a true *bandido* in the good sense of the word: a very tough motherfucker. But Poli was a known *bandido* in Colombia before Pablo. Poli had a few years on him too. The attitude of a *bandido* is: "If it's out there and I want it – I'm *getting* it." These guys [like Pablo] were just playing at being narcos. If you aren't born a criminal, you're never going to become a criminal. You may do criminal activities, but deep down inside the real criminal's a criminal from the heart, not from his activities.

'A *bandido*'s a guy who'll kidnap you, kill you, *whatever*; he's just a badass. He doesn't need money to be a badass. He's a badass because he was *born* a badass. The people that were in the cocaine business back then were the lowest of the lowest of the lowest. You had to be a fucking criminal motherfucker to be in that business.'

And Poli more than made the grade as a fucking criminal motherfucker. Coming from a 'full-on Medellín' background – a broken home in a low-class *barrio* – Poli got into cocaine circa 1975/'76. When he first arrived in Miami in 1978 as an illegal immigrant off a boat from Bimini, he was doing piffling kilo deals with Cubans. Bimini, a chain of islands in the western Bahamas, was the cartel's favoured jumping-off point to Miami, because Colombians didn't need a visa for Panama, and from Panama they didn't need a visa to get to The Bahamas. It was also only 92 kilometres away from the United States: an easy trip for people smugglers.

'At that time in the late 1970s, cocaine still had not reached the elite American consumer. It was dog eat dog. Poli survived that business in Colombia, came to America, and started dealing with the Cubans. They'd try to rip him off and he'd kill them. He was not psychotic; he was just very determined and possessed a functional mind. He had very strict rules and you didn't cross the line on his rules.'

But after meeting Bia, he was selling 100 keys in California to Brian Livingston. It was a mutually beneficial arrangement. Poli supplied and protected Bia. She provided him with a client that couldn't get enough merchandise. He didn't need to be moving more. Poli's style was to keep a low profile, kill a few people, remain a *bandido* and stay under the radar, all while making serious money.

'He'd hit the fucking jackpot,' says Luis. 'Poli was just cruising. He was not giving coke to any Cubans. In Miami back then, there were a lot of ripoffs and piece-of-shit types willing to rip off anyone – even Poli – to make a fast buck. They'd be king for a week or a month at max. He didn't need to be dealing with Cubans in Miami, or Colombians for that matter.'

Bia was also the ideal middle person. For Poli, she meant 'less heat or no heat'.

'We were never close,' she says. 'Poli protected me because I made money for him. That's the biggest reason. My life was completely separated from [the cartel]. Poli was only a supplier, not a friend. He was a real gentleman to me. But he always protected me from everything; he didn't want heat on me.'

For an emotionless killer with an iron grip, Poli had a tremendous sense of humour and loved to laugh. Having grown up in Medellín, Bia had a tough personality and could fend for herself, but Poli wouldn't allow any harm to come to her and would kill anyone who tried. Even so, she knew the business relationship had its limits – and drawbacks.

'When people knew Bia was working with Poli, nobody wanted to work with her, because they knew they could have a problem with Poli,' says Luis. 'You didn't fuck with that guy. He was a different breed. His look and the way he carried himself just let you know that he was not a person to mess with.

'It was like that scene in *Hannibal* when Hannibal Lecter picks up the FBI agent Clarice Starling in that pig pen surrounded by those Italian man-eating hogs, and the hogs just back away from him. Poli had the same presence as Hannibal Lecter; he instilled fear. So Bia never went to work with him on a daily basis. She knew that with Poli you should hang out with him for maybe five minutes, ten minutes, then count your blessings that you didn't get fucking shot up while you were with him.'

14

Sucking Tit for Milk

THE END OF THE 1970s and the beginning of the '80s was the high point of the market price of coke in America, and nowhere more than California. The US–Mexico border had yet to open up to cocaine smuggling and allow the future Mexican cartels a direct pathway from Tijuana to Hollywood.

By the time Bia was selling to Brian Livingston, a consignment of 100 kilos was fetching over $60,000 a key. That in turn would be broken up into half-kilos and sent to other dealers in all corners of the United States – Nevada, Hawaii, Alaska – where it would be cut multiple times to amass enormous profits once it reached the street. As an example, a kilo that cost $3000 in Colombia could be worth $250,000 once it had been cut. For that $6.2 million of cocaine, Bia paid Poli the wholesale price of $55,000 a key. That worked out at $700,000 profit for Bia from just one plane trip.

Poli in turn was getting much of his coke at cost price of $45,000 plus freight from José Antonio Cabrera Sarmiento aka 'Pepe', a major mover of merchandise in Florida, as well as having Pepe bring in Poli's own merchandise at $2000 to $3000 a key plus freight. Pepe would routinely load up his Merlin with 500 keys and fly from Colombia to an airstrip in Okeechobee, a two-hour drive from Miami.[70] As a high-ranking member of the Medellín Cartel, Pepe was one of the richest cocaine smugglers of the era but, fatally for him, one of the most indiscreet. He wore a bracelet that had 'PEPE' spelled out in diamonds. He paid for Rolls-Royces and yachts in cash. This flashiness saw him come up on the radar of US law enforcement and he spent most of the early 1980s being arrested, skipping bail, indicted, on the run or in jail.

'Pepe was under the umbrella of Medellín,' says Luis. 'He had his own cooks in kitchens in Colombia where they produced the coke. He was 47 years old back then. Poli was in his 40s too. So both men had been around for a long time [in the business] and were independent branches of the cartel. Poli had his own tailor-made cocaine manufactured in Colombia and he would bring it in Pepe's plane. His stuff was marked "357" because of the .357 Magnum he carried.

'So if we sold 150 kilos, 75 was Pablo Escobar's, 50 was Pepe's and 25 was Poli's, because Pepe also transported for Pablo. When Poli hooked up with Brian, he was selling a lot of Pepe's merchandise. But Pepe's loads were usually around 500 to 700 keys because he had a Merlin and he'd come straight in. On those he was doing 250 to 300 for Pablo and 50 for Poli. Pepe would take Pablo's shit and give it to Pablo's own distributors in Miami and just charge them a transport fee.'[71]

One of the cartel's distributors was Griselda Blanco Restrepo aka 'La Madrina' (The Godmother), a sociopath made famous by various documentaries and films. She would eventually be gunned down outside a butcher shop in Medellín in 2012 after being deported from the United States.

'Griselda came from very low on the social totem pole. At the beginning she was a distribution/sales arm for Medellín; an important sales outlet. But I'm sure she brought in some units of her own on the trips they sent to Miami, and she had other ways of bringing her own merchandise through other contacts she had that had routes into the States. Not too many people had transport routes. The Medellín Cartel and the Cali Cartel had the routes [into the United States] and anybody else that had transport was transporting for them. The people that were running transport from the northern coast of Colombia were mostly doing it for Medellín. There were not too many independent *oficinas* at that time.

'Then as Griselda grew and the volume of sales grew, she started feeling she owned Miami and the people in Medellín started to cut her off. She created her own sales and distribution organisation here in the States. She was head of a complete organisation with sources of supply in Colombia. The money got to her head so she started problems with other groups and came into conflict with Pablo. Then she killed a cousin of the Ochoas: Marta Saldarriaga Ochoa. Griselda made a lot of money and when you invest your money in problems and in conflicts, your problems and your conflicts are as big as what you invested in them – if not bigger. She invested a lot in creating havoc and vendettas.

'In truth, she was built up to be more than what she was. Griselda was scared shitless of Poli and his group. She knew that before she was even born, Poli had already killed 22 people in Medellín, half of them cops. Griselda wanted no part of Poli. *Nobody* wanted any part of Poli. If he went right, she went left. It was like a contest between a fucking tiger and a tied-up donkey. She knew she was on the losing end of that one. She may have the most violent, the most psychopathic [of the narcos in Miami], but Poli had further reaches into old Medellín; deep, *dark* Medellín. She knew that no matter how many people she hired she could not get to Poli. But he could get to her. She respected him. They both came from Medellín, but he was already killing when she was sucking tit for milk.'

15

Blue Boxes

The Medellín Cartel is thought of in the west as having always been under the centralised control of Pablo Escobar, but in reality it was a loose agglomeration of suppliers and transporters, all of whom were ferrying loads for each other to the United States.[72]

'It was a bunch of entrepreneurs *from* Medellín,' says Luis. 'The moneymakers in the Medellín Cartel were the Ochoa brothers, The Mexican, Fernando "El Negro" Galeano, Gerardo "Quico" Moncada, "Mono Abello" [José Rafael Abello Silva], Pepe Cabrera, Carlos Lehder, Pablo Correa, and the Pereira group, which was Octavio Piedrahíta – a transporter for Medellín who owned a football club in Pereira – Fernando "Marulo" Marulanda and "Mono Lopera" [José Vallejo Lopera]; I worked with all these guys. It was loosely knit but it was tight between Pablo, the Ochoas and The Mexican. The others were transporters or earners.'[73]

Escobar, as was his arrangement with Cabrera, would simply request a certain amount of weight be carried on routes to the US mainland. Escobar freighted his own coke on his own planes – the cartel was said to have as many as 55 planes at its disposal – but he also muscled in on other smugglers' routes and, if they didn't cooperate, he had them killed.

'If someone had a good route Pablo would go to them and say, "Take 200, 300, 500 kilos of my merchandise on your route."

You're not going to say no to Pablo. I was doing it with El Negro Galeano. He was my main contact and introduced to me by a friend of mine [from the cartel], Luis "Miki" Ramírez.'

Ramírez was an earner for the Medellín Cartel. He'd started out in the late 1970s/early '80s buying coke from Leticia, the southernmost city in Colombia and the capital of the department of Amazonas. He was also a close associate of Leticia cocaine heavy Evaristo Porras Ardila aka 'Papá Doc'.[74]

'Obviously part of that merchandise was Pablo's. When you got to be a certain size [as a trafficker], you got a phone call. Pablo was *Pablo*, don't take anything away from what he did. He was feared and he was a hell of a guy. But there were people that were there in Medellín before you even mentioned the Medellín Cartel.'

Like Bia's supplier, Poli. Says Luis: 'He was the only guy who ever defied Pablo.'

This was not an insignificant thing. The cartel's Jorge Ochoa once told PBS television program *Frontline*: 'You couldn't confront Pablo Escobar, because you knew what would happen: you would die.'[75]

'When the heat came down on Pablo, he called Poli to help him on a job,' explains Luis, who heard the story secondhand through an intermediary. 'This was later, in 1991. What I heard was Pablo wanted Poli to kill somebody for him and he had no reason to kill the man. Poli said, "No, you've got the wrong guy. I'm not for hire like that." Pablo started to get a little feisty and Poli said, "You know what? Let's end it right here. You take mine" – and he gave him his gun – "and I take yours and let's go for it. Right *now*." And Pablo says, "*No, no, no, no, no. Tranquilo*, settle down." So that was that. Pablo almost got offended but he still respected Poli.

'Now the way I see it is that Poli did that just to remind Pablo, "You can't have me kill for you with all your bodyguards and all your money. Remember who I am, because with me, it's one-on-one. If that's the way you want to go right now, that's the way it is with me. It's *you* and *me*. Forget about all these fucking bodyguards. For you to be at my level, it's got to be you and me if you want to do it like a man.

'Now if you want to do it like a fucking pussy or a chicken, then you can have your bodyguards kill me. But if you want to do it the way you know it's done, the way you know I've lived my life, then we're going to die under the rules of my life, which I know you understand is *our* life: the life of a *bandido*." Anybody else, Pablo would have fucking shot him right then and there. But he had too much respect for Poli. Being a *bandido* is a whole other culture.'[76]

*

The amount of money being made by the cartel was staggering. Production costs on a kilo of cocaine were minimal, about $1200 to buy 500 kilos of coca leaf from farmers in the Andes to turn into paste, then base, then refined cocaine or cocaine hydrochloride in its kitchens. In 1978/'79, a million or a million-and-a half pesos would buy you a kilo of pure cocaine in Colombia, around $3000. Getting it to the United States cost another $5000 per key. But once in Florida, it sold for upwards of $40,000, much more if you got it to New York, Los Angeles or San Francisco. By 1980, the price in Miami was $50,000 and each year it seemed to be getting higher. So there was astronomical profit to be made even before the cocaine was cut.

'Pablo Escobar, the Ochoas and The Mexican formed a group: The Mexican was the military arm of Pablo; Pablo with his cousin Gustavo controlled a lot of routes and under them were Pablo's partners Fernando Galeano and Gerardo Moncada; and then the Ochoas established the first distribution networks in the States. The first cocaine that arrived in Miami came wrapped in duct tape in the shape of soccer balls. If they were airdropped they'd be put in a plastic-type condom and also wrapped. Geometrically that's not the most efficient way to pack.

'The Ochoas came up with the idea to do boxes, which packed neater and maximised space on any plane or boat. So Pablo handled part of the organisation, the Ochoas handled the distribution, and The Mexican handled a lot of the kitchens and labs and the military part of it. And then they each *grew* themselves. The Mexican had clients, routes and suppliers of his own. Pablo also had suppliers and kitchens of his own, which he shared with the Ochoas and The Mexican, just like The Mexican shared his kitchens with Pablo. They were all interwebbed but they each had their own private routes that they didn't share with anybody.'

In 1984, after the cartel saw its processing plant in the jungle, Tranquilandia, burned to the ground in a Colombian Government raid, The Mexican started his own kitchens, making the purest cocaine available anywhere.

'The Mexican probably had more money than all of them at one given time. He was a fierce, *bad* motherfucker. He was worse than Pablo. He had very good cocaine. Each brand [of cocaine] belonged to a different group and these brands gained recognition because of how good they were. The Mexican had "Centavo" and "Reina"; those were marks of cocaine that hit the market. They were *fantastic*. So then [the cartel] all went under the Centavo brand. Of maybe 3000 kilos of Centavo, a thousand belonged to Pablo, a thousand belonged to The Mexican, and a thousand belonged to the Ochoas. The Medellín Cartel had the blue boxes, *las cajitas azules* – everybody wanted the blue boxes. In fact, blue boxes were so in demand other groups started to pack their merchandise in blue boxes. They were all having a great run and the market got flooded.

'Medellín wasn't the only cartel but it was the *major* cartel. The Cali Cartel was functioning but not as heavy as it did in the late '80s, early '90s. In the early '80s it was the Medellín Cartel, without a doubt. The Mexican was going to nail Cali. If they didn't shoot him first they had to bring in United States helicopters to get rid of him.[77]

'What made Pablo really wealthy was his association with the Ochoas, which opened up the cartel's distribution. You can't do everything yourself. The best example of a group that ran their business with administrative skills and business acumen are the Ochoas. They were the most level-headed and smartest. They didn't let the money go to their heads in a totally reckless way. They were able to make the money and keep it. Since Fabito had come to the United States and lived in Miami, he initiated the distribution inside the country and he had a lot of contacts for the sales. But then since everybody wanted cocaine, after a while *everybody* had cocaine contacts.'

16

Stalin in the Flesh

Luis was in way over his head surrounded by such hardcore criminals, but he didn't care. He was having the time of his life being Bia's live-in companion at Brickell Key while miraculously still holding down the insurance job.

When one day Poli brought 100 keys to Bia's apartment in a bunch of suitcases, he met Luis for the first time. They got on immediately, Poli enchanted by Luis's trustworthiness and sense of humour, Luis in awe of Poli's confidence and swagger.

'He was a very dangerous man. Poli wasn't serious; he was *very fucking dead serious.* I thought it was *fantastic.* Hang out with really cool people that have the power of life and death over other people? Make millions of dollars? Fucking pretty cool. I never got scared with Poli and killing people. Not that *I* killed people, but I knew that he did that. I didn't know exactly *when* he was killing people. It wasn't my call.

'I'm not going to kidnap kids but if we had to kidnap someone because he didn't pay, yeah. Poli killed people because they owed him money, because they did something wrong. He wasn't just randomly killing people like a psychopath. If you go to him, and you take five kilos from the man and you don't pay him, you know, you *should* be shot. You knew *exactly* what you were getting into.'

Not everyone in the cartel liked Luis, though. Bia had made an acquaintance called Joel (pronounced *ho-el*), yet another ex-cop from Medellín who was very close to Poli and also working for the cartel in Miami. Luis describes him as 'a volatile person, a wildcard, a wild, crazy sonofabitch. Those guys in Medellín were the scum of the earth – fucking killers. They'd whack people every day. They were from the low end of the totem pole and had risen on that totem pole by not being nice guys. At that level nice guys end up dead.'

Poli wanted Joel accompanying Bia on her trips out west and she wasn't happy about it, but they began travelling together by plane. Cocaine would be sent from Florida to California by car, and they would fly over to arrange sales and collect money. Joel was primarily there as 'protection'.

'I had seen Joel in some places in Medellín,' says Bia. 'We were not friends but he used to go sometimes to discos that we went to. It was a surprise to see him in Miami. I never knew his last name.'

Tensions boiled over on a selling trip to Los Angeles.

'They got to the LA Hilton one day,' says Luis. 'Joel was a good-looking guy, always well dressed, with expensive clothes, but he was rough around the edges and he spat on the rug of the hotel. Sometimes he was whacked out of his fucking brain [on cocaine]. But no matter how whacked Bia was, she never lost her cool. Bia got pissed and she told Poli and Joel got mad. One day [during the trip] Joel was high as a fucking kite and he left behind a fucking briefcase with $250,000 in the lobby. The bellhop had to retrieve the briefcase for them.

'So Bia had certain complaints against Joel: that he was a pain in the ass to travel with because he got a little drunk on the plane, sometimes a little obnoxious, a little loud. So Joel told Poli, "Why don't we whack Bia and we keep the client?" Poli said, "By no means." He told Bia, "You continue working with Brian and Joel will also work with Brian, but *separately*."'

What Luis wasn't to know was that when Bia had bought the life-insurance policy from him, she'd done it not just to help him out but because she actually believed she was going to get killed by Joel to take over her connections on the west coast. He found this out much later through Bia's brother, Arturo. In truth, the only thing truly stopping Joel killing Bia was Poli, who was even scarier than Joel – if that were possible.

'Joel was a very low-class person,' says Bia. 'He dressed sharply but he had no manners and I told Poli that I didn't want to travel with him anymore. Joel didn't like it but Poli told him if he did something to me he was a dead man, so I never heard from him again.'

*

The way Luis describes being with Bia, life – and Miami itself – opened up to him like a pop-up book.

'It was like a dream. Nothing in my life was mediocre. Suddenly everything's possible. You want a fucking house in Monaco? We can have a house in Monaco. Just got to do a couple of trips. Everything was possible. What made life difficult was no longer a problem, which was *money*. Money was never a problem. Anything you wanted, you bought. You never had to ask the price. When you don't have a budget, it's amazing. Gifts. Watches. Jewellery. Clothing. You hopped off the real world. Miami in the '70s and '80s was restaurants, nightclubs – Regine's, Ménage, The Mutiny, Alexandre, Faces in the Grove, Scaramouche, Cats, Ensign Bitters – champagne, cocaine, dancing, disco, *fucking*. It was like another planet. I hopped on this fucking spaceship and went to another planet.

'Miami was *crazy*. There was a side to Miami, the "cocaine cowboys" shit, and I was right in the middle of it and didn't even know it. I'd lived a very sheltered life. I didn't even know black people. I didn't even know Hialeah. I was hanging out on Key Biscayne with Key Rats [a term for people who grew up in Key Biscayne]. Then I met the most beautiful girl, the richest one, and the most dangerous guy. These guys, Poli and Joel, were real gangsters. Money's money whether you rob banks or hijack planes. It's your *business*. But Poli was worse than all of the other cocaine cowboys put together. Bia told me, "This guy has a reputation *from* Colombia."

'Poli wasn't just some fucking idiot that hopped on a boat and came to Miami and killed a couple of guys the other day because they stole a couple of kilos. No, this motherfucker had killed a lot of people *in* Colombia. He'd killed a lot of policemen because the most corrupt people in Medellín were the cops. He was feared *in* Colombia by the people that were feared *in* Colombia. So I knew that with Poli I was with, fuck, Stalin himself in the fucking flesh. And that gave me such a *feeling.*

'He was one hell of a fucking guy. Poli's word was his bond. You make a promise to God, and you fail it, lightning hits you. He was the cat's meow. He feared nobody. He'd pull out his gun and if you were quicker, all the power to you. If not, you were down. And he'd just leave you there like nothing had happened. He did not fool around. If you owed money 11 o'clock Tuesday and it didn't come around, he didn't give a flying fuck about the money. Poli always had money; he could take money from someone else. You can keep your fucking money. You're *dead.*'

17

Disco Champagne

Luis hadn't been with Bia for long, just a matter of months, but his long-suffering parents had come to accept their long-haired, tearaway son was lost to the dark side. It was the early months of 1979 and there would be no salvation in the insurance job for Luis. Their attitude was to embrace him rather than disown him altogether.

'[*Sighs*] They kinda, you know, they kinda *suspected*. They knew something was going on. I wasn't doing a 9 to 5. But they felt it was better to keep me close than throw me out of their house. I was never a well-grounded person. I didn't ever have strong convictions: I want to study hard, I want to be a doctor because I plan to have a family and get married and I think by the time I'm 45 I should have my own practice and when I'm 60 I'm going to retire because I want to buy a yacht. *No*. I wasn't thinking about *tomorrow*.

'So they were worried, very worried, obviously. They didn't know the extent of it, by no means. Not even the fucking law knew what we were doing. So they knew I was being kept and that I was living with Bia. She helped disguise it a lot, put it that way. Nobody figured that Bia, a woman, could be a big-time cocaine dealer. She was just a rich girl from Aruba, and I was with her.'

The law, however, did catch up with Luis.

'I was in a black Porsche 911 SC Targa with a guy called Randall Ghotbi in a backstreet in Coconut Grove, going to Brickell to Bia's apartment.[78] We were partying in The Grove. Randall was from one of the richest Jewish families in Iran. The Shah had just been kicked out, the Ayatollah came in and the Ghotbi family came to Miami and to New York. They pulled $400 million out of Iran.

'Bia and Jorge Lopez were in one car, and Randall and I were in the other. And I get pulled over by the cops and we had, like, an ounce of coke on us. I gave it to Randall and he dumped it out his window. I got taken in for DUI. So Randall goes to Bia's and tells her and Jorge that I'm at the station, and that's when Bia opened up a briefcase with like $300,000 in it – bundles and bundles of hundreds in rubber bands – and sticks her hand in and gives Jorge a wad of cash, "Get him out." *Boom.* Jorge goes down to the station and bails me out, but then we have to go back to that area in The Grove to look for the ounce of coke. And we found it.'[79]

*

It wasn't long before Luis managed to fuck up a good thing with Bia because of his major weakness: women. Bia was out west in San Francisco and had left him the keys to her place at Brickell Key.

'She found out that I fucked this real-estate lady. I rented an apartment for Poli close by on 1450 South Bayshore Drive and Brickell, and I invited her to Bia's apartment and Poli was there. We were having a party, snorting coke and drinking, and Arturo Gálvez, Bia's brother, ratted on me: he told Bia that I was having a party at the apartment and fucking a girl. Bia dumped me.'

It was their first fight but Bia, to be fair, was entitled to feel aggrieved: Luis had had sex with another woman, his real-estate agent, in Bia's own apartment. They got back together briefly but the relationship was too high octane on a daily basis for it to survive long term.

'There was a lot of physical sexual attraction so that always kept things going. We argued over petty stuff but mostly we were just enjoying our partying together. We would go to dinner and drink and then come home and continue drinking and snorting and have great sex. Then the next day we would be hung over and then relax. It's not like life was hectic and we had a lot of things to do all the time.

We'd just wake up and do whatever we wanted. We were constantly shopping for her kids, who were living with their grandmother in Aruba. We were enjoying life all round and travelling to New York to San Francisco to LA to Aruba.'

Bia found another boyfriend, a cocaine trafficker from Santa Marta in northern Colombia, and ended up moving to Lake Tahoe, on the border of California and Nevada.[80]

'I always wanted to keep Luis out of all that, as well as doing drugs,' she says. 'Mostly it was a good relationship but I ended it because he drank too much. I loved Luis but I couldn't handle the trouble he created. My life and business were completely separate. There were too many dramas due to alcohol. I always had a soft spot for Luis in my heart, but couldn't accept the way he drank and got crazy. Then there were the incidents at Xenon in New York and Faces in Miami. He got kicked out from both clubs.'

For Luis, his nightclubbing life is all a bit of a blur. He went with Bia to the world-famous Studio 54 on West 54th Street in New York before it closed in 1980 but says, 'I got bored and I went to sleep in some bleachers they had upstairs. Everybody who ever went to Studio 54 makes a big deal out of it, but I really didn't see it as that big of a deal: it was just a disco like any other disco. Great music, lights flashing and weird people walking around. What I really wanted to do was fuck Bia in the balcony area and since Bia didn't want to fuck I decided to sleep. I think I'm the only guy that ever went to Studio 54 and took a nap.'

Luis can't recall what happened at Xenon (like Studio 54 a super-trendy nightclub but on West 43rd) yet remembers what happened at the private Faces in the Grove at Mayfair Mall, Coconut Grove, south of Downtown Miami.

'We got so whacked out on Dom Pérignon, well, I did, that I started dancing on the dancefloor, took off my shirt, start swinging my shirt. Then suddenly I go to our table, I take the fucking bottle out of the champagne bucket, put it on the table, and take that bucket in the middle of the dancefloor, and just go, *whhhaaa*, threw all that ice on the dancefloor and everybody starts to slip and fall. It was raining disco champagne.

'And they suddenly turn on the lights and the bouncers come in and they grabbed a friend of mine, Jaider Esparza, and they just picked him up and threw him against a brick wall [*laughs*] and he had nothing to do with it.[81] Bia and I slipped out like nothing.'

She was singularly unimpressed.

'I don't like that type of behaviour. I don't like scandals. That was the main reason our relationship ended. At Xenon Luis got kicked out for the same reason as Faces: he threw the champagne bucket with ice-cold water and ice to the dancers to cool them off. After I left him and he began to work with Poli, he began to do drugs.'[82]

'Two party animals cannot blame it on each other,' says Luis, trying to remain philosophical about a woman whose primal sexual fire haunted him for decades. 'Bia broke up with me because, for a person like me, it's not good to be with a person like her. For a person like Bia it's not good to be with a person like me. We just fed into each other's craziness. That's *reality*.

'So I moved out of Bia's, took a studio apartment at 2100 South Bayshore Drive and went to work with Poli. He was actually *with* me when I was fucking the real-estate lady. *He* wanted to fuck the real-estate lady. I said, "No, no, this is my girl." He said, "I want to tell you something. Friends are to keep. Girls are to share." The bodyguard who was there with us, he thought Poli was going to shoot me, because I had denied him the right to fuck this girl.'

It was the start of the best training Luis could ever get in the coke trade.

'I never changed as a person. I guess I was always amoral when it came to money. But I never thought about it. When I met Poli, if it would have been anyone less, maybe I wouldn't have gotten into the business. In a way I was enchanted by his sense of "strictness to a code" – *you don't pay you die*, for example.

'A life of extremely high danger among extremely dangerous people comes with some magnetism. I was romanced by the danger but not *part* of the danger. These people put me in a *trance*. And it was the basis for the 25 years that I was never scared and never thought I would get arrested. I thought that feeling was going to last forever.'

Bia's new boyfriend, meanwhile, got busy with a pair of scissors.

'The guy turned out to be complete fucking idiot,' sneers Luis. 'He was so jealous that he went through all Bia's photo albums and cut me out of every photo she had. Every picture of Bia and me together, he cut me out. You know how many girlfriends I've had in my life and they've had ex-boyfriends? You think I ever cut a girlfriend's ex-boyfriend out of a picture? What a fucking *asshole.*'

18

Drive, He Said

WORKING FOR POLI AS a chauffeur was a straightforward job. He needed someone who spoke English, had a driver's licence, owned a car and 'didn't look like a lowlife thug'. But Luis's new boss wasn't Miss Daisy. If Poli ever got pulled over by the police, Luis explains, 'There would have been a shootout immediately. He wouldn't have handed over his licence. He would have given them a .357 fucking Magnum bullet in the head and driven away.'

It was a tense time to be a drug trafficker in Miami. At 2.30pm on 11 July 1979, two Colombian assassins in a 'war wagon', a Ford Econoline van with gunports, painted with the words 'HAPPY TIME COMPLETE PARTY SUPPLY' on the side and filled with weapons, bullet-proof vests and ammunition, pulled into the parking lot of Dadeland Mall in Kendall, in southern Miami, got out and coolly walked into Crown Liquors, where Luis and Bia used to 'buy two, three thousand dollars' worth of liquor for the apartment. Cases of Château Haut-Brion 1964; I mean, *unfuckingbelievable* wine.'[83]

They immediately opened fire with machine guns, killing Colombian fugitive Germán Jiménez Panesso, 37, and Dominican bodyguard Juan Carlos Hernández, 22. Morgan Perkins, 18, a store clerk caught in the crossfire who attempted to escape, was again shot in the car park while the gunmen were making their getaway. It was a bloodbath. Dade County assistant medical examiner Dr Charles

Diggs told *The Miami Herald*: 'I started counting bullet holes in one of them – and gave up.'[84]

Bia, knowing Luis was already becoming intoxicated by the business, had a word to Poli to protect her former boyfriend and not let him get killed.

'She asked Poli to take care of me. She felt, *fuck*, if I was going to be out there [in the coke business] it might as well be under the wing of a guy that's not going to let me get taken for a ride.'

So Luis, behind the wheel of a four-door silver Lincoln Continental, became a driver in a three-piece suit 'like an insurance salesman' with his New England Mutual card on him at all times. If he had to talk to the cops, 'I was an innocent-looking guy.' He remembers his first day.

'I picked up Poli from Charter Club [condominium] on Biscayne Bay, where he was living. He had just gotten up. He had showered, was in his boxers, and he had one of the girls putting talc on his feet, like a valet, helping him get dressed. He was very pampered. "La Rola" was his best friend; she was his confidante.[85] He trusted her with his life. But he had young girls with him all the time; they were sex companions.

'Poli would dress, like, *unbelievable*: a blue suit with an open silk shirt, a vest, and a fucking gold chain with a solid-gold jaguar with two emerald eyes. He'd wear one of those blue velvet hats; a Patek Philippe thin gold watch with a nice gold ring, a diamond pinkie ring. Almost dressed like a pimp. Not my style. You see this guy, you'd say, "What the fuck?"'

Each subsequent day followed a loose routine: Luis picked up Poli at 10am and they had a typical Colombian breakfast – a thin *arepa* (flatbread) spread with a little butter and a sprinkle of salt and accompanied by a drink of hot chocolate – in whatever apartment he was staying in.

Poli kept apartments in Charter Club, Key Biscayne and South Bayshore, alternating constantly for safety. He was well aware the heat was on him. Florida's biggest law-enforcement agency of the time, the Dade County Public Safety Department (later the Metro-Dade Police Department), had recently formed, albeit only to shut down four weeks later, an 18-man Special Homicide Investigation Team – the

'SHIT Squad' – to probe 24 drug-related homicides involving Latinos going back to November 1978.

A Latino policeman from the unit known only to Luis by the name Poli gave him – 'El Colorado' (The Red One or Red), for his red hair and Irish looks – was causing trouble and had raided one of Poli's apartments, hauling everyone inside for questioning down at the station – including Poli's children and the maid. It was all part of a Miami-wide police harassment policy, but Poli was apoplectic at this mortal affront to his dignity. It was now personal between him and El Colorado.

Armed with nothing but service-issue .38 calibre revolvers or .45 Colt semi-automatic pistols – unlike the movies, there were no long guns or shotguns stored under blankets in the trunks of their cars – Miami cops were poorly equipped for a war with Colombians toting machine guns, but all the more determined.

'I knew Poli had a battle with a Dade County cop called El Colorado. Colombians back then would hire lawyers after being arrested or taken in for questioning, but Poli never hired a lawyer after El Colorado hauled him in. He must have been so humiliated he ordered a hit on El Colorado instead. Poli moved every three months. He slept in one place one night, another place the next night.'

After breakfast, it was off to a meeting.

'Poli was never on time. If you told Poli, "Listen, we'll meet at McDonald's on 79th Street at 11 o'clock," he'd show up at one. It's because by being late for so many meetings he avoided getting killed so many times. He never hung out with a lot of bodyguards. He was very smart that way. He knew that alone he'd hide better and he'd keep a lower profile. He kept it "small" and that's part of the reason he never got killed in Miami. It was hard to find Poli.'

Lunch was usually at Mike Gordon's Seafood Restaurant, Joe's Stone Crab or The Forge 'and we'd spend $1000, $2000 like nothing', staying for hours and sometimes ordering four bottles of Château Lafite. Luis would have a couple of toots with his boss after lunch and they might go shopping.

'Poli would go into clothing stores and buy $8000 worth of clothes. He just said, "Drive," and I drove.'

When it was time to drop off Poli, they'd have dinner together and hang out a bit before Luis went home to sleep. He'd come by the next day and start all over again. When he wasn't chauffeuring Poli, he'd run errands.

'He once had me go to the airport to pick up some fucking duffel bags in a locker that were full of grenades and silencers and machine guns. So I went to the airport, looked around, made sure everything was good because I'm not a fucking idiot, I know it's not fucking Bibles, I opened up the locker, pulled out the duffel bags and here it is. There were no metal detectors. It was 1979. You could walk in an airport with a gun back then. I made sure nobody followed me on the way back. He said, "Did you look inside?" and I said, "No." And he asked me, "Didn't you wonder what I was sending you to pick up?" I said, "I don't wonder." My job was not to wonder. That was a big test.'

Other times Luis would work as a drug mule in tandem with Bia's brother Arturo and a third person (whoever was available) on cross-continental commercial flights. They'd take three kilos apiece when there were small quantities of merchandise to move out to Brian Livingston. There were no sniffer dogs to contend with. It wasn't the age of sophisticated airport security, even though a quarter of all seizures of cocaine were happening at Miami International Airport.

'California was the ticket. It was just as profitable as bringing it from Colombia to Florida. We would take keys on Eastern Airlines in suitcases and in hand luggage to Brian. Anything we got [from Poli], 12 kilos, 15, 20, 30, we'd send to California. If it were a low amount, he'd send me and Arturo and one more [mule], each of us with three, four kilos, on a plane, hand luggage, *boom*, nonstop to San Francisco, we'd give Brian 12 kilos.

'Arturo was white, a good-looking guy, *young*. Poli wouldn't put on a [South American] Indian-looking dude or nothing like that. We flew separately, Arturo and me, although the same flight, different tickets. On the plane we acted like we didn't know each other. I always dressed sharp, trying to look like an insurance guy. Coat and tie; I would use a blazer. You wear a blazer and people think you're an Ivy League guy. A blazer's the best disguise. You can do anything with a blazer. You wear khakis and a blazer and you can rob banks.

You don't even need a mask. They'll just look at the blazer. They don't look at your face. Blazers are amazing. If you ever want to do something criminal, wear a blazer.

'Back then you could just wrap the shit up, like if it was a Christmas present, in your carry-on bag and take three kilos and put it through the X-ray machine and you'd continue. We put it through the machine, and that's it. I was never afraid. Went to Miami airport, Eastern Airlines, hopped on a plane, put it through, *boom*, gave it to Brian, checked into a hotel, waited three, four, five days for him to pay us the money and we'd come back.

'While we were in San Francisco, we'd go to restaurants, party and wait. If I was nervous I wouldn't have done it. It was just the right time, the right place. If you did that five years later, you'd be fucking shitting in your pants. But back then nobody knew about this shit. One time coming back from San Francisco, I had $230,000 in a box that I checked in as hand luggage, and [airport security] looked at it, they put their hand in, they saw it was money and they let me go. It was another *time*.'

19

Ballad of a Well-Known Gun

LUIS WAS ALSO SAMPLING Poli's own product: by the key. After following such a set routine with his employer every day, he developed a coke habit of his own: sharing eight to ten grams a week between four to six people. This was not street cocaine; it was the best of the best in Colombia. He'd only been working as Poli's driver for a matter of months, but already made a few hundred thousand dollars.

'It was pure, it was there and it was part of our lives. We would never run out. It was just shit you took out of a kilo. Grab a bunch, put it on something, chop it up, *let's go*. It was part of our going-out routine, drink, next thing you know, you're doing a couple of bumps.[86] It was great for sex. You do lines when you buy shit off the street and it's so cut you gotta do a line. Poli would never, *ever* do a line. That's bullshit. That's shitty coke. We would *never* do lines. We were taking it right from the kilo.

'Poli would take it with his two fingers, go like that [*sniffs*], that's it. One in each nose [*sniffs twice*]; that was pure shit. You don't care if you drop some on your shirt. You just shake it off. Or if there was some shit on a table because we were partying, a little spoon or a little knife, and the tip of the knife [*sniffs*], that's it. I never saw anyone roll up a [dollar bill] and do a line. Fucking do a line of that shit and your fucking eyeballs would pop out.'

And even though he and Poli were around each other constantly, and came to consider each other as friends, Luis was made to never forget who he worked for.

'Sometimes he was tough with me. The day I dropped $100,000 playing poker with him, I told him, "I'll pay you this afternoon," and it was like three in the fucking morning when I said that. The afternoon was in what, like, *nine* hours? And sure enough, Poli didn't go to sleep. Enrique, his brother, came by my apartment that morning to tell me, "You'd better get your ass over there with 100 grand. Oscar hasn't gone to sleep. He's waiting for you. For him a gambling debt is more *sagrado*, sacred, than any kind of cocaine debt. He is fucking furious, Luis. If you don't get there this afternoon like you promised he's going to fucking kill you." And I go, "You're kidding me?" He said, "No, I'm not. That's why I'm here. Don't think I'm here because I want to be."

'When I got to the apartment, Poli was in bed; not sleeping, *sitting* in bed. I went to shake his hand, he didn't shake my hand, he just said, "Leave it there." It wasn't until the next day that he called me. But at the same time he trusted me with his life because I was the only guy who knew where he slept. I rented him his apartments. To people like Poli, when you lay your head on your pillow at night, nobody can know where you do that. Nobody can know where you sleep. Because then you really don't have a life. And they'll kill you while you're sleeping.'

*

When Poli felt like a change of scene, he and Luis would go to nightclubs, Poli bringing an arsenal of weapons with him in his Antioquian 'man bag', a *carriel*. But they never went to The Mutiny in Coconut Grove, Miami's most notorious nightclub, an annex of the hotel of the same name.

'Poli would stay away from those places. He was too hot. The Mutiny was not for him. Cops used to hang out there just to see who was there. He was way beyond all that. They were just a bunch of wannabes.'[87]

One night they went to the nightclub Alexandre at the Omni International Hotel on Biscayne Boulevard.[88] The Omni was where Pablo Escobar stayed when in Miami.

'Poli always had his *carriel* with his machine gun, his MAC-10 and his .357, but on the way out of the disco he gave me the *carriel* with the MAC-10, the .357 and a 9mm.[89] When he put it on my shoulder, my fucking shoulder almost fell off. We walked out of Alexandre, took a cab, like *nothing*. I was oblivious to it. I was so into the lore.'

Though Luis estimates Poli killed 'at least' eight people in Miami, he only saw him fire his gun once.

'A .357 will never fail you. It'll never jam. It's a revolver and it's got a bang and Poli was a great fucking shot. If he pulled his gun, somebody died. One morning, I picked him up at his apartment at like seven o'clock. Which was strange; he wasn't an early riser. He was *pissed*. He got in the back seat and says, "Let's go here," and we drove to Fontainebleau Park, these apartments in the west part of Miami. So we go up to the apartment and inside that apartment was Oscita, his son, and a kid called El Negro.'

*

In the mid-1970s Miami had been a pot-smuggling hub, but with the explosion of the cocaine trade and a resulting problem of oversupply there was reduced demand for marijuana by decade's end. Cubans controlled the distribution of coke in South Florida, routinely ripping off Colombians who supplied the product and cutting pure cocaine to be on-sold at massive markup to other cities around the United States. Fed up, the Medellín Cartel had started sending its own people to Miami to take over the entire business by force. Every day, assassins were being smuggled in by boat at $1500 a head. It was war.

'Cubans have an ego that's bigger than the Colombian ego and the thing is when you've got two egos like the Cuban ego and the Colombian *coastal* ego they're the same thing: they're two coastal peoples. But the Cuban ego came up against the Colombian–Medellín–Antioquian ego; and *paisas* are smart.[90] They don't just have an ego; they have an ego *and* a brain. That's why the Colombians had to send people over to Miami just to kill the Cubans. These were not mellow Cubans. They were hardass Cubans; as bad as the Colombians. But the Colombians always had the upper hand because they had the element of surprise. They bring in some guy from

Medellín nobody knows on a boat from Bimini, he whacks somebody, he goes back to Bimini. They don't live here, so they have the home-turf guerrilla advantage. That was why Poli had brought Oscita and El Negro from Bimini to kill somebody, a Cuban that owed Poli money from an old debt and that Poli had a war with, but the Cuban wasn't dead.'

Oscita and El Negro, only 17 or 18 years old, had already been in Miami for three or four days to carry out the hit but nothing had happened. Poli was furious.

'He thought he had given them clear instructions to go out and kill the Cuban. Then he starts to realise the reason these motherfuckers haven't gone out to kill this guy is they've started smoking base, *basuco*. He sees the towel on the back of the door, so the smoke doesn't go out. Poli was so pissed that he was *blinded* by how pissed he was. I'm just sitting on the sofa and I'm holding his *carriel*. He had a gun with a silencer, a MAC-10, the fucking thing with a couple of extra clips weighed 20 pounds. Suddenly he starts walking around, and he says, "*Loco* [*sniffs*], do you smell something?" I go, "No, no, I don't smell anything."[91] He starts walking around and he sees little drops of shit on the floor.

'And they opened the bathroom door. "We have a dog." They didn't want him to see the dog. And a puppy comes out. These guys were so based out they didn't bother to take the dog out to shit. Poli was so pissed, he said, "Fuck this," sat down right next to me, reached down into the *carriel* and went, *fttt fttt*, fucking killed the dog with a silencer. And that's when I said, "*Okaaay*, this is going to be a hell of a day." What a way to start. Basically Poli told those motherfuckers, "Listen, you pieces of shit, you either take care of this or I'm going to take care of it, and I suggest you take care of it." It got taken care of, because I never heard of it again. Oscita and El Negro went back to Bimini the same way they came in.'

*

At the end of 1979, Poli abruptly left Miami with the hit on El Colorado not executed. Luis had spent just three months driving for the taciturn Colombian but their time together left more of a lasting impact on his life than Miami University, Georgetown, FIU, or anything Luis's parents ever said to their son.

Rolling Stone that September had published a piece called 'The Cocaine Wars' by *Miami Herald* reporter and future bestselling writer Carl Hiaasen, about Dadeland and the battle between cops and cocaine cowboys in Miami. What had been a problem confined to Florida became an issue of national concern.

'I saw that article on top of the coffee table in Poli's apartment in South Bayshore Drive. It's not like Poli hung out at a bookstore. I was the only guy besides his sister and another family member that knew where he slept. I just walked in and they were packing a suitcase and I saw they were putting in a couple of .357 Magnums, Poli's weapon of choice. His sister Estella said, "Oscar's going back to Colombia, this whole thing's got too hot with El Colorado." He left Miami because of that article. He knew his time was limited if he stayed. He was as hot as a pistol when he left.'

PART 4
THE NETWORK

20

Navia's 11

AFTER POLI WENT BACK TO COLOMBIA, Luis decided he'd had enough of driving cocaine cowboys to lunch and wanted to branch out into the business on his own. Bia had stopped selling to Brian Livingston after she met Manolo Varoni, so there was an opening to sell cocaine directly to Brian, with Enrique Peláez Monsalve, Poli's brother, coming in as his SOS, source of supply.

The San Francisco honeypot couldn't last forever, though, and Luis was smart enough to realise it. To get seriously rich and become a major player, what he needed to do was diversify his client base, broaden his supply chain and distance himself from the city's drug wars as much as possible.

If 1979 had been bad for drug violence in South Florida, 1980 was worse with the heightened tension created by street riots in Miami that May, then the 'Mariel Boatlift' from April to September when over 125,000 seagoing refugees from the port of Mariel west of Havana, including inmates from prisons and patients from mental hospitals, swamped the city.

Fidel Castro had allowed anyone who wanted to leave Cuba to reunite with their families in the United States and taken the opportunity to clear out Cuba's jails and asylums. A tent city sprung up under the I-95 overpass. Groups of *Marielitos* were joining the cocaine trade, buying weapons and causing mayhem. The crime rate in Miami went up 89 per cent, murders 20 per cent. A local TV station was broadcasting public-service announcements about what to do if you got caught in crossfire during a gun battle. At seafood restaurants down by the Miami River, DEA agents and dopers would often be sitting at adjoining tables, and if a load were successful the dopers would send over a celebratory bottle of Perrier-Jouët champagne to the agents. It was Little South America.[92]

'What really shook me up was when the Mariel Cubans came over in 1980,' says Luis. 'They were completely out of their minds. One of them, a debt collector, had the Grim Reaper tattooed on his chest and in Spanish it said: *Matar es mi vida. Muerte es mi destino.* Killing is my life. Death is my destiny. When he closed his eyes one eyelid had *te* and the other eyelid said *veo*: I see you.

'I wanted nothing to do with Miami. I was already going a lot to LA and avoiding Miami as much as possible. I knew how these Cubans were. I didn't want to sell cocaine to them. I was slowly transforming into Colombian. I was living with Colombians, my friends were Colombians, I was around Colombians on a daily basis. Bia never sold cocaine to any Cuban.

'There could have been good Cuban buyers in Miami, but I didn't know any of them. Anybody will knock anybody off, steal from you. The Colombians were suppliers; they weren't clients. I thought, "Why should I have to deal with Cubans when I have a decent American I'm dealing with in Brian Livingston?" I had a good thing going in San Francisco. These *Marielitos* in Miami weren't honest Cubans like my dad. They were fucking street guys who were out to cut your throat, steal your coke and let you get killed by the Colombians.'[93]

But to go national, he couldn't do it alone. So Luis started to build a handpicked team of suppliers, transporters and dealers to get the product into major cities across North America.

First, he began bringing in cocaine through new suppliers in Colombia. Second, he hired Bernardo Palomeque and Javier Mercado, two former *marimberos* (pot smugglers) from Cuba who were the antithesis of Mariel Cubans: they had a glamorous touring-car operation in Miami called B&J Racing. Bernardo and Javier, behind the wheels of Chevrolet Corvettes, Ford Mustangs, Chevrolet Camaros and Porsche 911 Carreras, had competed in high-performance races such as the Daytona 24-hour and Sebring 12-hour.[94] In turn, they subcontracted their Colombian associate, Francisco Moya aka 'Juanchi', a fellow *marimbero* from Santa Marta.

Third, Luis employed a driver, Diego Forero, for transporting loads out west by road. Diego was Cuban-American but 'totally Americanised' and spoke impeccable English: a huge asset if he were ever stopped by highway patrol. Fourth and finally, he recruited Leif Bowden aka 'Arlo' in Santa Cruz, Terry Wozniak aka 'Landshark' in Los Angeles, Roger Lisko in Orlando and Brett Spiegel in Tucson as buyers, with additional sales connections in Boston and Minneapolis–Saint Paul.

It was like putting together a team of bank robbers for one last job, just like in the movies. Along with his existing client Brian Livingston in San Francisco, Navia's 11 effectively opened up Luis's cocaine to seven cities and five states and laid the foundations for what would become a small- to mid-scale 1980s cocaine empire.[95]

*

The Colombians that began supplying Luis were the most crucial part of his powerplay.

Octavio Piedrahíta, a transporter closely affiliated with the Medellín Cartel, would become best known as the owner of football clubs Deportivo Pereira (of the same city) and Medellín's Atlético Nacional. But secretly he ran a profitable cocaine route with an airline called *Transportes Aéreos Mercantiles Panamericanos* or TAMPA, a cargo carrier from Medellín.[96]

'The Piedrahítas had a lot of merchandise in Miami and their main distributor was their cousin, Elkin 'El Negro' Mesa.[97] They had thousands of kilos distributed in Miami and I was one of the guys that sold merchandise for them. Each group had a *recibidor*, somebody who received merchandise. The distributor for the wholesaler was called a *repartidor. Repartidores* were nobodies that they sent from Colombia to Miami. They received the merchandise and distributed it to whomever they were told to. They'd didn't make money off the sale. A lot of them took a monthly salary. They'd come to Miami, the cartel would rent them a house and they'd receive $10,000 a month. Sometimes when things were slow or delayed they didn't have much work but they'd still receive their monthly salary.

'The ones that got the salary were usually the *caleteros*; all they did was stay and "babysit" the merchandise at a *caleta* or stash house. They would come with their family and all and look normal. They'd just sit at home and watch TV. *Recibidores* had opportunities to make more money; the office would send some kilos in their name at cost, pay freight and sell through the office's distribution network.

'The Piedrahítas became big. Octavio had many brothers and they sometimes worked independently of Octavio. I worked a lot with Fernando who was partnered with the other brother Orlando. Fernando was stationed permanently in Miami – and he received merchandise from Octavio and Orlando who were on the production and shipping end in Colombia. But Octavio was the brother with the most merchandise and the wealthiest. As a family, they weren't exactly good-looking people. They were mixed: [South American] Indian and black. Octavio was the best looking of all of them, like an Indian with green eyes. They invited me to their home in Medellín. I met their mother and all the brothers and spent a couple days as their guest.

'Nevertheless Octavio started doing well for himself since he was running the TAMPA route plus other routes; he'd smuggle shit into the United States and made a lot of money really quickly. He was a very wealthy guy in Medellín. His brothers had their own access to cocaine in Medellín and sometimes they used Octavio's transport and sometimes they used other people's transport.

'Sometimes Octavio was in good with Pablo Escobar, sometimes he wasn't. I think Pablo kidnapped him once and it was like a joke in Medellín that every time Pablo needed a little extra money, he would kidnap Octavio – until he finally killed him. I don't know if it was over a mess they got involved in or just for the hell of it. I guess Octavio was getting too big for his britches; acting too much like a big shot. He was flashy. A big gold chain and a Mercedes, all that shit.'

Luis's other SOS were two upper-middle-class Medellín families he met through Bia, relatives of the Ochoas of the Medellín Cartel. Their coke came branded as 'MM' (for Medellín and Miami).

For security reasons they cannot be named, as they are alive and well in Colombia and not known drug traffickers.

'They all knew I had contact with Bia's main connection, Brian. But they did not want to supply me while Poli was supplying me. They were very cautious. They came from a high status – not the "elite" Medellín class at the time, but they had *class* status. Poli on the other hand came from the most dangerous and violent neighbourhood of Medellín – either *barrio* Antioquia [Trinidad] or Guayaquil, which are both very tough places. So they didn't want to be anywhere close to what they knew was a very dangerous situation. They knew that any conflict or discrepancy with Poli, the outcome was death. It was as simple as that. So after Poli left Miami they started to supply me. For a while one of these Medellín families was my main supplier.'

*

By the end of 1980, Luis was about to make his first million but had the humility to realise none of it could have happened without Poli and Bia.

'I kind of expanded really quickly. I built up a sales network, quite a business, in a short period of time. When people realised that I had been Poli's chauffeur, driven him, sold his coke, moved coke for him with Brian, lived with him, been his trusted confidant who was with him every day, the offers came flying from the Ochoa brothers, the Piedrahítas, *everybody*. But we got more merchandise from Fernando and Octavio Piedrahíta than we did from the Ochoas' relatives and Poli's brother Enrique put together.

'Poli was so feared that when he went back to Colombia and I was a free agent, they figured I must be a good guy to work with if I'd survived working with him; for them it was a hell of a resumé or a great credential. They really believed in me. They knew I came from class and wasn't some rat right off the street, and they respected that I grew up with that code of honour that I learned from Poli. I worked with Poli all that time and there was never a penny missing. If there would have been any missing, I wouldn't be alive to tell the story.

'It all went back to Poli. They really respected that. That opened big doors and then people started giving me a lot of merchandise.

Nobody would dare approach me when I was with Poli; to them, they thought Poli may take it as, "Oh, you're trying to steal my client." That's the last thing any of these motherfuckers wanted to happen: Poli thinking they're stealing the client. They didn't want to have any issues with Poli, or *potential* issues. With Poli, any sort of problem, certainly you were going to get whacked. So people didn't exactly want to get whacked that much; they kinda stayed away.'

Cocaine, ultimately, was no different to any other franchise.

'I realised this business was great. I liked it. I was constantly moving merchandise. I wasted no time. I was moving anywhere between 100 to 200 kilos a month, which is a lot, and the business was growing. I started taking from Enrique, the Piedrahítas and the Ochoa relatives. They knew that I would sell 100 kilos for Poli so they started offering me 100, 200, 300 kilos. That's when I started to develop Landshark and the other guys. With all that merchandise I started giving some to Brian, some to Arlo, some to Landshark, some to Roger and some to Brett. You build up a client base. That's my entrepreneurship. I build you up. I make you competitive in your market with good price and good quality. I was receiving cocaine fucking *pure*. I only ever cut it once. I cut 80 kilos and I made 100. And I never did it again.'

Luis could have been forgiven if he had; there was so much money to be made. By 1979 the wholesale price of coke was $51,000 and, through 1980 and coming into 1981, Luis was selling a key for $58–60K to Brian and $57–58K to Arlo and Landshark. A kilo sold for about $55K in Miami. A typical key might then be cut into three lots by a buyer and resold for significant profit.

'Being a narco was a business to me. I wasn't a killer, I wasn't a bad guy; I was a businessman. Everybody gets into the business to make money. Nobody gets into the business to kill people. What happens is the business changes them and they become killers. What kept me alive was my ability to turn a profit for everyone. It wasn't a gun in my pocket, it wasn't that I had 50 armed guys, it wasn't that I was a badass motherfucking killer; it was my ability to get shit from point A to point B.

'I stayed true to the essence of the business, which was making a buck. Everybody veers off. Because they make a buck, they buy fucking weapons, they hire bodyguards and they go crazy and they kill people. If you stay true to the business, it's to make a buck. It's not to kill nobody.'

*

But, still, he also had to know when to turn on the gangster persona.

Terry Wozniak was a blond, blue-eyed, very good-looking Canadian from a wealthy background who had gone to the prestigious St. Andrews College in Aurora, Ontario. He had got the nickname Landshark for his acumen as a smooth-talking salesman and hustler. Before he met Luis, he'd been a nobody out on Key Biscayne buying from small-fry suppliers who simply didn't have what he wanted: 30 or 40 kilos to sell out west. He kept badgering Luis to let him have some of his coke and Luis was becoming irritated.

'Okay. Listen, motherfucker. What is it you can do?'

'I can sell it in California, Luis.'

'I'll start you out with a kilo. But, let me just tell you, if you lose it you're gonna die. You better come back with the money, otherwise you're going to have a serious problem. That's who we work with. We are fucking *killer* Colombians. I'm not going to kill you, I don't believe in that. But I do believe in it if you steal. So I won't be doing any killing but you will be killed. They will kill your family up in Toronto. I'll take a chance on you. It's up to you. You either sell and live or steal and die.'

'Yeah, sure, no problem, Luis.'

It was the start of a beautiful business relationship. Landshark would buy hundreds of kilos every few months.

'He kept up his end of the bargain and really expanded sales. He was pumping out some serious weight for a while there. Then he decided to retire and go to Costa Rica and married an Eastern Airlines stewardess that used to take kilos out west. In the cocaine business you've got to kill. It's the only way. If people are bad, if people think they can take you for a million dollars and live, they'll take you for a million dollars. A million is a very powerful incentive. And if people think they can get away with it, they'll do it. In that business you've got to kill them.

'Landshark ended up owing me $300,000. So in the end he did fuck me but I had made so much money by then it didn't matter. If I can absorb the loss and it's my money, no one gets killed. But when it's the Colombians' money, they will kill you. You pay for it with your life. You crossed their line, not mine.'

21

Dirty Work

IN NOVEMBER 1980, JOEL, who had stayed in America to keep selling Poli's product to Brian Livingston, was killed in San Francisco by a gang of Peruvians. There are no known newspaper records of what happened, but according to Luis the Peruvian group had tried to muscle in by selling to Brian and there was a confrontation, which ended up with Joel dead.

Furious, Poli brought in a new enforcer for his precious cocaine pipeline: Evangelista 'Mario' Navas Villabona, a Colombian from Bucaramanga who had been paroled from an Oklahama federal prison the previous month on a marijuana- and cocaine-trafficking conviction and issued with a deportation order back to Colombia, which somehow he'd managed to skip. He was in his late 20s, tall, dark, skinny, moustachioed, reasonably good looking, and dressed flashily in gabardine pants and silk shirts.

'Mario came to whack the Peruvians. Dangerous guy. He'd put one right between your eyes, no problem, real quick. He just showed up one day as Joel's replacement. Joel had been very close to Poli; there was no way Poli and Mario were not going to avenge Joel's death. Take *vengarse* – revenge.'

The problem for Luis having such a hothead in his midst was protecting his own access to the prize client they were sharing. Mario had taken over from Joel in handling Poli's product in California; but with Poli back in Colombia and not overseeing day-to-day operations, what was stopping Mario taking out Luis and keeping Brian all for himself? It was a volatile situation with potentially fatal consequences. Luis instinctively knew he was dealing with a cold-blooded killer who would murder him without a second's thought for exclusive access.

'Poli shared the goose that laid the golden eggs with his brother and myself. But with Mario coming in, it could've been a situation where greed and the sheer amount of money being made could have caused me trouble. I don't know if deep down Mario was happy, but he was totally comfortable with killing people and had no doubts at all when it came to having to eliminate somebody. But I felt safe somewhat because Poli simply would not have allowed anything to happen to me.'

Even more uncomfortably, Mario had moved into the same apartment complex at Venetian Islands in Miami where Luis was then living and wanted Luis to vacate.[98]

'He said, "You're heating up *my* building. I want you out of here as soon as possible. We both can't live in the same building."'

What saved Luis was the same thing that saved him every time: his fast-talking. Even when Mario decided Luis owed him $400,000 for no reason, he found a way to sidestep certain death.

'Mario said I owed him $400,000 because I took one load out [to San Francisco] and I gave Brian 100 kilos and I gave it to him at 58 [thousand] a key and Mario was selling it to him at 62. And because of me he had to lower his price to 58 and it cost him $400,000.'

Cocaine-dealer math is not like any other math. A meeting to iron things out was arranged one night at Luis's apartment.

'We started to drink and snort. I had a kilo at the apartment. We were listening to The Police album *Reggatta de Blanc* over and over again and snorting coke. And that's when we started getting sentimental. I said, "*Wait*, you know, Mario, I've always respected you and Poli a lot, you know, and I know how much you love guns.' And I had just been in San Francisco and had bought this fucking antique gun. I don't how much it cost me. I don't know if it was $5000, $7000, $10,000, but the fucking gun cost me some money. And I thought, "*Shit*, I'm going to make up with Mario. This whole thing with the $400,000." Usually when you owed Mario $400,000 you died rather quickly. With me, it was different. He let it ride. Mario liked me. I was no threat to him. I was a cleancut kid.

'So I gave him the gun. We were all coked up and everything. When he opened the fucking case, he went, "*Woooow*. You're incredible. I knew you were a good man. You've become a real friend." But, you know, when somebody gives you a gun you gotta give 'em one in return; it's just the karma. So Mario reaches in his back and he pulls out his 9mm Browning, 14-shot, he kept it locked and loaded, and he gives it to me and I didn't know what to do with it. So I put it in the closet. And then he says, "Hey, but this doesn't mean you don't owe me the 400; you still owe me the 400, but we're a little better now."'

The next day the gun went off.

'Sure enough, I went into the closet, *boom*, the fucking thing misfired. That's the real reason why I left the fucking apartment. I didn't know where that bullet went; probably through a dry wall into somebody else's apartment. You could trace the bullet to that gun that killed I don't know how many people. For sure it killed more than one.

'When I next met up with Mario, a few days later, he asked where I had been. He hadn't seen my car around the building for a few days. I said, "Don't you remember? You *asked* me to leave. Out of respect for you I left." I think that impressed him. He was never to know I'd really left because of the missing bullet.'

*

As long as Luis didn't step on Mario's toes, selling cocaine out west was a straightforward process. It was so easy, on one occasion a female friend of his did a mule run on a private Learjet from Miami to Seal Beach, northern California. She and her male companion pretended to be newlyweds with coke stuffed in their suitcases. They had confetti and champagne aboard the private plane to give the impression they were on their honeymoon – the works. Luis was a man for fine details, which is probably why he lasted so long in the drug-trafficking business.

'When I was in California I worked at maintaining a look, a *stature*. I always went to Wilkes Bashford, which was a very high-end men's clothing store, and that's where I bought all my Brioni suits. I met Sharon Chase there, a fashion designer. She was friends with Gordon Getty and Danielle Steel. She knew all the top chefs: Jeremiah Tower, Alice Waters.

'We used to go out to all the best restaurants; the greatest restaurants in America were in San Francisco. Back then was when the California *nouvelle cuisine* was taking off. Sharon gave me a lot of legitimacy, being with her. Hotel suites, the opera, champagne at all times, a Cadillac limousine with a chauffeur – over the top. We were a great couple. When I went to LA I would stay for a month at the Beverly Hills Hotel and take a bungalow in the back, take two bungalows; one of my guys would take one, I would take another and our bills there were $30,000, $40,000 a month, like easy.

'What saved me was my low profile; I look innocent. There's a guy I knew, Joey Ippolito aka "Joey Ipp", who later sold coke to O.J. Simpson.[99] But he wasn't doing it like I was. Joey was taking 50 kilos, selling it out west, with O.J. Simpson, the Playboy Mansion and James Caan. He was in a limelight situation. That's not what you're supposed to do when you're dealing dope. You're supposed to keep a low profile.

'I never hung out with those crowds that I knew would only bring heat. My double life was being a criminal, an outlaw, and not trying to get captured. I could not bring heat to myself by hanging out with O.J. Simpson and James Caan and being the guy that sold them coke. Are you kidding? How long was that going to last? It's like asking to be arrested. I would never do it like that; being out there in society and everybody knows I'm an Italian guy in the dope business like Joey Ipp.'

*

The real dirty work was being done getting the coke from Miami to point A (Jacksonville) to point B (Santa Monica) and driving back again: the Interstate I-10 corridor from northern Florida to California, a punishing round-trip of almost 8000 kilometres. Through a mechanic called Helios, who was married to Enrique's and Poli's sister Catalina, Luis had a two-passenger Ford pick-up truck customised with a hidden compartment for his Cuban-American driver, Diego Forero. A 'fucking beauty', it was designed to hold 400 keys but usually stored 220 to 250 for better concealment.[100] It had a flatbed in the back with a raised floor or false double-bottom.

'Helios was good at working with metals and was a welder and had once mentioned to Poli to buy a small welding shop in Hialeah so they could make silencers. The truck had a motorcycle in the back, always kind of dirty and full of mud so it looked as if Diego was doing motocross circuit, going cross-country with his motorcycle.'

Diego would pick up the merchandise in a designated parking lot. The Colombians would leave behind a car containing the coke, which Diego would then drive to another location, where he would switch once again (with the coke) into another car.[101] He'd then drive to his vegetation-shrouded home in Coconut Grove to a covered garage and unpack the merchandise during the night. There the truck would be loaded up for the big journey.

'He'd always have some girl go with him. He had a girlfriend called "Red" and she was a big girl. Not a pretty girl but not ugly. She was a hairdresser. Diego was a really stupid-looking, withdrawn, reserved, laidback and not very talkative guy – definitely had a peculiar way about him. Tall – not fat or muscular. Just long limbs and on the thin side. He didn't look like a cocaine transporter. You would never think he was involved in anything illegal. He was the perfect man for the job and the stash was so well made, if anyone grabbed it they would have to bring the dogs because you couldn't figure it out.[102]

'The I-10 went from northern Florida and cut through Alabama, Louisiana, Texas, New Mexico and Arizona into California. Diego used that road when he delivered to Landshark in LA. Diego delivered a few times to Brett in Tucson, but a lot of times Brett would come up to LA and pick up his stuff. Brett had a big farm in Georgia and sent some of his people down to Miami a few times to pick up and take back to Georgia. He had a distribution ring going all the way up to the Carolinas. Roger would also come down to Miami from Orlando with his own people. He was very careful and we would give it to him here and he would handle taking it back up north.

'When Diego was taking merchandise to Brian he'd take a more northern route, going up to St. Louis [Missouri] and cutting across west. Most smugglers from Florida took the easy route, which was the I-10, but that became very hot and it also became hot for bringing money back.

'The northern route put us right into the Santa Cruz area where we had Arlo, and a lot of times we would divide the merchandise between Arlo and Brian. Sometimes we took a trip specifically for Brian or sometimes we took a trip specifically for Arlo, but those were the two main clients I had out there: both big players, each moving 100 keys a month. At $60,000 a key, it was a lot back then. A large shipment of coke from Colombia was 500 keys. It wasn't like now when they're bringing up 20,000 keys at a time.'

*

Getting coke out west was a cinch. It was bringing the money back east that was proving tricky.

'Diego was stopped on his way back from California, somewhere in Alabama or Louisiana, and the local sheriffs confiscated $160,000, and it was *my* money. In reality, it was a ripoff scheme because all he got was a citation that such and such police station is holding $160,000 and he has 90 days to claim it, and if he doesn't it will be forfeited. I'm sure that piece of paper never got officially filed anywhere and the cops kept the money. They confiscated millions of dollars that way and kept it for themselves. They would just keep the form in their top drawer; nobody ever came back to claim the money when it was drug money, so the confiscation was never really recorded – it never existed. But that was typical. The sheriffs in that area knew that a lot of vehicles passing through were coming back with money from California to Miami.

'Last time I transported money back myself, I had bought a 1981 Mercedes 300 TD in Miami, brand new, yellowish beige colour. I loaded it up with about 90 kilos and Diego drove it out west to give to Brian. I had about $6.2 million that I had to bring back to Miami. And I loaded it all up in that fucking Mercedes, in the trunk, it was about five or six suitcases, small ones, big ones, with some idiot named Coca Bear from Miami, and I said, "Fuck, me having to drive with this fucking idiot and this money," but I didn't want to drive alone and

I had nobody else, and Diego had already driven the coke out west and he wasn't available.'

Coca Bear was a large-framed, buck-toothed, mixed-race Cuban dealer from Little Havana in Miami. He spoke loudly, was easily agitated, and had a heavy coke habit: hardly the ideal driving companion. Kind of like a stoned, strung-out version of the John Candy character in *Planes, Trains and Automobiles*.

'So I hopped in the car with Coca Bear, who was a complete jerk-off – we barely spoke – and leaving San Francisco on the way to Reno I almost drove off the fucking mountainside. I'm not the best driver in the world. Scared the shit out of that motherfucker [*laughs*]. Dumb sonofabitch fucking turned white. So he says, "I'll drive from now on."

'We went to St. Louis and then made it back to Miami. There was so much money being accumulated out west from my sales that I said to the Piedrahíta brothers, "I can't be transporting that money back to Miami anymore. I'm not going to do this anymore with Learjets, either. You need to set up a banker out west to take my money from now on. From then on, the money we made from sales was always laundered in LA.'

Many years later Luis discovered that the dopey Coca Bear – in cahoots with a dealer accomplice in Miami – had been planning to kill him sometime during the trip so he could steal the $6.2 million in the trunk.

'It was only when they found out some of the money was headed for the Piedrahítas that they decided to abort.'

22

Dead-Shark Eyes

He might have been getting richer, but the more coke Luis handled, the more he was putting up his own nose.[103] He had given up on Santana albums and recreational pot and was bingeing on his own merchandise. Doing cocaine 'was just part of my life'. He liked to play tennis when not on drug business and was partying heavily two or three times a week with his usual trinity of stimulants: blow, alcohol and hookers. He was already a multimillionaire, both through illegal means and legitimate business, and living it up.

With the help of his father and in partnership with Bia's cousin, Ernesto Gálvez, Luis had started a trading company/sugar-packing operation, Caribe Packing, in Aruba. Luis Sr had long ago cashed out of his Glades County and Moore Haven sugar interests and diversified into shipping companies Ship Operators of Florida and Florida Lines, registering ships in The Bahamas and Mexico. Lobo-Kane Inc., a New Jersey-registered company with links to Luis Sr's old friend Julio Lobo, had the licence to use the Hershey name in the Caribbean. In partnership with Caribe, Lobo-Kane's Hershey sugar was shipped from New Jersey to Aruba. Ernesto would distribute the sugar in Curaçao supermarkets and other stores throughout the Caribbean.

Caribe Packing was a chance for Luis to go straight and his father was right behind him, all the way. It was the only reason he got involved.

'He wanted me to be more conservative with my money, be more disciplined, not party so much, and the whole Aruba sugar thing was set up for me to expand on it. He really enjoyed Aruba; he loved the place. But it's like that old saying: You can lead a dog to water but you cannot make him drink.'

*

The real truth, kept from his father out of shame, was that Luis was a functioning drug addict who had graduated from snorting coke to smoking it with a beautiful neighbour from Key Biscayne: Katie Brooklyn, a willowy, slightly drugged-out 22-year-old brunette with a Mia Farrow–style *Rosemary's Baby* pixie cut.[104] Luis's driver Diego introduced them, much to Diego's dismay when the two instantly hooked up.

'Diego was kind of a hanger-on, my wingman is some ways,' says Katie. 'But he was the one who connected us. Luis was somebody I'd been aware of because he was a Key Rat, so I knew the name "Luis Navia". We grew up on the island together. Diego was also from Key Biscayne but he was different to Luis: there was a tenseness underneath; anger boiling under the surface. He liked being around all that stuff; the danger. Diego came from a good family. He liked to have pretty girls around him and everybody liked him, because he was a nice guy; he was funny, he was always very free with his cocaine. But I think he was extremely jealous and resentful of people like Luis, who were the real deal and got all the babes.'

Which was easy, with his endless supply of coke.

'Luis and I had a great time together. I loved that life. It was limousines. It was just like being rock stars but it was all drugs [*laughs*] and a lot more money. Most of our time was spent partying, going places. It really was like the Wild West in Miami: shootouts in the streets. Every day you would hear about mass murders; it was really nuts. The streets were just clogged with these bright red Porsche Carreras with these big fins on their back and [on the water] there were the giant cigarette boats. All these dealers didn't care who knew who they were. Nobody hid their money. They flaunted it and bought these really expensive things. It was a crazy time. We even bought a horse called Rocky.'

Luis laughs at the memory: 'We bought a fucking saddle that was worth more than the horse. We paid $7000 for the horse and $15,000 for the saddle. And the riding boots from Hermès, this and that. And then we forgot we owned the horse, we were so based out, we didn't pay the bills for the hay for the horse. The bill for the hay was $4000. They repossessed the horse.'

In return for all of Luis's largesse, Katie taught her boyfriend how to smoke freebase or, in their case, high-class crack.[105]

'Luis would boil some water, get a test tube, put some coke in it to heat up in the water, making sure to turn it frequently, and once the coke was melted he'd add baking soda. The coke then turns into rocks. You put it on a plate, stick it in a water pipe, take a suck, and smoke accumulates.

'Oh, my God,' recalls Luis. 'Your heart feels like it's going to fucking pump right out of your chest and your mind goes like a slingshot to the fucking *moon*. The feeling of euphoria is just *booooosh*. Then that's the feeling you continue trying to chase the whole night; you'll never get that same feel from the second one. But you keep basing and it does a number on your head. When you're young and basing, sex is fucking pretty wild too. It's degenerate. You come up with all kinds of weird shit. I never got into homosexualism [sic], but we would always have lesbians, two or three women, shows and stuff like that. You sit there for a while and then you just talk shit for hours. You're solving the world's problems. High, fucking, talking about sentimental shit, the world, *anything*, you name it you'll talk about it.'

By mid-1982, Luis was freebasing 'all the fucking time' with Katie.

'We would go two, three days staying up, smoking the stuff; that's what it does to you,' remembers Katie. 'One time at Luis's apartment, his mom turned up and saw us totally strung out and started screaming at me, calling me a *puta*. Really, *really* embarrassing. His mother was shrieking at me, "You come from such a good family, what are you doing?" She knew my dad and my mom.'

Luis was also experimenting with a variation of freebase, what Colombians called *basuco*. You take some coke, put it in a sock or coffee filter, put acetone in it, heat it up with a blow dryer, and what's left is base cocaine. You mix it with tobacco out of a cigarette, light it, it melts a bit, and you take a hit.[106]

'When I was with the hookers and the girls, it was mostly cocaine. It was with Brian that we would smoke freebase in a glass pipe. Base was nasty. Brian was completely hooked on base.[107] When he was on base he could hardly talk; his eyes were just wide open, kinda paranoid. Mario loved *basuco*. Poli would usually do a snort but he would also do some *basuco*.

'When you start on that shit, you do not stop. I can tell you that when I smoked base you hallucinate, without a doubt. It gets to a point where you start hearing things, you start seeing things, you get super-paranoid, especially since you're already in a paranoid state because of what you do for a living. One time I was out in California, north of San Francisco, at Diego's house and we're smoking base and he took a machine gun with a silencer and just fired right into the fucking bushes. There was a forest behind the house. He was convinced there were people out there coming to kill us.

'Another time Brian had a house on a golf course and it was made of wood with a wooden, steel-type roof. A fucking golf ball hit the roof of the house. *Fuck*. It's a miracle we didn't die of a stroke. We used to take turns peeking through the blinds.'

*

Katie had started freebasing in 1980, well before Luis, and was making it with baking soda. By 1982 she admits she had a 'very big addiction problem'.

'I really knew how to do it. When I had access to cocaine that's how I wanted to do it; I didn't want to snort it. When you could freebase it, why would you want to snort it? So much better. *Oh, my God*. It's like your brain gets hit with a freight train. It just is so powerful. That's why people love crack. It's the same thing. It's a really great high; I don't recommend trying it [*laughs*].'

And even though everybody was getting wasted, Mario and Enrique decided that she was a bad influence on Luis because she'd taught him how to smoke freebase. It was okay for them to do base, just not Luis's girlfriends. They gave her an ultimatum.

'One day they told her she can't go out with me anymore. That if she does, they're going to kill her.'

She didn't think twice: 'Luis and I were never real serious. It was all drugs, really. We hung out maybe close to a year, then the Colombians kinda freaked out because Luis didn't do base prior to me and now he was doing all the product and not being as reliable. I had to get out of the relationship or be killed. It was in this really nice apartment out on Key Biscayne. I had been partying with Luis and Mario and a bunch of other guys came in. They were like shadows. The feeling that came off of them was so negative and dark and scary. They had dead-shark eyes. Black, bottomless eyes like sharks.

'I hate to say this, but they all look the same, the Colombians: real dark. Black eyes, black hair, dark skin. I didn't really want to look at them long enough to really take in who I was looking at, because I intuitively knew that this stuff I should not be observing; that these guys could kill me. They didn't care. They would kill people without even thinking about it. It was *zero* respect for human life. You just didn't want to meet their eyes. Plus, being a good-looking American girl, I didn't want to give the wrong impression. I was just real cautious with them. I did not like them.

'The atmosphere in the room changed when they came in. If you're in the water, a dark ocean, and suddenly a giant shark went by you, and you feel the cold current – that's how I felt with these people. They took a look around and they pulled Luis into this other room and left the door open. They're talking in Spanish and English and I heard Mario tell him, "If you don't break up with her or get rid of her, we will. You can't do this."

'Mario was nuts. *Scary*, *scary*, *scary*. When you're on coke you're a bit paranoid, right? Hearing that and feeling that, and I really do feel I could have been killed that day because these guys were crazy, I left. I needed to get out of there. If I hadn't, the guy was so unstable he might have just shot me or killed me right there. They were very, *very* bad people.

'I had no shoes on. My heart was racing through my chest and I was all the way on the east side of Key Biscayne and my family's house was on the west side, so I was walking across the island which is a couple of miles, and the sun was out, and after being up for days on cocaine and just that feeling of incredible humiliation and abject terror that they were going to come after me and I was going to be killed, it was horrifying.

'For days afterwards I was afraid one night somebody was going to come through the window and just quietly slit my throat because I knew too much or whatever. I was very scared. And then I couldn't get in touch with Luis. He had stopped taking my calls. And I now know it was to protect me. He needed to totally end all contact with me or they would have come after me. Luis is very spacey and stuff but he's a really good guy. Everybody loves Luis.'

As for Luis, he was told in no uncertain terms: *This shit is over. Pack a bag. You're out of here.*

'And they took me and sent me off to San Francisco, to the Miyako Hotel, a Japanese hotel.[108] Enrique came with me. He respected my father and did not want to see him suffer watching his son's life flushed down the toilet. The place had paper sliding doors, wooden floors, Japanese food. Back then it was very unknown. A small but very cool place. All the rooms had saunas. So these motherfuckers stuck me in a sauna for a month and dried me out till I didn't want to smoke base no more. There were no withdrawal symptoms; maybe there was an urge to go out and have some drinks because that's what initiates everything with me. Never in my life did I do coke if it wasn't after three or four drinks. Same with freebase: it's drinks, coke and hookers, in that order. They cleaned me up and Katie and I never saw each other again.'

She completely quit cocaine one day in 1986.

'The night before, I was smoking freebase with a guy and clearly heard a voice saying, "One more hit and you are dead." I stood up and walked out of that house right then and there, even though there was still quite a bit of cocaine left. That voice, which I now think was God, of course, terrified me. I went into rehab that morning. Later I found out that the guy I was smoking with died that night of an overdose.'

23

Night Train

MEANWHILE, MARIO WAS BUSILY preparing to assassinate the Peruvians. Luis's $400,000 debt hadn't been paid. He was still happily going out to San Francisco, safe in the belief he didn't owe Mario anything. Or so he thought. His new *lavador* or money launderer in LA, a Colombian called Vicente Blanco who had become a close friend, freaked when he found out.

'Are you fucking nuts, Luis?'

'He's my friend. Nothing's going to happen.'

'*No*, man. With a guy like that you don't even argue.'

Vicente gave Luis the money for the debt immediately.

'I mean, I would have paid Mario eventually, but time went by and I always told him, "It's not like I owe you 400. You didn't *make* 400; it doesn't mean I *owe* you 400." That went on for a while. If it weren't because he liked me, he would have killed me.'

*

Luis got a call to go a stash house in Kendall and pick up 180 keys of cocaine from the Piedrahítas. 'El Tigre', a Piedrahíta family member, was taking care of the merchandise. When he arrived with Diego, they found a room with no furniture and a bedroom. Inside were 80 kilos marked with one brand, 100 kilos marked with another, and about 300 more kilos also marked differently. It was a sizeable lode of coke.

'And I said to myself, "*Whoaah*, this is fucked up." I'm a good guy but, fuck, I know where all this merchandise is. I could pick up my 180 kilos and talk to a fucking *bandido* and tell him, "Hey, I know a house where there's 500, 600 kilos, go hit it." Sure enough, a few days later, El Tigre was found dead in that house and they stole the merchandise.'

Mario was called to 'clean up the body, clean up the mess and make sure that El Tigre's body went back to Colombia for the funeral'. He was also paid $250,000 to 'recoup the merchandise', which meant killing the people who killed El Tigre and getting a percentage of the value of the missing cocaine. Mario had already taken care of the Peruvians. Nine dead bodies in San Francisco and LA. All dispatched while he was as high as a kite.

'It's not a lightweight job there. Well, fuck, you know, the Peruvians shouldn't have killed Joel. Why the fuck would you want to kill Joel? And you think you're going to *live*? Humans are fucking stupid. I know Mario killed the Peruvians. I remember we had to go get him out of a fucking motel room where he was holed up with hookers and he was beating them up.

'Here's Mario, all fucking strung out, based out, with no shirt, in the room. I walk in, he's got a fucking gun strapped on to his hand with duct tape and smoking with the other, and a couple of hookers are all banged up. Somebody got the call, I think it was Diego, to go get him some more shit because they were running out of it, and when Diego walks in there he sees a whole scene with Mario having beat up the hookers. He comes back to me and Brian and tells us, "This guy's fucking out of control. The cops are gonna come down on that place. We gotta get him out of there. This guy's gonna burn us to hell."

'Mario wouldn't allow anyone to go in there except me, because he didn't feel threatened by me. So I had to bring him some more shit, some fucking liquor, started drinking with him and gave him some Valium to calm his ass down. He paid off the hookers, let them go and I just sat there and talked with Mario for seven hours till it got darker and he calmed down completely and went to sleep.'

*

In March 1982, Luis invited Mario over for an early Easter ham dinner at his parents' place. It was awkward. To say his guest was a little rough around the edges was an understatement. Being a Colombian too in Miami at this time carried something of a stigma in certain social circles, so Luis introduced Mario to Luis Sr and María as 'a friend of mine from Venezuela'.

Mario was emotional at how he was being treated. Used to being seen as an outcast, it meant a lot to him to be accepted by a family from a different socioeconomic background to his own.

'I can't believe you invite me to dinner, Luis,' he said quietly, turning to him while they were seated next to each other at the table. 'You don't judge people by who they are. We're friends. Equals.'

Luis was just 27 and a millionaire five times over when his father died that September. A pimple had come out on his nose that turned cancerous and it spread quickly to his lungs and pancreas. He died 17 days later. Luis Sr refused care. He went quickly. Luis went to the hospital every day while he was sick but wasn't there when he died. He was selling a car and collecting some money – just going about his normal everyday business – which he regrets to this day.

'The only two friends of mine from the cocaine business that ever met my dad were Mario, Poli's brother Enrique and Fernando Piedrahíta. Enrique and Fernando were both ushers at my father's funeral and helped to carry the casket. My relationship with my dad was always good; not super-affectionate, but he was a good man. He went the way he wanted to – *quickly.* He never needed any taking care of. I couldn't see my dad any other way.

'My dad was always working; my mother also believed that money is the solution to all things in life. My mother was very materialistic. I was not brought up correctly; I was not *led* to bad things but I was not straightened out. You put braces on people to straighten out their teeth. They should have applied heavy braces on me – and they didn't. So yeah, I regret not being there when he died, but that was me being very immature. I've been badly structured, badly trained. I was let loose to do whatever I wanted. But I'm not the kind to blame my parents. It is what it is.

'I lived in a society that was *super*-superficial; money was everything to the people on Key Biscayne. We grew up thinking money was *everything*. I saw nothing morally wrong with smuggling. A lost kid anywhere can be snatched up by anybody. You can lose your son or daughter if they're not well structured and a little weak. Nowadays with drugs, you start out doing a little drinking, going to South Beach, a couple of discos, you get in with the wrong crowd and you're *gone*. That's what happened to me.

'You've got to be totally out of your mind to be thinking like I was thinking at the time. My priorities were messed up. Where's this person going with all this? I was never grounded, and I think that's what shocked my dad. But then, what was he going to do? There was no stopping me. I was buying Ferraris, Porsches, running with major, *major* motherfuckers that disrupted society, killed cops, killed people. But I should have just forgotten about everything else and just been concentrating on my dad.'

I feel for the first time in our conversations that Luis, the tough-guy narco, is showing me a side of his personality he rarely shows anyone. He's truly opening up. I want to push him more. So I put it to him directly: Your father was such a strong figure in your life but in a sense I'd argue you betrayed his values by entering a life of crime.

'Without a doubt. And I completely tarnished the last name. It was a complete fuck-up.'

Luis pauses. There's a real note of emotion in his voice.

'I don't think about it, because if I thought about it I'd be so guilty that I wouldn't be able to function.'

Laura, whose manner in person is strikingly different to Luis – calm, measured, discreet – doesn't quite buy her brother's account of his parents not having straightened him out properly: 'Luis was very rebellious and overall he had a good relationship with our parents; he loved them very much. But Luis was his mother's favourite. She would protect him on many occasions and help him hide the truth from my father. My father was always very frustrated with Luis. He squandered so many opportunities that were given to him because he wanted to party. My father was an earnest, respectable and honourable man. Luis was the complete opposite in terms of temperament.'

*

At 10.40pm on Thursday, 7 October 1982, in Jacksonville 555 kilometres north of Miami, Mario boarded the *Silver Star*, the Amtrak No. 82 service to New York City, under a false name, armed with a Browning semiautomatic and a MAC-10, and holding $5000 in cash. With him were his 24-year-old sister, María Isabel Navas Villabona Ramírez, and his sister's two children, nine-month old Juan Fernando Ramírez and three-year-old Zuli Ramírez. They had a six-by-ten-foot first-class sleeping compartment and Mario went to sleep in the top bunk.

Before dawn the next morning the train was just outside Raleigh, North Carolina. The compartment was dark, the blinds were closed, but Mario was hallucinating on cocaine, possibly after smoking base. He thought he saw hands under the blinds. He was hearing voices. He was startled by some coloured lights. An argument broke out between him and María. In his own mind, he saw the compartment door open and twice opened fire at the door with the machine gun, thinking he was under attack. The conductor called ahead for police and, after stopping in Raleigh and evacuating the other passengers, the carriage was detached by Amtrak employees from the rest of the *Silver Star*, which eventually went on to Manhattan.

For the next three days Mario, firing his weapons periodically and unpredictably for no apparent reason, was at the centre of the biggest siege outside a prison in American history up to that date: with Raleigh police officers, snipers, news crews, Special Weapons and Tactics (SWAT) teams, firefighters, emergency personnel, county sheriffs, highway patrolmen, state investigators and two dozen FBI agents, including Frederick Lanceley, who taught the hostage-negotiation course at the FBI Academy in Quantico, Virginia, all massed outside.

Agents Gary Noesner and Spanish-speaking Raymundo Arras from the FBI Crisis Negotiation Unit, communicating through a speaker that was installed outside the door of the carriage, had offered Mario food and water but got no response. It was stiflingly hot during the day, freezing cold at night. Mario, naked or dressed only in shorts, either remained silent or was cursing to himself. He was suicidal. When he did talk, amid the crying of Zuli, he gave his name as 'Mario Rodríguez'.

Attempts to get intravenous fluids into the carriage via a tube passed through a bullet hole in the compartment door failed, because it wouldn't fit through the exit cavity. When food and water finally got to the hostages it was too late to save the baby boy, who died on the Sunday after two days without water. María had been shot in the forehead above the left eye on the Friday by her completely based-out brother. Her putrefying corpse smelled so bad it was attracting flies.

The stand-off ended close to dawn on Monday, when not long after midnight Mario passed Zuli out the window to agent Arras after 33 hours of negotiation in Spanish. After consulting with the man he called his *padrino* (godfather), New York attorney Paul Warburgh, who was speaking to him through a bullhorn, Mario surrendered. He emerged at 5.45am from the train dressed in a black leather jacket, maroon satin shirt and blue jeans.

'My understanding was that he started smoking base sometime after the train left Miami, and by the time they were in North Carolina he was whacked out of his mind,' says Luis.[109] 'Base makes you very paranoid when doing too much of it. You start to hallucinate – especially when you live a life where you have cause to be paranoid, like Mario's. Base puts you in a very dangerous state. At first it's euphoric, then it gets weird, and you don't stop until there is no more – and when there is no more you've got to knock yourself out with booze and Valium. At least that's what I did. If not, the withdrawal is nasty. Mario was a casualty of addiction while Joel was a casualty of war.'

Mario, then 29, was charged with two counts of first-degree murder and one of kidnapping. At trial, in 1984, it emerged he had been to jail in October 1974 and was convicted for trafficking under the name 'Mario Navas' in New York in July 1976.[110] The defence in the Amtrak case claimed Mario was an insane schizophrenic but it wasn't accepted and he was sentenced to life, convicted for first-degree murder of baby Juan and involuntary manslaughter of his sister. The prosecutor, District Attorney J. Randolph Riley, had sought the death penalty. When the jury foreman announced he'd been found guilty, Mario blew them a kiss.

In prison, fellow inmates would taunt Mario by mimicking the sound of a steam train.

*

Luis was talking on a payphone in San Francisco to his mother back in Miami.

'She'd told me to open up a newspaper, so I went to a newsstand. Mario's picture was on there. He had half his body hanging out of a window with a machine gun in his hand or something.

'"Hey, isn't that the guy you invited to dinner?"

'I was freaking the fuck out. I was thinking this could be a major problem here. I didn't make a big deal out of it.

'"*No*, Mom. He looks like him. My friend's Venezuelan and the newspaper says this guy was *Colombian*. *No*, *no*, *no*. That's not the same guy."

'"Oh, *okaaay*."'

PART 5
WILD WEST

24

Santa Marta Gold

In October 1982, following Luis Sr's death, Laura Navia, 24, married her brother's *lavador* Vicente Blanco, 40, in a small wedding in Panama City. Luis had introduced the pair to each other over dinner in Miami and they'd fallen in love. The newlyweds went to live in a penthouse in a 20-storey luxury apartment building in Santa Marta on La Costa Caribe, the Caribbean coast in Colombia's north. That Christmas, they invited Luis and his grieving mother, María, to stay for the holidays.

A picturesque but sprawling historic city of half a million people in the tropical banana-growing department of Magdalena, Santa Marta has five beautiful aquamarine bays, boasts scores of white-sand beaches, and is hemmed in by the snow-capped Sierra Nevada de Santa Marta, all of which makes it a popular place for tourists. It's also a major hub for drug trafficking and has been since the 1970s, being situated smack-bang in South America's most storied region for high-quality marijuana cultivation.

Coming not long after the death of Luis Sr, Christmas and the New Year should have been an opportunity for the Navias as a family to come together, pause and reflect on the passing of the great man. But Luis had his mind elsewhere.

Caribe Packing, a company that had started off as 'a clean, small deal', would after Luis Sr's death and Luis's buying out of the partners, be used as a front for cocaine trafficking to the US Virgin Islands and Puerto Rico. Luis would bring in refined sugar from Colombia, pack it, export it to the rest of the Caribbean under the Hershey brand and 'put some merchandise inside the sugar' that went to Saint Thomas (in the Virgin Islands) and Puerto Rico.

'Caribe had *been* legitimate. We bought used packing equipment from the Lobo-Kane operation in Pompano Beach, Florida, and set it up in Aruba. The plan was never to transport coke. I never did anything criminal with sugar while my dad was alive. Lobo-Kane was no longer involved. I only did it once or twice, then I got really scared. It wasn't much because I was trying it out. We only did one shipment to Puerto Rico.

'I was gone a lot. I was living in San Francisco most of the time, LA. I thought I had God by the beard. I thought I had hit the jackpot and was on my way to becoming an international fucking millionaire entrepreneur, and I was completely mistaken. But I was making money. I had some nice cars and I lived in nice places and I travelled.'

He was also eyeing an altogether different deal, the first and only pot smuggle of his career: 35,000 pounds or 17.5 tons of 'Santa Marta Gold', the best dope in the world, for which he stumped up $150,000 to Javier Mercado as starter capital for the purchase of the weed in Colombia and to organise transportation to the United States.

Javier and his American partner, Bernardo Palomeque, had already pulled off their first coke smuggle from Santa Marta for Luis: 160 keys purchased direct from the Medellín Cartel's Miki Ramírez, a close confidant of Pablo Escobar and Fernando Galeano.[111] Javier and Bernardo, sailing from Miami, picked up the load on a Defender boat called the *Happy Hooker* off Santa Marta, then came back through The Bahamas and into Miami, mooring it at the marina of the Rusty Pelican restaurant, right at the entrance of Key Biscayne, which overlooks the Miami skyline. It was hardly the world's most incognito smuggle but this was the early '80s.

Their Colombian liaison, Francisco Moya aka Juanchi, had taken six to eight months to deliver the merchandise from Miki Ramírez, and in the end it had been more hassle than it was worth, but it was a momentous event: Luis's first independent smuggle into the United States. This time Juanchi was promising a quicker turnaround.

As a *marimbero*, pot was his bread and butter and he had connections to the Dávila family, arguably the most successful and powerful marijuana traffickers in northern Colombia.[112] A steel-hulled 100-foot fishing trawler called *Cristal* was ready to go with an Ecuadorian captain who'd been paid $35,000, while Javier's crew in Miami was all set to receive the goods 200 miles off the coast of southern Georgia, north of Florida. They'd pay the balance. For $10-a-pound cost price, the pot would sell wholesale in America for $200 a pound, so 35,000 pounds would bring in $7 million minus $2.5 million for expenses: a $4.5 million profit.

'I had never done pot [as a smuggle] before in my life,' says Luis. 'My end of the deal was I put up the money to buy the pot, to come up with the expense money to get the show going. The pot was going to cost about $350,000, but $150,000 would get us going and do the trip.'

Finding the cash wasn't a problem. Luis had millions stashed away in safety deposit boxes in Aruba and Miami, half a million secreted in the attic of his dead father's house, another half a million packed in a mid-sized Zero Halliburton suitcase in a spare bedroom, more in small fire-resistant safes, and $250,000 on his person as play money. He was so flush he bought an apartment in Grove Isle for $250,000 in cash, with everything in it, sight unseen, when an indicted neighbour needed to get out of town quickly. But he had an important caveat stumping up the money for Juanchi.

'I actually wanna *see* the shit. I've never seen pot like that. I want to go.'

Juanchi and Javier thought he was crazy, but they acquiesced and Luis, dressed in blue jeans and a double-pocket khaki shirt with Lucchese cowboy boots, was picked up in Santa Marta by two or three of Juanchi's sidekicks to be driven to the jungle. Leaving Santa Marta, they travelled 100 kilometres south to the town of Fundación and then wound 165 kilometres east to just south of the city of Valledupar.

'It was no man's land. We were far in the middle of fucking nowhere is where we were. They didn't know where the fuck they were going.'

From there they were close to Venezuela and the Sierra de Perijá. When the road stopped they switched from the car to mules, getting higher and higher into the mountains, crossing rivers in areas controlled by groups affiliated with *Fuerzas Armadas Revolucionarias de Colombia – Ejército del Pueblo* or Revolutionary Armed Forces of Colombia – People's Army, better known as FARC. Inevitably, they were ambushed and held for ransom.

*

To give some historical context, there is an importance difference between the Colombian guerrillas, probably the best-known guerrilla group in the West being FARC, and the Colombian paramilitaries or *paras*.

'The guerrillas are left wing, "We're doing it for the liberation of the people," which is a fucking bunch of bullshit because they've murdered innocent people. The paramilitaries are right wing, *against* the guerrillas. It was Carlos Castaño Gil who started the paramilitaries when the guerrillas killed the Castaño brothers' dad.[113] The victims are the innocent *campesinos*, the peasants of the countryside. The guerrillas go into their town and they've got to feed the guerrillas. And then the guerrillas leave and the paramilitaries come in and they find out that they fed the guerrillas, so they kill them for feeding the guerrillas. They're both complete, total pieces of shit. But the group that kidnapped me never identified themselves as FARC.

'In Colombia there was a time called *la época de la violencia* or *La Violencia*, which was the conservatives against the liberals, and it was nasty. There were a lot of killings.[114] So Colombia has a long history of political killings. And from that era the guerrillas were born. They wanted a government free of the grip of the oligarchs, established families and right-wing money people.'

And in the process of loosening that grip, they opened up huge swathes of Colombia to cocaine production: land that the national government in Bogotá simply had no control over.

'For 50 years Colombia has been plagued by FARC and other guerrilla groups kidnapping politicians and businessmen and killing people. The major cocaine cartel in Colombia is FARC; they sell to *everybody*. They have a huge presence in Peru and Ecuador; they supply the cartels. They've been working directly with the Mexicans for years now. Ecuador is *flooded* with guerrilla cocaine. When I lived in Colombia I could never go from Bogotá to Santa Marta by car, because in the middle you'd get stopped by the guerrillas and kidnapped or killed.

'Then the paramilitaries with their drug money created armed militias and each one of those groups had 6000 men armed to the teeth, controlling certain areas. The paramilitaries claimed that they were never involved in drug dealing, but they were exporting tremendous amounts of product out of the Urabá area. If you think I've exported shit, they've exported 30,000 times more than me: millions of kilos. They've killed *thousands* of people.

'During the time of Andrés Pastrana Arango, the worst president Colombia ever had, he gave FARC an area of about 42,000 square kilometres, like the size of Switzerland, a no-conflict zone; it was a peace territory.[115] And all FARC did was set up cocaine labs and produce cocaine that supplied them for the next fucking 20 years. It was one big fucking cocaine lab.

'FARC supposedly disassembled but they just franchised their cocaine-growing areas and their labs through smaller criminal groups. They didn't reintegrate into society.[116] South America is still fucking the Wild West. Nobody's done a Netflix series on the Colombian guerrillas. They're the major suppliers of cocaine to the world.'

*

Luis handed over $20,000 in cash – it was all he had – but realised he could make a deal with the *comandante*, whose name was Camilo.

'One thing I clearly remember is that the people I was with told me that theirs was a non-violent group, so it was probably a mellow offshoot of FARC. I got in survival mode and said, "Let's make something good out of something bad." If I had just frozen up and melted down, they would have buried me out there. I said, "*Comandante*, we're here to buy pot. I don't need to buy it from them. I can buy it from you. We can all make money here."'

'Okay, let's talk,' Camilo replied. 'How much are you looking for.'

'Thirty-five thousand pounds.'

'By all means.'

The contract was thus sealed verbally and Luis and Juanchi's men were released.

'When I got back to Santa Marta, I told Juanchi and Javier, "The good news is I'm back. The bad news is we're not buying your pot. We're buying the pot from the guerrillas." I traded in my cowboy boots for some rubber boots the *comandante* had. That sealed the deal. I came down with red eye from being up there in the fucking jungle.'

The smuggle went ahead as planned, the boat being loaded up at night, and there was an entourage of a dozen people in three boats who wanted to be there when it happened on the water, including the owners of the load and their assistants. But Luis was told not to come due to a problem he had with a swollen knee, an injury from skiing and tennis. Juanchi thought it best he stay behind and manage the radio in Juanchi's apartment with Juanchi's wife. For him, it was another fortunate twist of fate.

'When they were loading in the ship at night in Bahía de Cinto, Juanchi went to the onload of the merchandise. A bunch of my friends went in three open fishermen to help. Santa Marta has five bays but there are very rough, ragged, sharp rocks at the point of each bay; it's surrounded by rocks. It was too rough, the waves hit. So two or three of the boats tipped.

'Everybody was in the water. One of the boats sank. The smart people were the ones who stayed in the middle and didn't try to go into land, because the waves were so rough that you would get banged up against the rocks. There's huge fish in there; not so many sharks, but huge groupers, and a lot of these people when they got cut up by the rocks obviously got eaten by the fish.[117] Five people died that night.'

The *Cristal* carrying the 35,000 pounds of marijuana managed to make it out of Bahía de Cinto and sailed north to the Windward Passage between northwest Haiti and eastern Cuba to The Bahamas, but the USCG cutter *Dauntless* intercepted the load east of The Bahamas and impounded the dope.

The fact the load never got to the drop-off point in the ocean off Georgia didn't matter to the guerillas. A deal was a deal. A furious Juanchi was forced to hand over to the guerrillas the $150,000 Luis had originally given him and come up with the $200,000 balance. It had been an expensive disaster.

'That's when I decided to continue doing only coke. It was too risky to send boats loaded with pot; they were too slow. It was better just to airdrop 500 kilos of coke and be done with it.'

25

The Spaghetti Incident

Surprisingly it wasn't through the two impeccably lineaged Medellín families connected to the Ochoas that Luis got the biggest break of his fledgling drug-trafficking career. Rather it came through their practically unknown narco associate Camilo Zapata aka 'El Halcón' (The Hawk), an independent operator who was using the smaller Pereira Cartel, a syndicate based in the city of Pereira, west of Bogotá, as his SOS.[118]

It was through Halcón that Luis was introduced to Pereira duo José Vallejo Lopera aka 'El Mono' or 'Mono Lopera' and Fernando Marulanda aka 'Marulo', as well as the unaffiliated Alberto Barrera aka 'Paco', a transporter who was sourcing a lot of his coke from the Medellín Cartel.[119]

Halcón, Mono, Marulo and Paco were not household names in the drug business in Colombia, but they were all major players inside or intimately connected to Medellín, the crucible of the cocaine industry, all four men having squared away tens of millions of dollars, if not hundreds of millions, in Swiss bank accounts. Working with Bia and Poli, Luis had been a couple of degrees removed from the top players in the cocaine trade. He'd got a degree closer with the Piedrahítas and the two Medellín families, who'd started supplying him while Luis was still in Miami. But now he was dealing directly with cartel heavies on their home turf on a first-name basis.

The South Florida Drug Task Force, an interagency initiative set up in 1982 by President Ronald Reagan and helmed by Vice President George H.W. Bush, had been tremendously successful, at least initially, in stopping loads from Colombia, and practically shut down The Bahamas and the rest of the Caribbean as a viable route into Florida. In just over a year, cocaine seizures went up 54 per cent, some eight-and-a-half tons being interdicted.

Much of that was down to an expansive radar system – radar balloons, mobile radar on USCS boats and planes, military radar including airborne early warning and control system (AWAC) aircraft, conventional aviation radar – but it was not foolproof: low-flying small planes and small boats could still evade detection.[120] The states further west along the Gulf of Mexico (Alabama, Mississippi, Louisiana, Texas) and unradared Mexico, not yet a narco state but ripe for exploitation with its corrupt police force and military, seemed like a much better back door into the United States, so the cartels were ideally looking for a transporter who could get their merchandise over the gulf and across the 3145-kilometre US–Mexico border with a minimum of fuss, loss and wastage.

Luis was their man. But formalising business deals with the cartels often required lunch dates and one such occasion required Luis to come to a ranch or *finca* outside Pereira. When he got there, the unnamed cartel boss, a large man dressed in an untucked polo shirt, was serving spaghetti with tomato sauce; not slow-cooked tomato sauce but the bottled commercial variety. It was just Luis, the cartel boss and a couple of his henchmen.

'Spaghetti and a bottle of fucking ketchup: Colombian ketchup. I was shocked but *fine*. We're eating; we finish lunch. Then he taps me on the shoulder, "Hey, I want you to come look at something." So we went out to a shelter with metal roofing behind the dining room. They'd park tractors there, farming equipment. And I see a guy being held down on a concrete floor by two or three guys. His legs were tied. One guy was holding his legs, one guy on each arm and shoulder, and one guy pouring water on his face. He was being waterboarded. I go, "What the fuck is going on here? What did he do? Did he steal a thousand kilos?" and he goes, "*No*, *no*, *no*. He stole beef.

He's a cattle thief." Stealing cows was a serious business in Colombia back then. In the Wild West, if you stole cattle they'd shoot you or hang you on the spot. In Colombia I was in the Wild West. I was back in 1865 USA.'

The cartel boss took Luis aside to explain why the cattle thief was being tortured. A young man in his mid-30s, he'd claimed he'd been stealing cows for a restaurant that was owned by one of the cartel boss's friends. But when he brought this friend to meet the cattle thief, the cattle thief was asked to identify him and couldn't. He got caught in a lie.

'It all started going south for him after that,' says Luis, matter-of-factly. 'I said [to the cartel boss], "Listen, I really don't need to be here looking at this. This is not my business. We just had lunch." He never insinuated that if I ever lost a load it would happen to me, but they ended up waterboarding the guy a little more. Then he said, "Take him away."

'By now they'd tied up his hands as well and they threw him in the back of a Toyota truck and they took him out into the field and put two in his head. They weren't going to shoot him there and get blood all over the truck. They buried him somewhere on the farm. Then we went back to the dining room and talked about doing some trips.'

Though he remains somewhat disturbed by what he saw that day, Luis shrugs it off as part and parcel of running a cartel in Colombia in the 1980s.

'It did put me off buying farms and having cattle. I didn't want to deal with farm managers. I didn't want to deal with employees who stole cows from me. If you stole cocaine from me, I just turned you on to the fucking owner of the cocaine, the *oficina*. I didn't want to complicate my life. But to me that kind of torture is nothing. If I would have been in that [torturing] business I don't believe in "partial" shit. I'd just grab the guy and fucking cut his leg off. "Okay, motherfucker, your leg's gone. You want to lose another leg?" That captures your attention real quick.

'Waterboarding is CIA bullshit. Waterboarding is fucking Boy Scouts. *Come on.* If I were ever to be tortured, waterboard me. That's the best torture in the world. Bad torture? Imagine some guy grabs you, another guy grabs your right arm, and they take a fucking chainsaw and just go *whaaack* and cut your fucking leg right at the knee. That's the first thing they do. No waterboarding. No *nothing*. You lost your leg and there's blood coming out. You tell me. What do you prefer? That or waterboarding? It's just what they use when they don't wanna leave any marks. Real torture? They take a fucking chainsaw and just chop your leg off. Or they put a fucking piece of fucking steel right up your ass and put you on a barbecue and they fucking twirl you around until you fry to death.'

26
Kilo of Thorns

THROUGH HIS DEALER FRIEND ARLO, Luis had been introduced to an American called Greg Lazzara, who'd run charter boats in Hawaii before falling in with Arlo and his doper crowd in Santa Cruz and becoming a sort of errand boy. Luis also would later use Greg for collecting money from his clients in California and Florida. While out west, Greg had made a contact with an American called Pino Fatone.[121]

'Greg was from New Jersey,' says Luis. 'Rough around the edges; kind of a heavy-breathing, hyper, very intense guy that nobody wanted around. Greg had a friend, Pino, a dope dealer, who introduced me to a guy called "The Doc" and he had the connection to Rafael Caro Quintero [aka 'El Príncipe'] and "El Cochiloco" [The Crazy Pig, Juan Manuel Salcido Uzeta] of the Guadalajara Cartel.[122] The Mexicans were just starting to get into coke. You see it in *Narcos: Mexico*. I was never introduced to Caro Quintero personally but we've been in the same room in Puerto Vallarta.[123]

'It was all arranged through The Doc. He worked with Caro Quintero big time. *Weed*. Then they started working coke with me and this was apart from the [Miguel Ángel] Félix Gallardo group. I only met The Doc once, in Tucson. Some other smuggling was done with a group I met through my brother-in-law, Vicente, who never got into drugs. His sister, Andrea, who was also a money launderer,

Luis Antonio Navia and his parents, Luis Sr and María, photographed in Havana a few years before the 1959 Cuban Revolution. Luis Sr was the right-hand man of sugar baron Julio Lobo y Olavarria. *Courtesy of Luis Navia*

Luis Sr and María with Meyer Lansky's 'gambling representative', lawyer Julius E. Rosengard, and Rosengard's wife Emma at Lansky's Havana Riviera hotel. *Courtesy of Luis Navia*

The impeccably attired Navias step out in Havana in the 1950s. Says Luis of his father's style: 'Always the best suits in New York. Tailor made. Ties from A. Sulka or Countess Mara. Shirts all monogrammed.' *Courtesy of Luis Navia*

Luis and his sister, Laura, at Hyannis Port, Massachusetts, circa 1962. They were photographed inside 'Camp David', the art studio of Julius Rosengard. *Courtesy of Luis Navia*

Luis, Laura, Julius and María, Hyannis Port, circa 1962. Julius's chauffeur is in the background. *Courtesy of Luis Navia*

Luis graduated as a senior from the all-boys Belen Jesuit Preparatory School in Miami in 1973. He can be seen in this page from the yearbook at right in the top-right photograph, wearing a Coca-Cola styled 'Cocaine' t-shirt.
Courtesy of Luis Navia

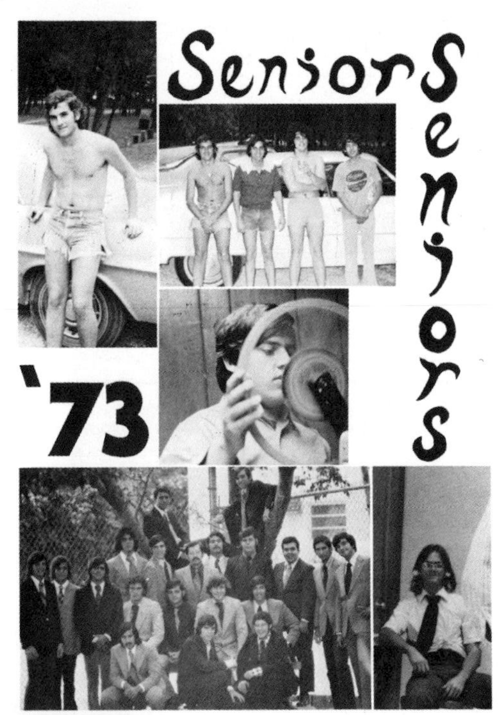

Luis was being groomed for great things in the world of business by Luis Sr. He took his only son to New York for a meeting with the law firm Milbank, Tweed, Hadley & McCloy, 'the top lawyers in the nation, the lawyers for the Rockefellers'.
Courtesy of Luis Navia

Luis during his short stint at the University of Miami.
Courtesy of Luis Navia

Luis with Latin American roommates Pablo an~~d Iván~~ at Georgetown University, Washington, DC, where he first sold cocaine: nine ounces or 255 grams.
Courtesy of Luis Navia

Luis was first introduced to the Colombian cocaine cartels through his Aruban girlfriend, Bia Gálvez, who had high-level connections in the Medellín Cartel. *Courtesy of Luis Navia*

Luis: 'It was instant fucking lust with Bia.' *Courtesy of Luis Navia*

Luis at a hotel in Beverly Hills, California, circa 1980/'81. His cocaine-trafficking career had just begun. *Courtesy of Luis Navia*

A newsprint picture of the arrest of Colombian enforcer Evangelista 'Mario' Navas Villabona after the deadly Amtrak siege in North Carolina of October 1982. *Photographer unknown*

A candid photo of the late Oscar Peláez Monsalve aka 'El Poli', reputedly one of the few men in Colombia who ever stood up face-to-face to Pablo Escobar. This photograph was recovered from one of his *caletas* or stash houses by Miami-Dade detective Roberto Diaz in 1979. *Courtesy of Roberto Diaz*

In an attempt to go straight and emulate his late father, Luis briefly owned/leased 22,000 acres of sugarcane in Florida. But he became involved in a fraud that sparked a United States Customs Service investigation, Operation Bittersweet, and ended up walking away from the sugar business altogether. *Courtesy of Luis Navia*

Luis's friend Lucchese crime-family figure Joey Martino was executed by his mob colleagues, encased in a cement-filled drum and dumped in a canal. Luis: 'I had a lot of dealings with the Lucchese group: somewhere around 6000 kilos. We used to have breakfast with 'em in Miami every other day. We used to sit down, typical mob style, you have nothing to do, you sit down for breakfast like Meyer Lansky did with his buddies. Coffees, Danish, this and that, and come up with something.' Their smuggling route to San Francisco was called 'Tony Bennett'. *The Martino Family*

Luis partying in the late 1980s with friend Richard Booth and girlfriend Lisa Cushing, who went to live with Luis in Colombia but didn't adjust well to life in South America. Lisa was later killed in an air accident. *Courtesy of Luis Navia*

Luis looking sharp in Bogotá, Colombia, 1989. He was now a pure narco but a man permanently on the run. *Courtesy of Luis Navia*

introduced me to a guy they called "El Tío", The Uncle.[124] Like "The Doc", I never knew his real name.'

Moving from pick-up trucks and fishing boats required a bigger capital investment in transport, so Luis bought his first plane, a 1977 beige Fairchild Swearingen SA26-T Merlin IIB twin-engine turboprop, for $500,000 out in Los Angeles, with Paco taking a 50 per cent share.

'The Merlin was a huge fucking plane; it stuck out – like it was bigger than the hangar. It stood real high. It looked like a fucking spaceship. It was not your typical smuggling plane: more an executive type, a big turboprop for private business. Most of the coke transported on the Merlin was through Paco. He had a lot of routes. His main sources of supply were Marulo and Mono through Halcón, and Pablo Correa of the Medellín Cartel.'

Luis kept the Merlin at small airports in Burbank, California, and Fort Lauderdale, Florida, and had two pilots, a *gringo* called Gordon 'Goo' Gray and a Colombian called Alejandro Álvarez, fly it to airstrips at Montería, southwest of Cartagena, and Aguachica, a flatlands rice-growing region northwest of Bucaramanga, to pick up the dope.[125] They'd also make occasional airdrops in The Bahamas. Each load from Colombia was about 600 to 700 kilos. The Mexicans handled the crossing logistics. The Doc took care of things once it was over the border.

'We started doing Rafael Caro Quintero's airstrip at La Peñita de Jaltemba, north of Puerto Vallarta, through a connection I met through Vicente Blanco. We hit that strip between eight and 12 times. We also used the Merlin to do some airdrops in Cancún to some of [the Medellín Cartel's] people. We hit Cancún eight to ten times with Miki Ramírez's merchandise. We also landed the Merlin a few times in Spanish Cay in The Bahamas. Alejandro flew into La Peñita and Spanish Cay.

'Goo was The Doc's and Pino's pilot. He was a crazy American, a great bush pilot. He was a great fucking pilot. *Period.* People in Colombia found out about how good he was as a pilot. He had to abort a mission, a Douglas DC-6 he was on; he landed off Cabo San Lucas in Baja California and he was stranded in the sea and he ended up in hospital. We did a few runs where Goo would airdrop in The Bahamas, come back in the morning, restock and refuel and fly out to Mexico – a 12-hour trip each way. Eventually problems arose between me and him and Greg Lazzara, but as a pilot he was amazing. Best bush pilot I've ever seen.'

*

And so quite by accident, Luis, using Puerto Vallarta as an operational base, became a pioneer of moving coke through Mexico in the early 1980s. A lot of Americans had been smuggling grass since the '70s, of course, and pot in Mexico was still a very valuable export. During one work trip he was introduced to a pot-smuggler *gringo* living up in the mountains of Puerto Vallarta, a friend of Rafael Caro Quintero whose marijuana-growing skills were made globally famous in *Narcos: Mexico.*

'He was a connoisseur of pot. He was like a hippie, a throwback from the '70s. I didn't catch his name. I went up there with my brother-in-law, Vicente, and this guy gave us some cookies to eat and he said they had marijuana in them. Brother, on the way back I started to hallucinate like I would have taken acid. I looked next to me, Vicente was driving, and I saw my father. I looked down at Vicente's legs, I saw my father's legs.

'Not too many smugglers were doing what I was doing; that I guarantee you. Nobody really had a plane like the Merlin. The Colombians, yes. The Mexican [José Gonzalo Rodríguez Gacha] and Pablo Escobar had a fleet of planes. [The Honduran narco] Juan Ramón Matta Ballesteros was already in Mexico working with Pablo, and bringing coke up to the Mexicans, and his partner was [Cuban narco] Alberto Sicilia Falcón.[126] But I was the only independent smuggler doing it.

'But to tell you the truth, each trip on the Merlin when I was dealing with Greg, Pino and Goo was a fucking royal pain in the ass. The trips I did without them were fine. The plane was great. On one trip these idiots fucking landed somewhere in the middle of the desert up in northern Mexico and had some mechanical problem, and I had to send two Mitsubishi MU-2 airplanes, "Rice Rockets", small little jets with turboprops, with mechanics from Miami with spare parts to fix the Merlin.[127]

'They had to jack up the plane and the whole thing was high risk, because how do you explain being in the middle of a desert fixing a plane that had no flight plan? It was either that or burn the Merlin. You know how much those fucking repairs cost me? About $100,000.'

*

The Doc was also using smaller piston-engine planes to airdrop in the Arizona desert. One particular airdrop had gone awry, some of the merchandise literally hitting cactuses on the way down. The cartel was not happy and had the punctured bags returned to Medellín.

'That was through Mexico with a crossing in Arizona; final delivery in LA. The bottom line is that we delivered in LA but some bags had cactus thorns in them.'

A meeting was arranged at El Pomar, the ranch of the SOS, Pablo Correa Arroyave, who became 'very wealthy and moved a lot of cocaine, *huge*' before he was killed by Pablo Escobar in 1986.[128]

Luis believes that Correa at one point was moving more coke to the US than Escobar and it had become an intolerable situation for the Medellín Cartel boss. When it came to coexisting with Escobar, 'you got too big, then bye-bye'.

'Correa told Paco he wanted to meet the man responsible for the route. So I went to meet him in Medellín. I booked into the InterContinental and was picked up by some of his guys. It was a very nice retreat he had on the outskirts of Medellín that had a professional cycling track: *pista de ciclismo*.'

It was then that Luis claims 'El Patrón' himself, Pablo Escobar, who also had some of his cocaine being transported, turned up. Los Pablos, the two Pablos, were in the same room with Luis. [129] The Cuban kid from Key Biscayne who'd sold croquette sandwiches for 50 cents a pop had come a long way.

'You can't have kilos with fucking thorns in them [*laughs*]. That's the power these people had: a kilo that's out in the desert. They took it back to Colombia just to show me. Pablo's coke was on all the trips but we never had a personal business relationship. So Pablo came in with ten fucking Suburbans and Jeeps with a bunch of his guys. Then the first group of his guys came in, then the second, and then he came. He always had what they call *anillo de seguridad*, which are security rings. The first group comes in, the second group comes in, you never know what car he's in.

'When Correa told me Pablo was on his way up to his office it was like nothing; he received a call on his radio and he said Pablo was coming up. I told him not to say anything about the thorns in the coke because I was kind of embarrassed, and worried if Correa did say something Pablo would say, "*Thorns?* What kind of fucking transport guy is this?" But Correa said, "*No, no, no. Tiene nada que ver con nuestra conversación.*" It has nothing to do with our conversation. Pablo was not there to see me; he was there to see Correa and I was not involved in the meeting that they had. But we shook hands when he came up and then they went into Correa's office.

'Most people from Antioquia, I don't know why, do not have a super-firm handshake. Pablo's handshake was medium-strength but firm. He was wearing jeans, tennis shoes and a plaid shirt with a pocket and a little notebook and a pen. The notebook fit in the shirt pocket.[130] He was courteous and I was courteous – "Pleased to meet you" type of thing.

'I was working with top people in Colombia at the time but just because Pablo Escobar walks in the room you don't try to make unnecessary conversation; you follow the lead. He was not there to see me and there was no reason for me to try to make it anything different. Of course, I knew who he was but Pablo back then was not the mythological figure he is today. At that given moment Correa was not Pablo's equal but he had a very significant amount of cocaine in the States. He was definitely a major player in the Medellín Cartel. I can forever say I was in a room with both of them. Two Pablos and a kilo full of thorns.

'That night Correa invited me to be his guest at the best disco in Medellín at the time, Kevin's, and then we went back to one of his houses with some girls and he assigned a few bodyguards to me.[131] The name of the head bodyguard was Chocolate. The next day one of Paco's private planes picked me up and took me back to Bogotá.'

*

As for the troubled Merlin, it eventually met its inevitable death in the blue waters of the Caribbean. It had simply run out of gas.

'The last time it flew Alejandro was shitting in his pants and so scared that he took off from Spanish Cay before they could top off the fuel tanks, so he had to land in the water. We call it *acuatizar* in Spanish. The plane is now part of a fucking reef off a Haitian beach.'

27

River of Blood

LOSING A LOAD OF marijuana or cocaine didn't necessarily mean certain death, as it's often made out in Hollywood movies about drug trafficking. It was far from a murderous free-for-all – or at least it wasn't till it devolved into all-out war in Colombia between Medellín, Cali and the government in Bogotá in the late 1980s and early 1990s. There was a degree of tolerance exercised among the cartels when it came to seizures, water landings or other screw-ups – of a sort, anyway. It was part of the business.

'You know the base of it, how it really works? You've got to keep your word, pay your bills and never lie. Anybody can lose a load. But you have to face up to it. There's a saying in Spanish: *La cara del santo hace el milagro*. The face of the saint makes the miracle. You lose a load, you go right to the owner and tell them, "Listen, I lost a load and it happened like this. Right now I've only got $700,000 but here it is; that's good money. The rest I'll pay back." That builds up your goodwill.'

No amount of goodwill, however, can save you when you steal a load, are *suspected* of stealing a load or someone simply wants you dead. Especially when that someone is Pablo Escobar. He might have dressed like a computer nerd and been awfully polite to Luis when they met at Pablo Correa's home, but Escobar was a mass murderer directly linked to the deaths of two of Luis's closest friends in the cartel: Mono Lopera and Paco Barrera.[132] Both men dreamed of a life outside the drug business: they wanted to go to live in Paris, for different reasons. But El Patrón would never let them leave Colombia.

*

Mono, who was 'early 40s, very good-looking, well built, blond, blue-eyed, almost six-feet tall', was cooking super-high-grade cocaine under the brands 'Cocos' and 'USA' in Ecuador and 'making a lot of money'. He owned a Spanish abode in La Candelaria, the colonial part of Bogotá with its narrow cobblestoned streets. Mono's home, a kind of retreat, had an unassuming entrance with two large wooden doors. Behind it were manicured gardens, rooms filled with antiques and exquisite furnishings, butlers, maids.

'You would walk the sidewalks and see these huge wooden doors and not realise that there were beautiful palatial homes behind them. Inside it was like another world. Back in the 1980s nobody really took a liking to that, but Mono did because he had that sense of art in him, so he bought one of these homes and completely renovated it. He used to just go there and hang out and get away from it all; it was like his retreat. It was just a great feeling to be behind those closed doors in the cool weather of Bogotá and listen to the sounds of the birds and the peacefulness that he had created there.

'Mono's idea was to one day leave Colombia, go to Paris and study French for a couple of years, take his family. That was his dream. He had some beautiful farms in Pereira, one called Marruecos [Morocco] with a large yucca plantation. The yucca fields were totally manicured. At that point he was a serious player in the cocaine export business. He was shot when he was visiting Medellín. I was told Pablo killed him. Either shot in the head or in the kidney. He was not taken hostage and tortured. A typical thing Pablo would do is hold you and you would have to basically beg for them not to torture you and ask for a quick death. He would take a good chunk of money from you before that happened.

'All I ever heard was that Pablo did not like that Mono was growing so big so fast and from knowing of his desire to educate himself more, his love for the finer things in life and his love for the arts, wanting to go to Paris and learn French, that was probably too much for Pablo to swallow and he did not see eye to eye with that.

In the end it could have been envy. But Mono was somewhat involved with the Cali people and maybe that's why Pablo killed him. Pacho Herrera became Pablo's main enemy.[133]

'Pablo was an even-tempered guy but when he got something in his head he was determined to carry it out. I have friends with strong ties to the old groups of the Medellín Cartel and the general word is that Mono was getting too big and his death was a result of differences with Pablo. Some personality differences must've come into play. I can see a situation where Pablo started taxing him a little more and demanding certain conditions and Mono said no and that's why he was killed.'

*

But it was the murder of Paco that shocked Luis the most for its sheer brutality. Paco, from Bucaramanga, was killed on a farm in Magdalena Medio Antioquia. His right-hand man, Pedro Pablo, had told Luis what happened. Luis had eventually bought Paco out of his share of the Merlin before it was ditched off Haiti, and together they did a bunch of trips from an airstrip in Montería, Colombia, airdropping in the Florida Keys and Cancún.

'With Paco I must have done close to 20 tons; that's a *lot* of trips. He became my main partner in Colombia. Paco accumulated about $140 million in a short period of time but he wasn't a badass or prone to violence. He was one of those guys that had it in him to better himself, to learn another language, to study. He said to me, "It gets to the point where you have that much money, you have to be ready to kill to protect it, and since I'm not ready to kill I'm going to retire."'

Like Mono, he'd already bought an apartment in Paris and was planning to move there with his girlfriend, Viviana, to get away from the cartels altogether.

'If you're gonna retire you should *tell* nobody you're gonna retire. They never let Paco retire. He would accumulate merchandise from a lot of people. And then he would just shoot it out on the different routes he had and then he would call you and tell you, "Listen, tonight, 300 of your kilos are going to Miami," for example.

'But a lot of the time he would take 300 kilos and not tell you they were going to Miami. And he'd send them to Miami, sell it there, and then with that money he would buy merchandise and replace your 300 kilos. That's a no-no. You're finagling. That rumour went around and it caught up to him. It's not like he owed somebody $20 million but Paco was riding a very fucking thin line. He was in somebody's scopes.

'People just got a little bit too jealous of him, and that's a problem also. And that's why I always made sure not to come across as too educated or an *I'm-better-than-you* type. A lot of people didn't like that about Paco. "Oh, so he can come, he can make $140 million, and he finagled a little bit, and we gave him a pass on that, and now he's just going to retire and go to fucking Paris, and now he thinks he's better than all of us?" *No, no, no, no.* Somebody may not like that.

'So when he called a route and people found out their merchandise was being sold in Miami because it all has markings [on the coke], Pedro Pablo in combination with somebody else kidnapped him. I've always suspected he had a hand in and profited from Paco's death. Rumour said it was Pablo Escobar [who ordered the hit] because Paco had finagled the merchandise. Since he was not a violent man they took most of his money. They took $80 million. And he gave it up. And they said that they were going to let him go. And they never let him go. I remember Pedro Pablo telling me about what had happened. They picked up his ass, they tied him up, they took all his money, and they killed him. The day they told him, "Okay, you can go," he went to wash his face in the river, and the guy who was there, when [Paco] bowed down to wash his face, *thwaaack*, chopped his head off.

'Think of it: in the mountains, in Colombia, in the middle of nowhere, a river running, and Paco, after days of being kidnapped and paying the ransom, going to wash his face and the guy next to him just pulls out a machete from its sheath. I can picture the guy with the machete, and *whooom*, the head just floating down the river. The ugly part is it takes more than one whack with a machete; it's not a katana and the person doing it is not a trained samurai.

'Every day is a thin line between life and death. In that business you can be dead the next minute. You look at somebody the wrong way. You say the wrong thing. You come across the wrong way. You think you're better than they are. There's so much planning: they can either whack you then and there or wait six months and whack you.'

28

Sugar King of Palm Beach County

PERHAPS LUIS REALISED HIS own longevity in the business wasn't guaranteed, so, as he had done all his adult life, he kept one foot in criminality, the other in respectability. The defining characteristic of his drug-trafficking career to this point had been walking this tightrope of self-identity. It still ate away at him that he hadn't proved he had the nobler makings of a real businessman to his father when he was alive; someone who could make it in proper commerce, not the illegitimate alt-world of cocaine smuggling.

Even in death Luis Sr continued to define how his son thought of himself; matching up to him seemed impossible to Luis through crime. But if he could somehow get a foot in the door of a real business and give it time to grow, he might actually stand a chance of proving he was a worthy inheritor of the Navia name.

Luis's ticket, or so he thought, was taking a stake in Wall Street sugar-trading company Lobo-Kane, run by Julio Lobo's nephew Gustavo Lobo and an Irish-American called Gerald J. or 'Gerry' Kane. Before his death in 1982, Luis Sr had introduced Gerry to his son and Lobo-Kane was already involved in the Navia family's concern in Aruba, Caribe Packing. Gustavo and Gerry didn't know, however, that Luis was using Caribe to traffic cocaine in the US Virgin Islands and Puerto Rico.

'I had given Gerry about $400,000 and the idea was to buy

50 per cent of Lobo-Kane. I think the contract was for $1 million. They thought it was money that I inherited from my dad. My father was known as a person that brought a lot of money from Cuba – and he did – but most people thought he brought over a lot more than he actually did. My dad was a very conservative man. He built up his sugar reputation over many years of hard work. I didn't inherit a lot from him. I inherited his name. But after he died I got the big idea of, "I'm going to invest in Lobo-Kane."'

Problem was, before he knew it, Luis was back to his old tricks – only this time he was playing 'the whole sugar game'. His impulse control was clearly poor.

'My original plan had been to become a legitimate businessman and get out of the other business. But I met this black guy from Trinidad called Mike Laburd, a businessman who lived in Toronto.[134] When I went to visit him he had his office on Bay Street, which is the Canadian equivalent of Wall Street. He was involved in international commodities trading and had some kind of plan to falsify paperwork after we imported sugar and left it in the States. He needed someone to sell it in volume for him, which was where Gerry came in.

'I thought it was a great idea. We weren't hurting anybody; it's not like we were lending people money and putting people in debt on mortgages that you knew they wouldn't be able to pay back and then you would have to come around and take their homes. It was a business where really there were no victims; the only victim was the US Government not getting their share of tax.

'I do not have that line [sic] of what's good and bad in business; business is business and government tariff laws are more crooked or more corrupt than anything else, so I had no reservations about contrabanding sugar. Compared to what I did every day for a living it was like nothing. I made a mistake playing international businessman after my dad died. He would never have gone for any of it. Apart from it being illegal, he would have told me how rough the sugar business is. But we were making more money doing the fucking sugar than the coke.'

*

The scam worked like this: in the early 1980s the United States Department of Agriculture (USDA) heavily subsidised the sugar industry through the federal price support program. A pound of raw American-grown sugar was worth 22 cents to a farmer in the US when sold to a refinery. Once refined, the wholesale price was 28 cents. But outside the US, a pound of raw sugar was only worth four or five cents, sometimes as low as three cents. So it was against the law to sell imported raw sugar in the US – if it came into the country, it did so under the strict condition it was refined and re-exported within 90 days. Importers would then claim a generous rebate or 'drawback' on the duty they paid to bring it in. This system kept American refineries in business and safeguarded the livelihoods of American sugar growers.

Luis saw an opportunity for Lobo-Kane to make a few easy million. He and his partners would buy dirt-cheap sugar in the Dominican Republic, export it to the US and pay the 2.8-cent-per-pound duty set by USDA, have it refined at Godchaux-Henderson Sugar Refinery in New Orleans (costing them no more than five cents per pound), then re-export it to the Caribbean and claim a 99 per cent rebate on the original duty and any export credits.[135]

Only his sugar wasn't actually being re-exported. Lobo-Kane falsified papers, passed off the sugar as American-grown, and sent it to a company called New York Bakeries which bought it at 21 cents a pound, seven cents cheaper than the going rate for American refined sugar. Lobo-Kane would pocket both the rebate and any credit on the falsified bills of lading (documents showing it had been sent for export by ship), plus the 12 cents difference between the cost of the imported refined sugar and the sale price to the bakery.

'Mike handled the sugar export and re-export part. I hooked him up with Gerry, who handled the selling of the sugar part and keeping the books. They started to put the whole thing together and they needed a capital infusion from me – $3 million – to get it going.'

Godchaux-Henderson was a subsidiary of Great Western Sugar Company, Dallas. They had bought the refinery from Luis's father's old friend, Julio Lobo, when he was offloading assets after the Cuban Revolution. Access to the refinery was limited and lucrative.

But because of the Cuban connection, the Navia name carried some weight.

'Drugs are the fastest way for poor people to make money. I did the sugar contraband thing only because I had a structure of sugar behind me that cost millions and millions. Wherever I went, smuggling followed me. Here I am trying to go legit by getting into the sugar business, but tempting situations are put in front of me. Everywhere I stepped, I was stepping into a smuggling pond. It's like Mr Magoo; everywhere he went he was surrounded by accidents and came away without so much as a scratch. I was the smuggling Magoo. So I went to Louisiana and personally met with the president of Godchaux-Henderson. It's not easy to get a slot in a refinery; they're reserved for the big players in the sugar industry. You can't just be anybody and go to Godchaux-Henderson and ask them to refine 10,000 tons of sugar for you.'

*

While Luis was buying Lobo-Kane a sugar company called L-Bis Industries fell in his lap.[136] L-Bis, based in Lake Harbor, Palm Beach County, Florida, had been started by a man called Lambert Bisonte who was the son-in-law of Thomas Vilgrain, 'one of the pioneers of the sugar business in Florida, a Florida cracker'.[137]

Bisonte had got into financial strife after borrowing tens of millions from banks to funnel money into another business he had, a goat farm in Darby, Montana, and began defaulting on his payments. He was now looking for a partner to come in and buy a stake in L-Bis. The deal involved 22,000 acres of sugarcane, half of which would be owned outright, the other half leased long term.

'Lambert believed in the future of goat cheese. He was trying to sell L-Bis because the banks were going to take it. He'd milked the company and put the money in the goat farm in Montana. L-Bis was a sugar-growing operation but it "rested" the sugar land by growing rice. So it had a rice mill and the rice it produced and milled was mostly exported to Haiti. It was $60 million in debt.

'While people in Miami were buying raceboats and thinking about hookers and going to The Mutiny, even though I was completely fucked out of my brains doing drugs and drinking and partying like an animal, I still had some kind of vision of what I wanted to be in life: which was to follow my dad's footsteps and be a legitimate businessman. So I went to Lambert and said, "I'll buy it. I'll give you $400,000 under the table for you, and we sit down with the banks, you back me up on everything and I'll commit to the banks and put in $5 million in new capital to restructure the company."[138]

'The deal with Lambert was to buy the business and take him out of the equation. That way he would be free of all obligations and debts that L-Bis incurred under his ownership. I was down in Florida busy with the whole L-Bis acquisition and my smuggling operation, so I let Gerry and Mike handle the sugar smuggling. But I needed somebody to help me out with L-Bis.'

The man Luis chose was Jaider Esparza, who'd been thrown out of Faces in the Grove in a case of mistaken identity when Luis had decided to dump a bucket of ice cubes on the dancefloor. Jaider was a short, skinny Cuban with beady eyes who made a habit of drinking a bottle of Crown Royal whisky every day.

'I needed Jaider because he knew how to work with banks. He was ex-CIA; one sharp dude. He'd got shot in the leg in the Bay of Pigs invasion and was a "player", although not in the drug business. He spoke with a Cuban Southern accent and wouldn't hesitate to shoot you. He was armed at all times: a gun holster on his ankle and some kind of self-defence knife in his left pocket.'

He was also a conman wanted for fraud.

'He started a computer-leasing company in North Carolina in the late '70s/early '80s when large-capacity computer systems were very expensive. He would lease these computers to big companies and it turns out he was scamming banks for huge amounts of money. He would offer the computers to companies that were doing payroll services, for example, leave them the computers and use those leases to get money from the banks to buy more computers, and I think a lot of those leases were false – it was like a Ponzi scheme. From what I heard, a lot of these leases didn't exist; he just pocketed the money. He was hiding from his problems in Miami and owed the IRS quite a lot of money. But he was an agile guy business-wise.'

So Luis and Jaider hit the road in Jaider's Cadillac or took planes. Luis made sure to bring plenty of cocaine with him for his personal use.

'I did not know the extent to which he was indebted to the banks and in trouble with the banks, but I said, "You help me buy this operation and I will help you solve your problem with the IRS." So Jaider was key as a front man for wheeling and dealing with these North Carolina and Florida hicks. We went to Charlotte and met North Carolina National Bank [NCNB].[139] We sat down with First Bank of Clewiston, Florida. There was another bank in Dallas. Using my dad's good name they thought I was the heir to his sugar interests in Miami. They refinanced $60 million in loans and we bought L-Bis Industries. The banks gave me $60 million – and I was a coke dealer, a smuggler.

'In Charlotte, after Jaider and I closed the deal in Memphis, it was like I was the leader of the Boy Scouts. I had 20 girls following me everywhere I went. *Everybody* wanted my cocaine. I ended up getting laid with three, four chicks in the room; we fucking had a great time.'

Luis was now the part owner/part leaseholder – at least on paper – of 22,000 acres of prime Palm Beach County sugar country.

'I went up to the mill various times, of course, and rented an office but was hardly involved in the business at all. I was drinking a lot and snorting a lot. Jaider and I were doing a lot of partying. Over-the-top spending money and living large.'

But almost as soon as he'd got into the sugar industry, Luis decided to get out. If he couldn't do justice to his father's name in his father's business there was no other option. For him, it was simply a matter of honouring Luis Sr's legacy, a point of integrity.

'Smuggling was my territory but sugar was *his* turf. When it came to sugar, I had to be like my dad – honourable and impeccable – or not be in it at all. The minute I had to walk *his* turf in *that* sugar land, I had to walk it like he walked it. Which wasn't my style. Not being corrupt. Not smuggling. I had to do it the right way; not be flashy or associate with shady Trinidadian businessmen from Toronto. So it was a great plan but I had a lifestyle that was incompatible with it. Carrying out the plan and my lifestyle were on a collision course with each other.

'It hurt me a lot to have to turn my back on it. Looking back, I was crazy not to have dedicated myself to L-Bis. My dad used to drive to Clewiston and stay three, four days a week. I should've moved up there, bunkered down and been an everyday, present, hands-on owner and learned the sugar business and been involved.

'I put together that whole L-Bis acquisition because it was a big deal to me: so I could say to myself I was as big as my dad and he would be proud. My intentions were good – they *were*. I wanted to get into sugar and get out of the coke. It was because of his name that we got that land. The only time I've ever felt guilty or reflected on what's right and wrong is when it comes to my dad. All my life I never gave a flying fuck about anything else. Of course Lambert wanted it back so I returned the company to him and never looked back.'

Yet not before using the last days of his ownership of L-Bis to launder money.

'I took full advantage of the situation at hand. Buying L-Bis gave me the opportunity to move other monies around. I laundered what was a good chunk of change – $4 million – to Aruba using some of the other companies that I owned independently of L-Bis. I also paid Jaider what I owed him. Back then people were not really that in tune with money laundering, and me having a sugar operation in Florida, being partners with a Wall Street sugar brokerage firm, and having a packing operation in Aruba associated with one in Pompano Beach created the perfect climate for me to launder.'

*

But for the first time, the feds were circling. While Lobo-Kane was scamming drawbacks in New Jersey and offloading contraband sugar to New York Bakeries, a long-running USCS investigation into the sugar industry called Operation Bittersweet, based out of New York, Baltimore, Miami and New Orleans, was wrapping up.

Lobo-Kane hadn't been the only sugar company fiddling the books: in fact, the practice of defrauding the US Government through bogus rebates and bills of lading was widespread: dozens of companies had been complicit. Some 250,000 to 500,000 tons of foreign sugar had being dumped, tens of millions of dollars had been stolen, and

Lobo-Kane's creative accounting had led to a tip-off, which resulted in Luis receiving his first subpoena. He hired a lawyer, Tom Wolfe of Miami law firm Shutts & Bowen.

Lobo-Kane was indicted for 'aiding and abetting, false claims, false entry, smuggling and uttering false bills of lading', and Luis was summoned to appear in a courthouse in New Orleans before a grand jury. But not before Gerry Kane, just 54, had a heart attack and Mike Laburd fled to Trinidad.

'The subpoena came in the mail and Gerry dropped dead on his front lawn in Staten Island. Thank God, because if not he would have blamed me for everything and I would have been indicted and gone to jail. I would have been *fucked*. Mike ran. He flew the coop. They never caught him. If they had, he would have fucking electrocuted me too.'

Luis said he gave $30,000 for the purchase of the sugar when the real figure had been $3 million. Lobo-Kane would eventually plead guilty to five counts of illegally importing 1.4 million pounds of sugar. Gustavo Lobo claimed innocence and agreed to an early plea deal while the Kane Estate admitted wrongdoing, Gerry's pension fund being garnished to pay fines.[140] Overall, Operation Bittersweet nabbed 12 companies and 11 officials in what amounted to a $50 million nationwide fraud on sugar import fees.

In hundreds of newspapers around America, Associated Press ran with the story of Lobo-Kane's downfall.

SATURDAY, AUGUST 3, 1985

SUGAR CONCERN ADMITS FRAUD

NEW ORLEANS -- A New Jersey concern has pleaded guilty to five charges of fraud in connection with the 'Operation Bittersweet' crackdown on illegal sugar operations. Lobo Kane Inc. of Linden, NJ., entered the plea in federal court. Customs agents said the company agreed in plea bargaining to return to the government $250,000 in illegal profits.

> The company also was fined $30,000. The indictment said Lobo Kane bought millions of pounds of sugar for export, filed false claims that it would be exported and then diverted the sugar back to the United States for resale at the higher domestic price. Lobo Kane was charged with submitting at least 45 fraudulent claims, resulting in $250,000 customs duties being refunded to Godchaux-Henderson Sugar Refinery.
>
> The government said Godchaux-Henderson had nothing to do with the scam.

As for Luis, no further actions were taken against him, because with Gerry and Mike gone, there were no witnesses to corroborate the government's case.[141] Caribe Packing was shut down and he walked out of the sugar business being owed millions (his share of the contraband profits that Gerry had kept) but a free man. To celebrate, he went drinking with Tom Wolfe on Bourbon Street in New Orleans.

'The first thing I did when I got out of the grand-jury room was I told Tom, "Let's go hit a bar." And I said, "I need to buy something as a reminder of this." So I bought a beautiful painting of the Mississippi River. I flew home with that painting as a reminder of that grand jury. It's still hanging in my sister's apartment. And I never contacted Gus Lobo or any member of Gerry Kane's family again.'

PART 6
WAR ZONE

29

Five Units of Fercho

By his own admission, Luis 'got spooked by all the sugar legal shit' and threw himself back into something decidedly less dangerous – cocaine trafficking – with a new sense of purpose. He'd found his groove as a smuggler and barely had to lift a finger to make a lazy million: the systems were in place, the right connections had been made, his Colombian suppliers were eager to move more of their product, and demand in the United States was at a peak – despite inroads made against the industry by President Ronald Reagan's war on drugs.

From Pereira, Montería and La Costa Caribe in Colombia he was moving thousands of kilos through Miami, Mexico, The Bahamas and Jamaica. Luis, now one of America's major drug smugglers yet unknown to law enforcement, had perfected the art of the route – though not without taking considerable risks. The Achilles heel of any cocaine-transport operation is unreliable personnel, someone flipping. Or it's volume – smuggle too much and the chances are you're going to be noticed.

'But for every load that gets caught, 50 make it through. It's ridiculous. You're in this business for so long that you just find the right person in the right place. You develop all kinds of friendships all over the world. You go wherever you have those friends. You've just got connections. Your whole network in life is dedicated to the export and trafficking of cocaine. That's how it is. Time, dedication and reliable contacts, like any business.'

*

Luis's main client was now El Tío in Mexico, who started moving big weight. After receiving Marulo's coke from Colombia he crossed it over into San Diego through Tijuana in Baja California. Another Mexican contact, Eduardo Fonseca, known by the moniker 'El Compadre', The Godparent, smuggled into McAllen, Texas, from Reynosa in Tamaulipas.[142] He was working directly with the Mexican federal police, the *federales*.

'Tío turned out to be a fucking goldmine. He had his own connections at the border. He had cars cross over and paid off officials. I had lost the Merlin so we rented a plane, a Cheyenne, and a pilot, 'Romerito', from Vicente Wilson Rivera González, one of the original cocaine producers from Leticia.'

Each load was 700 keys and Luis did 30 trips, nearly half of them to Guaymas, Mexico. And that was just one plane. He ended up operating a fleet of seven private planes, some bought, others leased – a Rockwell Turbo Commander, Beechcraft King Air, Piper PA-42 Cheyenne, Piper Navajo Panther, Cessna Titan, a Cessna Conquest and a Learjet 25 – and would variously keep them in hangars in Venezuela, California, Mexico and Colombia. In total, he moved more than 55 tons, or over 50,000 kilos, on small aircraft from Colombia to the United States in the late 1980s.

Fernando Marulanda would emerge as one of Luis's chief suppliers during this period.

'Marulo was a big, heavy-set guy, bald, about six-feet tall; he must've been 250 pounds. By any standards he was definitely on the heavy side. His nickname was "El Gordo", The Fat One, though I never heard anybody use the term *gordo* about him in the bad sense. As was his nature, he was always "moving with a purpose" – 24 hours in a day wasn't enough. When we first met he'd just come back from Ecuador, where he had been kidnapped and tortured by the police. He was hung by the tip of his thumbs and beaten bad. They'd discovered one of his cocaine labs. His partner Mono Lopera had arranged for the ransom to be paid and everything to be taken care of.

'Marulo was always buying farms and converting them into beautiful cattle ranches or places where he kept his showhorses; they were unbelievable.[143] He was known in Colombia for having beautiful *fincas*, just like the Ochoas. After Mono died Marulo became the top dog in Pereira and somehow he managed to keep out of harm's way. On one trip we airdropped off The Bahamas and there was like 400 units [keys of cocaine] on that trip. It wasn't a lot. But Marulo said that there were also five units of something he'd marked "Fercho", which is a nickname for Fernando – and he made it very clear to us that it was different; it was heroin. We took it and we gave it to somebody in Miami on his behalf. We never did it again.'

Did that bother you?

'I don't think about it much – heroin wasn't my daily business and Marulo just put those units on the trip. It was meaningless. I was not interested in opening a market for that and I don't think Marulo did too good either on the selling end or on the supply side. Cocaine is just as bad as heroin; it's just a different high. The only difference being cocaine was the drug of all the successful New York bankers and Hollywood movie stars; all the discos were full of cocaine people: dancing, having a great time. Cocaine was equated with discos and outlandish lifestyles. Heroin was equated to some junkie shooting up in an alley. But you can get just as addicted on freebase as you can on heroin.'

*

Having successfully kicked his own freebasing habit after his enforced self-isolation at the Miyako Hotel in San Francisco, Luis had turned his energies to spending his own money on the things he loved: cars, hookers and fancy hotels.

'At one point between Miami and San Francisco I had 14, 15 cars. I had a blue Bentley, a black 1981 Ferrari 308 GTSi, a 1957 MG, a 1965 Mustang, a 1962 Corvette, a four-door Vanden Plas, a couple of Jaguars, three Porsches, three Mercedes-Benzes. I kept most of them in storage, one at Diego Forero's and one at my parents' place.

'I'd give hookers $15,000 like *nothing*. Me and a friend of mine, Richard Booth, a salesman for Southern Wine & Spirits of America, would call up Moonflower Escorts in Miami Beach and they'd send girls over. I was the only customer who had credit. After one three-day spree with a dozen hookers we paid them $45,000. One day we threw $60,000 down the trash chute because $30,000 were false bills and we didn't want to get caught with them. We made a mistake and instead of ripping up 30 we ripped up 60 and threw away $30,000.[144]

'Nobody *ever* paid for dinner. I never went out to a dinner that was less than $900. I always picked up the bill. Every day I'd pick off something I liked in a boutique, like a $400 shirt. One day I walked into a store and I said, "What the fuck is this?" It was a cane made out of rhinoceros dick. "Wow, cool. Let's take three of those." They were $500 each. I'd go to San Francisco and buy all kinds of weird art. In Tucson, we'd stay in hotels for *months*. To pay a $50,000 bill at a hotel was nothing. You just spend money recklessly every fucking day, plus all the collateral expenses for your entourage.

'I had a friend called "Dave the Slave"; he was our gopher. He had a daughter. So for the birthday present, the baptism, we gave him a kilo of coke. But the truth is the craziest thing I ever wasted money on was just paying bills for trips where merchandise went missing. They were losses that I assumed so that people weren't killed. And we weren't making money like Pablo Escobar who *owned* the merchandise. We were only making a percentage on the transport. We weren't making $10 million a trip; we were making a million.'

*

Luis might have had money to burn but one of Navia's 11, Javier Mercado, was living way beyond his means on Star Island in Miami and looking to bring more coke into the United States to fund his extravagant lifestyle. To do so he was cutting some important corners in the process.

'Javier and his partner Bernardo Palomeque had made a lot of money and they retired for a while. They were both hitting it hard in the late '80s. Bernardo had a Gold Rolex with diamonds and his name engraved on it, a gold bracelet with his name, a chain with diamonds and a fucking flying eagle on it. He had a long-stretch Mercedes with a bar in the back. He was out of control. Then he started snorting coke, drinking a lot and hanging out with this young Cuban girl. It fucked up his marriage.

'Javier was a really good-looking guy, suntanned, tall, green eyes, a really bright guy; he used to date the most beautiful Venezuelan beauty queens. He'd had a very successful pot run with Bernardo and Juanchi and was a reckless motherfucker. He had everything going for him, but I think he was so desperate and so burnt out he was making a lot of bad decisions without thinking. He overextended himself. He was almost bankrupt. So after not seeing each other for a while, I ran into Javier and told him that I had just bought a Conquest II for $850,000 in Oklahoma. He suggested we keep the plane in Venezuela where he had connections with ex–Venezuelan Air Force pilots and commercial pilots.

'The Conquest for its speed and size – not being big and easy to keep on the ground – is probably the best airdrop-smuggling plane ever. Not as comfortable as the Merlin for executive comforts, but a lot better for airdropping. I would take care of the SOS in Colombia after moving down there and he would take care of the operations in the States, which included the airdrops to The Bahamas as well as the receiving of merchandise in California from El Tío and El Compadre. That's one thing I told Javier. "El Tío doesn't even know our name – we send merchandise to him and he pays us. That's the best-case scenario. Anybody has a problem, nobody knows who's who." The worst thing you can do is work with a person when he knows your name.'

*

The pilot Javier organised to fly the Conquest was actually a co-pilot, a Panamanian-Chinese called Chang aka 'El Chino'. Javier's regular pilot had never flown a Conquest and Luis's group didn't have a certified Conquest pilot who could step in. El Chino had recently been sent to flight-safety school to learn the aircraft's systems. Different types of aircraft have their own landing gears, hydraulics and instrumentation that require familiarisation before flying. Javier assured Luis that El Chino knew these systems and was ready to go. There was no time to waste. They needed a good bush pilot and quickly. The problem was that El Chino had never passed the course.

'Sure enough, the fucking plane lands in the desert outside of Monterrey, Mexico, they unload the merchandise, the merchandise leaves, suddenly the blades of the plane they feather, they go sideways, and you have to pull a switch under the seat to unfeather the blades so that the plane can go forward, so it can have grab.[145] These motherfuckers, El Chino and his co-pilot, they couldn't find the switch to unfeather the blades. The engines ran, everything was on, but they could not unfeather the blades and couldn't move forward.

'Supposedly if you go to flight-safety school you know the systems and it's the simplest of all things. It turned out to be a little switch under the pilot's seat. The Mexican Army was coming down the road. El Chino and his co-pilot were like, "We cannot leave this plane here." So they burned the fucking plane. The army arrested some of the Colombians and Mexicans receiving the load; they were put in jail. It was a complete fuck-up. The only good thing was we saved the merchandise. But I lost my plane.'

So Luis simply went out and bought one in better condition in Missouri. Every fledgling business needs its equipment.

'I bought the second Conquest with my own money and paid a little over a million with some odds and ends to bring it to $1.2 million. Obviously I was pissed but there was so much money coming in from the merchandise, we could always afford to buy a new plane.'

30

Body in a Barrel

MANY TIMES DURING THE writing of *Pure Narco*, Luis referred back to *Wiseguy* by Nicholas Pileggi. It was clear he identified very much with Henry Hill, a low-level hood in the Lucchese crime family, one of New York's 'Five Families' of La Cosa Nostra, who after decades in the yoke of the mob went into federal witness protection to save his and his family's life.

'The reason Henry Hill had to rat those people out is the minute he gets arrested, the first thing they do is they don't support his family, they don't give his family the pension that you deserve, because if you're sitting in jail and your family is religiously getting $10,000 to $15,000 a month with no problem, you don't rat nobody out.

'The American mafia used to have some very honourable, business-minded people involved. They laundered their money in America and they made America great. The mafia was little when New York was little: New York grew, the mafia grew.[146] They went into Las Vegas and created casinos. But real honour is when somebody gets busted and somebody goes and says, "This is your pension. You will have this for the rest of your life." That's why it's so incredible when you work for a company like FedEx or Coca-Cola for 30 years. You retire and they give you a pension, they give you a pay cheque. They're *there*. Even the US fucking Postal Service has a better retirement plan than crime.

'But these guys in *Wiseguy*, they think they're going to get ratted out, they even tried to kill Henry's wife; [the scene with] Jimmy the Gent [played by Robert De Niro] in the Garment District. So that's what it is. That's what I would tell people. The mafia ain't no fucking company. They're a bunch of cutthroats. There's no honour. There's none of that.'

Luis knows this not from the movies but from personal experience, after going through one of the strangest interludes in his drug-smuggling career: when he worked for the American mob in South Florida and met a man called Joseph Martino aka 'Joey', an 'earner' for the same Lucchese crime family Henry Hill was forced to rat on. Martino had become Luis's good friend after being introduced by Javier Mercado and Bernardo Palomeque.

'We hit it off right away. Joey was not a highly educated man; he just had a great personality and all he wanted to do in life was make money and live as well as possible. With Joey it was always coke, but I know that before he was involved in pot. He didn't do anything all day. All he did was plan his small goals: go to breakfast, visit with his girlfriend and then go to dinner with his wife, Joyce, hang out at Turnberry Isle during the weekends and suntan next to the pool. A ladies' man.

'You could say it was a shallow life but that's who he was: a very outgoing, very funny guy. He was happy living between his apartments in Miami and New York City. He was a great-looking Italian: black straight hair, clean-shaven. He was always well dressed, but kept it casual: he would wear those sports jogging sweatsuits a lot of the mob guys used to wear, with nice white tennis shoes.

'Joey hooked me up with the Lucchese group. Anthony Accetturo and Frank Suppa were the heads of the Lucchese family down in Hollywood, Florida.[147] We started working the Jamaican route. I had a lot of dealings with the Lucchese group: somewhere around 6000 kilos. We used to have breakfast with 'em in Miami every other day. We used to sit down, typical mob style, you have nothing to do, you sit down for breakfast like Meyer Lansky did with his buddies. Coffees, Danish, this and that, and come up with something.

'We called it "Tony Bennett", this trip that we were doing to

San Francisco. I met quite a few of the Italian guys. I was bringing in loads for them. But I wasn't connected to them like Joey was, because that was all he did; that was his thing. The Lucchese group used a small twin-engine plane, piloted by a guy named Bob, a Florida hick. They had a refuelling stop in Jamaica and I would load 'em up in Montería and we did a bunch of trips right into Fort Lauderdale Executive Airport. They had it paid off and they had local Hollywood police in their pocket also. When Paco was still alive we did eight to ten runs. The other guys I did that route with were Halcón and the Ochoa relatives from Medellín.'[148]

But in January 1988 Martino and a fellow mobster called Steve Cassone were arrested in possession of 20 keys. In exchange for a lenient sentence, Joey pleaded guilty and got ten years. Cassone got five. That June, while on bail, Joey left his home in Turnberry to go out for breakfast and get a shave at a barbershop, stopping his Mercedes at a phone booth outside a drug store in North Miami. He felt he was being watched. He made a phone call, his beeper went off, and he returned to the phone booth again. It was a short conversation. He waved at whoever he thought was watching him and then left west on 183rd Street. It was the last time he was seen alive.

'Joey got arrested because he started dealing with an undercover cop. He was set free on bail and when the Lucchese group read the indictment, they realised he was selling the merchandise to this undercover cop at 16 and he only told them 13.[149] So between that and the fact he was gonna sell 'em out and turn state's evidence, [the Lucchese group] invited him to a meeting where they killed him. They clubbed him over the head with an ashtray, I believe, something like that.[150] They put him in a 55-gallon barrel and they dumped him in the river at Hialeah.'[151]

It wasn't until 1994 that what was left of Joey's body was discovered, FBI divers fishing out the drum from its resting place in 15 feet of water. His skeleton was wrapped in plastic and his feet had been encased in cement. He could only be identified through dental records and the watch he was wearing. They'd entombed him with his gold Rolex.

*

Joey's death deeply shook Luis; not just for its savagery and clinical execution but the fact it exposed him to a greater risk of being double-crossed or even eliminated himself.

'The Lucchese group wanted to continue working with me, because they reached out after Joey went missing. The Italians, they always wanna have their fuckin' hook into you.[152] I was always with Joey but I'm not part of no fucking mafia. That's your deal. I'm an independent contractor. I'm not part *of* the Medellín Cartel. My back-up and source of supply is Medellín, different people. I ain't no fucking Yakuza, I ain't no fucking mafia, I've got enough troubles. That's why I let Joey Martino deal with them.

'These guys all want a piece of your hide. One tries to kill the other one, one's trying to cut the other one out. If you just turn your back for a minute they'll take your clients. You're dealing with the sort of people that if you slip up and they have the chance to kill you and gain advantage from your death, they *will* kill you. And if they don't kill you they will steal a load if they can get away with it.

'Joey always told me to "Cover your ass, cover your back, because these guys are ruthless" and he was right: he ended up dead. So I figured without Joey being there these guys are *bad*; they would not hesitate to kill me. I'd send them a trip and they'd kill me, they'd keep the trip, and it's *over.* I was looking at it from a business point of view: I had no guarantees of any kind, no security, it didn't feel right. After Joey was missing a week, two weeks, I said, "He's *dead.*" His wife was going crazy. I said, "I'm gonna get the fuck outta here. This is just going to get bad."

'I bought myself a little time and didn't send them the trip. Then, since they had nobody to work with, they started reaching out to some other group and I heard they all got popped in Louisiana. There's no honour in the mafia anymore. They're a bunch of fucking conniving hoodlums, thieves, no-gooders. Pablo Escobar killed his partners, the partners killed other guys, everybody's killing everybody. It's a bunch of bullshit.'

31

Going Down

Joey Martino's disappearance ultimately convinced Luis to leave Florida and the United States for good. He wouldn't live in Miami again for nearly 20 years. A traffic incident that got out of hand simply confirmed his decision.

'Around the time Joey went missing I was living in Grove Isle, Miami. I had a two-door Jaguar XJS. I was with a woman called Annette Soudry, driving out of La Crepe St Michel restaurant in Coral Gables. Annie was a French-Moroccan model: skinny, tall, crazy hair. She spoke French. Her English was all French style so that even added more to the exotic. Annie was in the front seat and a guy called Billy Basto was sitting behind her and Annie's sister, who was Billy's girlfriend, was sitting behind me on the left-hand side of the car.[153] Billy was a Vietnam vet. He had issues with authority figures.

'So we drive out of the restaurant and I get pulled over. I hardly ever had a licence; it was either suspended because of speeding or it was expired, but sometimes back then you could talk to the cop and pay a fine on the spot. I had driven without one for so many years that it was very much of a pain in the ass for me to go stand in line and get one. So I'm talking to this cop nicely, handling the situation in a nice way, and this guy, Billy, pushes the front seat forward, gets out of the car and hits the cop's partner – the other cop that was there.

'All hell breaks loose and they just start pounding on Billy with nightsticks, and in the matter of a minute, another squad car was called and Billy's ear was almost completely torn from the side of his head. So they held us both in custody. I remember being fingerprinted. I got out right away because I posted bail and there were no real charges against me, but Billy got lost in the system for three or four days before his family found him and bailed him out of a Dade County holding facility.'

*

Moving to Los Angeles seemed a wise idea. Luis flew west, brought over his new girlfriend, a pocket-sized blonde heart attack called Lisa Cushing, and for something different decided to open an art gallery, Navia Gallery on 665 North La Cienega Boulevard, West Hollywood. His plan was to hold an exhibition of Colombian art as its maiden show.

'I felt that Joey's partners had something to do with his death. So it was a good time for me to get out of Miami. It was always my dream to own a gallery because I was into art. I'd been buying art since 1979 when I first went out to San Francisco. It was also a good way to launder money.

'Money laundering is nothing to me; more than anything you're just avoiding taxes on what you sold, because obviously what you're selling is not legal. And that's what I did for a while until I had to close it. The gallery wasn't open that long but for the time it was open I laundered $6 million, $7 million. All this shit [drug money] that I got from El Tío, it could have been $10 million, $12 million, easily.'

The scam, like all of Luis's scams, was simple enough. At the time the Colombian artist Fernando Botero was hot on the West Coast.

'You have a guy in Colombia make a replica of a Botero for $500 and sign "Botero", and you buy a bunch of emeralds that are worth $500 and you bring them into the country, bring it through customs, and you declare your Botero painting at $300,000 and you declare the emeralds at $2 million. It was mostly emeralds that nobody could really put a value on. Who would say they were not real back then in 1987? You're at the airport, clear customs, fill out the forms for the high amount of money, you hire security services transport to take it from the airport to the gallery the next day and then you "sell" [the painting] for $500,000, $700,000, whatever, and you sell it to somebody in the Philippines.[154]

'Ferdinand Marcos had just been overthrown and back then there were a lot of Filipinos coming into LA. You insure it and you send the fake painting in a very secure insured transport service to the Philippines to, er, "Joaquín Wang Pie". These people didn't exist. Who was going to find out if Joaquín Wang Pie walked into the gallery, paid me cash, and he left to the Philippines and I sent him his painting? Or Joaquín Wang Pie bought his painting and left? Where's the painting? I dunno. I guess in Joaquín Wang Pie's apartment in Malibu Beach. Back then you could do all that shit. You can't now.'

But any sideline in fine art was going to be shortlived under the circumstances. Joey's disappearance, legitimate fear of the Italian mob putting a hit on his life, and the unfortunate traffic incident with the police in Miami had all been dramatic enough. What tipped Luis over the edge were murmurs of a DEA operation in the southwest.

'That's when the feds indicted 132 people along with The Doc in Tucson. Greg Lazzara and Gordon Gray were really worried and were convinced we were going to get indicted – typical Greg getting overexcited; he was a borderline nutcase and a social misfit – but I took the situation seriously enough and saw the possibility was there. I was already planning to move to Colombia but that put the lid on the bottle. I left for South America sometime around late August 1988, and Greg and Gordon came down after me. I never got a clear answer on how bad that got or how close it was going to get to me.'

Luis wasn't going to take his chances. He instructed his Miami-based corporate attorney Reid Constable, who'd represented him in his sugar dealings, to start offloading the bulk of his substantial property portfolio – million-dollar lots in Mashta Island, Key Biscayne; a house in Bayshore Drive, Coconut Grove; two apartments in Grove Isle and one in Turnberry; four rental apartments; and a vacant lot in Vail, Colorado – and missed his own party at the gallery. A Honduran woman and later lover of Luis's called Daniela Villareal managed the gallery in his absence.[155]

'I wasn't able to go. I was already in Colombia. From there I sent a bunch of painters to do that first exhibition but I have a *photo*. People drinking, hors d'oeuvres and bullshitting.'

*

When Luis touched down on an Avianca flight at Matecaña International Airport in Pereira, he had specific instructions from Fernando Marulanda: carry a soccer ball as your carry-on luggage. That way, a paid-off policeman would know who he was and yank him out of the line for passport control.

'I never went through immigration. I never registered as coming into Colombia. A couple of Marulo's guys picked me up at the airport and I stayed at a hotel in Pereira for two or three days.'

From there he went straight to Bogotá, moving into an entire-floor apartment on Calle 1A, right next to the American's ambassador's house on Avenida Carrera 3 in the posh neighbourhood of Los Rosales. His living room looked into the ambassador's backyard: an ironic choice of address for a man running from stateside justice, even though Luis didn't necessarily see it that way.

'I thought of it as living in a foreign country. It wasn't "on the run" like these Americans who write these books – "I had to live in a fucking apartment and share it with five illegal immigrants" or anything like that. When you're at a certain level in society, when you've got money, you *blend* in. You've got high-level friends, no one suspects you, everything's easy. You transfer from one country to the other. You just have to get the right paperwork.'

He even brought down his girlfriend, Lisa following him on a separate flight along with her pampered bulldog, Floyd.

'She had green eyes and she was wild. *Playboy* wanted her to do a centrefold, but she turned it down and she was with me at the time, so really didn't need the money. Fuckin' rock 'n' roll to the max. I mean, this girl would put on boots and a miniskirt, dance, *fuck*. Talk about a head-turner. She was a cool chick.'

But Lisa with her elaborately moussed and sprayed 1980s hairdo was not quite made for Colombian life and nor was Floyd. She only lasted four months.

'I felt protected down there, definitely. There was no extradition and Pablo Escobar was fighting for no extradition. Pablo declared war on a country because of no extradition. He said, "I prefer to have a tomb in Colombia than a jail on the other side."[156] They had to fight that war but it got out of control. It became a real war. In Pablo's eyes it was like when the Americans fought the Germans or the Arabs. You blow up planes, you blow up cities. It was a crazy time. The whole country suffered.

'So Colombia was definitely not for Lisa and there was not the kind of strength in our relationship to keep it together in a place that was foreign to her in every sense and not to her liking. The dog was accustomed to Evian water, so he gets to Bogotá and we go to one of the farms in Represa del Sisga, northeast of Bogotá, and he drank some water from a creek or something and he got a stomach infection. He died really violently. When Floyd died, Lisa said, 'I'm not happy here," and I said, "I understand." And that was it: she left.'[157]

Luis was nearly 33 years old, newly single, exiled and living far from home in what was effectively a war zone, with a dead bulldog on his conscience. He had all the money he'd ever need and still had an appetite for partying and fast women, but something was missing from his life. It was time for him to get serious and stop messing around with models, hookers and *Playboy* centrefolds. All wayward men, fugitive coke traffickers included, need to meet a nice girl sooner or later.

32

The Night They Shot Galán

IN THE FIRST SIX months of 1989, there were 2338 murders in Medellín and the cartel was arguably at the peak of its destructive power. Pablo Escobar, who had made *Forbes* magazine's list of the world's billionaires for three years running with a personal fortune of over $3 billion, was doing whatever he could to stave off the threat of the Colombian Government reinstating extradition – and that meant incredible levels of violence.

His biggest threat was a popular politician called Luis Carlos Galán Sarmiento, the candidate for the PLC or Colombian Liberal Party (*Partido Liberal Colombiano*), who was running on a platform of no mercy and a return of extradition for the narcos who were destroying the country from within. Escobar's beef with Galán was also personal: in 1983 Galán had pushed for Escobar's removal from Colombia's Congress, ending his political career before it had even started.

Luis's plans that northern summer were just to relax, so he headed up from the cool highland climate of Bogotá to the drier Santa Marta for some sun and sand.

'I went for a vacation and to see my sister. So I'm at the beach at La Cangreja and I see this young, beautiful, blondish Colombian girl getting into the water from the back side. Beautiful figure, cinnamon-white skin. I said to the guy I was with, "If I were to go for a Colombian girl, it's going to be somebody like that." I waited for her to come back out and she sat down with her friend.'

Her name was Patricia Manterola, she'd just turned 20 and was on spring break from her marketing and publicity studies at a college in nearby Barranquilla. Luis was about to deploy an early version of the pick-up art of 'negging'.

'I was tanning,' Patricia remembers. 'And the guy said, "Hi, does somebody have sunblock?" He came right up next to us. I took the one that I had, the Hawaiian Tropic, and passed it to him. And he said, "*No*, *no*, *no*. I want the *other* one." He took it! The Bain de Soleil. It's French, more expensive.'

Says Luis: 'I just started putting that shit on, all over me, using up half the bottle [*laughs*]. And she complained I was using up all her suntan lotion. I really liked her. She didn't like me at first but I just kept hitting on her.'

Patricia: 'I'd never seen this man in my life. I was like, "My God, he's Cuban, *whatever*." He went off to the water with my suntan lotion and I never saw him again. He was so . . . oh, my God, I don't know. I should have turned . . .' she pauses, reflecting for a moment. 'No, *no*. Everything happens for a reason. The next day I was at this house party and another friend of mine came up to me and said, "I want to introduce you to somebody from Miami." It was him: the guy from the beach who took my tanning lotion. I was like, "I cannot believe this." Luis was something *different*. Maybe that attracted me. It wasn't easy for him to get me.'

But he wouldn't be deterred.

'Patricia was a beautiful girl – a *knockout*.'

*

Patricia Manterola was born in Barranquilla, Colombia, on 19 July 1969 to Juan and Gladis Manterola. Of Spanish descent, Juan was a well-known attorney while Gladis's wealthy family ran farms on huge estates on super-prime land in and around Santa Marta: avocado, rice, banana, African palm, cattle ranching. In fact, they were one of the original families who started the paramilitaries, the *Autodefensas*, against the guerillas. Extortion was always a problem in the wilds of northern Colombia, and the Manterolas were not only personally well armed but hired private security guards.

'Since the time of my grandfather, who was a cattle rancher, we always carried a gun in the Jeep, along with a radio. Every car had a gun. We had to defend our land. So a lot of people like my grandfather, my uncles, the family of my grandmother, with other landowners we had to pay people to protect us from the guerillas. They always wanted more money; they killed people that worked for us.'

Says Luis: 'Patricia was a very clean girl from a good family, which I really liked. Her parents had divorced when she was six. She had two brothers. She didn't do drugs and didn't have an alcoholism problem. Juanchi, who also came from a good family in the area, knew of her and told me, "Man, you picked a real doozy there. But her uncles are going to kill you." Patricia was a clean kid from another generation. She's 13 years younger than me. She didn't grow up in that whole cocaine era.'

'I never did any kind of drugs,' she insists. '*Any*. I saw all the drugs in the world but I never tried it. Everybody knows that I don't do drugs. I went to the best high school in the city and one of the best colleges in Barranquilla. My friends were far from that business and there were no cartels in Santa Marta.'

*

On one of their first dates at La Escollera, a disco in Santa Marta, Luis turned to Patricia at about 10pm apropos of nothing and asked her to come with him to a farm called 'Panorama', owned by local marijuana-smuggling identity Juanchito 'Juancho Caterpillar' Noguera near Aracataca.[158] It had a well-known illegal airstrip, a 'hot' place for law-enforcement interest.

'"Patricia, would you accompany me?" I said. "I've got to go see a friend of mine about something." Gordon Gray had taken off in the new Conquest a few hours earlier and was airdropping in The Bahamas. I wanted to get on the radio and see if everything was good.'

'I said okay,' she recalls. 'I didn't know what was going on; I knew something was going on but not exactly what.'

The way she tells it, Patricia had no idea at that stage Luis was involved in cocaine. He planned to have her home by her father's curfew of two in the morning. They got in their car with a chauffeur and one of Juanchi's bodyguards and drove, with another car containing two more bodyguards tailing behind.

'So we're on our way to the farm and suddenly we hear on the fucking radio, "They just killed Galán."'

*

It was 18 August 1989. At 8.30pm at an open-air rally in Soacha in southwest Bogotá, Pablo Escobar's political nemesis, Luis Carlos Galán Sarmiento, had been assassinated on the orders of Escobar and other conspirators.[159] Up to 18 *sicarios* had been lying in wait. The military were going to any farm that had an airstrip and were on their way to the entrance of Panorama. It was a state of emergency and the cartels were firmly in the government's sights. Escobar's greatest fear, extradition to the United States, was immediately legalised by President Virgilio Barco Vargas. In the coming weeks, tens of thousands of people would be arrested, cocaine kitchens destroyed, and countless weapons, vehicles and aircraft seized.

Says Luis: 'The whole country had gone into lockdown. It was martial law. The fucking army started putting up roadblocks everywhere and we were outside the city limits of Santa Marta on the way to this farm in the backlands. We were past the point of no return; we couldn't turn back. They were arresting everyone on the highway. So we just had to get into the farm and, *fuuuccckkk*, we were stuck at the farm.

'Goo was on his way back from airdropping and there was nothing else we could do. We couldn't ask him to go somewhere else and land. What the fuck are we going to do with the plane? If we'd stayed the army would have hit us at the farm, we would have all gone to jail, they would have confiscated the plane, we would have been royally fucked. From above, if they'd had any army helicopters they would have spotted the plane *immediately*. We had to get the fuck out of there quickly.'

Luis and Patricia were parked next to the runway at Panorama and twiddling their thumbs in banana land in the middle of nowhere. Nothing was happening. It was an anxious wait and fog had rolled in.

They burned some tyres in barrels to get some fires going so Goo could see the dirt strip. Soon, dawn broke.

Luis: 'Goo comes back from the airdrop and it's daybreak and he's trying to land and the ceiling is too low.[160] He's trying to come down to spot the strip and it's very dangerous, because when the ceiling is that low and you're going that fast, you're coming down and, before you know it, the fog clears and you're so low that you may hit the ground or the treeline. It's like being in a fast-moving vehicle blindfolded, then suddenly the blindfold gets removed and there's nothing but the ground, trees or hillside in front of you. A pilot's worst nightmare.

'So it takes a very good pilot to land when there's a low ceiling and fog. We were on the radio guiding him in, giving him references because it was extremely dangerous even for an experienced bush pilot like Goo. We were all on edge as there was a good chance he wouldn't make the ceiling and land – and he *had* to land the plane. There was no other option. He was out of fuel and there was nowhere to go because of the situation with the military. If it would have been five more minutes, ten minutes, that he couldn't land because of the ceiling being too low, he would have crashed and died.

'He followed the instructions of one of the guys who handled the airstrip there and knew the area. Goo was flying 95 per cent by radar. "By radar" in the sense of what this guy was telling him, not what the radar was telling him. He couldn't see shit while coming down to land. Miraculously, he managed to pull it off. The plane came back with no seats or anything, because when you airdrop you take out all the seats so you can put in the extra fuel.

'A guy called "Moñón" Dangond had a strip called "La Y" in Ciénaga so we asked him if we could go from Panorama, make a little hop over to Ciénaga [26 kilometres sou'-sou'-west from Santa Marta], and keep the plane in one of his hangars.[161] We had to make it a short hop. We couldn't be flying around and we needed a place where there was a hangar so we could hide the plane, put the call letters back on, get our Venezuelan pilots who'd flown it to Colombia back on board and get the fuck out of there.[162] It took a lot of convincing for him to agree but he was close to Juanchi and our whole group. He said he'd let us do that for a few days but that was as much as he could allow, given the circumstances.'

'Luis was afraid; everybody was really worried,' says Patricia. 'But I didn't really care; everything back then was an adventure.'

Luis: 'I think I was more scared than she was. I feared for my life. So here I am with Patricia [*laughs*] and she hops on a fucking plane that just came from airdropping 800 kilos in The Bahamas and smells like gas [petrol]. Goo was like, "Who the fuck is she?" I said, "She's my girlfriend." And then I hear, "I'm *not* your girlfriend!" [*laughs*]'

Eventually Luis and Patricia got to the airstrip in Ciénaga, they took a car into the city and Patricia was able to return home to her worried father with a ready-made story: they'd been stuck all night because Galán had been assassinated.

'It was a hell of a way to start a relationship,' says Luis. 'This was like our first date. It *was* our first fucking date.'

Patricia still can't believe it either: 'I never imagined I was going to be Luis's girlfriend, let alone his wife.'

33

Two Toucans

PATRICIA'S ATTORNEY FATHER JUAN MANTEROLA was a traditional man who wanted to know the parents of the man his daughter was dating, and if he didn't like the sound of them, he simply forbade her from dating. That was that; this was rural Colombia, after all, where people sometimes get shot over family squabbles.

Her two polo-playing uncles, Fabio and Antonio, were also fiercely protective of their niece and well known in Santa Marta for settling differences with bareknuckle fists, rather than guns. If they found out that she was going out with somebody 13 years older, a man not from Colombia who nobody knew, least of all an international cocaine-smuggling felon, there could have been a major scene. The only solution for the star-crossed lovers was to pretend nothing was going on.

'We had to hide the relationship from my family,' says Patricia. 'They knew *everybody* in Santa Marta. Nobody knew about us, not even my close friends. Only Luis's friends knew about it. At the beginning I didn't have any clue of what he was doing; at that time the only problem I could have had was with my family about his age.'

While newly installed US President George H.W. Bush was telling Americans in his first televised address from the White House that 'victory over drugs is our cause, a just cause', Luis moved to Barranquilla to be closer to Patricia's college dorm in front of Parque

Washington and into a newly built high-rise hotel called Dann on Carrera 51B. The Colombian national football team stayed there during qualifiers for the 1990 FIFA World Cup in Italy.[163]

'We stayed in Barranquilla for about nine months. There was a lot of movement and action at the hotel. I'd see the players in the dining room and invited them to dinner. It was a great time in my life. I was in my early 30s, I was in Colombia, I had the Conquest, and I was working with Juanchi in Santa Marta and his group while renting the plane out to different drug-smuggling groups and making very good money. Juanchi and I were moving heavy weight.

'Patricia had a lot of guys after her so I wanted to make sure I discouraged that activity. I always had the concierge delivering stuff to her: flowers, teddy bears. Making sure she got home from school. Sending her food from the hotel if she wanted to eat something. Other guys knew who I was, so it wasn't like they were too anxious to get involved with Patricia.

'I used to hang out by the pool and one day I bought a couple of toucans and just built a big white cage in the lawns of the hotel to put my birds in there. I had a welder come over and put together the whole fucking thing. *Bam boom ba*. Back then you could buy toucans on a street corner. I used to do whatever I wanted. It was like my backyard. The owner came up to me and said, "What are you doin'? You're turning my hotel into a fucking zoo now?" I didn't ask permission. I was spending $3000 a week staying there, which was a lot of money in Colombia. I was the king of the hotel.'

But Patricia still wasn't sure Luis was the right man for her.

'I almost broke up with him. My behaviour was like a child's. "I don't want this, I don't want that." So one day I was in a corner fruit store in Barranquilla and I said, "I don't want you anymore." I turned around and started walking away from Luis and he was so mad he took a tomatillo, a small tomato, and he threw it, and I don't think he meant to hit me, but it hit me in the back. I screamed. The guy from the fruit store, who knew me, came at him with a machete. Luis went running down the street [*laughs*]. I was so angry with him but I was more worried that the guy from the fruit store would catch up to him and kill him.'[164]

*

From Barranquilla, Luis and Patricia moved to Bogotá at the height of the cocaine wars, with Pablo Escobar fighting the Colombian Government and the Cali Cartel on two fronts.

Luis had a front for his cocaine operation, an office at the World Trade Center on Calle 100 under the name *Asociación de Macadamia de Colombia* ('Macadamia Association of Colombia'), a sly nod to a 700-acre macadamia farm in Costa Rica he'd bought as an investment in the early 1980s. He had a personal secretary, Clara Macias, and an assistant, David Santos.[165] Patricia got her own apartment in case her family ever visited, while Luis stayed in his next to the ambassador's residence. She spent most of her time, however, over at Luis's. His bright idea was to buy her a $10,000 mobile phone (they were dear at the time) for when her dad called.

'My father always called me at seven in the morning and I couldn't stay in Luis's apartment because my father would call,' Patricia remembers. 'So he bought me this phone and got me another one for my car. I could then answer my phone in his apartment so my dad would think I was at home. We had a life like "normal" people. We moved around in the art community of Bogotá. We were neighbours of the United States ambassador; the view from our apartment was the ambassador's garden.'

Says Luis: 'We lived in Bogotá when the bombs were going off.[166] At no time did I say to Patricia, "Let's leave Bogotá," because of the bombs. We were in it and we could have run away from the violence just like anybody else, but we stayed. I just never thought it would happen to me. Thank God nothing ever happened to us.'

Patricia only realised something was not quite right in Luis's affairs when he told her they couldn't go to Miami.

'One day he told me he couldn't go back there. I think Luis always felt like he had to be on the run. But I was more aware about Luis's situation than he was; he liked to think that he spoke good Spanish in Colombia, but he didn't back then. He likes to think he is Colombian but he's not. He always looked and behaved like a foreigner and had the accent to go with it [*laughs*]. People were always asking him, "Where are you from?" And, you know, you didn't want to have that kind of attention when you had a fake identity and were living in the country illegally. My friends, my closest friends, maybe they suspected Luis was in the business but we never behaved that way or gave them reason to think that. But some people knew, for sure. If we got invited to things like weddings, we'd go but we'd just go to the party and that was it. It's not like we were going to dinner parties every week.'[167]

Their age difference was never an issue early in the relationship but on a chartered flight to Cuba, they were handing over their passports to military police who had boarded the aircraft to make immigration checks. Patricia collected the passengers' passports and handed them over.

'Who is Luis Navia? Where is he?' said the policeman. He was flipping through the pages of Luis's fake Colombian passport.

'He's *there*,' Patricia replied, nodding in the direction of the seat where Luis was drinking Scotch and laughing with his pals.

'Lady, get your daddy to come here.'

34

Death at Dog Rocks

MEANWHILE, LUIS'S MILLION-DOLLAR CONQUEST was a workhorse. He would bring it down to Colombia from its base in Caracas and do four trips at a time – two to Mexico, two to The Bahamas – to minimise flying times in and out of Venezuela.

'That plane probably did 15 trips, maybe 18. We made about $12 to $15 million with the Conquest alone. We always made money in Mexico. But on a few Mexico trips we were selling merchandise at $8000 a key when the price was 12.'

Deep in his own financial straits, Javier Mercado came forward with a proposal.

'Luis, Tío is taking too long to cross the merchandise [over the border]. We send the shit up to him in northern Mexico and he takes 30 to 45 days to cross?'

'It's fine. He always comes through.'

'We can do it much better. Let's work with Juanchi. We can airdrop in the Florida Keys, have my guys pick up and we can have our merchandise in a week. The next day we're in Miami.'

Luis was against the idea because smugglers from Santa Marta were 'disorganised'. But he gave in because he trusted Javier and wanted him to continue running operations in the States.

'He was a very able, intelligent and well-seasoned smuggler and knew how to solve problems. But we lost six trips back to back and I took a heavy hit. Even if you lose the merchandise you've still got to pay the pilots.'

Javier became increasingly desperate for a successful load. When the Conquest got to Pereira from Venezuela for one of Marulo's loads, he got on as a co-pilot when the designated co-pilot wouldn't make the trip because of safety concerns over failure reports (an aviation term for engine or system problems with the plane).

'When the engines reach certain hours of flying time you need to bring them in for scheduled maintenance; you should not push that. Javier hadn't spent adequate money on maintenance as required by the hours the engines had on them. So when the Venezuelan pilots got off, they said that the engines had some mechanical reports. The Colombian pilots got on and after a few minutes of checking out the systems, the co-pilot said he would not fly on the plane with those reports unchecked and pending. That's when Javier said he would go as co-pilot and somehow convinced the Colombian pilot, Junior Dangond aka "El Gordo", to go along with him.'

Luis got on too, just for the hell of it. The departure was timed for mid-afternoon so they would arrive in The Bahamas after sundown. The waiting boats would then pick up the cocaine during the night.

'Just out of pure adventure, I said, "Shit, I'll go with Javier. I'll go in the back; I'll go as a kicker."'A kicker is the passenger whose job it is to drop the merchandise out of the aircraft. 'And in the back of the plane, there was a black skinny guy from Barranquilla, a mechanic called Noel Cervantes aka "Kaliman".'

The four men were ready to take off when there was a commotion on the tarmac. El Gordo turned off the engines. Fernando Marulanda, who was there to supervise the onloading of the merchandise, wanted Luis off the plane and sent over his enforcer, Carlos Arturo Patiño Restrepo aka 'Patemuro', to forcibly remove him.[168]

'Get *off* the plane, Luis.'

'What the fuck, Fernando? Why? What's the problem? Javier's going.'

'If you die, who's going to pay me?'

'Okay, *okay*. Yeah, I guess you're right.'

And so Luis got out of the plane and watched his Conquest with

700 keys on board fly off into the skies above Pereira, bound for the Caribbean.

'A plane has to be in perfect shape when you're going to go down to airdrop. Planes aren't designed to go down, slow down, pull back the power, open the back door and throw shit out the back. Sure enough, they went down, they slowed down the power, the engine failed, *boom*, the fucking plane cartwheeled it right into the ocean at Dog Rocks in The Bahamas and all three of them died: El Gordo, Javier and Kaliman.

'Some of the merchandise was retrieved; they handed it to us in these fucking pails full of saltwater and cocaine. Javier's brother was down there, coordinating the receiving end with the boats on the water. He was on the radio and heard the whole thing. That was the last plane I owned. In the end, because of all the bad decisions Javier made, because he was so desperate, he fucking died. Desperate people do desperate things that result in fatal consequences. You don't hop on a plane that the co-pilot hopped off, although I was crazy enough to go along for a ride. I lost my Conquest that cost me a million dollars and another million in my share of the merchandise. But Marulo saved my life. I'm alive today because of Marulo.'

It was also the day Patricia found out what Luis really did for a living. He was a broken man. He'd lost $2 million in two planes, as much again in coke, and another friend was dead. Somehow, through it all, he was still alive. It was as good a time as any to get married, the couple formalising their relationship at Notaría 45 in Bogotá. There was no ceremony but they celebrated afterwards at an Italian restaurant.

'In Spanish we say, *nos casamos a escondidas*: we got married secretly,' says Patricia. 'I just sent a message to my dad and my little brother that I was married and that was it. Nobody in my family knew about Luis's business; only my brothers suspected it later on. Luis never looked or behaved like people who were in that business, we had friends who weren't in that business, and he had a really nice cover with the office in the World Trade Center. That's the funny thing: if you knew him at the time you would never have believed that he had something to do with drugs. Luis *never* talked about cocaine. But the day Javier died he was crying. He was completely destroyed and drunk. He told me everything. We were together by then. I was in love.'

PART 7
SCARFACE

35

Felony Favours

IN 1991, THROUGH AN INTRODUCTION by Fernando Marulanda, Luis began working for a Colombian drug lord called Luis Hernando Gómez Bustamante aka Rasguño, one of the heads of the North Valley Cartel – what Luis calls 'Northern Valley' – a criminal organisation that would become world renowned as the usurper of the Cali Cartel. Rasguño had only started out in 1987 but within three years was a major player, with up to 800 men working for him at any one time. His personal cocaine brand was Rolex.

'I moved merchandise for Rasguño to the Caribbean – airdropping off Tampa, as well as The Bahamas and into the Florida Keys, as well as water transport in fastboats into the Cancún area in Mexico for delivery to Houston.[169] We moved a lot of merchandise for Northern Valley and I became key transporter for that cartel.'

They also became unlikely friends, Rasguño borrowing one of Luis's aliases in Colombia – Julio Guzmán – for himself.

'Come January, everybody [in the cartels] changes his name, because you start the year with a new name. You don't want to be the same guy who got hot last year. So we were talking, I was ready to leave for the airport, and Rasguño says, "Oh, by the way you can't use Julio Guzmán anymore. I said, "What? [*laughs*] Er . . . *okay.*" What are you talking about?" He goes, "Yeah, that's going to be my name this year. Dr Guzmán." I was like, "Okay, I'll call you later and tell you who I'm going to be this year."'

Picking a name was no laughing matter. You needed to keep up to date with aliases in the cocaine business – or you could lose your life.

'When he was still alive, The Mexican, Rodríguez Gacha, moved about 2000 kilos to La Guajira. Some [South American] Indian guy at the strip where they received the 2000 kilos was like, "Who the fuck is this? Who is sending this shit from the interior? Some fucking idiot called Andrés? Who the fuck is *Andrés*? Fuck this guy." So they plotted to steal the 2000 kilos and they did. It just so happens that that year Rodríguez Gacha changed his name to Andrés. And sure enough, when you steal 2000 kilos from Rodríguez Gacha, the military arm of the Medellín Cartel, he sent his fucking group to La Guajira and they just killed, I don't know how many fucking Indians, 40, 50, 60, 70 fucking Guajiran Indians. "Who the fuck is Andrés?" *Okaaay*. Here we go. They found out who Andrés was real quick.'

*

Rasguño, born in 1958 in El Águila in the northernmost part of the Valle del Cauca, 'El Valle', was based near Pereira in and around the city of Cartago, and got his nickname, which means 'Scratch', for the scar on his left cheek which was left behind from a bullet that got way too close; according to folklore, Rasguño had laughed it off as only a scratch.

North Valley was probably the third biggest criminal syndicate in Colombia, behind Medellín and its original overseer, Cali, but would eventually attain complete dominance of the Colombian cocaine trade in the mid-1990s. At its height it accounted for 60 per cent of all cocaine transported to the United States, moving 500 tons in total.

It wasn't an easy time to be a drug trafficker in Colombia. Pablo Escobar was on the run from Colombian and US special forces, kidnapping high-profile targets and terrorising the main cities with car bombs and assassinations. His Medellín Cartel partner The Mexican was dead and the Ochoa brothers had given themselves up to the Colombian Government and confessed to criminal activity, in exchange for no extradition and imprisonment on heavily reduced sentences. In the vacuum left behind by the rapidly disintegrating

Medellín Cartel leadership, Cali and North Valley began thriving. Business was booming for Luis.

'Northern Valley was Orlando Henao Montoya, Rasguño, Iván Urdinola. The three of them ruled that whole valley and they were a very violent group. Rasguño had a hell of a reputation for being extremely violent and volatile, though I never saw that violence first-hand. Everyone in Colombia feared Rasguño big time, just as much as Pablo Escobar. He *was* the Northern Valley Cartel.

'While the [Cali Cartel's] war with Pablo was going on, Rasguño controlled the entrance to El Valle from the northern point at Cartago. He had to filter out all the people that Pablo may send into Valle del Cauca through Cartago, the gateway to El Valle.[170] You know how many people were killed coming in from Medellín through Pereira into Cartago to go into El Valle? Fucking *hundreds* of people died. Every day someone died. Kidnappers would be chopped up – *ba ba ba ba ba ba* – stuffed in burlap sacks and thrown down the Río Cauca. Rasguño had everything [audio] taped. The whole fucking city was phonetapped. A taxi driver picked up some guy who didn't look right? *Boom*. Dead. It was like nothing.

'Rasguño was very organised, not off the wall, not crazy, had everything calculated. That's why these narcos become so powerful and so successful and why they last so long. Anybody that does business with Rasguño you knew what you were getting into. He didn't say he was a saint. He was very honest, strict and upfront and you knew it. You fuck up, you pay or *die*. I highly respected him.'

*

Marulo's introduction of Luis to Rasguño was no small thing. In fact, introducing colleagues to each other in the drug business carries a great deal of responsibility, danger and financial risk.

'You don't do felony favours.[171] For somebody to do that, there has to be a lot of trust and confidence that the person's going to perform. There's no upside for them if you lose a load; they'll get charged for it. If anyone fucked up a load it could have been massive.'

Luis had a smuggling route with El Tío from the department of Risaralda, Colombia, into Tabasco, Mexico, with Rasguño providing the merchandise plus a pair of valuable Beechcraft King Airs.

'King Air 300s cost $4 million each in Colombia. So $8 million in equipment, plus, say, $5 million in merchandise, you're talking $13 million if the shit hits the fan. To us it was one more deal. Those planes Rasguño had, they left right from Pereira International Airport: each plane loaded up with 1300 kilos. They didn't leave from a fucking clandestine strip or nothing. You paid off the tower, *boom*.'

Fucking up a load involved a heavy hit indeed.

'El Tío lost a 400-kilo load and I paid up $2.4 million, just not to have the hassle. We handed it to them in LA and Rasguño's people lost it. They got busted, somehow, whatever. But still, he didn't like to lose. So Rasguño charged *me*. He charged me $6000 per kilo, not at cost; I already had some transport expenses factored into that $6000. So $2.4 million.

'The smart thing to do is pay the man and continue working with him. If I didn't pay him, Rasguño would either have ended up killing El Tío or they would have grabbed him, then El Tío would have said, "Let's get Luis out of the way; how much do I owe you, $2.4 million? Okay, we'll work direct now." Or they would have grabbed me, forced me to pay and got me to tell him El Tío's name and how to get in touch with him. He sends his people to talk to El Tío, hooks up with him, starts working with him, tells him I didn't pay, so El Tío has to pay, then Rasguño collects from both ends. That's how people are – not necessarily Rasguño, mind you, who was always honest with me. But it's a fucked-up business.

'So sometimes you take a loss because you're going to make more in the future. You've got to play it smart. You've got to realise that against these big animals a little rabbit has no chance. I just didn't want to be in a bad situation. I analysed it and realised that paying up would be better, and in the end at least I continued working with El Tío and made my money. There's a lot of things you know after so many years of working with people.

'But the great thing about this business is that on one trip a hundred units can yield a million dollars: $10,000 profit per unit. We really started to hit Belize heavy on the airdrops in 1989/'90 with Miki Ramírez and later on with Rasguño. I was doing a lot of airdrops off Tampa as well as Mexico trips. We were hitting it *hard* in '91. The Gulf War had broken out so [the US military] moved out some of those AWACs to the Middle East and we just banged those lighthouses a lot with Rasguño, with Miki who was getting his merchandise from Fernando Galeano. Pablo Escobar was still alive at that point.

'That was when we started doing the boat trips to Cancún. I opened up Cancún to Rasguño; I created that route. By "opening up", I mean I gave Rasguño the idea and he financed the buying of the first boats and the set-up of the operation in San Andrés. We were taking 700, 800 units per trip. That was my route, my people, my idea. I invented it. I bought the boats with Rasguño's money, I had the contacts, I took San Andrés captains and crews to Pereira to meet him. I was already doing a lot of airdrops to Cancún, but airdrops became a little dangerous because of radars out of Panama and stuff, so we decided to go by water.

'These boats were undetectable. They were almost like submarines, they'd be so low to the ground. Two trips we lost because we got with a storm and he didn't charge me for those trips, but he kinda kept it on the back ledger. But Rasguño's guys did go in and rough up the crew to make sure it wasn't bullshit and the loads had actually been lost.'

36

The Wake

By mid-1991, Pablo Escobar had surrendered conditionally to the Colombian Government, agreeing to imprisonment at his own \$5 million custom-built prison in Medellín called *La Catedral* (The Cathedral). It was a sweet deal: the jail was patrolled by guards he controlled on land he owned, on the guarantee he would not be extradited to the United States. In June, Colombia had passed a law in the Constituent Assembly to rule it out once again. The drug lord's sentence would be five years but he would last only 13 months before breaking out in farcical circumstances.

Escobar's jail was less a penitentiary and more a functioning luxury clubhouse for playing soccer and screwing whores. More alarmingly, he was using it as a base to continue directing his crumbling but still very powerful criminal empire with total impunity. And that meant having senior figures in the cartel visit him in person, including Luis's friend Fernando 'El Negro' Galeano and Galeano's partner Gerardo 'Quico' Moncada.

On 3 July 1992 the pair went to visit Escobar over the issue of 'taxes', or kickbacks, to the big boss but never came back.[172] They were shot, their corpses dismembered and then burned to ashes.[173] A day later their brothers, Francisco Galeano and William Moncada, were also killed. The already erratic and paranoid Escobar had lost the plot.

'There were three people who were supposed to go visit Pablo when Galeano and Moncada got killed: Galeano, Moncada and one other. I can't name him. Bad motherfucker. He used to buy all our merchandise from the trips we did up to the States with Miki Ramírez, Galeano and Pablo. Plus receiving thousands of keys a month from other groups. He's a billionaire. He was selling all of Galeano's merchandise before Galeano died.

'Anyway, he didn't show up to that meeting. He was supposed to go. He was smarter than that. He never went. He's one that fell through the cracks. Everyone says that he's been working with the DEA for many years, doing some kind of shit that nobody even knows about. Some people say he's an asset for Mossad [the national intelligence agency of Israel], a very rich and connected person. He's definitely very tight with the US Government, some kind of aid to antiterrorism; he's a wearing a super-bulletproof coat. He is a totally different animal.'

Luis's friend Miki, a powerful figure in the Medellín Cartel, who himself was due to visit Escobar, turned up at Luis's and Patricia's apartment in Bogotá upon learning of what had happened to Galeano and Moncada. He ordered a band of *mariachis* play while he mourned.

'Miki cried for El Negro at my apartment with *mariachis*. He had *mariachis* there for fucking almost a day and a half. The *mariachis*' lips were bleeding. We were drinking, he was crying. It was like a wake.'[174]

Remembers Patricia: 'He wouldn't allow the *mariachis* to stop. The *mariachis* could not sing anymore. And I had to speak to Miki and say, "Please, let them rest. I'm going to order food so everybody's going to eat." I was the only woman in the house and I had to get some [food] orders. And he said, "Okay." The *mariachis* stopped, everyone was relieved and nobody knew what to do. He was in pain. He'd just lost his friends.'

Luis: 'After that, Pablo called Miki and said, "Come see me." He had to go talk to Pablo at *La Catedral*. He was at my apartment in Bogotá before he left and he told me, "I may not come back." He was freaking out. You can't say no to Pablo Escobar. If you say no they're going to come kill you anyway. Miki was always very concerned. Everyone used to go and visit Pablo up there. He had to pledge his allegiance. You were 100 per cent with Medellín or you were going to traffic with Cali. Obviously he said Medellín.'

When Miki returned from the 400-kilometre journey to Bogotá he went straight to Luis's and Patricia's apartment. He was shaken.

'This is getting very fucking crazy, Luis. It was very dangerous. I didn't think I was going to make it out of there.'

Later that July, with Colombians up in arms at the killings of Galeano and Moncada, the country's new president César Gaviria ordered Escobar be moved to a military prison in Bogotá. There was a major stand-off and Colombia's deputy justice minister was kidnapped while attempting to negotiate Escobar's surrender. When Gaviria dispatched special forces to raid the prison, Escobar cut the electricity and used the subsequent confusion and chaos to stage his famous 'escape' from *La Catedral* to become a fugitive from justice yet again. It was so easy he practically walked out with his band of loyal *sicarios*. He was making a mockery of everyone.[175]

And that was precisely when Miki and his friends, including Galeano's brother Rafael and paramilitary leaders/brothers Fidel and Carlos Castaño Gil with funding from the Cali Cartel, decided to form the vigilante group Los Pepes, *Perseguidos por Pablo Escobar* or People Persecuted by Pablo Escobar.

Los Pepes wanted to take down Pablo for good.

*

Effectively a state-sanctioned death squad or terrorist organisation and beginning in January 1993 and running through to the end of that year, Los Pepes killed over 300 people either closely or loosely connected to Escobar (including total innocents who had nothing to do with him at all) yet allegedly had the full support of the reorganised and US-trained Colombian police special-operations units known as Search Bloc or *Bloque de Búsqueda*.[176]

Hunted on the ground and surveilled from the air, the corpulent, unkempt Escobar retaliated with more killings and car bombs, but he was in a dragnet from which there was no escape. It was the beginning of the end of the Medellín Cartel, the criminal organisation that had given Luis his start in cocaine. Miki himself, who Luis says 'worked two sides of the coin' – the cartels and the police – stood to directly benefit.[177]

'Miki was definitely at war with Pablo and had full government support: bodyguards with all the credentials and machine guns. The sort of weapons only government agents can carry legally. We were handling a lot of Fernando Galeano's merchandise and I was close to Miki, but I never felt I would ever be a target of interest to Pablo.

'Miki is actually a *fantastic* guy. He's a better salesman than I am and I'm a great salesman. He's fat, gregarious, he puts you in his pocket immediately. He's a fantastic, lovable con artist. Legal business, illegal business, *sideways* business, whatever business, he's just one of those guys. He's always been a great friend to me.'

He also gave Luis his narco nickname, 'El Senador' (The Senator). They were at Luis's apartment and were about to make reservations at a local restaurant when Miki said, "There's no need to make reservations, we just go." At the time, Patricia was pregnant with her and Luis's first child. Luis remarked that if he ever had a son, Senador Navia would be a good name. So Miki called up the restaurant and made the reservation under the name Senador Navia, they got in, and the pair had a good laugh about it. It was that simple.

'Nobody really knew the real reason why Miki called me "Senador" but I always dressed well. I usually dressed in khakis with a white or blue shirt and always threw in a pink; always did like pink shirts. One day I met Orlando Henao's brother Arcángel, "El Mocho", and Rasguño at Rasguño's office and I was wearing a really nice off-white linen suit and a white linen shirt, with a Dunhill blue-and-beige tie with perfect matching shoes. Mocho and Rasguño didn't dress so great.'

El Mocho had got his nickname, which means 'The Amputee', because he was missing an arm due to a birth deformity.

'Mocho goes to Rasguño, "Look at this guy. *El Senador*. He looks like a senator. We look like we work for *him*." And then Rasguño goes, "I know, I *know*. Don't remind me. I may have to kill him if you remind me twice." Rasguño was always kidding around: "I'm going to kill you, motherfucker." But they were words of endearment. He would never say that to anybody else. He'd just kill you.'

*

Affection had its limits. One day Luis made a terrible *faux pas* with Rasguño from which he was lucky to escape with his life. Rasguño was a portly man who enjoyed his food. After his own appetite, whatever goodwill Rasguño had for Luis was always going to be a secondary consideration.

'We shared an apartment together in San Andrés. San Andrés is a free-trade zone 150 kilometres off the coast of Nicaragua.[178] There you can buy American canned goods, Campbell's Soup, all the shit that you can't in the Colombian interior because there are no taxes on the island. Patricia would sometimes come over and cook for them. They'd get really bored in San Andrés with the food there, since they weren't at their farms with their servants, wives and cooks.

'So I come in and someone had bought all this Latin food, Colombian canned goods. Rasguño wasn't there. He was out. And I go, "What the fuck is all this Colombian food? We should be buying American food. We're in San Andrés." So I threw away all that Colombian food and I bought American food but it was *his* fucking food. Who in their right mind throws away somebody's food, let alone Rasguño's?

'So he came back to the apartment and saw I had thrown away his food; imagine, the leader of Northern Valley Cartel blowing off his top to the max. He put the word out: "Bring me that motherfucker right now. I'm going to kill him. This time for real I'm going to kill this motherfucker." Juanchi went looking for me. He finds me and says, "You're dead. Ras is *fuming*."

'So I get back and Arcángel Henao is sitting on this La-Z-Boy, looking at this whole scene of Rasguño chewing me out to the max. Red, ready to fucking bust a fucking chair over my head. Mocho is laughing. Rasguño is blowing his top. Everybody was just like *shaking*. They figured he was going to shoot somebody. You're talking about people that have killed thousands of people. And you know what he said? "So now I know why they call you Senador. You're so fucking high class you can't eat Colombian food because you're in San Andrés. Okay, motherfucker, you're not going to be El Senador no more. You know who you're going to be? You're going to be 'El Emperador'. You're not a senator, you're a fucking *emperor*.'

'Don *Ras* . . .'

'What I'm going to do, from now on, *every fucking boat* that leaves from this island I'm going to tell the captain your name. And the boat's not going to be named *Esmeralda* or *Quico 1* or *Mary 2* or *Island Girl 4*, it's going to be called *Emperador.* It's going to have your fucking name on it and I'm going to tell the captains that the owner of the merchandise is Luis Navia, El Emperador. If by any chance on any of these *El Emperador* boats we lose the merchandise, I'm going to charge you for it. So maybe that'll get you going when you've got the fucking *gringos* on your ass again.'

'Man, don't do that.'

'Sure enough, Rasguño put "El Emperador" on the boat. From then on, *El Emperador* hit like ten or 12 times. Usually those boats would go with 1600 kilos: of that, 1000 were Rasguño's, 600 were Mocho's, but 200 of Rasguño's were Orlando Sabogal's, "El Mono", who was Rasguño's right-hand man. He hated me and wanted to kill me. He would not have hesitated putting three in my head. He was jealous of my friendship with Rasguño.

'So Rasguño was like, "If they lose a load, everybody's going to charge their percentage on the boat to this man right here, The Emperor!" Now I'm saying yes to everything Rasguño is saying. I'm not going to go against this guy, being who he is. In the end, no *El Emperador* boat ever lost the merchandise. It's a miracle that I threw away Rasguño's food and I'm alive."

*

But Luis still felt like he was trusted and liked enough to be able to call on Rasguño for personal favours. After Escobar's escape, a meeting was arranged in Cartago between Rasguño, Luis and three major traffickers: Hernán Prada Cortés aka 'Papito', Silvio Bernal and José Orlando Sánchez Cristancho aka 'El Hombre Del Overol'.[179]

'They asked me to take them to see Rasguño. Papito was originally a member of the Medellín Cartel, but when people knew that Medellín was going down he asked me to set up a meeting with Rasguño. So I took Papito and Silvio to see him and Orlando tagged along. Papito and Silvio had the same worries and wanted to secure a right-to-live ticket after the war was over.

'Papito and Silvio were partners and shipping huge amounts to Mexico, 6000, 7000 kilos at a time, hundreds of thousands of kilos; at that time they were worth $500 million each, easily. Silvio used to be a gem trader in New York in the early 1980s; very elegant, educated, sharp, one of the smartest guys I ever met. He had a very successful relationship with a group of Mexicans affiliated with Arturo Beltrán Leyva of the Beltrán Leyva brothers, a very big cartel group in Mexico.[180]

'So Papito and Silvio didn't want any trouble and were open to working with Northern Valley. They knew the intimate friendship I had with Rasguño and that I was not the type of person that would set 'em up, take 'em to Rasguño and they'd all end up getting tied up and killed. That's a move, where if you wanted to double-play anybody, they'd all end up dead. You'd take 'em to a set-up. They trusted me as a loyal, honest, non-violent intermediary. They put their lives in my hands.

'These people aren't dumb. They're extremely wealthy, very powerful drug people. And they chose me to go talk to Rasguño. In life, generally, I've always been able to deal with people. Either the worst or the best, I've always had a pleasant demeanour for both. When I'm around you can put your guns down, we're here just as friends. They met with Rasguño, everything was cool and everything went forward. Rasguño started to work with them, being their SOS on these big loads.

'They were all in Rasguño's pocket. All the guys from Pereira, like Patemuro, Marulo's bodyguard, became very rich. He made hundreds of millions of dollars. I mean, think about it. You send 1500 kilos. After you transport the dope for your clients, you end up with 400 kilos free for yourself after the Mexicans take their cut. Four hundred kilos, you just made $6 million, $10 million. They did that five to ten times a month. Rasguño would do *ten times* that much.'

37

Real Crazy Motherfuckers

PABLO ESCOBAR AND RASGUÑO weren't the worst of the narcos Luis got to meet in Colombia. In fact, they were lightweights compared to some of the demented serial killers getting about in the cartels of the early 1990s.

One of them was Jairo Iván Urdinola Grajales aka 'El Enano' (The Dwarf), an evil cocaine and heroin trafficker from El Dovio in Valle del Cauca, who was once described by DEA agent David Tinsley in *The Washington Post* as 'the most feared trafficker in Colombia and worldwide as far as Colombians are concerned. He may be the most violent criminal on the face of the earth. He has an insatiable appetite for violence.'[181]

Urdinola was certainly renowned for butchering people in the most horrific manner possible: chainsaws, the works. In the Valle del Cauca he was responsible for the decapitations and mutilations of hundreds of victims, whose bloodied, mangled corpses regularly flowed down the Río Cauca as a warning to his rivals. Their fingertips would be burned or cut off to prevent identification.

For that reason, even Rasguño, who wasn't shy of chopping up somebody on a whim but better humoured than most cartel leaders, didn't want anything to do with Urdinola. However he was okay with Luis working with him, as long as he was kept out of their affairs. Luis and Urdinola set up a meeting in a car dealership that Urdinola owned in Cali.

'Iván was a very powerful person that you did not want to fuck with. He used to charge everybody for every loss. He never took a loss. Even if it was his fault, it was always *your* fault. I knew he was violent and vicious, a dangerous guy, but it was a dangerous business. Most people I dealt with were like that; I mean, with the most powerful SOS cartel leaders and such, you don't become that way by being a "nice guy". It was an *adventure* to deal with them. If you were in the dope business and you weren't dealing with psychopaths, then you weren't really in the dope business. That's what made it exciting; at least to me it was really exciting.

'There are no words to explain the adrenalin of doing business with these people, talking to them on a daily basis and dealing with them when they're in a good mood and when they're in a bad mood and knowing how to handle those situations. That's extreme living, to say the least. You are never tougher than the Mexicans. You are never tougher than the Colombians. You always have to remember that. You are just an idiot, a fucking bug that they can just swat any time they want.

'When I was in Mexico, I always told myself: I am in the land of Mexicans. They are the bosses. You can never act as a bigger shot than your hosts. You are nothing compared to these cartels. I was very sure of what I was doing and I knew that if I were to have a problem with Iván it would not be through dishonesty or leading him to believe one thing and doing something else.

'Still, you're dealing with volatile personalities and you never know: you can be very honest, suddenly have a problem, and one of these maniacs gets up on the wrong side of bed and just decides he doesn't want you around anymore and that's the end of the story. But if you sat around and thought about that all the time, then you're in the wrong business.

'Wall Street bigshots don't sit around all day thinking about how much they could lose; they think about how much they're gonna *make*. Losing cannot be part of the formula when the stakes are so high. It's like a profession and you decide what your specialty is going to be. My specialty was big numbers and when you deal with big numbers you deal with big sources of supply, and most of the time the big sources of supply are extreme-personality types.

'I got used to that. Very few Colombians would deal with someone like Urdinola on a one-to-one basis like I did and work huge numbers that would scare the hell out of most people. I always thought the bigger the better. It gets to a point where you're too big to fail. You'll probably be killed quicker for losing 50 kilos than you will for losing 5000. It's like the big banks; they're too big to go bust.'

But as is the way with many killers, Urdinola had a soft side. He could also be generous. After the meeting in the showroom was over, he spontaneously handed Luis the keys to a brand-new BMW M535i. A chauffeur drove it for him from Cali back to Bogotá. Luis was happy to accept the modest gift.

'Not long after that I did a trip to the Florida Keys for Iván in one of his planes – 600 kilos, but the fucking coke hadn't been packed right. There had been a mix-up where my waterproofed coke was sent to Mexico and the unprotected coke was sent to the Keys. So we did the airdrop and *boom* – the coke got splattered all over the Caribbean Sea. But Iván didn't charge me for it. It was unheard of. He made somebody pay for it or replace the merchandise; I guarantee you. The bags were all ripped open. The cocaine was full of saltwater. My connection in the Keys, Jorge "El Gordito" Cabrera, had to pick that shit up and put it in pails to give it to these people who received it as proof.[182] But, sure enough, I talked to Iván and he said, "I don't want to listen to you anymore. I'm not going to let you whip out a pencil, because the minute you whip out a pencil we all lose. You know what: give me back my car.'

'Oh, shit. You know, *er*, the car's a little beat up.'

'You lose my merchandise, now you tell me my car is beat up?'

'Iván, you won't believe it, man.'

*

Luis told him the embarrassing truth. There had been an incident in the car park of a condominium in Bogotá, outside the apartment of his pilot friend Gordon 'Goo' Gray.

'I went there to hang out with Goo. He's a good cook and he made dinner and we started drinking and snorting. Patricia wasn't totally pleased but she knew I liked to get together with my friends and drink and have a few snorts and talk shit all night. Goo's wife, Phoebe, had a really good-looking friend and she was trying to hook me up with her but she wasn't at the apartment that night.[183] The next day Patricia called and said, "Okay, time to come home."'

'When Luis didn't come home and I woke up in the morning I was so worried,' she remembers. 'I started calling everybody. "Is Luis at your house? Is Luis with you?" And Phoebe called me. She said, "Hey, don't worry, Luis is here, he spent the night here with Goo, and they were drinking. They're asleep now and then they're going to eat something."

'There was no jealousy; other women don't bother me in the least. I was sure nobody could stand him like me [*laughs*]. I was tired because I was taking care of Luis all the time. I was just a child but I was always like, "Please don't drink too much. Please don't do the coke." He *lovvves* coke. He didn't want to stop doing it. I always wanted him to stop.'

Luis continues: 'Being my usual rebellious self, I said, "No, I want to stay." So Patricia drove up to come get me and I kept saying no, that I wanted to stay and continue partying with Goo. When she got there, she called from downstairs from the guard house and she must've told the guard something because the guard let her in, so she was still pleading with me on her phone to come downstairs.'

Patricia: 'Luis didn't want to leave. I was really tired. I said, "Hey, let's go. It's enough. It's not your house. You can continue drinking and doing whatever but in your *own* house."'

Luis: 'I kept saying, "No, I'm not going." Patricia knew Goo had the penthouse and it had a balcony. So she was like, "If you don't wanna come downstairs, come out to the balcony and see what it's going to cost you for being such an asshole."'

Luis went to the balcony clutching his phone.

Patricia: 'And I was *soooo* mad, I took the keys of my car, I saw his car and I smashed into it. I completely destroyed his car [*laughs*]. The worst part was I destroyed mine too.'

In fact, Patricia was so incensed she rear-ended Urdinola's BMW four times with her own BMW, while Luis was watching on aghast. Hearing the story told in full, Urdinola let out a big laugh.

'Give me the story again, Luis. It sounds like my wife. Just fix the car up and send it back to me. That's the funniest story I've ever heard. You're one crazy sonofabitch.'

Luis's wife didn't find it so funny. Patricia was so upset she left Luis for a month and, in her own words, 'hid' from him at a friend's apartment. His drinking and coke habit had become too much for her to handle and she was over it.

'He waited for me every day while I was there, and I was like, "I don't want to know anything about you anymore, Luis. *Anything.* I'm tired. We're done." But a friend of ours got us together. When I came back I needed a drink: I ordered a Buchanan's on the rocks and told him: "You know, you have to take care of me." Luis promised he wouldn't drink for a year. And he did it. That's why I went back to him and our relationship survived.'

*

In early 1993, around the time Gilberto Rodríguez Orejuela and Miguel Rodríguez Orejuela of the Cali Cartel began negotiations with the Colombian Government to surrender peacefully and stop trafficking, in exchange for reduced jail time and keeping their spectacular wealth, Luis began working with a blond, blue-eyed Cali figure called Claudio Endo aka 'Mono Endo'.

'A fucking psychopath, a *maniac*. You talk about maniacs. Claudio was known to be a fucking psycho killer. That motherfucker would go and chop you up with a saw himself. He was nuts and wired. His eyes were always bloodshot, so they were red, white and blue. I just had a knack for dealing with nuts, I guess, I don't know. What I did was completely insane, but it was perfectly normal for me to go to Cali and work with someone like that. He was regarded as even more of a psychopath than Iván and more volatile.

'The Cali Cartel was trying to cut a peace deal with the government and part of the peace plan was to stop working, so they asked everyone to stop working.[184] Claudio said, "Fuck you. That's easy for you to say; couple of fucking old geezers that already have $10 billion. I'm still making my money. I still need to work." So he continued working. I did five or six trips with Claudio to Cancún to my people, 5000 kilos, when nobody was doing nothing. That's a lot of merchandise. We just whacked it like nothin'. *Boom boom boom.*'

That's when he got a phone call from Miki Ramírez.

'Senador, *please*, I beg you, stop working with Mono Endo. You're my friend. I don't want to see you die. Believe me, with Mono Endo you're going to end up dead. With me, there's no problem; you can lose a load. You're my friend. You're not his friend.'

'I agree.'

'So come home, come back to Bogotá, and I will open up the *oficina* just for you. I will give you what you need. But *stop*. Stop immediately with Mono Endo.'

It was sage advice. Endo was targeted and killed a year later by the Cali Cartel, who had sent a gang of *sicarios* to assassinate him at his *finca* outside Jamundí in the Valle del Cauca, just south of Cali. He was depicted being killed in season three of *Narcos* being dragged behind a car on the orders of Cali's Hélmer Herrera aka 'Pacho'.[185] The incident never happened. Instead Endo was shot between 50 to 100 times with machine-gun fire at close range. But the end result was the same.

'They just came in and shot him up in the bathroom of his farm. He locked himself in there and they just whacked him. Real crazy motherfucker.'

*

As for Iván Urdinola, in April 1992 he was arrested on a trafficking charge following a raid of 300 police and sentenced to four years and seven months' jail (an initial, much tougher sentence of 17 years was reduced because he confessed to sending cocaine to the United States). His equally feared younger brother Julio Fabio gave himself up in March 1994.

Urdinola was all set to walk free two years into his sentence but he was then rearrested and charged in relation to the August 1991 acid torture and brutal murder of an army officer called Ricardo Petersson, who'd had an affair with Urdinola's wife Lorena Henao Montoya, the sister of Orlando, while in Cali. Petersson was slit from his stomach to his throat and thrown in the Río Cauca, like most of Urdinola's victims. Still behind bars, Urdinola was murdered by poisoning in 2002.[186] Ten years later, Lorena was assassinated by *sicarios* on a motorbike.

There are few happy endings in the drug business in Colombia.

38

The Prisoner of Cartago

In May 1993, Luis did lose a load: a small but significant one in the scheme of things and for those who impounded it, when a boat called *Top Gun II* was intercepted by the US Navy hydrofoil USS *Hercules* some 200 miles west of Key West, Florida, with 375.5 kilos of 94 per cent–pure cocaine aboard. The two offloaders were detained and delivered into the custody of the USCS.

That year Luis was getting most of his work transporting for Rasguño, but was involved in a sideline as a supplier with his old smuggling friend from Santa Marta, Francisco Moya aka Juanchi. They'd rendezvoused the previous year in San Andrés with a group of smugglers Juanchi knew from the Florida Keys, but to Luis they were strangers and this had made him nervous. Juanchi's contacts were using a fleet of vessels from the Keys city of Marathon to pick up Miki Ramírez's cocaine that had been airdropped off the west coast of Florida, then bringing it back to the Keys and taking it to Miami for distribution. The *Top Gun* smuggle was the ninth and last.

'We had sent Juanchi's cousin to oversee operations in Miami and Tampa and receive monies and make sure merchandise was distributed, and he'd come running back to Colombia because he got hot. So we knew we were already hot. We were hitting the South Florida area from three angles: the east side, airdropping in The Bahamas; the west, airdropping off Tampa; and then from Cancún we were also sending merchandise up to Mississippi and Louisiana. At the same time we were working the Mexican border and delivering merchandise to LA.

'*Top Gun* was a trip that we did from Colombia to Cancún,' says Luis. 'It was a double offload. We had a large blue twin-engine inboard fastboat that Rasguño had bought in Buenaventura. And we loaded that boat with about 1200 kilos, dropped off 800 kilos off Cancún, received more fuel and continued to drop off 400 kilos more a little further north to Scorpion Reef [Arrecife Alacranes], north of the Yucatán Peninsula. The captain really didn't want to do the second leg of the trip and I don't blame him. After the two guys on *Top Gun* picked up the load, they were chased by this *huge* hydrofoil. It was like a building behind them. And they were busted.

'That was a logistical mistake. I should never have done a double smuggle. When you get to a place and you're handing off merchandise, that's it; the crew wants to go back. You should just deliver and go back but with a double smuggle you can pick up heat doing the first load and not know it, so you're already on fire on your way to the second drop-off.'

Luis was rightly spooked by what had happened.

'I was concerned, obviously. I knew that these people were going to talk. But I was living my life as if I had already been indicted. I knew I was hot; I'd been hot for years. What I did not know was that these people knew my name. Those fucking idiots that came to San Andrés from the Keys, I didn't know them. Juanchi knew them. I was not too happy meeting these people. I think one of them was already undercover.

'Juanchi got high and fucked up on coke and shit and my name must have slipped out. When you're drunk and high on coke, you talk about this shit, you think this guy's your best friend, and sure enough I told Juanchi,. "Why the fuck are you working with these people from the Keys who know your name, when we are working with El Tío from Mexico? He doesn't know who we are. He doesn't need to know our names. He knows that if he steals from us he's going to die. Yeah, he might take 30 days to pay us but he pays us and he doesn't know our *names*."'

Luis didn't know it yet but his cover was blown.

*

Things, however, were about to get a whole lot worse. Patricia was five months pregnant and staying at the Ritz-Carlton in Cancún. Andrea Blanco, the sister of his brother-in-law, Vicente, was also with Luis in Cancún but there was a problem.

'Andrea was losing her mind; she ended up in a psycho clinic. Basically she started talking shit about me. She didn't say that I was stealing but worse: that I was talking bad about Rasguño, that I was downplaying him, saying I was the boss and he was a gopher for me. Imagine – totally ridiculous. Never in my life have I ever done that. I respected Rasguño and it was an honour to be working for him.'

'She was a little bit nuts,' says Patricia. 'Andrea left a message for Luis with the front desk of the hotel, "The DEA is after you." And Luis and I took everything and we ran. And we went to Playa del Carmen as a precaution and nothing happened. But we didn't know that nothing was going to happen.'

The damage had been done, however, and word got to Rasguño that Luis had been badmouthing him. Luis got a call from Juanchi.

'You should fucking leave the country, right now. He's going to kill you. He's fucking pissed.'

Luis was mortified; they might have had their differences and business was business, but above all else he considered Rasguño a friend. So rather than fleeing to Southeast Asia, he jumped on a plane to Colombia and met the head of the North Valley Cartel at his *oficina*. Instead of talking things out, Luis was kidnapped and kept for 21 days at a *finca* outside Cartago.

*

'When they grabbed me, they put me in the car with a policeman from Pereira, one of Rasguño's bodyguards and some other Ras guys. On the drive over I was looking out the window to the pastures of the Valle del Cauca and my vision was going past the horizon and taking my mind away from the situation I was in. I was in a state of limbo. What's going through your head is that you're going to die. If you are taken in – you never walk out alive. What are you going to do? Turn into a Walter White?[187] That was very fictitious, that *Breaking Bad* shit. You took your lickings and you kept on ticking. I never for one minute thought that they were going to torture me; none of that stupid stuff, no. I just thought they were going to put a bullet in my head and it's over after you pay.'

Based on nothing more than a rumour, he'd been kidnapped and Rasguño had a legitimate pretext for doing so; but Luis believed there were overriding strategic motivations at play.

'They were already planning to do it, to take over my route and all this shit. Rasguño never takes somebody in, holds them, and lets them go. That's not good business. He wouldn't have let anybody else live. The reason he let me live was I wasn't a violent guy. That's what saved me.'

In other words, Luis wasn't the kind of trafficker who could do a couple of trips, make $20 million, and use part of that money to avenge his kidnapping. Rasguño was after a ransom: calculated through loads for the cartel that had been lost and cocaine Luis had bought himself on credit. It was an expensive tab sheet.

'He told me I couldn't leave until we squared off accounts. That's when everybody thought I was going to get killed. Even if you clear your accounts, you die anyway. The only thing you hope for is that they don't torture you. Rasguño did a complete audit. Believe me, if he would have found out that any of the shit that was said by Andrea was real, I'd be dead. I'm alive because I didn't steal from him.

'I had merchandise on different trips I had bought on credit and the merchandise that was en route hadn't been *coronado* yet – which means to get it to its destination and get paid. Rasguño's bill came out to $4 million. Cartels don't have fine print in their contracts. Money's a very powerful tool; you need to use it. I'd rather pay up than see somebody killed or be killed. If you don't pay, you die.'

*

Coming up with that kind of money quickly took some doing and fast-talking. Luis paid what he could in property deeds to apartments he owned in Bogotá and land he owned in San Andrés, plus cash and stakes in future loads, while his wife offered land she owned in Santa Marta, her car, art collection and jewellery. Juanchi also had to pay Rasguño but wasn't held.

'For a week I was in a daze,' says Luis. 'I didn't know what the fuck was going on. It was a nice farm with a pool. Rasguño's people would bring in some books in English. For the first three days I was handcuffed to a bed in an apartment, but the rest of the time I just stayed by the pool at the farm.

'I volunteered all my assets and my money and everything. I was the largest landowner in San Andrés. I had incredible lots down by the water where I was going to build a marina, I had lots on Santa Catalina, lots in Providencia – and that's what paid part of the $4 million.[188] They went to my apartment in Bogotá. They were very decent with Patricia. When Rasguño snatched me, she was seven months pregnant. Patricia said, "Take my paintings, take my jewels." They were worth a lot of money. His men said, "*No, no, no.* We don't want nothing of yours." Then they let her see me.'

Patricia, just 24, displaying a courage belying her years and not knowing whether she would be killed herself, met the cartel's lawyer in a café in a Bogotá shopping mall called Centro 93 to make arrangements for the payment of the ransom. Then 15 days after Luis had been taken, she flew to Pereira and fronted up at the *finca* in Cartago with 'a long list' of how she and the father of her unborn child were going to pay: properties, land, paintings, cars. Luis's personal secretary Clara Macias was with her, having helped put together the list.

'Rasguño was so ashamed when he saw me. All of them were.'

'When she showed up,' adds Luis, 'they couldn't believe it. No one does that. Patricia went to Cartago seven months pregnant. They were embarrassed because they'd never have expected a woman to show up. In most of these cases when that happens to someone's partner or husband, the women and everybody start hiding all the assets. They don't want to give up anything. They say the exact opposite of what Patricia said. Which was, "Take everything but just give me my husband back." She's got her grandfather's balls. Rasguño really liked Patricia. Rasguño's people thought she really didn't deserve me; that she had to put up with a lot of shit from me. They saw that she was a straight shooter.'

Patricia remembers it vividly: 'Rasguño told me, "*No, no, no.* Take your car. I don't want *your* things. That is not necessary." He promised me that he'd respect Luis's life and I explained to him, "He's not from Colombia, he doesn't have a brother, he doesn't have cousins, he doesn't have a family, he only has a sister and a mother in Miami who are never going to come to Colombia to ask what happened, so you can never expect *represalias* [retaliation]." No one was going to avenge Luis or do something like that. That's why I was there and they knew me. I really wasn't afraid because I think they are people with honour. They have this code that nobody really understands. They do respect some things.'

*

Any thoughts of escape were crushed when Rasguño's cold-eyed number-one henchman Orlando Sabogal Zuluaga aka 'El Mono' or 'Mono Sabogal' paid a visit. He made the situation very clear: Luis would be killed if he so much as even contemplated escaping. If El Mono had his own way he would have turned Luis into a colander from bullet holes, but Rasguño wasn't allowing any harm to come to him.

'El Mono *haaaated* Luis,' says Patricia. 'I cooked for El Mono and Rasguño in San Andrés. I'd always been nice to them and showed them respect. Luis and I were the opposite of the kind of people you normally see in the business. We were well educated. If you understand a bit about the social classes in Colombia you will know that some people don't treat each other with respect. I was never like that. My grandfather and my great-grandfather came from Spain and they taught us to respect the people who have less than you or work for you. You don't have any right to mistreat those people. So I always was very polite; more than polite. I tried my best. So because of the way we treated Rasguño and El Mono, they treated us with respect in the moment we needed it.'[189]

Eventually Luis felt confident enough to break the ice with the three *sicarios* who were guarding him.

'I got bored with the rice and beans every day and we used to send out for pizza. The old me came back. I created an ambience around me of laughter. Everything was a joke. Then that led to the hitmen taking me out to the pizzeria and Rasguño found out because he owned the pizzeria. Then taking me out for phone calls to my attorney Reid Constable about my macadamia farm in Costa Rica, and Rasguño found out because he had the phone company tapped. Then taking me out to get a driver's licence, and Rasguño found out because he had the motor registry tapped. I'd been in the country so many years I wanted a Cartago driver's licence, for the hell of it. Rasguño had that whole town wired.'

The three hitmen even came to like Luis and asked him for work.

'They were like, "Señor Navia. Don Luis. *Senador.* Eh, what do you mean you want a driver's licence? Dead people don't drive; you could be dead in an hour. You may be delusional, but we really like you. Usually when it comes time to kill someone we're holding, they tell us, 'You do it.' And this time nobody wants to do it. We're gonna flip. We're gonna draw straws. It's a problem between you and El Patrón and if he calls the order, we're gonna do it. We're going to kill you but we don't want to do it."

'They knew I had great connections in Mexico and I told them that if I got out of this situation I'd probably just go to Mexico, and they told me that they would love to come work with me. I mean, who the fuck thinks of a driver's licence when he's handcuffed to a fucking bed and they're going to kill him any moment? Usually when you're tied up and you convince a bodyguard who's holding you hostage to take you out for pizza, when you come back you're dead and the bodyguard's dead. The three guys that were holding me, they were scared shitless. I mean it's a miracle Rasguño didn't fucking kill them all. But he knew I was innocent. I was so naïve that I was kidnapped and I still didn't realise I was kidnapped. I was thinking of pizza.'

*

On the third week of Luis's imprisonment, the reparation had been paid and he was free to leave.

'Bets were on in Colombia: this time he's not coming back from a kidnapping by Rasguño. It doesn't happen. Rasguño kidnaps you, then you've got to wish for a quick death, he takes as little as possible and he leaves your widow with something to live on. But I came back. It was like a ghost coming back. And when he let me go, most people would get in a taxi and hightail it to the next country. I took the taxi to the local hotel in Cartago that he owned and I checked in under his name. My bill was under him: *Luis Navia as per Hernando Gómez.*'

Luis requested a private audience with Rasguño and he came to visit Luis in his hotel room. Rasguño was carrying a Harley-Davidson branded black-leather briefcase.

'Man, you've left me broke,' he told the North Valley Cartel leader. 'I have no money. Can you lend me $100,000 in the meantime?'

'You know what, Luis,' Rasguño snarled. 'I'm going to give you what I have in my briefcase. Do me a favour. *Please.* Get the fuck out of town.'

Patricia had flown into Pereira and hailed a taxi to take her to collect Luis in Cartago.

'I felt a little bit afraid. If they were going to kill us, it was going to happen then. But everything was okay. Rasguño's bodyguards were like, "Good luck with the delivery of the baby," [*laughs*] and they hugged me. They told me they were going to miss Luis. When we were alone in the taxi back to Pereira, I was really scared. I thought: "They could kill us here on this road." I was only going to feel safe on the plane back to Bogotá. Luis never lived by the rules. Not even after he was released after being held for almost a month, he stayed in Cartago asking to talk to Rasguño. Anybody else would have left immediately.'

Inside the taxi, Luis opened the leather case to see what was inside. It was $50,000. When he got home, Rasguño called.

'*Motherfucker.* You didn't even pay the bill!'

'Well, it's *your* hotel, Ras. I thought the least you could do was put me up for a couple of days.'

*

On 2 December 1993, with nowhere left to run, Pablo Escobar was shot three times by the *Policía Nacional de Colombia* (PNC or Colombian National Police) on a Los Olivos, Medellín, rooftop at Carrera 79B #45D-94: one bullet in the back of his right leg, one in his back and the *coup de grâce* through his right ear. Photos of his bloated, shoeless body twisted in its last repose on a bed of blood-spattered, broken terracotta tiles went around the world. The Medellín Cartel was over.

Luis found out the news Escobar had been killed at Cartagena airport through a corrupt army officer.

Three weeks later, on 29 December 1993, at Clinica del Country private hospital in Bogotá, Luis became a father for the first time. He and Patricia had a daughter, Juliana, and she was premature but a healthy 3700 grams. He cut the umbilical cord.

'Patricia was there, you know, having the baby, *boom boom*, and I grabbed the baby and I tell Patricia, "Patricia, *wow*, this is amazing, this is beautiful, my God, she's beautiful, she looks just like . . . *me*." Patricia thought I'd said she looked just like her. When she heard that she looked like me, Patricia fainted [*laughs*]. *Boom*, they had to come in with oxygen and everything. That'll knock out anybody. So Patricia has the baby and we get home and we start getting presents in packages from [the mail company] Servientrega. Cartago is known for its embroideries.'

As Patricia unwrapped the presents, there were some unfamiliar names on the cards: 'El Diablo' (The Devil), 'El Búho' (The Owl) 'El Caballo' (The Horse). She was puzzled.

'Luis, who's Caballo?'

'Oh, that's the guy who first chained me up when I was kidnapped, but let me out the first night when I went out to have pizza.'

'*Wha?*'

'Yeah, he's one of the hitmen you met. He crucified one of his victims and skinned him alive and sprayed him with alcohol.'

'Oh, okay. Well, this nice embroidery is from him for our newborn daughter. Who's Diablo?'

'Well, that's another hitman who killed seven people when they tried to kidnap Rasguño.'

'Oh, well he sent a nice little pillowcase for our baby. And who's Búho?'

'Baby, you met them. These were all the hitmen who had me in custody.'

He still shakes his head about it today.

'These guys were fucking killers and they sent embroideries to my wife.'[190]

New Year's Eve was just days away and Luis had survived a true *annus horribilis* – the *Top Gun* bust, a kidnapping and extortion,

Escobar's death – and emerged somehow as a father. Yet, bizarrely, there is no residual animosity to the man who'd put him through so much: Rasguño.

'Once Medellín broke up and Pablo got taken down, Northern Valley kind of split from Cali. Miki Ramírez knew [the Colombian Government] were going after Cali, so he didn't know what was going to happen with Los Pepes. He knew they were going to come after his ass. The government took away his security. So when the DEA went directly after Cali, that gave Northern Valley a window. Rasguño was kind of the one that took over and Northern Valley became the biggest cartel in Colombia. But it was because of Rasguño I saw my daughter. It touches my heart and I'll always love him and I'll always do whatever I can for him.'

PART 8

BLAME IT ON CANCÚN

39

Fire in the Lake

KNOWING HIS NAME HAD likely been leaked and USCS or the DEA was onto him meant one thing to Luis: selling his remaining assets, packing up the family and leaving Colombia. His next destination, naturally, was Mexico. The cartels were being brought to heel in Colombia but in Mexico it was still very much anything goes and the perfect place to hide. He spoke the language, had been moving drugs into the country since the early 1980s and the *federales* could easily be bought off.

So in March 1994, he arrived on a Colombian passport in his own name transiting Mexico City to Cancún, a beachside city in Quintana Roo he knew very well. His wife, infant daughter and their maid followed him in June. He began openly living as Luis Navia, Colombian, but also had a Mexican alias and fake passport under the name Luis Novoa Alfandari. He even bought a coffee company, Café Koba, and started buying beans from local growers and roasting and blending them to supply the city's then-booming hotel sector and its American clientele. Luis was selling 20,000 kilos of coffee a month. But the main game was always cocaine.

'I never looked like a narco or acted like a narco. Juliana had just been born and I was thinking about the future, organising my future trips with my SOS, which was Hernán Prada. He had the merchandise but no sea transport to take the merchandise to Cancún, so I put

Hernán in touch with Alfredo or "Api", the brother of Mono Abello. Mono was probably the sixth most important member of the Medellín Cartel and also affiliated with the Coast Cartel.[191] Api had fastboats for transport in the Caribbean. Cancún became such a profitable port of entry for cocaine that everybody and his mother started to send shit there. It became one of the biggest if not *the* biggest route at the time. Cancún was fun and games by daytime, but by night thousands and thousands of kilos were coming in. We did a bunch of trips. We did three trips in the last six months of '94. We were back in business.'

Prada Cortés, a Colombian but US resident who was a big mover of merchandise in New York, had fled the country in 1989 after an FBI investigation into his cocaine distribution network resulted in a federal arrest warrant.[192] In Colombia his silent partner was Edgar Guillermo Vallejo Guarin aka 'Beto el Gitano' (Beto the Gypsy), a fellow ex-Medellín alumnus and major cocaine trafficker to Europe, and together they were getting merchandise from the department of Boyacá in Colombia from people unaffiliated with any cartel but associates of The Mexican, the late José Gonzalo Rodríguez Gacha. They sent over a *sicario* called 'Wálter'. It was the first and only time Luis ever had his own bodyguard.

'He actually looked just like The Mexican. The night we brought in the first trip the turtles were nesting in the sand. Wálter and I were there, eating Domino's Pizza. He had been a hitman for The Mexican but was a fucking awesome guy. Our suppliers wanted the maximum protection possible for me. We got along great. For Wálter it was a relief to be around a non-violent family guy. He felt very at ease. If he had to have it out with six Mexicans, he'd walk out alive and the six Mexicans would be dead. He was very good at what he did. After I'd made the first trip I brought Patricia over to live in Cancún and we never went back to live in Colombia.'

Says Patricia: 'I was so happy. Luis bought Café Koba and finally we were doing something different. In Bogotá a lot of people had bodyguards – armed escorts or *escoltas* – even people who had nothing to do with that kind of business had them; I had friends that had bodyguards and they were just wealthy, legal businesspeople. Back then kidnapping was very common. Before and after Pablo Escobar fell, there were militias that had all the structure but no bosses to follow and they became kidnappers, *secuestradores*. And we always had the guerrillas. I think it was the worst time to be in Colombia.

'So Café Koba was a good business and I helped in sales, expanding the business. Our partners were third-generation, very prominent coffee people. Luis played golf and was occupied with the coffee business and his macadamia farm in Costa Rica. Right now I feel like I'm talking about a world that has been completely trashed for the last 20 years and it might be hard for you to understand how me and Luis were able to live in that world and not be completely absorbed by the criminal side of it, but that is part of Luis's magic: he makes you feel like anything is possible.

'Everyone's concept of the cocaine business is that it's full of ugly people but it wasn't like that. I understand people who have never been to Colombia thinking that, but you'd find really nice, high-class people being involved. We never got involved in "ugly things". We never had a gun in my house, ever. *No*. Luis was always against guns. I don't think I've ever seen him holding a gun.'

'It was the best years of my life,' says Luis. 'We lived in a very nice house on the beach. We planted coconut trees in the big yard we had, went for beach walks every day, enjoyed life with my wife and my kid. South and Central America was my playground. I could go anywhere. I knew where to go, how to go, and as *what* to go.

'All the people that I knew in Mexico that were in the drug business, on the Colombian side, were all very well-to-do, high-level people. They had kids, the whole family atmosphere. It's different when you're an American with no cultural interactions. I wasn't a deadbeat. I moved in high society freely. To me it was no problem. We'd go somewhere and we were in like Flynn. That's an art that I had. A lot of people can't do that. They just can't adapt.

'Americans on the run in Mexico or South America have a hard time. But I adapted [*clicks his fingers*] immediately. The whole nine yards. The kids in school. The apartments. The car, the credit cards, the bank accounts, *everything*. Nobody in Mexico thought I was in the drug business. I was just a very rich Colombian guy who partied like an animal. That said, you have to be sharp and on your feet. It's not easy.'

Richard Booth, his old friend in mischief from Miami, agrees: 'Luis would always have to get up and just leave his belongings and move somewhere else. He really was a very bright guy at what he did to stay ahead of the game for 25 years.'

*

How to properly answer a phone call from a drug lord is one such skill only 25 years of experience can give you.

One day Luis answered the phone: it was Hernán Prada Cortés asking him about Alex DeCubas aka 'Coco' or 'Mario', a fellow Cuban-American cocaine trafficker on the run in Colombia. An ex-champion high-school wrestler with a hulking frame and connections to Félix Chitiva and Miki Ramírez, he was a fugitive from a drugs indictment in Florida, had recently left Brazil, and invested $2 million of his own money in a clandestine project to build a homemade narco submarine.[193]

'Hi, everything good, Luis?'

'Yeah, Papito. I'm good.'

A lot of people in the drug business get killed because people lie, badmouth their rivals, harbour jealousies, or completely make up stories to protect themselves and get other people killed instead. In the drug business every phone call is important. It pays to speak the truth, every single time.

'Hey, you know Coco?'

'Yeah.'

'What kind of guy is he? Is he legit? Does he know what he's doing?'

'Yeah, definitely. He knows what he's doing. He's been a smuggler all his life.'

'Would he steal?'

'*No*. Without a doubt he would not steal. If he has a loss, he'll own up to it.'

'Okay, because I was thinking of working with him.'

'He's an excellent guy. You're in good hands, Papito. He knows what he's doing.'

And that was that. But a few weeks later, Luis got a message to call Lester Delgado Cabrera aka 'Pinky', the cousin of El Gordito (Fatty),

Luis's Cuban *recibidor* in the Florida Keys.[194] He was in Bogotá. Pinky, also a Cuban, was a very relaxed, almost bohemian cocaine trafficker with a shabby dress sense and Harry Potter eyeglasses, who'd got his unusual nickname for the advanced case of psoriasis he had. He'd be shedding skin all the time.

According to Luis, before Pinky arrived in Colombia he'd been on the lam in the United States and then Rio de Janeiro, where he was sharing a house with DeCubas and a blond, blue-eyed American from Islamorada in the Florida Keys called Steve Smit aka 'Chepe', another fugitive. All three travelled on fake Dominican Republic passports.

Pinky's specialty was trafficking coke to England and mainland Europe on sailboats, usually 500- to 600-kilo loads, and using a Dutchman and Brazilian national called Godfried Hoppenbrouwers aka 'Pappy' as his logistical brains. Pinky and his Cuban-American colleague, DeCubas, got their coke from Pablo Escobar's former associate, Félix Chitiva, who in turn was getting his coke from Miki Ramírez and later Los Mellizos in northern Colombia.

'The three of them finally ended up in Bogotá because obviously they needed to get the work, and Colombia was where all the connections were. When they lived in Brazil, Alex would just hire hookers all day and Pinky used to put on his backpack just to walk and get away from that madness. I guess he was kind of depressed. He missed his mother a lot and knew that he wasn't going to be able to see his family anymore, being on the run. He could live off his backpack. When they got to Bogotá they again all lived in the same house. Alex started using his contacts to do his airdrops in the Keys and he also began building the submarine. Pinky concentrated on the sailboats to England and Chepe was very mechanically inclined and he worked with Alex on the sub.'[195]

'Hey, Luis,' said Pinky, down the line. 'I really want to thank you for what you did. You saved Alex's life.'

'What do you mean?'

'Well, when Papito called you, Alex was tied up. They'd had him tied up for a week or two. We lost a load in the Keys. It was a set-up. Papito wanted to see if you'd say Alex was prone to stealing loads.'

*

Wálter lived in the same apartment complex where Luis and Patricia had a townhouse/villa but Luis also kept a third apartment where they just talked and Luis would take his hookers. But the close proximity allowed him and Luis to get to know each other quite well, beyond their professional relationship.

'Wálter was at our villa on and off but he was always around; he never made his presence felt and he was a very respectful, calm person. He had a wife and daughter in Pereira. They owned a party supply store: ornaments and stuff for kids' parties, first communions. He felt they were safe there and he wanted to set himself up financially and get his family away from all the madness and live normally. He always carried a SIG Sauer P226 9mm; a great gun, easy to handle and accurate. He used to tell me it was special because it was German-made. I think it took 15 rounds. He also had an AK-47 hidden somewhere.'

But Patricia found out about the bachelor pad. She showed up, confronted Luis and left in a huff when one of his girlfriends was hiding in the shower. Wálter turned to him. He was about to teach Luis a very valuable lesson about the drug trade: it's all about protecting the business.

'Listen, I've been through a lot of things in life. And I've never been so scared as today. I am more scared of your wife than I've been of any man I've ever had to kill. This is not going to leave this room but let me tell you: this can never happen again, because if down south in the *oficina* they found out that I let you have a girlfriend and that in the process of you having a girlfriend your wife found out and we caused her any kind of emotional damage, they're going to kill me.

'Your wife is a very decent, classy girl. Believe me, I've seen it happen where these girls lose their fucking top and call the *oficina*. My lifespan would be the time it takes a hitman to come from Bogotá to Mexico City to Cancún and blow my brains out. After they killed me they'd probably kill that girl and dump her in the mangroves and get rid of the problem. You, they won't kill. You're not supposed to have girlfriends. You're supposed to be a family man because we're moving tens of thousands of kilos through here and there can be no waves. This has to be a very calm lake. There can be no fires in the lake.'

40

Chasing a Ghost

ROBERT HARLEY JR WAS born in Philadelphia, Pennsylvania, on 11 March 1965, the youngest of three children and the only boy with two older sisters. The Harleys were 'buffet Catholics' because they weren't especially religious and picked of Catholicism what they liked, while ignoring what they didn't like. Both his late parents, Italian-Irish mother Violet and Dutch-Irish father Robert Sr, were from the coal-mining region of Pennsylvania.

Violet worked for the US Navy while Robert Sr was an oilman for the Phillips Petroleum Company, so when his father got promoted they'd find themselves moving. Harley had a peripatetic childhood, switching between Pennsylvania, New York, Ohio, South Carolina and Florida. By 1979, when Luis began his cocaine career with the Medellín Cartel, 14-year-old Harley was going to St. Thomas Aquinas High School in Fort Lauderdale, 30 minutes up the I-95 from Miami, and working at a marina downtown called Pier 66.

'I was living in Fort Lauderdale when all this business really started taking off. South Florida in the late '70s was wide open. I graduated high school in 1983 and went to college at the University of Pennsylvania back in Philadelphia. My undergraduate major was in economics and finance. It doesn't make sense but I knew after freshman year that I didn't want to do that. I didn't know what I wanted to do for a living but I knew I didn't want to do *that*.

'Growing up in Fort Lauderdale I had a US Customs agent who lived two houses down from my family and I had an ATF agent – Alcohol, Tobacco and Firearms – who kind of lived diagonally from us, so I saw those guys fairly regularly.[196] And I liked being in Florida. I liked being on the boats, being around marinas and airplanes and all the rest of that, and I don't really remember exactly how it happened but in my junior year of college I started applying to federal agencies. I got interviews and went through the application process with multiple different agencies; I even got interviewed by the CIA at one point in Philadelphia.

'DEA actually offered me a job first in the fall of 1986 but at the time everybody was going one of two places for DEA: New York City or Puerto Rico. And I got an offer from Customs subsequent to the interview process from DEA. It was to go to Key West and literally that's how I ended up with Customs in Key West versus any other agency. It was about geography. Everybody starts at the same pay grade and goes through the grades at the same rate. In those years Customs and DEA was essentially the exact same job.'

By March 1987 Harley had enrolled in a 16-week course at the Federal Law Enforcement Training Center (FLETC) in Glynco, Georgia, to learn the ropes as a special agent. Six months later there was four weeks of 'boat school', where rookies were taught how to drive boats for interception.

Harley calls it 'FBI Lite because Customs wasn't nearly as regimented in those years as the FBI was. FBI agents in those days were still kind of suit and tie. Customs agents worked in the ports, airports and seaports. And you weren't ever going to wear a suit and tie doing that kind of casework. So the academy was a little more lax. Myself and one other guy in my class were the youngest by far. Most people were in their early 30s. We were both 22. So it was really unusual for them to take people that young, but there was a huge expansion because of what was going on in South Florida at that time.'

The Florida Keys had long been a hotbed of drug-trafficking activity with whole families of 'multigenerational smugglers', as Harley calls them, involved. There were so many smugglers in the Keys, agents would scour through high-school yearbooks picking out suspects. For the first couple of years as a USCS agent he was on the water.

'I was a boat driver. In those days there wasn't a marine officer position – the agents actually drove the boats when we were doing interdictions. It was two or three a week. It was very hectic in the beginning. By about '91 or so, because they put so many assets into the Gulf and the southeast coast of the US, it forced the smugglers into Texas, Arizona and southern California. There were still a lot of loads going into the Gulf of Mexico into '92 and '93. There was straight-on interdiction going on – boat patrols by Coast Guard, Customs, Fish and Wildlife, so there were coastal patrols, there were coastal radar installations on top of condominiums.[197] That's when BLOC, the Blue Lightning Operations Center [in Miami], was set up and that was starting to pick up the near-shore activity.[198] So you weren't having airdrops 20 miles offshore and the boats running it in.'

Instead, smugglers, including Luis and his *recibidor* friend El Gordito, were forced to make airdrops way out to sea. Serendipitously, cocaine bales float.

Continues Harley: 'There's a NOAA weather buoy way out in the Gulf of Mexico and it was outside of most radar range.[199] It was definitely outside of all fixed-radar ranges. And only if there were Coast Guard aircraft and other spook-type aircraft up would you ever know that an airdrop took place out there. That started probably in '91, '92. I think they called it the Coke Machine. That's a long trip, though. That's not easy smuggling for the guys doing the boat end of the deal. Around that time there were also a couple of airplane crashes and I think that had an effect on the willingness to do those long aircraft trips from La Guajira to the north side of Cuba and back, because you're kind of pushing those aircraft to the outer limits of their capabilities.

'In those years, to me, I felt interdiction was pointless. I don't think anybody knew exactly how much was coming in. Really, the way to stop it was to dismantle an organisation and it wasn't until '92, '93, when we changed our focus away from interdiction and towards actually working up the chain and dismantling organisations, *that's* when I think we really made a big impact.'

*

In October 1991 Harley met Mary Adair, a shorthaired, tanned blonde from San Jose, California, while she was holidaying with her family in Key West. They fell in love.

'Her father was a captain of the Santa Clara California Police Department and he retired. One of his daughters lived in the Keys. They were there visiting. His youngest daughter, Mary, was there on vacation. And I met her through her father, Robert. We were drinking together at Fat Tuesday on Duval Street, Key West.'

Things really were that simple for Harley. He was like a fair-haired version of Mitch McDeere from John Grisham's *The Firm*, with the perfect girlfriend in tow. By 1992, he and Mary had moved in together. The same year Harley heard the name 'Navia' for the first time.

'We had a series of smuggling incidents where we caught the boatloads coming in. We prosecuted some of the folks on the boats and some of the boat drivers, the vessel operators, and a couple of those we were able to move up from them to the next level; kind of the mid-level brokers on the States side. It was myself and one or two other agents doing independent cases at the time that ended up intersecting when we started interviewing that next level of broker on the US side, not the foreign side. That's a different hierarchy. In the US a broker is not as important as he is overseas. It just means he's a guy who's got a contact that has cocaine. I can remember at least two or three different interviews where separate brokers gave us the name "Navia" and we were able to put it together. Eventually I put together "Luis Navia".'

Harley had a partner working with him called Carol Libbey. Originally from New Jersey, she graduated with a criminal justice degree from Northeastern University in Boston then joined the USCS in Fort Lauderdale in 1983, before transferring to Miami in 1989. As part of the Miami Investigative Drug Asset Seizure Group (MIDAS) she later worked as an asset forfeiture agent. According to Harley, her 'abilities to research things was excellent'. So excellent she turned up a photo from one of Luis's two traffic arrests in Dade County/Metro-Dade. These were the days when such records weren't automated.

'I said to Carol, "We *have* to find a picture and a way to identify the guy because otherwise we're chasing a ghost,"' says Harley. 'The worst thing that you can do is to chase a ghost, because you can never prove that this is the person you are talking about. It was critical. But Carol was very tenacious. She's a lot more serious and can be a lot meaner than I am.'

Libbey: 'Bob had an informant that told him that there was this arrest, so he had already looked in Coconut Grove's [law-enforcement computer] system and there was nothing, as well as the national system. So I decided to look in Metro-Dade's system, which at the time had jurisdiction over the entire county.[200] And I went down and went into their system and it came up with two arrests. It said [Luis's] name, the date, and next to one of the arrests it had a number. I asked what the number was and they said, "That's an archived file." So I requested the archived file.

'The next day Bob came with me and we went back, they pulled the file and there was really nothing in there except this picture. One of the arrest records was already destroyed. Every so many years they would destroy all their records. You didn't save it for anything. So it was an old snapshot. In the old days you would get your picture taken with a Polaroid camera. We had to take a picture of *that* picture.

'It took quite a few tries. It wasn't easy. All this digitalisation we have now was still in its infancy. They actually told us, "You're lucky because this should have been destroyed a year ago." You have to understand, back then DUI was not a big deal. DUI you would take the guy and you would put him in the drunk tank for the night and release him the next day. It wasn't like today, where it's "DUI, *ohmigod*, we have to arrest him and prosecute him to the full extent of the law." Nobody cared back then.'

Harley: 'We finally had a photograph of Luis. It was old, black and white, not great, from the late '70s. But we *had* a photograph. It was his arrest photo for a DUI. Then I could take it back to those brokers and do photo line-ups and say, "Point out Luis Navia to me." That's when we knew exactly who he was. That put a name and a face to a real person.'

*

By now Luis had been formally identified and indicted along with a group of other narcos in the Florida Keys and Miami, but the magnitude of what was about to come down on him was still a secret.[201] It was time to make a tentative approach to his family. So Harley and Libbey knocked on the door of Luis's elderly mother's house in Miami and introduced themselves. María, then in her late 70s, got the shock of her life but didn't come out. Luis's sweet-natured, softly spoken sister, Laura, who had divorced from the womanising Vicente Blanco in 1990, was also at the house and remembers meeting the two USCS agents outside.

Harley: 'They were very standoffish. It was non-confrontational. I was very polite and courteous. They took my business card and I was just telling them, "He needs to call me because I think things can go badly and I can make them better."'

Laura: 'I was quite concerned for Luis and my mother. As you can imagine, that situation was incredibly concerning.'

Libbey: 'They didn't like us. I know that's hard for you to believe because we're such nice people, but they didn't like us. They didn't tell us anything: "He's not here. Get off our property." [*Laughs*] Needless to say his mother and sister were not going to give us a picture. Luis had left the United States by then.'

Luis is vague about how quickly the news of Harley's visit got to him in Mexico, but he brushed it off as a mild nuisance and he kept the whole thing from Patricia.

'It's not like my mother and sister were completely oblivious. Laura married a Colombian and he was involved in money laundering but they were elegant, well-to-do, high-class people. *Everybody* was involved in cocaine back then. Like in Saudi Arabia, you know, most people are involved in oil. In Colombia, most people were involved in cocaine. Bob was hoping I'd reach out to him, cooperate and become a snitch. That's why they give you a business card. I was already acting like a fugitive. I had left the United States. I figured I was already indicted and a wanted man. Yeah, it wasn't the best news but it wasn't *news*.'

41

Dead in the Water

After surviving Colombia during the hunt for and takedown of Pablo Escobar, living by the beach in Cancún was so uneventful and placid the most tumult Luis experienced was at night while he was asleep. He tossed and turned and would often talk while unconscious, waking with no memory of the nightmares he'd been having.

It would be a stretch to say this drug trafficker was haunted by the faces of people he'd known who had met violent deaths or with the guilt of shaming his family – Luis simply has no recollection of what passed through his mind – though it's possible. His physical health had also started to deteriorate.

'I took these herbal pills that were supposed to give you energy and cut down your eating habits. I was in pretty good shape, walking a lot, but I took these fucking herbal pills on the recommendation of a friend of Patricia's who was a weightlifter and bodybuilder and I had an allergic reaction with the joints in my body. Some days I couldn't even move. I couldn't get out of the car.

'It was really weird. It came to a point where they almost had to call for a wheelchair to get me out of the cab from the airport. In Bogotá I always used to stay at Papito's house; we were very close friends. He took me to his doctor who would analyse your physical being with pendulums. The doctor recommended all these fucking pills: chelated magnesium, shark cartilage, a bunch of shit.'

Around that time Luis was due to fly from Bogotá to Cancún via Costa Rica.

'At the last minute I was delayed for whatever reason and I had to change my trip and I flew via Cuba. *Boy*, when I got to Havana the state security agents really gave me the fucking treatment. They took me into a room. I have never in my life been so scared as I was there. I actually said to myself, "I may never, *ever* get out of here and nobody will ever know where I am," because I came into Cuba with a Mexican passport.

'A lot of Mexican *narcotraficantes* like El Señor de los Cielos, Amado Carrillo Fuentes, would meet their Colombian connections in Cuba.[202] I never met Amado, but we did some loads for him through an associate who paid us in Houston. The Cubans felt there was something fishy about me. They started giving me the tenth degree, and the 11th *and* the 15th.'

Luis explained he had just come from Bogotá, lived in Mexico City and owned a fledgling coffee business in Cancún. He was simply in transit and wanted to go visit one of the many coffee companies that operate in Havana. He'd prebooked a room at the five-star Meliá Cohiba Habana, right on the seafront.

'They interrogated me for about eight hours, till the morning. And I really thought I could kiss my life goodbye. Finally they let me go. The Cuban security agents drove me to the Meliá Cohiba, and they gave me a big presidential suite. And I knew it was totally bugged. They actually thought I was going there to meet with some kind of Mexican.'

The next day he toured Old Havana and went to a coffee business but he knew he was being watched.

'I was so scared the next day I went to the airport early. The plane took off at seven, I was there at five. I wanted to get home for Christmas. I was exiting [immigration], ready to get on the plane, and the lady who stamped my passport said, "So you're Mexican, *huh*?" And she said it in such a way that was like, "We know *exactly* who you are and we're letting you go but you can't fool us." I freaked out. When I got to Cancún, since I was running a day late because of the mix-up with Costa Rica, the guy that used to receive me in immigration wasn't there.'

Luis was about to learn a tough lesson. As former USCS agent Robert Mazur wrote in his book *The Infiltrator*, one of the cardinal rules of using a false identity is to 'stick as close to your real-life experience as possible in order to minimise the number of lies you have to spin'. Luis had strayed too far from his real-life experience.

'They could easily have discovered in Havana that I wasn't really Mexican; now I get to Mexican customs with a Mexican passport as "Luis Novoa Alfandari", and you know, you can fool someone with a Mexican accent if he's not Mexican but if he's Mexican it's pretty tough.

'I'd never lived in Mexico as a Mexican. I always had my Colombian passport. I was Luis Navia but Colombian. Mexicans thought I was Colombian. So I was in line as Luis Novoa Alfandari and a little upset from the whole episode in Havana, and the guy at the immigration desk starts talking fast. He asked me a question and I didn't really understand it, he was talking so fast, and by mistake I said, "*Cómo?*" And that was it. I was dead in the water. Mexicans don't say *cómo*, which means "what". They say *mande*.'

His weakness in Spanish dialects had finally caught up with him. A rapid-fire conversation ensued, with the officer trying to catch out Luis on his local knowledge. According to Luis's passport, he was born in Mexico City. The officer tripped him up quickly on a geographical question.

'What *delegación* were you born in?' he said, referring to the local word for borough.

'Polanco.'

'That's not a *delegación*, it's a shopping district.'

Luis had to think fast. His salesman instincts kicked in. But instead of making up a story like he would normally do, he did something totally out of character: he straight out confessed.

'Listen, you are right. I'm not Mexican. The reason I use this Mexican passport was simply for *commercial purposes* to expedite matters to avoid the lengthy visa process. I had no time to get a visa. I'm Colombian. I'm in the coffee business. I own Café Koba here in Cancún.[203] I live here. My wife is waiting for me outside. I am not in some weird business, as you may think. I just use this passport as it's easier to travel through Central America. So let's do this. Because of your time lost and all the inconvenience I've caused you, why don't you come to my house on the day before Christmas? I'm going to be with my family, have somebody come early in the morning, we'll work this out for 10,000.'

Luis laughs at the memory.

'He thought I meant 10,000 *pesos*.[204] When he came to my office at Café Koba, I gave him an envelope with 10,000 dollars inside and he almost flipped backwards. He offered me whatever I needed, a federal police escort to the Belize border, *anything* I wanted. He asked me if I could give his niece a job. After that, he was always there for me. But I'd been very lucky. I should have avoided the diversion in Cuba and turning up in Cancún without my immigration guy to receive me – all for trying to get home for Christmas. Always have your priorities straight when you're a fugitive. Your number-one priority is not getting caught.'

42

The Board Meeting

It was the summer of 1995 and Luis was about to turn 40. He was living with his beautiful 26-year-old wife and infant daughter in a villa on a Mexican beach and had the best chance of his life to go straight. More than enough money was coming in from the night-time *panga* smuggles to finance his retirement many times over, Café Koba was doing well in Cancún, and a long-held passion project to build a multimillion-dollar 'binational macadamia operation' in Central America was starting to take shape. It was the perfect time to call it quits on crime.

'I had a great business in Café Koba. I would come home, have lunch, go out with Patricia and Juliana, go to the movies. Patricia had made good friends. We had a beautiful life.'

His 700-acre macadamia farm in the shadow of the Arenal Volcano in Costa Rica had proved a shrewd purchase for a block of land he'd only visited three times and Luis fancied himself as a Panama hat–wearing macadamia baron. But not being a hands-on owner had created problems. The way he tells it, some of his investors had been selling shares and stealing money.

'Costa Rica wasn't exactly my cup of tea. I always felt they were a bunch of fucking rats and Costa Ricans were too in bed with the Americans. I didn't like Costa Rica. The caretaker–manager was doing jack shit. I was living in Colombia at the time and I sent some

Colombian financial guys to look at what was going on down there. They came back and said, "You got a great piece of fucking land, it's all on a lake, it's worth a lot of money, and they're not working it to its full potential and this guy is basically skimming off the top. Whatever money you sent down there he's stealing part of it to live and part of it is going into the farm.'

Luis was so angry that for the first time in his life he contemplated killing a man.

'That would have come back to haunt me. That's it. I would have been *fucked*. Believe me, I wanted to. He stole from me, he deceived me, he lied to me. I put my faith in him. I thought this was going to be my way out of the cocaine business. I was planning to retire, that's where my future was, macadamia and coffee, and this guy backstabbed me.'

So Luis brought in his attorney, Reid Constable of Miami law firm Horan, Horan & Constable, to buy back stock and take a controlling interest in the farm and kick out the partners.[205] At the same time he commissioned a study of the macadamia industry in Mexico, initiated plans to build a processing plant, and had the grand vision of creating a Costa Rica–Mexico macadamia cooperative 'to open up Mexican macadamias to the world'.

Unlike his brief foray into sugar in the early 1980s, this time around he thought he was going to retire from cocaine for good, buy a turboprop, shuttle between his holdings in Costa Rica and Mexico, stick with coffee beans and macadamia nuts rather than coca leaves, do the right thing by his young family, and finally make good on the Navia name and do his father proud.

And then, just like that, it all fell away.

*

'When Reid went to a board meeting to present the takeover proxies and to exercise our control of the company, 51 per cent of the shares, an attorney that sat on the board of directors of Ilhabela Mac SA told him, "Did you know your client, Luis Navia, is indicted on drug charges out of Key West, Florida?" Reid had to leave that meeting. That was it. It was over.'[206]

Luis was on a payphone in Cancún when he got the news.

'Did you know that you were indicted by the US Government?' Constable asked him down the line from Miami.

'Reid, *Reid*, that's impossible. I've never been to Key West.'

'General Noriega had never been to the US either and he got indicted in Miami. I recommend you give yourself up.'

Luis didn't quite know how to react. He knew there was every chance he'd been indicted, but he'd not had it confirmed until that moment.

'I was freaking the fuck out. It was life-changing. I didn't tell Patricia right away. We had a baby. She kinda knew that I had an issue when I first left [the States], but we didn't talk about it, you know, it was just normal.'

This time he had no choice but to tell her about Harley.

'I wasn't angry with Luis,' she says. 'Just upset because I was really happy in Cancún. I had a one-year-old daughter and I thought we could finally make a life there as a family.'

43

The Firm

ROBERT HARLEY MIGHT NOT have left Key West but he knew 'almost exactly' where Luis was on a couple of occasions in Costa Rica and Mexico. The problem of bringing him in was a matter of interagency resources, along with myriad political and legal complexities.

'I did not go [down to Mexico] but [other] people did: DEA and Customs have people "in-country". But getting one of our agents in a foreign country to go run down a lead is not the easiest thing in the world, because they get a hundred of those a month. And convincing them that *this* lead is more important than all the other leads they need to run down is the trick. Attempts were made [to capture Luis], but I always felt they were a day late and a dollar short, each time. And it's just a function of getting people to do what you want them to do and they don't have to do.

'Keep in mind too, some places are easier than others to get people picked up and sent home. There are legal systems that are more complicated than others and legal systems that are more corrupt than others, and sometimes even though there's an opportunity you can't translate that into action. It's just not going to work.'

Instead, Harley had a better plan.

'We went a little more overt and went after his business records.'

*

'Carol Libbey's job was to identify potential assets for seizure and to exploit investigative avenues that you can get from assets,' says Harley. 'She really put the effort in. She was in the weeds. She is an excellent agent in looking at things microscopically, numbers and details. She was critical in putting together all of Luis's business stuff – like Ilhabela Mac – and then identifying Reid Constable as the resident agent for all of that.'

Libbey: 'I was in the Asset Forfeiture Group, which works with all the other [law-enforcement] groups in a parallel case to the criminal case [concentrating] on all the assets. We knew if Luis was involved with all these drugs, then there had to be assets, and that's how I got into it, trying to track him down through the assets.'

Harley: 'We found that Luis had assets and then he liquidated assets, bought new assets and then liquidated those assets, and it was because of how the business was going for him essentially. So Carol would come with the leads and then she and I, or me or some other agent, would take that [information] and start doing the interviews, questioning everybody and turning the heat up to see what would fall out.'

It was Harley who'd spoken to the directors of the macadamia plantation in Costa Rica and, as he puts it, 'shook up the world for Luis. I knew that, because Reid Constable just about passed out.'

More was to come. Harley paid a visit to Horan, Horan & Constable in Coral Gables, right near the University of Miami School of Law, and directly accused Constable of knowing Luis was a drug dealer and of laundering money.

'Reid Constable knew Luis was a dope dealer. He knew *exactly* what his client was. And Reid made money off Luis's business practices. He was the agent for the attempts to legitimise Luis's profits. Luis thinks that he was shielding Reid from it, but I've got news for you: Reid hired Vernon Dolivo, who at that time was one of the most expensive attorneys in Miami and they hung up all of the grand-jury documents that we wanted from that law practice.[207] We ended up with maybe a quarter of the documents that I knew existed that would have proved all the money laundering that had gone on.'

Libbey: 'This was a time when [attorneys] didn't ask questions: he had money, he hired me, I'm just going to do what my client tells me to do because he's paying. Whether Reid Constable fully participated in anything more than moving the assets and turning a blind eye, I don't know, but he definitely didn't want to know.'

Luis, however, maintains Constable knew nothing about his cocaine trafficking.

'He never suspected that I was in the drug business. Truthfully, he did *not* know and I will always maintain that Reid did not know; I cannot understand why Bob Harley doesn't believe that. I was just a rich guy because my dad was rich. Reid only knew about my money background from my dad's sugar business. He represented me in the buying of the 22,000 acres in Florida, so he was always exposed to sugar money. The one mistake I made was bringing him to visit me in Cancún. I should never have done that. Security-wise that was a big mistake. He should never have known where I lived.

'Reid played hardball with Bob. He didn't cooperate. He thought it was an abuse on Bob's part to be treating him the way he treated him; that he was an innocent victim, which he was, and Bob didn't believe him. Just because he didn't cooperate doesn't mean he's guilty. The government expects everyone to cooperate and if you don't and make them "work" for their information, they get pissed. It's a perfect example of the federal government's abuse of power. Reid did not know anything about any of my illegal businesses – at all. They treated him as if he did. They declared him guilty before ever proving him guilty and made him go through hell. If the federal government have a hard-on for you, they can destroy your life. And they destroyed his life.

'You know, they go in on riot mode, guns blaring, knock the door down, and they take all the papers in the law firm, your partners get freaked out; who the fuck wants a partner being investigated by US Customs? His partners probably thought he was money laundering for me and never told them anything and was making millions, which was not true. Bob unfortunately destroyed Reid's law practice in Miami, and Reid also suffered a heart attack. They destroyed him and then he had to scale down and move to Sarasota and open up a smaller law firm with his new wife.

'I don't know what the fuck happened there. Bob fucked it up for Reid. But then again, Reid fucked it up for himself. You're dealing with the US Government, the most powerful entity in the world. The chances of surviving a federal indictment are 97 per cent against you. They can say whatever they want and the burden of proof is on you. You know how much it cost the law firm to defend Reid? It was tremendous. Hundreds of thousands of dollars.

'I feel very bad about what happened because I was a drug dealer. Reid was innocent. Bob came at him hard. It's one of those things that still haunts me. It's a nasty thing what happened to Reid Constable. That's one of the things I fucked up, that I feel really bad about and I wish I could someday make good on it and make it up to him.'

*

Harley won't hear a word of it.

'Reid Constable destroyed himself. Did he have a heart attack? Yes he did. Did he quit the law practice? Yes he did. He didn't die *destitute*. He retired from Coral Gables to, like, Fort Myers in a gated community and sold his partnership in an incredibly successful Coral Gables law firm. So that's no crocodile tears for anybody.'

You don't buy his story of innocence?

'*Never.* Still don't. One of the other partners ran interference for Reid. He's telling me, "I don't think Reid would have been involved in those kinds of things." I said, "*Really?* Where do you think Luis Navia, who couldn't come back to the United States to conduct business, was getting his money from? [*Laughs*] I mean, is that not in essence this bullshit that Reid didn't know? Your client can't come to the States and he's going there [to Mexico]?

'Reid knew Luis grew up on Key Biscayne. Luis was a US citizen. Reid travelled far to pick up money to go buy businesses for him. What did you think it was? There's no way that Reid Constable was in *any* way innocent of knowing what this was all about. And to this day I have no idea how much money the firm or Reid made off of all that transactional work, because those are records that they refuse to produce. They fought us tooth and nail about every document we asked for.[208] My argument was, "If you were innocent, prove it to me."

'Horan, Horan & Constable was a legitimate firm but they did illegitimate work and made a ton of money by simply turning a blind eye. And there's no way you don't know. So as far as I'm concerned, did Reid launder Luis's money? Yeah, he did. Could I positively prove he knew the source of funds? No, I could not. All I could prove was he had to travel foreign [sic] to conduct all of the transactions with a United States citizen. We're talking millions but not hundreds of millions.'

Luis doubles down in denying Harley's allegations: 'Reid did *not* know I could not come back to the United States. A lot of people decide to move to Mexico and are not fugitives. Reid never picked up money; I used transfers. Supposedly you are innocent until proven guilty, aren't you?'

*

Luis should have turned himself in to the authorities but going back to the United States wasn't an option. He just continued what he was doing and began taking the benzodiazepine Xanax to help him sleep and reduce his anxiety.[209]

'That indictment started in 1991.[210] The US Government has five years to pull the trigger. If Bob hadn't indicted me in 1995 he would have lost the opportunity. Once you're indicted, all you can do is either turn yourself in or work harder. In the end I was already under indictment, I woulda gotten picked up and fucked anyway. They would have taken away the macadamia farm because my indictment was there. So in the end everything worked out.'

Once again, the Navias were packing their bags.

'The three of us left Cancún in a hurry. Wálter went back to Pereira. This time I was really scared. I moved out, went and stayed at a hotel while I sorted some things out and within a week I'd left for Mexico City.'

PART 9
MAGOO IN MEXICO

44

Dinner with Alberto

For Luis, moving from Cancún to the biggest Spanish-speaking metropolis in the world, a city of 20 million people, meant four things: getting a new identity, finding a new apartment, buying a new business and trading in his boardshorts and Hawaiian shirts for something better suiting the weather and his new social circle: a suit and tie.

Fortunately, by the start of 1996 he had more than enough money to buy as many fake passports as he liked. Luis was keeping his millions in offshore accounts plus his usual standbys (safety deposit boxes and real estate), laundering through consulting companies, and still kept at least a quarter of a million in cash at home.

'I had different people doing the passports. I had a guy in the Dominican Republic, I had a lady in Guatemala, I had somebody in Colombia. It's difficult to get really good passports. You can get a fake passport for $1000. You can get one for $500. A decent set will cost you $10,000, but to that you add the bank accounts that go with a good passport, the credit cards, and before you know it you're looking at $50,000 on the low end. I went back to my original roots of being Jewish. I changed my name to Louis Anton Naviansky Bonavia.'[211]

But one Mexican passport wasn't enough. He also splashed out on a set of Guatemalan passports for his family to have for safekeeping. Patricia wanted no part of it.

'Luis tried to make me change my name so many times. We went to Guatemala and he was trying to get me to take a fake passport. I said no. Never. *Neh. Ver.*'

Holed up with their maid in a rented luxury bolthole in the *colonia* of Interlomas, an outlying upmarket neighbourhood ringed by shopping centres, their relationship had hit the skids. Luis hadn't stopped drinking or quit the business, as she'd hoped he would, and the showdown between Reid Constable and Robert Harley in Miami had spooked him enough to start drinking more. While he'd successfully kept his promise to Patricia back in Bogotá not to drink for a year and then given himself licence to have a tipple occasionally, his idea of helping himself long term wasn't to check into rehab or join Alcoholics Anonymous. It was to go on two-day binges every 30 days.

'I would only drink once a month. I decided I might as well limit my fuck-ups to 12 times a year.'

But at least the new legitimate business was promising: Industrias Guantex de México SA de CV, a manufacturer of surgical gloves, household gloves and condoms. His co-partner was a relative of Mexican multibillionaire Carlos Slim Helú.[212] Their business cards had the words 'USA Flex' as a logo, with an American flag in between. An ironic choice of graphic for a man on the run from US justice.

'Unthinkable it's on the card.'

*

In Mexico City Luis met Alberto Sicilia Falcón, a Cuban narco kingpin who, operating as a heroin and marijuana trafficker out of Tijuana in the 1970s with a trusty Great Dane by his side called Skipper, was widely regarded as the first of Mexico's major drug bosses. He's one of the main characters in the first season of the Netflix series *Narcos: Mexico* (in which he is portrayed as a flamboyant homosexual) and James Mills's gargantuan 1986 book on international drug trafficking, *The Underground Empire*. A former CIA-trained, anti-communist operative in Miami by his own reckoning, Sicilia Falcón would go on to bring large amounts of coke into Mexico with Juan Ramón Matta Ballesteros, a Honduran who worked with the Medellín Cartel.

'Alberto was the big boss before Amado Carrillo Fuentes,' says Luis. 'Playing with the CIA is one thing. *Being* the CIA is the only way you can survive. Playing with the CIA you're going to get burnt. And that's what happened to him.'

In real life, Sicilia Falcón wasn't shot in the head as portrayed in *Narcos: Mexico*. Nor was he as open about his sexuality. He went to jail in 1975 and escaped the following year from the Palacio de Lecumberri prison in Mexico City through a tunnel he had personally financed from a property adjoining the jail, decades before El Chapo dreamed up such a thing. But he was arrested days later and sent back to prison. He wrote a book about it in 1979 called *El Túnel de Lecumberri*.

What actually happened to Sicilia Falcón in the 21st century has long remained a mystery and when I spoke to Luis he could not shed any light on the matter, other than they met and had a 'bunch of encounters'. There are some scattered online mentions in the Spanish-language press of Sicilia Falcón being released from prison in 1998, but Luis insists he was introduced to him outside prison in 1996 through a friend, a jetset refugee from the 1970s, Denisse Zavala, the daughter of a very famous Cuban-Mexican film actress.[213] He says their meeting took place at her home in Tecamachalco, Mexico City.

'Denisse knew *everybody*; she knew Alberto back from the days before he went to jail, when he was Alberto Sicilia Falcón, the leader of the Mexican cartels. She had some balls on her. When I needed to travel sometimes with my Mexican passport, she would come with me. She could pull me out of a hot situation. I was concerned about travelling with a Mexican passport so I felt more comfortable going with her. I took her to Bogotá. We travelled through Belize. She loved adventure.'

Luis also alleges Sicilia Falcón's criminal partner when they met was Francisco Sahagún Baca, former head of the much-feared but defunct Division of Investigation for the Prevention of Delinquency (DIPD). Sahagún Baca had been right-hand man to the notorious chief of police in Mexico City, Arturo 'El Negro' Durazo Moreno.

The only problem timeline-wise is Sahagún Baca disappeared in 1989 following his arrest on drug offences in Michoacán state, a mausoleum later being built for him in the city of Sahuayo with the name 'Francisco Sahagún Vaca'. However, it is empty. There was no funeral, nor is there any official record of his death or burial in the civil registry.[214]

'Sahagún Baca was a dangerous character to say the least; a vicious killer. He'd had the free run of Mexico City under Durazo. There were nights that they would go out and shoot the vagrants and the beggars living on the street – like a cleansing of vagrants. I hung out with Francisco and Alberto for the good part of two years. Alberto and I used to meet almost on a daily basis at the Centro Santa Fe shopping centre and have a coffee and Danish.

'There was no publicity that he was released from prison; a big figure like that who escaped. He was the first guy to escape from a Mexican prison – it wasn't El Chapo. Alberto was a big deal in Mexico. He wanted a Colombian connection. I also met him in early 1999 in Chetumal [in Mexico] where I gave him $35,000. He needed it. He was not doing well financially.

'The strange thing is we became good friends and he didn't have too many people he could trust or relate to because of his notoriety in Mexico. His protector was "El Azul": Juan José Esparragoza Moreno.[215] El Azul was the true *consigliere* or ambassador between all the groups; a very powerful man and the smartest operator in that whole Mexico scene.

'Meeting with Alberto, talking to him, hanging out with him, you would *never* think he was nothing but a full-on straight man: a real ladies' man. But I guess he had that fucking wild, crazy touch to him. He did not want to be *known*. We put together a couple of deals. We probably did three trips; that's it. I didn't trust him 100 per cent. It was merchandise that was already in Belize and I renegotiated it. I gave it to his people and they delivered it in Houston, but we only spent a year doing that together.

'The first trip we just sold the coke in Mexico. I wasn't about to risk it crossing the border with him; I didn't know how good his connections were, so we just sold it in Mexico. Later in Chetumal I paid him some money for things we did while I was smuggling in Jamaica. But we made a friendship. Finally I hooked him up with

Sergio Perdomo, an associate of José Orlando Sánchez Cristancho. They handed over $200,000 as an investment for a load.'[216]

*

So what really happened to Alberto Sicilia Falcón?

One of the biggest challenges in writing this book was verifying many of the claims Luis made and his accounts of meetings with people who were either dead or had disappeared. Understandably those criminals who *were* alive weren't going out of their way to lead documented lives, for all sorts of reasons. It is certainly not unheard of in the drug world for traffickers to undergo drastic plastic surgery to evade scrutiny, sometimes with fatal results.[217]

Luis also didn't want me contacting every narco he knew; understandably there were personal-safety issues for both of us if word filtered out that an Australian writer was working on a big-time drug trafficker's memoirs. The whole project was top secret while we were writing it. But Sicilia Falcón presented a particularly unique situation: for someone made so famous by Netflix, it seemed incredible that no one seemed to know whether he was dead or alive. It was one of those rare situations where not even Google could help establish his mortality.

Fortunately I was able to locate a former colleague of his from the 1970s, an American from Albuquerque, New Mexico, called Brian Dennard, and Sicilia Falcón's sister Mercedes (or 'Mercy' for short), who is based in Mexico. It turns out her brother, one of the most legendary but reclusive narcos of all time, died at his home in Mexico City on 24 May 2011 from a stroke.

Luis remembers Sicilia Falcón's house was 'up in the mountains, up in the hills, a wooded area with curving roads behind Santa Fe in the middle of fucking nowhere. He had 16-year-olds as his attendant, gardener, houseboy. I never saw him with any women.' Patricia, who was with Luis, similarly remembers it being 'a little bit like a castle'. During a dinner conversation about the levels of violence in the Bible and the Koran, Sicilia Falcón whipped upstairs and brought down his personal copy of the Koran for the Navias to inspect. He was a rare breed of narco.

Dennard, who got to meet the Medellín Cartel's Pablo Escobar, Carlos Lehder and Jorge Ochoa, says this is true: 'When I first met

Alberto Sicilia Falcón, we talked about Aleksandr Solzhenitsyn all afternoon, played backgammon and talked some more about Roman history and the dictator Sulla.[218] Alberto and I spent more time talking history – Roman, Russian, Greek – than we did about the "monkey business". He was really a brilliant thinker. The house had two pitched roofs, so it looked like one of those old pointed bras like Madonna wore. He called it "The Bra".'

Mercedes Sicilia Falcón also confirms the general location: 'When my brother got out he lived a bit with my ex-husband and me; he lived a bit in the city. Yes, he lived in Contadero, and yes he did have a gardener that was a young guy. He lived for a while on Calle División del Norte in Contadero, and then went further into the mountains.'

Contadero is right behind Sante Fe. It is three kilometres from Centro Santa Fe mall, the biggest in Latin America.

When I told Mercedes that Luis was insisting their meetings happened in the late '90s, she initially responded that her brother was housed in Santa Martha Acatitla prison in Mexico City with his hawk Homero (yes, a *hawk*; I was shown a picture of it behind bars), and she later picked up Sicilia Falcón from the maximum-security Altiplano prison in Almoloya de Juárez, outside the capital, upon his release in 2001.[219] It's the same jail where El Chapo escaped through a tunnel in his cell in 2015.

'I never met Luis or heard my brother speak of him. No one until you, Jesse, has ever contacted me about anything related to my brother's life in or out of prison. Many people have written false things about Alberto; even *Narcos: Mexico* lied. I guess someone that might have met my brother either in jail or out of jail might have invented that he was killed in Tijuana.

'The only real thing *Narcos: Mexico* got right was Skipper the Great Dane, and the fact that my brother was educated. My brother never acted or walked or talked or dressed like a homosexual. I never saw him at home or anywhere kissing or being with men. I did see him with ladies. I picked up Alberto when he was released from Almoloya. I have been really mad at all the crap that's been printed about him and all those shitty people making money out of it.'

Brian Dennard says similarly: 'Alberto was always a bull of a man. The idiotic portrayal of him in *Narcos* is absurd and insulting.

He was a fun guy: smart, intellectual, charismatic and my friend. In a world full of very, *very* bad and dangerous people, he was unique in his intellectualism and cultured persona. There were never any wild parties at his homes. The only thing valid was when in one scene a huge Great Dane walked through. The portrayal of a swishy gay Alberto was ridiculous; though he was bisexual, you would never peg him as gay if you met him.'

But he was eccentric, sometimes conducting meetings while sitting on the toilet.

'He would not use anything but Amino Pon soap.[220] Whenever you came to see him – business or pleasure – he would ask you to bring as many bars as you could bring. It was a fixation of his. Amino Pon smells wonderful and leaves your skin without a soapy residue. Worth every penny. He had a tailor who made him sort of safari outfits; quite a few three-piece suits. He had a barber who came to cut his hair. In his bathroom he had a toilet that was on a very high pedestal, so you were at eye level with him.

'One time when I went to the house in Mexico City, there was a turkey wandering around the yard. Alberto told me that they were going to fatten him up and have him for a feast. About two months later I was back in Mexico City again and we were sitting in his office when the turkey came walking in and jumped up onto his desk. *Gobble gobble*. I asked Alberto, "So what happened to the plan for the big feast?" He said, "Well, he has become a member of the family and quite a good watchdog, plus Skipper gets along with him like a brother, so we have cancelled his execution and given him a name. Meet Arturo."'

*

So could Sicilia Falcón actually have been given leave from jail before 2001?

'Everyone wants to make money out of my brother's name,' says Mercedes. 'The only time Alberto was able to leave jail was in 1985 when our mother died, and that was only with a huge police detail and only for two hours. I ask myself how [Luis's alleged meeting with Alberto] happened if my brother was in jail at that time, and my dad and I saw my brother every day. Alberto had all the green areas redone and taken care of in the jail. He had lots of things done in jail to try to keep it looking nicer.'

I told Luis what Mercedes said, but he was adamant things happened the way he tells it. Making money was certainly not a motivation in him mentioning Sicilia Falcón to me – he was gaining nothing from it; if anything, it was only muddying what had up to that point been a clean, reliable story.

'I'm not lying, Jesse. Everything I tell you is true. *Period.* Either she's covering for him or she never really knew that he was out. For security reasons sometimes it's better not even to tell your family. It's *Mexico.* I was with Sahagún Baca when there was a cemetery stone with his name on it and he was supposed to be dead. I'm telling you I was *with* Alberto Sicilia Falcón.

'As far as I know he wasn't in jail. If he was sneaking in and out of jail, that's a whole different story [*laughs*]. I didn't keep tabs on him that well. It proves the reality of the Mexican system [*laughs*]. There's no fucking way in the world the men I met were imposters. In my business there are no imposters. I respected Alberto. I found him to be a *hell* of a cultured guy, a highly educated man.

'He dressed in grey flannel pants, Oxford button-down shirts, nice sweaters, a pinkie ring, and carried a beautiful gold Dunhill lighter. In that business it's very rare to find a guy like Alberto Sicilia Falcón. He knew the Greek classics. He was a very interesting guy, a hell of a personality, a very good-looking man. A class act.'

But to someone reading this, Luis, wouldn't it give them pause to call your credibility into question?

'I hope they do because they will call the credibility of the Mexican Government into question. Sicilia Falcón was out of prison. There may be a guy serving time for "Luis Navia" in a prison in Mexico who is not Luis Navia. He's being paid $20,000 a year to say he's Luis Navia. Luis Navia's actually out! That's very typical in the Mexican system. I'm not about to make a fool of myself by printing this. I'll go toe to toe with anybody on anything I have ever told you. With all due respect to his sister, I was *with* Sicilia Falcón. Even from the half-crippled way he walked with a cane, there ain't no imposter who could be him. Dying in Mexico is all paperwork.'

Says Mercedes: 'My brother's health was very good. He was healthy and strong. Eight years before he died prostate cancer was detected, which he beat. But before he died frontal-lobe brain cancer was found. He went into surgery and 80 per cent of that cancer was extracted. He had a heart attack three days before his forehead bone was to be rebuilt. Before all that he just enjoyed his life with my dad, my daughter and his six German shepherds and his hawk.'

Did your brother have a cane?

'No, he did not. He only had a very small limp in one foot: the foot that was rebroken several times after all the horrible tortures he went through when he was apprehended; all of that due to the fact that he was loyal and never gave up any names of anyone.[221] He put in almost 20 years in jail just with my parents and me by his side.'

Did he know Sahagún Baca?

'He did know that sonofabitch but not as a friend, not as an associate, not as an acquaintance. He was just the cop in charge of all the instructions, all the tortures, and of everything that was done to him. That's it.'

So Sahagún Baca was actually one of the people involved in torturing your brother?

'Giving orders.'

And was his hawk named after Homer of *The Iliad*? Was your brother into Greek classic literature?

'Yes, he was, and also Greek mythology and Roman. He spoke several languages and learned many of them through books not teachers. My brother was also a great cook and painted.'

*

The truth was I was starting to doubt Luis and it was troubling me greatly, mostly because there was no way I could independently check off some of his claims. This was not the first time in my career I'd had such a crisis of confidence; it's part of the job of being a journalist or biographer. Sometimes a story *is* too good to be true.

Then, not less than 24 hours later, Mercedes contacted me again and said her brother was released in 1994, not 2001: a seven-year difference that made Luis's story totally feasible. It was quite the *volte face* – and left unexplained.

'My brother was released in 1994 after being inside since 1975 and completing his time. He was inside for 19 years.'

I thought you told me he was released in 2001?

'No, I said our *father* passed away in 2001.[222] Our mother passed away in 1985. My father and I picked him up from Almoloya de Juárez prison.'

Sicilia Falcón's sister had also changed her tune about Sahagún Baca.

'It was Florentino Ventura who was the cop in charge of all tortures regarding my brother.[223] Sahagún Baca came after all the tortures my brother went through.'

Okay, so it is possible that Luis met Alberto Sicilia Falcón in 1996–'98 when he said he did, if he were released in 1994?

'Maybe he met my brother afterwards; I just don't know that for a fact. What I do know for a fact is that my brother had nothing to do with anyone or anything related to that lifestyle.'

I read Luis her quote.

'What lifestyle? The narco lifestyle or the homosexual lifestyle?'

So you think Sicilia Falcón could still be alive?

'*Possibly.* In Mexico the limelight will get you fucked. If Denisse Zavala admitted to you that she introduced me to Alberto Sicilia Falcón she'd have *federales* looking at her up the yin-yang. But it could well be that he died of cancer – a journalist would have to check hospital records of the exams Mercedes says he underwent, although he could register in the hospital with a false name. I would say he's dead, but in Mexico you never really know.'

Robert Harley was right: Luis's life really does read like fiction.[224]

45

Airdrops and Raindrops

MEANWHILE LUIS CONTINUED TO bring loads into Cancún but it was getting increasingly complicated. The glory days were over. Alcides Ramón Magaña aka El Metro ('The Subway'), a high-ranking lieutenant of the Juárez Cartel's Amado Carrillo Fuentes, had come in as the owner of *la plaza* or the exclusive smuggling territory. To work in Cancún smugglers now needed official permission from either him or his boss, Carrillo. Both were working with Rasguño.[225]

Metro was a former policeman, like a lot of Mexican drug lords, and once reputedly headed antinarcotics for Mexico's Federal Judicial Police, the PJF or *Policía Judicial Federal*. At the same time he was working as a driver/bodyguard for Carrillo and saved his boss's life on 24 November 1993 after a machine-gun attack by the rival Tijuana Cartel's Arrellano Félix brothers, Ramón and Benjamin, at the Ochoa Bali Hai restaurant at Avenida Insurgentes Sur 1524, Mexico City. Five people died.

Now Carrillo's favourite and a big, bearded man of over 240 pounds (110 kilograms), Metro was running the southeast cell of the cartel from Cancún in cahoots with the corrupt local governor, Mario Ernesto Villanueva Madrid, who received kickbacks in the tens of millions during the 1990s: reputedly $500,000 for every load of cocaine passing through the state of Quintana Roo.

'We were working Cancún, and El Compadre in Reynosa said to cancel operations because Metro had taken over Cancún and he wasn't about to work with Metro; we had to cool off a bit. It was a very volatile situation. The end result when you deal with Metro is that somebody gets hurt. All those trips we did in Cancún, all those airdrops, all those boat deliveries, all that shit, we were doing directly with the *federales*. We worked directly with them and the army; we used to send big gasoline trucks into Cancún and move out all the merchandise in other vehicles and go through the Reynosa–McAllen crossing into Houston. We were working heavily with the Gulf Cartel.'

But an associate of Luis's, a Cuban known only as Sigfredo, didn't follow the Juárez Cartel's script.[226]

'El Compadre had a very good relationship with the *federales*. But when Metro got to Cancún you *had* to work with Metro. El Compadre said, "Listen. I'll do something else but right now Cancún is off the books." I went to El Compadre's daughter's wedding in Monterrey and that's when Sigfredo said, "No, I'm still going to continue working Cancún with my guy in Guadalajara."

'Soon after, Sigfredo went missing. They grabbed him at a deli, forced him into a car, took him somewhere, then tortured him and fucking chopped him into pieces. His head was found somewhere around the beach in Punta Sam and his legs 100 miles away in Chetumal. They fucked him up bad. So we didn't work Cancún. El Compadre was a smart man. He wasn't in the business to have that kind of headache.'

*

With his fondness for hippie clothes and bad case of psoriasis, Pinky Delgado might have been the oddest-looking drug trafficker with the best name in the history of crime, but his sailboats operation to Europe had proven exceptionally lucrative.

A white, blue-eyed Cuban fugitive called Pedro Jiménez aka 'Flaco' (Skinny) had been working for Pinky in England, where he would meet the sailboats filled with cocaine.[227] Flaco, who knew Luis from his time in Cancún, told Luis about the run he was having with the sailboats and in turn offered to introduce him to his European fixer, Nick Fisciatoris aka 'Nick the Fish'.

A Greek and American dual citizen, Nick the Fish was a classic, old-style, pot-bellied mafia figure from New York, but had been living in London since the 1970s. He owned properties in Manhattan, Canada, London and Greece. He was a renowned figure on the British illegal-gambling and horse-racing scene (it's been said he'd spent $50 million on gambling alone), one of the biggest drug wholesalers in the country, and Flaco's point man to the big buyers in England and mainland Europe. He and his pals also lived it up – hookers, fine dinners, all the cocaine it was possible to hoover – sometimes blowing up to $30,000 a night.

Luis was busy enough in Mexico City but the idea of expanding into Europe and making even more money appealed. So he asked Flaco to set up a meeting and Fisciatoris flew out to Cancún to meet Luis, bringing with him a violent British criminal associate straight out of a Guy Ritchie movie, Kenneth Regan, who had a profitable racket selling counterfeit passports. As one British law-enforcement agent later put it: 'Half of the UK's major crime figures were travelling the globe on them.'

Luis: 'Nick the Fish was a very elegant dresser. Not the Italian silk-type look; Oxford or Ivy League. Clean cut, well shaven, smoked a lot. He was one hell of a character. He always had a tremendous wad of cash in his pocket. We all did, but that's one thing I always remembered about Nick: he *always* had a big wad. His middle name might as well have been "Cash". Mobsters don't believe in wallets; they believe in rubber bands. Nick always carried his wad in a rubber band. I never saw him use a credit card. Nick was a classy guy but you did not want to piss him off. He always covered his ass by speaking from payphones; nobody knew where he lived – he was no fool.'

Unlike what is portrayed in *Narcos: Mexico*, business dates between high-level narcos didn't involve sharing a bottle of Scotch. That's a Hollywood cliché.

'In my experience, I went to a lot of meetings in the daytime and never were we drinking Scotch or anything else. In Colombia that was not looked upon favourably. Mexico was a little bit more relaxed but partying was at night after meetings.'

It was a propitious occasion, in any case: Fisciatoris offered to facilitate the right introductions – for a fee. In return, Luis offered to get him cheaper cocaine by cutting out middlemen. They parted ways with a handshake and a mutual commitment to begin planning their first operation together.

*

'The next time I actually worked Cancún was when El Compadre's partner Jesús Aburto, who was working with [the Sinaloa Cartel's] Ignacio "Nacho" Coronel Villareal, told me, "I've got a green light to work through Chetumal. We can bring the merchandise in through Belize."'[228]

A green light meant Metro was getting a financial cut of all the coke moved in his *plaza*. Nacho was giving him 30 per cent. Belize is about 500 kilometres south of Cancún. Chetumal is right on the Belize–Mexico border.

'I said to Jesús, "Man, are you sure? You got all this covered with Metro?"

'"We're covered with Metro. We've got permission, Luis. Everything's cool."

'"Okay, no problem." So I went ahead and gave the signal and had 800 kilos sent to my *recibidores* in Belize. *Perfect*. The fucking trip started out wacko from the start. The Colombians got there with the load. There was so much work going on that there were boats out there all the time. Belize City is a small town; all those offloaders know each other. But the Colombians, *my* Colombians, they gave it to the wrong guy. I was in Chetumal but communicating with my people in Belize. They confirmed that they gave it over but they gave it to "Raindrops".'

Raindrops is the alias of Belizean gangster James Swan.

'I said, "I can't believe this shit. *Fuck*." I got Raindrops' number and called him. At first he didn't want to hand over the merchandise. Imagine that shit. I said, "Listen [*laughs*], let's get one thing straight here. I'm working for a group of people that if you don't hand over the merchandise, you're going to *die* and your whole family's gonna *die*. *Everybody's* gonna die. You're not going to be able to kill any one of us.

We're going to kill all of *you*. That's a fact. It's not something I'm coming up with.

'"Unfortunately, you're not going to die so quick. You're going to have to tell us where the merchandise is. So it's up to you how long you want to live under fucking *tremendous* pain and suffering. It's going to happen within a week. So I'm going to call you tomorrow. You have 24 hours to think about it. I'll call you tomorrow. I'm your friend. Believe me, I don't want to do this. But it's going to happen."

'I called him back the next day and said, "Listen, we'll pay you the pick-up fee. And as a gesture of good faith we're going to give you five extra kilos." Raindrops was like, "Okay, man, it was a hassle, you know. Give me the pick-up fee and 15 kilos." I said, "You got it. Give us the merchandise. The pick-up fee our guy was going to get, it's yours. You did your job. We're going to give you 15 kilos."

'Sure enough, after that he was on me to work with him, he wanted to continue picking up, and Raindrops and my guy in Belize partnered up. I continued working with my main source in Belize and it was the first trip after the Raindrops incident when I personally went to Cancún again to supervise the trip. We had the merchandise and I went to talk to Metro. And that's when it happened, getting put in the fucking crocodile thing.'

46

The Crocodile Thing

Cancún was now ground zero for coke in Mexico and all the deprivations and excesses of the cartels.

'At night it was the complete underworld. Kilos of cocaine coming in, heads getting chopped; it was a rough scene. Cancún became the number-one port of entry for merchandise in Mexico at that time. Metro was moving tens of thousands of kilos.'

In March 1997 Luis, travelling under one of his many aliases, and Patricia, seven months pregnant with their second child, checked into the CasaMagna Marriott Cancún Resort. He'd told Patricia it was a vacation but it was anything but. Once he got to their room he called a female contact, his liaison with Metro. She didn't answer. But he knew where Metro was likely hanging out with his goons: a hotel he owned.

'So I went over to this hotel in Punta Cancún [the hotel zone] and I order some drinks to see if I can spot Metro or one of his men. And suddenly one of them, this guy called Gil, shows up.'

Gil was Metro's transporter. Shown a photograph by me, Luis believes Gil may be Gilberto Salinas Doria aka 'El Guero Gil', a notorious Mexican narco who worked for Metro and the Juárez Cartel in Playa del Carmen and Reynosa in the mid to late 1990s.[229] He cannot be certain.

'I'd heard he killed some people on the border; a doctor and his family or something.'[230]

Luis explained to Gil he had some merchandise in Belize and was trying to get hold of Metro to talk about it. In truth he wanted to make sure Jesús wasn't lying to him about getting the green light. Metro was busy but Gil suggested they have some drinks, so Luis agreed and they did some coke and began playing pool in the hotel bar.

Over the table, Luis told Gil he'd made arrangements for the Belize coke, some 600 kilos, to be delivered into Metro's *plaza* at Chetumal. One game followed another and for the hell of it their last game was played for money: $250,000 deducted from the cartel's transport retainer if Luis won or 50 kilos 'off the top' of Luis's coke at $5000 a key if Luis lost (about $100,000 wholesale but worth $650,000 in Houston).

Luis managed to lose the game, explained he had a busy schedule the next day and said goodnight. It was 11pm.

*

'Next day I wake up, I had a tennis game at eight in the morning at some nice clay indoor courts. Then I went over to the Café Koba office and I said, "Let me go make a phone call." There was a Pemex gas station in front of Café Koba. Jesús Aburto, who was with me, was getting gas. I go to the payphone and I'm dressed in my tennis outfit, all in white, and suddenly some fucking guy grabbed me by the back, grabbed my hair, because I had long hair, fucking yanked out a piece of my hair, and then hits me. *Boom boom boom*, on the side of the head.'

When he opened his eyes, startled from the blow, Luis saw Metro himself standing over him with two of his *sicarios* by his side. The Subway was unmistakable: fat, full beard, thick black medium-length hair. Jesús was standing by the petrol pump filling up his car, almost oblivious to what was happening.

'What the fuck's going on?' said Luis, spluttering like a man does when he's just been kinghit by Mexican *sicarios* who've come out of nowhere.

'You're working here without permission.'

'What do you mean? Of course we have *permission*. Look, Jesús is right there by the car!'

Luis has total recall of what happened next.

'It happened so fast. They wanted to stick me in their car. Luckily Metro had a [Chevrolet] Tahoe or a [GMC Yukon] Denali, smaller than a [Chevrolet] Suburban, a two-door SUV. If it would have been a four-door I would have been fucked, because they would have thrown me in the car, left, and those two to three minutes were the difference between life and death for me at that point.

'They started trying to put me in the car and I said to myself, "If they put me in that car, I'm dead. I'd rather they shoot me here than they put me in that car." So when they tried to fucking put me in I flipped around, almost did a backflip, I couldn't fucking believe it. Then they hit me in the back with the butt of a fucking AK-47 but my adrenalin was pumping so hard I was still shaking and moving and avoiding getting put in the car.'

Luis had to do some quick thinking. His heart was pounding.

'Let's calm down. Let's fucking calm down here. Look, Jesús is right *there* and he can explain this whole thing. Have Jesús come *here*. We're going to talk this over and if we need to go with you, we'll go with you. The only thing I ask is I ride in the front seat with you, so we can talk.'

'You kidding me, Colombian man?' Metro replied. 'Now you're asking to ride in the front seat. You want to drive too?'

Jesús was told to leave his car at the pump and brought over. Luis got in the front of Metro's SUV, Jesús in the back, with the two *sicarios* beside him, their caps on backwards, the unofficial uniform of hitmen in Mexico. Metro was at the wheel. Luis began pleading for his life.

'Metro, I came here yesterday. I tried to reach out to your lady but I couldn't find her. I went to the hotel and then I ran into Gil. We started drinking, we started snorting, we played a pool game and I lost $250,000.'

'What kind of fucking cockeyed story is that? You expect me to believe that? You're working here without permission. This motherfucker in the back is going around me.'

Luis turned around to Jesús.

'"What the fuck, man? I thought you told me you had this all squared away." I realised then that this motherfucker hadn't squared away shit. He was trying to score one on Metro, slip one in without paying a fee. The guy he was working for was Nacho Coronel – high level, very powerful – so Metro couldn't exactly whack him, but whack me, *yeah*. Right then and there I was a low guy on the totem pole and if they had to blame somebody, they'd blame me. So I said, "Call Gil."'

*

There wasn't any time to waste. Metro had driven to a cement theme park called México Magico on Kukulcan Boulevard, at the entrance of which was a huge, 30-foot-high pink piñata. The nearby lagoons were full of crocodiles.

'Metro used to take people there and throw them in there. That was *known*. We got there and right before we drove off the road to the crocodile enclosure, he kept dialling Gil and I said, "Let me use my phone," and I called Gil a few times and finally he answered and I passed him to Metro.'

The car had stopped right in front of the crocodiles, which were lying in the bright Yucatán sun. Luis was perspiring from the certainty his luck had finally run out.

'I have the Colombian here,' said Metro from the front seat. 'I'm going to throw him to the crocodiles. The only thing that's going to be left of him are these fucking white tennis shoes he's wearing.'

'What the fuck are you talking about, man?' said Gil over the phone.

'The Colombian with the trip in Belize. He's trying to go around us. I'm going to fuck him up.'

'*Noooo*. Don't do that. *Noooo*, man. He owes me $250,000.'

'What?'

'Yeah, last night we were playing pool. He's got to give me 50 kilos in Cancún. That's the deal. Fifty kilos at $5000 a kilo is $250,000.'

Metro turned to Luis, shaking his head in bewilderment.

'So it *is* true,' he said, laughing. 'You're fucking crazier than I am.' There was a pause. His little joke had cut through the tension in the air like Bee Gees on a dancefloor. It meant one thing: Luis would live another day. 'You know, Colombian man, today's your fucking *day*, motherfucker. I'm going to have a drink on you tonight.'

*

When they pulled up to the grand foyer of the CasaMagna and opened the door for Luis to get out, Metro was all smiles.

'Enjoy your evening. *Relaaax*, Colombian man. We'll talk tomorrow. Now I'm going to talk to your fucking partner back here, this piece of shit lying fucking sonofabitch. I'm going to have to call his boss and see what we do with him.'[231]

And he drove off, with Jesús and the two *sicarios* in the back seat. The most terrifying episode of Luis's eventful life had ended, again, with him somehow still breathing. The Magoo of blow had outdone himself.

'There's no words to describe what it's like to get put in a car in Mexico with Mexicans of a cartel that you know kill people every day. Metro was killing people. He was psychotic. He was a psychopath. He *is* a psychopath. He was killing people indiscriminately *every fucking day*. Any tip he got, anybody working, anybody that he *thought* was working, anybody that he *thought that he thought* was working, got whacked. I lost $250,000 playing pool and that's really fucked up. But it saved my life. If I would have gone to bed that night, wouldn't have gone out to the bar and just got up and played tennis, I would have been dead.'

Patricia remembers when he got back to their room at the CasaMagna: 'His face had changed. Really *changed*. He was so afraid; he was in shock. It was a different kind of fear.'

47

Out of Breath

TWO MONTHS LATER, on 30 May 1997, Santi, a son, was born at Hospital Angeles in Mexico City. Luis cut the umbilical cord again. Things weren't going well in his marriage with Patricia, but the impending arrival had brought them closer than they had been for a long time: going to the doctor together, buying baby clothes and sharing the excitement of bringing a new life into the world.

The due date had been the 27th and when it didn't happen they went out with friends to the Ochoa Bali Hai, the same restaurant where the Juárez Cartel's Amado Carrillo Fuentes had survived a machine-gun attack by diving under a table. Luis got really drunk.

'I was feeling a little dizzy, probably did a couple of snorts, and I called over the maître d': "Bring me oxygen." He was like, "What do you mean?" So I said it again: "Bring me oxygen." Imagine, you're at a restaurant and you're so drunk you ask for *oxygen*. The restaurant didn't have any oxygen but I was a guy who always got what I wanted.

'So sure enough the maître d' arranged it somehow, called the paramedics, fire rescue, some shit like that, and they brought over to the table one of those little, long green oxygen canisters with two wheels. And I put on my oxygen mask and started to breathe oxygen and continued drinking. Patricia got insulted. Nine months pregnant and she left with a couple of her friends, and I stayed there in the restaurant continuing to party out with my friends and then finally got home. That was the extent of my craziness.'

Says Patricia: 'We were in a really bad situation at that moment. It had been bad for over a year. The only thing that was keeping us together was the fact I was pregnant. I had lost patience with him. I didn't want to be involved in anything to do with him. He travelled a lot and I didn't care. Every time I was happy to see him leave. I was tired. I didn't want him anymore. I'd had enough. I wasn't in love.'

Their relationship, like the out-of-shape Luis himself, had run out of breath.

*

So the last thing Luis's and Patricia's struggling marriage needed was to move all over again, but that's exactly what happened when, with the apartment lease up for renewal, their landlord got suspicious about the bona fides of 'Louis Naviansky'. This time around, Luis's fake passport and birth certificate weren't going to cut it. With Robert Harley on his tail and a single phone call to the US Embassy enough to bring down everything, there weren't a lot of options left. Cancún was all but closed off because of Metro.

'It was really weird. You never know where the heat's going to come from. I really felt the heat from this motherfucker. I had to renew the lease and he knew I was one of the principal owners of Guantex, so I don't know why the fuck that guy got suspicious about me. I was Louis Naviansky, Mexican Jew, but I had no real paperwork to back that up. He knew I was not Mexican. A Mexican knows when you're Mexican and when you're not Mexican. My partner didn't know anything about my narco background, so I couldn't go to him for help. I got a little scared. And I said, "You know what? I better fucking leave."'

It was a wise decision. The USCS had been 'a week away' from nailing him. Contrary to Hollywood movies, not every US fugitive is actively tracked down with singular purpose by a lone federal agent whose every waking moment is spent thinking about nabbing the bad guy. It's simply a matter of using in-country resources (agencies, informants), if they are available, to effect arrests.

'Mexico is not that easy to work in and I got poor support there,' says Harley. 'We were about a week behind when Luis got word that we knew exactly where he was living. I finally got DEA in Mérida or Cancún to get with our people and they had pretty much figured out where exactly he was living in this particular apartment. I think that's the only time we were just about to be hands-on again. Understand that I had other indictments with other people that we were also looking for; so it wasn't like a Tom Hanks film where I'm the only person and I'm following Luis around the globe. It simply is not like that. There's no way I could devote that kind of energy to Luis Navia to the exclusion of all the other responsibilities I had. That's not how it works.'

Says Luis: 'The DEA and US Customs have got all the time in the world. They've got time on their side. They're in no rush to bring me in; I'm already indicted. They're just looking to find out more. These guys get a salary; they couldn't give a flying fuck. If it takes Bob Harley eight more months to pick me up, that's eight more months at $7000 a month. These guys, from the day they start to the day they finish, they're only thinking about their retirement. The biggest thought of a government agent is not catching the bad guy; it's making sure they get the best benefits they can from the government. Time to them is the clock clicking up to retirement.'

*

Luis went down to Colombia that December to see Juanchi about expanding the business, and came back through Panama City. It was while he was in Panama that he got a phone call from Juanchi.

'Listen, before you go back to Mexico, "Fresh" wants to talk to you. Call Fresh.'

It was a name he hadn't heard for years. Fresh, a wiry, dark-skinned black boat captain from San Andrés whose real name was Cordelio Vaceannie James, was one of his transporters from the early 1990s when he was working with Rasguño. He supplied boats and captains from San Andrés to work Cancún and when Rasguño severed his relationship with Luis, Fresh kept the connection. He was living in Panama.

'Using my route they did 44 trips at 1600 kilos a load – that's over 70,000 kilos. He was freaking the fuck out. These guys were working Fresh to the bone. He had to fake a heart attack and go to Panama to stop working with Rasguño. He figured he already had enough money and wanted to work at a slower pace and do his own trips, and get away from the pace and crazy workloads of the big *oficinas*.

'Rasguño Inc. – the Northern Valley Cartel – worked 24/7 all over the world. Fresh must have had $80 million stashed away and he was a *nobody*. I never saw a penny. So he stole from me. He did something he shouldn't have done. He went behind my back with Rasguño. He was always short-changing people.'

Luis got him on the phone.

'Fresh, it's Luis.'

'Ah, Senador, I really need to talk to you. I've got a great connection in Jamaica. We want to start working. We need your source of supply.'

'Right, *okay*, but you owe me. Because of me you met Rasguño. You did 44 fucking trips to Cancún, Fresh. So according to my figures you owe me quite a bit of money. I'm on my way back to Mexico. I'm going to spend Christmas there. If you want we can meet in Panama in two weeks.'

Commissions are another part of the drug business little known to the outside world. If you introduce two people who then go on to work together, you can demand to be remunerated handsomely on each load.

'But they're very difficult to enforce and most of the time they pay a few times and then they just completely forget about you and the two parties continue working and they leave you out of the loop. That's what happened when I took Silvio Bernal and Hernán Prada to see Rasguño. They started working these big loads to Mexico but I never saw a penny. You might get paid once or twice but rarely ever again.

'So unless you were in a really, *really* strong position to make them pay, it was all one big clusterfuck. You could kill them but usually commissions were totally trampled on. In the end, Fresh paid me $1.2 million for the Rasguño trips – around $25,000 per trip for 44 trips – and then he gave me $200,000 to buy merchandise at cost for the first trip we did in Jamaica. The only reason Fresh paid me is he needed me to be a source of supply. I would also take care of the Colombian side of things, which Fresh never really liked handling himself.'

PART 10
CATCH ME IF YOU CAN

48

I Don't Like Cocaine (I Love It)

A MAN ON THE RUN from US Marshals who speaks functional Spanish, desires a Central American climate, and demands a certain level of Latin American creature comforts without having to get around in a moving convoy of armed private security guards has limited options after Colombia and Mexico. Costa Rica? Too many Uncle Sam–loving *gringos*. The Republic of Panama is one place he might end up, and it's where, in March 1998, Luis rented an apartment in the Edificio Miraluz on Calle Ramón H. Jurado in the seaside neighbourhood of Punta Paitilla.

It had been almost ten years since the pockmarked, crooked General Manuel Noriega was captured during the US invasion but Panama was then and remains today a roost for international fugitives. Officially, though, Luis was there for a legitimate reason: to open a Panamanian outlet of his Mexican rubber-gloves business, Guantex International SA. Unofficially, the landlord issue back in Mexico City had him deeply worried and he'd moved for one thing only: moving more cocaine.

'It was a good place for me to start exporting rubber gloves to South America through the Colón Free Trade Zone. I had a legal reason to go there. But after talking to Fresh I had more of a reason to live in Panama.'

Luis couldn't have been closer to temptation, either, his neighbours in the Miraluz building being Fresh and Fresh's light-skinned black cousin from San Andrés, Sonny Bowie, a transporter for the Los Mellizos Cartel in northern Colombia, 'the largest coke organisation at the time – extremely violent, vicious and a lot of heat on them'. Sonny, who practised a voodoo-like religion called Santería and kept a separate room in his apartment for the god Chango, handled logistics for the cartel's ship smuggles through his company, Sea Trade International.[232] Panama was also where Los Mellizos had a law firm, Pérez, Carrera y Asociados, represent their front companies that owned the ships.

*

Fresh's prize contact in Jamaica was the ponytailed and bearded Leebert Ramcharan aka 'The Indian'. Born in 1959, he was of sub-continental Indian origin but a Jamaican citizen: tough, smart, hands-on and in full control of the coke business out of Montego Bay. In 1998, he was unknown. By 2004, Ramcharan had made the list of top-ten drug kingpins under the US Foreign Narcotics Kingpin Designation Act, being named by President George W. Bush. He was personally responsible for moving about 15 tons of coke.[233]

Luis, organising cocaine runs from Colombia to Jamaica, Belize and Mexico with Fresh, as well as getting 'a little piece of the action' with Sonny Bowie, began shuttling between Panama and Jamaica for the better part of the year, living part of the time in Ironshore, Montego Bay. Fresh had a nearby villa just out of town.

'I did about 12 trips with Ramcharan and Fresh. I had my own villa with a butler and maids and all the hookers you could wish for, and a separate villa where I took a girlfriend of mine from San Andrés when she visited.

'Ramcharan basically ran Montego Bay. He had a lot of money and was moving a lot of product. He was the biggest player in Jamaica. He had a house up on the hill that looked like a hotel. He thought he was invincible. He had the finest strip club there, the Flamingo Club on Sugar Mill Road. The Flamingo was in an old sugarcane plantation and it was kind of rustic, but it was really nice and it had a jerk hut in the back with great jerk chicken and jerk lobster.[234]

'Ramcharan was a tough guy, no fucking pussy; he would get

down and dirty. One night at the club there was a fight; he went up to a guy and fucking smashed a bottle right across his fucking head; half his face. He ended up with like 17 stitches in his hand; the other guy ended up with like fucking 35 stitches on his face. He had muscle with him. If they had to put someone down, they put 'em down.

'Jamaicans are a tough group. They are not friendly island bongo players. Jamaicans are mean motherfuckers and that comes from the days of the slave revolts and all that. Most Jamaicans drive around with a machete in their car and they will not hesitate to use it. If there's a problem, they'll get out and have it out with a machete. It is no place to wander off. You just don't take a ride with your girlfriend and "see Jamaica". It's getting better but when I was there people that went to Jamaica stayed in their hotel, all inclusive, and didn't go out.'

*

A long-planned smuggle with his Greek-American contact Nick Fisciatoris had also come to fruition. The cover load was unusual.

'We had a delivery of cactuses to Belize. They'd been imported *from* Holland – they were cultivated there – but we'd changed the paperwork to make it look like they were Mexican cactuses being exported to Holland. We'd spent a lot of time looking for cactuses in Mexico and we could not find them – of course we couldn't find them. Those kinds of cactuses are grown in greenhouses in Holland.

'I remember going to Belize with Fresh when the cactuses arrived and him not wanting to eat at the restaurant at the hotel. He said, "Why don't we just go out the back of the hotel to the dock and we fish for our meal? There's great fish here; parrotfish." I was like, "Are you fucking crazy?" And he went out and actually caught six parrotfish with his fishing line and sinker. And we cooked them in the room. That was something that was so against Luis Navia. I was all about going to the hotel dining room and champagning it. But that's the kind of guy Fresh was.

'In the end the cactuses sat in Belize for about six months. The merchandise was meant to go back to Holland packed in the cactuses. They were ornamental round cactuses that we experimented with – we took out the insides of the cactuses and left them in soil and they could survive for almost a month without completely withering away: half a kilo in each cactus.

'We had that whole situation worked out with Nick over in Holland – he was going to receive it – but Hurricane Mitch came in and just sat on top of Cancún and Belize for I don't know how many days and flooded the warehouse, and all the fucking cactuses died. So then we had to divert the merchandise; it was sitting in Cancún for so long. I said, "Let's just send it to Miami." So we aborted the export operation to Holland and the merchandise was sent to Miami and that's when 350 units got busted by the DEA.'

49

The Separation

WHEN HE WASN'T IN Belize disembowelling Dutch cactuses and packing them with cocaine, or in Jamaica moving thousands of kilos for the Montego Bay mob, Luis was still going down to Colombia from his home base in Panama City. In Bogotá he had an unexpected reunion with Oscar Peláez Monsalve aka Poli, a man he hadn't seen for almost 20 years since he'd left Miami in a hurry.

'I was meeting some Mexicans in Bogotá and I saw Poli at Pepe Cabrera's casino on Avenida Carrera 15 and Calle 98. I found out he was there and I went to see him. He was glad to see me but, overall, he was a very dry guy. Don't think he was overly friendly. We spent time together, we spent a couple of hours talking, and then we hopped in his car. He had two guys with him and his .357 under his thigh. He said, "I'm going to give you a gift" and he went by a club he knew and he picked up two nice chicks and he dropped me off at a hotel. He made sure his hookers gave me a great time. And I didn't see him again. I left the next day.'

Luis also slotted right into Panama life like nothing was up, taking Juliana, now four, to school, coming home at night to have dinner, and doing his husbandly duties in hosting the in-laws who'd come to visit from Colombia. But by now there was no escaping the truth: his marriage to Patricia was in crisis. Guantex International SA existed in name only. It was no more than a cover for Luis's cocaine trafficking. He had no intention to go straight.

Patricia had been unhappy for some time but hadn't let on how she was feeling. Now she was ready to pull the trigger. Leaving a relationship is difficult at the best of times, moreso when your husband is a wanted international felon and running out of people he can turn to, let alone trust. But Luis had run out of excuses for his behaviour.

'Luis promised me that when we went to Mexico City he would start a legal business and stop the cocaine – and he didn't. So one day I found out he was continuing and for the first time he'd started keeping these things from me. I'm not stupid. I was so sad and in that moment I was thinking, "I don't want this."

'I was sure I didn't want that life anymore. I wanted to be a normal person: go to the movies, take care of my husband when he came back from his job. I was really tired of everything. I had two kids. Always something would happen and we'd have to move. I tried to make Luis drop the cocaine, "Let's do something different. Let's go. *Drop* it." We had the coffee business and the latex-gloves business and I thought everything was going to be fine, but after two years of everything being good I realised that he never stopped.

'I always thought that I could make him change; we talked about him retiring many times. So after what happened with Rasguño, when he bought the coffee business in Cancún and the factory in Mexico City to make latex gloves, which was a very good business, I believed that he was retired. I always told him that money wasn't the most important thing, but then I realised that Luis never did it for that; it was the adrenalin.'

He's prepared to concede she has a point.

'That's true. I wasn't hooked on the cocaine business; I was hooked on making a lot of money. I always wanted to retire. But *how* did I want to retire? I always thought big. Patricia thought I was expanding the gloves business immensely in South America through the Colón Free Trade Zone. But when she got to Panama she saw I was still trafficking. The gloves were never sent. She realised I had no intentions to stop drinking or retire. Guantex was a great business but with Leebert Ramcharan we started making millions.'

*

Money wasn't enough for Patricia to stay. It never had been. She just wanted a husband. She stuck out the year and left Panama to spend Christmas and New Year's in Cabo San Lucas, Mexico.

'We went back to Mexico but she stayed and I returned to Panama,' says Luis. 'We did not travel together because I was using a different last name. I was in Panama for about a month and I called her to come down and that's when she said she wanted a separation.'

Patricia remembers it well: 'We were more apart than ever at the end of 1998. We were talking by phone and he said, "I'm not drinking, I'm going to the gym." I'm a very healthy person and I had urged him to go: that it was a good thing for him to do for himself. He told me he was going. But he was fatter than ever when I saw him in Cabo San Lucas. Fat and drinking whisky. When he moved to Panama he also started doing coke again because of the kind of people he was with. I was shocked. "Oh, my God, everything's a lie." In that moment I took the decision. I needed to stop. So I decided to leave him.'

Luis: 'She told me, "No, I've decided to leave you. I'm not going to continue to be a gypsy all my life. I see that you're not going to change. You're going to continue working and drinking, the same lifestyle. I'm through with this life."'

Patricia: 'He was asking me if I wanted to go to Madrid or Barcelona. I said, "No, I don't want to." He said, "But why? You want to separate?" And I said, "Yes." I didn't have the balls to tell him directly. I wanted to say it but I couldn't say it. He said it before I did.

'It was the *drinking*. I think Luis has this recklessness to him because of the drinking. It was a crazy kind of life. You can do anything. You have a lot of money, all the opportunities, beautiful people, the parties. But to survive you have to be someone like me. I never did drugs. I might drink two, three glasses of wine if I go to a dinner, or a little bit of champagne, but that's it. So my head was always clear.

'Luis never fit the profile of a narco. I thought he was going to realise the life was not good for him to continue being in the business, but that was my problem – you think you can change people. You think, "Because he loves me he's going to stop drinking. Because he loves me he's going to stop doing coke." People only change after they decide they want to do it. When you really love and care for someone and they drink and do coke again and again and *again*, you start hating them. I always told him, "You are amazing when you're not drinking and doing coke." We could have been a perfect couple if not for that. I didn't see him for a year after that.'

50

The Postcard

LUIS WAS POLEAXED, BUT only momentarily. For the first half of 1999 he dealt with his existential pain the same way men the world over deal with break-ups.

'Then shit, I went into a depression. I went through a little bit of a hard time there so I hit on this girl, Michelle, who I knew from her working at the Davidoff store. There's a saying in Spanish, *un clavo saca a otro*: one nail takes out another. The best way to recreate your old girlfriend is to get a new girlfriend.'

It was instant lust. Michelle was a Xerox of Luis's estranged wife – just ten years younger. She had the looks of a 1980s swimsuit model – high thighs and slits for eyes – and liked to try out moves from the *Kama Sutra*.

'A girl can have a great body but she doesn't have the sexuality. Michelle was a very hot girl. Sex and exoticness just came out of her pores. She was, *whooah*, one hot situation there. Nicely built, nice ass, nice tits, on the white side with dirty blonde hair and very voluptuous, very sexual. I had to fuck Michelle three times a day. I'd come home and she'd have the room all lit with candles and a beautiful bucket of champagne and roses and she used to give me a super-massage with oils. Michelle was like, "I read this, let's try this." *Whooah*. What the fuck. The body lubricates itself and it's open for this type of sex and, you know, anal sex and front sex, whatever.

'She showed me how to hold off coming. She'd put ice on my balls. I had no Viagra back then; it didn't exist. It was just something in your head. It was crazy but it was beautiful. It's great to experience that. Some men never experience that. It was a fucking trip with her. I didn't have time to be reading no fucking *Kama Sutra* when I was dealing with Nick Fisciatoris, Elias Lemos and fucking freighter loads of cocaine in the daytime.'

*

But he had plenty of time to think about the mistakes he'd made. While they were still together, Patricia had begged Luis to stop taking drugs and drinking and agreed to move to Panama on the condition their relationship would improve. But the night she arrived from Mexico City they'd got their maid to put the kids to bed and gone out to the Davidoff cigar store to smoke with a pair of boisterous Mexicans.

'She gave me a chance. She held up as much as she could. It started to go bad when we were in Mexico already and I was drinking a little too much, and after Santi was born she expected me to settle down a bit and I didn't. Patricia came to live in Panama with the kids and the Mexican maid. But the day I picked her up at the airport I was with these two tall Mexican guys from Guadalajara, with the fucking boots and the big Mexican belt buckles with *toro* and the horns, and we were drinking and snorting and this was the day she arrived. Like nothing changed. I was drinking with two Mexicans I ran dope with. *Hello.* Weren't you supposed to quit?'

Away from the family home, Luis had no problem drinking a bottle of Scotch a night with a friend. He might have had a bottle of Finlandia vodka and a can of Mott's Clamato for the hangover the following evening. He wasn't a faithful husband either.

'I didn't brush it in her face. But Patricia knew that I would go out with Juanchi and when I went to Cartagena and San Andrés, we were fucking partying out. Our informants that we had all over the place said, "Shit, your wife just arrived on a flight." I go, "What?" We had to clear out the apartment, this and that, *ba ba ba*, and we were fucked up, but in the end when she got to the apartment it was just me and Juanchi drinking by ourselves, no hookers, no nothing like that. Still, she wasn't happy about it.'

So you were still partying with prostitutes?

'I partied with hookers for 25 years. *Jesus Christ.* It was like a lifestyle.'

Patricia told me she never found out about the affairs. If Luis had been cheating too, it doesn't particularly bother her.

'I never found out anything, so he was intelligent in that case. If Luis went on a trip and something happened one time with another woman, it's not important. He wouldn't have to tell me. I just don't want to know. The problem is when you have a relationship parallel to your own relationship. I never saw that kind of behaviour in him. I never lost time thinking he went to San Andrés and he fucked somebody. I don't care. I knew he wanted to be only with me.'

When it came to extramarital sex, says Luis, there was a kind of unspoken understanding between them when he was away from home.

'I was always a party animal. That's what fucked me up. I was always unfaithful to girlfriends but only in party mode. I've never been unfaithful to true love. I've been unfaithful to physical *need*. Physical need is like taking a piss. True love is something else. I wish I'd been a different person and wasn't addicted to drinking and snorting. When I didn't drink I was never unfaithful. I wasn't one of those "dry snorters" that snorts coke without drinking. I always drank and *then* I did coke. And then when you do the coke you drink more.

'Some men are just womanisers and get a steady girl on the side and get her an apartment, that kind of situation. I never did that. That's ridiculous. Fucking give your money to another home? Whatever money you have you bring it home. I only got out of whack when I travelled somewhere with my buddies, we were at a hotel and we'd start drinking, snort cocaine, and then you call hookers. It's cheaper to have a hooker. Those fucking lovers that you keep on the side cost you a fortune when they want to go haywire. A hooker doesn't even know what your name is. You're Julio one day, Alex the other, Pepe, fuck knows.'

*

Back at the Miraluz building in Panama after one of his trips, Luis visited Sonny Bowie's apartment. Sonny opened the door and invited him inside. The candles were burning brightly in Sonny's shrine to Chango.

'How are you, Sonny?'

'Everything's fine, Luis. But listen, Senador, while you were gone INTERPOL came and asked for us.'

'INTERPOL? What are you talking about?'

'INTERPOL came to the building. They were asking about you, me and Fresh. They were asking for Luis Navia, American. But don't worry because I've already consulted with Chango.'

Luis was in Panama under his travelling name, Novoa.

'Sonny, I'm out of here. Everything may be cool with Chango but that does not sound good at all to me.'

Luis called his maid over to Sonny's apartment and asked her to pack him an overnight bag.

'I didn't even go back to my apartment. I went to a hotel, registered under another name, I hung out for a few days. Just hearing that comment of Sonny's, I was out of there. I knew he and Fresh were hot. All my life I always fled and avoided and really took seriously any kind of law-enforcement involvement. That was something I didn't fool around with. I left the Miraluz building but I stayed in Panama for a while, renting somewhere else under another name, and kept a very low profile. I had to wrap up certain business with Fresh and that's when I left for about three months to Jamaica.[235] When I came back I went to see Michelle at the cigar store. I asked her, "Do you want to come with me to Europe?" I didn't tell her exactly what was going on. We stayed in Panama for another two weeks, very low key. Then I got my passports and we flew to Madrid via Santo Domingo.'

Before he left there was one last thing to do. Luis had long toyed with the idea of sending Robert Harley a fine silk necktie from Ecuador, and even paid for David Santos, his occasional personal assistant in Panama and Colombia, to pick one up from a men's boutique.

But there was no time for that now. Luis had a picture he'd taken in Cuba in the early 1990s. In it he was seated, dressed up like a yacht captain (complete with white cap), with two men either side of him:

one in the garb of an African dictator and the other an Arab emir. In the background was a 100-foot yacht.

He picked up a pen and began writing on the reverse side. The inscription was brief and deliberately provocative from an international fugitive to a federal agent. Luis signed off with a cheeky nom de plume, a nod to Meyer Lansky.[236]

> *Bob*
> *Dollar for dollar, dictators and Emirs are still the best investments!*
> *Saludos*
> *Meyer*

And then he walked out the door, leaving instructions for it to be sent when David went to pick up some money in the United States. The thinking behind it was simple enough but diabolically mischievous.

'I wanted Bob to get it with a Miami postmark.'

A couple of weeks later at an office building in Key West, the men and women of the United States Customs Service were turning up for another day's work when a huge laugh reverberated around the office.

'I have a sense of humour,' says Harley. 'I thought it was cheeky and funny. None of this was ever personal. I never took it personal. But I'm surprised we ever found it. I think he just sent it to "US Customs, Key West, Florida".'

51

Burnt Out

GREEK BUSINESSMAN ELIAS LEMOS, the 53-year-old owner of Callisti Maritime, was a friend of Nick Fisciatoris. Like Nick, he spent a bit of time in London, living in Eaton Square, but was based permanently in Milan, where he was staying at the Hotel Manzoni on Via Santo Spirito.

Elias was looking to get into cocaine and had the family money to do it. His billionaire cousin Costas Lemos of Greek shipping company CM Lemos, who died in 1995, had been one of the wealthiest ship magnates in the world. Elias wasn't exactly cut from the same cloth and in 1998 was taken (along with a group of associates) to the High Court of Justice in London to face a claim on the tort of conspiracy by Bankgesellschaft Berlin AG. The judge found against him.

'Elias was a legitimate ship owner who had a tendency towards illegal businesses,' says Luis. 'He was always fooling around with cash. The attractive thing about shipping is the incredible amount of cashflow. At the end of the year there can be losses, you can be working at a loss, but the cashflow is so tremendous that it doesn't matter. The motivation [for any dope smuggler] is the incredible amount of money that you make.'

And because of Sonny Bowie's troubles with INTERPOL and British law enforcement having recently come down on Pinky

Delgado's sailboat operations, Elias had his opening to get started as a partner in a major international drug-smuggling operation.

Jorge García, who'd been promoted to Los Mellizos' head of operations, met Luis in Barranquilla to gauge his interest in taking over shipping responsibilities from Sonny, who had been arrested in Panama and sent back to Colombia. A pot-smoking Colombian-American narco with a nervous tick called 'Willie' had introduced them, and in turn Jorge then met Elias, who was eager to please. The cartel needed ships – and they needed them urgently.

So when Luis arrived with Michelle in Athens from Madrid in September 1999, Luis again using his Mexican passport, Elias was busy looking for vessels to buy. Two Greek hoods – 'Lefty', a friend of Lemos, and 'Greek Peter', a close associate of Nick Fisciatoris – had been entrusted with a sizeable budget to scout for new vessels for Los Mellizos.

'We were definitely planning some big things with them. I was going to bring in new routes with Lefty and Greek Peter, and Los Mellizos were going to buy the ships and supply the merchandise. In Greece it was easy to be a Mexican because nobody knows what a Mexican looks like or talks like. I had just come out of a great winning streak in Jamaica. We were going up in the world. We were doing freighters.'

But Luis was under no illusions about who he was about to work with. The tale of cocaine trafficker Gustavo Salazar Bernal aka 'Macabí' is an example of the dangers faced by anyone who crossed the Mejía Múnera brothers.

Intelligent, capable, industrious, smart and good-looking, Gustavo liked to play tennis at his country club and was involved in the cocaine business. A bona fide criminal but not a murderous one, he owned a boat factory and built fastboats for Los Mellizos, quickly going from nothing to having $20 to $30 million in the bank. Then, says Luis, his whole attitude changed. Gustavo thought he was a bigshot. When there was a discrepancy over 5000 kilos stashed somewhere, Gustavo and the Mejía Múnera brothers had a firm difference of opinion. Gustavo didn't back down.

'Gustavo was never a killer. He was never a true outlaw. That is something you're born with. People make a lot of mistakes. Sure enough, one day Gustavo was waiting to catch a plane, and some guy came up to him and said, "Sir, do you want to get your shoes shined?" He said, "Yeah, might as well. I'm waiting here." So the shoeshine boy bent down, opened up the shoeshine box and whipped out a fucking 9mm Browning with a silencer and just clipped three or four bullets in his head. That was the end of this big shot, Gustavo Salazar Bernal. They make the big mistake of thinking that because they have a lot of money they're big criminals. *No*. You're still the same idiot. On top of that, before they killed Gustavo, they killed his brother Fernando.'[237]

*

The year 1999 would go down as a bad one for ship smuggling in northern Colombia.[238] Starting with a tip-off and crucial lead-up investigations from British intelligence, four 1970s-built vessels – the *Cannes*, the *China Breeze*, the *Castor* and the *Pearl II* – were all busted by British and American forces on the high seas, each carrying significant multi-ton loads of 'merchandise' from the Caribbean Sea to European waters.[239] VAW-125 Tigertails, sophisticated radar planes equipped with Hawkeye technology, were deployed. In total 13,689 kilos (just over 15 tons) were seized and with the *China Breeze* and *Pearl II* alone, there had been 19 arrests in the United States and the Netherlands.

Though there was some dispute over what cartel was responsible for each ship – it was later revealed the DEA and USCS were at odds over the origin of a number of cocaine loads – Los Mellizos were directly linked to at least two of the four. They were heavy blows: the cartel simply didn't have enough ships in reserve to cover all its losses. They'd need to buy new ships outright.

Luis, however, had only minimal knowledge of what was going on with the law-enforcement interest in the Atlantic.

'I didn't know about those ships going down; I didn't know they had lost that many ships. I knew that they'd had some problems [with their ships], I just didn't know specifically which ones. I only knew any of this was going on because of Nick Fisciatoris. We made certain moneys from Nick. Sonny had started to buy a couple of these ships.

While I was in Panama, Sonny used to let us participate in some of his dealings and take us in on some of his profits, and we used to take Sonny in on some of Fresh's and my Jamaica trips. Were we really involved? *No*. Not directly. We made money because Sonny gave us commissions. He was already trying to get away from buying ships in Panama and buying them in Greece and we helped him out with a bit of that.[240] I remember him talking about the *Pearl II*.'

*

Luis, with ships now supplied by Elias Lemos of Callisti Maritime, was promising to get the Mejía Múnera brothers' coke through to the Port of Rotterdam without a hitch.

'When Sonny got arrested and was out of commission, that's when Jorge García came to me to take over. Los Mellizos never knew Jorge came to me. Sonny was hotter than a pistol. What he would do was take his ships from Panama to Suriname to pick up rice – Suriname is an exporter of rice – and from Suriname he would head out to Europe. Los Mellizos already had it down pat, picking up rice in Suriname. But that whole Panama–Suriname pick-up route was burnt out. Suriname was still a good place for smuggling but when that ship left from Panama, even though it was empty, you knew [the DEA] kinda knew it already.'

What Luis brought to the Mellizos organisation was a bold new approach. His innovation in their criminal enterprise was to work the shipping routes in reverse, so as to evade suspicion.

'When we sat to talking, I told them, "Listen, this makes all the sense in the world because that's where we work *backwards*." Come from Greece, go to Brazil, come up that coast, you hit me in Guyana, we never come into this fucking hot Caribbean area. They really liked that.

'So I had no ships coming out of Panama or Colombia or Venezuela. I had ships coming in from Europe down to the Brazil–Venezuela region to drop off goods from Europe and Africa and pick up sugar in Brazil, iron ore and aluminium in Venezuela, then going back out towards Europe. The ships never entered the really hot zone between Panama and the northern coast of Colombia and western Venezuela.

'We would hit and pick up in the eastern Venezuela–Guyana area, which from there in a few hours you are already in the Atlantic. We would hit the ships with the cocaine around 6pm when they were already miles offshore and by midnight they were into the Atlantic. There was *no one* out there.

'We were making $5 million a trip. You don't make that kind of money off legal cargo. Dope business is astronomical. You get it in a suitcase in cash and there's no bullshit about it; it's there. On top of that, the Colombians paid for their ships and we got to *keep* the ships. So we got a free ship and we could have ended up having a bunch of free ships.'

52

Under the Gun

ELIAS AND LUIS HAD a ship: the *Suerte I*. In Spanish, *suerte* means 'luck'. The 7546-ton bulk freighter had been bought in December 1999 at the bargain price of $2 million under its former name the *Aktis*, but it wasn't seaworthy and Elias had called it in to dock in Piraeus, Greece, for $400,000 of urgently needed repairs, much to Luis's annoyance.

As this was Callisti Maritime's maiden joint venture with Los Mellizos, there was a lot riding on its success and no latitude for further fuck-ups. Elias and Luis were charging the cartel $5 million for the voyage plus expenses, but these expenses were blowing out. For almost six months, along with Elias's partner Filippos Makris, the trio had lived at the luxury Four Seasons Astir Palace Hotel in Vouliagmeni, 45 minutes south of Athens, and racked up tens of thousands of dollars in hotel bills, mostly in bar tabs.[241]

Apart from his work commitments during the day, shopping with his Panamanian girlfriend, Michelle, and bracing walks along the coastline, Luis rarely left the hotel and was taking medication to help calm his already frayed nerves over the delays. But for the first time in almost a year he had got to see Juliana and Santi, now aged six and three, who stayed with Patricia at the Astir over Christmas and New Year's. Juliana even became good friends with Elias Lemos's son. Luis took happy snaps of his children clambering over the *Suerte* as it was moored in Piraeus and at the Callisti end-of-year party.

In Luis's initial conception of the *Suerte*'s grand smuggle, the coke would be offloaded from Venezuela to Spain no later than July. The ideal time to hit the Galician coast was actually even earlier: June, when the sun went down at a reasonable hour. This was because by August, people were swimming at beaches until 10pm.

So the whole operation was running months late and encountering conditions that weren't conducive to industrial-scale drug smuggling. After all, when you're trying to keep a low profile without alerting the police, Galician fishing boats are expected to return to shore at certain times of the day, like commercial fishermen on trawlers everywhere. It's important to look normal.

'Fishing boats go out and fishing boats come back,' explains Luis. 'There's travelling *times*. If you're smuggling with a fishing boat, you can't come back at the wrong time. You've gotta play the logistics right. Basically because of the delays we were all under the gun.

'When Elias told me that he was bringing the ship to Greece I thought it was going to be in the country for a month not *six* months. We had planned to be down in Venezuela by March. Bringing the *Suerte* into Piraeus was a big mistake. But once we realised that mistake, we were too far into fixing it and did not have the time to move it.'

*

By 2000 Luis had been working full-time in the cocaine business for 22 years and had made $100 million 'easily', but he'd wasted nearly all of it or had it taken away from him. The bare truth was that he was having cashflow problems yet operating to a different standard of liquidity than most people.

'My situation was very reckless, the lifestyle. The other guys in Colombia would invest their money in land, real estate. I was a man with no solid foundation. Being a fugitive and having no solid ground, you're just all over the place. It eats you up alive. I always had $20,000 in my pocket or in my room for spending and for shopping. I was always going shopping with Michelle and buying things and I was even looking to buy an apartment in Vouliagmeni. I mean, in that business being "broke" is worrying that you only have five to ten million dollars. I had access to a checking account that always had $50,000 to $100,000 available; at least $50,000 that I had direct quick access to.'

Complicating the financial situation further, Willie, who'd become involved with the group after replacing Pedro Jiménez, had audaciously filched a $400,000 introduction fee for setting up Elias Lemos with the cartel's Jorge García.

A Miami-born US citizen with Colombian heritage, Willie came from a wealthy family who lived in Key Biscayne and had known Luis since at least the early 1980s. But that hadn't stopped Willie asking Elias for a commission. The money ended up coming straight out of an $800,000 kitty Los Mellizos had provided to tide him and Luis over for the six months it was going to take to get the smuggle up and running.

'Willie and I were good friends but he was greedy with the $400,000 he took from Elias. It was taken very prematurely. It was a commission on a fucking trip that hadn't happened. This happens sometimes. These fucking idiots meet the Colombian connection, they get friendly and they get fucked.

'Willie convinced Elias to send him $400,000. There was no stipulation anywhere that Willie was supposed to get $400,000 for an introduction, but he pressured Elias so much that Elias gave in. By the time I got to Europe there was already money being transferred for the buying of the *Suerte*, and in one of those transfers Elias gave Willie two transfers of $200,000. I was *extremely* pissed. I was supposed to have $150,000 at least for my expenses when I got to Europe, but the payment of the $400,000 to Willie left us all cash short in Greece.

'Because of that, financially we started off the whole venture depending on Jorge and Los Mellizos for everything – and that's not how it's supposed to be. Then Nick Fisciatoris took another $400,000 from Elias. With that $800,000 that was paid to Willie and Nick we could have made three or four million dollars buying merchandise. We were living great but I wasn't the happiest camper. I just wanted to finish what we were doing with the *Suerte* and go back to Colombia. I knew these big ships were too much of a paper trail.'

*

The protracted delays were also starting to attract the attention of corrupt local cops.

'Some government-connected thugs were hitting up Elias for money because they had suspicions about the *Suerte*. Nick even punched Elias in the face – *boom* – at his cabana at the Astir Palace. One day I saw Filippos Makris with a black eye and he told me that these thugs went to the Callisti Maritime office and brought along some taekwondo guy, who put a kick to the side of his face. I met some of these government dogs and they obviously knew what we were up to. We had to play it down as much as possible and that's when Elias and I thought it best to get out of Athens and go to Milan and stay with his friend Baron Massimo Paonessa.'[242]

Baron Paonessa owned a company with an interest in a granite quarry in Venezuela.

'Massimo had a diplomatic passport from The Vatican. One day we got drunk and he goes into his secret safe room, and inside a safe he whips out like this fucking Masonic outfit from the 1600s, secret-society shit. Massimo had some connections in Venezuela through granite. We were going to start exporting granite from Venezuela and put the granite in the ships with the coke. With Massimo we had also spoken about putting together $50 million and a group of Swiss banks and we were going to make a move to corner the Mexican and Central American coffee market; buy up a lot of the production, a lot of the futures. That would have put a dent in coffee roasters in America that use coffee from the region in their blends.

'We were always scheming. We had big plans. I later found out from law enforcement that they knew about this granite thing and for a while there, when they used to listen in on our phone calls on the Venezuelan end of the smuggle, the numbers were so huge they thought maybe we were referring to the granite, which, in real life, ships in thousands of tons.

'Massimo's wife or his girlfriend was this redhead from Calabria and she was definitely connected to the 'Ndrangheta [the Calabrian mafia], who are really off the wall. They will eat the Sicilians for lunch. They were just starting to get heavily involved in cocaine. Today they control the cocaine coming into Europe. And that's the kind of connections Nick Fisciatoris had and the kind of shit that we were looking at because we were looking at bringing coke into Italy with the 'Ndrangheta. It was a whole different ball game. The 'Ndrangheta is a very closed unit. They are vicious. They give the Russians a run for their money – that's how bad they are.'

*

While in Milan, Luis and Elias also met a Dutch-Indonesian yacht captain and associate of Greek Peter. The captain owned a 40-foot yacht moored in southern Portugal and was planning to rendezvous with the *Suerte* off the Azores, where he would pick up a 500-kilo load for shipment to England.

Luis even went further afield to Paris a few times to have 'another meeting with some other fucking mobster from London about selling more coke . . . that's what we did all day: think about transporting more coke', and stayed at the Hôtel Plaza Athénée on Avenue Montaigne, while Elias went on to London. His hotel bills came to $30,000, paid for by Callisti Maritime.

'I refused to meet with any Colombians in Europe. I avoided London. I never went there. They told me they had cameras in London. I said, "What the fuck am I going to do in a fucking country where you walk into the airport and they've got cameras and eye surveillance. Are you crazy?"'

He didn't do much sightseeing in Paris either.

'Why leave a hotel? The hotel is the best place in any city. You go to any city in the world, why the fuck would you leave the Ritz-Carlton or the Four Seasons? What are they going to show you? You want to see the Louvre? You don't need to go to no museum to see a painting. You can *imagine* a painting. I went into the Louvre once, you know, I walked in, I said, "Yeah, okay, fine, fucking-A, super, dynamite, let's get the fuck out of here. Let's go to a real museum. Let's go to a fucking classic restaurant where they have some kind of recipe from the 1600s or something." *That's* interesting.

'Like New York. For me, the best museums in New York are the fucking Jewish delis. Pretty soon there's not going to be any of them left. In Europe, same thing. We used to go to this restaurant in Paris called Fouquet's.[243] It was right near the Plaza Athénée. The Arc de Triomphe was down the block. I passed by, I looked at it, said, "Yeah, well, this looks really cool," and that's it, *gone* [*laughs*]. You think I even bought a souvenir? Fuck that shit.

'I went to the Eiffel Tower, and I looked up, I said, "Wow, that's really cool, let's go have some drinks, let's go to the bar, let's spend seven hours in a fucking fancy restaurant drinking champagne." My idea of tourism is to check into a fucking super-incredible hotel, hit the hotel bar and the dining room, and pick an incredible restaurant and knock the hell out of that restaurant every night. 'Cause I don't go to a lot of restaurants. I pick the best one and go there 17 fucking times. Then everybody knows you, everybody knows what you want, where you want to sit, what you drink. I'm very strange in that way.'

When they returned to Athens, Nick Fisciatoris had been busy wheeling and dealing. He'd set up a meeting with the Russian mob. They wanted to buy 50 tons of cocaine, had 'unlimited' demand and would take delivery of the merchandise in Albania. Luis even had the opportunity to buy 15 Russian military submarines through mob connections in Greece, but 'they wanted us to buy all 15 and where the hell are you going to keep 15 submarines?'

53

The Heat

MORE THAN THE DELAY with the departure of the boat or the shortfall in his kitty, what was bothering Luis the most was the attention they were getting.

'Elias really fucked up by bringing the *Suerte* to get fixed in Athens, where *everybody* knew him. He should never have opened up the office there. They all clinged on to him. Greek law enforcement was shaking him down. Nick was shaking him down. The heat we picked up in Greece I blame completely on Elias.

'But, saying that, Nick also brought the heat. Nobody needed to know that Nick was in the mix and somehow or other people put it together that Nick and Elias were together on the *Suerte* deal. And obviously once that was figured out it was quickly figured out that I was the South American connection.

'Elias was not a gangster. He was just someone very well connected in the shipping world that had decided to transport coke. I thought he had everything under control and he was totally okay under the cover of being a legit Greek ship owner. But he was not a natural-born gangster like Nick, or a guy like myself with 20 years of smuggling experience.

'I just wanted to get the *Suerte* out of Piraeus and get the whole trip done, then regroup with some of the other Greeks that Nick introduced me to. Some of them had their own ships and with others we were going to buy ships and work them together, but definitely not in Piraeus.

'I said to Elias, "You should have taken this fucking boat to get fixed in Alexandria, Egypt." Nobody would have even known it was there. We could have told everybody we were still in the process of buying it. It was sitting right there in Piraeus, when everybody in town knew Elias. So we were blown. We were already hot in Greece. It's a shame, that, it's . . .'

He trails off. There's almost misty-eyed whimsy in his voice when Luis thinks about what went wrong.

'I think Elias fucked it up. These guys completely fucked up a good thing.'

*

By the time Luis and Michelle flew into Caracas from Milan in June 2000 and met Jorge García and his fellow Los Mellizos associate Iván de la Vega Cabás, then moved on to Puerto Ordaz, he was walking into a trap.

'I'd already had a couple of close calls in Caracas. We used to keep our planes there, including the Conquest. I didn't want to go back there. So I said to Elias, "This is fucked up. I'm already over here, I've already crossed the fucking puddle, for me to have to cross back, you know, *fuck*. I didn't like travelling. For me, each time you travel under a Mexican passport it's a risk. So, sure enough, I get to Venezuela and these guys were expecting a Greek. Nobody knew I was "The Greek". Nobody knew I was Mexican, nobody in Venezuela knew anything about me except Jorge, but he didn't tell anybody.'

Luis was taking Prozac to help relieve his anxiety.

'You can be taking it and you can be head-deep in shit and you think everything is fine. Willie had warned me: "There seems to be something going on. Stop taking the Prozac. That shit dulls your nerve endings. You need to be sharp, man. I've heard some fucking rumours. I'll keep you posted."'

They got their warning but didn't abort when they had the chance.

'You know it's funny,' Jorge said when he got a moment with Luis. 'We were riding around the other day and there was a car following us.

We stopped the car and we went up to the people in the car. "What the fuck are you doing following us?" It turned out they were some guys from the UN.'

'What? United Nations?'

'Yeah, there's a lot of foreigners here because of the port, the steel; they were guys from the UN.'

'Were they American?

'We don't know. They said they were Canadian.'

'Man, are you sure? What the fuck? That's crazy.'

Days later, Jorge came to Luis again.

'Luis, we found a device on one of our cars. We just hired a taxi and put it in the taxi and told the driver to drive it to Maracaibo.'

'And that's when I said, "I'm out of here. This is very strange." I was having trouble finding my passport and went back to Caracas. But the *Suerte* had come into Puerto Ordaz. I was on another fucking planet.'

PART 11

AN INFILTRATED SITUATION

54

The Phone Call

IT WAS 16 AUGUST 2000 and another stinking hot day in Maracaibo. The only thing worse than being stuck in Venezuelan heat is being stuck in the same heat in handcuffs in the back of a black Suburban outside a police station.

Luis was staring intently at the *gringo* with the skinny white legs and Hawaiian shirt. The door opened and Luis could now see him more clearly. Very handsome, tall and well built, the American had a lean jaw and burry moustache.

Eric J. Kolbinsky was a former investigator and later corporal from the Organized Crime Division (Vice & Narcotics) of the Department of Public Safety in Durham, North Carolina. He'd joined the USCS in 1987 and for his first posting was stationed 'down on the border' in Laredo, Texas, then transferred to Wilmington, North Carolina.

In 1991, Kolbinsky switched again, this time to the DEA in Atlanta, Georgia, as a special agent and first went down to Colombia in 1998. The night before he arrived that November, a fellow DEA agent called Frank Moreno was shot in the chest and killed during an altercation outside a nightclub in the Zona Rosa district of Bogotá. As Kolbinsky remembers: 'The bullet clipped his aorta, exited his back and struck an individual across the street in the head, killing him also.'

Bienvenidos a Colombia. Welcome to Colombia.

Kolbinsky was sent to the DEA Resident Office in Barranquilla in the department of Atlántico. His primary duty was liaison with local antinarcotics police in Santa Marta, 100 kilometres by road to the northeast. He spent a lot of time at the port. The cartels would hide cocaine in loads of bananas or even under bulk carriers carrying La Guajira coal.

'They would attach what we call "parasitic compartments" to the hulls of the ships; like a torpedo tube that they'd weld on to the hull.[244] So divers were always diving these ships prior to them leaving to make sure they weren't full of cocaine. As a rule the DEA very seldom got involved in any sort of enforcement activity. We were always in the background. We had armoured vehicles but we were still restricted where we could travel by road.

'When we went out on operations we were always well prepared; we had tons of cops or military with us. So we weren't shooting out with the bad guys in Colombia – moreso doing jungle ops, where if you get fired on, you fire back in self-defence – but in a regular law-enforcement effort on the streets. We would hang back and advise, that sort of thing. It was still dangerous but not as dangerous maybe as earlier times [with Pablo Escobar]. But where else can a grown man play Cowboys and Indians?'

Luis thought Kolbinsky looked like the Hollywood actor Sam Elliott. He was gentlemanly and mellow in a hippie kind of way: 'He wasn't this redneck motherfucker at all.'

'Hey, Mr Navia, how are you?' Kolbinsky said politely in his gentle Carolinas drawl, as his USCS partner from Houston, Special Agent Vicente M. Garcia, got in the other side of the car. Luis was now sandwiched in the back of the SUV between the full might of American antinarcotics enforcement: DEA and USCS.[245] 'You're being held on suspicion of drug trafficking. We're going to take you back to the United States for a charge Customs has on you for a load you brought into the Keys.'

Luis had spent over a decade running from American authorities, five of them as a fugitive. For him, the United States was a place he could never return.

'I don't know what you're talking about. I'm a Mexican. Luis

Novoa. I want representation from the Mexican consulate. I want a lawyer.'

'Listen, we know you're Mr Luis *Navia*. You're originally from Miami. You're indicted in the Florida Keys. There's no sense in you denying it. We're going to take you back to the US. Let me put you on the phone to someone who knows you.'

Kolbinsky dialled a number on his cell then handed it over. A man's voice came down the line. He too was on his cell. Luis knew immediately who it was. Under American law, Kolbinsky had to hand over his detainee to the agent who'd had him originally indicted, even though the DEA's plan had been to allow Luis to go back to Europe and arrest him there.

'*Er*, hello?'

'Hi, Luis. This is Robert Harley from the Florida Keys. I've been to your mom's house. You know I've been there asking about you. We have an indictment on you.'

'You've got the wrong guy.'

'Luis, *Luis*, listen to me. Your mother lives at Cypress Drive on Key Biscayne. We know who you are. C'mon. *Please*. Cooperate with the gentleman next to you. Make it smoother for yourself. There's no turning back here. Don't talk to anybody down there. Keep your mouth shut. I'll see you in Miami.'

In his gut Luis knew Harley was right. When he handed the phone back, Kolbinsky made the situation plain.

'Well, if you're not Luis Navia, and you're not a US citizen, I can't help you. I'm going to have to turn you back over to the Venezuelans.'

That meant being left with the cop who was threatening to cut him into a thousand pieces. It wasn't much of a choice.

When I asked Kolbinsky to describe how Luis processed being caught once and for all, he laughs drily: 'He was fine but going through some changes. The world was coming down around him at that point.'

55

The Butterfly Effect

FROM THE DEA END, the case against Los Mellizos had originated in Barranquilla, originally a one-man operation, with a so-called 'vetted unit' that was 'working' Iván de la Vega Cabás and the Mejía Múnera brothers. It was run by agents Angelo Meletis and Rick Bendekovic and they were mostly involved in wiretaps, but officially the focus of DEA activity in Colombia was to support local cops in bringing US cases against drug traffickers: whatever work the agency does gets prosecuted in the States.[246]

Vetted units, a kind of special taskforce, were part of the DEA's Vetted Unit Program, initiated in 1996, in which local police officers worked alongside DEA agents stationed overseas in investigative work and intelligence gathering. At the time, there were four such vetted units in Colombia, with over 100 members. Other units had been set up in Bolivia, Peru and Mexico.

But as with the CIA's fraught relationship with the FBI regarding intelligence, there was lack of information sharing and a great deal of rivalry going on between American law enforcement in Colombia, this time between the DEA and USCS.[247]

Senior Special Agent (SSA) Nigel Brooks worked Operation Journey from the USCS Office of Investigations in Houston, while his Spanish-speaking colleague in the investigations unit, Vicente Garcia, was sent down to Venezuela to actively monitor Luis on the ground.[248]

Garcia had previously been the case agent for the prosecution of the crew of the *Cannes* and even boarded the *China Breeze*, before 'we gave it to the DEA, playing nice'.

Brooks was born to a US serviceman father and British mother in Birmingham, England, in 1947, educated in Lydd, Kent, and came to America in 1965. He was drafted into the US Army in 1966, served a tour of duty in Vietnam and started his law-enforcement career in the early '70s with USCS as a sky marshal in Hawaii. He found it was far preferable working with the British, Her Majesty's Customs and Excise (now merged into Her Majesty's Revenue and Customs, HMRC), because it offered better protection for their informant.

'At the time of the *China Breeze*, I was the Acting Resident Agent in Charge [RAC] in Galveston, Texas. Subsequently, I moved to a three-agent group that ran Operation Journey. My partners were Senior Special Agent Denny Lorton and Special Agent Jay Sills.[249] I primarily took the lead because of my relationship with HMCE's National Investigation Service [NIS] and the fact that I was about to retire and was willing to fight for what I believed in. Younger agents could suffer consequences because of the politics involved.

'The NIS was the investigative arm of HMCE. They were roughly equivalent to the DEA but they also investigated other revenue-related crimes in addition to drugs; much like the US Customs Office of Investigations, which investigated drugs, money laundering, export controls, revenue fraud, and so on.

'We worked mostly with HMCE in both Colombia and Venezuela in order to provide complete protection for our source of information inside the organisation. Our relationship with DEA in this investigation was pretty adversarial, the reason being that we had recruited the informant who was inside the organisation, and DEA wanted control of the investigation. We had totally different philosophies of how the investigation should be managed.

'Because the organisation had stopped sending cocaine to the US, and was sending it to Europe, we worked with HMCE to identify and track the load vessels, allowing law enforcement in Europe to identify the receiving groups and make the arrests and seizures there. DEA wanted to be able to just seize the drugs at the source or as soon as they were loaded onto the ships.

'At that time, US Customs, DEA and the FBI had jurisdiction over drug enforcement. However, when it came to foreign investigations, DEA had that remit as they had attaché offices overseas.[250] DEA was incensed that we were running a source on their turf, and under normal circumstances we would not have been able to do so as DEA had primacy. By working with HMCE, we were able to get around that. There were a few occasions where the source's name was revealed to the Colombians, and that was potentially a huge problem due to the fact that at that time there was massive corruption in law enforcement down there . . . to this day I'm still surprised that the [Los Mellizos] organisation never figured out the identity of the source while [the investigation] was ongoing.'

Eric Kolbinsky admits the situation was normal: 'There were always fights about who was in charge.'

Robert Harley agrees but maintains there were no major issues.

'In every agency there are personalities that are difficult. One type of personality is not endemic to DEA or Customs. I tell people that assholes are equally distributed among agencies. It's just a fact. If you have 100 Customs agents, five of them are assholes and nobody can work with them. So if you happen to come into contact with them and that's your only frame of reference, that's what you're going to think about the agency. It's the unfortunate reality of humanity. Nigel Brooks [of Customs] and the others were investigating proactively trying to interdict a load going to Europe and Eric Kolbinsky [of DEA] ran into Luis as a fugitive while looking at other suspects in-country in Venezuela. It was unbelievable. We had an agent down there who actually went *with* the information. They did what needed to be done.'

*

So how had El Senador finally been caught?

Luis's theory about the phone tap in Galerías Mall being triangulated from Europe turned out to be wrong. American federal agents had been in Venezuela for four weeks due to a tip-off from the informant and Luis had been walking around right under their noses – only they hadn't known who he was until his true identity was discovered completely by accident in Puerto Ordaz. Not even their prize snitch had known who Luis was.

'We got a fingerprint off of a glass and that's how we identified Luis,' says Kolbinsky. 'There was a meeting when all of [the cartel] were there and that's when we got a fingerprint. Some unidentified individual showed up in the middle of this meeting. We had no idea that Luis was even supposed to be there. Whatever interception stuff that had taken place over [at the vetted unit] in Colombia, it was not relayed to us that there was anybody else supposed to be at that meeting in Puerto Ordaz.'

Brooks confirms this is true.

'Luis first came to our attention in July 2000 when the final preparations were underway by the organisation for the movement of cocaine to Europe on the *Privilege* and the *Suerte*.[251] He was identified staying at the Hotel InterContinental Guayana in Puerto Ordaz and was using a Mexican passport but with the name Novoa. HMCE and the *Guardia Nacional* got approval from the Venezuelan Government to monitor his phone in his room and through that monitoring determined that he was communicating with Elias Lemos in Italy, and making phone calls to the US, Spain, Greece, Colombia and Mexico.

'Elias was initially intercepted when Luis called him from the hotel in Puerto Ordaz. Much of the time he was being monitored, it appeared he was trying to get some financing. In addition to his interactions with Jorge García and Iván de la Vega, he was also in contact with Jamil Nomani – "Indurain". So I assume that his role was with the European end of the conspiracy. Our intelligence was so good that we knew names of vessels, geographic locations of onloads and offloads, and we were able to identify the exact location of the storage site on the Orinoco.'[252]

Once he had been identified, Luis's subsequent great escape in Venezuela was foiled by the latest high-priced electronic surveillance technology: a Harris Corporation mobile phone–tracing device or digital analyser called a Triggerfish.

'The DEA and US Customs located Luis in Maracaibo,' says Kolbinsky, who knew and worked with Steve Murphy and Javier

Peña, the DEA agents who took down Pablo Escobar and were made famous by *Narcos*. 'We had a Triggerfish, intercepting cell phones. They call it something else now [Stingray]. There's been a couple of generations of improvements since.

'We were sitting up in a hotel room in Maracaibo and we had the number dialled in. It works off the cell signals. Most traffickers knew we could track them by their cells so it made sense Luis was on a payphone. We knew he was in Maracaibo and were monitoring him whenever he and Iván did use their cell phones. We figured out which hotel he was staying in. The Venezuelans reinitiated surveillance at the hotel and followed him to the mall. When I went to the police station to meet him I knew his name already.'

Vicente Garcia, on his first overseas mission, had been following Luis all over Venezuela for close to a month, both on foot and with the Triggerfish, which was the property of the USCS office in Houston. Brooks had sent Garcia to South America with the device because all the other available equipment inside Venezuela was being used on other jobs. Its portability was a key feature.

'From city to city, carrying a large tracking device,' says Garcia. 'My job was just to follow him while I was there, to intercept phone calls. There was a convoy of us: just me and the *Guardia Nacional*. Wherever he went, we surveilled him. We were almost killed twice on the road between Caracas and Puerto Ordaz. There were some cities between that were just horrible places. We stayed at so many holes in the wall; it was crazy [*laughs*]. Navia would be on one floor of a hotel, and I'd be either one floor below or one floor above, almost in the same location he was, so that I could be able to use the Triggerfish. He never saw me.

'Triggerfish was an evolving technology. We had two types of phones: digital, which was barely coming on board, this was 2000; and analogue. The Triggerfish that I had could do analogue with no problem and could do digital limitedly.[253] That was one of the issues: Navia's phone was digital. So I had to be in very close proximity to him in order to be able to pick up traffic from his phone. There were concrete walls in some of these places. It was very difficult to monitor. Today you can get a handheld Triggerfish. Back then mine was the size of a suitcase. So you can imagine: I was dragging a friggin' suitcase with wheels on it all around Venezuela.'

*

Luis's fingerprints were sent through to Robert Harley and the indictment brought against him in March 1995 for cocaine smuggling in the Florida Keys was actioned.

'We had prints on file and it went back to those original arrests in Dade County,' says Harley. 'We had fingerprints from an old Dade County arrest.'

His 25 years in the drug business had come to an end over a pair of minor traffic offences uncovered by Harley's partner Carol Libbey all those years ago, back when, as she drily puts it, Luis was 'young and stupid'.[254]

If ever there is a better advertisement for the benefit of not drinking and driving than Luis Antonio Navia, I don't know what it is.

Says Harley: 'It was critical to proving he was who he was. It was an insignificant moment in his life that really mattered later on. You don't know how the butterfly effect is going to affect you 20 years from now, but it did with Luis. Fingerprints would be the method to confirm who someone is, especially if you're going to expedite their removal. In those days, the arrestee better be a United States citizen or you would have many hoops to jump through to fly them out immediately. This was pre–war on terror days when protocols changed and other nationalities were removed from foreign countries and flown to the US or Gitmo [Guantánamo Bay, Cuba] a bit more often. I was notified very shortly before his arrest, and didn't receive confirmation until he was on his way to Florida.'

*

Vicente Garcia of USCS in Houston was given the task of coordinating the arrest, while awaiting confirmation that arrest warrants had been approved by the US and Venezuelan Governments. Like a Mexican Ray Romano, dressed in jeans and a T-shirt, he blended in easily with the shoppers at Galerías Mall in Maracaibo. A pale *gringo* in 5.11 Tactical shorts and a baseball cap would have given the game away.

'There was a guy following him in the mall, and it was me. He didn't realise I was American. Eric Kolbinsky would stick out like a sore thumb walking around the mall trying to do surveillance: 6'4", blond, blue eyes. I had two *Guardia Nacional* officers with me. They were armed; I wasn't. We're walking and I'm on the phone with my [country] attaché and he's saying, "Don't lose him." And I said, "There are thousands of people in this mall. The only way I won't lose him is if I literally walk with him." And he said, "Walk *with* him." And I said, "Alright, we're going to get into something here." I was *literally* walking behind him.

'And he turned around a couple of times like he wanted to fight with me or something. I stopped, and he just looked at me [*laughs*] and I looked at him. I think he noticed the *Guardias* were a couple of steps behind me as well. He didn't know if he was going to get kidnapped or what at that point. He kept walking and we followed him until we got the okay to make the arrest. The United States cannot do law enforcement in foreign countries. We were there with the *Guardia Nacional* but we didn't do the actual hands-on.'

The man with half a dozen aliases and as many fake passports, 'The Greek', 'El Senador', was busted.

The US Government finally had their man. [255]

56

The Snitch

FATALLY FOR LUIS, THERE was a *sapo*, a snitch or confidential informant, within the Los Mellizos organisation itself and there had been going all the way back to the middle of 1999. He was a Colombian called Tommy Taylor.[256] An unknown second informant inside the cartel, a 'subsource', had facilitated a face-to-face and very risky meeting for Taylor with the Americans.[257] Taylor agreed to testify against the cartel, but only when its leaders had been arrested, extradited and were in the custody of the US Government.

'The whole case came about after the interception and seizure of the *China Breeze*,' says Nigel Brooks. 'We recruited Taylor as a CI from inside the organisation and from that time on had complete inside knowledge of their activities. He was high enough in the organisation that he worked with both Iván de la Vega and Jorge García, and interacted with other members of the organisation from Miguel Mejía Múnera on down. It enabled us to identify all of the main participants including the Mejía Múneras, De La Vega and García. His information was so precise that we had the INMARSAT numbers, cell numbers, onload and offload coordinates, and frequencies and codes used by [Los Mellizos].'[258]

More gallingly, Luis had met the cartel's mole when he arrived in Caracas. After the capture of the *China Breeze*, Taylor (along with the subsource) had been flown from Barranquilla to Houston to provide information on the impending *Pearl II* smuggle to Brooks and his USCS colleagues. They then returned to Colombia and carried on working for the cartel. USCS in turn shared their information with Britain's HMCE but not the DEA, such was the ongoing discord between the two stateside agencies.

'Using Taylor we had run one load into Amsterdam on board the *Pearl II* and had it successfully taken out by the Dutch Prisma team,' continues Brooks.[259] 'We beaconed the ship and monitored the onload off the coast of Venezuela using a British warship, HMS *Marlborough*. Myself and HMCE's drugs liaison officer [DLO] in Miami, Brendan Foreman, were at the command post in Key West at JIATF-East when the onload from the *pangas* took place. *Marlborough* was monitoring from over the horizon using their technical capabilities. The *Pearl II* headed to Africa with a legitimate load, then to Amsterdam where it was searched and the load found. Unfortunately the Dutch were premature and didn't wait for the offload that was to take place over Christmas on the dock.[260]

'This investigation was actually headed by US Customs in Houston with our co-equal partners from HMCE's National Investigation Service and their drugs liaison officers in Colombia and Venezuela. DEA also assisted, but due to the fact they had an extremely poor relationship with Venezuelan law enforcement, all coordination on intelligence was passed from Customs to HMCE and they handled any interaction with the *Guardia Nacional*.

'We worked exclusively with HMCE in Britain and their DLOs in Colombia and Venezuela, mainly because we had the same goal: identify the receiving end and allow the Europeans to take the enforcement action while we provided the intelligence. It was supposed to be strictly an intelligence-run operation with no US law enforcement contemplated.

'The DEA greatly resented the fact that we were running a source in *their* area, and we refused to grant them access; the reason being for the safety and security of Taylor and his family. We just could not allow the possibility of his identity being revealed. Once we identified Víctor and Miguel Mejía Múnera as the leaders of the organisation in early 2000, things became even more contentious with DEA because of the stature of those two.'

*

'Tommy Taylor was a fucking basehead from Barranquilla,' curses Luis.[261] 'He came from a good family but he was no good. And Iván was the idiot who brought him into the organisation to work in a gopher capacity. He didn't have any routes, *nothing*. He was just a gopher; Iván's assistant. It seems that they caught on to this whole thing and Tommy travelled to the US to see his daughter who was in college or something. They grabbed him at the airport and they shook him up, they scared him, and they flipped him.[262]

'When he came back to Colombia he was already working for the DEA. That's why he didn't know who I was. He didn't know who I was so he could never mention "Luis Navia". He just knew that Iván had a connection in Greece: "The Greek". Little did I know that Tommy had already infiltrated [Los Mellizos] and I walked into an infiltrated situation in Venezuela. When I got arrested and the news came out, a friend of mine that worked for the Mellizos who I'd known for years said, "Shit, it's *El Senador*!" He had no idea I was The Greek either.'

Luis might have got away with his role in the entire Los Mellizos conspiracy had he not handled the glass in Puerto Ordaz. As far as the international authorities were concerned, the figure Taylor spoke of, 'The Greek', was just that: a Greek.

'Navia's name actually never came up either in the Colombian end of the investigation or when they moved to Venezuela,' says Nigel Brooks. 'Taylor never spoke of him, but did identify everyone he was aware of. We used code for people's names and vessels. Vessels were "X" and individuals were "Z". When Luis arrived on the scene he was assigned Z-23, Miguel Mejía Múnera was Z-16, Víctor Mejía Múnera was Z-22, Jorge García was Z-1 and Iván de la Vega was Z-2. The numbers were not assigned in order of rank but assigned as we identified individuals.[263]

'Luis was identified because we were monitoring Jorge's phone and found him at the hotel that way. From that day on, all of his telephone conversations were intercepted . . . basically, *everyone* was screwing the Colombians. The Greeks were screwing them for money to fix their crappy rust buckets; even the Colombians were screwing each other by embezzling. But I guess when you're making hundreds of millions, who cares? We on the other hand had to follow policies and procedures and continually write reams of justification for money for travel, source payments and technical equipment. No wonder no one has yet won the war on drugs.'

As for Luis's suspicions that his hotel room had been broken into by unknown persons, he was right. A redacted intelligence document from the operation confirmed 'the GN [*Guardia Nacional*] gained access to the room and searched [his] luggage', however Brooks says he has no knowledge of Luis's passport being taken.

But why didn't Taylor know Luis's name? The DEA's Eric Kolbinsky has a good idea.

'Iván de la Vega shielded Luis from the others. They didn't need De La Vega if they had direct access to Luis.'

*

In exchange for his cooperation, Tommy Taylor was promised cash and sanctuary for him and his family in the United States, as well as provided with encrypted instant messaging and emails to maintain daily communication with the US and British agencies coordinating Operation Journey until its eventual conclusion.[264]

After the *Pearl II* in Amsterdam became the fourth vessel to be impounded, Taylor provided names, intelligence and phone numbers to tap, then later relayed the coordinates of the cartel's jungle stash sites after seeing them on Jorge García's computer. Intelligence stations were set up in Caracas, Maraicabo, Puerto Ordaz, Upata, Barrancas del Orinoco and Tucupita. With the *Suerte I*, Taylor was leading Luis, Jorge and Iván to their doom.[265]

'We located where all the big stashes were,' says Graham Honey, the supervisor in charge of Operation Journey for the National Investigation Service of Britain's HMCE, which was working closely with the *Guardia Nacional*. 'I can remember the day [our liaison officer in Venezuela] phoned up to say, "We've got it, we've got this big stash," and then they'd move from that one to another one and found even more drugs.'

Using the coordinates provided by their prized informant, American interagency taskforce JIATF-East took satellite images of the Orinoco buildings, docks and *pangas* from space. A meeting between the DEA, HMCE, USCS and Italian, Venezuelan and Colombian parties involved was held at the US Embassy in Caracas in late July to coordinate the takedown, not helped by Venezuelan President Hugo Chávez refusing American drug surveillance planes in the country's airspace.[266] Meanwhile in Italy, the *Raggruppamento Operativo Speciale* (ROS), or Special Operations Group of the Italian *carabinieri*, was working the Albanian angle with the help of anti-mafia public prosecutors in Lecce.

They were in the tiger's mouth but didn't know it.

57

Shitting Match

THE BRITISH, WHO IN Bogotá had their own version of the DEA, known as HMCE, had brought the Americans in on the investigation because they knew they weren't going to get any prosecutions in the UK. The difficulty they had was in proving the individuals involved had committed crimes in their jurisdiction, or establishing a direct nexus to the UK for the drugs being transported into mainland Europe. American antinarcotics agencies, however, had more sweeping powers. And so what would become known as Operation Journey was born.

'My main focus [when I went to Barranquilla in 1996] was on "El Caracol" [The Snail], Alberto Orlandez Gamboa, the head of all the North Coast [Cartel] at the time,' says Rick Bendekovic, former agent advisor to the DEA office in Barranquilla. 'We were able to take him down and he was extradited later.[267] The Brits were working a bunch of cases and included the DEA office in Greece at the time and US Customs in Houston mainly and Miami as well. We used to bring everybody in to certain strategy meetings. That had led to *China Breeze* and the *Pearl II*.[268]

'When we give something an operation name it's to target an organisation. Behind it is going to be, in a perfect world, as best-case scenario, a well-defined organisation at the end of the investigation, or at least it's going to be [a case of] "We suspect these people to be moving stuff" and want to build it into a dismantlement of a criminal organisation. That's what our operation names signify: a *criminal* organisation. The maritime world was complex.

'We were working with the Brits mainly with their technology. A couple of months into it, the Colombians had sunk their teeth into it completely, and it was expanding and it was pretty much all [the DEA] was doing in Barranquilla. Los Mellizos would later become that office's primary objective.'

But both Graham Honey of HMCE and Nigel Brooks of USCS contend there was major infighting between American agencies working the case, not dissimilar to the feud between the CIA and FBI before the Twin Towers attacks on 11 September 2001. The DEA was also resentful of British involvement. Pre-takedown meetings in DC, Galveston, Athens, Barranquilla and Bogotá had laid bare those divisions. Information sharing generally was at best poor and at worse non-existent, with all the problems coming from the DEA's end.

'There was a real shitting match between US Customs and DEA at the time,' says Honey. '[HMCE] always kind of stayed in the background but I like to think we had the lead intelligence all the time this was going on. We were way ahead of what the DEA were doing; we got pissed off with the DEA.'

Brooks agrees: 'We had a massive problem with DEA because they were extremely upset that Customs was running an operation with HMCE in what they considered *their* area: South America. While our strategy was to monitor onloads of cocaine and allow the vessels to head to their destinations, DEA wanted to take the loads as soon as they were received. They wanted *seizures*. The US has been very successful taking out huge loads, but all you get are the transporters and not the organisations receiving it. But we prevailed in our strategy.'[269]

Honey: 'I had the biggest pissing match with Jim Soiles, the DEA attaché in Greece, over the whole thing; we just didn't get on.[270] The DEA took credit for everything but trust me: they had very little to do with it. There were a lot of good guys within the DEA but that whole job we sat with them on a daily basis and they were way off what was going on. The Americans did a huge amount but their problem was they were in conflict with each other a lot of the time and we were trying to dice [sic] between all of the agencies.'

The DEA's Bendekovic concedes this is true: 'We had to stay in our lane. And we did. We put together what we had with what the Colombians had with our joint resources, and once the prohibition of extradition was repealed that was the most valuable tool we had [against the traffickers]. We set up those teams waiting for that repeal of the extradition prohibition. That became the critical tool. Intercepts, informants and all the traditional techniques of gathering evidence and identifying criminal activity, those are the same. They might change in nuance, but it's facing down time in a US jail that really spooked them and really got their attention.'[271]

58

Atlantic Crossing

THE BYZANTINE MACHINATIONS INVOLVED in the seizures of cocaine in the north Atlantic Ocean of 1999–2000 are worth a book on their own and cannot be explained easily, largely because there remain doubts about who owned what merchandise, who owned what ship and who could take credit for bringing it all down.

Gustavo Adolfo Gómez Maya, a narco from the northernmost Colombian department of La Guajira, was arrested for his role with the *Cannes* and the *Castor*, along with his female partner Ivonne María Escaf de Saldarriaga and three other Colombians.

Gómez Maya's client list included Los Mellizos and Beto el Gitano. After the *China Breeze*'s load was initially but wrongfully pinned on Gómez Maya, Iván de la Vega Cabás was subsequently positively identified as being behind the vessel's illicit cargo. Part of the load on the *China Breeze* was intended for Beto.[272]

Says Nigel Brooks of USCS: 'The *Cannes* and the *Castor* was Gómez Maya and *China Breeze* was [Los Mellizos].' But he disputes Gómez Maya was working for Los Mellizos: 'Our source was the person responsible for getting the ships and he told us that Gómez Maya was not affiliated with The Twins.'

For his part the DEA's Rick Bendekovic is adamant '*China Breeze* and *Pearl II* were [Los Mellizos]' and 'there might have been other charges but I know the strongest charges on [the indictment for Beto el Gitano] were the 4000 kilos on the *Castor*'.

Graham Honey of HMCE is not so sure either way: 'There wasn't just one group; there were several groups involved in all these loads. The difficulty with these groups, as we found through the years, is it's an informal arrangement. They all work together, they all did bits together, they may or may not have a part in a load . . . it was always difficult to know exactly who was doing what for who.'

*

What is not in doubt is that the *China Breeze* carried a crewmember working as an informant for the DEA office in Athens, who supplied the source with communications equipment and satellite-tracking devices. Another ship in the conspiracy, the *Regent Rose*, was purposely sunk by the cartel off Cartagena, Colombia, before it could be apprehended.

Says Brooks: 'Sonny Bowie in Panama was purportedly the owner of the *Regent Rose*. Los Mellizos were going to use the vessel to transport a load to Europe, but it was taken offshore and scuttled when they discovered that there was possible law-enforcement interest in it. Sonny had been arrested and was apparently cooperating; the organisation received copies of the debriefs and decided to scuttle the ship.

'Sonny had apparently been jailed in Panama and the organisation had received a copy of a confession by a Panamanian called Wellington Fong concerning previous cocaine smuggling by the *Regent Rose*. Based on this, Los Mellizos decided to make it disappear and use a Greek vessel instead.

'We identified the attorney in Panama [Roque Pérez aka 'Alejandro'] who had handled the paperwork for the purchases of the vessels the organisation was using. DEA approached him, which then led to Los Mellizos taking *Regent Rose* out to sea and sinking it.'[273]

Miami Express, an unmentioned ship linked to Gómez Maya, was captured by Spanish law enforcement in October 1998 carrying just over four tons. The intelligence on it had started with HMCE in Miami. Another vessel, the *Dawn*, had initially been set to go, which would carry a 'parasite' fastboat.

'The boat was to be launched with the cocaine aboard 90 miles from the Portugal–Spain border,' says Brooks. 'The *Dawn* had some serious mechanical problems and was replaced by the Greeks with the *Aktis* [renamed the *Suerte*]. It was on a six-month time charter for $279,000 – which was to be applied as a down payment on the purchase – and Los Mellizos had already invested money in the repairs in Greece. At the end of the time charter, the organisation had agreed to buy the vessel for $1.83 million.'[274]

*

Another enduring mystery of the conspiracy is why the *Suerte* and its sister vessel in Venezuela, the *Privilege*, were never loaded with cocaine. Jorge García and three accomplices were intercepted by the Venezuelan Coast Guard before they could reach the *Suerte* while the *Privilege* left port completely empty, despite some intelligence suggesting it was carrying a five-ton load.

Says Brooks: 'We never did find out if the attempt to intercept was a coincidence or intentional as the agreement with the *Guardia Nacional* was to let the load run . . . I don't think after some reflection that the attempted interception was a coincidence.'[275]

Colombian and Albanian newspapers reported that the *Privilege*, previously the *Misty*, was purchased in Belgium by two Albanians, Arbën Berballa and Aleko Durda, brother of notorious drug trafficker Frederik Durda aka 'Bull'.

Brooks confirms the vessel was bought in Antwerp, left from Ghent, and the original plan of Los Mellizos was 'to offload 500 kilos to a sailboat off Gibraltar, then head to the Adriatic to offload the remaining 5000 [to Italian and Albanian recipients] 20 miles offshore from Albania. The port destination for the *Privilege* was Ravenna, Italy.

'Because Los Mellizos had sources in the Albanian Government, we all agreed that the Italians would handle the Adriatic enforcement and HMCE would monitor the 500-kilo offload off Spain. The number substitution code for this smuggle was "ADRIOTECUN". This code was provided to us in March 2000 long before the actual smuggle. Frederik Durda was identified as being the Albanian controller for the load.[276]

'The *Privilege* was compromised and the organisation found out that there was law-enforcement interest in it while it was in port in

Venezuela. They decided to not use it and it was loaded with cargo. We were fully aware that its use for smuggling cocaine had been abandoned; however we had a huge problem with DEA. Customs was running the source and getting information in real time. So even though we knew it was not loaded, DEA convinced the Spanish that it had been and caused it to be boarded and searched.

'When that happened I received an email from a DEA agent in Barranquilla to the effect that "The Spanish boarded the *Privilege* and found five tons of coke; just thought you'd like to know". We had been advised by HMCE that DEA had encouraged the Spanish to take out the *Privilege* a day before and I personally called the Spanish case agent to advise them exactly where the false compartment was located. Of course, our source was correct – the *Privilege* did not have a load of cocaine.'[277]

*

It is widely believed that Los Mellizos had been tipped off from someone allegedly within or connected to an American agency working on the case, most likely the DEA in Colombia. Víctor Mejía Múnera was reported by Colombian newspaper *El Tiempo* to have called off the load.

Brooks: 'I do not know for sure that Los Mellizos got the information directly from DEA, but our source told us they were aware of law-enforcement interest. When the organisation found out about the law-enforcement interest [in the *Privilege*] it decided to just send it with legal cargo. Our source told us that it would not be used to carry a load, but DEA did not believe us and coordinated with Spanish authorities to have it boarded at sea and taken into the Canary Islands for a search.

'The European end of the *Privilege* and *Suerte* offloads were to be handled by Greek, Italian and Albanian organisations and there was some initial intelligence that payment for the loads was to be in the form of Eastern European arms, which would be transferred to the Colombian paramilitaries. The plan was to allow both vessels to load and proceed to Europe where they would be intercepted by European law enforcement.[278] Unfortunately the loading of the *Suerte* was stopped by premature enforcement action taken by the Venezuelan Navy who intercepted the *pangas*. We still do not know if it was a chance encounter or a deliberate act.

'The subsequent raids on the *finca* [at Doble Uno] and Orinoco location basically ended the operation. And the *Privilege* was boarded by Spanish special forces off the Canary Islands despite the fact that we had advised it was not loaded. Apparently DEA had misrepresented the intelligence to the Spanish who put a great deal of time and effort in unloading the legitimate cargo.'

*

So who were the hapless 'Canadians' from the United Nations who almost got their cover blown while tailing Jorge García in Puerto Ordaz?

No one has owned up, but it's most likely they were DEA agents. Intriguingly, a redacted USCS intelligence document states: 'Z-1 [Jorge] has a source in the GN [*Guardia Nacional*] who is reportedly a lieutenant who has told Z-1 that there are many DEA agents currently staying in Puerto Ordaz [PO] at a hotel there . . . we would suggest that any US personnel in PO keep a very low profile and gradually withdraw in such a way as to raise no suspicion.'

Clearly they weren't inconspicuous enough.

'Given the size of the case and the number of agencies involved, it perhaps was inevitable that it would end prematurely,' laments Brooks, who personally removed a tracking device from the *Suerte* when it was impounded in Galveston. 'Sigma was the HMCE team responsible for technical installations and placing trackers on vessels and vehicles. When it attempted to beacon one of the vehicles the organisation was using [a Ford Explorer] so that Los Mellizos' ranch [at Doble Uno] could be located, a security guard in the parking lot saw it and told Jorge García someone had been under his vehicle. I'm not aware there was any confrontation like Luis has described it.

'The surveillances for the most part were done by a special unit of the *Guardia Nacional* and while US Customs, HMCE and DEA did participate in surveillances I'm pretty sure they teamed up with the GNB. The tracking device was not an active tracker but one that recorded locations and had to be retrieved to download the information, so putting it in a taxi wouldn't have accomplished anything as it was not being actively tracked in real time. That said, there were a number of instances where the organisation saw things, vehicles, and individuals they thought suspicious.'

Graham Titmuss, an investigation officer at HMCE's National Investigation Service in London, who'd been coordinating the case among various HMCE DLOs going back to before it was even called Operation Journey, has no firsthand knowledge of any agents, American or British, pretending to be Canadian.

'At the time of the bust we were not sure where Jorge García was and the DEA were unlikely to know. Despite the DEA claiming all the credit for Operation Journey, it was run by HMCE and US Customs.[279] For my part, Journey became an extension of Operation Jezebel, the first seizure being on the *Pearl II*. Jezebel seizures were from the *Cannes*, *Kobe Queen*, *Goiana*, *China Breeze*, *Castor* and *Svetlana*.[280] But the story of the Canadians seems right. Unfortunately for us the DEA got involved in Venezuela. The DEA were not as covert as we wanted them to be, hence the premature arrests and no drugs being loaded on the *Suerte*.'

His colleague Barry Clarke, a retired HMCE investigation officer who went on to work for Britain's National Crime Agency (NCA), agrees: 'I would put a bet on them being DEA.'[281]

59

Nick the Fish

UNBEKNOWN TO LUIS, NICK FISCIATORIS, his well-dressed, chain-smoking, old-style gangster fixer in Europe, had been on the radar of British intelligence services. He had a close association with Irish cocaine kingpin Brian Wright aka 'The Milkman' (he always delivered) and his lieutenant Kevin Hanley, who were targeted in one of the UK's biggest antinarcotics takedowns, Operation Extend, which commenced in September 1996 and wrapped up in 2007 with the 30-year imprisonment of Wright. This was an operation that focused mainly on Pinky Delgado's operations – the transporting of cocaine from South and Central America to Europe by yacht – but involved law enforcement in the Caribbean, South Africa and Australia.

'Nick Fisciatoris was living in London in the 1990s and featured on a number of major drugs cases,' says Barry Clarke of NCA, one of Britain's most experienced cocaine intelligence agents, having been a member of HMCE/HMRC's operational cocaine team and head of cocaine intelligence.

'Nick lived in New York for years and came to London in the 1970s where he worked the casino circuit. Nick was on the periphery of a number of Branch 3 jobs in the early 1990s when he lived in a flat at the back of Harrods.[282] He was a shadowy figure who was a middleman and broker between UK criminal groups looking for bulk cocaine and suppliers in South America.

'The profits to be made in the early-to-mid-1990s cocaine market were enormous. Many criminal groups looked to cash in at this time. As is always the case, the three things that British organised crime groups – OCGs – struggled with were supply from source, transportation to the UK, and ability to launder huge amounts.

'One British group stood out as the most sophisticated and prolific. They were eventually dismantled and prosecuted but only after an investigation spanning more than ten years. We initially investigated and understood this OCG from a UK perspective, but in time we realised that the wider supply group was international and operated at the highest level.

'Nick's role was undoubtedly well connected – he was known to have travelled to Mexico, Venezuela and Miami during the mid-'90s trying to broker various deals – but he went on to become increasingly unstable and volatile; ultimately a liability. He was well known to HMCE/HMRC at this time as a fixer and broker, but he was never truly understood. We now know that he attempted to broker numerous importations into the UK from South America and Holland. He dealt with the Navia group, but it was Brian Wright that was the real power in London as he had the finance and status.

'The supply chain above and below Luis was working with some of the UK's biggest traffickers and criminals; albeit they probably weren't aware of each other on a day-to-day basis. They, like us, law enforcement, were involved in groundbreaking business.'

*

When Operation Extend blew up Pinky Delgado's sailboat racket in 1998/'99 and Brian Wright's right-hand man Kevin Hanley was arrested, Wright fled to the Turkish Republic of Northern Cyprus – which had no extradition.[283] Fisciatoris had been close to Wright but they were now estranged. Another associate, Kenneth Regan, who had 'corrupt access at Heathrow airport' and had come with Fisciatoris to Cancún to meet Luis in 1996, was also arrested and convicted for heroin trafficking in 1998. He subsequently turned supergrass for the British authorities.[284]

As for Pinky, he'd long disappeared into South America along with his gopher Flaco, the man who introduced Luis to Fisciatoris, and Flaco's replacement, Willie. Of Luis's direct acquaintances, only fellow Miamian Alex DeCubas got nailed in the Extend investigation but nearly two dozen people went down for combined jail terms of over 200 years. The *Suerte* disaster would be Nick Fisciatoris's last hurrah.

'In all honesty, we didn't establish the link between the Journey suppliers and Extend suppliers until long after the arrests, and only when the supply chain started to cooperate in the United States,' says Clarke. 'All we initially knew was that Pinky [Delgado] and Mario [Alex DeCubas] were the nicknames of the suppliers. Pinky had the contacts – in reality the "contract" – in the UK to move bulk cocaine every year. This was primarily to Brian Wright and Kevin Hanley, but with Nick Fisciatoris making the introductions and taking a brokering role. So Nick was linked to both investigations. I was aware of Operation Journey but I wasn't one of the officers leading the case.

'In the aftermath of Operation Extend, when we arrested many of his associates, Nick left the UK. I met him a short time after in Athens – DEA Athens informed me that Nick had turned up at their office and wanted to talk. I met him twice over two days, but he didn't say much that we didn't already know. He was clearly attempting to gauge how much evidence we had against him. He didn't mention Operation Journey and I couldn't push him as I was also very conscious of future criminal proceedings.

'Nick was really interesting to talk to; a fascinating character from another age. The British criminals viewed him as unstable, demanding and as a liability. He was often referred to as "the lunatic". He was an old-style criminal, very engaging and funny in a sinister way: straight out of a film set. Nick provided me with some background and filled in some blanks but he wasn't inclined to give us the whole story. In reality we never had enough evidence to charge him so he slipped away. We heard no more of Nick after that. I last saw him circa 2001, and he was in his 60s then so likely he is dead by now.'[285]

60

Clear and Present Danger

AFTER HIS TALKING TO in the Suburban from Eric Kolbinsky, Luis slept on a chair at the police station. The next day Luis, Iván de la Vega Cabás and Michelle Arias were flown by helicopter to a military base in the foothills of Caracas.

The cavalry was there to escort them. There were around 150 Venezuelan soldiers at the airfield when they left, aboard ten army helicopters. They'd come to Maracaibo from the capital specifically for the transfer. Iván was also headed for an American jail, an indictment being obtained by the United States Department of Justice five days before his capture in Maracaibo, charging him with conspiracy to import cocaine.[286]

The short journey gave Luis some time to think. Would he try to stay in Venezuela and get a lawyer? The process of formal extradition potentially would give Luis and Iván another year in the country, where they would cool their heels in jail. The other option was simply bribing someone. Luis had tried to bribe the Colombian cop with $500,000, an offer to which he gave momentary consideration, but he said his hands were tied.

When Luis offered a million, he was told the Americans were already involved and there was nothing they could do: 'There's no money deal here. It's far beyond that.'

The security situation on the ground was tense, with fears expressed

Los Mellizos could ambush their convoy with rocket launchers like something out of *Clear and Present Danger* and assassinate Luis, Iván, Michelle and everyone else before they cooperated.

In Caracas, trucks loaded up with confiscated cocaine from Operation Journey thundered through the gates of the military base. So he could have one last night with his girlfriend, Luis paid $200 to an army captain in exchange for a barracks room with an air conditioner.

Even under interrogation and scared for her life, Michelle held the line on Luis's cover story: that he was a Mexican businessman called Novoa.[287] Feeling remorseful, he gave her a thin, 22-carat gold tie-link chain as a parting gift. Luis also sent a soldier to buy him a new button-down shirt and clean khakis, as he knew sooner or later he was going to be photographed.

'I didn't want to look like a fucking bum. If I was going back to America I was going back in style.'

*

Luis got to make a phone call to Patricia in Mexico. The guard who let him use the telephone had a gun on him.

'It must have been two o'clock in the afternoon. I looked around and I said to myself, "I could yank this gun and shoot this motherfucker and make a run for it." But I knew I wouldn't get far because it was a mountainous area with difficult terrain and I wasn't in the best shape. I wasn't going to last long, especially with Kolbinsky's long legs.'

When the phone was answered, his estranged wife wasn't home.

'The maid picked up the call. Juliana was at school. Patricia wasn't there. The only one that was there was Santi.'

It was a poignant moment: the international felon being caught at last and not being able to tell his own son what was happening. All Santi could say was, 'Oh, *Papá*.' Tears welled up in Luis's eyes.

'It wasn't like I could have a conversation with him. He was three years old. When I spoke to him it was "*Googoo, gaga, Papá*." I didn't tell him anything. My family didn't know what I was doing in Venezuela. It broke my heart, thinking I might not see my son for 25, 30 years. I told him I loved him very much and that I hoped to see him soon. And that's when I decided I had to get out of this mess as soon as I could.'

*

Night had fallen in Caracas and a light-grey USCS Lockheed P-3 Orion was on the runway being readied for the three-hour trip to Florida, its red, green and white lights glowing in the darkness. Eric Kolbinsky and Vicente Garcia would accompany the two arrestees on the flight over.

Luis was ordered to make a final call to Los Mellizos in Puerto Ordaz, to pretend he was still in Maracaibo and 'to let them know we were not under arrest'. The man he spoke to on the other end of the line was Wilmer Joiro, a *sicario* from a violent family in the Alta Guajira and the right-hand man of Jorge García. Wilmer wasn't at all convinced by the ruse and would have already known Jorge had disappeared into the wilderness.[288] It didn't wash. When Luis got a moment alone with Iván, he suggested they pay the *Guardia Nacional* to escape.

'Listen, Iván, what we gotta do is get put in jail here in Venezuela, get $2 million, pay these guys off and get the fuck out of here and go back to Colombia. With two million bucks they'll let us go. We can fight this.'

'Are you fucking crazy, man?' Iván replied, totally incredulous at what he was hearing. 'You know what's going to happen to us when this thing comes down and the Mellizos find out we've been arrested? The first thing they're going to do is have us killed in jail. They're the ones that are going to kill us.'

'Iván, *Iván*, what the fuck are you talking about? We've been working for these guys, made them money.'

'Who do you think you're working for, Luis? If we stay in Caracas we're dead.'[289]

That was when the penny dropped. A man can watch only so many friends die and survive only so many kidnappings in the cocaine business before he realises the game is up. This time Mr Magoo had struck out for good.

'Now *that's* when I said, "Listen, I'm Luis Navia and I'm ready to go back to the United States. And fuck this shit."'[290]

Luis's former wife Patricia Manterola, daughter Juliana Navia and Luis at the beach in Cancún, Mexico, 1994. Says Luis: 'Cancún was fun and games by daytime, but by night thousands and thousands of kilos were coming in.' *Courtesy of Luis Navia*

USCS Special Agent Robert Harley (INSET): 'Attempts were made [to capture Luis in Mexico], but I always felt they were a day late and a dollar short, each time.' *Courtesy of Robert Harley*

Luis and son Santi in Mexico, circa 1997/'98.
Courtesy of Luis Navia

Luis and Juliana in Guatemala, 1998.
Courtesy of Luis Navia

The Houston conference for the seizure of the M/V *Cannes*, along with the impounded four tons of cocaine. This was a watershed moment in what would become the 12-nation Operation Journey. USCS Commissioner Raymond Kelly is in the dark suit.
Courtesy of Vicente Garcia

The M/V *Cannes*.
Courtesy of Vicente Garcia

A screen grab of a USCS PowerPoint presentation showing the four main targets in the takedown of Los Mellizos (The Twins).
Courtesy of Nigel Brooks

Some of the cocaine found on board the M/V *China Breeze*.
Courtesy of Vicente Garcia

The cheeky picture postcard Luis sent to Robert Harley while on the run in Panama. *Courtesy of Luis Navia*

Luis, Juliana, Santi and Luis's girlfriend Michelle Arias in Caracas, Venezuela, right before the takedown. *Courtesy of Luis Navia*

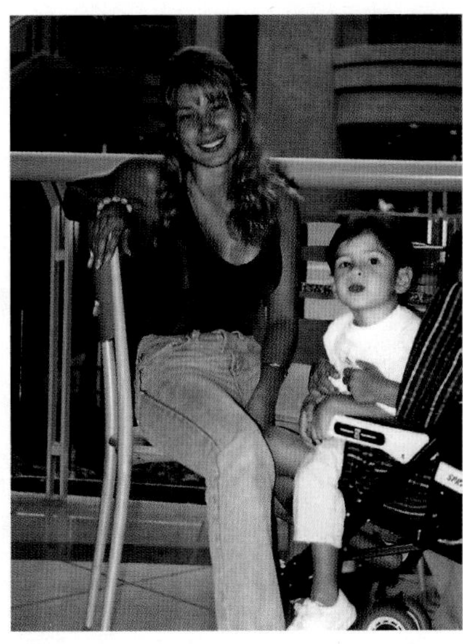

Michelle and Santi. *Courtesy of Luis Navia*

DEA Special Agent Eric J. Kolbinsky (SECOND FROM RIGHT) and USCS Special Agent Vicente M. Garcia (SECOND FROM LEFT) in Venezuela in 2000 with unidentified members of the Colombian National Police and Venezuela's *Guardia Nacional* prior to leaving Caracas on a plane for Maracaibo to arrest Luis. Both Kolbinsky and Garcia followed Luis through Venezuela prior to his arrest. *Courtesy of Eric Kolbinsky*

Kolbinsky at a cocaine lab in the Sierra Nevada de Santa Marta, Colombia, with a seized kilo. *Courtesy of Eric Kolbinsky*

A satellite view of the enormous Orinoco Delta, the location of jungle stash sites for an estimated 25 tons of cocaine. Says Luis: 'The Orinoco Delta, that is *huge*. It makes the Everglades look like a little fucking backyard.' *Planet Observer/Universal Images Group via Getty Images*

Guardia Nacional officers with part of the seized Los Mellizos cocaine in Puerto Ordaz, Venezuela. At the time it was the South American country's biggest ever coke bust. Operation Journey officially netted 22,489 kilograms or almost 25 tons. *Associated Press*

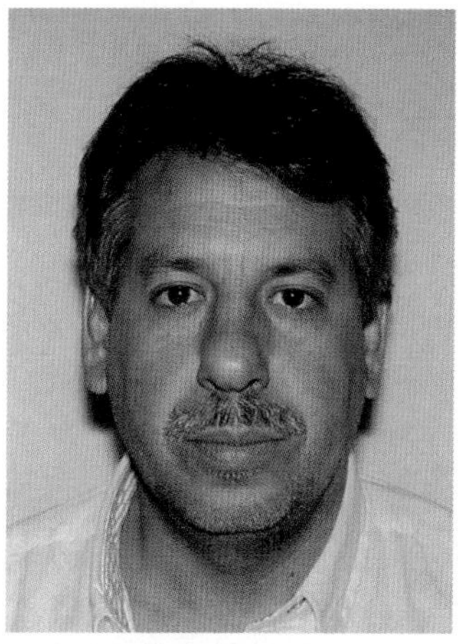

The photograph that marked the end of Luis's 25 years in the cocaine business. Says Luis: 'This was taken by Kapinsky [Eric Kolbinsky] before we left the military barracks in Caracas where I was being held with Michelle Arias and Iván de la Vega.' *Courtesy of Nigel Brooks*

A Colombian reward poster for Los Mellizos: drug lords and twin brothers Miguel and Víctor Mejía Múnera. *Associated Press*

Luis and alleged Jamaican drug trafficker Richard 'Storyteller' Morrison at Federal Correctional Institution, Coleman, Florida. While sharing a cell with Luis at the Federal Detention Center in Miami, Morrison would wake early each morning to tie his running shoes. Says Luis: 'He said to me, "You've gotta be *strapped*." He called tying his shoelaces being strapped. You never know when you're gonna have to fight. How are you going to fight somebody in a pair of fucking slippers?'
Courtesy of Luis Navia

Luis playing the drums for his prison rock band, Prizm.
Courtesy of Luis Navia

A post-release Luis enjoying being a dad again with a young Santi.
Courtesy of Luis Navia

Luis by the beach in Islamorada, Florida, November 2019.
Courtesy of Jesse Fink

The old devils. Luis and fellow cocaine smuggler Jorge 'El Gordito' Cabrera, Islamorada, Florida, November 2019. In 1995 El Gordito was famously photographed in Miami with Vice President Al Gore and at the White House with Hillary Rodham Clinton.
Courtesy of Jesse Fink

Eric Kolbinsky, Robert Harley and Luis Navia meeting together for the first time, St. Petersburg, Florida, November 2019. Luis bought Harley the tie as a gift. *Courtesy of Jesse Fink*

Luis and the man he affectionately calls 'Bob'. *Courtesy of Jesse Fink*

PART 12
SOWING THE SEEDS OF LOVE

61

The Business Deal

At 3am on 19 August 2000 Luis was taken for processing at USCS. At 5am he was taken to the Federal Detention Center (FDC) in Downtown Miami. The FDC, run by the Federal Bureau of Prisons (BOP), is a faintly Stalinist, featureless grey prison building where 1300 prisoners of all descriptions and offence levels are held awaiting trial, sentencing or to appear in court as witnesses: rapists, murderers, gang members, cartel figures, heroin addicts.

After changing into green jumpsuits, Luis and Iván de la Vega Cabás were put in general population with other prisoners on separate floors. Luis was given a government-appointed attorney who spoke to him in Spanish like a low-class Cuban, *cubanaso*, and he listened quietly downstairs in the interview room as his case file was being read out on not one but two cocaine-trafficking indictments: the original March 1995 indictment from the Florida Keys and new charges for his role in the *Suerte* smuggle. When it was over Luis spoke in English.

'What am I looking at here?' he said, shifting in his seat.

'*Un pingal de años*.'[291] A shitload of years.

Luis couldn't believe what he was hearing.

'When the lawyer said that, I said to myself, "I've definitely got to get rid of this motherfucker."'

*

It was high time to start interviewing different attorneys. Luis was on the same floor as legendary 'cocaine cowboy' Willy Falcón, who was back in the clink after beating serious drug-trafficking charges four years earlier.

'We were both on the tenth floor. He hadn't gone to trial yet as it took a long time for him to go to trial. At first they were both together, him and Sal Magluta.'[292]

The first lawyer Luis met he didn't like. Then Falcón recommended one of his defence attorneys, John Bergendahl, who agreed to sit down with him. What follows is Luis's recollection of their conversation.

'Luis, I could charge you $250,000 right now and take your case, but I've got to be honest with you. There's not much I can do for you. Your '95 indictment is 4600 kilos, there's confiscated merchandise, I know for a fact there's a few people from that old indictment who are still sitting in jail that would *love* to testify against you to get their time off.

'Plus, if we fight these guys, they'll bring in this Operation Journey indictment and make it into a formal indictment and there's 25,000 kilos of dope confiscated. Your co-defendant, he's going to testify against you. You don't have a chance. They're going to nail you. You could be looking at a possible life sentence here.'

'What do you mean "life sentence"? I didn't kill nobody.'

'You don't understand. Your level is way up there. Right now you're at level 43.'

Level 43 is the highest offence level under the *United States Federal Sentencing Guidelines*. In other words: life.

'Wait a minute. I told these people I'm willing to do ten years.'

'*Ten* years?'

'Yes. I'm willing to give them all my money, do ten years and that's it.'

'*No, no, no.* You don't understand. You're going to have to give them the money, cooperate totally, completely do everything they ask you to do plus more, and *then* you'll get ten years – and that's being extremely lucky.'

'What?'

'Yes. If you do cooperate the first time around, I doubt that you'll get something less than 14 [years]; you'll get 14 to 17 and that's with a great attorney with a great plea deal. And we could work something out like that, but you have no other choice. You need to cooperate. That's what Colombians do. Colombians treat this as a business. This ain't no mafia, this ain't no blood pact. You get caught, you cooperate, it's a *business deal.*

'Right now you are going to make the most important business deal of your life. That's why the US dollar says "In God We Trust". The only part where they mention God is on the dollar. To them, religion and dollars, it's the same thing. You've got to be sharp, you've got to be on your feet. If you've ever been sharp, this is the time to be sharp. There's no fucking up here.'

'*Wow.* Okay.'

*

When he got back to general population, Luis told Willy what had happened with Bergendahl. Willy suggested Luis get an attorney who specialised in deals; Bergendahl's own style was to fight cases.

'Willy was the first one who took me aside and said, "Listen, you better call yourself an attorney that specialises in doing plea deals. I do *not* suggest you take this to trial." And it was either him or someone else in the unit that recommended I hire Ruben Oliva to cut me a plea deal.

'So I called Ruben. He came across the right way. He's Cuban. I never wanted a Cuban attorney; I always wanted to go with a Jewish attorney – I always said to myself *Jewish* attorneys, *Jewish* accountants and *Jewish* doctors – and I had already given $35,000 to another attorney who was kind enough to return it. And Ruben charged me I think it was $100,000, and that was the most Ruben had ever charged in his life.'[293]

62

The Roadmap

SEVEN DAYS INTO HIS confinement at FDC, in the early evening of 26 August, Luis was eating dinner at a four-man table with 100 other prisoners in the common area. There was a bank of televisions at the front of the room showing the nightly news. A prisoner at his table finished chewing a mouthful and turned to Luis.

'Hey, isn't that you on TV?'

'I was like, "*What?*" I look up and go, "What the fuck?"A CNN special report comes on, all about Operation Journey. They fucking showed me and Iván getting off the plane in handcuffs, a map of Venezuela with arrows of ships going everywhere – three arrows to the US, three arrows to Mexico, four arrows to Spain, three arrows to Italy – and 25 tons of cocaine confiscated in Venezuela. *Major* drug bust. Everybody on the fucking floor turned around and looked at me. I hadn't even realised it.'

USCS Commissioner Raymond Kelly was addressing a roomful of journalists and photographers at a press conference in Washington, DC, flanked by DEA Deputy Commissioner Julio Mercado, Rear Admiral David S. Belz representing JIATF-East, and other men in suits. There was no mention made of the Mejía Múnera brothers, Jorge García, Sonny Bowie, Nick Fisciatoris, Willie, Elias Lemos, or anyone else involved in the conspiracy. Instead, bumbling Iván was being cast as the supervillain in charge of his own cartel, 'the De La

Vega group', with Luis his lieutenant.[294] Kelly described it as 'one of the most complex networks we have ever seen'.

'We wiped out a sprawling organisation whose tentacles reached around the world. Massive amounts of cocaine will be kept off the streets of Europe and America. And thanks to this global law-enforcement effort, we now have a powerful new blueprint for fighting the international drug trade.'[295]

For anyone watching at home, the import was clear: this was a historic takedown of one of the world's biggest ever cocaine-smuggling operations, right up there with the dismantling of the Medellín and Cali cartels. But for Patricia and Luis's family, it was the first time they'd heard he'd been arrested.

The following day, 27 August, Luis's 45th birthday, Operation Journey hit the papers.[296] His downfall was global headline news.

Reputed head of drug ring taken to US after arrest
The New York Times

12-nation effort breaks up Colombian drug operation
The Washington Post

Major drugs cartel smashed
BBC News

$1bn haul of cocaine seized in 12-nation operation
The Independent

US deals blow to cocaine trade as 25 tonnes seized
The Guardian

Luis's newfound celebrity at the FDC also caused quite a stir. Within half an hour a Special Operations Response Team (SORT), colloquially known as the 'Goon Squad', came and put him and Iván in solitary in the Special Housing Unit (SHU). They had to switch from green to orange jumpsuits.

'The Bureau of Prisons is a totally different entity to DEA, FBI, US Customs. FBI doesn't tell them more than they need to know. "This is a criminal. We picked him up on a drug bust, *ba ba ba*." BOP has its own rules and regulations. Their duty is to keep the prisoner *alive*. They don't get paid for dead bodies in custody. They have their own internal security team, Special Investigative Services, and they have to figure out if you're gang related, which cartel you belong to, and not to put you on a floor with another member of a rival cartel.

'So SIS put us in the SHU right away for 90 days because we were high-profile prisoners. We got separated right away. I was on one side and Iván was on the other. I couldn't see him. They wanted to find out everything about us and our affiliations before putting us back in general population. I had a five-man custody detail. Every time they moved me, five guys were assigned to me. Not moved me from floor to floor, but just to get some sunshine.

'Solitary was a relief because you get time for yourself. And I looked out my window and I saw the Hard Rock Cafe, bayside, the backside of Biscayne Bay, and I said, "Well, look at this, man. I come back to Miami and I got a penthouse." I was in the penthouse. It was the top floor and I was alone. The SHU is great when you're alone because you've got your own little apartment.

'When you've got to share it with somebody, well, then you've got to shit in front of somebody. You've got no privacy. But when you're alone in the SHU? *Fuck*, man, you start doing your push-ups, you set yourself. You get your breakfast, you eat, you relax, take a nap, then you do some push-ups, then you do lunch, then you ask the guard to let you out and go to the library for two hours and type letters to your girlfriends, shit like that. Then you come back, take another nap, do some more push-ups, then it's dinner, and you go to bed at nine o'clock and wake up at six. It's a routine. I got a little depressed but I was more concerned about getting out.'

*

It was upstairs in an attorney–client interview room at SHU that Luis came face-to-face with Robert Harley, the man who'd been looking for him for nigh on a decade. Ruben Oliva of Miami law firm Rojas

& Oliva, PA was representing Luis. There was no ceremony. No speeches. They all shook hands and got down to business.

'Bob was a gentleman. He looked like a small version of Robert Redford. Short, stocky, blond guy.'

So Eric Kolbinsky looked like Sam Elliott and Harley looked like Robert Redford and you'd had them both on your tail?

'*Exactly*. And I'm Dustin Hoffman.'

Laughs Harley: 'As long as you're not, you know, Hannibal Lecter, I am professional, civil and polite. This is what polite society demands of people. I didn't meet the plane from Venezuela because its arrival was sooner than my ability to drive to Miami from the Keys.

'Luis was a character from the first moment we met. He was joking from, like, minute one. He wanted coffee and we got him coffee. He was very much himself. He was not a wiseguy. He was literate, a thinker, he listened, he processed what was being said to him, and he asked relevant and intelligent questions. So I was like, "He's *not* what you picture a major narco trafficker to be." Luis is just not that person. It's an interesting thing. I don't think it's easy to put these people into a box. It's just not that simple. Not at that level.

'I had a very frank and adult conversation with Luis and I laid out a roadmap for him and told him, "You've got huge life choices ahead of you. You can die an old man in prison or you can be honest from day one and do what you can to salvage the rest of your life." Basically convincing him he needed to get on board right away. The choice was up to him.'

Luis could see he had a shot at freedom; he wasn't going to blow it.

'I remember Bob saying something like, "After this is over I just want you to relax and sell hot dogs on Key Biscayne. But whatever you do, do *not* lie to me." I realised I had one more opportunity. That I could actually get out of there. When you're in that situation and they tell you, "You have life choices to make," they're giving you an opportunity to have a *life*. If I had been a violent offender that scenario would have never happened. Bob would have never come to me on those terms. To these people violence makes all the difference in the world. They're in the drug business. They understand the drug business. They have a badge to be violent; we don't. When you shoot back, you've got a problem.'

63

Closed Doors

By now Operation Journey was all over the nightly bulletins in Colombia and Mexico, but Patricia had found out early. A Colombian friend of hers in Mexico City knocked on her door unannounced at about 8pm on the evening of 26 August 2000 and asked her to come to his car. They then drove a short distance and picked up another Colombian friend, parked in a side street, and turned off the engine.

'Patricia, we're pretty sure Luis has been taken by the DEA. We think he's now in the United States.'

Still, she was shocked when she turned on the TV a couple of hours later and saw the footage from Fort Lauderdale airport of Luis being escorted off the tarmac.

'The newsreader was the father of a friend of my daughter,' says Patricia. 'I was like, "Oh, my God." Even from a distance I knew it was Luis. I was just happy they didn't read out his name.'

*

The next day, the fallout on the Navia family was swift and devastating.

Luis's nephew Andrés Blanco: 'My grandmother woke me up with a newspaper in hand, screaming, "Read this and tell me it's not true!" But she also kept a paper bag full of cash that was always kept in her locked closet, which was called Fort Knox, where she kept anything valuable.

She had electronic shutters installed when my grandfather died. It was a literal period of darkness after the news came out about my uncle, because she kept the windows closed for weeks. She just hid away. She didn't want to see anyone. I think my mother, my grandmother and my brother Martin and I probably took the brunt of that.'[297]

Laura: 'It was horrible. My mother was hurt, ashamed of her son, and very upset. She locked herself up in her home and did not want to see anyone. She fell into a deep depression. She rolled down all the electric hurricane shutters and stayed in the dark. Friends would come to visit to check up on her, and she refused to answer. Simple tasks like going out to the market were incredibly difficult for her. She was too ashamed to be seen. There was a very severe and noticeable deterioration in her mental and physical health that started with Luis's arrest and imprisonment. At the same time, it brought her some peace, knowing that he was safe in prison. At least she knew where he was, and she could visit him.'

Andrés: 'When my uncle was arrested, a lot of things clicked for me. Looking back, I do remember feeling watched at our hotel in Caracas. We were at the pool and you know when you feel eyes are on you? I'm a relatively perceptive individual and I just remember being like, "That woman over there has been watching us." Later we found out all the phones were bugged.

'My uncle's saving grace was being arrested. He may not have been killed by anyone, but he was going to kill himself the way that he was doing drugs, drinking, smoking and being overweight. He was going to have a heart attack; die on the toilet. It was very embarrassing for my grandmother. I think that was the point of the beginning of a decline for my grandmother physically and mentally. I think that's when we started to see the first signs of Alzheimer's. Her cognitive skills suffered.'

Luis: 'My mother was shocked and she closed her doors to the world. She was a little embarrassed, I guess, but she knew I wasn't exactly on the right track. She and my sister both *knew* what I did. I was an adult. That was what I chose to do. They didn't know the specifics of the cartels I worked with, but they knew I wasn't an accountant in Bogotá.'

For Laura, especially, life was about to change dramatically.

Laura: 'The pressure from Luis's arrest was not easy to handle. It was a hard situation to explain to my children, family and friends, even though it was in the newspapers and on TV – how do you face that? It brought shame to us all. Even though Luis was away from us for many years, we considered him the head of the household since my father passed away. We had old-fashioned views of the "man in charge". My children always argue this and insist I am – they adamantly say that I am – but I don't see myself this way. They are very protective of me.

'To say my plate was full is an understatement. When I look back, it was a challenging time. I was working and carried the responsibility of not only raising my two teenage sons [as a single woman] but caring for my ageing mother as well. When in the midst of it, you do what you need to do to keep the boys in school and to keep life as normal as possible. Andrés and Martin were the source of my strength.'

Andrés: 'For my mother it was difficult because everything came down on her. There were attorney's bills to pay. She was the glue that kind of held everything together. The strength she showed during that period is astounding.'

Luis: 'It was very hard on Laura when I was in jail. Nobody helped her. Just like nobody helped Patricia. Laura also got cancer: she lost a kidney. So I've been surrounded by great women on both sides. She's a hero to me. She tells her kids, "Listen, your uncle's not perfect. But your uncle's your uncle, he's my brother, and he's been very good to all of us. So even though he's not perfect, *please*, respect him." She allows no disrespect and no bullshit.'

Laura: 'It's nice to hear my brother say that. He and I were brought up to be very close. Our parents always taught us we were one. This is how it still is; we are very different but unconditional with one another. I do not agree with the life he chose to lead. Many times, I did mention this to him, and he would always say he would quit the business soon. That being said, Luis is very loyal. Loyalty is important, and I taught this to my children. Family is family, and we need to be there for one another.'

*

At FDC, Luis was hardly to see his family over the coming months, but they came to visit him when they could: his mother María, sister Laura, nephews Andrés and Martin.

Laura: 'It was very difficult; I was in tears. Just thinking about it now I choke up. Those were incredibly difficult times. While it was good to see Luis, the circumstances were awful.'

Luis's estranged wife didn't have a visa to enter the United States and Juliana and Santi knew absolutely nothing about what had happened to their father.

Patricia: 'They thought he couldn't come to Mexico because he didn't have a visa. But he called all the time.'

Luis: 'The kids were small and going to school and had other things on their mind. I said to my family, "Listen, this is my problem, this is my time, I need to live in here, I don't need to be reminded of how nice life is on the outside." You're in *prison.* I knew people who had their family come visit them every fucking weekend. Who the fuck wants to put their family through that fucking torture? There was no life on the outside for me. I didn't want contact. I was happy in my prison. I was doing my own time. I don't need to see people. My world is the inside.'

Andrés: 'To watch my grandmother begin to deteriorate like she did and the struggles my mother had to go through to keep it all in order, we were the ones constantly visiting my uncle in prison. And when he needed money or something, the call came to us. My uncle tried to shield Patricia as much as possible from his time in prison. I don't think they ever visited him so they never saw the ugly side of it all. They never really confronted the fact he was in prison.'[298]

Patricia: 'Luis was always worried about his mother and sister. He's the kind of person who takes care of everybody. He always supported his mother and his sister and his nephews. The good thing for him is they weren't living in Colombia; they were living in Miami. My father found out the truth [about Luis] when everything was in the news. My mother is three years older than Luis. I think she always knew but she never told me anything. She came to visit us in Bogotá when Juliana was born, in Cancún a few times and in Panama. She cared about him, and I know she was worried about it.'

*

A couple of months into solitary, Luis felt confident enough to phone Patricia and ask her to travel from Mexico City to Colombia to talk with the heads of the cartels and, he says, 'recover monies owed to me'. He had no one else to turn to.

'I wanted to see where they stood. If they'd said, "Don't say anything, we'll cover your expenses but just hang in there," I would have hung in there.'

'He wanted money to pay the lawyers,' says Patricia. 'He wanted to know how they could help him. I think in that moment Luis wasn't okay [mentally]. He was desperate. He was crazy to send me down there. If I had told them he was thinking of cooperating with the US Government, they would have killed me right away.'

But she agreed to go. For a week, Patricia, showing a loyalty to Luis that probably wasn't deserved, shuttled between Cali, Pereira, Armenia and Bogotá attempting to get an audience with drug lords and paramilitary leaders.

'It was very difficult. I was crazy. *Imagine*. I don't know what I was thinking, really. I was worried about Luis but we were in it together when everything happened. Luis asked me to do it. Nobody wanted to do it. Not even Laura. I didn't think too much about it. I wasn't scared; maybe I should have been [*laughs*]. If someone asked me to do it again, maybe I wouldn't do it. They could have killed me if they'd wanted: "disappear" me. But I never felt like something was going to happen because Luis wasn't that kind of guy.'

Luis 'Miki' Ramírez, Francisco 'Juanchi' Moya, Hernán 'Papito' Prada Cortés, Fernando 'Marulo' Marulanda and others from Luis's two decades in the business in Colombia were all on her checklist.

'I tried to reach people. Everybody was afraid of meeting me. Nobody wanted to meet; maybe they thought I was with the [DEA], but I wasn't. I just wanted to do the right thing in that moment. Nothing worked, nobody showed.'

But word did get through to her eventually from an intermediary that she, Luis and the kids were safe; no one was in danger, whatever Luis chose to do going forward. Their message was simple: Luis should look out for himself and do what he needed to do to get back with his family. A couple of million that was owed to him, however, wouldn't be paid. No money would be forthcoming for lawyers' bills or anything else. Luis would just have to bear the financial and legal brunt of what was coming to him.

That still left the boss of all bosses at that time in Colombia: Luis Hernando Gómez Bustamante aka Rasguño. It was his word that mattered most and he was the only cartel leader whose blessing Luis felt was absolutely critical. For Patricia, he wasn't an easy man to find, embroiled in an intra-cartel war with North Valley rival Diego León Montoya Sánchez aka 'Don Diego'.

'I spoke with the *comandante* of a paramilitary group and he connected me to "Ras" when I was in Cali; I spoke to Rasguño on [two-way] radio.'

Their conversation was brief over the crackling audio line but she got the assurance she was looking for from a man who had held her own husband to ransom.

'Don't worry, Patricia. Everything's okay between me and Luis.'

64
Rule 35

THE MAN LUIS BELIEVES he owes his freedom to today was the man who hunted him down all those years: Robert Harley. The key issue was defining the word *leadership*.

'The guy who held the key to my liberty, to my freedom, was Bob. Was I a leader in a "leadership role"? *Leadership role* is really fucked up because your base offence level is 38 for the amount of cocaine. Anything over 150 kilos is base level 38: 150 kilos is *nothing*. For the US Government, a kilo is an immense amount of drugs. Then they add on two points for a manager role. Then they add three points for leadership, which is an extra ten years. So when you get to level 43, you're looking at life. In our business, you're looking at fucking mega years.'

Says Harley: 'This was the source of a lot of discussion. For the duration of my investigation of Luis, I believed him to be in a leadership role. Some of the attorneys from what was then called the 959 Group out of DC, which was the special prosecutions unit, still saw him [in] a leadership role.[299] But once the in-depth debriefing started to take place and we were able to verify what his activities were, it was very clear he was a broker; he was not the leader of an organisation. There were several layers above him.

'So are we going to charge a boat captain [for] leadership in an organisation that has 14 levels above him? No, we don't. Well, then why do we charge the broker in Colombia as a leader if he has three, four, five levels above him? This was my argument. It was literally a discussion about what does that term mean.

'Everybody who sat through all the debriefings, and you were able to then put that together with, say, murders that took place of people above or around Luis, you realised that he did not have the capacity to control the fate of anyone. So if you can't control other persons' fate, then how are you a leader? You are a worker. You're *part* of the organisation. He did have "enhancements" for his role. He just was not the leader of an organisation. He wasn't a cartel person. He was an opportunist from Key Biscayne, Florida.'

*

Negotiations went on for a year. Harley had never heard of the mysterious narco The Doc, the reason Luis left the United States in the first place, back in 1988.

'I never saw an indictment out of Tucson. The original prosecutor out of Miami, Pat Sullivan, and another one called Guy Lewis who originally indicted the case, had to deal with the 959 Group. One day these guys showed up after Luis had been brought in and we were starting to debrief him, and I had an altercation with one of them, a *major* discussion in the hallway about them showing up at the 11th-and-a-half hour and telling us how to conduct an investigation.[300] There may have been an indictment out of Tucson and the 959 Group never said anything to me or to Luis.'

Luis was in the FDC for a total of 13 months, three of those in solitary.[301] Situated right in the heart of Miami, it was a 'very accessible place for government agents', so he spent most of his time in interview rooms. One of the people who went to meet him was Barry Clarke of Britain's HMCE.

'I met Luis in Downtown Miami while we were trying to track down the suppliers of the Operation Extend cocaine ring in the UK and he was cooperating as part of the wider Journey case. He had not been on our radar during Extend. We knew that Brian Wright and Nick Fisciatoris had met with people in Paris, Mexico, Venezuela and elsewhere, but not who. Luis had some knowledge of those suppliers and confirmed some details for me – he was a very astute operator.'

He also shared a cell with Richard 'Storyteller' Morrison, an alleged Jamaican drug trafficker who refused to cooperate with the US Government and would wake up early each morning to immediately tie the laces on his tennis shoes so he was prepared in case of a fight.[302]

'We shared a two-man room. A certain bond is created when you room with somebody for months and months. He said to me, "You've gotta be *strapped*." He called tying his shoelaces being strapped. You never know when you're gonna have to fight. How are you going to fight somebody in a pair of fucking slippers? He built a great physique in prison.'

The debriefings dragged on for over a year and Luis wasn't at all confident of being able to convince Harley he wasn't a leader or organiser for the Keys indictment, especially taking into account the *Suerte* bust: the buying of the ships, the elaborate planning of the routes.

'I *was* an organiser. But in my case, those three [sentencing] points meant that instead of seeing my daughter when she was nine and my son when he was six, she would have been 19 and he would have been 16. I would have missed all their years growing up. I was looking at 20 years, possibly 25 or 27 – if not life. If you have two indictments, your sentencing guidelines go through the roof. My big thing was to get out in time so that I could spend time with them and I was with them during their teenage years.'

Some creative thinking was required. Luis's eureka moment was using Francisco Moya – Juanchi – the first name mentioned in the March 1995 indictment (Luis's was second) to his advantage. Luis went to Harley figuring he was going to get slugged hard only on the Florida Keys rap, because he was going to plead guilty to a technicality on the *Suerte* indictment. When a defendant pleads guilty to charges on a US federal indictment, they are prosecuted with what's called an 'information' instead. Put simply, it's a lesser rap.

'I said, "Bob, I will admit to you that all of my life I've been in a leadership role. But on this one [Keys] indictment, Bob, I wasn't. I would not lie to you. I can't afford to lie to you. This was Juanchi's deal. I never wanted to work with these motherfucking Cubans from the Keys; I didn't know these fucking idiots. One day I met them in

San Andrés; they knew my name because Juanchi gave them my name. I had just met them. Juanchi was the organiser on *this* indictment. So on this particular case that I am being nailed on, I was not an organiser. That's the truth.'

Harley didn't say anything.

'He let me sweat it right out.'

*

A couple of days later, Luis got a visit at the FDC from Ruben Oliva. What follows is Luis's recounting of the conversation.

'I got the best news I'd ever want to give you. Bob's going to take off "organiser": the leadership role.'

'I go, "Oh, my God. *Ooowhooah*." That's like if they would have told me, "You're free." I was brought in on one indictment, my first offence. And for being my first offence I got a reduction. In the end they never counted that Venezuela thing as a second offence. It was a one-count information.[303] I supplied information, the indictment's there, but they don't hit you with the full load of the indictment. My guidelines were only based on the Keys case – on one indictment, that's it.'

Says Harley: 'I'm not too sure, it would have been after his extradition to the US, but the [Journey] indictment was dismissed presumably due to his cooperation on the Journey case. As Luis started to cooperate all I did was put in the effort to corroborate what he had to say, verify that he wasn't screwing the government, and then when I got things that I thought were pretty critical I got them to other agents, agencies and prosecutors that I thought would use it to Luis's benefit.

'Most of my own efforts preceded Luis's indictment and arrest, and he cooperated immediately. But in the long run it's really about successful prosecutions for the government. I was honest and frank with him and I gave him the opportunity. I think he saw an opportunity and seized it. He's always been an opportunist. I pretty much made sure Luis got a fair shake. I testified on his behalf for Rule 35. I helped him get ingratiated with agents I thought could use what he had in his brain to help him reduce his sentence. He was on board, fully.'

Ruben Oliva was beaming. According to Luis, his attorney told him: 'So now we can go before the judge and we're looking at 11 years, but with a "5k1" it's nine years and then we can work on the Rule 35. You can be out of here in five years.'

*

What saved Luis from copping a full sentence for the Keys indictment was Section 5k1.1 of the *United States Federal Sentencing Guidelines* (aka a '5k motion' or 5k1, which applies before sentencing) and Rule 35(b) of the *Federal Rules of Criminal Procedure* (which applies after sentencing). In other words: cooperation. Under Rule 35, a term of imprisonment may be reduced 'if the defendant, after sentencing, provided substantial assistance in investigating or prosecuting another person'.

On 30 November 2000 Luis pleaded guilty to conspiracy to import five kilograms or more of cocaine (Docket No. 95-10007-CR-KING) and guilty to conspiracy to possess with intent to distribute five kilograms or more of cocaine on board a vessel subject to US jurisdiction (Docket No. 00-6308-CR-KING). The latter charge carried a maximum term of life and the amount of cocaine involved over the two indictments was 9375.5 kilograms or just over ten tons.[304]

But in exchange for his cooperation, pleading guilty early and accepting criminal responsibility for his conduct, he effectively went in front of the judge on 6 July 2001 as a one-time offender. Luis says the *Suerte* indictment did not count towards his sentence.[305]

'I was caught at the perfect time,' is how he explains it. 'It was the perfect moment. Timing was everything. The government needed cooperation from us. My original sentence was 11 years, and with my 5k1 – reduction before sentencing for the cooperation you've done up to the moment – I got sentenced to nine, *boom*, and then from nine is when you start working on your Rule 35. My Rule 35 gave me a reduction of four years. Why do you think Colombians that traffic such tremendous amounts of coke and kill so many people get out in seven years? Because they do Rule 35. They *all* cut deals. Cocaine is a *business*. Because it's a business at all times, you cut the best deal possible for yourself.

'I was Ruben Oliva's first major case. People were amazed what Ruben did for me, but I got my time off because I was a lot of help and because I was never a violent person. I did five years because I killed nobody. Did I ever order anybody to get killed? *No.* If I'd killed an American citizen I'd still be in jail. If I'd been suspected of killing Colombians, I would probably have done five more.'

The court also granted his request to undergo a drug/alcohol treatment program, which got him a year off his sentence.

'That's why you ask for that. They put you in a separate dorm and you go through the drug/alcohol treatment, which is just bullshit; you go to these classes and they talk about all this shit. Taking on Ruben Oliva was the best thing I did. Nobody could believe the great deal he got for me, and as a result he started getting all the major Colombian drug dealers as clients. Today he's probably the top cooperation lawyer in the country. He'll charge millions for a plea agreement like nothing.'

Things would turn out well for Harley too. Just over a week later, he married his longtime sweetheart Mary at the Hotel Bellagio in Las Vegas. Carol Libbey attended. His father, Robert Sr, was his best man.

65

The Typewriter Room

On 25 August 2001 Colombia's DIJIN, the *Dirección Central de Policiá Judicial e Inteligencia* or Central Directorate of the Judicial Police and Intelligence, launched a raid on two Bogotá apartments owned by Víctor and Miguel Mejía Múnera and used sledgehammers to uncover $35 million in cash that had been hidden behind interior wall cavities, the biggest such discovery in the world at the time.[306] The action came just days after the arrest of The Twins' accountant, Félix 'La Mica' Chitiva. It was the crowning moment of *Operación Horizonte*, a Colombian offshoot of Operation Journey. The money, wrapped in plastic, was stored in $100,000 bundles of $100, $50 and $20 bills. It took eight days to count.

The Mejía Múneras were nowhere to be found, having fled into the jungles of the interior. But soon news would emerge they'd bought for $2 million a paramilitary franchise called *Bloque Vencedores de Arauca* (Arauca Victors Bloc) from paramilitary leader Carlos Castaño Gil. Changing into army fatigues allowed them to smuggle even more cocaine, because being classified as paramilitary commanders rather than actively hunted down as drug lords gave the brothers better protection of their smuggling routes. The reason: the Colombian Government at the time was actively seeking an armistice with paramilitary groups it was fighting in northwest central Colombia, which would culminate in the Justice and Peace

Law (Law 975) of 2005. Bogotá newspaper *El Tiempo* declared the Mejía Múneras had 'mocked the government' by becoming *paras*.

Castaño's ACCU group and The Twins' bloc would be absorbed into another group called United Self-Defenders of Colombia (AUC), a murderous front for drug trafficking that was branded a Foreign Terrorist Organisation by the US Government.[307] After the paramilitaries in the jungles eventually 'demobilised' in their tens of thousands (a large number but not all of them), surrendering arms and confessing to war crimes in exchange for drastically reduced sentences and suitably comfortable 'jails' in which to serve their time, The Twins decided they didn't want to go into custody as part of the deal. They started another criminal enterprise, Los Nevados, and became fugitives.

So it wasn't long before the Mejía Múneras had a $5 million bounty put on their heads by the DOS. In 2004, The Twins were indicted for narcotics trafficking in Washington, DC and in 2007 they were named among the Most Wanted Drug Traffickers by the DOJ and Colombia's Most Wanted by DIJIN. That same year, they were declared Specially Designated Narcotics Traffickers by the USDT.

In 2008, Víctor was killed in a shootout with national police at a ranch over 200 kilometres north of Medellín, while Miguel was captured days later hiding in a secret compartment in a tractor-trailer and extradited from Colombia to the US the following year as a Consolidated Priority Organizational Target of the Organized Crime Drug Enforcement Task Force. He was indicted for multi-ton cocaine loads between 1994 and 2004 and sentenced to 14 years' jail by a New York court in 2016.[308]

*

Before dawn on 5 September 2001, Luis was sent in an air-conditioned bus along with other inmates for the 430-kilometre journey from the FDC to low-security Federal Correctional Institution (FCI), Coleman, outside Orlando.[309] It was the luxury express and Luis went out of the way to avoid the alternative.

'If you're a problem inmate and they want to fuck with you bad, they put you on something called "diesel therapy". That means they put you on a bus from Miami to Seattle, and you hit every fucking county jail there is in between. And that's the worst. Because you have to wake up at three in the morning, the bus takes off at five, you're in a bus all day, then the next day the same thing. That breaks a lot of people.

'You want to do your thing, *boom boom*, and then get assigned to your prison, your home. What prison you go to depends first on your level of security, where you have your family and where you request to go. That's if you're a nice guy and you cooperate. But if you fight the government and say, "Fuck you," and they give you 35 fucking years, you get shipped away wherever they want and they'll ship you to a penitentiary. The inmates own that place; the guards don't. In a US penitentiary you're going into *their* house. A guy that's doing life, what the fuck does he care? You look at him the wrong way, he'll fucking take his fork and put it in your fucking eyeball.'

*

As Luis's fellow prisoners were not the most dangerous felons in America, there was a low risk of being stabbed with a fork in the eyeball or being murdered while asleep in his two- or three-man cell or 'cube'. Was he ever worried about being the victim of a cartel revenge-killing while inside?

'No, *never.* They're not that stupid. You're dealing with smart men here. The cartels have killed a lot of people but they aren't killing Americans or committing more crimes in America to make their situation worse.'

Instead, over the next 108 months he concentrated on his rehabilitation.

'I would sit and type debriefings for hours and send it all to Ruben Oliva. I worked it myself. No attorney can work it for you. You've got to work your case yourself. I was totally dedicated to working on my time reduction.'

Some letters were even written in freehand, in Luis's neat handwriting. He signed each one 'A. Newman'. *A new man.*

'I *was* a new man. Information is knowledge and knowledge is money in this business. And that's why every day I used to rent the typewriter room at Coleman and from two to four I used to write my whole history and send it to Eric Kolbinsky and other agents. I worked hard at what I was doing. That was my job. Ruben did a great job because I did a great job for him. I was constantly sending memos. I sent him 100 to 150 memos to forward to the agents. I was building my whole Rule 35. I was working diligently every day, *typing*, *typing*, *typing*. It was like writing a book.'

He also got visits from the DEA and other agencies.

'It was more historical information that Luis was providing to us,' says DEA agent Eric Kolbinsky. 'Who he had done loads for, how much, when it was, that sort of stuff.'

But again there were no visits from his family, owing to their longstanding visa and passport problems from a decade of being on the run. Juliana and Santi still didn't know Luis was in jail, though he'd write letters and paint pictures for them. But his former Honduran lover from the Navia Gallery in LA, Daniela Villareal, visited often, six to eight times.

'For a year she would fly in from California and stay at a local hotel. For three days at a time she would come in every day at 8am and leave at four. No sex, no nothing. Visiting rights at Coleman is you sit at a table and buy snacks and you talk and you eat. She used to spend three days with me. Everybody there would be freaking out at this fucking beautiful six-foot-tall girl. I'm extremely grateful to her for doing that.'

*

So the obvious question is why, for all the time he was in jail, Luis's family didn't visit him and Patricia couldn't simply fly the 2000 kilometres from Mexico City to Miami. It wasn't like the Navias weren't thinking of him: they wrote him letters and he'd call them whenever he could.

In Mexico, it's a legal requirement that both parents accompany a minor and sign the application for a child's passport before an official. Prior to Luis's arrest in Venezuela, Santi Navia, who was born in Mexico City and was only a toddler, had an expired Mexican passport. Patricia tried to renew it without Luis, who was in Spain at the time, but she needed Luis's authorisation to be able to travel overseas with Santi. Her idea was that Luis could go to the Mexican consulate in Spain and sign a form giving her permission to travel with Santi alone (another legal requirement), but Luis, then in the midst of planning for the *Suerte* smuggle, only had fake passports on him in names that most clearly weren't Navia.

Of course, it was suicide to present a fake passport to a consular official, no matter how well it was made, especially so if Luis and Santi had different surnames on their documents. So Patricia asked a lawyer in Mexico if she could take Santi abroad with a Colombian passport (which he had through her Colombian nationality), but was informed that because her and Luis's son, then only three, was born in Mexico she needed to have him travel on a Mexican one. The former couple was in a bind. So Luis came up with a plan.

Patricia: 'I was told the person I had to see worked in the passport office and you gave them money. I didn't know it was a fake passport; I swear. They gave me the passport; everything appeared exactly as it should.[310] I travelled to Europe with the kids. Santi went to Spain, then he went to Venezuela. We entered Mexico with that passport. Time passed and after everything that happened with Luis in Venezuela, we were supposed to come to the United States to see him in jail.

'So when I went to the American embassy in Mexico City to get Santi's visa for the US – Juliana and I already had our visas – I was really confident about what Luis had told me: that Santi's passport had been issued by people who worked in the passport office. I never thought I was doing anything really wrong. But the Americans called me over and said, "You have a false passport." I said, "That's not possible." Then they found out Luis's name and they asked me why Luis was in jail. I was like, "Oh, my God." I thought everything that was happening had to do with him, but no: it was all because of the passport. None of it was my fault. But maybe I was stupid to follow the orders of my husband.'

Luis: 'They wanted to put Patricia in jail. That was one scary fucking moment. She had to stay in the US Embassy and I had to call Ruben Oliva. He had to pull all these strings, call [prosecutor] Pat Sullivan, and Pat had to call the embassy down there and tell them to keep the Mexicans out of it; that I was of valuable interest to the US Government. They didn't hand her over. Thank God my kids were young. In the end they took her visa, my daughter's visa and they never gave Santi his.'

66

God Exists

WHEN HE WENT INSIDE, Patricia moved to Argentina briefly with the kids to be with her Italian boyfriend, but they broke up and she went back to Mexico City. She was single for a year before she met Ignacio Bargueño, a broker for an investment bank. He was dark featured, handsome, blue eyed, square jawed, moustachioed and permatanned: every inch the total nightmare for any prisoner pining for his estranged wife behind bars.

But by now Luis had accepted everything was over between him and the woman he loved. He was happy that Patricia was with a good man. All he was concentrating on was surviving prison. His old cellmate at the FDC, Richard 'Storyteller' Morrison, would join him at Coleman but be housed in a separate unit. The experience proved much less stressful than Luis expected. Instead of *Escape from Alcatraz* it was more like the garlic-cutting scene in *GoodFellas*: certain luxuries could be had for a price but friendships came free. He hung out with Colombian and Cuban drug smugglers and had a right royal time.

'It was a little scary at first but I thought it was going to be much worse. Prison was the thing I feared most in life but I had the best, *best* time. I know that throughout my years in prison – the worst thing that I thought could possibly happen to me – I had somebody who helped me make those probably the best years. God exists. There's something out there bigger than you that actually cares for you, for whatever reason, and is by your side, helping you out and making these really bad times bearable and good.

'I had great friends all around me. We were fucking cracking up and cracking jokes all the time. I used to sweep the area in front of my unit and got $5.60 a month or something like that. I paid $100 for a bottom bunk. I had a commissary account with $400 a month.[311] A lot of people don't have a hundred bucks in prison; a lot of people don't receive a penny. Fifty bucks is a lot of money in prison. Four hundred was a lot; sometimes you couldn't spend it. A lot of people use their money because they don't want to eat the prison food. That wasn't my experience. I always found the prison food to be good.

'We didn't run the place; it was a federal prison. But whenever they had chicken, we'd buy up all the chicken and have chicken *paella*. We had any kind of food. We never brought in liquor, we never brought in lobster, we never did that; we weren't *ridiculous*. We knew we were in prison. I didn't need to eat a lobster. I've eaten 29,000 lobsters in my life. But I adapted very well and we lived very well. The only thing is we couldn't go nowhere and we weren't getting laid.

'The only person I had sex with while I was in prison was myself. Sex is overrated. You get horny and shit, you start looking at these prison guards. Some of them were nice. I kept notebooks. They all have portraits of naked ladies Scotch Taped onto them. But *fuck*, it gets wild in there. I saw a lot of Puerto Ricans. They tend to be degenerates. They don't care what they fuck. They'll fuck anything.'

For recreation, he played drums in a prison band called Prizm. Finally, after 25 years, his musical career had taken off – it was just behind bars.

'Like the prism of, you know, a triangle, the prism, Pink Floyd.[312] We played rock 'n' roll: Pearl Jam, Bush, Nirvana. I also played for the church choir and the country band. We had great instruments. The feds finance great instruments. I had fucking Pearl drums.'

The only real discomfort he encountered was asleep in his bunk. Luis was having nightmares. He'd often scream in his sleep and have to be woken up by fellow prisoners.

'They would tell me it was happening because of what I'd done in my life and it was like my demons coming back to haunt me, now that

I was away from it all. I don't know [*laughs*]; I don't remember. They thought it was because of the people who had been killed or tortured [during my time as a drug trafficker]. These people didn't really know me, but they figured, "This guy's freaking out and he was in the drug cartels and it's a withdrawal symptom from his past." Again, I don't know. I don't have that much time to be thinking about that shit. I was thinking of how I was going to make a living after I got out.'

*

Luis walked out of prison on 27 July 2005 on supervised release for a term of four years, under which he was forbidden from possessing a controlled substance or any firearms and had to submit to drug tests. He never did the in-jail drug/alcohol program, being released before he was due to start. His conditions were he could not commit another crime, associate with anyone involved in criminal activity or engage in informant or special-agent work without the permission of a court.

Between his conviction and release, September 11 had reshaped the focus of American law enforcement from drugs to terrorism and seen USCS merge with the Immigration and Naturalization Service (INS) and Federal Protective Service (FPS) to become United States Immigration and Customs Enforcement (ICE), under the aegis of the newly formed Department of Homeland Security (DHS).

'Before I knew it, five years were over. They went by quick. When you're sitting in prison, you think, "Fuck, five more years," but you keep yourself busy every day. I never had a sickness, never had a fight, never was picked on, never had issues with any other group, was always in a very good mood, never suffered from depression, always had my case going in the right direction. I was playing drums, I had a reading routine, I was in great health, I exercised a lot, I was in a right frame of mind, had no distractions, I was very *focused*.

'I had to be at my best with my dealings with the US Government, which isn't exactly a pushover; believe me, they're not nice guys. They don't give you any freebies. If you don't earn it, you won't get it. A guy called Randy Richardson picked me up. He worked for Bob Harley down in US Customs in Key West and since Bob was my arresting agent he sent Randy. That's not normal. The warden was freaking out.

They sent an ICE guy to pick me up? I was very fortunate. They could have made me sign deportation papers.'

Though he'd been conferred citizenship through his parents in 1968, Luis had never got around to claiming the official paperwork to prove it – a naturalisation certificate. He'd simply let it lapse, not thinking it would ever become a major issue, and it had become just that.

'Usually when they release you [from jail] into the world, if you can't prove American citizenship either they send you to a detention centre to be deported, or if you're a Cuban – they can't send you back to Cuba – they make you sign deportation papers.[313] That means that when the US opens relations with Cuba [which happened under President Barack Obama], they can send you back. The BOP didn't make me sign that because they thought Randy was there to take me to a detention centre. He wasn't and he didn't think about it. They didn't think he was going to take me to a Best Western and get me a room [*laughs*] so my sister could pick me up the next day. He also gave me a tour of Tampa on the way.'

As she had always been, through thick and thin, Laura was by her brother's side.

'My sons and I picked up Luis in Tampa, and we were so happy to see him.'

Luis can still remember the day she pulled into the car park: 'The first song I heard on the radio when I was driving with my sister and nephews down to Miami was "Sowing the Seeds of Love".'

Laura: 'I was not pleased with his hotel bill. Somehow he had managed to rack up $700 in phone calls in 24 hours.'

It was just another one of Luis's great escapes; perhaps the greatest in all the adventures of the drug world's Mr Magoo.

PART 13
FLICK OF THE SWITCH

67

Everything Kills People

For a 68-ton cocaine conspiracy (of which 25 were seized), Luis serving only five years in jail on charges that could have put him away for life seems outrageous – even if he cooperated. After all, the man transported at least 200 tons of cocaine over the course of his drug-trafficking career.

I ask Robert Harley if critics of these plea deals and light sentences handed out to drug traffickers are justified.

'They're missing the entire point of our criminal justice system. One, if the objective of our criminal justice system is to punish and rehabilitate people, then I'm here to tell you that we've been a success with respect to Luis Navia personally. Two, you cannot buy dope with the Pope. This is my rule. There's no way to make successful big cases with John Q. Citizen.

'The US Government *has* to get in bed with people like Luis Navia to dismantle global organisations. The only way you do that is with a carrot or a stick. So the carrot is we won't use the stick. And that is how you make successful cases. I couldn't tell you exactly how many individual cases, arrests and successful prosecutions Luis's cooperation resulted in, but the value to the US Government in the efficiency of investigations *far* outweighs any need collectively for society to have punished him for a longer period of time. In my world, that's a success story.

'So, in the balance, when you assign value to one direction or the other – either strict punishment or cooperation and doing Rule 35-type work – there's no way around it. There's a cost to incarcerating people and there's a cost to doing unproductive investigations with no information. In the big picture the US Government came out ahead in both respects.

'We punished Luis, incarcerated him, rehabilitated him, put him back out, and we netted *many* successful investigations because of the deal we made with him. It's a cost-benefit approach to jurisprudence. But I know a lot of people resent the fact that he was out in five years.'

Even Luis concedes he was fortunate.

'The criminal justice system is the criminal cooperation system, at least when it comes to the war on drugs.'

*

One of the first things Luis wanted to do when he got out was go down to Mexico City.

'I wanted to reunite with my kids and make it in the real world. I wasn't scared of going back to prison. I was scared of losing what I love most – my kids and family. Before, I had sacrificed them for the business.'

But to do that, he needed a real passport, not one of the seven fakes he'd used while on the run. Throughout his years as a drug smuggler, when using a real passport, Cuban issued, he'd travelled as a resident of the United States with a re-entry permit. So though he was raised and educated in the United States, was granted citizenship in 1968 through his parents, and had an American accent, as far as the BOP and ICE was concerned he was Cuban. He had insufficient American documentation.[314]

'Mary Kramer, my immigration attorney, told me to go to the passport office and show my parents' naturalisation certificates and some other paperwork I had, and give them the whole spiel on how I came to America in 1960. I only had photocopies. My alien registration card had a picture of me when I was five years old and the lady behind the counter said, "Yes, that looks like you," stamped the form and told me to take a seat. "You'll have your passport shortly."

I just happened to hook up with the person that looked at all of my paperwork and accepted what I said. Nobody could believe it. Ruben Oliva told me, "That's America! Today was the day your planets aligned again. Hold on to that passport, Luis, and don't you ever lose it, because you'll never get another one that easily."'

Luis, out of prison clothes and in his new garb of aviators and khakis, met his family in the lobby of a hotel in Zona Rosa.

'It was beautiful,' he says, with nostalgia. 'Patricia brought Santi and Juliana to the hotel and of course I was at a group of payphones at the side of the lobby in front of the gift shop. As usual I was working the payphones. It was an incredible moment, very emotional, a lot of happiness. Santi was kind of lost because he would talk to me on the phone but he had never really seen me. I had always told my kids that I was working out my immigration issues to be able to travel to Mexico, and their immigration issues to be able to travel to the US. So he'd been very small the last time we saw each other. Juliana was very happy too but she was more wary of me.'

For Santi it was effectively the first time he'd met his father: 'When we parted I was three, so I didn't have much of a memory of him. I grew up without him there but I knew he was *somewhere*. I was excited. I'd only found out he was coming the day before, so there was no preparation. I was wearing my school uniform. And I saw him and he looked just like the pictures I'd seen. I'd only really seen him in pictures since I was a baby. "Shit, that's *him*." We walked up to each other and hugged. It was a great feeling. I was very happy. My mom left and then we went up to his hotel room and I had to do some homework and he was helping [*laughs*].'

Patricia: 'They were happy but Juliana was a little bit weird. It wasn't easy for Juliana and Santi. They grew up not having a normal attachment to their father. I never knew when they were going to be reunited again. With Luis gone, Ignacio had become the father of my kids. Juliana would say to him: "You're going to walk me down the aisle when I get married." But I never let them forget their real father. I always put a photo of him next to their beds. They needed to know that they had a father; that he was a good person; that he loved them.

'I always spoke highly of Luis. In Latin America, when people get divorced things can get nasty. But I think you always have to be civilised. So it wasn't like they saw him last week and they were speaking to him again today. When kids don't see their father for such a long time it's natural there is going to be stilted conversation.'

Juliana: 'When my mom first told me he was coming, at first I was like, "*What?* What do you mean?" I started crying. It was like this ball of emotion that came over me. I just didn't believe it. I was crying but I also didn't know how to feel. I would talk to him on the phone, but it's not the same. I always had an *idea* of my dad because Ignacio was my father figure. So for me he was this person that would call me on the phone or I'd get cards from him.

'When we finally met at the hotel I was standoffish because this was someone I was supposed to know and have a connection with and I didn't feel like that. I could see how excited he was to see me and he was very happy and loving, but I just didn't have that connection. It had fallen away. I had become used to my father being this faraway figure and I was okay with it. It wasn't something that was missing.'

*

Luis stayed in Mexico City a week, using a taxi from his hotel to drive Santi and Juliana to school and taking them out to dinner and tenpin bowling. If the kids pressed him on why he'd been gone so long, he just stuck to the story: he'd been having 'immigration problems'.

Juliana: 'I felt wary of him. I didn't really understand why immigration problems could be so big for my dad not to be with us. I have memories of me when I was little getting into a fight with my mom, and I would just cry and want my dad to be there. I would sometimes pretend to be calling him on the phone. "I'm on the phone with my dad!" And obviously I wasn't. It was really hard.

'I remember this one time I was in third grade and it was Father's Day. And even though I had Ignacio [as a stepfather] it wasn't the same. And there was this song they made us memorise about your dad – 'Hoy Tengo Que Decirte Papá' ['Today I Have to Tell You Dad'] – and I'd just *cry, cry, cry, cry.* I would sing it, hold my tears back, then just go to the bathroom and cry. I also had a book in first grade that they gave us – this big, thick book, a Father's Day gift, 100 blank pages – but I didn't have anyone to give it to. So every Saturday or Sunday when I was feeling really sad, I'd think about my dad and write him letters.'

Understandably, given everything she had been through, Patricia also had mixed feelings of her own seeing Luis just turn up after being away so long.

'I looked at him and my first thought was, "Oh, my God. He's become shorter." [*Laughs*] You know when people take a pill and it makes them shrink? He looked so old: short and old. That was my first impression. That's the *truth.* "I can't believe I was married to him. He's so fat and so old." [*Laughs*] In that moment it was different. When a man is young, at 30, 35, 40, 42, 43, they look the same; you're not going to see much difference. Luis wasn't like that anymore.'

*

Reintegrating into Miami society was easier than Luis expected. His family stuck by him and no friends walked away from him for his drug past; as he tells it, it was an open secret that he worked in the drug trade.

'Everyone knew me from what I was before; they all knew what I was into. I came back and I was the same guy I've always been. The business never changed me.'

His family's travel ban was eventually overturned through the US embassy in Mexico City and ICE, and Santi came to Miami for Christmas in 2008, with Juliana following shortly thereafter. Luis would play them Neil Young's 'Cinnamon Girl' and 'Ohio' in the car. That same year both his children received US citizenship. For the next three years, Luis was just a regular single dad in Miami raising two small kids – except he was also making up for lost time. Unlike everyone else, they still knew nothing of his narco past.

'When they went to live with him in Miami, he cooked for them and he treated them like they were babies,' laughs Patricia. 'Sometimes he treats Santi like a baby; he forgot he's not a baby. He's very protective of them.'

Luis: 'I took them to school every morning. They did their first communion. I signed them up to do catechism. Took them to rowing practice. Took my son to karate and all the karate championships. I was really into it with him. I'd cook dinner for them every night, make them breakfast, make their school lunch. They lived with me. Patricia gave me that. It gave her a little time to have her relationship with Ignacio.'

Clearly your children mean everything to you, Luis. So you can't avoid this: What would you say to someone who had lost a child to cocaine? (In 2019 the son of one of Luis's cousins had overdosed on cocaine cut with fentanyl, which had rattled him and made him deeply uncomfortable when he attended the funeral.)

'I am sincerely sorry; I am. But the reality is you could have lost them to an automobile accident, you could have lost them to an overdose of Xanax, you could have lost them to a bad vaccine. In my opinion, alcohol is worse than cocaine. What are we supposed to tell the parents of a kid who loses his life because he was drinking? Go sue Johnnie Walker Black?'[315]

Do you feel remorse?

'Not completely. I don't feel any remorse for trafficking cocaine. I did something illegal not something *immoral*. Look at the people who smuggled pot and now it's legal. Legality has nothing to do with morality. I don't swallow that for a fucking minute. Slavery was legal. Today, people pay their workers $5 an hour or less. They're worse than anybody. I would have been immoral if I'd tortured people, stolen from people, killed people to steal from them, been a liar, brought some Albanian girls as hookers on a ship that was coming back empty from transporting a load to Europe. I didn't do any of that. I consumed my own product. I *believed* in my product.

'Where I feel remorse is for the pain I caused my family and those families that have suffered from or lost a loved one to cocaine abuse. I should have studied, become a professional and not gotten involved in that business. So my answer is how can you feel complete remorse if you did that for 25 years? I was totally convinced that it was my business and it was a good business and we were providing a product that society *wants*.

'It's an entertainment product. Did Joseph Kennedy feel any remorse for the victims of overdosing on alcohol?[316] *No*. Do the cell-phone companies feel any remorse because some motherfucker got cancer of the brain from using a cell phone? *No*. Do the pharmaceutical companies feel remorse because they put out a drug called OxyContin and half the nation got hooked on fucking heroin because of that? *No*. It's a *product*. God put the coca plant on this earth. It's just that some fucking degenerate white man went to Peru and made it into a powder and put it up his nose, when it was never intended to be used that way. *Everything* kills people.'[317]

68

Team America

'WHEN I GOT OUT OF PRISON, my family still lived in Mexico and I could have gone back to Mexico or Bolivia or Ecuador and with what I knew about how the system, DEA and other agencies work, and their limitations, I could have lived in Bolivia and done small loads to Europe – where even if my connection there got caught, there would be little chance of Europeans coming for me in Bolivia.[318]

'Europeans are not proactive like Americans in going after people overseas. Also American prosecutors are not taking cases where the dope does not end up in the United States. Working big and being part of the largest multinational smuggling operation with Los Mellizos brought the heat and problem to me. So knowing that, if I'd wanted to get back into the business I would have established some kind of legal business and worked small: 30 kilos every 90 days to Europe or Eastern Europe and net for myself $300,000 every 90 days. Exporting it and making it into another country is easy. It's the selling that has become a little difficult. But I didn't want that – my drug days were over.'

*

Over the following years Luis went down to Colombia and Panama dozens of times and quite judiciously won't reveal exactly what business he was involved in, or his precise role in the war on drugs beyond his Rule 35 efforts. The information remains strictly classified.

But he has cogent words of advice for any ex-narco contemplating going over to the other side.

'Undercover work, what they call joining "Team America", is effectively drug dealing with a licence.[319] If things go well a source can make a lot of money; you're rocking 'n' rolling. You're back in the drug business; you're a drug dealer again, at a high level. You're not an informant in Miami, dealing grams – you're dealing with major loads and shit like that. But don't think the DEA sets you up and you're covered with beautiful IDs.

'You don't have a badge. It's your responsibility to report if you see anything of interest. They just throw you out there. You've got to work that shit yourself. They do jack shit. You live or die. A drug dealer knows what he's in for. It's crazy out there. I think the drug business is a great business. It's a moneymaking business – but with big money comes big risks. The problem is there are too many informants and your life expectancy is very short. If you want to be in the drug business you're playing with fire. When I started in cocaine there were not nearly the amount of informants out there, and the DEA did not have the kind of information they have today: all of which they have gathered over the course of the last 30 years. It's not the same game from when I was involved; if you're in the drug business now, chances are you'll get burned.'

Depending on who pays the bill, good money can be made being a so-called 'asset' – the rewards are lucrative, in the millions – but payment is often held up by bureaucracy and paperwork. It is believed, however, that the DEA caps payments to informants at $250,000.[320] The really big money for ex-narcos is working privately on Rule 35s for cartel leaders already in prison.

'There's a lot of money on the table. If you're well hooked up, you can do it. It's the exception, not the norm. If you wait for the DEA to pay you you're fucking dead in the ground. They might ask an informant to go out there to be a drug dealer, but they don't finance him like a drug dealer. With Rule 35s, money can be made from another angle. It's the guy in jail who pays. Informants get a retainer and they go to work. But it's not as easy as it sounds. To keep it legal you need the defendant's [case] agent and prosecutor to approve this "third-party cooperation". This approval is becoming tougher to get from prosecutors. It largely hinges on defendants with money being able to effectively "buy" their freedom.

'When it is approved, sometimes the guy in jail has the information and they need feet on the ground: a sharp person to carry through the operation and be a liaison between DEA agents and the operation itself. The informant has to work hand in hand with the DEA and a lot of people simply don't get on with agents. So the informant has to have their trust. The guy in jail will hire a person who knows the business and won't get agents pissed off or double deal. It's legal but it's a grey area; the best thing is not to do it.

'Team America work is the other side of the coin. Supposedly one is legal and one is not. It's a business. You're still working for the same dollar. An informant has got to be able to flick that switch. When they go completely to the other side, it's a complete 180; but they're still at the same side. Personally, I can be Mexican, Colombian, cop, narco, bad guy, good guy, [American] Indian, cowboy. It's all the same shit to me. I've been in this business 45 years: 25 one way, 20 the other.'

Luis agrees the DEA is more prepared to risk the lives of ex-narcos and civilian Colombians and Mexicans in the war on drugs than its agents in the field. A lawyer representing major cartel figures in Miami told me: 'The American criminal justice system runs on informants. That's what it relies on.'

'Why risk the life of an agent when the DEA can just risk the life of somebody that's not an agent?' says Luis. 'Government agents don't risk their lives. Nobody's going to kill them. Colombian cartels know exactly who works for the DEA, ICE or FBI. They've got all that information, they've got all their data, but they're not going to kill one of them because if they do kill an American the DEA is going to go after them immediately. So that's going to put an end to your business.

'The cartels let DEA agents exist. They know what clubs they go to, they've got hookers working that fuck 'em. Agents have got it made in the shade. They get double pay when they're in Colombia. They live like kings down there. They're white guys with great moustaches; they're getting laid left and right. They carry a gun and a badge and they have a great time. And *everyone* knows they're a DEA agent.

'I'd tell any Colombian who's considering going to the other side, "You better know what you're doing being an informant because you're definitely disposable if you're not American." The DEA can't go around losing the life of an American. That's a major fuck-up and a major career block. That's why they'd rather use Colombians. Most of these confidential informants or CIs are Colombian.

'There have been meetings where the Colombian [CI] thinks he's signed up when he's not really signed up. It's really a no-lose situation for the agency. It's tricky. A lot of these Colombians are doing it so they can get their visa, but the DEA is right upfront with them: they don't guarantee anything. If you do something spectacular, yeah, they'll put in for some money and a visa but in the meantime it's a case of "See what you can do". They send them out there and they have to come up with *something*.

'You can't have a source who's a *gringo*, who's an American citizen, and because of your recklessness he gets killed. Then you've got a problem. Then you've got a *career* problem. That's why when a DEA source goes down there [to South America] they have to be very careful. A DEA agent can't just tell them, "Hey, go down to Colombia and get fucking killed." That agent will be doing paperwork for the next ten years and they'll be doing it out of somewhere like Bumfuck, Utah.'

69

Smoke and Mirrors

IT WASN'T UNTIL 2009 when Juliana was 15 and Santi 12 that they found out about what Luis did for a living between 1978 and 2000. He and Patricia, who a year later with Ignacio was given a permanent residency visa to join her children in Miami, had been putting it off for as long as possible.

'We were afraid because they didn't grow up in that kind of [narco] life; they went to an American school in Mexico City,' says Patricia. 'I'd always told them not to smoke, not to do drugs, and being their father Luis was so worried to tell them; like *crazy worried* about what they were going to think of him.'

Says Luis: 'I told them because there's no reason why a father shouldn't see their kids for five, six years. You just don't fucking disappear for six years. I was truthful with them. I didn't want them to think that their dad didn't visit them because their dad was out partying in Europe and not thinking of them.

'So I sat them both down and said, "Listen, I have to be truthful with you guys because I don't want you to think I never loved you or I put you on a second level or you were second to anything. The reason I didn't see you for six years is that I was in jail. I couldn't visit you because I *couldn't* visit you. I went to prison for a situation that you can google my name and find out. It was a mistake I made in life.

'"When I was younger I got involved in some illegal business and in the end because of some business dealings in Greece, they finally caught me and I went away. That's why I didn't see you. I love you both most in life. I couldn't see you because physically I was in jail and could not get out. The only thing I ever thought about while I was in jail was you guys."'

As a 12-year-old boy, Santi absorbed the news reasonably well – there's some coolness cachet having a cartel figure as a father, even though he never let anyone know about it – but Juliana didn't receive it kindly.

Juliana: 'I never told any of my friends or anything. In Miami I knew a couple of people whose parents used to be in the cartels, but it wasn't something that we talked about. I did know this one boy whose father actually knew my father – he was part of the Cali Cartel – and he would always brag about how his dad was in the cartel, how he was in prison in Orlando, and this was before I found out about my dad. I always thought it was super-weird that he would talk about that.

'Somehow jail came up with Dad. I was like, "You weren't there for us." I would get really mad when Dad would reprimand me because in my mind I always had that idea he didn't have the *right* to reprimand me and my brother because he didn't raise us. In my mind the only person who could yell at Santi and me was my mom. And then my dad exploded: "I wasn't there for you not because I didn't want to be there for you but because I *couldn't* be there for you. I was in jail!"

'I stopped and I stared and I was like, "Oh, my God." I was shocked. It was a big, *big* change for me to come to Miami to live with my father, someone I didn't really know; I was 15. I was going through all sorts of changes. Deep inside of me, and I still feel this way, I kind of resented my dad for not being there my whole life. And it's not his fault. But me finding out that jail was the reason he wasn't there for me kind of put a small dent in our relationship at first. Then, as time went by, finding out he went to jail made me understand more why he hadn't been there; it made things better. Not that I approve of what he did because I don't. But it kind of gave me peace in a sense because I knew the real reason.'

Patricia: 'Juliana needed time to understand. In the beginning, she wasn't okay. There was distance between her and Luis and she was judging him in some ways. I told her, "A lot of people make mistakes; we all make mistakes. You need time to recover from this but your father paid a price. He loves his liberty." Now, because she took the time to know him, I think finally she can be okay with her father. Luis is a great father; an amazing father. He missed a lot of their childhood and I think that makes him really sad, mostly because he missed Santi growing up.'

Luis's nephew Andrés is one family member who isn't totally convinced Luis and Patricia played it right.

'I always thought it was very weird that his children were shielded from this, relatively significantly, up until they moved to the US and then things were kind of explained.'

But Luis is unapologetic: 'That's what you do. How are you going to tell a six-year-old kid you're in jail? Why would you tell them that? What benefit is that going to bring? I'm the one who knows when they're ready and they were ready at the right time.'

So what lesson do you think you passed on to your kids?

'They've *seen* it. You don't become a drug trafficker nowadays. Today is not the right time for drug trafficking. That era is over. Part of the reason I did what I did was timing. Everything in life is timing. I happened to be in a situation where all the dots connected perfectly. I became a drug trafficker at the highest level because I started at the highest level with Bia Gálvez and the Medellín Cartel: suitcases full of millions of dollars. It's a money game. If Bia had been dealing grams I would never have continued in the drug business. I could make more money selling life insurance. I wasn't living in a fucked-up apartment in Hialeah full of cockroaches. I never had to go out and sell grams in Liberty City [a working-class neighbourhood in Miami with a high concentration of African Americans]. I was hit, like, *boom*. Studio 54. Learjets. That's why I got into it. I'm not ashamed of what I did.

'So yeah, I wasn't a doctor or a lawyer; my kids accept that. We now have a great relationship. They think I'm a gifted person in the sense that I can play both worlds: the legal business world and the other thing. And while I was in the other thing I still maintained a very straight persona and image. They admire me in the sense of, "There's nothing you can tell my dad that he hasn't seen or hasn't done."'

Juliana: 'I know Dad loves me and I love him. I feel I judged Dad harshly at the beginning and even now I feel like I'm kind of harsh on him just because sometimes I don't like the attitude he takes. Yeah, he has some things to be proud of but I don't like the fact he flaunts [his cartel associations]. It bothers me that he's flaunting something like that. He loves the rush. He's very easygoing. I admire a lot of the traits that my dad has. He did an amazing job with me and my brother; especially with me back then. I could be a big pain and he had all the patience in the world. We have very similar personalities. It was just nice to see myself in my dad.

'When I think that he missed mine and Santi's childhood it makes me really sad. My dad is the best dad in the world. For everything he's gone through and we've gone through [as a family], he could have easily forgotten about us and not cared. I think it's something super-respectable and admirable that the first thing he did when he got out [of jail] was to get his papers in order to come to see us in Mexico and bring me and my brother to Miami. He always put his family first; he always did it for his family. Yeah, he made a lot of mistakes. But he always had our best interests at heart. And I think that's everything that my dad does: he does it with the interests of my brother and me at heart.

'I think what my dad needs to get from this whole experience [of writing the book] is to get his drinking under control, because I feel a lot of the mistakes that happened in his life could have been avoided if he wasn't drinking. I see a pattern over and over that is affecting his life: whether it's Mom and Isabelle or me and my brother. He needs to get healthier. I also know I need to be nicer to him and not to be so judgemental. I'm very proud of him. Nobody's had the life that he's had. It's an unbelievable life and he should be proud of it. I just feel he thinks of those people that ran the cartels as role models or as heroes. But they're not. And I feel that's something that he needs to realise.'

*

Luis, what do you think Juliana and Santi would say is your best quality as a father?

'That I'm always thinking of them, that I do everything for them, that I think of them first, and I struggle to make it better in life to give them a better life, and to show them that hard work and discipline goes a long way. I make every effort for them to have a good education so they can become professionals and I would never, *ever* tell them to get into the drug business. I've always been good to my kids, I've always been good to their mother, and I've always been good to everybody around me in the drug business. Yes, it was illegal but I've always been very honest in my illegal business – unlike a lot of people who are very dishonest in their legal business.'

When you were a drug trafficker do you think you failed them as a father?

'*Yes*. The minute Juliana was born, that's it; I should have quit. Thank God nothing happened but I put everybody in danger by being in that business. I should have bought a couple of McDonald's franchises and laid back. Patricia would have been completely supportive if we'd done that. She never knew about my excessive spending. She never had control over the money. I should have said, "Sweetheart, stash it all. Don't let me spend." But I didn't have a game plan or a life plan. That's what I tell Juliana and Santi: "You've got to have a life plan." The cocaine business is all a bunch of smoke and mirrors. In the end you're going to get super-fucked. It's not a totally bad business, it's just high risk; I have a lot of nostalgia for it.'

70

The Forbidden Apple

FOR A MAN WHO ESCAPED DEATH so many times, life after jail was not so kind to Luis and he suffered a string of personal tragedies and hardships.

Patricia's and Ignacio's move to Miami to be with Luis, Juliana and Santi saw them have a son, Sebastián, a year later.[321] But Sebastián was only two when Ignacio, aged 50, suddenly and unexpectedly passed away. The circumstances cannot be divulged.

'He was an excellent man,' says Luis. 'I was so fortunate to have him in my life. What hurt me so much about Ignacio dying was that my kids lost a great, *great* father. He was a killer-looking guy. He should have been in fucking Mexican soap operas. He was the opposite of me. I'm social havoc. I pray to Ignacio every night. I've cried for Ignacio more than I have for my dad.'

At time of writing, Sebastián was nine and Luis had taken the small boy under his wing. Fully bilingual, he's a bright, intelligent, even brilliant child; and Luis dotes on him.

Says Patricia: 'Luis has a very special relationship with Sebastián. I think it's because of all the time Luis missed with Santi. He didn't see Santi from the age of three through to nine. I don't see him as a father. For Sebastián, his father figure is Santi. But Luis is very special to Sebastián, for sure. Sebastián loves him.'

Luis, however, sees himself as a father to Sebastián 'without a doubt'.

Who's right? I don't know, though Patricia is best placed to say. But on a personal level it's very touching to witness this veteran tough-guy narco be so fond of and clearly disarmed by a child who is not even of his own blood. It says a lot about Luis's character and his goodness that he regards it as his moral duty to be the boy's guardian when his real father, Ignacio, cannot be here.

When I had dinner with the Navia family at Patricia's home in Brickell, Luis spent a lot of time with Sebastián talking about mathematics and aliens. Patricia's new husband, David Donald, a rock musician, was away on tour.[322] The evening was totally normal, apart from a social call midway through from one of Luis's old cartel friends in Colombia: one of the big bosses who'd done his time and was now a free man. It was akin to getting a call from Tony Soprano. When Luis answered his cell phone in Spanish, his voice changed. It became much deeper, more *macho*. He left the room to continue the conversation. His past – as much as he was trying to escape it – was still very much a part of his life. It would always be with him.

'I consider Sebastián my son. In the first week in catechism when he was seven, we asked him, "What do you think, God and all this?" and he goes, "Oh, it's all fake news. It's all different dogma presented in different ways just to take money from the different groups. Religion is a business. It's all fake news."

'Sebastián's lived experiences that you and I have never lived. He's seen things. His soul has been opened to dimensions we don't know. His father died unexpectedly and he understood that at age six. And when you understand things like that, your mind starts to try to find answers elsewhere; places where you and I have never had to go to, thankfully – maybe unthankfully. Maybe if more people suffered more intense situations, then they wouldn't be such idiots and such morons.'

So why was it okay for him to find out about his dad's death so early and your kids not to find out you were in jail?

'You couldn't hide Ignacio's death because there was a mass, the parents and everybody – it's obvious. My kids were in Mexico. They had no reason to know. They spoke to me every day. Sebastián never spoke to his dad again. You can't say, "Your dad's on vacation."

In that kind of situation you've got to break out because there ain't no coming back. *Remember* – I was coming back.'

*

In 2017, Luis's mother, María, died aged 95. As with the death of his father, Luis Sr, it left him with some conflicted feelings, though there had always been great love between them.

'She was the one who brought us up. I'm not going to say she was a bad mother. But her style maybe wasn't the kind of style I needed to make me into a more formed and disciplined individual. My mother was not that disciplined. She never worked. A lot of mothers that had a rich husband, like she did, always wanted to go out and do something on their own. She wasn't like that. Is it good or is it bad? I can't say. It is what it is. But maybe that wasn't the best type of mother a person like me needed.

'My mother knew what I was doing; it was *obvious* what I was doing because I was living in Bogotá. She used to go see me down there because she was my mother; she loved me unconditionally. She knew I had some illegal moneys coming in, yeah, but also she felt I was involved in legal business. She didn't want to realise the whole picture and I gave her no reason to realise it; to her I was a very respectable legal businessman that had a lot of money, though she worried she would one day get a phone call that I was dead. She'd tell me, "This is not the type of thing to do forever, just get out. Get out while you're ahead." But I didn't listen to anybody.'

So when you look back on your life, who do you feel loved you the most?

'Laura. My sister has always had an unconditional love for me, in good or bad, you know [*pauses*]. It was only the two of us siblings. She's always been there for me, even at my lowest. *Totally*. I love her two sons, my nephews, Martin and Andrés, as if they were my own. She and my mother never saw the nastiness of the business.'

Laura: 'We never knew the reality, the true extent, of Luis's business. We were in la-la land when it came to this. Honestly, we were somewhat stupid. After what I know now, I look back and am disgusted. The writing was on the wall, but I guess we didn't want to admit the truth to ourselves. Luis's past business and life is not an easy subject for me. It brought my family so much pain and anguish that I have asked my brother on numerous occasions not to bring up the past. He is lucky to be able to start a new life.'

Andrés: 'My uncle's eccentric. He tends to put his foot in his mouth, speaks before he thinks, says things to be outrageous, likes to push buttons. When you have an argument with Luis, come at him with the truth and expect to have a discussion about it, he'll fly off the rails and you'll have a fight. But within an hour or two he's calling to apologise. He's got a very good heart but the maturity of a 25-year-old – maybe less [*laughs*]. My mother, Laura, is probably the complete opposite. More measured; a more sensitive personality. They couldn't be more different in that regard. They're probably polar opposites. My mother took care of my grandmother right up until the very end. My grandmother didn't want to be put in a home and my mother made sure that wish was honoured and took care of her with the help of some nurses. She was with her every single day.'

Laura: 'Luis is outgoing, loud, and speaks his mind; quite an extrovert. He's ever the life of the party; an anything-goes kind of person which in the right setting can be a lot of fun. In spite of his boisterousness and mischievousness, he's always a noble person. He's very loyal and is a good friend. Luis is more like my mother, whereas I am more like my father. I'm a quiet, reserved individual.

'I want to say that Luis and I had the same upbringing; however, being a woman at that time, I was held to a very different standard. There were different expectations at the time. Luis was given opportunities I was not given. Had I had the chance to go to Georgetown instead of him, I know I would have made the most of that incredibly privileged situation, which he squandered to party. Luis got away with things I would never have.'

*

Luis's relationship with Isabelle Meneses came about when she threw him a party on leaving jail in 2005. They'd known each other for decades, meeting the first time as teenagers, and she has never made any secret of her disapproval of Luis's criminal career. She never knew Luis when he was a cocaine trafficker but opened her heart to him when he came out of prison. She was totally against him doing this book and was the only person in his inner circle apart from his nephew Martin who would not be interviewed.

'I fell in love with Isabelle the day I met her,' says Luis. 'She was like the girl your mother tells you is the kind of girl you should marry: beautiful, very intelligent. She says the biggest crime I committed was not getting out of the drug business the day I had my first child: exposing my kids to that shit.'

Luis now has a strained relationship with Isabelle's family because of his drinking and has 'said a couple of things that insulted the whole family and I really fucked up'. On one occasion she straight up called him a 'functioning psychopath'. He's *persona non grata* at Meneses family events.

As he puts it pithily: 'I ate the forbidden apple, which was bringing up my past in front of her family.'

*

Throughout the writing of *Pure Narco* I couldn't help but think Luis retained lingering feelings for Patricia – not necessarily romantic, but a deeper, loving attachment. It would be understandable, given what she did for him as a wife and continues to do as a presence in his life. The regret he feels for what he put her through must be hard to live with sometimes.

Their daughter, Juliana, regards her as a hero: 'I think my mom did an amazing job by always keeping my dad's image in my brother and me. I always had a picture of my dad on my nightstand and we had photo albums of him. Any time I would bring him up or ask about him, she was always there to tell me stories about him. She would *never* avoid the topic. I don't know anyone else who would do that for their kids with their dad being in that situation. I could understand if my mom didn't want to talk about it. But she did. She didn't want us growing up thinking we didn't have a dad, even though he wasn't there. He was always there in my mind. If it wasn't for her I feel that it wouldn't have been as easy as it was for my brother and I to go back into a relationship with him.'

Luis agrees: 'Patricia did such an incredible job with the kids. She was the key – not just in the way she handled them but always speaking good about their dad. I'm sure she went through some really tough times, and in the toughest moments is when she proved how amazing she is. She continues to be beyond amazing. There's not enough I can say about the quality of woman that Patricia is. I've been blessed to have her as the mother of my kids.'

Do you still love her, Luis?

'Yes, in the true sense of the word. She is the mother of my kids and I realise that I've been very fortunate and blessed to have her in my life, but we could not live together as man and wife. But I probably love her more now than ever before.'

Patricia: 'You don't stop loving people but you start loving them differently. I love Luis, of course. I care about him, of course. But I also love his girlfriend. She's amazing. Isabelle's the best person in the world for him. I tell him, "You have to take care of her," if they have a fight or something. "If you break up with her, I'm going with her." I'd take her side, not his.'

71

There Is No War

PART OF HELPING THE US GOVERNMENT fight the war on drugs, of course, is testifying against your former associates. For decades it's been an accepted part of the cocaine business that when American law enforcement is circling, or a cartel has already been brought down, negotiation and counternegotiation in and out of the courtroom is all part of the game.[323] Luis has been called up as a witness in some major cases that went to trial.

'I spoke the truth. The government let me go under the condition that I would help them in the future and I kept my word to them. They respect that. When I testified against a former associate – I won't name him – I told the court he was my friend, that he was always a gentleman. I could have sat anywhere in the courtroom and I went and sat right behind him and we spoke. He turned to me and said, "I appreciate that you've been truthful."

'With another associate I looked at him straight in the face and I testified, right then and there. He stole a trip from me and I assumed a million-dollar debt; most of the debt was my profit. I've always been very truthful in court. In that case, that individual got what he deserved. It's over, buddy. Wake up. Smell the coffee.

'While I was in the business I was under the threat of death every day of my life. If you lost a load, we're going to kill you. If you don't pay us, we're going to kill you. So, okay, kill me now for testifying.

I'm not scared of dying for being involved. I've been under the "You're gonna die" cloud for 20 fucking years: the cloud of death, torture and possible fucking life imprisonment. So what's more "You're gonna die" cloud? That's how I look at it. If you're scared of dying, then don't get involved in this business. What the fuck's wrong with you? You're not joining a fucking convent. You're joining a drug cartel.

'The cartels are winning forever and ever. There is no war. It's *nothing*. It's all a big joke. It's a big pay cheque for the people in the DEA. They are not stopping drugs at all. The only way to stop the drug trade is when cocaine in South America is more expensive than cocaine in North America. To me, the DEA is a private enterprise involved in drugs but with permission to do so. The DEA is the fourth cartel and they are as powerful as they are because of the information they have. They could never get this far with good old-fashioned police work. *Impossible.*

'The DEA's perfect scenario is to grab a guy who thinks he's hot, a boss, and they offer him leniency, no jail time, citizenship, if he cooperates, so they can catch a bunch of people. What they want to do is look at the networks working inside their country. For example, find a guy in Colombia who's sending shit to Mexico. Tell him you have a G2.[324] [The DEA will] put up the plane, they'll put up *everything*.

'You [the informant] go down there, the Colombian guy puts up the 2000 kilos to put on that G2, they'll fly it over to Mexico (they've got their own pilots), then they'll work the local contacts and work the case for three or four months, and all those phone numbers they get – Joe calling Bill and Bill calling Peter – before you know it, they've got tremendous intel on the [drug-trafficking] network going on in their country.

'The only way to do that is through true infiltration. Police work is very difficult. Starting from scratch and being a policeman? *No*. You've got to have a guy who's an ex-drug dealer who knows somebody that knows somebody that knows somebody that *connects* you. And then you've got to watch out. You can't paint it too fucking pretty because then everybody will know it's a set-up. That's the only way police agencies work. It's the only way they're going to have big arrests and be able to justify a pay cheque. That they end up doing some damage? *Yes.*

They put away whoever is working at the time. But soon enough somebody else comes in and takes their place [*laughs*]. It's a no-brainer.

'America will never win the war on drugs. This is all *bullshit*. The drug business is growing because of simple economics. I remember when people used to send 100 kilos of cocaine like it was some incredible thing. The Mexican loads today are 20,000 kilos at a shot. When I started, the Medellín Cartel was at its peak. When I ended, the Medellín Cartel was nowhere, it was dead. Five fucking cartels – Medellín, Cali, Northern Valley, Coast, FARC – went down the drain. The Mexican cartels took off like fucking bats out of hell.

'The Colombians now are working to India, Sri Lanka, China, Europe, Australia. It's harder to get cocaine from Colombia to China than Colombia to Miami, obviously, but the amount of money coming into Colombia is still *unbelievable*. The profits are through the roof. The Colombians left the US market to the Mexicans – they send the Mexicans the coke but they let the Mexicans handle distribution. It's incredible what's coming into the US. I'm not saying there aren't Colombian groups working the US – they're doing it through the Caribbean: Haiti, the Dominican Republic – but today it's all about globalisation. Everything is about distribution and consumption and getting it to the end user, as it always has been. The business will never end. It will *never* end. People will never stop doing drugs. Cocaine is a nasty drug but it's a great business. It will be around forever.'

*

I ask Luis what he'd do if he were in charge of American drug policy and what he'd do to end the war on drugs. Interdiction or interception of drugs from source to the street doesn't seem to be working. Nothing does. In 2016, the US Government spent $4.7 billion on interdiction efforts in Central America – nearly 20 per cent of the total federal budget for drug control.

'The key is education. Education can lower the numbers of people consuming drugs, but there has to be better educational programs so people avoid becoming addicted to alcohol and hard drugs in the first place. We have had educational programs in place for 30 years now but consumption of drugs is still growing.

'We have a country of 300 million. You can't do here what you do in a country of 30 million; those lower population numbers are manageable on a social level. Lower population and fewer drug users means drug-rehabilitation programs are easier to implement. So there has to be a change in mentality here in the United States. We need to try to make the whole sequence a lot less violent in all aspects. To get a better hold of and control on the tremendous violence that is associated with the transport, distribution and selling of cocaine, you need to decriminalise.

'Now I could take the dollar figure that it would cost to buy all the coca leaf [in South America], and buy all the coca leaf there for a lot less money than it takes to run the DEA. You take $3 billion, buy up all the coca leaves in Colombia and Peru, and burn it. That's *it*. There's no cocaine for anybody. There's no cocaine this year, motherfucker. Do it through the Department of Agriculture, so you're not buying cocaine, the powder; you're buying the leaf, an agricultural product.

'I told this to the US Government in a debriefing. It's like when United Fruit used to corner the fucking banana market. They used to buy up *all* the bananas in Central America so there were no bananas for anybody to export. The price of bananas would shoot up. The US Government makes the public believe you get rid of drugs by burning confiscated drugs. *No*. You get rid of drugs by buying it at the farm level *and* burning it.

'But can you imagine what would happen if there was no cocaine? The reaction from dealers in the urban cities when you tell them they've no crack or coke to sell? What do you think? They're just going to go and take a job at 7-Eleven? They're gonna go apeshit. And then they're gonna run into the suburbs, kidnap your wife, steal your car, put a hot iron in your baby's back, take your jewellery, and then you have a crime wave that's shooting out of the urban centres into the suburbs. The DEA lose their jobs and their pay cheques and their pensions, and have to switch from their laidback cushy jobs to becoming city cops, so they don't want to hear about that. They told me: "Shut up and don't you ever say that again." And they know it's true.

'So it all gets back to education. You have to educate people *not* to snort cocaine. The solution is going to be all through education.

There's no violent solution to this. So buying up all the coca leaves doesn't solve shit, it just creates another problem. But it would solve most of the problem of cocaine supply. America could have the most educated country in the world but we have a country full of morons, where eighth graders don't even know how to do math. American college kids binge drink. You ever seen a Korean, Hindu or a Pakistani go to college here and binge drink? No, they're binge studying.'

72

Crossing the Line

WHEN I ASKED ROBERT HARLEY where he ranked Luis in the company of famous American cocaine traffickers Max Mermelstein, George Jung and Barry Seal, he replied: 'He's right in the middle of that range of people. We're talking 100-plus loads of 750 to 1000 kilos apiece. Maybe more. And I mean *real* loads, that's 500-plus [kilos each time]. That's a lot of product.'[325]

Where does Luis rank himself in their company?

'We were all up there as far as amounts of cocaine.[326] They were the first ones who went to Medellín and met with Pablo Escobar. I was there for many years and met all these major players also, including Pablo. The difference is they got caught early. And then of course they become famous. Barry Seal, he got caught real quick, started working for the US Government, he got killed and *then* he became famous.

'Seal did his thing, though I probably handled more merchandise than he did. The thing is, I've always been black or white. I never worked for the DEA when I was smuggling. I never worked for *any* law-enforcement agency when I was smuggling. When I was a drug smuggler, I was a drug *smuggler*. For 25 years I never got caught and flipped and went down there [to South America] working for the DEA, like Seal did. Seal got popped three years into his working endeavour. That's when he started going down there for the DEA.

'I wasn't caught until Operation Journey. I had a very long run. Most people don't have that run. I look at Willy Falcón and Sal Magluta. They started in 1978 and were arrested in 1991. I went from 1978 all the way to 2000 without being caught. I never killed anybody, I never carried a gun; I didn't need to. I was backed by the most vicious, feared people in the business. With that kind of firepower behind you, you don't need to carry a gun. The only time I ever held a gun was with Mario; it fucking misfired. I always maintained my sense of humour, and I remained independent.'

Would he name himself, Mermelstein, Jung and Seal as America's most successful cocaine traffickers?

'No, because we all got caught. Or we're dead. The most successful cocaine traffickers are the ones we've never heard about. People in Colombia, Peru, Miami, Maryland or New York, who smuggle drugs and they make $10 million and they buy a car dealership and make $50 million from the car dealership. Nobody knows what they did, and they have a beautiful life. That's the most successful kind of drug smuggler. Silvio Bernal, who I took to see Rasguño, has worked since 1975 and to this date has never been indicted and is worth at least a billion. You've got to be a fool to do what I did.

'Everybody in Colombia was shocked when the bombs started going off in the 1980s and the problems began with Pablo. The whole business started getting bad connotations. Up to then, in Miami, everybody wanted to hang out with the cocaine dealers. Even after the cocaine-cowboy massacre in Dadeland, still, *fuck*, The Mutiny was going full blast. Everybody wanted you to be at their parties: high society, film stars, *everybody* – cocaine dealers were movie stars. We were the life of the party. In Colombia, we got invited to the best parties. Then, when the shit started getting violent with Pablo, it was "Keep away". Attitudes towards us changed and now nobody wants to be associated with a drug dealer or a smuggler.

'The word narco has been trashed. Remaining true to the narco business is not being a killer; it's trafficking cocaine. In Colombia in the early 1980s, before all this shit started to happen, narcos were accepted in society. Narcos were just "colourful" people who were invited to society parties and it was always great to have the narco come. You not only brought the good dope with you but your interesting character too. That's when nobody knew about the violence. There was always violence, a hit is a hit, but it was kept in the background and conducted in a more civilised way. Cutting off the heads of ten or 15 people, that's taking it to another level. Narcos were not killers, like today. Basically they were just rich guys doing a business that nobody really knew about; it was a new business and there was even a song written about it: 'Cómo Lo Hacen' by Frankie Ruiz. The lyrics go: *Cómo lo hacen? Yo no sé. Cuál es el negocio?* "How do they do it? I don't know. What's the business?"[327]

'And now, because of all that violence, because nobody stayed a true narco, everybody started to get weird and violent, fucking kidnapping and cutting heads, nobody wants to have nothing to do or be associated in any way with the word narco. You're no longer a pure narco; you crossed the line. They started to fuck it up years ago. If you want to be a part of a criminal element in society, keep it professional. If they'd just kept it on a business level, narco wouldn't be so terrible now. Nobody wants to be close to a narco today. We're bombarded with so much negative media on the word narco, but if you can see a positive side to it, then that would be me.'

PART 14
THE BELLY OF THE BEAST

73

Stockholm Syndrome

MAKING HUNDREDS OF MILLIONS in the drug trade isn't all it's cracked up to be, according to Luis, who still uses valet parking at his apartment building when he can just as easily park himself; old habits die hard. You see, when you get that rich, chances are you'll be kidnapped or killed.

'It's a great idea to make $100 million in the drug business but the best idea is to get out. We were just so caught up in who we thought we were: that we were untouchable, that we were these amazing businessmen handling huge amounts of money, juggling the cartels on one side with trying to do legal stuff on the other, that we lost sense of reality. If you make $100 million and stay in [the drug business], you're staying in an element that is totally murderous, conniving, thieving. You're dealing with people that will cut your head off, will kidnap you; you're in a very violent criminal environment. And if you do have $100 million and it's stashed away, believe me, there are people that will try to take it from you.

'Maybe getting involved in cocaine was my own way to rebel for being so mad at myself for not actually having become the person I knew I was given every opportunity to become. I've always been mad at myself for that. So by taking it to these extremes, that was my way to rebalance my life as much as possible and expunge that inner disapproval of myself. It was my way to slap society in the face and show them that I was making huge amounts of money by not being a doctor or dentist or lawyer or traditional businessman. I loved that. And while I was active in that business for all those years, I was proud of my business and I loved my business. I was very happy being in that business. To me it was the best business in the world. I never thought of the moral aspects of it.

'But after so many years of being inside this crazy, socially unacceptable, off-the-wall business I was then affected with a sort of Stockholm Syndrome where you start relating to your captors. And I hate myself for being so reckless with money. So when I look back, the biggest thing that I got out of all that, staying in the business for so many years, was being *alive*.

'If you have $100 million, even $10 million, you should get the hell out of Dodge. A lot of money can bring you a lot of problems. More money, more criminal mentality. More money, more criminal activities. More money, more criminal elements surrounding you at all times.

'The problem originates with mindset. If you say, "I'm going to get into the business and when I make $5 million I'm out," if you get out there's no problem. It's when you stay in and betray your original plan and say, "Just a few more trips and then I'm out," *that's* when you slowly start changing your mindset, lose focus and become out of touch with reality.

'If people know that you have $100 million and you're not a badass sonofabitch with badass genes who won't saw them to death, they will come after your money. They will eat you alive. Maybe that was my saving grace: that I never had that much at one time that people wanted to go after me, or that I was always working for someone who had more. Even if people *thought* I had that much – and many did – I always continued working for people that had a lot more than I did and were verified cut-your-head-off types. That's why people never really came after me: because of the people I worked for.

'If I'm honest with myself, I failed at the business. My cocaine days were a failure. As a drug trafficker I was very much a success because I smuggled in a lot of trips and I lost very little. But I got into the business to become a very rich man, a billionaire, and I played it wrong. My only failure was as a money saver; I don't have $100 million. I was a lousy administrator. I made the biggest mistake ever: not separating the lifestyle and the drugs and the partying from the business.

'In the cocaine business it's very hard to have partners. There are few people that you can really trust. I was always concerned with getting caught so I felt a partner could be a liability. He gets caught he knows everything about you. So it was very hard to do everything I was doing by myself, not get caught, keep a family, stay alive, make money and expand the business.

'Although I'm a believer in God, money was the ultimate. My goal in life was always to have lots of money. Money is my driving force. It always has been and there's a direct correlation between money and happiness in my life. When I have no money, I am a very unhappy character. When I have money, I am very happy. But money's very cheap, you know, in the sense it's something you can count. That's how cheap it is. How can you count your family's life or the life of a loved one? There's no counting that. How do you count love? When you can count something, it's a very cheap commodity.

'So the best thing that happened to me was getting arrested. Because since I didn't do the right thing for myself, someone else did it for me. My life was going nowhere. In the end I lost 90 per cent of my money but I've been blessed in other ways. My family loves me, they accept me, they cradle me. Nobody I know has that. I'm still paying for past mistakes – but always thankful that each day I learn and I'm healthy.

'A friend of mine in Miami is being deported to Colombia. He's sitting in an immigration detention centre in Louisiana. He was here working with the government; he was signed up with the DEA. He's got an awful situation on his hands with his family, with his deportation. If he gets deported it's a death sentence.[328] If you work with the law and you're not an American citizen, they can turn on you tomorrow morning, just turn their face and say, "We never met you. Leave the country." And that's it: you're *fucked*. If you're Colombian, you should only be an informant if you're willing to lose it all and you don't know how to do anything else. This guy produced so many cases for these people. No one from the government has gone to bat for him and he's in a fucking jam.

'So yeah, I have to work for a living and wake up at six and deal with construction workers – they're a more hardcore group than the drug cartels – but I have good health to do it; that's a blessing. I keep my day job because consulting for the government has a very limited upside. It's a business that if I concentrate on, it will work. I can build it up to be something good.'

74

Collateral Damage

LUIS HAS A NEW APPRECIATION of the country that naturalised him.

'I feel American but not 100 per cent 'cause I'm not. I'm a mix of different cultures. I'm very Colombian and I'm very much American and I'm a little bit Cuban. But my heart is between the US and Colombia.'

Society has been incredibly generous to you given the death and destruction you dealt in by trafficking cocaine.

'I was incredibly generous to law enforcement. I didn't get anything for free. My aid to law enforcement merited my discount in time, because my testimony and the incredible amount of information I provided in the end benefited society; if you think removing criminals from the street is a benefit to society, I helped do that. But I don't think my testimony dented the supply of cocaine in the world at all, and I don't think El Chapo's capture will dent the supply of cocaine in the world at all.'

*

Somewhat surprisingly, the conviction and sentencing of El Chapo in 2019 actually irritated Luis. He never met El Chapo, but he did do 'a few trips in the mid-1980s with a Colombian whose main guy was El Chapo; however, no one knew him by that name. In the early days they called him 'El Rápido', The Fast One, because everybody used to take a long time and he came up with his tunnels and he was handing merchandise over in four days. El Tío would take 30 to 45 days. You'd send it to Mexico with El Chapo and in *four* days it would be in LA.'

So what annoys you about his sentence?

'They talk so much about El Chapo and how bad he was and, yes, obviously in that business you have to be bad, but he was from complete poverty, no shoes, dirt floor. He came from a very poor family in Badiraguato, Sinaloa, and he was in a situation in which he had to do what he had to do to get ahead in that area: marijuana and eventually poppies were being grown and he was surrounded by people who were in that business. He was a sharp guy and he succeeded in that business. He had no education. It's a rough business and it's a rough world. He had to do what he did. It was his only way out.'

But he chose to be a killer, Luis.

'When you get to that level you have to be, just like when you get to be president you have to order drone attacks on innocent people. It's kill or get killed and you know it. The world is full of violence. I loved doing what I did. I treated cocaine as a product that needed to be moved, just like coffee. My business model was getting contraband from point A to point B and, yes, that contraband created collateral damage – sad, bad, *whatever* – but that was my business model: transport and logistics and trading a bit.[329]

'I stuck to what I felt very comfortable with; I never got really involved in any other part of the business, even the money-laundering side. So killing, *no*. It takes a special soul to do that. I was not that guy. You should never, *ever* change who you are. You should never let anything change your true self. Circumstances change a lot of things about us, but there are some lines you don't cross.

'I got into it for the money and, yes, I did a lot of drugs, yes I know some people got whacked, but I never crossed *that* line. I was never a bad guy. I never tried to become a bad guy and I won't pretend to be. If I'd become a bad guy I would have been dead, *immediately*. These people smell if you're scared. They're wild animals. They never sensed fear in me because I stayed *myself*. I was nuts, of course. It's not normal for a kid with a good background to get into the cocaine business and for that business not to change them. But I just remained who I was. I always kept that very clear in my mind. That's what saved me.[330]

'Don't get me wrong. If somebody got killed, somebody got killed. It's not like I went apeshit over it, but it was never in me to approve it and that was not me or my business model or my life model. I saw a lot of it – not with my own eyes – but I *knew* a lot of it. I knew it was going on. People get killed every day. People overdose. The military will go in and kill a lot of innocent people. Even the US Government – to kill one Taliban leader they drone a fucking place and they kill 40 or 50 innocent people. That's a known fucking *fact*.

'The government is working with snitches all the time.[331] They risk the snitches. They put 'em out there. They know they're gonna get whacked. Some of them do, some of them don't, I can't generalise like that. But the government is just another side of the same coin. They've just got a badge. My business model was not to kill; my business model was to export cocaine. Killing was collateral damage. It was not the core of my business model to go out and kill other human beings like it is when you're part of the military.

'Who I really detest are the politicians that go to school, go to the Ivy League colleges, take classes in public policy and ethics, educated men who know the difference between right and wrong, and yet they're elected into office to serve the people and they are corrupt. That's the worst crime of all: educated people doing bad to the people that elected them. I just did bad to myself.

'I'm an educated man who got into a business that I shouldn't have gotten into or I should have gotten out a lot sooner. I'm not going to get into the part about how the drugs harmed other people: that's a whole different thing. But I should have seen the difference. The real big punishments should go to educated people who know the difference between right and wrong that are caught betraying the public's confidence and who are corrupt. There's a lot of money out there that could be put to a lot of good use in the public sector and it's siphoned off to corrupt politicians. They are the worst criminals.

'I crossed a line when I began killing myself by indulging in the product. Cocaine is a bad motherfucking drug; it's dangerous and completely destructive to yourself and your family. By getting involved in my own product I killed the essence of my business, which was making money. If I hadn't consumed the product and not been drinking and not been partying, I could have turned $15 million into billions. I only harmed my family and myself through the worst weapons: drugs. They will make you suffer for a lot longer than any gun wound or gunshot will.

'So it's a big moral thing there. It's what happened to me. That's how I failed. I would never say to anybody, "Do cocaine." I've never seen a guy that smokes pot come home and beat up his wife. Alcohol is a whole different scene, a very dangerous and nasty drug, and when you mix it with cocaine it's total destruction.'

75

The Heaven Part of Hell

ON 28 MARCH 2018, Luis went to a reading by the American crime author T.J. English at Books & Books in Coral Gables for his book about the Cuban mob, *The Corporation*. Luis had always been fascinated by 'The Cocaine Wars', Carl Hiaasen's 1979 *Rolling Stone* article that had spooked Oscar Peláez Monsalve to leave the United States so abruptly, and had only recently learned that Poli had died since their brief meeting in Pepe Cabrera's Bogotá casino.

Luis was feeling nostalgic for his cocaine days and the quiet, impassive killer who had been his guide and teacher. The well-known gun of Medellín hadn't been quick enough pulling out his trusty .357 Magnum during an attempted carjacking outside a bank. Poli had clocked the gunman on the passenger side, where his girlfriend was sitting. He just hadn't seen the second killer behind him. He'd been shot dead at almost point-blank range.

In 'The Cocaine Wars', Hiaasen had interviewed a group of Dade County detectives and one of them was Roberto Diaz. Luis was sure Roberto and Poli would have known each other from the cocaine cowboys era.[332]

'Jesus, it's a war,' one of the cops had told Hiaasen. 'The Colombians have got the money, they've got the mobility, they've got the manpower. It's unbelievable. If the Cubans want to hit you, they'll take you out to the Everglades, shoot you in the back of the head and dump you there.

Not these assholes. They like shooting people in public, in the busiest shopping centre in Miami. They don't give a shit.'

So, after the reading was over, Luis got talking with some retired detectives from New York and Miami, told them he wanted to contact Diaz for this book, and they promised they'd put the two in touch. A few days later, Luis's phone rang. It was Diaz.

'Hey Luis, I got your number from my buddies. How can I help you?'

'Well, Roberto, I think we may know someone in common. His name is Oscar Peláez.'

There was a long silence on the other end of the phone.

'Oscar *Peláez*? Luis, how do you know Oscar Peláez? What exactly did you do for him?'

'I was his chauffeur. I used to secure the apartments where he went to sleep at nights. "Poli" they used to call him.'

By now Luis was convinced Diaz thought he was a Colombian hitman – with good reason. If you drove for Poli, you also knew how to use a gun.

'Luis, when you were with Poli did you ever hear the name "El Colorado"?'

'Yes.'

'How did you hear of El Colorado?'

'Well, I knew Poli wanted to kill him.'

'Do you know who El Colorado was?'

'No, I have no idea who he was.'

'Luis, *Luis*. I'm El Colorado. We raided one of Poli's apartments after a tip-off.'

Instantly, Luis had a flashback: Poli had been looking for El Colorado to whack him and had brought people from Colombia over to do the job. Luis just didn't know who El Colorado was or why exactly the two men had been at war. Now, to his horror, he was speaking to the target of his own boss's assassination plan and had implicated himself through being his employee.

Suddenly everything he'd long suspected had become very clear. Poli wanted to kill El Colorado solely because of the raid on his apartment: being held and photographed, the confiscating of photo albums, the roughing up of Poli's family. It wasn't a case of a dirty Miami cop stealing merchandise. Diaz's raid had been a personal affront to Poli. He was out for *vengarse* – revenge.

'Shit, Roberto . . . I knew he had a hit on El Colorado. But I really didn't know El Colorado was *you*. Yeah, I was Poli's chauffeur but I was also working as a salesman for New England Mutual Life Insurance.'

'Poli had a hit on me, Luis. I can't say the Dade County police department had a hit on Poli, because a police department doesn't put hits on people, but if we would have run into him, we would have gunned it out right then and there because we knew who he was; we knew what kind of character we were dealing with. And you were Poli's *chauffeur*?'

'Yeah, that's right.'

'In other words you were driving a fucking hearse, Luis. You would have been right in the middle of a fucking gun battle. You would have been dead. Nobody would have walked out of there alive.'

When he ended the call, Luis was rattled. He phoned his lawyer, Ruben Oliva, immediately.

'I asked him if I could possibly have some trouble from that association: like an attempted murder charge. Usually in that business, when you're a chauffeur you're very good at the wheel and you're also a hitman if you need to be. I was driving a fucking time bomb. Ruben said not to worry, nothing's happened: "Poli's dead. There's no gun, there's no victim."'

A few weeks later Luis met Diaz at his office and took a photo of Poli from Diaz's collection on the condition he never showed anyone. On seeing the famous Dade County cop in the flesh for the first time, Luis knew he was talking to the one and the same El Colorado.

'He looked Irish: red, freckly, tall, strong. Roberto's a tough dude. I was looking at a guy that my boss was going to kill. He didn't want to show me pictures of Poli. All these years had passed, I'd told him Poli was dead, and he was still hesitant to let me take a picture. I had to give him my word that I knew Poli was dead. He thought it could have been a vendetta after many years; and I'd walk in there and shoot him. He still thinks Poli's *alive*; that's how much of a cop he is.

Roberto knew what he was dealing with. He knew he was dealing with the devil himself.'

*

To this day Roberto Diaz remains haunted by his time on the frontline of the cocaine wars. He and his team were the real *Miami Vice*. He was happy to talk for *Pure Narco* but against the wishes of his wife, who wanted no part of it – understandably.

Luis and I sat down with the former detective at Cayo Esquivel, a seafood restaurant in Miami. Diaz had retired in March 1985 at the age of 32 and become a private investigator. He looked like a beefed-up Chuck Norris: neatly combed blond-red hair, a short-cropped grey beard flecked with red whiskers, icy blue eyes. Solidly built and standing six feet tall, at 67 he still looked formidable, with a big chest, big hands and forearms like small torpedos.

A resident of Westchester in the western part of Miami, a Donald Trump–voting Republican and a Christian, Diaz drinks but has never smoked and never touched drugs. He was born in Cienfuegos, Cuba, his parents of French-Swiss and northern Spanish stock.

'I'm the only Cuban guy with red hair,' he jokes. 'When the Dadeland shooting happened none of the police departments down here were ready for what came afterwards. I had a Colombian source that told me that there were two Colombian groups warring in Dade County. The source told me that one group had a truck and that they had made it bulletproof. The source told me that the two groups were armed with machine guns and hand grenades. I believed my source and wrote a memo to my captain with what the source told me. I was told that the source was full of shit. No one at the time had any idea that the Colombians were capable of having these weapons.

'Sure enough, the day of Dadeland, I was off [duty] and got a call from my sergeant telling me to come in because of the shootout at Dadeland. They had found the abandoned "war wagon" nearby. From then on it was one homicide after another, oftentimes multiple homicides. No one was prepared for what the Colombians did. One detective from homicide, Mike McDonald, who has since died, was on his way home driving on the Florida Turnpike when two speeding cars went by him, one on either side of his car, with guys hanging out the window firing MAC-10s at each other. He was caught in the middle of this and he's got a little .38 calibre revolver. Hits were being done in the open, in shopping-centre parking lots, at intersections. Bodies dumped on the side of the road.

'The same Colombian source gave me the info on Oscar Peláez. It must have been good [intelligence] and the source must have said that Poli was a big player for homicide to have initiated an investigation on him. We went after him and got him and his family at his house. They were all brought into our office and interviewed. The same source later contacted me and told me that Poli had put a hit on me. I guess Poli was pissed because we disrupted his operation or style of living. I notified my command staff verbally and by memo, but again, none of them took it seriously. I certainly did but no special watch order or protective detail was assigned to me.

'The Anglo mentality was that these Colombians were just a bunch of yahoos. The command staff didn't think these people were as well organised as they were. They knew the firepower they were using but, typical of the time back then, the command staff just didn't do much by way of arming us with adequate firepower. It was me, myself and I – that was it. I obviously took it very seriously knowing what these guys could do.

'Life went on, we kept investigating, Colombians and Cubans kept getting killed. We were spread so thin that we didn't have time to concentrate on one particular person. We were not prepared for these types of investigations. Our focus was investigating homicides; it was a whirlwind of stuff happening and we were trying to catch up. We were outgunned and outmanned. We were *way* behind the eight ball: guys with a six-shot versus guys with a MAC-10. So the tactic was just to make life miserable for these pricks, harass the shit out of these people, and try to put a stop to the killings.'

*

Diaz doesn't deny roughing up Poli.

'There could have been a couple slaps upside the head. *Bam bam*. It was to put the fear of God in him. "We know who you are.

We're going to fuck you over, you miserable piece of shit. You think you rule the streets here? Get the fuck back to Colombia, you fucking Indian." We brought his whole family into the homicide office. The Colombians were very on the move; they kept different stash houses. They were no fools. They were *prepared.*

'I don't know how many people Oscar Peláez killed or had killed but, from what Luis has told me, he was a real bad guy. During the time we investigated Poli, as far as I can recall, none of us knew how bad he was or that he was feared by any of the other Colombians. One Colombian, Conrado Valencia Zalgado aka "El Loco Martel", was extremely dangerous and violent. I had his photo and when we showed them to witnesses – the few we could find – they would flinch and knew who he was and how violent he was.

'We were constantly working. I remember guys sleeping at the desks in the homicide office, working countless hours, going home to shower, flopping in bed, and being called two to three hours later because there had been another drug-related homicide. So when I was given Luis's phone number all these years later and I spoke with him I was suspicious. But he was very forthcoming and honest.

'Luis is a very non-typical narco. He's really a rare species; he's not a lowlife. He has class and pedigree – unlike the Cubans who came in the Mariel boatlift who were bad motherfuckers. He reminds me of these little coral fish who live among poisonous coral. And if any other fish touches that coral they get poisoned. But these little fish are immune from any of that poison. Luis lived among these killers, these heavy hitters, and he had some scary times. He was able to survive that; not a lot of people can do that.

'When Luis verified that Oscar Peláez had put a hit on me, it blew my mind. I kind of flashbacked to when the source told me that Poli had put a hit on me. I was hesitant to meet with Luis because of this, but, again, he was very open with me so I accepted meeting him. I was not aware that Poli called me El Colorado. My friends used that nickname for me and some still do.

'The *Rolling Stone* article didn't change the way we did our investigations. I just remember that all cops in general were frustrated with all the crap that was going on. We just kept doing our jobs.

But I was surprised that Luis said it caused Poli to leave Miami. Go figure that the power of the pen caused him to leave town. Luis told me that Poli was killed by some street thugs in Colombia when he was ambushed in an apparent attempted robbery. [*Pauses*] I hope so.'

Luis's memory of the stone-cold killer remains untainted, even with the knowledge of how close he came himself to being killed in a shootout with Dade County police.

'I feel bad about working as a driver for Poli, because if he'd killed Roberto, I would have burned in some kind of fucking hell. It's a miracle Roberto's alive. His saint should be Carl Hiaasen because if it weren't for that article in *Rolling Stone* Poli would have never left and Roberto would very possibly now be dead. This is, like, *Pulp Fiction* shit [*laughs*], let me tell you. I now love them both. But in my book, Poli's no psychopath. And I will fucking defend him and his honour. Nobody can tell me differently. If he's in hell, it must be the heaven part of hell.

'I knew who he was but there was something about him that touched me. He's been a big influence on my life. I loved Poli. I cry sometimes. I get really sentimental; I've shed tears for him. I still haven't met anyone that matches him – in terms of the way he lived his life. Every time I hear the Elton John song "Ballad of a Well-Known Gun", it reminds me of Poli.[333] He was black and white. There was no fucking grey area there. He was one of a kind.'

76
Crooked Road

Luis speaks of being afflicted with Stockholm Syndrome in relation to his time in the cartels yet it could also apply to his unusual relationship with American law enforcement. Seeing the Danny DeVito–like Cuban-American walking alongside the nearly 200 centimetre–tall Southerner Eric Kolbinsky, you would never think one had put handcuffs on the other 20 years ago.

The two men are now good mates. They bonded after Luis got out of jail and the pair began working together on a bunch of historical drug cases that ended in successful prosecutions. Like Robert Harley, Kolbinsky lives in St. Petersburg, Florida, and is happily married to Lorena, the sister of Carolina Gómez, a former Miss Colombia and Miss Universe runner-up. She's 20 years younger than he is and, like her sibling, very beautiful. He jokes that 'the agents who went down to Colombia always came back with a Colombian wife, even the married ones'.

Luis and I drove four hours from Miami to St. Petersburg to see Kolbinsky and spent an evening bar-crawling downtown. Michael Diorio, a retired agent for the Department of Homeland Security, also joined us.

'It's not like I have a lot of friends; it's not like I *knew* a lot of people,' admits Luis. 'Eric's my friend; one of my very few friends.'

At a celebration in Miami for Kolbinsky's retirement and

65th birthday in 2017, Luis turned up. He walked into a crowded room of law-enforcement officers of every shade and hue.

'DEA, FBI, ICE, policemen – they were *all* cops. I felt like one of them. When I was there, they went around and asked everyone what relationship they had with Eric, and when they got to me, I was the last guy. I told them, "Eric and I were in the same business. I was a smuggler and he was a cop. We were both in the drug business."'

To this day Kolbinsky doesn't go anywhere without a firearm and is fully badged up, even when walking with his and Lorena's toy Pomeranian. When he heard the news that Luis was publishing his life story, he was thrilled.

'I think it's great. I think it's awesome. He's a character. Luis rolled with most of the major players back in the day. He really is lucky to be alive, in the sense that it's not a job you normally retire from: most people end up dead or in federal prison for the rest of their lives. He got lucky. Luis just spent a few years inside and lived. He never screwed anybody over. I guess he was an honest dope transporter.'

The fan club is mutual, even if Luis steadfastly refuses to pronounce Eric's surname correctly. Invariably it leaves his mouth as 'Kapinsky', is stored in his phone as such, and he doesn't seem to care when you correct him on it. It's become a sort of running joke.

'Kapinsky's a slim, good-looking guy. He's got more pussy than any drug dealer I've ever met. He partied out more than I did. It's a miracle his dick is still on his fucking body.'

'Ever since I arrested him I've been babysitting this guy,' Kolbinsky joked wrily as we watched Luis stagger out of yet another bar in what locals call 'St. Pete'. At one point during the night, Luis, emboldened by alcohol, had got up on an empty stage where a band had set up their equipment, sat down at the drum kit and started bashing out a solo. One of the band members had to step in and take the drumsticks away from him. 'He lives in the past. It never leaves these [narco] guys.'

Their unusual friendship, I believe, speaks volumes about Luis's character. In some ways he is a model example of prisoner rehabilitation. But in the eyes of many he will always be a criminal – including, it should be said, Luis's own. That is fair enough. He may talk up his non-violence as a factor that separated him from other narcos, but the fact is inescapable: he chose bad over good. That, arguably, was his worst crime of all. Fifteen years after he'd got out of jail, I often got the sense he didn't quite know what he truly was at heart: law-abiding American citizen or South American *bandido*. There's an inner struggle of sorts going on and it's being played out every day. In one unguarded moment, Luis admitted as much.

'That's the hard part – finding out who my true self is. Still having trouble figuring that one out. To tell you the truth I'm a little scared of myself. I'm scared of what I'm capable of.'

It was this man I felt great fondness for; stripped of all his bluster and artifice and just laying it down as real as he could. The man concerned only with making money and talking up his cartel pals I never related to or cared for. It was a welcome sign that for Luis's storied criminal past he was just like the rest of us: still searching for meaning and purpose and now coping with a life where his every whim wasn't accommodated. He'd lived in a complete bubble for most of his life: a self-confessed spoiled child of rich Cubans who'd seamlessly evolved into a spendthrift American cocaine trafficker. Until now, the true value of money had never really hit home. Now he was facing hard reality. The narco fantasy was well and truly over.

*

Luis also remains on good terms with the man who brought him down, Robert Harley, though it's clear to me over lunch at Dr. BBQ in St. Petersburg that their relationship can never be much more than jailer and prisoner. They might have been buddies in another life and under different circumstances, but they made moral choices that sent them on separate paths, and their sense of right and wrong runs deep and in opposite directions.

After putting off retirement, Harley is now employed by the DHS's Homeland Security Investigations division (HSI) and doubles as a supervisor in the Department of Justice's Office of Professional Responsibility (OPR) or internal affairs unit, which investigates attorneys employed by the DOJ. His official title is Resident Agent in Charge, ICE, OPR, Tampa.

He and Kolbinsky have just physically met for the first time and the two men have an easy rapport typical of agents serving the same government master. But, by contrast, there's an air of hesitancy and caution about Harley when he's around Luis. From where I'm sitting this seems totally understandable, not least because of the fact Harley is still an active agent and there are rules and protocols to follow when meeting ex-convicts (though Luis does do his best to break the ice by buying Harley a tie adorned with Texas state flags on it for old times' sake, which he is very happy to receive). Defining their friendship depends on which of the pair you ask.

'Every once in a while I'd meet Luis at Cracker Barrel in Florida City and have a cup of coffee, whatever, just to talk,' says Harley. 'People would call me, agents from other agencies and ICE, and say, "What's the deal with *him*?" and I would tell them the back story.'

Luis: 'Bob is straighter than Eric but we have a great friendship. He's a career guy, sharp. I've met his wife. A federal agent does not normally come around with his wife and introduce you to his wife; you being an ex-cartel guy. They do that because they trust you. These guys put away a lot of people in jail.'

'That's true,' replies Harley. 'I am straight. I am honest, frank and fair. But the job doesn't define me. I'm a career person. Over 33 years you start to judge character and Luis is an opportunist. He benefited from making bad choices and doing criminal activity but at the root of his person, is he an evil person? Some people do things for the money and the thrill, but it doesn't make them an evil person. It makes them a *criminal*. Some people are evil people but not all evil people are criminals. Luis does not pose a threat to me or anybody else. He's not that kind of person.'

Would you call yours a friendship?

'That would be a little odd. I'm not sure about a friendship. It's an odd relationship and I think this is why: I was always honest and I never made it personal. I was not mean or rude or arrogant. I just laid it out, matter of fact. I think a good person doing bad things responds to that type of relationship, if you follow my logic.'

Why did Luis do it?

'It's adrenalin, purely. This is all about the art of the deal and being on the edge of all that craziness. He enjoyed the thrill of it all and a little bit of the risk and the excitement, and let's face it: the money, the women, the drugs. He enjoyed all the carnal pleasures of being in that business.'

His nephew Andrés Blanco thinks Luis romanticises his life. Would you agree?

'I do think Luis romanticises his life too, but I think, in fairness, *everyone* does. That is the coping mechanism for the average human. The dysfunctional human is the one that focuses on all their negativity in their life and drives themselves into depression. The rest of us rationalise our bad behaviour so we can move forward. It's absolutely true; this book is a way for Luis to, I don't know [*pauses*]. . . put a good spin on a kind of dark life.

'Everyone finds a road to personal redemption. I think Luis saved his life. He has a sense of humour as a defence mechanism for himself – and it works. Was he violent? *No.* The people that he worked with? Yeah, *absolutely.* Do you impute the violence to him, though, as a member of the organisation? If you don't pull the trigger, what is your culpability? I don't know. These are big questions with no answers from me.

'Luis is not threatening; he's unassuming and self-deprecating. He's not dumb and he's inoffensive for the most part. He comes across as a joker and a businessman. Somebody you'd be willing to conduct a business transaction with. And I think that has served him well. That's the only reason he's alive. But he's not innocent by any means. These were bad moral choices by him. It wasn't like he woke up one day and said, "You know what [*laughs*], I'm going to be a drug smuggler." The road's a lot more crooked than that. I ended up where I am because of a sequence of events. But I very well could have been somebody different. And I came from a good family in South Florida with a great education. So what does that mean?

'I'm not a moralist; I don't do the job because of the morality of it all. I'm not an ultra-conservative. I am a *pragmatic* person. This is what the law is. This is what I was hired to do. It's a contract relationship between me and my employer. I never passed a value judgement on the people that we were chasing unless they committed what I considered to be the "personal crimes". If you rape somebody, if you beat up somebody, if you shoot somebody, if you kidnap them, if you threaten them, to me that changes the nature of the crime. And I've absolutely met people that I thought were just faulty human beings that were bad for society. Luis is not like that. These are people that commit crimes of opportunity.

'It's about *greed*. It's not because they make these moral decisions. It's exciting. There's a risk factor involved. There's a risk–reward relationship that they can't get away from. I've seen Luis probably a half-dozen to a dozen times; texted and talked to him by telephone dozens of times, maybe as much as a hundred times. And that's an accurate account of the relationship.'

*

Harley did send Luis a kind text the day after their lunch of ribs and tacos in St. Petersburg. It wasn't just a courtesy thank-you note but a word of advice. Luis wasn't selling hot dogs on Key Biscayne like the still-active ICE agent had once hoped – he was yelling at guys called José all day on a speakerphone from the driver's seat of his car. It was time for a change; a re-evaluation or reloading. It was a plea: *don't sweat the small stuff.*

'When I think about your life, Luis, I really believe things came together in such a way to allow you a giant second chance. It was your intellect and effort, to be sure, but don't discount the gift of karma you've been given. Life is good and you're here and healthy. Enjoy it whenever possible.'

Of course, Harley was right. It struck a chord with the rehabilitated narco. There was a moment on the roadtrip when I felt I saw a side of Luis I had never seen before. We were coming through a tollbooth on the Everglades Parkway and he handed over a ten-dollar note to a chinless, moustachioed collector wearing a Florida Turnpike Hawaiian-style shirt. The collector's nametag said 'HARVEY'. Harvey took the money, diligently counted out the change for the $3.25 toll and cheerfully said, 'Have a great day,' to Luis.

Harvey, who appeared to be a simple man, did his stultifyingly boring job day in, day out in a tiny, cramped box surrounded by a swamp full of crocodiles in the middle of nowhere. When we pulled away from the booth, I turned to Luis and said, 'You know, mate, your life could be a lot worse. You could be sitting collecting coins in a tollbooth in the Everglades like Harvey.'

The look on Luis's face was hard to describe, but one of realisation, peace and acceptance. The truth had finally hit him in the unlikeliest of places. After we got back to Miami, Luis called me to ask if we could hit some yoga classes together before I left to fly home to Australia. Maybe there was more to his life than making money, after all.

77

On the Hook

THE BIG MYSTERY IS how much money Luis still has: onshore and offshore. He surely has money *somewhere*: his kids went to good private schools, his ex-wife is living more than comfortably, and he admits 'I've always lived well' and 'Whenever I'm short three or four thousand dollars, three or four thousand dollars appears'; but, reasonably enough, he wouldn't tell me how much he'd managed to *keep* from his drug days or where he kept it.

'It's not very good to share that information. I don't want to get into that. Nobody had to sell nothin'. It's an *unanswered answered* question. But my late brother-in-law, Vicente, lent me money and helped me out a lot.'[334]

Equally I asked him several times to give me an accurate figure of how much he'd *made* over the course of his criminal career – he'd quoted me anywhere from $80 million to $120 million – but he couldn't settle on one number.

'I don't think he knows; I don't think we know,' says Robert Harley. 'Here's the problem. In his job, the job Luis had in the operation, he was on the hook in both directions. He's on the hook to get the product and if the product is lost he's the one that's on the hook for paying the bill, because the owners of the product rarely go without being paid. So he might have made millions of dollars but it also cost him millions of dollars, because there were plenty of loads that were taken *off*. Just the ones in the Keys I can think of, off the top of my head there's at least seven or eight that were taken off and maybe there were a dozen that were successful. So what really is the profit margin in that? I'm not sure.

'And you have to picture that the finances in those days were a little different to today. You were still talking about having to get cash collected from all the distribution points, consolidated and smuggled back out and into Panama, Colombia or Venezuela. So even if you have a successful load, you're still not going to get 100 per cent payoff – and you're going to use it to downpay for the next one anyway. Luis made millions but, in the end, I don't know. I don't believe he has any money stashed anywhere. I truly believe that. I'm not saying it's impossible but I never saw that kind of money trail.'

Either way, I couldn't help but feel maybe Luis, El Senador, had got away with the greatest smuggle of his career. Are his millions hidden away or is he really what he says he is: just a hardworking regular guy who gets up at 6.30 in the morning and comes home at night exhausted to unwind on his deck with a few grapefruit vodkas? Is he both? Is he less Mr Magoo and more Keyser Söze from *The Usual Suspects*? Only he knows.

I was curious to know if his views about money had changed at all, now that he had his family around him, safe and well. He'd had incredible wealth and blown it. He'd led an exciting life and been imprisoned. He'd completed a full circle from civilian life to criminal life and then back to civilian life again. What does being 'rich' now mean to him with the benefit of hindsight? Had he actually realised there was another path to happiness and contentment?

'You should have at least $2 million stashed away earning interest and have some sort of ongoing concern returning $20,000 a month. With that, $2 million in a bank account and no mortgage on your home, you're good to go. You don't need $50 million. Some people don't need money and are very bohemian. Some people think living in a hammock under a tree is very nice and comfortable. I don't. I need to live in a nice place. I don't know; different strokes for different folks. But I'm a rich man in that I have my kids, I have my family, I know people that did a little time in jail and they managed to keep

$20 million, but they've lost family members to cartel violence. I'm very rich and very fortunate for what I have.

'The US Government did me a favour by picking me up because I was so far gone and into Neverland that I would have never gotten out on my own. I was living in the belly of the beast. I would tell anybody if you have the opportunity: *go to school*. The moral of my story is to get an education; there's a lot of money to be made legally. It might not be as fun or so fucking adrenalin-driven as cocaine, but it's a very tough world out there in this business and if you have half a brain you have *options*. Take the education option. You're going to make more money by going to school and becoming a professional, working at it, and putting your heart into it. I put my heart into it *and* I risked my life for what I did. So risk your life for what you're going to do, motherfucker, and you will be very successful in today's world because intelligence and hard work are rewarded.'

*

Luis Antonio Navia spent his life trying to escape responsibility, escape mundanity, escape his father's expectations, escape reality. He did that through criminal enterprise, alcohol, drugs, hedonism, sex and the pursuit of material wealth via legitimate and mostly illegitimate means.

The beast makes us all believe that to be happy we constantly have to have *more*. But the more successful he was as a drug trafficker, the more dangerous the job became. Even when materially he had everything he'd always wanted, he was never satisfied and his health suffered as a result. Luis didn't see it then, but he was creating his own prison. The beast had swallowed him up. There was no way out, whichever way he turned. A man can spend his life on the run from the law but he cannot evade hard truths about himself.

Luis's goal in life was to make hundreds of millions of dollars, ostensibly as a way of filling the vast shadow left by his father and masking his own feelings of inadequacy for not finishing university or making it as a businessman in the real world, yet it was something he could never achieve. He made the money but he couldn't fill the shadow. That's because a criminal life cannot deliver a man prestige and dignity; the accumulation of money itself cannot either. But a regular job, his devotion to his two children and his ex-wife's child, and his uncommon willingness to confront the demons he still lives with have all delivered Luis humanity, humility and honour that are beyond price. He has now filled the shadow. His is ultimately a true redemption story.

Being on the run with no endpoint is no life at all. It was time to come in. It was time to own his mistakes and take responsibility for them. It was time to cut the most important business deal of his life. The person who held the key to his own freedom wasn't Robert Harley, Eric Kolbinsky or anyone else in American, British or European law enforcement. It was Luis. He'd held that key all along, only this time he finally believed it, backed himself and went for it.

Luis's 25-year adventure as a narco came to a close because the choice facing him was clear: certain death in Colombia or going back to the United States and facing up to all the things he'd spent his life running away from. In the end, ironically, federal prison in Coleman and a humdrum construction job became sweet freedom from an illusion he'd sold himself: that a selfish life can be lived without consequences. It took Luis losing everything – his money, his reputation and, most of all, his liberty – to escape the beast.

Boom.

EPILOGUE

The Icepick

A TYPICAL DAY ON A construction site in Miami, Fort Lauderdale or the Florida Keys is a far cry from Luis's 1980s cocaine heyday. His Miami is not the art-directed neon cityscape of Michael Mann, but traffic jams on the interstate, industrial lots, print shops, hardware stores, and a cast of tough-looking Cubans and Dominicans who aren't doing their jobs properly – all of which boils his blood.

He's perpetually on the phone, whether in his car or out of it, worries constantly, and has a major texting problem behind the wheel. Many times I had to yell out 'LUIS!' to stop him running up the back of a car while he was checking Google Maps or asking Siri to dial the number of a contractor. To meet him, you would have no idea he'd been a multimillionaire hundreds of times over. He acts, looks and talks like a stand-up, normal Hispanic American, but has an endearing habit of charming cashiers when he pays a bill. After having dinner with me and Santi one night, he left the restaurant, walked two blocks to a Mexican *paleta* store, then returned with a coconut ice cream for the young girl who had served him. He retains an easy charm around women. It all betrays his past. El Senador ain't dead yet.

'I wake up at seven in the morning and meet some welder in the hot sun and get under a fucking pool deck that's 100 degrees down there, and fucking make it through a manhole to show this motherfucker where he has to clamp a piece of steel to, so that he can weld a railing on the outside. Or go to a building and have to go up seven or eight flights of stairs, because there's no elevator yet to see the conditions on the eighth floor to see where we're going to anchor a louvre.'

It might be a comedown, and honestly it probably is, but from where he's been Luis is just glad he's alive, free, has his marbles and kneecaps and is still able to walk. He's an unlikely embodiment of the American dream. Civilian life, however, still took some getting used to. As we were wrapping up work on the book Luis called me from Miami International Airport while checking in for a business flight to the Caribbean. After years of smuggling coke through airports around the United States, he'd finally been detained by Transportation Security Administration agents.

'I put my briefcase through the TSA check and everything was fine but then got to the gate and reached into the side pocket of my briefcase to get my boarding pass, felt something and it was a fucking icepick. I was going to throw it away but I figured the right thing to do was hand it in, because I'd already passed security. If I'd thrown it in the garbage somebody could have picked it up or cameras would have caught me throwing it away. The TSA chief, the assistant TSA chief, six TSA agents, Miami police and everybody came on the scene when I handed it in. Everybody and their mother took pictures of my driver's licence and my passport.'

'That's a murder weapon, sir,' said one of the cops. 'Have you ever seen the movie *Basic Instinct* with Sharon Stone?'

'I don't remember seeing it but I'm sure I'll watch it when I get back home.'

It had been a stressful situation and they eventually allowed Luis to board. But doing the right thing hadn't panned out quite as he'd expected.

'I'll soon find out if I get put on some kind of terror watchlist. In the computer I'll forever be the guy that tried to sneak an icepick past security at Miami airport, even though I voluntarily handed it in. Lesson learned. Always check your bag before you travel in case you have a murder weapon inside. In the old days if I'd found an icepick in my bag I would have just thrown it in the garbage, wiped it clean of fingerprints and walked away. So I guess I am reformed.'

Months later, a warning notice duly arrived from the Department of Homeland Security, letting Luis know he'd violated title 49, Code of Federal Regulations (CFR), section 1540.111(a) of the Transport Security Regulations. He wasn't criminally sanctioned but had been temporarily barred from going through the quick line at the airport. When Luis texted Robert Harley about it, concerned about the ramifications, he got the reply: 'You've been on a lot worse lists.' It was a slap on the wrist, even though it was the US Government that had failed to detect his banned item.

'My whole life has been a security checkpoint walking through with an icepick in my briefcase. Burning the candle at both ends until one day, *bingo*.'

The question, though, needs to be asked: Why'd you have the icepick in the first place?

'Miami welders are a rough crowd.'

Narco Nicknames

El Azul The Blue One
El Búho The Owl
El Caballo The Horse
El Caracol The Snail
El Chapo Shorty
El Chino The Chinaman
Chupeta Lollipop
El Cochiloco The Crazy Pig
El Compadre The Godparent
Cuñado Brother-in-Law
El Diablo The Devil
El Enano The Dwarf
Flaco Skinny
Gitano Gypsy
El Gordo/El Gordito The Fat One or Fatty
El Halcón The Hawk
El Hombre Del Overol The Overall Man
La Madrina The Godmother
El Mejicano/El Mexicano The Mexican
El Metro The Subway
La Mica The Monkey (The Female Monkey)
El Mocho The Amputee
El Mono/La Mona Blondie
El Negro Blackie
El Padrino The Godfather
Patemuro Wall Kicker
El Patrón The Boss
El Poli The Cop
El Príncipe The Prince
El Rápido The Fast One
Rasguño Scratch
El Senador The Senator
El Señor de los Cielos The Lord of the Skies
El Tigre The Tiger
El Tío The Uncle

Characters

Not all the people mentioned in the book are listed here but these are the main ones. Typically, Spanish surnames are double-barrelled, but not all. The father's surname (patronym) comes first, then the mother's (matronym). In the book proper, characters with Spanish surnames are generally first referenced by the patronym, eg: Pablo Escobar. Here we have listed both names where known or relevant. Aliases or nicknames, common among drug traffickers, are also used where known and some characters are only known by their aliases or nicknames. Pseudonyms are noted. – JF & LN

The capos (cartel bosses and major cartel figures)

B

Alberto Barrera aka 'Paco' Colombian. Independent transporter reputedly beheaded by the Medellín Cartel in the mid-1980s.

Griselda Blanco Restrepo aka 'La Madrina' (The Godmother) Colombian. Major trafficker for the Medellín Cartel. Arrested in 1985 in California. Sentenced to three concurrent 20-year sentences in 1986 but released in 2005. Killed in 2012.

C

José Antonio Cabrera Sarmiento aka 'Pepe' Colombian. Major trafficker for the Medellín Cartel. Arrested in 1985. Sentenced to 30 years' jail in 1986. Believed to have been released in the 1990s for his cooperation in the trial of Panamanian dictator General Manuel Noriega. Now deceased.

Rafael Caro Quintero aka 'El Príncipe' (The Prince) Mexican. Guadalajara Cartel leader. Arrested in 1985 for the murder of DEA agent Kiki Camarena, he was sentenced to 40 years' jail but released in 2013 on a legal technicality. An arrest warrant was reissued but he remains on the run in Mexico and in the top ten of the FBI's Most Wanted Fugitives.

Carlos Castaño Gil Colombian. Paramilitary leader and member of Los Pepes. Assassinated by his brother José Vicente Castaño Gil in 2004. Vicente is believed to have died in 2007.

Pablo Correa Arroyave Colombian. Major trafficker and partner of Pablo Escobar in the Medellín Cartel. Killed by Escobar in 1986.

E

Claudio Endo aka 'Mono Endo' Colombian. Major drug lord affiliated with the Cali Cartel. Killed in 1994.

Pablo Emilio Escobar Gaviria aka 'El Patrón' (The Boss) or 'El Padrino' (The Godfather) Colombian. Most notorious narco in history and boss of the Medellín Cartel. Killed in 1993.

G

Luis Fernando Galeano Berrio aka 'El Negro' (Blackie) Colombian. Major trafficker and partner of Pablo Escobar in the Medellín Cartel. Killed by Escobar in 1992.

Luis Hernando Gómez Bustamante aka 'Rasguño' (Scratch) or 'Ras' Colombian. Leader of the North Valley Cartel. He was first indicted in the Southern District of Virginia in 1997 and offered a surrender deal by the DEA at the Cartagena Hilton in December 1999. He rejected it because he refused to become an informant. Arrested in Cuba in 2004 after travelling on a fake Mexican passport, he was extradited to Colombia in 2007, then extradited to the United States in 2007. He was sentenced to 30 years' jail in 2013 for trafficking 550 tons of cocaine, among other charges. Believed to be currently imprisoned at the FDC in New York.

Gustavo Adolfo Gómez Maya Colombian. Major trafficker who worked as a transporter for different cartels. Extradited in 2001 and sentenced to nearly 14 years' jail in 2002.

Joaquín Archivaldo Guzmán Loera aka 'El Chapo' (Shorty) Mexican. Sinaloa Cartel leader who can safely claim to be the most famous narco since Pablo Escobar. After a decade of being a fugitive in Mexico, he was arrested in 2014, escaped prison in 2015, was recaptured in 2016, extradited to the United States in 2017, and sentenced to life in prison plus 30 years in 2019.

H

Arcángel de Jesús Henao Montoya aka 'El Mocho' (The Amputee) Colombian. North Valley Cartel leader and brother of Orlando Henao Montoya. Arrested in and extradited to the US from Panama in 2004, he was sentenced to nearly nine years' jail and released in 2012.

Orlando Henao Montoya aka 'El Hombre Del Overol' (The Overall Man) Colombian. Original head of the North Valley Cartel. Killed in prison in 1998.

M

Fernando Vicente Marulanda Trujillo aka 'Marulo' Colombian. Major trafficker and boss of the Pereira Cartel. Extradited to the US in 2010. Sentenced to 17 years' jail in 2013 for drug trafficking and money laundering.

Miguel Ángel Melchor Mejía Múnera aka 'Pablo Mejía' Colombian. Head of Los Mellizos Cartel with brother Víctor. Named in FBI's Most Wanted Drug

Traffickers in 2004. Captured in 2008, extradited to the United States in 2009 and sentenced to 14 years' jail in 2016.

Víctor Manuel Mejía Múnera aka 'Chespirito', 'Sebastián' or 'Pablo Arauca' Colombian. Head of Los Mellizos Cartel with brother Miguel. Named in FBI's Most Wanted Drug Traffickers in 2004. Killed by the PNC in 2008.

Gerardo Moncada Cuartas aka 'Quico' (Kiko) Colombian. Major trafficker and partner of Fernando Galeano in the Medellín Cartel. Killed by Pablo Escobar in 1992.

O

Fabio Ochoa Vásquez aka 'Fabito' Colombian. Major trafficker and one of the five main heads of the Medellín Cartel and the youngest of the Ochoa brothers. Arrested in 1999, he was extradited to the US two years later. In 2003, he was sentenced to 30 years' jail.

P

Oscar Peláez Monsalve aka 'El Poli' (The Cop) Colombian. Independent distributor aligned with the Medellín Cartel. Now deceased. Not to be confused with Colonel Oscar Peláez, former chief of the investigative branch of the PNC.

Carlos Octavio Piedrahíta Tabares Colombian. Major transporter for the Medellín Cartel. Killed in 1988.

Hernán Prada Cortés aka 'Papito' Colombian. Major trafficker for various groups including the Medellín Cartel. Arrested in Colombia in 2004, extradited to the United States in 2006 and sentenced to 28.5 years' jail in 2009.

R

Leebert Ramcharan aka 'The Indian' Indian-Jamaican. Major Caribbean drug lord. Arrested in Jamaica in 2004, extradited to the United States in 2007 and sentenced to 37 years' jail in 2008.

Luis Enrique Ramírez Murillo aka 'Miki' (Micky or Mickey) Colombian. One of the biggest Medellín Cartel figures of the 1980s and '90s, he turned against Pablo Escobar and became one of the driving forces of Los Pepes. Jailed for various offences, he is now walking free and lives in Bogotá.

Alcides Ramón Magaña aka 'El Metro' (The Subway) Mexican. Major drug lord and lieutenant of Amado Carrillo Fuentes in the Juárez Cartel. Arrested in 2001, he was caught alone in Villahermosa, Tabasco, by Mexico's Special Operations Airborne Group (GAFES), the same unit that caught Rafael Caro Quintero. He'd shed 20 kilograms and shaved off his moustache to try to slip the dragnet. Sentenced to 47 years' jail in 2007.

José Gonzalo Rodríguez Gacha aka 'El Mejicano' or 'El Mexicano' (The Mexican) Colombian. Major trafficker and one of the five main heads of the Medellín Cartel. Killed in 1989.

S

Orlando Sabogal Zuluaga aka 'El Mono' or 'Mono Sabogal' Colombian. Right-hand man for Rasguño in the North Valley Cartel. Arrested in Spain and extradited to the United States in 2006, sentenced to six years' jail in 2010. Died of colon cancer in 2020.

José Orlando Sánchez Cristancho aka 'El Hombre Del Overol' (The Overall Man) Colombian. North Valley Cartel leader and former right-hand man of the Cali Cartel's Rodríguez Orejuela brothers. Shares a nickname with Orlando Henao Montoya, but he is the 'fake' Overall Man and Henao is the 'real' one. Arrested in 2001 on money-laundering charges, he was extradited to the United States in 2001 and was jailed until 2006, whereupon he returned to Colombia. However he was re-extradited to the US in 2017, on bank fraud and money-laundering charges, making him the first Colombian drug trafficker to be extradited twice. Sentenced to eight years' jail in 2018.

Alberto Sicilia Falcón Cuban. Major drug lord and pioneer of cocaine trafficking in Mexico. Sent to jail in 1975, he escaped but was caught days later. Released from prison in 1994 and died in 2011 in Mexico City, according to his sister, Mercedes.

U

Jairo Iván Urdinola Grajales aka 'El Enano' (The Dwarf) Colombian. Major drug lord and leader of the Cali and North Valley cartels. Killed in prison in 2002.

V

Edgar Guillermo Vallejo Guarin aka 'Beto el Gitano' (Beto the Gypsy) Colombian. Major trafficker and silent partner of Hernán Prada Cortés. Arrested in Spain in 2008 and jailed in the United States. Released early and returned to Colombia where he survived an assassination attempt in August 2019.

José Vallejo Lopera aka 'El Mono' or 'Mono Lopera' Colombian. Major trafficker and partner of Fernando Marulanda of the Pereira Cartel. Killed by Pablo Escobar in the mid-1980s.

Z

Camilo Zapata aka 'El Halcón' (The Hawk) Colombian. Trafficker affiliated with the Pereira Cartel. Now has interests in cattle ranching and farms and lives in Medellín, Colombia. Pseudonym and fake nickname.

Other narcos (low- to mid-level cocaine traffickers and/or cartel figures)

B

Sonny Bowie Colombian. Transporter for Los Mellizos Cartel. Briefly jailed in Colombia and rumoured to have died of cancer.

C

Félix Antonio Chitiva Carrasquilla aka 'La Mica' (The Monkey or The Female Monkey) Colombian. Accountant for Los Mellizos and former trafficker for the Medellín Cartel. Arrested in 2001, extradited to the United States in 2002 and sentenced to 30 years' jail. Released in 2008.

D

Alex DeCubas aka 'Coco' or 'Mario' Cuban-American. Major trafficker. Arrested in Colombia in 2003. He was sentenced to 30 years' jail but was released in 2012.

Iván de la Vega Cabás Colombian. Low-level operative of Los Mellizos and based in Venezuela at the time of Operation Journey. Arrested in 2000, sentenced to just shy of 20 years' jail (reduced to 10.5 years) in FCI Loretto, Pennsylvania, and released for deportation in 2009. Now lives in Barranquilla, Colombia. Suffered a heart attack in 2019 and believed to have survived.

Lester Delgado Cabrera aka 'Pinky' Cuban. Major trafficker. Never caught. Whereabouts unknown but believed to be in Brazil.

'The Doc' American. Major trafficker. Based in Tucson, Arizona. Real name, whereabouts and fate unknown.

F

Nick Fisciatoris aka 'Nick the Fish' Greek-American. Fixer and major drug wholesaler based in Europe. Believed to have died in 2012.

Eduardo Fonseca aka 'El Compadre' (The Godparent) Mexican. Luis's *recibidor* in Reynosa, Tamaulipas, Mexico. Whereabouts and fate unknown. Pseudonym. Real nickname.

Diego Forero Cuban-American. Transporter for Luis in the 1980s. Pseudonym.

G

Bia Gálvez aka 'La Mona' Aruban. Distributor for the Medellín Cartel. Pseudonym. Real nickname but she doesn't like it.

Jorge Enrique García Molinares aka 'Cuñado' (Brother-in-Law) Colombian. High-ranking transportation chief in the Los Mellizos Cartel and superior to Iván de la Vega Cabás. Reported directly to the Mejía Múnera brothers. Escaped the Orinoco Delta with the help of indigenous people, was arrested in Spain in 2002 and became a key informant for Spanish judge Baltasar Garzón. Believed to be walking free in Europe. Whereabouts unknown.

Gordon Gray aka 'Goo' American. Bush pilot for Luis in Colombia and Mexico. Pseudonym and fake nickname.

J

Cordelio Rodolfo Vaceannie James aka 'Fresh' Colombian. San Andrés–based trafficker. Killed in 2018.

'Joel' Colombian. Right-hand man of Poli. Killed in 1980 in a cartel-related revenge assassination. Real name unknown.

K

Angelos Kanakis Greek. Chairman of Callisti Maritime. Sentenced to seven years' jail in 2000 and fined €50,000. Whereabouts and fate unknown.

L

Elias Lemos Greek. Shipping magnate, owner of Callisti Maritime. Sentenced to 18 years' jail in 2000 and fined €250,000. Lost an appeal against his sentence in 2011. Whereabouts and fate unknown.

Brian Livingston American. Cocaine dealer. Believed to have died of cancer in jail in 1992.

M

Filippos Makris Greek. Ship owner and shareholder of shipping company J. Lemos. Sentenced to seven years' jail in 2000 and fined €50,000. Whereabouts unknown.

Joseph Martino aka 'Joey' Italian-American. Mobster in the Lucchese crime family. Killed in 1988.

Javier Mercado Cuban-American. Major trafficker and partner of Bernardo Palomeque and Francisco Moya. Killed while airdropping at Dog Rocks, The Bahamas, in 1990. Pseudonym.

Francisco Moya aka 'Juanchi' Colombian. Major trafficker and partner of Bernardo Palomeque and Javier Mercado. Sentenced to seven-and-a-half years' jail in the Netherlands and the United States for cocaine trafficking and was released in 2017. Turned his hand to farming tilapia and now lives in Santa Marta, Colombia. Pseudonym and fake nickname.

N

Evangelista Navas Villabona aka 'Mario' Colombian. Enforcer/*sicario* for Poli. Died of natural causes in prison, date unknown.

Jamil Nomani aka 'Indurain' Bangladeshi-Colombian. Recruiter of shipping crews for Los Mellizos. He was married to a Colombian and lived in Colombia. Whereabouts and fate unknown.

P

Bernardo Palomeque Cuban-American. Major trafficker and partner of Francisco Moya and Javier Mercado. Never jailed, he lives in Miami. Pseudonym.

S

Adler Berriman (Barry) Seal American. Former TWA pilot and smuggler for the Medellín Cartel. Murdered by the cartel in 1986.

T

Tommy Taylor Colombian. The snitch inside Los Mellizos. Believed to be living under witness protection in the United States. Pseudonym.

'El Tío' (The Uncle) Mexican. Luis's *recibidor* in Tijuana, Baja California, Mexico. Real name, whereabouts and fate unknown.

W

'Willie' Colombian-American cocaine trafficker. Never apprehended. Whereabouts and fate unknown. Real nickname. Not to be confused with Willy Falcón.

Brian Wright aka 'The Milkman' Irish. Major trafficker and associate of Nick Fisciatoris. Arrested in Spain in 2005, he was sentenced to 30 years' jail in 2007. Released in 2020.

US and UK law-enforcement agents

B

Rick Bendekovic American. DEA agent in Colombia and former DEA country attaché to Spain. Now retired.

Nigel Brooks British-American. USCS agent in Houston, Texas. Now retired.

C

Barry Clarke Briton. HMCE (later NCA) officer. Now retired.

D

Roberto Diaz Cuban-American. Dade County Public Safety Department (later Metro-Dade Police Department) detective. Now retired. Pseudonym.

G

Vicente Garcia American of Mexican descent. USCS agent in Houston, Texas. Now retired.

H

Robert Harley American. USCS (later ICE) agent in Key West, Florida. Still on active duty.

Graham Honey Briton. HMCE officer. Now retired.

K

Eric Kolbinsky American. DEA agent in Colombia. Now retired.

L

Carol Libbey American. USCS agent in Miami. Now retired.

T

Graham Titmuss Briton. HMCE officer. Now retired.

Historical figures

B

Fulgencio Batista y Zaldívar Cuban. Former president of Cuba. Overthrown by Fidel Castro in 1959. Exiled from Cuba in 1960, he died in Marbella, Spain, in 1973.

C

Fidel Alejandro Castro Ruz Cuban. Former prime minister and president of Cuba. Died in 2016.

Hugo Chávez Venezuelan. Former president of Venezuela. Died in 2013.

G

Luis Carlos Galán Sarmiento Colombian. Former presidential candidate in Colombia. Assassinated in 1989.

César Gaviria Colombian. Former president of Colombia.

Ernesto 'Che' Guevara Argentinean. Cuban revolutionary. Executed in La Higuera, Bolivia, in 1967.

L

Meyer Lansky American. New York mobster. Died in 1983.

Julio Lobo y Olavarria Venezuelan-Cuban. Sugar magnate. Friend of Luis Navia Sr. Exiled from Cuba in 1960, he died in Madrid in 1983.

N

Richard Nixon American. Former President of the United States and neighbour of Luis Navia Sr. Died in 1994.

R

Charles 'Bebe' Rebozo Cuban-American. Richard Nixon's best friend and neighbour. Friend of Luis Navia Sr. Died in 1998.

Julius E. Rosengard American. Lawyer and gambling representative in Cuba for mobster Meyer Lansky. Friend of Luis Navia Sr. Died in 1974.

T

Santo Trafficante Jr Italian-American. Florida mobster. Died in 1987.

Luis Navia's family members, important business associates, friends or girlfriends

A

Michelle Arias Panamanian. Luis's former girlfriend in Europe and Venezuela from 1999 to 2000. Lives in Panama City. Pseudonym.

B

Sebastián Bargueño Manterola American. Second son of Patricia Manterola. Half-brother to Juliana and Santi Navia. Lives in Miami. Pseudonym.

Andrés Blanco American. Luis's nephew. Son of Laura Blanco and Vicente Blanco. Brother of Martin. Pseudonym.

Laura Blanco (née Navia) Cuban-American. Luis's sister. She divorced her late husband Vicente and now works as an executive for a major government authority. Lives in Miami. Pseudonym.

Martin Blanco American. Luis's nephew. Son of Laura Blanco and Vicente Blanco. Brother of Andrés. Pseudonym.

Vicente Blanco Colombian. Luis's brother-in-law. Died in 2017. Pseudonym.

María S. Bonavia Cuban. Luis's mother. Died in 2017.

Katie Brooklyn American. Luis's former girlfriend in early 1980s Miami. She hasn't touched a drug of any form since 1986 and now lives a quiet life running a pottery studio in Vermont. Pseudonym.

C

Reid Constable American. Luis's former corporate attorney. Lives in Sarasota, Florida. Pseudonym.

Lisa Cushing American. Luis's girlfriend when he first went down to Colombia to live permanently. Died in a plane crash in the early 1990s.

K

Gerald (Gerry) Kane American. Part-owner of Lobo-Kane with Luis. Died in 1985.

L

Mike Laburd Trinidadian-Canadian. Businessman who allegedly engineered the Lobo-Kane sugar scam. Whereabouts unknown. Pseudonym.

M

Patricia Manterola Colombian. Luis's ex-wife. Widow to defacto partner Ignacio Bargueño who died in 2013, aged 50. Now remarried. Lives in Miami. Pseudonym.

Isabelle Meneses Ecuadorian-American. Luis's girlfriend after being released from prison. They were estranged at time of completing the book. Lives in Miami. Pseudonym.

N

Juliana Navia Colombian-American. Luis's daughter. Lives in Miami. Pseudonym.

Santi Navia Mexican-American. Luis's son. Lives in Miami. Pseudonym.

Luis Navia y Cuscó Cuban. Luis's father. Died in 1982.

O

Ruben Oliva Cuban-American. Luis's defence attorney.

Acronyms

959 Group Field-enforcement group of the DEA's Special Operations Division
AB *Armada Bolivariana de Venezuela* (Bolivarian Navy of Venezuela)
AE *Armada Española* (Spanish Navy)
ACCU *Autodefensas Campesinas de Córdoba y Urabá* (Peasant Self-Defence Forces of Córdoba and Urabá or Peasant Self-Defenders of Córdoba and Urabá)
AGC *Autodefensas Gaitanistas de Colombia* (Gaitanista Self-Defence Forces of Colombia)
AUC *Autodefensas Unidas de Colombia* (United Self-Defence Forces of Colombia or United Self-Defenders of Colombia)
AWAC Airborne early warning and control system
ATF Bureau of Alcohol, Tobacco, Firearms and Explosives
BACRIM *bandas criminales* (criminal bands)
CIA Central Intelligence Agency
CFR Code of Federal Regulations
CI Confidential informant. Also called asset or confidential source (CS). In UK agency parlance, may be referred to as 'sensitive intelligence'; in Colombian drug lingo, *sapo*; pejoratively, snitch
CNN Cable News Network
CNP *Cuerpo Nacional de Policía* (National Police Corps), Spain
BANDES *Banco de Desarrollo Económico y Social* (Bank for Economic and Social Development), Cuba
BLOC Blue Lightning Operations Center (part of USCS)
BOP Federal Bureau of Prisons *see also* **SIS**
DC District of Columbia
DEA Drug Enforcement Administration
DHS United States Department of Homeland Security
DICI *see* **DIJIN**
DIJIN *Dirección Central de Policiá Judicial e Inteligencia* (Central Directorate of the Judicial Police and Intelligence), Colombia
DIPD *División de Investigación Para la Prevención de la Delincuencia* (Division of Investigation for the Prevention of Delinquency), Mexico. Sometimes referred to as *Dirección* (Directorate)

DLO drugs liaison officer (Her Majesty's Customs and Excise, UK)
DOJ United States Department of Justice
DOS United States Department of State
DUI Driving under the influence
FARC *Fuerzas Armadas Revolucionarias de Colombia – Ejército del Pueblo* (Revolutionary Armed Forces of Colombia – People's Army)
FBI Federal Bureau of Investigation
FCC Federal Communications Commission
FCC Federal Correctional Complex
FCI Federal Correctional Institution
FDC Federal Detention Center
FIU Florida International University
FLETC Federal Law Enforcement Training Center
FPS United States Federal Protective Service
FWS United States Fish and Wildlife Service
GCHQ Government Communications Headquarters, UK
GNB *Guardia Nacional de Venezuela* or *Guardia Nacional Bolivariana* (Bolivarian National Guard of Venezuela or Venezuelan National Guard)
HMCE Her Majesty's Customs and Excise, UK
HMRC *see* **HMCE**
HSI Homeland Security Investigations division of DHS
ICE United States Immigration and Customs Enforcement
INMARSAT International Maritime Satellite Organisation
INS United States Immigration and Naturalization Service
INTERPOL International Criminal Police Organisation. Also abbreviated as ICPO-INTERPOL
IRS Inland Revenue Service
JIATF-East Joint Interagency Task Force – East. Now absorbed into JIATF-South
Los Pepes A Colombian vigilante group formed by prominent narcos to terrorise Pablo Escobar and his associates. Stands for People Persecuted by Pablo Escobar. In Spanish, *Perseguidos por Pablo Escobar*
MDLEA Maritime Drug Law Enforcement Act
MIDAS Miami Investigative Drug Asset Seizure Group (part of USCS)
NCA National Crime Agency, UK (formerly **SOCA**)
NCNB North Carolina National Bank
NDDS Narcotics and Dangerous Drugs Section of the DOJ
NIS National Investigation Service (HMCE)
NOAA National Oceanic and Atmospheric Administration
OCDETF Organized Crime Drug Enforcement Task Force
OCG Organised crime group
OPR Office of Professional Responsibility of DOJ
PA Professional Association
PD Police Department
PLC *Partido Liberal Colombiano* (Colombian Liberal Party)
PNC *Policía Nacional de Colombia* (Colombian National Police)

PJF *Policía Judicial Federal* (Federal Judicial Police), Mexico
RAC Resident Agent in Charge
ROS *Raggruppamento Operativo Speciale* (Special Operations Group), Italy
SHIT Special Homicide Investigation Team (SHIT Squad)
SHU Special Housing Unit (Federal Bureau of Prisons)
SIS Special Investigative Services *see also* **BOP**
SNO Statement of No Objection
SOCA Serious Organised Crime Agency *see also* **NCA**
SOD Special Operations Division of DEA
SORT Special Operations Response Team
SOS Source of supply
SA Special Agent; also *Sociedad Anónima* (Anonymous Company), equivalent to Inc. or Ltd.
SA de CV *Sociedad Anónima Capital Variable.* Equivalent to Inc. or Ltd. in Mexico
SSA Senior Special Agent
SVA *Servicio de Vigilancia Aduanera* (Customs Surveillance Service), Spain
SWAT Special Weapons and Tactics
TAMPA *Transportes Aéreos Mercantiles Panamericanos* (Pan-American Mercantile Air Transport). Later became known as Avianca Cargo
TSA Transportation Security Administration
UM University of Miami
UN United Nations
UNODC United Nations Office on Drugs and Crime
USCG United States Coast Guard
USCS United States Customs Service
USDA United States Department of Agriculture
USDT United States Department of the Treasury
USMS United States Marshals Service
USN United States Navy
USS United States Ship
WITSEC United States Federal Witness Protection Program (Witness Security Program]
WMJX 96X FM
WHYI Y100 FM

Gazetteer

A

Aguachica City in Colombia

Almoloya de Juárez Town outside Mexico City, Mexico. Location of Altiplano maximum-security prison

Alta Guajira Peninsula in the Colombian department of La Guajira

Amazonas State of Venezuela

Antioquia Department of Colombia

Aracataca Town in Colombia

Archipelago of San Andrés, Providencia and Santa Catalina Department in Colombia. In Spanish, *Archipiélago de San Andrés, Providencia y Santa Catalina*

Armenia City in Colombia

Arrecife Alacranes (Scorpion Reef) Reef in the southern Gulf of Mexico

Aruba Island country in the Caribbean off the coast of Venezuela. An autonomous country of the Kingdom of the Netherlands, along with the Netherlands, Curaçao and Sint Maarten. Dutch and Creole speaking

Atlántico Department of Colombia

Azores, The Archipelago in the north Atlantic Ocean and autonomous region of Portugal

B

Bahamas, The Country in the Caribbean. English speaking

Bahía de Cinto (Bahía Cinto) Bay in Tayrona National Natural Park, Colombia. In Spanish, *Parque Nacional Natural Tayrona*

Baja California State in Mexico

Bal Harbour Oceanside village in northern Miami

Barrancas del Orinoco Town in Venezuela

Barranquilla City in Colombia

Belize Country in Central America. English, Spanish and Creole speaking

Bimini District of The Bahamas, made up of North Bimini, East Bimini and South Bimini islands

Bolívar Department of Colombia
Bogotá Capital city of Colombia
Boyacá Department of Colombia
Brickell Neighbourhood and financial district adjoining Downtown Miami
Brickell Key Man-made residential island in Brickell
Bucaramanga City in Colombia
Buenaventura Port city in Colombia

C

Caldas Department of Colombia
Cali City in Colombia
Canary Islands (Islas Canarias) Archipelago in the Atlantic Ocean off the coast of northwest Africa. Autonomous community of Spain
Cancún City in Mexico
Cape Sable Cape in the Everglades National Park. Southernmost point of the continental United States
Cape Verde Island country located off the west coast of Africa. Portuguese speaking
Caquetá Department of Colombia
Caracas Capital city of Venezuela
Cartagena City in Colombia
Cartago City in Colombia
Cauca River River in Colombia. In Spanish, *Río Cauca*
César Department of Colombia
Chetumal City in Mexico
Ciénaga Town in Colombia
Ciudad Juárez Border city in Chihuahua, Mexico. South of Texas. Base of the Juárez Cartel
Coconut Grove Neighbourhood in central Miami
Colón Free Trade Zone A free port at the entrance of the Panama Canal
Contadero *Colonia* of Mexico City
Coral Gables City in Miami-Dade County, south of Miami
Cordillera de la Costa Mountain range in Caracas
Córdoba Department of Colombia
Costa Rica Country in Central America. Spanish speaking
Costa Caribe, La (The Caribbean Coast or the Coast) Caribbean coast of northern Colombia. Shortened to *La Costa*
Curaçao Island country in the Caribbean off the coast of Venezuela. An autonomous country of the Kingdom of the Netherlands, along with the Netherlands, Aruba and Sint Maarten. Dutch and Creole speaking

D

Dade County County in Florida encompassing Miami. In 1997 it changed its name to Miami-Dade County
Dadeland Commercial district of Kendall suburb in Miami
Delta Amacuro State of Venezuela

Democratic Republic of São Tomé and Príncipe Twin-island country located off the coast of west Africa. Portuguese speaking
Dog Rocks Reef in The Bahamas
Downtown Miami The central business district of Miami

E

El Águila Town in Valle del Cauca, Colombia
El Dovio Town in Valle del Cauca, Colombia
Envigado Town outside Medellín, Colombia. Location of Pablo Escobar's *La Catedral*
Essequibo *see* **Guayana Esequiba**
Essequibo River River in Guyana. In Spanish, *Río Esequibo*
Everglades, The Region of tropical wetlands in southern Florida
Everglades National Park National park in southern Florida. Constitutes 20 per cent of the entire Everglades

F

Facatativá City in Colombia
Florida Keys Archipelago in southern Florida
Fortaleza City in northeastern Brazil
Fort Lauderdale City in Florida
Fundación Town in Colombia

G

Galicia Autonomous region of northwest Spain
Galveston City in Texas
Georgetown Neighbourhood of Washington, DC. Location of Georgetown University
Grenada Country in the Caribbean. English speaking
Grove Isle Man-made residential island in Miami
Guadalajara City in Mexico
Guantánamo Bay Location of US naval base and detention camp in Cuba. Known as 'Gitmo'
Guatemala City Capital city of Guatemala. In Spanish, *Ciudad de Guatemala*
Guayana City Port city in Venezuela. In Spanish, *Ciudad Guayana*
Guayana Esequiba Region of western Guyana claimed by Venezuela
Guayaquil Capital city of Ecuador
Guaymas City in Mexico
Guyana Country in northeast South America, formerly known as British Guiana. English speaking

H

Haiti Country in the Caribbean. French and Creole speaking
Havana Capital city of Cuba
Hialeah City in Miami-Dade County, Florida
Hollywood City in Florida, between Miami and Fort Lauderdale

Houston City in Texas
Hyannis Port Town in Massachussetts

I
Interlomas *Colonia* of Mexico City
Ironshore Suburb of Montego Bay, Jamaica

J
Jacksonville City in Florida

K
Kendall Suburb of Miami
Key Biscayne Island town in Miami
Key West Island city in the Florida Keys, Florida
Keys, The *see* **Florida Keys**

L
La Guajira Department of Colombia
Lake Harbor Town in Florida
La Peñita de Jaltemba Beach town in Mexico
Lecce City in the Apulia region, Italy
Leticia City in Colombia
Liberty City Neighbourhood in central Miami
Little Darby Island Island in The Bahamas
Little Havana Neighbourhood west of Downtown Miami
Los Olivos *Barrio* of Medellín. Location of Pablo Escobar's death
Los Rosales Upmarket *barrio* of Bogotá

M
McAllen Border city in Texas. North of Tamaulipas
Magdalena Department of Colombia
Magdalena Medio Antioquia A sub-region of the department of Antioquia in Colombia
Maicao Town in Colombia near the border with Venezuela
Maiquetía Port city in Venezuela. Location of Simón Bolívar International Airport, servicing Caracas
Manaus City on the Amazon River in Brazil
Maracaibo City in Venezuela. Location of Luis's arrest
Marathon City in Florida
Mariel Port town west of Havana
Mariusa National Park National park in Venezuela's Orinoco Delta. In Spanish, *Parque Nacional Mariusa*. Also *Parque Nacional Delta del Orinoco*
Mashta Island Neighbourhood in Key Biscayne
Medellín City in Colombia
Melbourne City in Florida
Mérida Capital city of Yucatán in Mexico

Mexico City Capital city of Mexico. In Spanish, *Ciudad de México*
Miami Beach Oceanside neighbourhood in central Miami
Miami-Dade County *see* **Dade County**
Miami River River that runs through Downtown Miami
Michoacán State in Mexico
Montego Bay City in Jamaica
Montería City in Colombia
Monterrey City in Mexico
Moore Haven City in Florida

N

Naples City in Florida
New Orleans City in Louisiana
Norte de Santander Department of Colombia
Northern Cyprus *see* **Turkish Republic of Northern Cyprus**

O

Okeechobee City in Florida
Orinoco Delta A large, flat region of tributaries at the mouth of the Orinoco River
Orinoco River River in Colombia and Venezuela. In Spanish, *Río Orinoco*
Orlando City in Florida

P

Palomino Town in Colombia
Panama Country in Central America. Spanish speaking
Panama City Capital city of Panama. Not to be confused with Panama City, Florida
Pereira City in Colombia
Piraeus Port city in Greece
Playa del Carmen Resort town in Mexico
Polanco Upmarket neighbourhood of Mexico City
Pompano Beach City north of Fort Lauderdale
Port of Rotterdam Port in the Netherlands and the largest in Europe
Puerto Ordaz Town in Venezuela, part of Guayana City
Puerto Rico Island territory of the United States, located in the Caribbean
Puerto Vallarta Resort town in Mexico
Punta Paitilla Neighbourhood of Panama City
Punta Sam Residential community in Cancún

Q

Quantico Town in Virginia. Location of the headquarters of the FBI Academy
Quintana Roo State in Mexico

R

Raleigh City in North Carolina

Represa del Sisga Dam northeast of Bogotá
Reynosa Border city in Tamaulipas, Mexico. South of Texas
Risaralda Department in Colombia

S

Sahuayo City in Mexico
St. Petersburg City in Florida
San Andrés (Isla de San Andrés) Island off the coast of Nicaragua. Part of the Colombian department of Archipelago of San Andrés, Providencia and Santa Catalina
San Nicolas City in Aruba
Santa Fe *Colonia* of Mexico City
Santander Department of Colombia
Santa Marta City in Colombia
Santo Domingo Capital city of Dominican Republic
Sierra Nevada de Santa Marta Mountain range in northeastern Colombia
Sierra Parima Mountain range in northern Brazil and southern Venezuela
Sierra de Perijá Mountain range in northern Colombia and western Venezuela
Sinaloa State in Mexico
South Beach Oceanside neighbourhood in central Miami, just south of Miami Beach
Star Island Man-made residential island in Miami
Sucre Department of Colombia
Suriname Country in northeastern South America, formerly known as Surinam. Dutch speaking
Tabasco State in Mexico

T

Tallahassee City in Florida
Tamaulipas State in Mexico
Tampa City in Florida
Tecamachalco *Colonia* in Mexico City. Shortened from Lomas de Tecamachalco
Tijuana Border city in Baja California, Mexico. South of California
Tolú Resort town in Colombia
Trinidad and Tobago Twin-island country in the Caribbean, close to Venezuela. English speaking
Tucupita City in Delta Amacuro in Venezuela's Orinoco Delta
Turkish Republic of Northern Cyprus An internationally unrecognised state in Europe and considered part of the Republic of Cyprus. Recognised only by Turkey
Turnberry Isle A residential resort in North Miami. Now the JW Marriott Turnberry Resort & Spa

U

Upata City in Venezuela
Urabá A sub-region of the department of Antioquia in Colombia

US Virgin Islands Island archipelago territory of the United States, located in the Caribbean. Officially named Virgin Islands of the United States. The main islands are Saint Croix, Saint John and Saint Thomas. Previously known as the Danish West Indies

V

Valencia City in Venezuela
Valle del Cauca Department of Colombia
Valledupar City in Colombia
Vedado Upmarket neighbourhood in Havana
Venetian Islands Chain of six man-made residential islands in Miami
Vouliagmeni Upmarket seaside suburb of Athens, Greece

Z

Zulia State in Venezuela

Operation Journey: By the Numbers

Vessels captured

Name: M/V *Cannes*
Flag: Panama
Seized: 14 January 1999, off Jamaica
Cocaine haul: 3803 kilos

Name: M/V *China Breeze*
Flag: Panama
Seized: 27 May 1999, off Puerto Rico
Cocaine haul: 3880 kilos

Name: M/V *Castor*
Flag: Panama
Seized: 31 May 1999, off Venezuela
Cocaine haul: 4000 kilos

Name: M/V *Pearl II*
Flag: Panama
Seized: 23 December 1999, in Amsterdam
Cocaine haul: 2006 kilos

Name: M/V *Suerte I*
Flag: Malta
Seized: 17 August 2000, off Grenada
Cocaine haul on ship: none
Cocaine haul on land in Venezuela: 8800 kilos

Name: M/V *Privilege*
Flag: São Tomé and Príncipe
Seized: 31 August 2000, off Canary Islands (Spain)
Cocaine haul: none
Total official cocaine seizure: 22,489 kilos (24.78 US tons)

Arrests by vessel

China Breeze: 5 (United States)
Pearl II: 14 (The Netherlands)
Suerte I: 13 (Venezuela), 2 (Italy), 1 (France), 8 (Greece)
Total arrests: 43

Nations involved

Albania
Belgium
Colombia
France
Greece
Italy
The Netherlands
Panama
Spain
United Kingdom
United States
Venezuela

Glossary

A

Acuatizar To ditch or land a plane on water

Aeropuertos clandestinos Clandestine airports or illegal runways

Anillo de seguridad Security ring

Arepa A kind of flatbread made of corn flour, water and salt. Popular in Colombia and Venezuela

Asset Confidential informant or source, often handsomely paid

Assistant US Attorney Federal prosecutor representing the US Attorney

Avenida Avenue

B

Bahía Bay

Bandido Bandit or outlaw

Barrio Neighbourhood (Colombia). *See also* **Colonia**

Base *see* **Freebase**

Based out Stoned on base

Basuco A variant of base

Bisturí Scalpel

Blanco White

Bloque Bloc or unit

Blow Cocaine

Broker Law-enforcement slang for go-between or middleman in a cocaine deal

Bump Snort drugs, usually cocaine. *See also* **Toot**

Burnt out or **burnt** Past its usefulness; fucked; 'this guy's burnt'

Bush pilot Pilot of small planes who is skilled in landing on illegal runways or airports in remote areas

C

Calle Street

Cajitas azules Blue boxes. Refers to cocaine packages owned by the Medellín Cartel, Colombia

Caleta A residence used for storing cocaine. Alternately used as a term for a secret compartment in a room that is designed to facilitate a quick escape. *See also* **Stash house**

Caletero Minder of a stash house. *See also* ***Caleta*** and **Stash house**

Camiseta Literally, shirt. Cuban slang for 'wife beater' singlet

Campesino Peasant

Capo Drug lord

Carabinieri Military police (Italy)

Carriel A kind of 'man bag' used in Antioquia, Colombia. Worn on the side with a shoulder strap, buckle and closed cover

Caterpillar Brand of marine diesel engine

Cell phone Mobile phone

Cigarette or **cigarette boat** *see* **Go-fast boat**

Ciudad City

Clean No drugs on board

Cocaine cowboys Catch-all term used to describe drug traffickers of the late 1970s/early '80s period in Miami when drug-related violence between Cubans and Colombians and among Colombians themselves was at its peak. Also used as the title of a well-known documentary on the subject

Colonia Neighbourhood (Mexico). *See also* ***Barrio***

Comandante Commander (paramilitary)

Compadre Godfather, godparent, co-father

Consigliere Italian mafia term for advisor or right-hand man

Contador Accountant

Contrabandista Smuggler

Coronado Literally 'crowned' but in drug-trafficking parlance means to get cocaine to its destination and get paid

Crack Cocaine mixed with water and baking soda or ammonia and heated until a mass forms that hardens when dried. Commonly smoked

Croqueta Croquette

Cubanaso Low-class Cuban

Cubano Cuban

Cube Prison unit or cell

Cut Adulterate pure cocaine with an additive to increase profitability

Cuida carga On-board controller or guard of cocaine load

D

Debriefing Post-mortem of actions or decisions made during a particular law-enforcement event or operation. Can also refer to a verbal or written record of a cooperating witness or defendant

Delegación Borough (Mexico)

Department Political subdivision in Colombia, of which there are 32

District Attorney Chief prosecutor at state or county level

Dope Can be used to refer to any kind of drugs including cocaine but commonly marijuana

Doper Another word for ***Narco***

E

Eduardoño A Colombian boat ideal for smuggling. *See also* **Open fisherman** and ***Panga***

Eight ball Eighth of an ounce or 3.5 grams of cocaine

Enhancement An increase in punishment in a criminal penalty

Escolta Escort or bodyguard. *See also* ***Guardaespalda***

F

Fastboat see **Go-fast boat**

Feds US federal agents

Federales A 'Spanglish' word for Mexican federal police or other federal agencies

Finca Ranch or farm

5k1 or **5k motion** Refers to section 5k1.1 of the *United States Federal Sentencing Guidelines*, which allows for a reduction in a custodial sentence for cooperation prior to sentencing

Flipped Became an informant

Freebase Similar to crack but purer and more dangerous to make. Cocaine typically mixed with water, ammonia and ether

G

Gitano Gypsy

Go-fast boat A narrow, multi-engine-powered, V-shaped boat designed for fast speeds on open water. *See also* **Fastboat**

Gordito *see* ***Gordo***

Gordo Fat

Grand jury A body under the US federal legal system that must approve an indictment before it is initiated against a person

Green light Permission to move drugs through an area on payment of a commission

Gringo Foreigner or American

Guardaespalda Bodyguard. *See also* ***Escolta***

Guero Fair-haired, white or blonde in Mexican Spanish

H

Heat Police or DEA attention

Hot In danger or peril

Hotter than a pistol Under surveillance

I

Indictment A formal charging document in the US federal legal system that requires grand-jury approval before being initiated against a person. It essentially means there is enough evidence to proceed to trial

Indian Indigenous South American

Information A formal charging document in the US federal legal system that does not require grand-jury approval but will go to a magistrate or other judicial officer before being initiated against a person

J

Jai alai Pronounced 'hi lie'. An indoor sport of Basque origin popular in Miami in the 1970s and 1980s

K

Key Kilogram (kilo) of cocaine; also a reef or low island, as in Key Biscayne or Brickell Key (synonymous with cay or *cayo* in Spanish)

Key Rat Person who grew up in Key Biscayne

Kicker Passenger whose job is to throw cocaine out of a plane over a designated airdrop spot

Kitchen Cocaine processing facility or coca-paste refinery

L

La Catedral Pablo Escobar's tailor-made prison in Envigado, 'The Cathedral'

Lam *see* **On the lam**

Lavador Money launderer

Level 43 The maximum offence level of the *United States Federal Sentencing Guidelines*

Load Consignment of cocaine for delivery by boat or plane

Loco Crazy

M

Macho Masculine

Mafia An organised crime group with strict hierarchy and codes

Mariachis Group of musicians playing mariachi music from Mexico

Marielitos Immigrants from Mariel, Cuba, in the Mariel Boatlift. Also referred to as 'Mariel Cubans'

Marimberos Marijuana smugglers. Typically refers to smugglers from northern Colombia (La Guajira, Barranquilla, Santa Marta) but can also refer to Cuban smugglers in Miami

Mellizos Twins

Merchandise Cocaine

Mestizo Mixed race

Miranda rights (Miranda warning) Verbal notification by law enforcement of one's legal rights, such as the right to remain silent

Mothership Main vessel in maritime smuggling operation

Mona Blonde or fair-haired (feminine, Colombia)

Mono Blond or fair-haired (masculine, Colombia)

Mule A low-level cocaine courier

N

Narc DEA agent or any counternarcotics law-enforcement official. Not to be confused with ***Narco*** or ***Narcotraficante***

Narco or ***Narcotraficante*** Drug trafficker. *See also* **Doper**

Narcotráfico Drug traffic

Negro Black

O

Oficina Office. In drug-trafficking lingo, it refers to the central office, day-to-day operational headquarters, or enforcement and collection arm of a cartel. Most commonly they act as SOS (source of supply) for transporters

On the lam American slang for flight from justice or arrest

Open fisherman Another name for a centre-console fishing boat with an open-deck layout. *See also* ***Eduardoño*** and ***Panga***

P

Padrino Godfather

Paella A slow-cooked rice dish of Spanish origin commonly made with meat, beans, seafood and vegetables

Paisa A native of the northwest of Colombia (Antioquia and other departments)

Paleta A kind of Mexican ice cream on a stick, like a popsicle

Panga Outboard-powered fishing boat. *See also* **Open fisherman** and ***Eduardoño***

Paras Paramilitaries

Patrón Boss

Pinga Cuban slang for 'dick'

Pista de ciclismo Cycling track

Playa Beach

Plaza Exclusive smuggling zone or territory

Popped Killed

Pot Marijuana

Puta Bitch or whore

Q

Queso Cheese

R

Recibidor Receiver of merchandise

Repartidor Distributor for wholesaler of merchandise

Represa Dam

Represalias Retaliation

Rola The feminine for a native of Bogotá (masculine, ***Rolo***)

Routes Tried-and-tested aerial or nautical pathways for drug smuggling

Rule 35 Refers to Rule 35(b) of the *Federal Rules of Criminal Procedure* under which a jail sentence can be slashed 'if the defendant, after sentencing, provided substantial assistance in investigating or prosecuting another person'

S

Sagrado Sacred or holy

Sapo Literally frog or toad. Snitch or informant

Secuestradores Kidnappers

Screwy Not right

Sicario Hitman
Snitch Informant
Spook Spy
Stash house A residence used for storing cocaine. *See also* **Caleta**
Suerte Luck

T
Takedown Final stage of operation
Taken off An unsuccessful load that has to be paid for. As in 'taken off' expected profit
Team America DEA slang for source or informant (as in 'he joined Team America')
Thai stick Cannabis plant (leaves, buds) twisted into a compact, cigar-like cylinder for smoking
Third-party cooperation Euphemism for an informant privately hired by an inmate to help get a reduction in sentence. *See also* **Rule 35**
Toot Snort drugs, usually cocaine. *See also* **Bump**
Toro Bull
Trip *see* **Load**

U
Unit see **Key**
US Attorney Chief federal prosecutor

V
Vengarse Revenge

W
Weight Large amount of cocaine
Whacked Killed
Wiseguy Mobster or member of the mafia
Working DEA slang for building a case against someone or an organisation

Criminal Organisations

The following are drug cartels and mafia groups Luis worked for, was connected to or supplied directly or indirectly between 1978 and 2000. Names of individuals mentioned were active during this period. – JF & LN

Colombia

Medellín Cartel (*El Cártel de Medellín*)
Leadership: Pablo Escobar, Ochoa family, José Gonzalo Rodríguez Gacha
Notable figures: Carlos Enrique Lehder Rivas, Luis Fernando Galeano Berrio, Gerardo Moncada Cuartas, José Rafael Abello Silva, José Antonio Cabrera Sarmiento, Pablo Correa Arroyave, Diego Murillo Bejarano

Cali Cartel (*El Cártel de Cali*)
Leadership: Rodríguez Orejuela brothers, José Santacruz Londoño, Francisco Hélmer Herrera Buitrago
Notable figures: Victor Patiño Fomeque, Juan Carlos Ramírez Abadía, Claudio Endo

North Valley Cartel (*El Cártel del Norte del Valle*)
Leadership: Orlando Henao Montoya, Luis Hernando Gómez Bustamante, Diego León Montoya Sánchez, Wilber Alirio Varela Fajardo
Notable figures: Juan Carlos Ramírez Abadía, Jairo Iván Urdinola Grajales, Carlos Alberto Rentería Mantilla, Arcángel de Jesús Henao Montoya

North Coast Cartel or Coast Cartel (*El Cártel de la Costa/El Cártel de la Costa Atlántica*)
Leadership: Dávila family (Santa Marta), Nasser family (Barranquilla), José Rafael Abello Silva (Santa Marta), Alberto Orlández Gamboa (Barranquilla)

Pereira Cartel (*El Cártel de Pereira*)
Leadership: Fernando Marulanda, José Vallejo Lopera, Carlos Arturo Patiño Restrepo

The Twins Cartel (*El Cártel de Los Mellizos*)
Leadership: Mejía Múnera brothers

Mexico
Juárez Cartel (*El Cártel de Juárez*)
Leadership: Amado Carrillo Fuentes

Gulf Cartel (*El Cártel del Golfo)*
Leadership: Juan García Abrego, Osiel Cárdenas Guillén

Tijuana Cartel (*El Cártel de Tijuana)*
Leadership: Arrellano Félix family

Guadalajara Cartel (*El Cártel de Guadalajara*)
Leadership: Rafael Caro Quintero, Miguel Ángel Félix Gallardo, Ernesto Fonseca Carrillo

United States
Lucchese crime family in Florida (La Cosa Nostra or Sicilian mafia)

Italy
'Ndrangheta or Calabrian mafia

Jamaica
Leebert Ramcharan organisation

Albania
Durda brothers organisation

United Kingdom
Brian Wright organisation

Spain
José Ramón Prado Bugallo aka 'Sito Miñanco' organisation

Acknowledgements

Jesse Fink

Thank you first and foremost to the law-enforcement agents involved in Operation Journey, Luis Navia's capture in Venezuela, and the ongoing fight against international cocaine trafficking who agreed to be interviewed for *Pure Narco*. This book could not have been written without the benefit of their collective experience in the frontline of the war on drugs.

My thanks to active ICE agent Robert Harley; retired USCS agents Carol Libbey, Vicente Garcia and Nigel Brooks; retired HMCE agents Barry Clarke, Graham Honey and Graham Titmuss; retired Metro-Dade Police Department detective Roberto Diaz; and retired DEA agents Eric Kolbinsky and Rick Bendekovic.

Eric, especially, was incredibly generous to both Luis and me during our time together in Miami and St. Petersburg, Florida, read a rough early draft and kindly agreed to write the foreword. You're a legend, 'Kapinsky'.

Roberto vetted the chapters on Poli and the cocaine cowboys era while Vicente, Nigel, the two Grahams and Barry took the time to carefully check the chapters on Operation Journey for accuracy, for which I'm hugely appreciative. Nigel also went beyond the call of duty, not only in reading a full draft but supplying images and background information on Operation Journey, including redacted intelligence documents, redacted emails from Tommy Taylor, and his own written summary of the takedown. I can't thank you enough, Nigel.

Thanks to Luis's family – Patricia Manterola, Santi Navia, Juliana Navia, Sebastián Bargueño Manterola, Laura Blanco and Andrés Blanco – for answering my phone calls as well as your kindness, hospitality and generosity during my stay in Miami.

My thanks also to Katie Brooklyn, Bia Gálvez, Richard Booth, Brian Dennard, Mercedes Sicilia Falcón, Gary Noesner, Peter Walsh, and all our pseudonymous and anonymous sources in and out of the cocaine trade.

It would be remiss of me not to mention our stellar support team at Penguin Random House Australia: Alison Urquhart, Patrick Mangan, Justin Ractliffe, Alex Ross, Bonny Maddah, Benjamin Fairclough, Louise Ryan, Emily Hindle, Lucy Ballantyne, Alice Richardson and Nerrilee Weir. It was Ali who originally commissioned *Pure Narco*. This is our third outing together and she has been the single biggest champion of my writing career. I look forward to us publishing more books.

In the UK, thanks to Kelly Ellis and Ciara Lloyd at John Blake Publishing. In the US, thanks to mapmaker Alicia Freile at Tango Media.

Lastly, a note of gratitude to Luis. His is a complex, confronting and oftentimes unsympathetic story but I believe he is a good man at heart, despite his character flaws and myriad mistakes. We're all imperfect. It takes a true *bandido* to own up to it publicly. I tip my hat to you, my friend.

Luis Navia

Patricia, you have been a blessing in my life from day one and raised three of the most incredible kids: Juliana, Santi and Sebastián. I love the four of you.

Laura, you are the most amazing sister a brother could wish for and I am blessed to have Andrés and Martin as my nephews.

CL, thank you from the bottom of my heart for the wonderful gift you gave me that came at the right moment; 2005 was a great year! V for victory and love!

Luis Emilio González Chávez, thank you for your loyalty and friendship over the years.

Ruben Oliva, thank you for your total support and guidance during the most important negotiation of my life.

And to Jesse Fink, thank you for piecing together this 25-year (make that 45-year) rollercoaster ride.

Bibliography

Articles (Print and Online)

Longer pieces from *The Washington Post* and *Omni Magazine* were especially useful in reconstructing the Amtrak siege in Chapter 6. – JF & LN

'A 14 años de cárcel fue condenado alias El Mellizo en Estados Unidos', no byline, *W Radio Colombia*, Bogotá (Colombia), 7 January 2016

'The afterlife of Pablo Escobar', Jon Lee Anderson, *The New Yorker*, New York, 26 February 2018

'Alleged drug baron held in Florida', Lenny Savino and Wanda J. DeMarzo, *The Miami Herald*, Miami, 27 August 2000

'A poco más de 20 años, aún queda la duda sobre la muerte de Amado Carrillo, el "Señor de los Cielos", líder del Cártel de Juárez', no byline, *Vanguardia*, Saltillo (Mexico), 4 September 2018

'Arbitron to reissue Miami survey in wake of 96X diary tampering', Marc Kirkeby, *Record World*, Vol. 35, No. 1626, New York, 2 September 1978

'Art market: painting withdrawn from sale after artist declares it a fake', Dalya Alberge, *The Independent*, London, 19 May 1993

'Asesinado Juan Manuel Gaviria Vásquez, testigo "estrella" de E.U. contra clan de Los Mellizos', no byline, *El Tiempo*, Bogotá (Colombia), 28 July 2009

'Así destrozó la vida y la honra a muchos inocentes el prevaricador Garzón', no byline, intereconomia.com, Madrid, 19 February 2012

'The avalanche of cocaine hitting Europe', no byline, *Spiegel Online*, Hamburg (Germany), 9 November 2019

'The avenger: in Colombia, a father has taken on a drug baron with a vicious reputation to get justice for the brutal killing of his son – and so far dad is winning', Douglas Farah, *The Washington Post*, Washington, DC, 26 March 1996

'BACRIM in Venezuela', no byline, insightcrime.org, Washington, DC, 7 April 2015

'Baltasar G. tras Castaño', no byline, *El Tiempo*, Bogotá (Colombia), 6 February 2004

'Bartell to tighten control', Ray Herbeck Jr, *Billboard*, New York, 18 February 1978

'The bell tolls for him', Sean Rowe, *Miami New Times*, Miami, 31 July 1997

'Big smuggler of cocaine is arrested, Mexico says', Tim Weiner, *The New York Times*, New York, 14 June 2001

'Billions of dollars of cocaine are smuggled into the US by sea every year, and the Coast Guard says it can only stop one-quarter of it', Christopher Woody, *Business Insider Australia*, Sydney (Australia), 20 November 2018

'Bizarre plea fails to cut prison term', no byline, *The South Florida Sun-Sentinel*, Deerfield Beach (FL), 16 Jan 2002

'Brazil's cocaine trade leaves widespread violence in its wake', Anabel Hernández, *Deutsche Welle*, Bonn (Germany), 27 August 2019

'Capturan en Tabasco al *capo* Alcides Ramón Magaña', Jesús Aranda, *La Jornada*, Mexico City (Mexico), 14 June 2001

'Capturan hombre de confianza de "Los Mellizos"', no byline, *El País*, Cali (Colombia), 3 January 2005

'Car bombs in Colombia kill 25, injure 150', Douglas Farah, *The Washington Post*, Washington, DC, 13 May 1990

'Charles "Bebe" Rebozo, 85, dies', Richard Pearson, *The Washington Post*, Washington, DC, 10 May 1998

'Clear and present danger', Simon Carr, *The Independent*, London, 25 November 1998

'Coast Guard seizes record amount of cocaine', Associated Press, *The Arizona Daily Sun*, Flagstaff (AZ), 13 May 2001

'"Cocaine cowboy" deported to Dominican Republic after his bid to stay in US fails', Jay Weaver, *The Miami Herald*, Miami, 19 November 2018

'Cocaine cowboys', Jack Anderson, *The Washington Post*, Washington, DC, 22 June 1980

'Cocaine in Germany: the "South American tsunami"', Volkmar Kabisch, Jan Lukas Strozyk and Benedikt Strunz, dw.com, Bonn (Germany), 28 December 2018

'A cocaine story', Alfred Peza, *AIM*, Tirana (Albania), 15 March 2001

'Cocaine surge to Europe fuelled by new gangs, violence: report', Axel Bugge, reuters.com, London, 14 December 2018

'The cocaine wars', Carl Hiaasen, *Rolling Stone*, New York, 20 September 1979

'Colombia arrests 10,000 after slaying', Associated Press, *The New York Times*, New York, 21 August 1989

'Colombia capo may be first ever extradited to United States, twice', Victoria Dittmar, insightcrime.org, Washington, DC, 7 March 2018

'Colombia captures head of drug traffickers', Xinhua News Agency, Woodside (NY), 1 March 2006

'Colombia commemorates 30 years without Luis Carlos Galán as questions remain', Adriaan Alsema, *Colombia Reports*, Medellín (Colombia), 18 August 2019

'Colombian criminal arrest reminder of dissolved cartel's influence', Leonardo Goi, insightcrime.org, Washington, DC, 28 March 2017

'Colombian drug smuggler gets 30 years in prison', United Press International, *The Orlando Sentinel*, Orlando (FL), 8 October 1986

'Colombia elites and organised crime: "Don Berna"', Jeremy McDermott, insightcrime.org, Washington, DC, 9 August 2016

'Colombia-led multinational operation seizes 94.2 tonnes of cocaine in 105-day period', Helen Murphy and Luis Jaime Acosta (Peter Cooney, editor), reuters.com, London, 30 April 2019

'Colombian police capture reputed drug lord', Reuters, *The Christian Science Monitor*, Boston (MA), 29 April 1992

'Colombian police seize $35 million/US-raided raid finds bags of cash in walls of two Bogotá apartments', John Otis, *The Houston Chronicle*, Houston (TX), 26 August 2001

'Colombian, 31, gets life in Amtrak siege case', United Press International, *The New York Times*, New York, 29 February 1984

'Colombia's drug trade', no byline, *Colombia Reports*, Medellín (Colombia), 26 June 2019

'Columbia [sic] drug lords vie for cocaine trade control', Bernd Debusmann, *The Globe and Mail*, Toronto (Canada), 2 August 1988

'Convicted cocaine smuggler posed with Mrs. Clinton, Gore', Terry Frieden, CNN, Atlanta (GA), 23 October 1996

'Cops puzzled over drug submarine', Andrew Selsky (Associated Press), *The Washington Post*, Washington, DC, 30 September 2000

'Corruption in Venezuela has created a cocaine superhighway to the US', Nick Paton Walsh, Natalie Gallón and Diana Castrillon, CNN, Atlanta (GA), 17 April 2019

'Court sentences Jamaican drug boss to 37 years', no byline, reuters.com, London, 24 May 2008

'Cuban sugar-wolf', Drew Pearson, *The Panama American*, Panama City (Panama), 23 April 1956

'Customs: more cocaine seized on ship in Philadelphia than estimated', Associated Press, WITF, Harrisburg (PA), 27 June 2019

'DEA feels better about Venezuela after raid succeeds – the 16 arrests and seizure of 10 tons of cocaine eased fears that the country would not co-operate with US agents', Associated Press, *The Orlando Sentinel*, Orlando (FL), 26 August 2000

'Decomisan en Venezuela más de cinco toneladas de cocaína', Reuters, *El Mundo*, Madrid, 21 August 2000

'Desperado at twilight – book chronicles life of Lauderdale's Jon Roberts', Chauncey Mabe, *The South Florida Sun-Sentinel*, Deerfield Beach (FL), 1 January 2012

'Drug arrest removes big shipper, agents say', Lenny Savino, Knight Ridder Tribune News Service, *Sunday Star-News*, Wilmington (NC), 27 August 2000

'Drug barons like Howard Marks always claim to be Mr Nice. Don't fall for it', Tom Wainwright, *The Guardian*, London, 13 April 2016

'Drugs bust hits 32 countries in one swoop, Customs and intelligence forces unite to arrest thousands in Caribbean', Christina Lamb and Jeremy McDermott, *The Sunday Telegraph*, London, 26 November 2000

'El desayuno está a bordo', Jorge A. Rodríguez, *El País*, Cali (Colombia), 12 September 2000

'El lujoso apartamento que enfrenta a dos narcos', no byline, *El Tiempo*, Bogotá (Colombia), 28 June 2015

'El ocaso de un oscuro personaje: Arturo Durazo, el implacable', Carlos Álvarez, *La Prensa*, Mexico City (Mexico), 30 November 2018

'Escobar: 17 años de historia del criminal', no byline, *El Tiempo*, Bogotá (Colombia), 2 December 1993

'Esta es la confesión que Rasguño hará en E.U. [US]', no byline, *El Tiempo*, Bogotá (Colombia), 22 March 2007

'Eureka jury names drug "kingpin"', no byline, *San Francisco Examiner*, San Francisco (CA), 2 April 1986

'Ex contador de "Los Mellizos" dice que en Ralito delinquían sin control alguno', Asdrubal Guerra, *W Radio Colombia*, Bogotá (Colombia), 16 June 2008

'Fact and fiction in the war on drugs', Prospero, *The Economist*, London, 1 September 2016

'Family fights in court over Cuban sugar mills', José de Cordoba, *The Wall Street Journal*, New York, 4 April 1999

'$5,000 found in train compartment', no byline, *The Washington Post*, Washington, DC, 13 October 1982

'Former KXGO owner indicted in Humboldt cocaine-ring case', Peter Sibley, *Times-Standard*, Eureka (CA), 2 April 1986

'4-year fight in Florida "just can't stop drugs"', Joel Brinkley, *The New York Times*, New York, 4 September 1986

'Gang boss linked to Colombian drug lords: US documents tie Quebec Hells Angels leader to cocaine traffickers', George Kalogerakis, *The Vancouver Sun*, Vancouver (Canada), 3 May 2002

'Gjykata spanjolle: "Kolumbiani, ortaku dhe furnitori i Frederik Durdës', Habjon Hasani, arkivalajmeve.com, Tirana (Albania), 1 May 2008

'Glades co-op directors are re-elected', no byline, *The Clewiston News*, Clewiston (FL), 17 December 1964

'Godfather for hire', Yudhijit Bhattacharjee, *The New Yorker*, New York, 30 July 2018

'Granja venezolana escondía operación masiva de contrabando de cocaína', Associated Press, *Critica*, Panama City (Panama), 28 August 2000

'Guilty plea in sugar fraud case', United Press International, *The Town Talk*, Alexandria (LA), 2 August 1985

'Guilty: The Milkman – international cocaine smuggler who always delivered', Ian Cobain, *The Guardian*, London, 3 April 2007

'"Head of the snake" cut off: global drug boss arrested', Knight Ridder Newspapers, *Deseret News*, Salt Lake City (UT), 27 August 2000

'Historia de "narcoficción"', Jorge A. Rodríguez, *El País*, Madrid, 25 September 2000

'Home-grown coca plagues Colombia: toxic cocaine byproduct spreads addiction to young', Michael Isikoff, *The Washington Post*, Washington, DC, 9 January 1989

'Honduras elites and organised crime: Juan Ramón Matta Ballesteros', Steven Dudley, insightcrime.org, Washington, DC, 9 April 2016
'How dealing cocaine in Colombia led to mortgage fraud in Aventura', David J. Neal, *The Miami Herald*, Miami, 1 October 2018
'How drug lords make billions smuggling gold to Miami for your jewelry and phones', Jay Weaver, Nicholas Nehamas and Kyra Gurney, *The Miami Herald*, Miami, 16 January 2018
'Imprisoned drug trafficker's dad, son plead guilty', Ann W. O'Neill, *The South Florida Sun-Sentinel*, Deerfield Beach (FL), 6 June 2003
'An incursion into Venezuela, straight out of Hollywood', Julie Turkewitz and Frances Robles, *The New York Times*, New York, 7 May 2020
'Indictments charge sugar-export scam', Associated Press, *The Orlando Sentinel*, Orlando (FL), 22 June 1985
'In brief', no byline, *Broadcasting Magazine*, New York, 2 August 1976
'Interpol's Mexican chief kills two, commits suicide', UPI Archives, United Press International, Washington, DC, 18 September 1988
'Interview: Jorge Ochoa' (transcript from 'Drug Wars' series), *Frontline*, pbs.org, Medellín (Colombia), 2000
'Interview: Juan David Ochoa' (transcript from 'Drug Wars' series), *Frontline*, pbs.org, Medellín (Colombia), 2000
'Is this the new Medellín Cartel?', Adriaan Alsema, *Colombia Reports*, Medellín (Colombia), 5 June 2019
'Italy: international drugs bust highlights Albania's role' (original source: Agenzia Nazionale Stampa Associata, Rome, in Italian), *BBC Monitoring European*, London, 10 February 2001
'José "El Mono" Abello regresó a Santa Marta y ya fue objeto de un atentado que presagia otra guerra', no byline, *El Tiempo*, Bogotá (Colombia), 3 September 2008
'Julio Lobo: el millonario a quien el Che le propuso dirigir la industria azucarera en Cuba', no byline, cibercuba.com, Havana (Cuba), 11 November 2018
'Jury finds Noriega guilty on 8 of 10 counts, Noriega guilty on 8 counts', Richard Cole/Associated Press, *The Morning Call*, Allentown (PA), 10 April 1992
'Jury sentences convicted Navas to life in prison', United Press International, *Technician*, Raleigh (NC), 29 February 1984
'La generación de la mafia', no byline, *El Tiempo*, Bogotá (Colombia), 9 September 2001
'La policía abandonará esta semana el registro del "Privilege" si no halla droga', Jorge A. Rodríguez, *El País*, Madrid, 12 September 2000
'Las gambetas de "Micky"', no byline, *El Espectador*, Bogotá (Colombia), 18 October 2008
'La tumba vacía de Sahagún Baca, primo de Martha, y los cárteles de Michoacán', Francisco Javier Larios Gaxiola, elregio.com, Monterrey (Mexico), 15 July 2018
'Long day's journey into fright', Ronald K. Siegel, *Omni Magazine*, Vol. 11, No. 3, New York, December 1988
'Los carteles de la coca', no byline, *Semana*, Bogotá (Colombia), 16 March 1987

'Los celos enfermizos del "Mellizo"', no byline, *Semana*, Bogotá (Colombia), 1 February 2014

'Los errores en la protección al informante que delató a "Los Mellizos"', no byline, *El Tiempo*, Bogotá (Colombia), 28 January 2016

'"Los Mellizos", el mayor clan del narcotráfico desde Pablo Escobar', no byline, *La Razón*, Madrid, 13 February 2004

'Los narcogemelos', no byline, *Semana*, Bogotá (Colombia), 1 October 2001

'"Los Nevados", el nuevo cartel de "Los Mellizos" Mejía Múnera que declaró guerra al estado', no byline, *El Tiempo*, Bogotá (Colombia), 15 December 2007

'Major drugs cartel smashed', no byline, *BBC News*, London, 27 August 2000

'Marijuana and meth are getting more popular in America, but cocaine has declined', Carolyn Wilke, *Science News*, Washington, DC, 23 August 2019

'Mexico arrests accused drug cartel kingpin', Chris Kraul, *The Los Angeles Times*, Los Angeles, 14 June 2001

'México: duro golpe al narcotráfico', María Elena Navas, *BBC Mundo*, London, 13 June 2001

'Mexico's Interpol chief dead in suspicious "suicide"', no byline, *Executive Intelligence Review*, Vol. 15, No. 9, Washington, DC, 30 September 1988

'The Mexican poppy eradication campaign', Peter B. Bensinger (administrator), *Drug Enforcement*, Drug Enforcement Administration (United States Department of Justice), Washington, DC, February 1977

'Miki Ramírez: de delator a capo del narcotráfico', no byline, *El Tiempo*, Bogotá (Colombia), 4 July 1996

'Mob figure's slaying surfaces after six years', Gail Epstein and Amy Alexander, *The Miami Herald*, Miami, 1994 (exact date unknown; from clipping)

'Navas believed to be cocaine importer', no byline, UPI Archives, United Press International, Washington, DC, 14 October 1982

'Navas is convicted: sentencing set today', *Wilson Daily Times*, Wilson (NC), 28 February 1984

'Noriega found guilty on eight of 10 counts', *Tulsa World*, Tulsa (OK), 10 April 1992

'Norte del Valle Cartel', no byline, insightcrime.org, Washington, DC, 17 November 2015

'Notorious drugs baron dubbed "top, top man" who smuggled £5million worth of cocaine into Britain hidden in watermelons is jailed for more than 17 years', Harriet Arkell, *The Daily Mail*, London, 3 October 2014

'Officials: mobsters', Warren Richey, *The Fort Lauderdale Sun-Sentinel*, Deerfield Beach (FL), 19 August 1994

'Officials seize $35 million in drug money', Associated Press, *Times-News*, Twin Falls (ID), 26 August 2001

'$1bn haul of cocaine seized in 12-nation operation', Jan McGirk, *The Independent*, London, 27 August 2000

'Opposition leader upsets Colombia's plantation owners with science: sugar kills more people than cocaine', Adriaan Alsema, *Colombia Reports*, Medellín (Colombia), 11 June 2019

'Over 50 tonnes of cocaine seized at Antwerp's port in 2018', Oscar Schneider, *The Brussels Times*, Brussels (Belgium), 11 January 2019

'Pablo Escobar: ¿qué escribía en sus libretas?', no byline, *La Prensa*, Lima (Peru), 2 December 2016

'Pair get life terms in murder', Henry Fitzgerald, *The Fort Lauderdale Sun-Sentinel*, Deerfield Beach (FL), 23 January 1997

'Personality spotlight: Pablo Escobar Gaviria: Colombian cocaine king', UPI Archives, United Press International, Washington, DC, 20 June 1991

'Police officer, member of the cartel' (in Greek: 'Αστυνομικός, μέλος του καρτέλ'), no byline, *Ta Nea*, Athens (Greece), 28 August 2000

'Reputed head of drug ring taken to U.S. after arrest', John H. Cushman Jr, *The New York Times*, New York, 27 August 2000

'Revelará Rasguño nexos con narcotraficantes mexicanos', Notimex (news agency), *La Jornada*, Mexico City (Mexico), 20 July 2007

'Security concerns mount as drug smuggler's trial nears', David Gibson, *The Fort Lauderdale Sun-Sentinel*, Deerfield Beach (FL), 30 November 1986

'Sentencia de 47 años de prisión a Ramón Alcides Magaña [sic], "El Metro"', no byline, *Proceso*, Mexico City (Mexico), 21 June 2007

'Sicarios acaban con la vida de Cordelio Vaceannie', no byline, *Semanario El Extra de San Andrés*, San Andrés (Colombia), 5 February 2018

'Sicarios intentaron matar a excapo del narcotráfico "Beto el Gitano"', no byline, *El Tiempo*, Bogotá (Colombia), 16 August 2019

'The siege, the gunman and the FBI negotiator', Phil McCombs, *The Washington Post*, Washington, DC, 16 October 1982

'The sleaze connection', Guy Gugliotta, *The Washington Post*, Washington, DC, 22 September 1991

'A Spanish-speaking gunman holding two young children hostage told. . .', Craig Webb, UPI Archives, United Press International, Washington, DC, 10 October 1982

'Sugar concern admits fraud', Associated Press, *Asbury Park Press*, Asbury Park (NJ), 3 August 1985

'Sugar smuggling is under investigation – dealers are accused of evading US import quotas', Anthony M. DeStefano, *The Wall Street Journal*, New York, 21 June 1985

'Suspect's detention extended', Ellis Berger, *The South Florida Sun-Sentinel*, Deerfield Beach (FL), 29 August 2000

'13 firms linked to major fraud in sugar trade', Mary Thornton, *The Washington Post*, Washington, DC, 22 June 1985

'There's no business like drug business', Nicholas Pileggi, *New York Magazine*, New York, 13 December 1982

'Thomas Leroy Wolfe', no byline, *The Oklahoman*, Oklahama City (OK), 2 November 1985

'Trafficker's guilty plea ends lengthy drug case', Larry Lebowitz, *The Miami Herald*, Miami, 17 June 2003

'Trafficker sentenced to 20 years in prison', Ann W. O'Neill, *The South Florida Sun-Sentinel*, Deerfield Beach (FL), 23 July 2003

'Traffickers-turned-"paras" find way to foil extradition', Gerardo Reyes and Steven Dudley, *The Miami Herald*, Miami, 8 September 2006

'Train gunman yields child, then gives up, with 2 dead', Associated Press, *The New York Times*, New York, 12 October 1982

'12-nation effort breaks up Colombian drug operation', Rick Weiss, *The Washington Post*, Washington, DC, 27 August 2000

'23 plead guilty in sugar scam', Kevin McGill, Associated Press, New York, 11 July 1985

'Two from ship's crew charged in $1 billion cocaine bust at Port of Philadelphia', Virginia Streva, *PhillyVoice*, Philadelphia (PA), 19 June 2019

'200 years for cocaine gang', Paul Cheston, *The Evening Standard*, London, 14 June 2002

'Two sugar companies owned by Lobo family are declared bankrupt: Olavarria & Co., Galban Lobo Co. say $25 million lien precludes possibility of settling debts', no byline, *The Wall Street Journal*, New York, 17 November 1966

'Un mese appostati sull'Orinoco il carico era nascosto sott'acqua', Daniele Mastrogiacomo, *La Repubblica*, Rome, 10 February 2001

'USCG sets new record for cocaine seizures', Richard R. Burgess, *Sea Power*, Vol. 42, No. 11, Washington, DC, November 1999

'US court condemns Colombia drug trafficker "Rasguño" to 30 years', Taran Volckhausen, *Colombia Reports*, Medellín (Colombia), 3 December 2013

'US deals blow to cocaine trade as 25 tonnes seized', Jane Martinson, *The Guardian*, London, 28 August 2000

'US unloads record bust of 20 tons of cocaine', Adam Tanner, reuters.com, London, 24 April 2007

'Venezuela raid nets 5 tonnes of cocaine', Gabriella Gamini, *The Times*, London, 22 August 2000

'Venezuela: Chávez backs international anti-drugs push', *Oxford Analytica Daily Brief Service*, Oxford (UK), 28 September 2000

'Venezuela: National Guard confiscates two more tons of cocaine' (original source: *El Nacional*, Caracas, in Spanish), no byline, *BBC Monitoring Americas*, London, 24 August 2000

'Venezuela: police seize five tons of cocaine in international operation' (original source: *El Nacional*, Caracas, in Spanish), no byline, *BBC Monitoring Americas*, London, 20 August 2000

'Venezuelan raids net record cocaine haul', Alex Bellos, *The Guardian*, London, 26 August 2000

'The voice of reason', Sierra Bellows, *Virginia Magazine*, Charlottesville (VA), Winter 2010

'VAW-125's Tigertails', Troy Miller, *Wings of Gold*, Vol. 28, No. 4, Falls Church (VA), Winter 2003

'War on drugs has helped cocaine traffickers conquer swathes of Central America, study suggests', Harry Cockburn, *The Independent*, London, 1 April 2019

'Women in law enforcement', no byline, ice.gov, United States Department of Homeland Security, Washington, DC, 3 October 2018

'The world's deadliest criminals: Colombian cocaine cartels', no byline, *The Miami Herald*, Miami, 8 February 1987

'Young Amtrak hostage taken to foster home', UPI Archives, United Press International, Washington, DC, 14 October 1982

Books

The following titles between them provided interesting background into the sugar and/or cocaine trades, the DEA and the war on drugs, the American mafia and Colombian cartels, pre-revolutionary Cuba and Latin America, and other aspects of Luis's story. Some personal recommendations: Enrique Cirules's book *The Mafia in Havana* is an essential resource for background on the mob in Cuba; William C. Rempel's *At the Devil's Table* is the go-to book on the Cali Cartel (and formed the basis for season three of *Narcos*); while Peter Walsh's *Drug War* is an excellent primer on the British law-enforcement aspect to Operation Journey. – JF & LN

A Brief History of Cocaine (Second Edition), Steven B. Karch, CRC Press, Boca Raton (FL), 2006

American Desperado: My Life as a Cocaine Cowboy, Jon Roberts and Evan Wright, Crown Publishers, New York, 2011

The Art of Doing: How Superachievers Do What They Do and How They Do It So Well, Camille Sweeney and Josh Gosfeld, Plume, New York, 2013

At the Devil's Table: The Untold Story of the Insider Who Brought Down the Cali Cartel, William C. Rempel, Random House, New York, 2011

Big Deal: The Politics of the Illicit Drug Business, Anthony Henman, Roger Lewis and Tim Malyon with Betsy Ettore and Lee O'Bryan, Pluto Press, Sydney (Australia), 1985

The Bullet or the Bribe: Taking Down Colombia's Cali Drug Cartel, Ron Chepesiuk, Praeger Publishers, Westport (CT), 2003

The Cocaine Wars: Murder, Money, Corruption and the World's Most Valuable Commodity, Paul Eddy and Sara Walden with Hugo Sabogal, Century, London, 1988

Colombia's Narcotics Nightmare: How the Drug Trade Destroyed Peace, James D. Henderson, McFarland & Company, Inc. Publishers, Jefferson (NC), 2015

Dangerous Liaisons: Organized Crime and Political Finance in Latin America and Beyond, Kevin Casas-Zamora, Brookings Institution Press, Washington, DC, 2013

The Dark Art: My Undercover Life in Global Narco-terrorism, Edward Follis and Douglas Century, Gotham Books, New York, 2014

DEA: The War Against Drugs, Jessica de Grazia, BBC Books, London, 1991

Down by the River: Drugs, Money, Murder and Family, Charles Bowden, Simon & Schuster, New York, 2002

Drug War: The Secret History, Peter Walsh, Milo Books, Preston (UK), 2018

El Túnel de Lecumberri, Alberto Sicilia Falcón, Compañía General de Ediciones, Mexico City (Mexico), 1979

Full Circle: The Remarkable True Story of Two All-American Wrestling Teammates Pitted Against Each Other in the War on Drugs and Then Reunited as Coaches, Chuck Malkus and Jerry Langton, Simon & Schuster, New York, 2018

Gang Land: From Footsoldiers to Kingpins, The Search for Mr Big, Tony Thompson, Hodder & Stoughton, London, 2010

Gangsters of Miami: True Tales of Mobsters, Gamblers, Hitmen, Con Men and Gangbangers from the Magic City, Ron Chepesiuk, Barricade Books, Fort Lee (NJ), 2010

Hotel Scarface: Where Cocaine Cowboys Partied and Plotted to Control Miami, Roben Farzad, New American Library, New York, 2017

Hunting LeRoux: The Inside Story of the DEA Takedown of a Criminal Genius and His Empire, Elaine Shannon, William Morrow, New York, 2019

The Infiltrator: My Secret Life Inside the Dirty Banks Behind Pablo Escobar's Medellín Cartel, Robert Mazur, Back Bay Books, New York, 2009

Inside Central America: Its People, Politics and History, Clifford Krauss, Summit Books, New York, 1991

Killing Pablo: The Hunt for the World's Greatest Outlaw, Mark Bowden, Atlantic Monthly Press, New York, 2001

Los Jinetes de la Cocaína, Fabio Castillo, Equipo Nizkor, Bogotá (Colombia), 1987

Loving Pablo, Hating Escobar: The Shocking True Story of the Notorious Drug Lord from the Woman Who Knew Him Best, Virginia Vallejo (translated by Megan McDowell), Canongate Books, Edinburgh, 2018

The Mafia in Havana: A Caribbean Mob Story, Enrique Cirules, Ocean Press, Melbourne, Australia, 2010

Miami Babylon: Crime, Wealth and Power, A Dispatch from the Beach, Gerald Posner, Simon & Schuster, New York, 2009

Narcoland: The Mexican Drug Lords and Their Godfathers, Anabel Hernández (translated by Iain Bruce with Lorna Scott Fox), Verso, London, 2013

Pablo Escobar: My Father, Juan Pablo Escobar (translated by Andrea Rosenberg), Ebury Press, London, 2016

The Politics of Drug Violence: Criminals, Cops and Politicians in Colombia and Mexico, Angélica Durán-Martínez, Oxford University Press, New York, 2018

Raising Cane in the 'Glades: The Global Sugar Trade and the Transformation of Florida, Gail M. Hollander, University of Chicago Press, Chicago (IL), 2009

Richard M. Nixon (*The American Presidents* series), Elizabeth Drew, Times Books, New York, 2007

Stalling for Time: My Life as an FBI Hostage Negotiator, Gary Noesner, Random House, New York, 2018

The Sugar King of Havana: The Rise and Fall of Julio Lobo, Cuba's Last Tycoon, John Paul Rathbone, Penguin Books, New York, 2010

The Takedown: A Suburban Mom, a Coal Miner's Son, and the Unlikely Demise of Colombia's Brutal Norte Valle [sic] *Cartel*, Jeffrey Robinson, St Martin's Press, New York, 2011

The Underground Empire: Where Crime and Governments Embrace, James Mills, Doubleday & Co., New York, 1986

Wiseguy: Life in a Mafia Family, Nicholas Pileggi, Simon & Schuster, New York, 1985

Documentaries

Cocaine Cowboys, Billy Corben (director) and Albert Spellman (producer), Rakontur, Miami (FL), 2006

Declassified: Untold Stories of American Spies (Episode 305: 'The Norte Valle [sic] Cartel'), Domini Hofmann (executive producer and director), CNN, Atlanta (GA), 2019

The Godfather of Cocaine, William Cran (writer, director and producer), *Frontline*, PBS, Boston (MA), 1995

The Invisibles, Sherry Fynbo (executive producer), Beyond Entertainment, Sydney (Australia), 2020

Pin Kings, Jon Fish (producer), Brett Forrest (writer) and Victor Vitarelli (executive producer), *Sports Illustrated*, New York, 2016

The True Story of Killing Pablo, David Keane (director and executive producer), History Channel (A&E Networks), New York, 2002

Documents, Research Papers & Monographs

'American gambling activities in Cuba anti-racketeering', confidential memo sent to FBI director from Legat, Cuba, United States Government, Washington, DC, 25 June 1958

'America's habit: drug abuse, drug trafficking, and organized crime', Irving R. Kaufman (chairman), report by the President's commission on organised crime to the President and the Attorney General, Washington DC, 1986

'Auto de procesamiento', Juzgado Central de Instruccion Numero Cinco Audencia Nacional Madrid, Sumario 7/03, Contra la Salud Publica, Administracion de Justicia, Madrid, 5 February 2004

'The Cali Cartel: the new kings of cocaine', drug intelligence report, Drug Enforcement Administration (United States Department of Justice), Washington, DC, November 1994

'Colombian drug trafficker sentenced to 40 years in prison', United States Immigration and Customs Enforcement press release, Washington, DC, 24 April 2012

'Colombian paramilitary leader extradited to the United States to face US drug charges', United States Department of Justice Office of Public Affairs press release, Washington, DC, 4 March 2009

'Colombia: the shape of trafficking to come?', no byline, *International Narcotics Review*, DCI (Director of Central Intelligence) Crime and Narcotics Center, Central Intelligence Agency, Langley (VA), June–July 1995

'Confidential informant communications', Nigel Brooks, redacted emails from Tommy Taylor, United States Customs Service, Washington, DC, 2000

'Confidential: Operation Journey update as of 6/6/00', Nigel Brooks, redacted intelligence document, United States Customs Service, Washington, DC, 2000

'DEA Congressional Testimony: statement by Thomas A. Constantine, administrator, Drug Enforcement Administration before the Senate Foreign Relations Committee, Subcommittee on the Western Hemisphere, Peace Corps, Narcotics and Terrorism regarding international organized crime syndicates and their impact on the United States', Drug Enforcement Administration (United States Department of Justice), Washington, DC, 26 February 1998

'Domestic implications of illicit Colombian drug production and trafficking', Richard B. Craig, *Journal of Interamerican Studies and World Affairs*, Center for Latin American Studies at the University of Miami, Vol. 25, No. 3, Miami, August 1983

'Drug control: DEA's strategies and operations in the 1990s', report to congressional requesters, Norman J. Rabkin (editor), United States General Accounting Office, Washington, DC, July 1999

'The Drug Enforcement Administration's international operations (redacted)', audit report 07-19, Office of the Inspector General, United States Department of Justice, Washington, DC, February 2007

'Ecuador prosecutes landmark money laundering case', unclassified diplomatic cable, United States Embassy, Quito (Ecuador), Public Library of US Diplomacy, wikileaks.org, no headquarters, 3 March 2008

'The FCC's broadcast news distortion rules: regulation by drooping eyelid', Chad Raphael, *Communication Law and Policy*, Vol. 6, No. 3, Mahwah (NJ), Summer 2001

'Former Miami-Dade County resident sentenced to more than 8 years in prison for bank fraud and money laundering schemes', Drug Enforcement Administration press release, Kevin W. Carter, Special Agent in Charge, Drug Enforcement Administration (United States Department of Justice), Miami, 27 September 2018

'FY 2017 performance budget congressional submission', Drug Enforcement Administration (United States Department of Justice), Washington, DC, 2017

'Head of drugs gang convicted', HMRC news release issued by The Government News Network, London, 2 April 2007

'A history and analysis of the Federal Communications Commission's response to radio broadcast hoaxes', Justin Levine, *Federal Communications Law Journal*, Vol. 52, Washington, DC, 2000

'Human rights in Mexico: a policy of impunity', Ellen L. Lutz, Americas Watch Committee (Human Rights Watch), New York, June 1990

'Impact of the South Florida Task Force on drug interdiction in the Gulf Coast area: hearing before the subcommittee on security and terrorism of the committee on the judiciary United States Senate', 98th Congress, first session on the scope of the drug problems in Alabama and other Gulf states, Mobile (AL), 28 October 1983

'The interface between extradition and asylum', Sibylle Kapferer, Legal and Protection Policy Research Series, Protection Policy and Legal Advice Section, Department of International Protection, United Nations High Commissioner for Refugees, Geneva (Switzerland), November 2003

'International extradition and the Medellín cocaine cartel: surgical removal of Colombian cocaine traffickers for trial in the United States', Steven Y. Otera, *Loyola of Los Angeles International and Comparative Law Review*, Vol. 13, No. 4, Los Angeles, 1991

'Juárez Cartel leader sentenced in Manhattan Federal Court to 27 years in prison for importing more than 200 tons of cocaine into United States', United States Attorney's Office press release, United States Attorney Southern District of New York, United States Department of Justice, Washington, DC, 2 December 2009

'Judgment, between Bankgesellschaft Berlin AG et al. and Elias Dimitris Lemos et al.', The Hon. Mr Justice Creswell, High Court of Justice, Queen's Bench Division, Commercial Court, 1996 Folio 1681, Royal Courts of Justice, London, 22 January 1998

'Leadership protection in drug-trafficking networks', David C. Hofmann and Owen Gallupe, *Global Crime*, Vol. 16, No. 2, London, 2015

'Life of a cell: managerial practice and strategy in Colombian cocaine distribution in the United States', Joseph R. Fuentes, dissertation thesis, City University of New York, New York, 1998

'Maritime security report', Office of Ports and Domestic Shipping, United States Department of Transportation (Maritime Administration), Washington, DC, November 2000

'Mi historia en prisión', Iván de la Vega Cabás, self-published, Barranquilla (Colombia), 19 May 2010

'Nicolás Maduro Moros and 14 current and former Venezuelan officials charged with narco-terrorism, corruption, drug trafficking and other criminal charges', United States Department of Justice press release, Office of Public Affairs, United States Department of Justice, Washington, DC, 26 March 2020

'Mafia & Co: the criminal networks in Mexico, Brazil and Colombia', Juan Carlos Garzón (translated by Kathy Ogle), Woodrow Wilson International Center for Scholars Latin American Program, Washington, DC, June 2008

'Muy señores nuestros', letter by Julio Lobo announcing the appointment of Luis Navia Sr as vice-president of Galbán Lobo Trading Company SA, Havana (Cuba), 11 March 1957

'The narco threat to US security: Venezuela's criminal regime fuels regional instability', Ambassador Roger F. Noriega (Retired), statement before the Senate Caucus on International Narcotics Control US Counternarcotics Strategy, Washington, DC, 11 June 2019

'Navia draft debrief', Barry Clarke, notes of interview with Luis Navia, Her Majesty's Customs and Excise, Miami, 2001/'02

'Nota de prensa sobre la "Operación Ostra"', Ministerio del Interior press release, Ministerio del Interior, Madrid, 15 September 2000

'Operation Journey', briefing presentation transcript, William Ledwith, chief, International Operations Drug Enforcement Administration and Jeffrey Casey, executive director, Office of Investigations, United States Customs Service, Washington, DC, undated (circa August–September 2000)

'Operation Journey: a blueprint for the future, Special Agent in Charge, Houston, Texas', Nigel Brooks, Microsoft PowerPoint presentation, United States Customs Service, Washington, DC, 2000

'Origins of Operation Journey', Nigel Brooks, typewritten summary of Operation Journey, private document, Houston (TX), 2002

'The regression of a country', Camilo Castellanos, *El Embrujo*, Colombian Platform for Human Rights, Democracy and Development, Bogotá (Colombia), November 2009

'Re: M/V *Suerte I*, attention: Mohamed', fax to Coastal Maritime Inc. (Colombia) from Angelos Kanakis of Callisti Maritime Inc., Piraeus (Greece), 2 May 2000

'The speed of light', print advertisement for Michelob Light Racing Team, Anheuser-Busch, St. Louis (MO), 1980

'Structure of international drug trafficking organizations: hearings before the permanent subcommittee on investigations of the committee on governmental affairs United States Senate', 101st Congress, first session, Washington, DC, 12–13 September 1989

'Treasury targets Colombian drug traffickers', United States Department of the Treasury Office of Foreign Assets Control (OFAC) press release, Washington, DC, 30 August 2007

'United States of America v. [redacted]', Criminal Docket for Case [redacted], United States District Judge James Lawrence King, United States District Court, Southern District of Florida, Key West Division, Key West (FL), 3 March 1995

'United States of America v. Iván de la Vega Cabás', Judgment in a Criminal Case, Case Number: 1:00-6274-CR-HUCK, United States District Judge Paul C. Huck, United States District Court, Southern District of Florida, Miami Division, Miami, 18 January 2002

'United States of America v. Iván de la Vega Cabás', Amended Judgment in a Criminal Case, Case Number: 00-CR-6274-PCH, United States District Judge Paul C. Huck, United States District Court, Southern District of Florida, Miami Division, Miami, 26 February 2008

'United States of America v. Luis Navia', Judgment in a Criminal Case, Case Number: 00-6308-CR-KING, United States District Judge James Lawrence King, United States District Court, Southern District of Florida, Miami Division, Miami, 19 July 2001

'United States of America v. Luis Navia', Unopposed Motion to Transfer and Consolidate This Action to Lower Number Case, Case Number: 00-6308-CR-DIMITROULEAS, United States District Judge William P. Dimitrouleas, United States District Court, Southern District of Florida, Fort Lauderdale Division, Fort Lauderdale (FL), 27 October 2000

'United States of America v. Néstor Suerte', Memorandum and Order, Criminal Number: 00-0659, United States District Judge Kenneth M. Hoyt, United States District Court, Southern District of Texas, Houston Division, Houston (TX), 4 June 2001

'U.S. Drug Enforcement Agency and counterparts from other nations announce developments in large anti-drug operation', rush transcript, CNN, Atlanta (GA), 26 August 2000

'U.S. officials say they have stopped major Colombian cocaine network', rush transcript, CNN, Atlanta (GA), 26 August 2000

'White House fact sheet: cooperation between the United States and Colombia on counter-drug programs', The White House, Washington, DC, 30 August 2000

Motion Pictures/Streaming Series

Inside the Real Narcos, Stuart Cabb and Will Daws (executive producers), Channel 4, United Kingdom, 2018

Loving Pablo (aka *Escobar*), Fernando León de Aranoa (writer and director, based on the book *Loving Pablo, Hating Escobar* by Virginia Vallejo) and Javier Bardem, et al. (producers), Pinguin Films/Dean Nichols Productions/ Millennium Films, et al., Spain, 2017

Pablo Escobar: El Patrón del Mal, Carlos Moreno and Laura Mora Ortega (creators), Caracol Televisión, Colombia, 2012

Narcos, Chris Brancato, Carlo Bernard and Doug Miro (executive producers), Gaumont International Television, United States/Colombia, 2015

Narcos: Mexico, Chris Brancato, Carlo Bernard and Doug Miro (executive producers), Gaumont International Television, United States/Mexico, 2018

Televised News Reports/Online Videos

'A billion dollars' worth of cocaine seized', *CTV News*, CTV Television, Scarborough (Canada), 26 August 2000

'Cocaine: why the cartels are winning', *The Economist*, YouTube, London, 23 August 2018

'Colombian police kill major drug trafficker in raid on ranch', AP Archive, YouTube, London, 21 July 2015

'USA: Colombian drug ring: arrests', Associated Press Television News and United States Customs Service Video, Story Number 192665, AP Archive, London, 26 August 2000

'World's largest drug bust in Mexico', AP Archive, YouTube, London, 22 July 2015

Websites

archives.gov
bop.gov
cbrayton.wordpress.com
colombiareports.com
courtlistener.com
dea.gov
derechos.org
directnews.gr
drug.addictionblog.org
elregio.com
extradicion.com.co
familytreenow.com
fas.org
fiscalia.gov.co
forbes.com
formatchange.com
fredmitchelluncensored.com
govinfo.gov
hndm.unam.mx
ice.gov
inmatereleases.org
insightcrime.org
interpol.int
jaimemontilla.com
justice.gov
knightcenter.utexas.edu
law.cornell.edu
marinetraffic.com
medellinabrazasuhistoria.com
medellinliving.com
mercado.com.pa
murderpedia.org
narconews.com
newspaperarchive.com
ncjrs.gov
offshoreleaks.icij.org
opencorporates.com
pbs.org
pepes.exposed
planespotters.net
proyectopabloescobar.com
racingsportscars.com
reuters.com
sanctionedlist.com
saltwatersportsman.com
shipspotting.com
sortedbybirthdate.com
state.gov
treasury.gov
sudnews.it
sunshineskies.com
tovima.gr
tni.org
tradewindsnews.com
travel.state.gov
ufdc.ufl.edu
unodc.org
wikileaks.org
wired-gov.net
zougla.gr

Endnotes

1 Debriefing is a law-enforcement term that refers to a review or rundown of actions taken during a particular event or operation, such as the takedown of a criminal conspiracy.

2 A full list of all the Spanish words used in the book and their meanings, as well as drug-trafficking slang, can be found in Glossary. Diacritics or accent marks are frequently used but familiar geographic names such as Mexico and Mexico City are spelled without accents.

3 It was no fault of Wright, who evidently spent a great deal of time trying to verify the claims his subject was making and apparently even cautioned Roberts not to include his war tales in the book.

4 Perhaps wisely, Luis has made a general habit of shying away from all forms of social media but he did once join Facebook. 'The only friend I had was "Popeye",' he laughs, referring to Pablo Escobar's chief *sicario*, the late Jhon Jairo Velásquez Vásquez. Popeye died of cancer in February 2020.

5 As 'Louis Navia'.

6 US tons. A metric ton is 1000 kilos. A US ton is 907.185 kilos.

7 Luis changed his plea after initially pleading not guilty. 'You plead not guilty to everything,' he jokes. 'That lasts for about a month.'

8 Isabelle Meneses is a pseudonym. All the members of Luis's family and inner circle have been given false names for their protection, apart from his deceased parents. All pseudonyms used in the book are indicated.

9 A lifelong partyer and Scotch drinker, in recent years he has observed a rule of not drinking alcohol during the 40 days of Lent.

10 Mr Magoo was a cartoon character voiced by actor Jim Backus for 40 years. The myopic, elderly Magoo got into calamitous situations but always managed to come out on top through dumb luck; perhaps why Luis identifies with him so much.

11 An eerily prescient joke, given the COVID-19 pandemic in 2020.

12 The kidnapping, brutal torture and murder of DEA agent Enrique 'Kiki' Camarena Salazar by the Guadalajara Cartel in 1985 bears out that statement. Camarena's story formed the basis for the first season of *Narcos: Mexico*.

13 In Spanish, *mono* is literally 'monkey', but in Colombian Spanish it is used to refer to Caucasians or a white person with light hair. The feminine is *mona*.

14 Since 2003, ICE has been part of the United States Department of Homeland Security (DHS).

15 Ignacio Bargueño is a pseudonym.

16 In reality, though, it's probably best known around the world for being used in the title of an Enya album. Sadly Venezuela, physically a very beautiful country, is not a destination visited by many tourists and its economy has now all but collapsed. It is not just a failed state but a narco state. Former US diplomat Roger F. Noriega used the very term in testimony to the Senate Caucus on International Narcotics Control in Washington, DC in June 2019. A CNN report earlier the same year revealed 240 tons of cocaine was crossing the border every year from Colombia to be transported north. In March 2020, Venezuela's president, Nicolás Maduro Moros, was indicted by the United States on charges including narco-terrorism and cocaine trafficking. A $15 million reward was offered for information leading to his arrest and/or conviction. A coup attempt by US mercenaries was foiled two months later.

17 The *Post* gave it the full treatment: raids on 'snake-infested bunkers' filled to the brim with cocaine as 'monkeys looked on from the trees'.

18 A key is drug slang for a kilo. The figure of 68 tons was based on estimates that informants provided to the DEA. European cocaine prices in 2000 fluctuated depending on where the drug was sold, but these were the prices contained in an official USCS PowerPoint presentation. According to data from the United Nations Office on Drugs and Crime (UNODC), a gram was worth $138 on the street in Finland, but $33 in the Netherlands. At December 2019 prices a kilo of cocaine in Colombia would cost $1000 and fetch $70,000 on the street in Europe.

19 It was made up of separate settlements/processing facilities Pascualandia, Coquilandia, Villa Coca, Tranquilandia I, Tranquilandia II and Tranquilandia III.

20 In the calendar year 2017, the Federal Criminal Police Office of Germany announced that 639 tons was confiscated globally (similar figures were recorded in 2018 and 2019). An accumulated 41 tons was seized at the port of Antwerp in Belgium in 2017, 50 tons in 2018.

21 A description used by USCS in a PowerPoint presentation to describe De La Vega's role in the maritime transportation organisation.

22 What Luis calls 'Northern Valley' is commonly called North Valley Cartel. *El Cártel de la Costa* operated out of the Colombian cities of Santa Marta and Barranquilla, as well the Dutch protectorate of Aruba.

23 Drug slang for kilograms.

24 In fairness to Mermelstein, who as part of WITSEC died in 2008 while living under an assumed name in Kentucky, his second wife was Colombian: Cristina Jaramillo.

25 The Cartel of the Suns (*El Cártel de los Soles*), a group that emerged from inside the ranks of the Venezuelan military during the presidencies of Hugo Chávez and Nicolás Maduro Moros, is now allegedly one of the most powerful cocaine cartels in the world. Says Luis: 'They are fucking exporting more shit out of Venezuela into northern Africa and Central America than ever before.' The Cartel of the Suns was named in the US indictment against Maduro in March 2020.

26 It has also been claimed that Brazil is the world's second biggest consumer of cocaine, after the United States, with 1.46 million users. A gram of coke in Brazil costs six to ten times less than it does in the US.

27 Bikers remain heavily involved in cocaine distribution.
28 Perhaps an underestimate. At the time of Luis's arrest the average salary for a DEA special agent was roughly $100,000.
29 Colombians also call Medellín the 'City of Eternal Spring'.
30 Explains Luis: 'I always use a Jewish name. All my fake Gmail accounts are under Jewish names.'
31 An alternate spelling seen in news reports is Kalisti.
32 Other departments where Los Mellizos had influence were Antioquia, Magdalena, La Guajira, César, Santander, Norte de Santander, Boyacá and Caldas.
33 Chitiva, from Barranquilla, turned against Escobar as the Medellín Cartel crumbled. He is tall and dark with black straight hair, bushy black eyebrows and long arms. La Mica, which means 'The Monkey' but in the feminine, was a nickname Chitiva picked up in high school: 'You look like a female monkey.'
34 Luis's *modus operandi* was to keep his true identity secret, even though Víctor had met Luis at Luis's Bogotá apartment in 1993 and knew his real name. Víctor had wanted to send cocaine to Cancún, Mexico. 'There was a reason for that. I was already a fugitive. I did not want the heat travelling across to me in Venezuela.'
35 A pseudonym.
36 Says a former girlfriend: 'Luis was never someone you looked at and thought, "*Wow*, what a good-looking guy!" But there was something about him. He was very confident and flirtatious and funny and sweet. He was a very elegant gentleman, very suave, and knew how to treat a lady: with much respect and attention.'
37 Galicia in Spain's northwest has long been a hot spot for the smuggling of contraband in Europe.
38 A pseudonym.
39 The fake passports were Dominican, Colombian, Panamanian, Mexican, Guatemalan and Venezuelan, including some doubles.
40 All pseudonyms.
41 Juliana, born in Colombia, was given a visa for 72 hours. Santi had no problem: he was born in Mexico.
42 Luis believes they met.
43 A Greek report claimed it was $200,000.
44 Oddly, the fact that the boat and captain shared the same name was completely coincidental. Single-name Hispanic aliases are *de rigueur* in the Latin American drug trade, even for Bangladeshis. Jorge García had another story to Luis's: Nomani was 'Indian' (subcontinental) and the Filipinos were recruited by Nomani's brother in the Philippines. Former USCS senior special agent Nigel Brooks confirms Nomani was Indurain's real name. He is referred to as 'Nomadi' in Spanish court documents.
45 In 2002, as part of extradition proceedings against Hells Angels member Guy Lepage from Quebec to Florida, it was revealed by a confidential informant or CI to the DEA that Los Mellizos had been sending tons of cocaine to Quebec. The Hells Angels would send trucks filled with cash to Miami as payment. Lepage was mentioned in Spanish court documents.
46 Los Mellizos had already delivered a substantial amount of 'weight' under the radar into Europe (one report claimed ten tons a week in the US and Europe).

47 Explains Luis: 'The *oficina* is a main office for each cartel that handles SOS [source of supply]. They would give me the merchandise in Colombia and I would use my different routes to place the merchandise in the States. So the *oficina* acts as headquarters for day-to-day operations as well as debt collections, keeps track of merchandise in different countries as well as merchandise en route, and also keep tabs on representatives they have in different countries distributing the merchandise. They have an accounting department, a collections department, a transport department. Some outfits are bigger than others. In all my years I always dealt directly with the head person of a particular *oficina*. My *oficina* always worked different routes at the same time.'

The most famous *oficina* is Medellín's La Oficina de Envigado, which after the death of Pablo Escobar became a cartel in its own right under Diego Fernando Murillo Bejarano aka 'Don Berna', doling out cocaine as well as assassinations. A lawyer representing a roster of cartel bosses who spoke on condition of anonymity says it was effectively 'the accounts receivable department of the Medellín Cartel. It controlled all of the street gangs; whole neighbourhoods.' In 2019 there were reports out of Colombia that La Oficina de Envigado has combined forces with paramilitary group *Autodefensas Gaitanistas de Colombia* (AGC or Gaitanista Self-Defence Forces of Colombia) aka *Clan de Golfo* (Gulf Clan) aka Los Urabeños, along with the Santa Marta–based Pachenca gang and *Clan del Oriente* (Clan of the East) from Magdalena Medio Antioquia to form a new super-cartel. Says Luis: 'La Oficina de Envigado existed while Pablo was around. But that was always a collections office as well as a hit office.'

48 Not as far-fetched as it might seem. Historically, coca plantations have been successful in Formosa (Taiwan), the island of Java in the Dutch East Indies (Indonesia), Okinawa in Japan, and Ceylon (Sri Lanka).

49 The amount impounded altogether on the ground in Venezuela is unclear. A number of reports claimed five-and-a-half tons in plastic barrels were found on an island in the delta. The coke was apparently hidden under a camouflage tarpaulin on a platform built above mangrove roots. Another report said two tons were confiscated in a separate raid in Barrancas del Orinoco. Another report said two-and-a-half tons was found on the abandoned farm in two pits. A collective figure of ten tons was also given. Luis estimates that of the 25 tons amassed at the fishing camps 15 were seized in the raid.

50 Other *guardaespaldas* (bodyguards) and *sicarios* (hitmen) were 'Gardel', 'Nando', 'El Tío', 'Popeye' (no relation to Pablo Escobar's henchman Popeye), 'Tuso', 'Chino' and 'Dinastía'. All were named in Spanish court documents.

51 Not technically true. Mobile phones are triangulated not landlines. Triangulation is a technique by which one can determine a mobile phone's location by measuring the strength of its signal from the nearest mobile-phone tower, drawing a coverage radius from that tower, and then measuring the strength of its signal from second and third mobile-phone towers, again drawing a coverage radius around each of the towers. Where the three radial circles intersect pinpoints the location of the phone.

52 An identical copy was later recovered from Iván de la Vega Cabás.

53 The boat's captain, Néstor Suerte, was convicted in the United States after Malta, where *Suerte I* was registered, waived its jurisdiction over the vessel and consented to its boarding and searching, as well as the application of

American law under the Maritime Drug Law Enforcement Act (MDLEA). This is done by issuing a Statement of No Objection (SNO). Suerte contested that the US had no jurisdiction over him to bring him to trial. A trial court agreed but it was overturned on appeal. Suerte then pleaded guilty and received a sentence of time served. The Filipino crew was repatriated to the Philippines.

54 Who 'they' were is unclear, though a BBC report quoting *El Nacional* newspaper in Venezuela said 'those arrested [in Operation Journey] were transferred to the Counternarcotics Command's [*Comando Antidrogas*'s] headquarters where they are being questioned in the presence of the officials of the Prosecutor-General's Office so that a case could be opened against them and they could be placed under the orders of the appropriate courts'.

55 His biographer, John Paul Rathbone, estimates it would be equivalent to $5 billion today.

56 Luis Sr was a supporter of Batista; Luis believes his father and the dictator knew each other. Batista's daughter Marta María Batista Fernández was a friend of Luis's sister Laura when they both lived in Miami, meeting at Miami-Dade College.

57 He gave them back to Rosengard when he fled Cuba in 1960 to protect the jewels. Luis says his father's plan was never to emigrate to America permanently: 'We thought we were going back.'

58 It is an irony not lost on Luis that Nixon created the DEA by Executive Order in 1973.

59 The company filed for bankruptcy in 1966 over tax debts.

60 The mill eventually closed down in 1977.

61 Fidel Castro went to the same school in Havana before it was moved to Miami after the revolution.

62 Claudia Betancourt is a pseudonym. Omar, another pseudonym, had a drug- and people-smuggler friend, real name Julian Brown, whose family owned the Compleat Angler Hotel in North Bimini, where Ernest Hemingway stayed from 1935 to 1937 and wrote *To Have and Have Not*. 'The Browns ran Bimini for *years*,' says Luis. 'They were smuggling pot way back in 1971, '72, '73. Julian was in jail in the US in '75. Unheard of; back then, that was an incredible crime. He was Omar's best friend. The hotel burned down in 2006, with Julian inside. Julian tried to save the merchandise they had stashed up in the roof; coke not pot. He died in the fire.' A second brother, Frank, was electrocuted in 1970. A third brother, Ossie, was beaten to death with a lead pipe during a home invasion in 1996. A fourth brother, Spence, died on the Browns' boat, the *Alma B*, after it capsized off South Bimini in 2000. The patriarch of the family, Captain Harcourt Neville Brown, died of natural causes in 1997.

63 A pseudonym.

64 Andy later married Marivi Lorido, a friend of Luis's sister, Laura. Luis sold his new car, an Audi Fox, to Andy's brother, René, a jai alai player who got caught up in a match-fixing scandal in 1979. Clau, Luis's girlfriend, was a good friend of Marivi. Technically, Luis was still living at home with his parents but using the rental property as his animal house.

65 It's worth pointing out that Bia has a conflicting story to Luis's about how he found out she was a dealer: 'That life for me is finished. I'm a very private person. I don't talk much about my past. I have lived a fulfilling life. I enjoyed

it very much. But I never used a gun in my whole life and I never menaced anybody.' Luis is adamant his version is the truth and as he described. It was the only thing they disagreed on during the writing of this book. Says Bia: 'Luis's story about the Learjet and the emeralds is not true. What I said to him was that I sold emeralds and that's why I travelled to San Francisco. I used to take Learjets to carry money. He never saw an emerald or the other stuff.'

66 Colombian magazine *Semana* effectively said as much in 1987: *Es la organización criminal más peligrosa del mundo*. 'It is the most dangerous criminal organisation in the world.'

67 Roland and Andreina are pseudonyms.

68 Fabio Ochoa, along with Pablo Escobar and Fabio's distributor in Miami, Rafael Cardona Salazar, is said to have ordered the assassination of Barry Seal.

69 Manolo Varoni, Peter Sharwood, Marcos Geithner and David Patten are all pseudonyms.

70 Pepe (a common Spanish nickname for José) also had a business relationship with a Miami pilot called Jack DeVoe, who ran a small fleet of Piper Navajos under the name DeVoe Airlines from Miami to a constellation of smaller cities in Florida and Alabama: Key West, Orlando, Melbourne, Jacksonville, Fort Lauderdale and Tallahassee. It called itself 'The On-Time Airline' and it proved to be just that for Cabrera. The US Government later calculated that DeVoe had done over 100 smuggling runs from Colombia via Little Darby Island in The Bahamas to Florida, transporting three-and-a-half tons in wing fuel tanks and using eight to ten contract pilots. DeVoe made millions each month. He was arrested and sent to jail for 30 years in 1984, his airline shut down altogether.

As for Cabrera, after he was sentenced to 30 years in prison in 1986 for trafficking more than eight tons of cocaine, he was named 'one of the top five cocaine smugglers in the world' by a Florida state prosecutor and among the 'world's deadliest criminals' by *The Miami Herald*. More convictions on trafficking and racketeering charges followed. He eventually cut a deal with the US Government to testify against Panamanian dictator General Manuel Noriega and was released from jail early, as well as being granted immunity from further prosecution and being allowed to keep part of his fortune. He is now deceased.

71 In the documentary *Cocaine Cowboys* Jon Roberts claimed Rafael Cardona Salazar aka 'Rafa' or 'Rafico' 'really controlled almost every kilo of coke that came into this country through the people from Medellín' and 'there was nobody higher than him for the Medellín Cartel in this country'. Luis says the claim is 'a bit exaggerated – but *yes*; at that point Rafa was the cartel's main guy, the high-level point man, in the United States representing the Medellín Cartel: Pablo and the Ochoas. This was the early '80s to approximately '84. But there were associates of Medellín – Pepe Cabrera, for example – who didn't give their complete load to Rafa to distribute.' Cardona was murdered in Medellín in 1987.

72 In 1989 a US Senate subcommittee, the Permanent Subcommittee on Investigations, declared as much: 'What is commonly referred to as the Medellín Cartel is actually made up of approximately 200 individual trafficking groups which ally themselves in order to coordinate different phases of cocaine production, transportation and distribution.' Joseph R. Fuentes's excellent 1998 doctoral dissertation thesis, 'Life of a cell', defines

a cartel in Colombian practice as being 'a geographically closed area in which are grouped a loose federation or coalition of major drug-trafficking organisations that have formed alliances for the self-serving purpose of reducing the risky nature of the business in which they participate'.

73 Quico is the standardised spelling for Moncada's nickname in Colombia, but Kiko is also an accepted variant.

74 Leticia is located on the border with Brazil and Peru. Porras died in 2010.

75 Says Luis: 'Jorge is a very smart man; very charismatic; great people skills. To be able to handle Pablo and The Mexican, the Cali Cartel, the Castaño brothers and everybody else that followed, you can imagine what sort of organisational ability and intelligence Jorge has. That ability to handle people is an art form.'

76 A doctor friend of Luis, who shall remain nameless, makes an interesting observation: 'Escobar and the other violent narcos needed to believe in the delusion that they were *bandidos* – kind of like Robin Hoods that were helping the poor – in order to assuage their malignantly narcissistic egos. Luis is, at his essence, a very good person with high morals and many regrets now; there's a good degree of shame and guilt there – the opposite of the psychopathic serial killers with whom he associated for so many years. It's like the excitement and the fact that one could die at any second became an even more powerful drug than money or cocaine for these guys.'

77 During a 15 December 1989 shootout with Colombian police in a banana grove outside Tolú, on the Caribbean coast south of Cartagena, The Mexican, aged 42, his son Freddy Rodríguez Celades, 17, and their bodyguards were cut to pieces by AH-6 Little Bird light attack military helicopters equipped with miniguns. Its recreation was one of the best scenes in *Narcos*. Almost exactly four years later, Escobar himself, 44, would be slain in another shootout with Colombian police.

78 Randall Ghotbi is a pseudonym.

79 Lopez, the one and same from the radio scam, is now deceased.

80 A pseudonym.

81 A pseudonym.

82 Says Bia: 'Luis came to water my plants at the apartment, so that was the way he found out what I did [dealing cocaine]. Poli came to my place and told him about [me dealing]. I never wanted Luis to get involved in anything. I got pissed off with Poli about that and he apologised.' Replies Luis: 'I don't remember Poli coming to the apartment and telling me that. If I was in Bia's apartment watering the plants and Poli came over and I opened the door for him, believe me: that meant I already knew she was involved with cocaine. How could I have been partying with Poli and all that and not know anything?'

83 Some reports claimed three assassins were involved.

84 It was later revealed to be a hit connected to Griselda Blanco's organisation. Two gunmen, both Colombians, were identified.

85 *Rola* is a slang term for a woman from Bogotá.

86 Slang for snorting.

87 A statement that would seemingly contradict a claim in Roben Farzad's book about The Mutiny, *Hotel Scarface*, that anybody who was anybody in the cocaine scene in Miami went to the hotel.

88 The Omni Hotel is now the Hilton Miami Downtown.

89 The Ingram Military Armament Corporation-10.
90 *Paisa* is a term for people from the northwest of Colombia, particularly Medellín.
91 *Loco*, meaning crazy in Spanish, was one of Luis's many nicknames, because of 'my demeanor in general – funny, off-the-wall comments, drinking, partying'. Another was 'La Luisa' because of his long hair. 'Not very many people from Colombia and in the business had long hair; it was just me and Fabito Ochoa.'
92 As one DEA agent puts it: 'South Florida is the gateway to South America, and all the shenanigans that go on in South America are just as prevalent there. It's the fraud capital of the United States in terms of different scams and credit card business, and there's always issues with corrupt cops down there. Miami is a sunny city full of shady people. Everybody's working a fucking angle.'
93 Being Cuban also had its advantages, especially after the release of *Scarface* in December 1983. Says Luis: 'A lot of Miami started getting developed with dope money. But up until *Scarface* Americans didn't know much about Cubans. For all they knew Cubans were *¿Qué Pasa, USA?*, the [PBS-produced bilingual] TV show with Rocky Echevarría [aka Steven Bauer] who did the movie *Scarface*. That's the reason Andy Garcia went to LA to become a movie star – because of the success that Rocky was having – and then he surpassed Rocky. Americans thought Cubans were working in hotels or superintendents of buildings. Now they were fucking cool, dangerous, another type of level; like the equivalent of Don Corleone but Cuban. So it elevated Cubans to a position of intrigue. You went to San Francisco and said, "I'm a Cuban from Miami," that was like saying, "I'm a gangster."'
94 Says Luis: 'When he was racing for [B&J Racing] Bernardo drove a Mustang and Javier drove a Corvette. We went to the first [sports car] Grand Prix of Miami in 1983.'
95 Diego Forero, Leif Bowden, Terry Wozniak, Roger Lisko, Brett Spiegel, Bernardo Palomeque, Javier Mercado and Francisco Moya are all pseudonyms. B&J Racing is also a fake name.
96 Octavio Piedrahíta was later indicted for money laundering in Florida and was behind a massive 1762-kilo cocaine seizure in 1982 in Miami. It has been claimed that Piedrahíta organised the 30 April 1984 assassination of Colombian politician Rodrigo Lara Bonilla but the Ochoa brothers have blamed Pablo Escobar. In 1983 Bonilla, then Minister of Justice, accused Escobar, a member of the movement *Renovación Liberal* (Liberal Renewal) who harboured ambitions of becoming president of Colombia, of being a drug trafficker. Bonilla was also behind the raid on Tranquilandia in March 1984. Piedrahíta was assassinated in 1988.
97 Says Luis: 'Mesa was killed, I believe, in Miami around 1983, '84.'
98 Luis had several apartments in Miami during this time: Biscayne and 21st, Venetian Islands, The Palace on Brickell Avenue.
99 Ippolito, who died in 2006, was a well-known New Jersey mob identity and southern California restaurateur who raced speedboats. He was mentioned in a 1980 ad for Michelob Light Racing Team. He was probably most famous for his friendships with Caan and Simpson, and in the 1980s and '90s served separate jail terms for marijuana and cocaine trafficking.
100 Helios and Catalina are pseudonyms.
101 Says Luis: 'The Colombians later began delivering with drop-off cars. They would just drop off a car at a parking lot, hand you the keys, you'd go get the car, do your thing and return the car the next day.'

102 Ironically, in the mid-1980s the truck was eventually busted carrying a load of 60 kilos but Diego managed to slip away from the police and escaped. Says Luis: 'The truck was parked outside a restaurant and some kind of freak situation happened and a police dog smelled the coke or something and suddenly the truck was surrounded by cops and hauled away. A dog just happened to smell what was inside the truck. It was not that Diego was being followed. He saw the commotion and the truck being hauled away, all from a distance; that's why he was never arrested. Later I heard that they now use the truck in police presentations to show how drugs are being hidden in vehicles.'

103 According to Luis, sampling your own product wasn't regarded highly among the higher echelons of the cartels: 'Most of those high-level guys, if they did [snort], they did it very privately. On the Coast [in Colombia] there was more snorting among the high-level guys. There's more of a party atmosphere there; people are more happy-go-lucky. Pablo Escobar didn't really like it. He'd have a beer; he'd smoke. He loved to smoke pot. A couple of his hitmen would get really high. Even Popeye talked about it. The Mexican, I believe, didn't snort coke.'

104 A pseudonym.

105 Says Luis: 'It's essentially the same thing as crack; although we used a propane torch, which gives a very clean burn, and pure base. As opposed to crack, which when it gets to the street is not as pure and is usually smoked in a smaller pipe with a simple everyday lighter.' Freebase is commonly made with cocaine, water, ammonia and ether. Crack is commonly made with cocaine, water and baking soda or ammonia.

106 The reason he and Katie are still alive is that they were smoking quality coke, even if it were mixed with other things. In Colombia, what's also called *basuco* ('Colombian crack') is much lower quality: typically crude or low-grade coca paste mixed with gasoline, kerosene, solvents, sulphuric acid, brick dust, and other additives/chemicals. It's cheap on the street, highly addictive and frequently lethal.

107 Luis believes Brian Livingston died of colon cancer in prison. There is a report from northern California's *Times-Standard* on 2 April 1986 of a William Brian Livingston, 38 (described as 'one of Humboldt County's biggest cocaine dealers'), being indicted by a federal grand jury in Eureka (CA) for 'managing a large-scale cocaine ring' at Fieldbrook, 465 kilometres north of San Francisco on the Pacific coast. He had surrendered to authorities in San Francisco after a three-year investigation by the FBI. The article states Livingston, then employed by Record Plant Recording Studios in Los Angeles, had 'distributed a total of at least 88 pounds [40 kilos] of cocaine in Hawaii, San Francisco, Las Vegas, West Palm Beach [FL] and Humboldt and Sonoma counties' with sales totalling $2 million and 'most of the cocaine [coming] from Florida'. Assistant US Attorney Peter Robinson is quoted: 'I am confident [Livingston] is the largest cocaine dealer prosecuted in Humboldt County.' Another report published the same day in *San Francisco Examiner* says Livingston 'operated from 1976 to 1983'. This individual would appear to be the one and the same Brian Livingston Luis knew and worked with and he believes it is, confirming Livingston's Record Plant employment and Humboldt County residence, though it cannot be verified with 100 per cent certainty. A death record for Sonoma County, north of San Francisco, lists one William Brian Livingston as passing away on 26 October 1992 with a birth date of 14 June 1947. So this person would have been 38 in April 1986: the same age as the William Brian Livingston indicted in Humboldt County for cocaine trafficking.

108 Now the Hotel Kabuki in Japantown at 1625 Post Street, San Francisco.
109 According to Ronald K. Siegel in a 1988 piece for *Omni* magazine, Mario was doing coke in the carriage and the sound of him sniffing was recorded 64 times on tape. Siegel, a psychopharmacologist, recreated the incident for the judge, complete with artificial heat, a legal cocaine substitute, chemicals (putrescine, cadaverine) designed to replicate María's decaying corpse, and sounds from audio tapes of the siege. He concluded: 'Under the right conditions any brain will hallucinate.' Siegel died in 2019.
110 It was also revealed Mario had married a woman called Estella in a New York correctional facility. Marriage records indicate he married a 'Soledad E. Bonilla Nocua'. Estella too was sentenced on cocaine-related charges in 1976, but escaped from prison in West Virginia in 1977. The couple had two sons, Freddie, then 13, and Angelo, 11. Luis believes Mario died in jail and this was confirmed by former FBI Crisis Negotiation Unit head Gary Noesner, who told me, 'Mario died in prison from a stomach [aortic] aneurysm. Not sure what year.'
111 Sometimes spelled 'Micky' or 'Mickey'.
112 Pablo Escobar's former mistress, the journalist and author Virginia Vallejo, has called them 'the kings of marijuana'. In August 2019 Camilo Dávila Jimeno was caught in Mexico and extradited to the United States for cocaine trafficking. His brothers Juan Manuel, Raúl and Pedro are considered the major hitters in the family, along with their cousin Eduardo.
113 His group was called *Autodefensas Campesinas de Córdoba y Urabá* (Peasant Self-Defence Forces of Córdoba and Urabá or ACCU).
114 'The time of the violence' or 'The Violence'. It was a catastrophic civil war that lasted from 1948 to 1958. Over 200,000 people were killed.
115 Pastrana served as president of Colombia from 1998 to 2002.
116 FARC announced a unilateral ceasefire in 2015 and, two years later, as part of a peace accord with the Colombian Government, handed over its weapons. It has re-emerged as a political party, *Fuerza Alternativa Revolucionaria del Común* (Common Alternative Revolutionary Force).
117 Grouper-on-human attacks are not unknown in the diving scene, especially by Atlantic goliath groupers, though there are no known reports of humans being killed by groupers. More likely the five poor souls were eaten by sharks or they died from their injuries or drowning, though it's a good story.
118 The name Camilo Zapata and the alias El Halcón are both fictional but the man is very real.
119 Paco is a common nickname for Francisco, but Luis says Barrera's first name was Alberto.
120 By 1986, cocaine smuggling in Florida had actually *increased* and George D. Heavey, a regional commissioner of USCS, would concede in *The New York Times*, 'We're overwhelmed. It's like fighting the Chinese Army.'
121 Greg Lazzara and Pino Fatone are pseudonyms.
122 Both Caro Quintero and El Cochiloco are featured characters in *Narcos: Mexico*. El Cochiloco was killed by the Cali Cartel in 1991.
123 However, The Doc did contact Luis when Caro Quintero was arrested in Costa Rica to see if something could be done for him. The date of the arrest was 4 April 1985. Caro Quintero was subsequently extradited to Mexico for his involvement in the murder of DEA agent Kiki Camarena. Today he is on the run. See Characters for details.

124 El Tío is not to be confused with Teodoro García Simental of the Tijuana and Sinaloa cartels. He also has the nickname 'El Teo', but it is spelled differently.
125 Gordon 'Goo' Gray and Alejandro Álvarez are both pseudonyms.
126 Matta Ballesteros aka 'El Negro' is another character featured in *Narcos: Mexico*. After being kidnapped by Honduran forces and US Marshals in 1988 while on a morning jog in Tegucigalpa, he was flown to the Dominican Republic and renditioned to the United States. Matta Ballesteros's removal caused riots in Tegucigalpa, and five people were killed. He was convicted of the kidnapping of Kiki Camarena as well as drug trafficking and remains in prison.
127 The MU-2 was manufactured by Mitsubishi between 1963 and 1986.
128 In the 2012 Colombian soap opera *Pablo Escobar: El Patrón del Mal*, Correa is shown being accidentally shot by two of Escobar's *sicarios* while tied to a chair. Says Luis: 'All I know is he was killed because of the differences he had with Pablo. He wasn't the only one that Pablo killed. [Hugo] Hernán Valencia was killed and I remember Alonso Cárdenas, a brother-in-law of the Ochoas, was killed. That was kind of the start of the "Everybody that worked big had to pay Pablo" era. It was almost the beginning of the [Medellín] collections office, which later became La Oficina de Envigado.' Valencia was shown being killed in the same episode of *Pablo Escobar: El Patrón del Mal*.
129 A third Pablo, José Pablo Correa Ramos, the former president of football club Deportivo Independiente Medellín, was assassinated in 1986.
130 According to the late Popeye, Escobar only used the notebooks to write down the names of the people he wanted assassinated.
131 Kevin's was Escobar's favourite nightclub.
132 Javier Peña, the DEA agent whose pursuit of Escobar formed the story for the first two seasons of *Narcos*, estimates he was responsible for over 10,000 murders.
133 Francisco Hélmer Herrera Buitrago aka 'Pacho' was a homosexual narco and one of the heads of the Cali Cartel, but probably best known outside Colombia as one of the main characters in *Narcos*. He is played brilliantly by Argentinean actor Alberto Ammann. Herrera also appears in *Narcos: Mexico*. According to William C. Rempel's book *At the Devil's Table*, Herrera's feud with Escobar started when Herrera refused to hand over a Colombian man Escobar wanted killed. The targeted man had murdered an associate of Escobar's friends over a love triangle gone wrong in New York and sought Herrera's protection.
134 A pseudonym.
135 There are also reports that the duty was much higher: $12 to $15 per 100 pounds.
136 The company's name has been changed.
137 Both pseudonyms.
138 Says Luis: 'You can buy the *assets* of a business – and *not* the business. In this case that was not permitted because the banks wanted somebody to buy the business and be responsible for the debts of the business; when you just buy the assets you are not responsible for any debts or obligations of the business.'
139 Defunct and since merged with other banks. Now trading as Bank of America.
140 After Kane's death, Lobo and his lawyers discovered the scam while going through company records. Said Lobo: 'I found drawback papers of questionable accuracy were being furnished in connection with a Canadian

export [of sugar] and that other documents ostensibly exporting sugar to the Caribbean were totally fraudulent.'

141 It's estimated $5 million was swindled by Lobo-Kane.

142 Eduardo Fonseca is a pseudonym. In English *compadre* is usually taken to mean friend but in Spanish can also mean godfather, godparent or co-father. As Luis explains: '*Padrino* literally means "godfather". But in Mexico *compadre* is used a lot more than in other parts of Latin America and it is usual in Mexico that two very close friends or associates call each other *compadre* as a term of endearment, which was the case with El Compadre. When I met him, the person that introduced us called him *compadre* – so I started calling him El Compadre – and later I was godfather at his daughter's wedding – *padrino de boda* (best man) – so then we were actually *compadres*.'

143 In Colombia, Marulo was also well known for dispossessing local farmers of their land through threats and intimidation.

144 Booth concedes he was there but strangely denies throwing money down a chute. He also claims, somewhat bizarrely, he didn't know what Luis did for a living: 'I never saw or heard of his business dealings because it could only hurt my reputation and career. I was shielded from that. One time Luis had fallen asleep and woke up. I was still going. He gave me, like, $10,000 and told me keep the party going while he left to conduct his business.'

145 Feathering means to pitch or angle the outer blades of the propellers so that they lie flat with the slipstream. Unfeathering means to regain normal pitch. When blades are feathered the plane can't be propelled forward. The blades need to have pitch for the plane to move.

146 Writing in *New York* magazine in 1982, Nicholas Pileggi reported that illegal drugs had gross sales of $79 billion in 1980. Or in the words of US Attorney General William French Smith: 'About equal to the combined profits of America's 500 largest industrial corporations.' It was the biggest industry in New York.

147 In 1993, Accetturo was convicted of racketeering and sentenced to 20 years' jail but got out in 2002. He's now in witness protection.

148 Halcón managed to get out of the business and is living to this day. Says Luis: 'He's living in Medellín off the fat of the land. He made a lot of money.'

149 The going price was $16,000 a key. Says Luis: 'The market was flooded. It was the '80s: everybody was bringing shit in.'

150 One report had Joey being bludgeoned. Another said he was suffocated with a cushion.

151 Four men were implicated in Joey's murder: Cassone, Oscar (also known as Irving) Schwartz, Fabio Decristofaro and Joseph Marino. In 1996 a group of Lucchese crime family wiseguys including Cassone, Marino, Frank Suppa and Anthony Accetturo, already in jail and wanting to secure a reduction on their sentences, testified against Schwartz and Decristofaro. The pair was sentenced to life in jail. Says Luis: 'Schwartz and Decristofaro were the ones who actually hit him over the head and clubbed him to death.'

152 Says Luis: 'Joey Ippolito was always being hooked, having to pay off a bunch of fat slobs up in New York that had nothing to do with what he was doing but expected payment. I've seen Anthony Accetturo Jr come and slap Joey Ipp's ex-partner, Eddie Trotta, at the restaurant Tiberio in Bal Harbour because he expected Joey's ex-partner to pay him for just being Anthony Accetturo's son.'

153 Annette Soudry and Billy Basto are pseudonyms.

154 A Botero fake of 'The Dancers' valued at $500,000 was withdrawn from a Christie's sale in 1993 after the artist called it a 'very vulgar copy'.

155 Reid Constable and Daniela Villareal are pseudonyms.

156 The actual quote (from 1986) was *Preferimos una tumba en Colombia a un calabozo en Estados Unidos* or 'We prefer a grave in Colombia to a jail in the United States.' Escobar and other narcos formed a terrorist group called Los Extraditables ('The Extraditables') to wage war on the Colombian Government over the issue of extradition. Extradition was first signed into Colombian law in 1979, instated in 1983, repealed in 1987, reinstated by presidential decree in 1989, repealed again in 1991, then reinstated permanently in 1997, but the treaty was declared invalid in 1998 by Colombia's constitutional court. Where the law currently stands is open to debate. A Miami lawyer told me: 'Officially there's no extradition. Unofficially there is. It's called "administrative extradition".'

157 According to Luis, Cushing died in a twin-engine plane crash in the Rockies of Colorado during a snow-skiing holiday circa 1991. No newspaper reports are available to verify this claim.

158 Says Luis: 'The *paras* later killed Juanchito. The shootout was at his farm. He was with a longtime friend and associate called "Mata Tigre". They died with arms in hand.'

159 Escobar *sicario* Popeye, who said 'the most successful' of all his 257 killings was Galán in the Channel 4 series *Inside the Real Narcos*, also claimed politician and former justice minister Alberto Santofimio Botero was allegedly behind it, along with José Gonzalo Rodríguez Gacha aka The Mexican. (Other rumoured participants have included elements within the Colombian military and intelligence services and the *paras*.) Santofimio was sentenced to 24 years' jail in relation to the assassination of Galán in 2007 but released a year later, then had his sentence reinstated in 2011. He was placed under house arrest in 2017. Says Luis: 'Santofimio was the one who got Pablo involved in politics and he was the root of all the problems that came afterwards. If Pablo had stayed out of politics I think things would've been different.'

160 Ceiling is an aviation term that refers to the height measured from the earth's surface to the base of the lowest cloud layer. Generally it means low cloud and a lot of fog. A low ceiling is highly problematic on illegal runways or *aeropuertos clandestinos* (clandestine airports), which are usually made of dirt, because of lack of illumination or lack of a clear approach from dwellings or uncleared vegetation.

161 Says Luis: 'Moñón ran Ciénaga – he had absolute power in that area and had large expanses of banana land, the big cash export crop.' His full name was Carlos Manuel Dangond (sometimes seen spelled as Dangon) Noguera. He died in 1991.

162 During a typical drug-smuggling run, a light aircraft legally enters a country's airspace, lands at a legitimate airstrip, lodges a flight plan with the local civil aviation authority, then stops at an illegal airstrip and picks up merchandise. The smuggler then replaces the assigned call letters (registration marks) on the plane – indicating the plane's country of origin (such as Venezuela, prefix YV) – with whatever a paid-off air-traffic control official tells the smuggler to replace it with (Colombia's prefix is HJ or HK). The official then reports the

plane is travelling to a false destination. The drugs get delivered, unloaded and the correct call letters are put back on the plane on its return to its country of origin. Some planes, though, do not work with any air-traffic control at all and fly in totally illegally.

163 There were two World Cup qualifiers in Barranquilla in 1989: the first on 20 August, two days after the murder of Galán, which was Colombia vs Ecuador. The second was 17 September, Colombia vs Paraguay.

164 Shrugs Luis: 'Where are bodyguards when you really need them? I almost get killed by a guy at a fruit stand with a machete but can survive the cartels.'

165 Both pseudonyms.

166 Two car bombs went off in Bogotá on 12 May 1990, killing 19 people, following on from hundreds of bombings throughout Colombia in 1989. Six people were killed in another car bomb in Cali. Probably the worst of all of Escobar's atrocities was the bombing of Avianca Flight 203 on 27 November 1989, killing 107 people in the air and three on the ground in the mountains outside Bogotá. Luis Galán's replacement and later Colombian president, César Gaviria, had been scheduled to be on board but didn't catch the flight from the capital to Cali.

167 For $5000 Luis had a Colombian-made passport that said he was born in Santa Marta: 'It was a very well-made passport. Five thousand dollars in Colombia back then was a shitload of money.' He also had a national identification card that was made to look like it had been notarised in 1968 when he was 13. 'That was a super-good one.'

168 The same Patemuro threatened to kill former Assistant US Attorney Bonnie Klapper during her prosecution of the Norte del Valle Cartel. In 2012 he was sentenced to 40 years' jail in the United States and ordered to pay a $5 million fine. The name Patemuro is a unique one. Says Luis: '*Pate* could refer to "kick" (*patear*) and *muro* to "wall". I do not know the origins of the nickname but the closest thing to the meaning would be "wall kicker", or maybe he played soccer and he had a very powerful kick. All these rich guys in Colombia had soccer fields on their farms and they were all soccer aficionados.'

169 Luis was mostly using a kind of open fisherman boat called an *Eduardoño*, which is named after the company that makes them: Eduardoño SA.

170 Rasguño gave an interview to Bogotá newspaper *El Tiempo* in 2007 in which he said he knew Escobar 'a little. But later we became enemies, because the guy was nuts. I did not go to Medellín to go after him, but I did take take two trucks with dynamite from him and two helicopters that were going up to Cali carrying weapons. I also used to call the cops and report cars. They almost did me in [sic] in Cartago on his orders. It was a police major from Cartago . . . when Escobar died I went to the Coast and said, "No more." But there are so many expenses that you have to go back. Maintaining your bodyguards and that deluxe lifestyle – which is not a good life at all – is very expensive.'

171 A criminal favour with no benefit involved.

172 The real reason was the discovery on one of Galeano's properties of a stash of over $20 million that had been withheld from Escobar and gone mouldy. In Robert Mazur's *The Infiltrator*, he writes: 'Moncada had hidden a mountain of money in a Medellín home to evade Escobar's efforts to finance a war against the Colombian Government and its efforts to establish an extradition treaty with the US.'

173 This was according to Escobar's chief *sicario*, Popeye. A 2017 film made about Escobar, *Loving Pablo*, depicted the two men being butchered with

a chainsaw. Mazur claims both men were hung upside down by their feet and tortured with blowtorches.

174 A 1987 non-government organisation report published in Colombia described *mariachis* thus: *la debilidad de casi todos los narcotraficantes*. The weakness of almost all drug traffickers.

175 William C. Rempel's book *At the Devil's Table* details a plot by the Cali Cartel to aerially bomb *La Catedral* while Escobar was inside, using MK-82 bombs sourced in El Salvador. It was foiled at the last minute but might explain the haste with which Escobar fled the prison.

176 The website Pepes Project (pepes.exposed) has released thousands of pages of previously classified documents concerning Los Pepes. Whether American law-enforcement agencies were also involved in these extra-judicidial killings is not proven, but it is widely believed to be true. Carlos Castaño Gil claimed before he died in 2004 that 'Los Pepes worked with the tacit cooperation of the US Government. The Colombian authorities did not oppose us either.' Another excellent website, Medellín Abraza Su Historia (medellinabrazasuhistoria.com), details that victims of Los Pepes included 'Alba Lía Londoño, music teacher of Manuela Escobar, the drug lord's daughter; Nubia Jiménez, nanny of Escobar's children; Alicia Vásquez, general services employee of one of his properties; and Juan Carlos Herrera, a minor who was a friend of [Escobar's son] Juan Pablo Escobar.'

177 A declassified 1995 CIA report stated that with the fall of Medellín and Cali 'Ramírez may be best positioned in Medellín to benefit from the fall of the Cali kingpins'. He ended up getting an amnesty for his Los Pepes crimes from the Colombian Government, but served jail time for creating paramilitaries in 1997 and money laundering in 2013.

178 It's just over 700 kilometres west-northwest of Cartagena.

179 Cortés is sometimes spelled Cortéz in news reports. Silvio Bernal is a pseudonym for a trafficker who has flown under the radar of law-enforcement authorities. Just to confuse things, 'El Hombre Del Overol' (The Overall Man) is a nickname Cristancho shared with Orlando Henao Montoya, the big boss of the North Valley Cartel. Cristancho is known as 'the fake Overol', Henao 'the real Overol'. According to folklore, Henao wanted to confuse authorities and ordered Cristancho take his nickname too. However, Luis disputes this: 'Cristancho was definitely part of the Cali group but never a power player. He was made out to be more [important] than he was. He was always devious and played both sides. It was never a pre-planned strategy between him and Orlando; I don't believe he and Orlando ever had that great a personal relationship.'

180 The pseudonymous Bernal, an associate of the Ochoa brothers of the Medellín Cartel, was also allegedly a money launderer but was never indicted or arrested. Arturo Beltrán Leyva was killed by Mexican special forces in 2009. His brothers are Carlos, Alfredo and Héctor. The Beltrán Leyva Cartel is a splinter group of the Sinaloa Cartel.

181 Pablo Escobar had a copy of a US indictment against Urdinola while 'imprisoned' at *La Catedral*.

182 During the writing of *Pure Narco*, the authors met El Gordito in Islamorada, where he is a wealthy landowner. He has plans to write his own book.

183 A pseudonym.

184 According to Rempel's *At the Devil's Table*, this proposal was formally made to almost 100 gathered cartel figures and roundly rejected by them at one of

Pacho Herrera's farms a short time after Pablo Escobar's death in December 1993.

185 As detailed in *At the Devil's Table*, a similar incident did occur in real life when Herrera brutally murdered a farmer who had made the mistake of hosting a group of Medellín Cartel *sicarios* at his farm. It was used as a staging post before their coordinated assault on a soccer match being played at Herrera's Los Cocos property outside Cali. The attack left 19 people dead. A vengeful Herrera made the farmer's capture and torture a personal crusade. Herrera surrendered to the Colombian Government in 1996. He was killed in jail in 1998.

186 Luis says the rumour is Lorena poisoned her husband but that it is not true. He believes Urdinola died of a heart attack.

187 The main character in the television series *Breaking Bad*, played by Bryan Cranston.

188 The main islands of San Andrés, Santa Catalina and Providencia make up the Colombian department of Archipelago of San Andrés, Providencia and Santa Catalina (in Spanish, *Archipiélago de San Andrés, Providencia y Santa Catalina*).

189 According to sources in Colombia, El Mono, who was born in Toro in the Valle del Cauca in either 1965 or 1966, died in 2020 from colon cancer.

190 Says Luis: 'After I got out they called me a few times saying they were offering their services at any time if I needed them and that they would like to come work with me.' El Diablo, real name Ariel Rodríguez, was tasered, beaten to death, dismembered and beheaded, and his body parts dumped in the jungle sometime in 2005. See *The Takedown*.

191 José Rafael Abello Silva aka 'Mono Abello' was in jail at the time, having been extradited from Colombia to the United States in 1989. He was sentenced to 30 years' jail but after cooperating was released in 2007. The following year, he survived an assassination attempt on a beach in Santa Marta by *sicarios* on board a jetski. The gunman had been aiming for Abello's head but instead shot him in the buttocks. Luis makes out as if it were the most normal thing in the world: 'They shot Mono in the ass. No big deal. It happens every day. People miss.' His brother wasn't so lucky. Api was assassinated in 1995 by *sicarios* allegedly working for Los Mellizos.

192 It is estimated that Prada Cortés's organisation sent 24,000 kilos of cocaine to the United States between 1988 and 2006. He moved a lot of weight for Medellín and Carlos Alberto Rentería Mantilla aka 'Beto Rentería' of North Valley.

193 Félix Chitiva has said that Los Mellizos were the first to successfully use submarines to transport cocaine. DeCubas later became well known in the United States through the ESPN magazine article/documentary/podcast *Pin Kings*. DeCubas sourced cocaine via Chitiva who dealt with Medellín. Luis, by contrast, says he had direct access to the cartel.

194 In 1995 Jorge Cabrera aka 'El Gordito' was photographed shaking hands with Hillary Rodham Clinton after donating $20,000 to the 1996 Bill Clinton–Al Gore presidential campaign. 'It was frickin' hysterical,' says Robert Harley. 'I remember seeing the pictures and going, "You have *got* to be shittin' me. That's American politics at its best.' The Democratic National Committee paid back the money. Cabrera was also photographed with Gore.

195 Smit (real name Wayne Dillon) began building the 30-metre, three-section, Russian-designed submarine in a warehouse in Facatativá, a city just outside Bogotá. It was designed to carry 10,000 kilos of cocaine. The facility was raided in September 2000. He wasn't there when the raid happened and managed to escape. Luis says DeCubas 'put up some initial money for the first submarine from earnings made from the airdrops they did off the Florida Keys and Los Mellizos ended up funding the rest'. Smit died inside a smaller, prototype, semi-submergible submarine off the coast of Palomino, La Guajira. 'He's still there; he's inside the fucking submarine that sank off the beach. I've been told by Alex he wanted to commit suicide; that he had no desire to continue living.' But Luis is not so sure: 'Here you have an American citizen that dies in a submarine that was going to be used for cocaine-transport purposes.'

196 It changed its name to Bureau of Alcohol, Tobacco, Firearms and Explosives in 2002.

197 United States Fish and Wildlife Service (FWS or USFWS).

198 A command-and-control centre for USCS radar in South Florida.

199 National Oceanic and Atmospheric Administration (NOAA). Harley estimates the buoy was 130 miles off the coast of Naples, Florida.

200 The Metro-Dade Police Department, formed in 1981, changed its name to Miami-Dade Police Department in 1997.

201 Says Harley: 'Most of the loads that led us to the cooperators who were able to identify Luis were incorporated into that original indictment.' The prosecutors' rap sheet listed nine smuggles using the ships *Carol*, *Lucky Star II*, *Bad Habits*, *Candy* and *Top Gun* from November 1991 through to May 1993. Of that nine, six loads were aborted and only three were successful. *Top Gun* alone ran four loads, three of which were aborted. Of a total of 4475.5 kilos, only 1475.5 kilos were delivered. It wasn't the most successful enterprise for Luis. He was contracted by the main conspirators after the failure of the first run on lobster boat *Carol*, which with 500 kilos on board had to turn back after mechanical problems upon leaving Marathon, Florida. The second load, 600 kilos on the *Lucky Star II*, was successful. It picked up the load after an airdrop 253 miles northwest of Marathon in the Gulf of Mexico, then rendezvoused with another vessel called *Shark*, near Cape Sable in the Everglades National Park.

202 Translates as 'The Lord of the Skies'.

203 Café Koba still operates in Cancún and has no association with Luis.

204 An amount of 10,000 pesos would be worth roughly $500. An amount of $10,000 would be worth roughly 200,000 pesos.

205 The law firm's name has been changed.

206 The company's name has been changed.

207 Vernon Dolivo is a pseudonym.

208 Says Harley: 'We did eventually get documents from the law firm, so we did see what companies [were created] and [what] investments were made and they were already liquidated.'

209 Sold in Mexico as Tafil.

210 Harley disagrees: 'The big indictment was 1995 but I think the first set of indictments were in '92 and early '93. That's when we started indicting the boatloads and he might have been indicted as an unnamed co-conspirator.' Nigel Brooks from USCS's Houston headquarters agrees with Harley: 'The Southern District of Florida docket shows the indictment was dated March

1995. While it's based on the 1991 case, Navia was not named in that case.' For confidentiality reasons the full details of the 1995 indictment will not be referenced in this book.

211 Luis had cards and IDs in various permutations: Luis Naviansky, Louis Naviansky, Louis Naviansky Bonavia, et al. Juliana was enrolled in school as Naviansky with a fake birth certificate.

212 *Guantes* is the Spanish word for gloves. Guantex was a name Luis came up with to denote 'glove technologies'. His partner had no knowledge of Luis's illicit activities.

213 Denisse Zavala is a pseudonym.

214 Durazo was jailed in 1986 but released in 1992. He died in 2000. Sahagún Baca was born with the matronym Vaca, but changed it to Baca. Sahagún Baca is the cousin of former first lady of Mexico Martha Sahagún Jiménez, wife of President Vicente Fox Quezada.

215 Former federal policeman Esparragoza Moreno, with ties to the Guadalajara, Juárez and Sinaloa cartels, remains one of the FBI's Most Wanted Fugitives despite unconfirmed reports of his death in 2014. He served prison time over the death of DEA special agent Kiki Camarena.

216 Perdomo, full name Sergio Hernán Perdomo Lievano, remains on the run from US justice. He is believed to be in Spain.

217 The best-known case of a narco having plastic surgery is Mexican drug lord Amado Carrillo Fuentes, who died in 1997 while undergoing a major operation. Another is Cali Cartel/North Valley Cartel figure Juan Carlos Ramírez Abadía aka 'Chupeta' (Lollipop), who was caught in Brazil in 2007.

218 Sicilia Falcón was also into Mikhail Bulgakov, Nikolai Gogol and Mikhail Zoshchenko. Sulla was the Roman general Lucius Cornelius Sulla Felix (138BC–78BC).

219 Santa Martha Acatitla is about a 30-minute drive from Centro Sante Fe shopping centre.

220 A discontinued Redken line of conditioning beauty bars.

221 Says Dennard: 'Alberto twisted his leg when he was being tortured, along with electrocuting him. He told me the whole story when I came to Lecumberri. He got the leg rebroken by doctors and reset and then started doing gymnastics to get back in shape.'

222 This is not true.

223 Ventura was a *comandante* of the PJF and later head of the Mexican division of INTERPOL. He was described by former CIA agent Pat Gregory in *The Underground Empire* as 'the most brutal man I have ever met . . . the most powerful police official in Latin America'. He killed Skipper the Great Dane during a raid on Falcón's home and later died by apparent suicide in 1988, though the circumstances – shooting himself in the head after murdering his wife and her friend in their car – were suspicious. There was only one witness and the witness's testimony was doubtful. The Medellín Cartel is believed to have ordered Ventura's assassination.

224 Luis and Mercedes subsequently contacted each other by email after an introduction by the author.

225 El Metro was another narco who underwent plastic surgery after he was named on Mexico's and the United States' Most Wanted lists. The DEA had a $2 million reward for information leading to his arrest. Next to nothing was known about him.

226 A pseudonym.
227 Not his real name. His first name is believed to be Franco and his surname cannot be disclosed. He is wanted on a case in Florida that similarly cannot be disclosed.
228 Jesús Aburto is a pseudonym.
229 Salinas Doria, a former policeman in the border town of Donna, Texas (near McAllen), was arrested in Mexico in 1998, then escaped, was rearrested in Venezuela, then sent back to Mexico in 1999. In 2007 he was extradited to the United States. In 2009 he was convicted of trafficking 200 tons of cocaine from Mexico to the US and sentenced to 27 years' jail.
230 There is no record of Salinas Doria murdering a doctor and his family.
231 Jesús wasn't killed but Luis is sure someone had to pay 'extra tax'. For the record, Luis went on to do some trips with Metro. As he puts it, a 'bond' had been created.
232 Sometimes spelled as 'Sony'.
233 Ramcharan was arrested in Montego Bay in 2004 as part of a takedown headed by the DEA's Kingston office and extradited to the United States three years later. He was sentenced to 37 years' jail (some reports say 35) in 2008.
234 The Flamingo Club was renamed the Tropigala. Jerk is a hot spice mixture from Jamaica that is rubbed on or used to marinate seafood or meat.
235 Fresh was killed at his daughter's home in San Andrés, Colombia, on 5 February 2018, reportedly aged 60 or 61, shot twice by an unknown assailant. He was dead on arrival at hospital from wounds to his skull and thorax. At the time of his death he was on a Colombian Most Wanted list. According to Luis, a member of Fresh's family got caught smuggling cocaine out of Santa Marta but never got permission from Los Rastrojos, a cartel that had emerged out of the ashes of the North Valley Cartel.

'The group was started in the interior of Colombia by North Valley's Wilber Varela, "El Jabón" ["The Soap"], when he was at war with [the now extradited and jailed] Diego León Montoya Sánchez, "Don Diego". They spread their presence to San Andrés to impose taxes on the people that were working.'

Los Rastrojos demanded Fresh pay a tax with land he owned and the balance in cash. Fresh flew from Montego Bay to San Andrés to confront the gang and told them he wouldn't pay. He was then told to insert a SIM in his phone and call the number of the gang's *oficina* in Medellín. He refused.

'If Fresh had stayed in Jamaica, he'd still be alive. He made a mistake I have never made: don't die for money. You can always make money again but you can't come back from the dead. They put a bullet in his head, easy, *done*, end of problem.'

236 Lansky died in Miami in 1983. For a time in the mid-1980s Luis had dated Lansky's step-granddaughter, Cynthia Duncan. Her grandmother was Lansky's second wife, Thelma, who died in 1997.
237 The date of the killing was 30 August 2001. The assassin was Jhon Freddy Orrego Marín, a figure associated with the North Valley Cartel. Rumour is it was a case of mistaken identity. Fernando is sometimes reported as Hernando.
238 According to a USCS PowerPoint presentation, 43 metric tons were seized in 1999. The figure was supplied by INTERPOL.
239 The dates of the seizures were 14 January (3803 kilos, M/V *Cannes*), 27 May (3880 kilos, M/V *China Breeze*), 31 May (4000 kilos, M/V *Castor*) and 23 December (2006 kilos, M/V *Pearl II*).

240 Luis says Sonny used his connections to buy the freighters *Regent Rose* and *Privilege*.
241 A Greek newspaper, *Ta Nea*, estimated it was 20 million drachmas, or about $70,000.
242 A pseudonym.
243 Located at 99 Avenue des Champs-Élysées.
244 Typically they carry a buoy and beacon in case they are released on the open sea, to allow for quick recovery.
245 Garcia denies there was a Colombian cop in one of the front seats: 'I don't remember any Colombians being there.'
246 At the time of writing this book Meletis was still an active agent and would not be interviewed without permission from the DEA. He texted me: 'As a result of being an active agent, I need to confirm with headquarters elements that the referenced investigation is completely adjudicated before I am authorised to release information pertaining to said investigation. As soon as I receive clearance I will let you know.' It never came. Joked another DEA agent: 'I think they wait forever to give you an answer and hope you give up.'
247 The FBI's intelligence gathering is officially restricted to the United States and the CIA's to overseas, though this is not always practically the case.
248 Brooks retired in 2001, Garcia in 2016.
249 At the time a senior special agent or SSA was one pay grade above special agent or SA. Says Brooks: 'SSA was used in US Customs to designate pay grade GS-13, which could only be gained through competitive announcement; you had to compete with others and be selected on merit. SA was pay grade GS-12. Usage was discontinued around 2007 when the grade for SA was raised to GS-13. DEA and FBI also had GS-13s and the advancement was without competition. Customs went to the same non-competitive advancement system as DEA and FBI and eliminated the "senior" from the special agent title. Now all federal criminal investigators have the same pay-grade structure regardless of agency: Customs (which is now Department of Homeland Security), FBI, DEA, etc. All call their criminal investigators "special agents".'
250 FBI and USCS also had their own attaché offices overseas, but according to Eric Kolbinsky, DEA was considered the lead office overseas. Garcia says that USCS 'back then had probably 50 offices. When I retired, we had 70 offices in 48 countries worldwide; more than any other agency or equal to the FBI.'
251 Both vessels were carrying tracking devices installed by HMCE.
252 The offices of Callisti Maritime were raided on 25 August 2000 and Elias Lemos was extradited from France to Greece in 2002. He was sentenced to 18 years' jail and fined €250,000 for his part in the conspiracy. Others arrested in Greece were Filippos Makris, Nikos Mavridoglou, Angelos Kanakis, Ioannis (Yiannis) Lemos, Constantine (Constantinos) Athanasios and Theodoros Fatsis. Baron Massimo Paonessa (a pseudonym) was arrested in Italy but his fate and whereabouts are unknown.
253 Nigel Brooks has a different recollection: 'The Harris equipment was analogue only and was not capable of intercepting digital; something that Harris did not manage to fix for a couple of years. Usually when you intercept a cell phone you do it by hooking into the cell-phone company. The Harris equipment is portable and has direction-finding capability too, but it is short range. Using the cell company, you don't need to be in proximity.'

254 There is some dispute about what arrest the fingerprints actually came from, and Carol Libbey could not confirm whether it was the Coconut Grove arrest in 1979 where Luis threw cocaine out of his car or the Coral Gables arrest in the mid-1980s when his friend Billy Basto assaulted the police officer. Both Luis and Harley believe the fingerprints came from the same arrest – Coral Gables – but Harley maintains on that occasion Luis was arrested for DUI, not driving without a licence.

'I think it was that but Luis gets the charge wrong. He wasn't the one who struck the officer. I think he was taken in because they charged him with drunk driving. The reason I think it's a DUI in my head is because the DUI would have been the potential felony charge. Driving without a licence is literally a traffic charge.'

Why would Luis remember the charge differently to you?

'For Luis, that is what he lived. So that's how he remembered it. That's probably true. But that charge was in Dade County because that's where we found the picture.'

Former Dade County detective Roberto Diaz (introduced later in the book) disagrees with Harley: 'DUI has never been a felony, especially for a first offence. Driving without a licence has always been a traffic offence for which the driver can be arrested. In either case, even back then, the subject would be taken to jail where a booking card would be created and a photo taken and attached to the booking card.'

255 'US Customs has jurisdiction with anything that has a nexus to the US border,' says Kolbinsky. 'If it came across the border or if it's coming across the border they have authority. Technically, once it comes into the US, then DEA handles it. But we also have legal jurisdiction to investigate overseas as well as they do. Over the years DEA was real territorial about the whole drug thing and the only agents with Customs who could work drugs were cross-designated with Title 21 authority, which is the federal statute that covers the drug laws. There used to be silly arguments all the time about that. But not so much anymore. Operation Journey was primarily a DEA operation.'

But he makes a concession: 'Unlike our people, [the British drugs liaison officers or DLOs for HMCE] readily passed [information] on to [US] law enforcement. We worked closely with the Brits. The Brits' dark side was intercepting a lot of satellite-phone traffic in those days. A lot of folks were very territorial. Partially since I had been with Customs, I wasn't that way. I saw the benefit of everyone working together. If you had the source then it was your case. Sometimes I felt I was excluded from information because my co-workers knew how I felt about sharing info.'

However in Peter Walsh's *Drug War*, the author quotes Nigel Brooks as saying that the FBI also had 'concurrent jurisdiction to investigation violations of the *Controlled Substances Act*'. This was enacted in 1982 by the US Attorney General.

Brooks disagrees with Kolbinsky's claim regarding DEA's primacy: 'Operation Journey was in fact a US–UK operation and it was developed by US Customs Office of Investigations Houston and HMCE's NIS. The operation name was given to it by HMCE and adopted by Customs and subsequently DEA.'

256 A pseudonym.

257 As Nigel Brooks remarked in his case notes: 'The source was a resident of Barranquilla, and his absence from there without just cause could have been a

cause of major suspicions on the part of the organisation. Because the security of the operation and the safety of the source were paramount, it was decided that all control and communications with the source would be handled from Houston, and that no face-to-face contact with the source would be attempted in-country. Due to the source's position of trust in the organisation, and the certainty that he and his family would be killed should his cooperation ever become known, it was decided that his identity would only be disclosed to law-enforcement agencies in Colombia having a strict "need to know".'

258 INMARSAT is an acronym for International Maritime Satellite Organisation, so 'INMARSAT numbers' refers to maritime communications by satellite. The devices used are commonly referred to as satellite phones or 'sat' phones.

259 Prisma was a special unit of the Dutch police set up to investigate cocaine trafficking.

260 A crewmember of the *Pearl II* subsequently turned informant.

261 Nigel Brooks does not share this view: 'All the time I knew him, I never was aware that Taylor used drugs.'

262 Brooks has a different story: 'Taylor came to us voluntarily following the seizure of the *China Breeze*. He reached out for us and we flew him from Colombia to Houston. We had no idea who he was or what his role was until that time.'

263 He'd also been given the name 'Leo' by Taylor in Operation Journey communications up to that point.

264 Brooks again: 'I also set up a backstop in case of an emergency or if Taylor needed to contact us or the law-enforcement folks in Colombia needed to contact him. I introduced him to HMCE DLO Hank Cole who was one of the DLOs in Colombia we dealt with directly.'

265 Jorge made it out of South America but was caught in Barcelona two years later, imprisoned in Cádiz, and became an informant, getting everyone in the conspiracy indicted in Spain. A Spanish-language report later claimed Jorge handed over 'several suitcases' of paperwork (including accounts) to Spanish judge Baltasar Garzón, documenting all of Los Mellizos' activities from 1994 to 2000. Garzón was famous for indicting Chilean dictator Augusto Pinochet. He officially indicted Luis as well as dozens of other Los Mellizos conspirators in a sealed indictment in the National Court of Madrid in February 2004. Taylor was also named in the indictment but not specifically identified as the snitch. Iván de la Vega Cabás, however, has publicly identified him. His real name will not be published in this book.

How was Taylor outed? Talk is that a loose-lipped DEA agent had revealed to his Colombian lover, a friend of the wife of Jorge García, that an investigation of Los Mellizos was well advanced.

'There was some pillow talk from one of the agents in Barranquilla that nearly caused some problems,' says Brooks. 'I never made an official complaint or report about it because I felt that it was not intentional and saw no reason for a DEA agent to be disciplined over it. One of the problems with running an investigation of this magnitude is one of control. We tried to control the various aspects, but other agencies like DEA pursued leads on their own and coordinated with other foreign law enforcement without our knowledge or consent. At the end of the case, DEA had thoroughly briefed the Spanish [authorities] and the examining magistrate [Garzón] had issued an indictment for most of the organisation and had included our informant in the indictment. This also happened with the Colombian authorities that also indicted him. So basically we had good reason to be concerned about our source [Taylor].

'In our case it was a constant effort to get funding for travel, paying expenses for the source, and getting him paid a reward. The two attorneys [out of Washington, DC] held up the payment for the case for a couple of years, claiming that if [Taylor] was to testify they didn't want the jury to be told that he had been paid for the information. Total bullshit. In fact after I retired I reached out to [Republican] Senator Chuck Grassley to ensure that the source was paid and that the US Government honoured its commitment.

'One of the other problems we had was that DEA was convinced [Taylor] was lying and convinced [the two attorneys from DC] that was the case too. The truth is that in all my dealings with [Taylor] I never detected a lie; the guy was always straightforward when we asked him questions and gave us a great deal of historical information about the organisation . . . [Taylor] was advising us daily of his communications and [our own] intercepts confirmed what he told us. We never advised him that his communications were being intercepted so it was a good way of ensuring he was not playing us.

'The [two attorneys] threatened to prosecute Taylor if he failed to testify before the grand jury in Miami. But they would not have been able to because when we debriefed him about prior acts we intentionally did not advise him of his Miranda rights; therefore nothing he said to us could have been used against him.

'Taylor even had to pay his own way to the US for himself and his family and was in default on the house he had purchased due to the fact that US Customs was reluctant to keep on paying him without approval from DOJ. The letter to Senator Grassley did the trick and he was paid for the information.'

The second informant inside Los Mellizos also now lives in the US. Both informants left Colombia immediately once Operation Journey took down the cartel in Venezuela.

266 Brooks: 'It's true that Venezuela was protective of its sovereignty over the use of US air assets, but without a doubt this case could never have been made without the complete cooperation of the *Guardia Nacional*. While DEA claimed that they were not to be trusted, the *Guardia Nacional* actually worked hand in hand with HMCE's DLOs and had the utmost integrity.'

267 El Caracol was arrested in June 1998 and extradited to the United States in August 2000. He was sentenced to 40 years' jail.

268 Brooks's account is slightly different: 'Following the seizure of the *Cannes*, I reviewed the classified message traffic about the seizure and determined that HMCE was involved, called my contact in London – HMCE's Graham Honey – and Operation Journey began shortly afterwards.'

269 In his case notes of Operation Journey Brooks characterised DEA's attitude to including HMCE in the investigation as 'openly hostile . . . DEA totally disregarded the fact that had it not been for the HMCE operation, the *Cannes* and the *Castor* would never have been intercepted.'

270 An attempt was made to contact the now-retired Soiles for this book but he did not respond. He went on to become DEA chief of global operations. In his case notes Brooks writes: 'In order to fully understand the problems between DEA, US Customs and HMCE in this investigation, I believe that it is necessary to view the relationship in the context of DEA Administrator

Thomas A. Constantine's 1998 congressional testimony. The Mejía Múneras were major targets of the DEA, but US Customs and HMCE had scooped them. DEA had no intention of playing second fiddle or equal partner with anyone. I would surmise that following the successful intercept of the *Pearl II*, and the resulting identification of Miguel and Víctor Mejía Múnera as being the leaders of the organisation, some very hard questions were probably asked of field offices in Colombia and elsewhere by DEA headquarters in Washington.' More damningly, he concludes: 'The Memorandum of Understanding between US Customs and DEA requires that in foreign investigative matters, the DEA country attachés represent Customs and service their requests for assistance. Throughout the investigation, DEA failed to comply with the requirements of the agreement.'

271 For a comprehensive account of the British role in Operation Journey and its information sharing with USCS, read the chapter 'Cocaine Armada' in Peter Walsh's excellent book *Drug War* (Milo Books, 2018).

272 Beto el Gitano was arrested in Spain in 2008 and extradited to the United States, where he was sentenced to 22 years' jail. His mugshot (along with Miguel Mejía Múnera's) appears on the DOS's website, under the heading 'Brought to Justice' in the Target Information section of the Bureau of International Narcotics and Law Enforcement Affairs' Narcotics Rewards Program. He was released early, whereupon he returned to Colombia and survived an assassination attempt in the Valle del Cauca in August 2019. An anonymous Miami-based lawyer euphemistically describes both Beto el Gitano and Miguel Mejía Múnera as 'highly respected' figures.

273 Pérez would be gunned down in 2001 while drinking coffee in an outdoor café in Panama City, a murder that has never been solved. Prior to his death, Pérez was approached by Brooks to cooperate. He declined. It was a fatal mistake.

274 Brooks quotes a price slightly less than Luis's estimate but is backed up by documentation sent between Callisti and the cartel.

275 Two of García's accomplices were later arrested and gave up the locations of stash sites. In his case notes Brooks writes: 'It is my opinion that the search and seizure of the *Privilege* was based largely on the urging of DEA.'

276 All three Albanians went to prison on long sentences but Frederik Durda escaped in 2005 when he visited his wife in a maternity hospital. He was recaptured a day later.

277 Brooks says USCS's battle of wills with the DEA all came down to the issue of 'control of the source and our refusal to allow DEA to document him or act as controllers. We were told continuously that the source was not being truthful and, while acknowledging that possibility, I had asked for any documentation which would prove that claim. It was never forthcoming.'

278 What is essentially known in law-enforcement parlance as a 'cold convoy'. Explains Brooks: 'Cold convoy is a term primarily used by US Customs to describe an investigative method that involves the tracking of a known subject or means of transportation to its ultimate destination. It is different from a "controlled delivery" in that a controlled delivery means a delivery of cocaine or some other illegal substance under the *control* of the law-enforcement agency. A cold convoy is the tracking and surveillance of a suspect or transportation means.

'So, for example, *Pearl II* is identified as the load vessel, HMCE installs a beacon to track the vessel, HMS *Marlborough* monitors the loading of the cocaine and the vessel is allowed to proceed while being tracked to its destination in the Netherlands. Law enforcement is provided enough information about the vessel so that they can make the search, seizure and arrests. The source of the information is not disclosed in order to protect the operation and continue the intelligence gathering. Whereas with a controlled delivery, law enforcement intercepts a load and the transporter agrees to cooperate and deliver the load under the supervision of law enforcement. The load is delivered and recipients arrested.'

279 Officially it was designated a joint investigation of USCS and the Organized Crime Drug Enforcement Task Force (OCDETF) in 2001, under the purview of the US Attorney General and DOJ. OCDETF utilises the resources of different law-enforcement agencies in the war on drugs, but primarily DEA.

'It was something I had no control over,' laments Brooks of the designation. 'I wanted to run the operation as a strictly intelligence op, passing info to the Europeans through HMCE for enforcement action.
A guy in our headquarters was monitoring the initial operation and without our approval or consent proposed it to "Main Justice" as a "Linear" project. By Main Justice I'm referring to Washington, DC, working for DOJ headquarters in the Narcotics and Dangerous Drugs Section [NDDS]. Linear was a program promoted by our headquarters and was aimed at dismantling major organisations.

'Main Justice assigned two attorneys from DC to the operation and that really began all of our problems because they wanted "dope on the table". I had already decided to retire in 2001 so was not in it for the glory but for the case. Unfortunately, in addition to turf wars, agents can really promote their careers with big significant cases, and that's what happened with Operation Journey. OCDETF is not primarily a DEA initiative; it is a DOJ initiative and every federal agency has an opportunity to sponsor an OCDETF case. It's more of a PR initiative than anything, and the problem with making a case like Journey [an] OCDETF [designated investigation] is that there are too many fingers in the pudding. Success claims a thousand parents. Failure is an orphan.'

280 A total of 50 tons was seized from those vessels, excluding the *Cannes*. In Baltasar Garzón's Spanish indictment the following vessels were named as part of the Los Mellizos conspiracy: *Miami Express*, *Goiana*, *Stiletto I* (aka *Madeleine* or *Polux)*, *Svetlana*, *Pearl II*, *Regent Rose*, *Kobe Queen*, *Scan Utrescht*, *China Breeze*, *Privilege* and *Suerte I*. Brooks told me Operation Jezebel, a major investigation that utilised the combined forces of British intelligence, military and law enforcement, was initiated from 'intelligence developed by HMCE's drugs liaison officer [DLO] in Miami, Martin Dubbey, from some information passed by FBI special agents Manny Ortega and Cesar Paz [in Miami]. They had an "in" with a business that was providing INMARSAT phones to dubious characters in Colombia. The phones were actually the prime communication method for the cartel between the ships and the organisations. The US could do nothing, but the Brits had much wider latitude. Martin tasked the UK's GCHQ [Government Communications Headquarters] with intercepting those communications and thus began Operation Jezebel.'

281 Brooks: 'HMCE, US Customs have varied responsibilities. The people involved in Operation Journey were criminal investigators. But there is also

the trade side, handling imports of merchandise, assessing duties, inspecting cargo and passengers: the side the public normally interact with at airports and seaports. While the uniformed and trade folks of HMCE were made part of HMRC, the investigative functions relating to drugs were rolled into the Serious Organised Crime Agency [SOCA], now NCA.'

282 According to former HMCE agent and Miami DLO Graham Honey: 'Branch 3 refers to the cocaine teams in the investigation division, which became the NIS of HMCE then HMRC.'

283 After being sentenced to 15 years' jail in 2002, Hanley was released in 2010 but sent down again for nearly 18 years in 2014.

284 Supergrass is a British term for snitch or informant. Regan went to jail, was released, then rejailed in 2005 after being convicted of the murders of five members of an entire London family, the Chohans, including two children.

285 An internet search of death records in New York pulls up a Nick Fisciatoris: 'NICK FISCIATORIS was born 17 June 1940, received Social Security number 071-36-6611 (indicating New York) and, Death Master File says, died 16 December 2012.' A 1940 birthdate would then be right. Notes Luis: 'He was a heavy smoker, a chainsmoker for years; he wasn't gonna last more than ten years.'

286 Zack Mann, a USCS spokesman, explained: 'The two were brought [to Miami] because the venue on conspiracy charges to import cocaine in 1998 and 1999 originated in South Florida.'

Nigel Brooks: 'The venue for the prosecution of Iván was based on my debriefing of one of the crewmembers from the *Pearl II* in the Netherlands. The informant had told us that the *Pearl II* had been used to smuggle cocaine into Fort Lauderdale in 1998. I pulled entry records and other Customs records showing that the vessel had been in Fort Lauderdale during that time. The crewmember (who had been on the vessel continuously since that Florida smuggle) verified what had happened and that the offload took place to go-fasts off the coast. He told us of three smuggling trips to Fort Lauderdale that year and I was able to verify that the vessel was in Fort Lauderdale on those occasions. That gave us the "venue" [location] for a US prosecution of Iván.'

Iván pleaded guilty, did not testify, paid restitution of $300 and was sentenced to almost 20 years' jail with supervised release when his sentence ended. But before he went away, he asked the court, in the words of *The South Florida Sun-Sentinel*, 'to be injected with anthrax, HIV, other viruses and the worst poison to prove he would survive because of his conversion to Christianity while in solitary confinement'.

On 9 October 2009 Iván was released from Loretto prison, Pennsylvania, after serving just over ten years. That December he was deported to Colombia. According to Luis, 'Iván lost his marbles to religion while inside [jail]. He is now in Colombia – never restored himself completely. He's living poor on the outskirts of Barranquilla.' He makes bizarre videos in Spanish on YouTube and claims he was kidnapped to United States in 'chains' by the DEA.

287 Michelle was deported to Panama City and not charged. Luis spoke to her one time from prison in the United States and never saw her again.

288 Wilmer Joiro is a pseudonym. He was not named in Baltasar Garzón's Spanish indictment. Luis believes Jorge was going to be assassinated by Los Mellizos: 'I think they would have killed him. He was going to get fucking whacked. He's alive because all this shit happened; because Tommy Taylor turned in the

organisation. He was too smart for his own good. I think he did a couple of trips behind [the cartel's] back. They were a little leery of Jorge. They wanted to do the *Suerte*; then they were going to call everybody in. They already knew "The Greek" was not Greek; that he was some Mexican guy. The Mejía Múnera brothers didn't know that I was the guy responsible for transport. The Mellizos didn't know who "The Greek" was either and I *knew* them. I wanted it that way because I knew that the Mellizos were so fucking hot. I knew Caracas was a hot situation. Once the *Suerte* left, they were going to call me in for a meeting, they were going to keep me, have me continue to buy ships in Greece and work with Elias. We had good plans going forward: we were going to be able to do at least eight trips a year – 50,000 kilos a year, easily – to Europe.'

Brooks has a different take: 'I think there may be some stretching of the truth here [from Luis]. To the best of my knowledge from Taylor, the Greeks just provided the transportation and were paid for that service. They didn't have the distribution organisation nor the supply organisation.'

289 A hunch that would seem to be well founded, according to an email sent by Tommy Taylor to USCS. In the email, dated 7 August 2000, before the *Suerte* raid, Taylor reveals Víctor Mejía Múnera had been tipped off by a corrupt Colombian lieutenant about a PNC (Colombian National Police) investigation into an Albanian group working inside Venezuela. A narco working for Los Mellizos called Pedro Vélez had been making phone calls to Albania, Jorge García and Luis. Víctor had had Pedro's phone records pulled and Taylor was of the view Víctor would have Pedro and Luis ('Leo') killed for the leak to the PNC: 'Of course Pedro will be killed and also Leo because [Víctor] told him that he wants to see Leo to give [him another] job.'

Says Brooks: 'By this time Víctor was so frustrated with the delays from the Greeks and the problems with communications security that [Taylor] felt he would probably have some people killed.'

290 Kolbinsky has a slightly different recollection of this exchange: 'I believe Luis had the conversation with Iván about the Mellizos before Garcia and I had him in the back of the SUV. That conversation I'm sure was a factor in his admitting he was Navia after I told him I had no choice but to return him to the Venezuelans if he insisted he was "Novoa". I distinctly recall him admitting he was Navia in the SUV. If my memory is correct, his exact words were, "Okay, you got me."'

291 Says Luis: '*Pinga* for Cubans is dick. Everything in a Cuban's life is his dick.'

292 Cuban-Americans Willy (or Willie) Falcón, full name Augusto Guillermo Falcón, along with Sal Magluta, full name Salvador Magluta, known together as Los Muchachos ('The Boys') were indicted with conspiracy to import and distribute 75 tons of cocaine between 1978 and 1991. They went to trial in 1995 but were stunningly acquitted in 1996. Later it was discovered they had bribed the jury foreman, Miguel Moya, with half a million dollars. He went to jail for 17 years in 1999. Three witnesses were also murdered.

The pair was reindicted in 1999 and Falcón took a plea deal on money-laundering charges in exchange for handing over $1 million, and dropping other charges such as obstruction of justice and jury tampering. In 2003 he was sentenced to 20 years' jail but released in 2017 and immediately went into detention awaiting deportation. After fighting extradition to his native Cuba because of fears he would be killed for his involvement in a 1990s CIA-supported plot to murder Fidel Castro, he was deported to the Dominican

Republic in 2018. Magluta, not so lucky, was sentenced to 205 years' jail in 2002, later reduced to 195, after money-laundering, bribery and witness-tampering charges all stuck. Says Luis: 'What saved Willy was that Sal's case involved a murder. When they separated their two cases Willy was able to sign a plea agreement and get 20 years.' Willy's younger brother, Gustavo, also indicted in 1991, went on the run for 26 years but was found by US Marshals in 2017, living under a false name in Kissimmee, Florida. He was sentenced to 135 months' jail in 2018.

293 Top cartel figures are today charged anywhere from $1 million to $5 million for a plea deal.

294 News reports that suggested Iván was 'CEO', 'drug kingpin', 'global drug boss' and 'the head of the snake' are utter nonsense. He was simply a gopher or go-between.

295 In Houston, Nigel Brooks was not so impressed with the historical revisionism on display. In his case notes he writes: 'A White House press release spoke of the joint investigation and the cooperation between United States and Colombian law-enforcement agencies. Nothing was further from the truth.' The press release, 'White House fact sheet: cooperation between the United States and Colombia on counter-drug programs', was issued on 30 August 2000.

296 Says DEA's Rick Bendekovic: 'It seems [the DEA] conflated several operations to make for a better story. The stats they listed were aggregated from several marine ops, including the *Transatlántico* seizure of 4600 kilos from M/V *Castor*.' Nigel Brooks agrees: 'The *Cannes* was not really Operation Journey although we included it – it was part of HMCE's Operation Jezebel. Even the *China Breeze* and *Castor* were part of Jezebel and it wasn't until we actually recruited the source that Journey came about.' For a full list of Operation Journey seizures, see Operation Journey: By the Numbers.

297 Martin Blanco chose not to be interviewed.

298 Luis disagrees: 'Andrés knew their visas were revoked and Patricia almost got arrested because of the fake passport. They saw the ugly side – she was raising two kids without their dad.'

299 A field-enforcement group of the DEA's Special Operations Division (SOD). According to a DOJ report, 959 Group is also known as the Bilateral Case Group or Bilateral Investigations Unit. Its sister group within SOD is called 960 Group or 960a Group, a Terrorism Investigations Unit.

300 Brooks believes they were the same two attorneys who caused him problems: 'In Houston we had massive problems with them because once DOJ gets involved we basically have to go through them; although investigative matters are the sole prerogative of the agency running the case. Usually, we would take a case to the judicial district that had jurisdiction and the attorneys from that district handle things. In the case of Operation Journey, DOJ took over the prosecution and have the authority to muscle in on a case being handled at the district level – that's probably what happened with Luis Navia and the Southern District of Florida (Miami). I can well understand the ire of a case agent in Miami and the Assistant US Attorney when two guys drop in from Washington, DC and try to take their case away.

'Once the case was taken down, I retired in January 2001 and US Customs was essentially pushed out of the investigation by DEA. There was one debriefing of De La Vega in Miami in which he lied about a previous smuggle using a vessel into the New York area. We knew it, and the Customs agent who debriefed him wrote a memo to that effect. [The two attorneys] had the memo suppressed because it would have totally destroyed any credibility should De La Vega have had to testify – he did not. After that Customs was no longer involved in the case.'

301 If a prisoner is housed in an FDC longer term and not in a regular prison, that usually means they are preparing to turn government witness: 'That means they are working on a Rule 35.'

302 Morrison was extradited from Jamaica in 1991, imprisoned for 22 years and deported back to Jamaica in 2013. He sued the Jamaican Government for wrongful extradition.

303 An indictment and an information are both formal charging documents under the US federal legal system, but only an indictment requires grand-jury approval before being initiated. According to Rule 7(b) of the *Federal Rules of Criminal Procedure*, 'an offense punishable by imprisonment for more than one year may be prosecuted by information if the defendant – in open court and after being advised of the nature of the charge and of the defendant's rights – waives prosecution by indictment'.

304 Brooks disagrees: 'The cases were consolidated and Luis pleaded guilty to both the 1995 indictment and the *Suerte* case.'

305 Luis submitted this statement as part of his sentencing deal: 'I have gained nothing by my criminal activity but instead lost everything, my self-esteem, my family, my liberty . . . I am guilty of the offence and express a sincere and profound sense of remorse and contrition for my actions.'

306 Now known as *Dirección de Investigación Criminal e INTERPOL* (Directorate of Criminal Investigation and INTERPOL or DICI).

307 It controlled huge swathes of Colombia: the North Bloc, the Bogotá/Llanos Bloc and the Central Bolívar Bloc in the country's south. Castaño was later murdered by one of his own brothers. The six-part documentary series *The Invisibles* includes an excellent profile and investigation of the AUC and its leadership.

308 On Colombia's Canal RCN network, an episode of a popular TV show called *Comando Élite* was devoted to the brothers. The DEA informant who gave up the location of Víctor and Miguel was murdered in 2009. His name was Juan Manuel Gaviria Vásquez aka 'Tocayo'.

309 Coleman is a Federal Correctional Complex (FCC), consisting of four prisons including Coleman-Low near Wildwood, Sumter County, central Florida.

310 Santi's name, date of birth and place of birth were all correct. Says Luis: 'It was a real one but pulled from the stack.'

311 An account set up for a prisoner so they can purchase everyday items in prison.

312 A reference to the album cover of *Dark Side of the Moon* (1973).

313 This was the case until 2017 when the United States abolished its 'wet-foot, dry-foot' policy, whereby if a Cuban citizen reached US soil without a visa, he or she could not be deported and could lawfully remain in the United States while applying for permanent residency.

314 Even though he got his passport in 2006, Luis didn't obtain a naturalisation certificate until 2009, back-dated to 1968 when he became a US citizen.

315 Luis may have a point. Even sugar kills more people than cocaine in the United States. Statistically 25,000 Americans die each year from health

complications related to sugar intake while 14,000 die of cocaine overdoses, usually mixed with an opioid.

316 Joseph P. Kennedy Sr, John F. Kennedy's father, was a major liquor importer in the 1930s, his company Somerset Importers bringing into the United States brands such as Gordon's London Dry Gin and Dewar's scotch whisky.

317 Austrian scientist Karl von Scherzer collected coca leaves on a scientific expedition to South America in the mid-1850s and gave them to Göttingen University chemistry professor Friedrich Wöhler. His assistant, Albert Niemann, successfully extracted cocaine in 1859.

318 Cocaine is not only decriminalised in Bolivia (up to 50 grams) but coca production is also legal. Selling and transporting cocaine, however, is illegal.

319 DEA slang for becoming a source, CI or asset.

320 According to a well-placed legal source in Miami.

321 A pseudonym.

322 David Donald is a pseudonym.

323 In October 1999 there was a meeting of 30 narcos and the DEA in Panama to nut out terms of their surrender. Rasguño was one of the attendees.

324 The Cirrus G2 Vision Jet.

325 Brooks is more sceptical: 'As far as the *Suerte* goes, Luis was a representative of the ship's owner. I don't believe he had anything to do with route-planning or distribution – the Greeks just handled the transport. Routes and onloads/offloads were all handled by the people in the organisation. In today's parlance I'd describe Luis as being a contractor. Luis would not have access to the onload/offload coordinates or codes used.' When I pointed out Luis had those codes in his possession when he was arrested by the *Guardia Nacional* in Maracaibo, Brooks doubled down: 'I was not aware that he also had the codes, but it would make sense as he was handling the crew replacement and would need to give them to the captain, etc. I know that Iván de la Vega had it in his possession when he was arrested . . . I still believe Luis was just a transportation guy when it came to Operation Journey. His role was to represent the owners of the *Suerte* to get the vessel where it needed to be; to make sure that the crew was changed and handle those things. Overall, Jorge García would have had the greatest knowledge of each smuggling venture from onload to offload.'

326 Mermelstein claimed under oath to have been responsible for trafficking 55 to 56 tons. He was also implicated in five murders, including Barry Seal's. Seal trafficked about 60 tons. Jung was only ever convicted for a ton of coke but, working as a transporter for the Medellín Cartel's Carlos Lehder, was responsible for a similar amount to Mermelstein and Seal.

327 The song, written by Raúl Marrero, was first released by Tommy Olivencia on his self-titled album on the Top Hits label in 1983. Ruiz was the vocalist. Marrero, Olivencia and Ruiz, all dead, were Puerto Ricans.

328 This individual, an extremely famous cartel figure, was arrested in 2001 in Colombia and extradited to the United States for drug trafficking. He was eventually deported to Colombia in 2019. For safety reasons he will not be described or named.

329 In 2000, the year Luis was arrested, the White House said in a press release: 'Each year, illegal drug abuse is linked to 52,000 American deaths and costs our society nearly $110 billion in health care, accidents, and lost productivity.'

330 This is true. Most of the top-tier Colombian narcos of the 1980s were from peasant or lower-class stock.

331 Luis is correct. The DEA used more than 18,000 sources between 2010 and 2015, according to a 2016 DOJ audit.
332 Roberto Diaz is a pseudonym. He requested one due to fear of reprisal – even years after Poli's death.
333 The opening track of John's 1970 album, *Tumbleweed Connection.*
334 Vicente Blanco died in 2017, two days after the death of Luis's mother. Their funerals took place the same day.

Index

FIGURES DE FANTAISIE

DU XVIe AU XVIIIe SIÈCLE

Cet ouvrage accompagne l'exposition *Ceci n'est pas un portrait. Figures de fantaisie de Murillo, Fragonard, Tiepolo...* organisée par le musée des Augustins, à Toulouse, du 21 novembre 2015 au 6 mars 2016.

Cette exposition a bénéficié du soutien de Médipôle Partenaires

ÉDITION
Musée des Augustins
Axel Hémery, directeur éditorial
Geneviève Ponselle, coordination éditoriale
Sandrine Bonnet, Alice Jego et Mathilde Naud, recherche photographique

Somogy éditions d'art
Nicolas Neumann, directeur éditorial
Stéphanie Méséguer, responsable éditoriale
Laurence Verrand et Sarah Houssin-Dreyfuss, coordination et suivi éditorial
Teddy Bélier, conception graphique
Anne-Marie Valet, contribution éditoriale
Béatrice Bourgerie et Mélanie Le Gros, fabrication

www.somogy.fr
www.augustins.org

ISBN : 978-2-7572-0998-1
Dépôt légal : octobre 2015
Imprimé en République tchèque (Union européenne)

Ill. de couverture : Michael Sweerts, *Garçon au turban tenant un bouquet de fleurs*, Madrid, Museo Thyssen-Bornemysza
Rabat 1 : Pietro Bellotti, *Un vieux chanteur*, Paris, courtesy galerie Canesso
Rabat 2 : Bartolomé Esteban Murillo, *La Jeune Marchande de fleurs*, Londres, The Governors of Dulwich Picture Gallery
4e de couverture : Jean-Baptiste Santerre (d'après), *Jeune Fille endormie à la chandelle*, Nantes, musée des Beaux-Arts

FIGURES DE FANTAISIE

DU XVIe AU XVIIIe SIÈCLE

MUSÉE DES AUGUSTINS

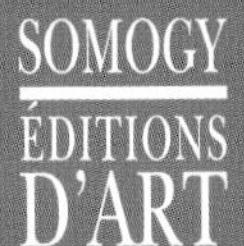

Comité d'honneur

Monsieur Jean-Luc Moudenc, Maire de Toulouse, Président de Toulouse Métropole
Monsieur Francis Grass, adjoint au Maire en charge de la politique culturelle
Monsieur Pierre Esplugas, adjoint au Maire en charge des musées

Commissariat de l'exposition

Axel Hémery, directeur du musée des Augustins
Melissa Percival, professeure d'histoire de l'art et de civilisation française à l'université d'Exeter, Royaume-Uni

Auteurs du présent catalogue

John Chu, conservateur au National Trust (Londres)
Petra ten-Doesschate Chu, professeure à l'université de Seton Hall (USA)
Axel Hémery, directeur du musée des Augustins
Melissa Percival, professeure à l'université d'Exeter
Martin Postle, adjoint au directeur des études du Centre Paul Mellon (Londres)
Bronwen Wilson, professeure à l'University of California, UCLA (Los Angeles)

REMERCIEMENTS

La véritable cheville ouvrière et tête pensante de cette exposition est Melissa Percival, professeure d'histoire de l'art et de civilisation française à l'université d'Exeter, qui a manifesté un enthousiasme communicatif du début à la fin de cette belle aventure. La réussite espérée de l'exposition lui reviendra de droit. L'université d'Exeter a immédiatement soutenu son action. Nous souhaitons remercier en particulier son Dean of the College of Humanities, Mr Andrew Thorpe.

John Chu, Petra ten Doesschate-Chu, Martin Postle et Bronwen Wilson ont apporté une contribution originale à la question de la figure de fantaisie.

Muriel Adrien, maître de conférences en études anglo-saxonnes à l'université Toulouse Jean-Jaurès de Toulouse, est une partenaire ancienne du musée. Nous lui devons l'engagement de l'Université à nos côtés dans l'importante traduction des textes anglais pour le catalogue. Elle est également l'organisatrice du colloque consacré à la figure de fantaisie à l'occasion de cette exposition. Nous associons à ces remerciements monsieur Jean-Michel Minovez, président de l'université Toulouse Jean-Jaurès, les enseignants et étudiants du CETIM, du DEMA et du CAS.

De nombreux prêteurs institutionnels et privés ont accepté de se séparer d'œuvres de tout premier plan pendant la durée de l'exposition. Nous leur en sommes infiniment reconnaissants :

- Aix-en-Provence, musée Granet : M. Bruno Ely
- Amiens, musée de Picardie : Mme Sabine Cazenave
- Anvers, Koninklijk Museum voor schone Kunsten : Dr Elsje Janssen
- Barcelone, Museu Nacional d'Art de Catalunya : M. Pepe Serra
- Belfast, Ulster Museum of Art : M. Tim Coole
- Besançon, musée des Beaux-Arts et d'Archéologie : M. Emmanuel Guigon
- Bologne, Pinacoteca Nazionale : M. Gianpiero Cammarota
- Bordeaux, musée des Beaux-Arts : Mme Sophie Barthélémy
- Brême, Kunsthalle : Prof. Dr Christoph Grunenberg
- Bruxelles, Musées royaux des beaux-arts de Belgique : M. Michel Draguet
- Caen, musée des Beaux-Arts : Mme Emmanuelle Delapierre
- Cambridge, The Trustees of The Fitzwilliam Museum : M. Timothy Potts
- Cardiff, National Museum of Wales : M. Oliver Fairclough
- Cortone, Museo dell'Accademia Etrusca e della Città di Cortona : M. Paolo Bruschetti
- Dijon, musée des Beaux-Arts : M. David Liot et M. Matthieu Gilles
- Douai, musée de la Chartreuse : Mme Anne Labourdette
- Dunkerque, musée des Beaux-Arts : Mme Aude Cordonnier
- Düsseldorf, Stiftung Museum Kunstpalast : M. Beat Wismer
- Épinal, Musée départemental d'art ancien et contemporain : M. Thierry Dechezleprêtre
- Falmouth Art Gallery : Mme Henrietta Boex
- Florence, Polo Museale di Firenze, Galleria Palatina-Palazzo Pitti : M. Matteo Ceriana
- Freising, Diözesanmuseum : M. Christoph Kürzeder
- Gênes, Musei di Strada Nuova, Palazzo Rosso : M. Piero Boccardo
- Gouda, Museum Gouda : M. Gerard de Kleijn
- Grenoble, musée de Grenoble : M. Guy Tosatto
- Haarlem, Frans Hals Museum : Mme Ann Demeester
- Karlsruhe, Staatliche Kunsthalle : Prof. Dr Pia Müller-Tamm
- Lecce, M. Luciano Treggiari
- Lille, palais des Beaux-Arts : M. Bruno Girveau
- Londres, Dulwich Picture Gallery : M. Xavier Bray
- Londres, The National Trust : M. David Taylor
- Lyon, musée des Beaux-Arts : Mme Sylvie Ramond
- Madrid, Museo Thyssen-Bornemisza : M. Guillermo Solana
- Marseille, musée des Beaux-Arts : M. Luc Georget
- Milan, Pinacoteca di Brera : Mme Sandrina Bandera
- Modène, Galleria Estense : Mme Nicoletta Giordani
- Montluçon, musée des Musiques populaires : M. Éric Bourgougnon
- Montpellier, musée Fabre : M. Michel Hilaire
- Munich, Bayerische Staatsgemäldesammlungen, Alte Pinakothek : Prof. Dr Klaus Schrenk
- Nantes, musée des Beaux-Arts : Mme Blandine Chavanne
- Narbonne, musée d'Art et d'Histoire : M. Bertrand Ducourau
- Olomouk, Zamek, Arcibiskupstvi olomoucké : Mgr Josef Nuzik
- Orléans, musée des Beaux-Arts : Mme Bénédicte De Donker
- Paris, Galerie Canesso : M. Maurizio Canesso et Mme Véronique Damian
- Paris, bibliothèque-musée de la Comédie-Française : Mme Agathe Sanjuan
- Paris, musée Jacquemart-André : M. Jean-Pierre Babelon et M. Nicolas Sainte Fare-Garnot
- Paris, musée du Petit-Palais : M. Christophe Leribault
- Pau, musée des Beaux-Arts : M. Jean-Pierre Melot
- Rancate, Pinacoteca Cantonale Giovanni Züst : Mme Mariangela Agliati-Ruggia
- Rome, Polo Museale Romano, Galleria Borghese : Mme Anna Coliva
- Rotterdam, Museum Boijmans Van Beuningen : M. Sjarel Ex
- Rovigo, Pinacoteca dell'Accademia dei Concordi : Prof. Enrico Zerbinati

- Rovigo, Seminario Vescovile : Don Bruno Cappato
- Salzbourg, Residenzgalerie : Dr Gabriele Groschner
- Strasbourg, musée des Beaux-Arts : M. Dominique Jacquot
- Toulouse, Fondation Bemberg : M. Guillermo de Osma et M. Philippe Cros
- Turin, Galleria Sabauda : Mme Annamaria Bava
- Udine, Civici Musei, Galleria d'Arte Antica : M. Romano Vecchiet
- Utrecht, Centraal Museum : M. Edwin Jacobs
- Valence, Museo de Bellas Artes : Mme Paz Olmos Periz
- Varèse, Museo Baroffio : Mme Laura Marazzi
- Venise, Fondazione Musei Veneziani, Ca'Rezzonico : Mme Gabriella Belli
- Vienne, Kunsthistorisches Museum, Gemäldegalerie : Dr Sabine Haag
- Vienne, Gemäldegalerie der Akademie der bildenden Künste : Dr Martina Fleischer
- Wurzbourg, Martin von Wagner Museum : Prof. Dr Damian Dombrowski

Nous souhaitons remercier les confrères, chercheurs et historiens de l'art qui nous ont aidés dans nos recherches : Sébastien Allard, Virginie Barthélémy, Ilaria Bruno, Adeline Collange-Perugi, Alberto Craievich, Raffaele De Giorgi, Guillaume Faroult, Marc Favreau, Florence Gétreau, Liesbeth Helmus, Neil Jeffares, Élisabeth de Jonckheere, Caroline Joubert, David Mandrella, Natalie Rigby, Gudrun Swoboda, Ludmila Virassamynaïken, Annie de Wambrechies, Joanna Woodall.

Pour leur soutien déterminant, nous ne saurions assez remercier M. Francis Grass, adjoint au Maire de Toulouse chargé de la culture, et M. Pierre Esplugas, adjoint au Maire de Toulouse chargé des musées ; Mme Marie-Christine Labourdette, directrice des Musées de France, M. Laurent Roturier, directeur régional des Affaires culturelles de Midi-Pyrénées.

Nos remerciements s'adressent également à Mme Sandrine Demoulin, directrice générale des Affaires culturelles de la Ville de Toulouse, et à Mme Pascale Samuel, conseillère pour les musées à la direction régionale des Affaires culturelles de Midi-Pyrénées.

C'est enfin une tâche bien agréable que de remercier l'ensemble du personnel du musée associé à ce projet, tout particulièrement Mme Geneviève Ponselle, pour la coordination générale de l'exposition et de la communication ; Mme Caroline Berne, pour la régie des œuvres ; Mme Ghislaine Gemin, pour les relations avec la presse et les réseaux sociaux ; Mme Caroline Latour, pour le multimédia et le site Internet ; Mmes Aurélie Albajar, Émilie Micouleau, Claire Ponselle, Marie Allaman et Jessica Rivière, pour leurs actions vers les publics et la programmation culturelle autour de l'exposition ; Mme Sandrine Bonnet, pour les demandes de prêts, aidée de Mmes Mathilde Naud et Alice Jégo, pour la documentation et les commandes d'images ; Mme Marine Désormeau, pour la relecture de l'ouvrage ; MM. Gérald Bégin et Benoît Darolles, qui ont assumé la charge administrative et le suivi financier de l'exposition ; MM. Hervé Gasquez et Tahar Boucif, pour le suivi des travaux ; Mmes Nouara Conte et Élisabeth Louer, MM. Norbert Bac, Christophe Bernet, Michel Carrière, Patrick Courtade, Tony Evans, Emmanuel Perrin, membres de l'équipe technique ; M. Mohamed Kesseiri, responsable de la sécurité ; Mmes Françoise Baumard et Catherine Vaquero, chargées du suivi administratif RH au musée ; ainsi que les agents de l'accueil et de la surveillance et tous ceux qui ont collaboré, à un titre ou à un autre, à la réalisation de cette exposition au sein de la mairie de Toulouse et de Toulouse Métropole, notamment Mmes Marine Barelli, Claire Coquemont, Fabienne Darasse, Assya Cazaux, Leila El-Mellouki, Pascale Gourney, Catherine Humbert, Maryline Odorico, Cathy Pedron, Élisabeth Ruffé, MM. Olivier Berthézène, Guillaume Boulesteix, Alain Bouzer, Greg Chorlet, Christophe Vauboin.

Toute notre gratitude s'adresse à nos fidèles animatrices de la fédération Léo-Lagrange pour l'animation des ateliers jeunes publics : Mmes Gabrielle Campana, Marie Deback-Rodes, Prissyla Deschaumet, Charlotte Dreyfus, Sophie Lasserre et Pascale Latour.

Les Amis du musée et sa présidente Mme Isabelle Saint-Pierre soutiennent l'action du musée depuis des années. Nous les en remercions chaleureusement.

L'exposition de Toulouse a bénéficié du mécénat de Médipôle Partenaires. Nous saluons leur engagement.

Nous englobons dans ces remerciements nos complices et partenaires fidèles toulousains, le centre culturel Alban-Minville, le lycée Saint-Sernin, l'Office du tourisme, le musée Paul-Dupuy, ou nationaux comme *Télérama* et la Fnac.

Nous tenons à saluer le travail d'Emmanuelle Sapet, scénographe, Teddy Bélier pour le graphisme, Daniel Martin pour les photographies, Laurence Verrand et Sarah Houssin-Dreyfuss pour la coordination éditoriale du catalogue, Emmanuelle Toubiana pour l'organisation des conférences de presse, la Cie du *Rêvoir* pour le parcours poétique et la collecte de rêves, Chad Kéveny pour l'atelier de peinture pour adultes ainsi que les intervenants (conte, spectacle vivant, animations) de la programmation culturelle du musée.

Après *Benjamin-Constant. Merveilles et mirages de l'orientalisme*, le musée des Augustins s'engage dans une nouvelle coopération internationale avec *Ceci n'est pas un portrait. Figures de fantaisie de Murillo, Fragonard, Tiepolo...* Un partenariat inédit entre la Ville de Toulouse, l'université d'Exeter (Royaume-Uni) et l'université de Toulouse Jean-Jaurès est à la base de ce projet original. Plus de quatre-vingts tableaux provenant de huit pays européens constituent un parcours riche d'enseignements. La force de cette exposition montre à quel point le patrimoine est un matériau vivant car ces hommes et ces femmes, ces enfants et ces vieillards de l'Ancien Régime sont nos contemporains et illustrent nos passions éternelles. Ils nous ressemblent et nous émeuvent par la poésie de l'évocation dont sont capables les artistes bien plus que par la précision photographique de leur regard. Cet échange fécond entre le passé, le présent et le futur est au cœur même du positionnement de Toulouse, qui s'est mise en ordre de marche dans l'optique du label Unesco.

JEAN-LUC MOUDENC
Maire de Toulouse, Président de Toulouse Métropole

AUTEURS DES NOTICES

AH : Axel Hémery

MP : Melissa Percival

ÉQUIPES DE TRADUCTION

De l'anglais vers le français des essais et d'une partie des notices

Encadrants : Muriel Adrien, Marie Bouchet, Xavier Cervantes, Catherine Delyfer, Marie-Jeanne Gauffre, Isabelle Keller-Privat, Amélie Josselin-Leray, Geneviève Lafon, Sylvie Maurel, Nathalie Rivières de Carles, Laurence Roussillon-Constanty, Pascale Sempéré, Nathalie Vincent-Arnaud.

Étudiants : Sophie Besançon, Marie Brun, Maya Coelho, Alexandra Cueille, Laure Dartiguepeyron, Ailbhe Johnson, Cyrielle Lahuna, Olivia Mur, Fanny Narcy, Catherine Pearce, Arnaud Pommereau, Agnès Potier, Caroline Réveillac, Edwige Thélisson.

ABRÉVIATIONS

Les mesures sont données en mètres

Cat. : catalogue

Cat. exp. : catalogue d'exposition

H. : hauteur

H.s.t. : huile sur toile

S.d. : signé daté

S.d.b.g : signé daté en bas à gauche

S.d.h.g : signé daté en haut à gauche

Fig. : figure

Inv. : inventaire

L. : largeur

SOMMAIRE

AVANT-PROPOS

Le projet de cette exposition remonte à cinq ans en arrière, alors que Melissa Percival, spécialiste de peinture française du XVIIIe siècle, professeure à l'université d'Exeter, travaillait à son livre remarqué, *Fragonard and the Fantasy Figure*. Il s'est matérialisé au cours d'échanges où le concept de figure de fantaisie s'est affirmé avec force comme un principe fécond de la peinture ancienne. Ce concept, partagé par les commissaires, n'est en aucune façon leur invention mais une construction élaborée à partir de catégories consacrées de l'histoire de l'art qui n'avaient jamais été systématiquement rapprochées jusqu'à présent. Bien loin du seul Fragonard, l'exposition couvre presque trois siècles de peinture européenne, du début du XVIe à la fin du XVIIIe siècle.

C'est cette exposition que nous présentons aujourd'hui au public toulousain. Elle est totalement inédite, aussi curieux que cela puisse paraître, bien qu'on y croise des problématiques envisagées par ailleurs sous l'angle du portrait, de la scène de genre ou de l'allégorie à l'occasion de nos expositions antérieures. Les habitués du musée retrouveront les figures isolées du caravagisme nordique (*Corps et Ombres. Le caravagisme européen*, 2012), l'expérimentation sur le visage (*Fra'Galgario, peintre de caractères*, 2004) et l'ambivalence entre le portrait et la scène de genre (*Petits Théâtres de l'intime*, 2011).

C'est également une exposition audacieuse et les commissaires sont conscients qu'ils prêteront flanc à la critique. Sur les quelque quatre-vingts tableaux retenus pour illustrer la figure de fantaisie, on dénombre également, à dose homéopathique, des figures de saints et de héros antiques ou bibliques, des représentations allégoriques et des portraits. Il nous a paru légitime de préférer l'esprit de finesse à l'esprit de géométrie, la licence poétique au pédantisme. C'est pourquoi l'exposition se caractérise par la diversité et l'ouverture. Diversité des lieux de création d'abord : huit écoles nationales sont représentées ainsi que les principaux foyers artistiques européens, de Rome à Paris, d'Utrecht à Londres, d'Anvers à Vienne, de Haarlem à Naples, de Séville à Venise... Diversité des mouvements et genres artistiques ensuite : on trouvera ici des giorgionesques et des caravagesques, des rembranesques et des *Bamboccianti*, des *Pitocchetti* et des peintres de *tronies*, des auteurs de têtes d'expression et de *fancy pictures*. En dépit de quelques absences regrettables (Titien, Rembrandt), les plus grands peintres sont présents avec des œuvres mémorables et attendues : Annibal Carrache, Frans Hals, Jordaens, Murillo, Fragonard, Greuze, Tiepolo.

Le plan même de l'exposition reflète cette volonté de panorama orienté mais libre de la peinture européenne en musardant autour des stratégies du regard et des expérimentations des peintres. Au point de départ, on trouve le modèle, réel ou idéalisé, et la façon dont il oriente le regard de l'artiste puis du spectateur par la séduction directe ou indirecte, ou ce qu'on pourrait appeler l'effet du regardeur regardé. On aborde ensuite des catégories de modèles absorbés dans une action, selon l'expression consacrée de Michael Fried (en particulier dans son ouvrage, *La Place du spectateur*), avec tout d'abord les musiciens, bruyants dans la réalité et silencieux dans la peinture. On se plongera ensuite dans un état plus méditatif avec des figures rêvassant ou philosophant dans des attitudes proches de l'abandon, la lecture étant propice à la fois à la concentration et à l'évasion. La conséquence extrême de cet oubli du monde est l'endormissement et la séquence des dormeurs est sans nul doute la plus poétique et surprenante de l'exposition.

La deuxième partie s'ouvre sur un éloge de la folie, l'action dérangeante de l'ironie et de la raillerie qui subvertit l'ordre du monde et permet à l'artiste d'énoncer un jugement moral. Cette section intitulée « Rires et sarcasmes » réveillera sans nul doute la galerie des personnages et notre public. Nous proposerons ensuite à ce dernier d'explorer une constante de ces peintres si différents en apparence qui est leur volonté d'expérimenter sur la matière première constituée par les carnations, les chevelures et les rides, ce que nous avons appelé le « Laboratoire du visage ». Nous conclurons par un phénomène partagé avec la littérature, le théâtre et l'opéra qui est le déguisement, pouvant aller jusqu'au travestissement et se manifester par la recherche d'un exotisme de fantaisie. Nous avons intitulé cette dernière section « Atelier du costume ». Ouverte par une courtisane vénitienne du XVIe siècle (mais est-on si sûr de son statut ?) de Paris Bordon, l'exposition peut ainsi fermer le rideau sur le magnifique portrait autrefois considéré de l'abbé de Saint-Non en costume espagnol de Fragonard.

Les essais du catalogue sont tous issus de l'Université britannique ou américaine. La raison vient d'abord de la genèse de ce projet et des disponibilités des uns et des autres mais ce choix permet aussi d'aller à la rencontre d'une histoire de l'art véritablement pluridisciplinaire, engagée dans les débats contemporains, rédigée dans une langue intelligible et qui ne se prend pas trop au sérieux.

Le redoutable honneur revenait à Melissa Percival de présenter l'objet même de cette étude. Dans son essai introductif, charpente de notre édifice moins fragile qu'il n'y paraît, elle définit patiemment les termes de notre équation. En partant d'une typologie voire d'une taxinomie, elle finit par parvenir à l'expression d'une poétique. Généralement (mais l'exception rôde, insatiable), une figure de fantaisie se présente sous la forme d'un buste ou d'une demi-figure en plan serré, au décor minimaliste, et où le peintre élabore une technique informelle et expérimentale. Melissa Percival balaie d'une plume alerte trois siècles de théorie et de pratique de la peinture. Une fois cette histoire résumée, elle s'attelle à l'exploration des métamorphoses du visage puis elle s'interroge sur l'identité des modèles et sur leur mise en scène et en action avant de conclure par une réflexion sur les rapports entre fantaisie et imagination.

Bronwen Wilson, historienne de l'art canadienne, professeure à l'université d'East Anglia à Norwich (Grande-Bretagne) et spécialiste de l'art de la Renaissance vénitienne, consacre son essai aux figures féminines, dites de courtisanes, dans la peinture vénitienne du XVIe siècle et à leur évolution jusqu'au caravagisme. Ces représentations posent la question, centrale dans toute l'exposition, de la richesse inépuisable des interprétations possibles des images. Il n'est pas anodin que des inventeurs de la « manière moderne » comme Giorgione ou Titien soient à l'origine d'archétypes telles la *Laure* ou la *Flore* qui transcendent toute tentative d'enfermement dans un genre précis et, par là même, se revèlent extrêmement influents.

Petra ten-Doesschate Chu, historienne de l'art néerlandaise, professeure à l'université Seton Hall (États-Unis), spécialiste de l'art du XIXe siècle et en particulier de Courbet, nous propose un essai sur le thème des représentations de dormeurs dans la peinture ancienne. Elle établit des parallèles, connus depuis l'Antiquité gréco-romaine, entre Hypnos, le sommeil, Éros, la petite mort érotique, et Thanatos, la mort, la vraie. Le dormeur est observé à son insu, ce qui fait de lui un pur produit de l'absorbement cher à Michael Fried. Il incarne aussi parfois le péché de paresse mais on lui pardonne beaucoup car il dort du sommeil de l'innocence. C'est finalement dans *Blanche-Neige et les Sept Nains* que l'auteure voit une métaphore de ce propos, Blanche-Neige et Dormeur symbolisant au sein de la même histoire deux attitudes face au sommeil.

Martin Postle, adjoint au directeur des études du centre Paul Mellon (Londres), ancien conservateur à la Tate Britain et spécialiste de peinture anglaise du XVIIIe siècle (Reynolds, Zoffany), consacre son essai à la représentation des vieillards aux XVIIe et XVIIIe siècles. Partant de considérations statistiques et sociologiques sur le vieil âge, il analyse la perméabilité entre les représentations de saints ermites et les têtes d'étude produites comme exercices dans les ateliers de Rubens et Rembrandt. Un véritable marché de collectionneurs se développe autour de ces sujets pittoresques que la gravure permet de diffuser à une plus grande échelle. Des peintres présents dans l'exposition comme Denner ou Nogari se spécialisent dans ce sous-genre. À la fin de la période étudiée, c'est le modèle lui-même qui impose sa personnalité, dépassant son rôle de vieillard dans une composition religieuse ou historique.

John Chu, conservateur au National Trust, travaille actuellement sur la *fancy picture* en Angleterre au XVIIIe siècle. Son essai traite d'un sujet très prisé au XVIIIe siècle, la représentation d'une jeune femme dans l'embrasure d'une fenêtre. Afin d'en montrer la cohérence, il choisit cinq tableaux peints en France entre 1715 et 1739. Cet angle d'approche lui permet ainsi d'évoquer les stratégies du marché de l'art et les échanges artistiques entre Paris, Londres et Berlin. Inventé par Rembrandt, ce sujet suspendu entre la rue et l'intérieur reste étonnamment figé au fil du temps.

J'espère que le public parcourra l'exposition et son catalogue avec le même plaisir qui a présidé à leur élaboration entre Toulouse et Exeter, dans une émulation enthousiaste et créative.

AH

LES FIGURES DE FANTAISIE. UN PHÉNOMÈNE EUROPÉEN

Cette exposition dévoile la fascination de l'art européen pour le visage et le corps humains pendant plus de deux siècles. Elle a pour thème principal un type d'œuvre qui a traversé les époques, les figures de fantaisie, où le sujet est présenté au spectateur en gros plan. Les détails contextuels tels que le décor ou les éléments narratifs sont relégués au second plan par rapport au personnage, à la position de sa tête, à la courbe de son front, son sourire ou sa grimace. Certaines figures sont engageantes ou séductrices, d'autres, méprisantes ou méfiantes. Leur charme subtil ou leur indifférence manifeste suscitent la curiosité, la complicité ou le désir du spectateur. Pour les artistes, souvent contraints par les exigences précises d'une commande (saisir une ressemblance, reproduire fidèlement une scène biblique ou mythologique), ces études informelles offraient un exutoire libérateur. Véritables expériences menées sur la matière humaine, elles étaient également l'occasion de déployer tout le brio, l'extravagance et l'humour que peut offrir la peinture. Ce qui naissait dans l'atelier avait du succès auprès des acheteurs, qui appréciaient la beauté et le mystère de ces « têtes » mais qui s'intéressaient aussi à leur étroite relation avec le processus artistique.

Si les *tronies* de Rembrandt et les figures de fantaisie de Fragonard sont bien connus du grand public, l'histoire, au sens large, des figures de fantaisie est moins claire. Des recherches récentes ont fait la lumière sur les *tronies* néerlandais[1], les *teste di fantasia* vénitiennes et bolonaises[2], les figures de fantaisie françaises[3] et la *fancy picture* britannique[4]. Mais les multiples liens entre les écoles et les artistes n'ont pas été établis à ce jour. Dans cette exposition, la figure de fantaisie est envisagée pour la première fois comme une entité distincte, qui se développa et se diffusa dans l'Europe entière. Le corpus que nous proposons est d'une grande diversité, mais sa densité et sa cohérence sont surprenantes : courtisanes vénitiennes de la Renaissance, portraits en buste de buveurs et de musiciens isolés de l'école caravagesque, vieillards barbus

1. Hirschfelder, Krempel, 2013 ; Hirschfelder, 2008 ; Gottwald, 2009.
2. Venise, 2006 ; Rovigo, 2010 ; Vérone, 2011-2012 ; Diane De Grazia, « Tiepolo and the Art of Portraiture », in New York, 1996-1997, p. 255-261 ; Dozza, 2001.
3. Percival, 2012.
4. Nottingham/Londres, 1998 ; Chu, 2014.

Joshua Reynolds, *The Strawberry Girl*, Londres, Wallace Collection

et Orientaux de la peinture nordique, vagabonds *pitocchi* des *Bamboccianti* et d'autres peintres naturalistes italiens, *Espagnolettes* de la France du XVIIIe siècle, études d'enfants sentimentales et émouvantes. La persistance de certains types de figures et leur récurrence dans différents pays et à différentes périodes de l'histoire sont particulièrement remarquables.

Deux problèmes d'ordre méthodologique se posent d'emblée à nous, le premier étant la nomenclature. Il s'avère en effet difficile de trouver une dénomination unique pour ce qui relève d'un phénomène original dans l'art européen plutôt que d'une catégorie distincte. Le terme « figure de fantaisie » a été délibérément choisi pour son exhaustivité : il comprend toutes les œuvres présentées ici sans privilégier ni exclure une école ou un artiste en particulier. En pratique, cependant, l'usage de l'expression « figure de fantaisie » était peu répandu durant la période dont il est question, et à peine plus commun au XIXe siècle[5] ; aujourd'hui, ce terme n'est pas partout bien compris. Mais le fait qu'il n'existe pas d'étiquette réellement appropriée ne signifie pas qu'il ne s'agit pas là d'un véritable objet d'étude.

De fait, le début de l'époque moderne ne manquait pas de termes pour désigner ces œuvres. Le plus commun était alors « tête », « teste » ou « head ». Le mot néerlandais *tronie* s'est imposé dans la deuxième décennie du XVIIe siècle. Cette dénomination désormais obsolète a pris le sens de « visage » – elle possède aujourd'hui des connotations quelque peu familières, comparables à celles de « trogne » – mais elle renvoyait auparavant au masque et, par conséquent, à la notion de représentation (peinte) du visage[6]. Ailleurs, les inventaires et les catalogues précisaient le terme d'origine, évoquant plutôt des « têtes de fantaisie », « têtes de caprice » ou utilisant l'équivalent en italien et dans d'autres langues européennes. On trouvait aussi fréquemment un titre simplement descriptif comme *La Dame au voile* (Raoux), ou plus évocateur comme *La Menaceuse* (Rigaud, cat. 9) ou *The Strawberry Girl* (Reynolds, fig. ci-dessus), qui faisait allusion aux circonstances dans lesquelles l'image avait vu le jour ou bien donnait un aperçu de l'état psychologique du sujet. Les graveurs qui reproduisaient les tableaux à l'intention du grand public se montraient souvent très inventifs dans la recherche de nouveaux titres. On notera également que le terme de « portrait » était assez souvent utilisé pour faire

5. Par exemple, Manet, attentif à la tradition, emploie le terme de « figure de fantaisie » pour décrire sa *Dame aux éventails* (Paris, musée d'Orsay), une représentation idéalisée et exotique de Nina de Callias.
6. *Cf.* De Pauw de Veen, 1969.

référence à toute peinture de tête, que ce soit ou non une œuvre de commande ou qu'un modèle ait posé ou non[7].

La seconde difficulté méthodologique, plus complexe encore, est celle du genre. L'histoire de l'art a tendance à penser en termes de types d'œuvres distincts, et les représentations de la figure humaine sont ainsi classées selon les catégories suivantes : scène de genre, portrait, histoire et allégorie. Bien qu'elles soient d'une utilité indéniable pour cataloguer et comprendre les différentes fonctions de la représentation, les étiquettes sont, dans le présent contexte, à la fois académiques et anachroniques. La première distinction entre les genres est à porter au crédit de Félibien dans la préface de ses conférences à l'Académie royale de peinture et de sculpture, en 1669, dans laquelle il établit une hiérarchie, accordant à la peinture historique la première place. Son objectif sous-jacent, et celui des écoles en général, était d'élever la peinture au rang d'art « libéral ». Mais les acheteurs d'art et, dans une certaine mesure, les artistes eux-mêmes ne faisaient pas grand cas de ces distinctions. Les œuvres que nous présentons ici ont été conçues en marge de l'institution, émanant peut-être d'un projet de peinture historique ou de portrait, mais avec l'objectif implicite de mieux comprendre l'expression humaine, d'étudier une pose, de transposer les traits d'un modèle en un type ou un archétype, ou encore de rechercher l'anecdote. Ce sont cette immédiateté et cette liberté vis-à-vis des conventions qui étaient appréciées des particuliers. Notre postulat est que la perméabilité des genres a fait partie intégrante de la pratique artistique durant toute la période considérée, et qu'elle n'a donc posé problème que plus tard. C'est précisément parce qu'elles se situent dans l'entre-deux des classifications traditionnelles que les peintures de cette exposition présentent un intérêt à nos yeux.

Plutôt que d'essayer de déterminer de manière trop normative ce qui est ou n'est pas une figure de fantaisie, nous avons opté pour une démarche plus ouverte, à l'instar de cette tendance ou préoccupation de l'art européen[8]. En choisissant les tableaux de cette exposition, les commissaires ont adopté une approche *a posteriori* : la plupart de ces peintures se composent d'un seul personnage, le plus souvent d'une tête, en buste ou à mi-corps. Lorsque les figures sont montrées en pied, le décor environnant est minimal et l'attention se porte intégralement sur la pose, l'attitude du personnage ou son état psychologique. En nous limitant aux spécificités de la figure individuelle, nous avons dû exclure les compositions de groupe qui y étaient associées. Ces liens sont plus évidents dans certains cas que dans d'autres : si des artistes tels qu'Alexis Grimou ont presque exclusivement peint des personnages seuls au cours de leur carrière, d'autres, à l'instar de Giacomo Ceruti, ont sans peine navigué entre la représentation du groupe et celle de l'individu. Les recherches sur la *fancy picture* britannique ont eu tendance à traiter de la même façon les figures individuelles et celles qui font partie d'un groupe, alors que pour la peinture d'Europe continentale, on parle spécifiquement de « tronies », de « teste » ou

7. *Cf.* Percival, 2012, chap. 1er.
8. Classer les figures de fantaisie est une tâche aux difficultés innombrables. L'étiquette « Gattung » (genre) choisie par Franziska Gottwald, 2009, semble trop normative, même si on ne l'applique qu'à la peinture néerlandaise. Dagmar Hirschfelder, 2008, adopte une définition plus souple mais, en choisissant Lievens et Rembrandt comme cadre pour son concept de « tronie », situer des artistes tels que Hals lui devient difficile.

Giorgione, *Garçon à la flèche*, Vienne, Kunsthistorisches Museum

de « têtes ». L'étude comparative de toutes ces traditions ouvrira la voie à de nouvelles perspectives de recherche.

Nous avons laissé de côté les peintures qui se prêtent à des interprétations iconographiques trop évidentes (la série des Lucrèce et des Madeleine, des apôtres, etc.). Nous avons fait quelques exceptions à ce principe lorsque l'iconographie est éclipsée par un détail tel qu'une chair flasque (Jordaens, *Figure d'apôtre (Saint Pierre)*, cat. 56), ou lorsque la figure est à ce point animée qu'elle en occulte la signification externe ou « transcendante » du tableau (Van den Hoecke, *La Sibylle agrippine*, cat. 72). De la même manière, notre sélection s'est élargie à des œuvres qui représentent des modèles clairement identifiés, mais dont la ressemblance n'est sans doute pas la principale préoccupation, les traits du modèle ayant plutôt été empruntés ou adaptés dans le but de créer un sujet fictif. Dans le cas des autoportraits, la figure du peintre revêt un caractère excentrique grâce à toute une gamme de costumes et d'accessoires. Le choix des figures de fantaisie a donc surtout été dicté par des considérations subjectives : une pose intéressante, une expression mystérieuse, un costume ou une technique picturale hors du commun, une marque d'humour, un élément retenant l'attention et suscitant la surprise.

On observe la concordance d'éléments formels, que ce soit dans la peinture d'histoire, de genre ou dans le portrait : une vue en gros plan de la figure humaine, tout à la fois individuelle et universelle, la représentation d'une personne vivante, animée, une imprécision générale quant au contexte ou à la raison d'être de la figure en dehors de son « être-là ». Nous avons pris soin de tenir compte des données empiriques derrière chaque tableau, bien que pour ce type d'œuvres les informations soient souvent limitées. Il existe à l'évidence une différence entre une esquisse préparatoire et un portrait de commande. Mais connaître l'identité du modèle n'apporte qu'un éclairage partiel sur les méthodes et les relations de travail de l'artiste. Aussi nous intéressons-nous ici plus volontiers aux diverses manières, parfois inattendues, dont le modèle a été utilisé, et nous avons souhaité mettre l'accent sur le caractère contingent de celui-ci.

Une histoire européenne

Cette exposition présente une anthologie des figures de fantaisie. Dans la mesure où nous cherchons à établir des liens entre des écoles et des artistes qui ont jusqu'ici été considérés comme distincts, notre approche est thématique et ne respecte pas de chronologie particulière. Cette méthode s'inspire également de l'intemporalité de ces tableaux qui, délibérément, ne sont ancrés ni dans un contexte ni dans un milieu spécifiques. Cela étant dit, il sera utile dans cet essai de revenir à des séquences temporelles afin de mettre en évidence des schémas, des étapes décisives et des périodes d'intense activité.

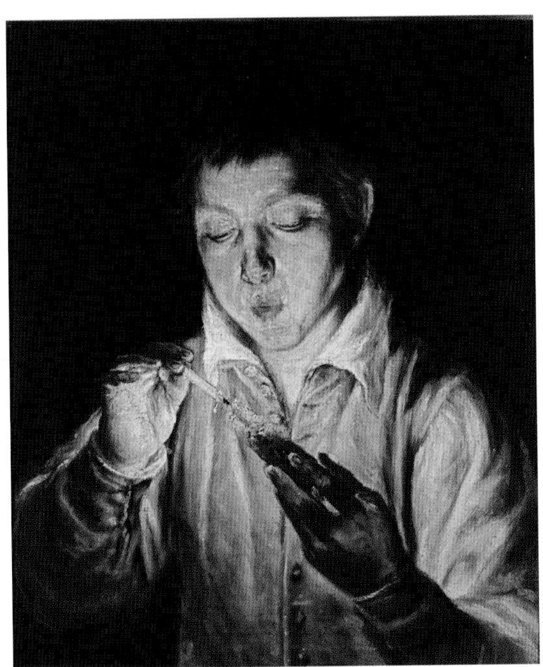
Le Greco, *El Soplón*, Naples, Museo di Capodimonte

La figure individuelle, en buste, existe depuis longtemps, au moins sous la forme d'icônes religieuses représentant le Christ, la Vierge Marie et les saints. Il était communément admis que l'objet matériel pouvait invoquer une présence divine (un pouvoir que les iconoclastes craignaient et dénonçaient), ce qui était un aspect particulièrement important de la pratique privée du culte[9]. Dans son étude fondatrice, *De l'icône à la scène narrative*, Sixten Ringbom montre à quel point les changements inhérents aux pratiques du culte entre la fin du XIVe et le début du XVe siècle ont contribué à intensifier le lien émotionnel avec les figures[10]. Il rend compte de l'essor de ce qu'il appelle « le gros plan dramatique », une nouvelle approche artistique où l'icône statique et conventionnelle prend vie et se charge d'émotions diverses.

La peinture séculière d'après modèle vivant destinée à des collections privées fait son apparition avec la peinture de chevalet à la fin du XVe et au début du XVIe siècle. Parmi les premiers exemples de figures de fantaisie, nous comptons les mystérieux bergers et musiciens à mi-corps de Giorgione (par exemple, le *Berger à la flûte*, Royal Collection, Hampton Court, le *Garçon à la flèche*, fig. page ci-contre) qui évoquent un monde pastoral de fantaisie érotique empreint de références à la mythologie classique. Dans *La Vieille* (1508-1510, Venise, Gallerie dell'Accademia), Giorgione traite la figure humaine de façon plus rustique. Titien a produit de nombreuses figures de femmes sensuelles à mi-corps et à demi-nues, créatures fictives mêlant types mythologiques ou allégoriques (Flore, Vanité), portraits de Vénitiennes de haut rang et modèles qui étaient peut-être des courtisanes. Le véritable intérêt de ces représentations ne réside pas dans l'identité du sujet, Titien cherchant plutôt à représenter un idéal féminin propre à susciter un désir érotique[11]. On trouve également cet idéal dans les œuvres de Palma le Vieux, Sebastiano del Piombo et Bartolomeo Veneto. Le *Jeune Garçon allumant une chandelle*, dit *El Soplón* (1570-1572, fig. ci-dessus), étude sensible et très intense du Greco, est un autre exemple

9. *Cf.* Belting, 2007.
10. Ringbom, 1997.
11. *Cf.* Goffen, 1997.

Pierre Paul Rubens, *Tête de vieil homme*, collection particulière

des premières figures de fantaisie. On ne peut pas non plus manquer d'évoquer les études expérimentales de demi-figures de paysans par Annibal Carrache, tel *Le Mangeur de haricots* (1580-1590, Rome, Galleria Colonna).

Au tournant du XVIIe siècle, le Caravage donne un nouvel élan aux figures en buste. Dans ses compositions de groupe religieuses et séculières, il rapproche les figures les unes des autres, rognant les corps de façon à mettre en avant le dos, les épaules, les mains et le visage. Ces raccourcis et cette proximité du spectateur, ajoutés à un clair-obscur saisissant, augmentent la charge psychologique de ses sujets, saints en prière ou en contemplation, tricheurs ou diseuses de bonne aventure. Le gros plan contribue également au naturalisme des tableaux, accentuant des détails tels que chair vieillissante ou ongles sales. Certains contemporains du Caravage trouvaient ses innovations choquantes car elles remettaient en cause l'intégrité de l'*istoria* ; mais pour le spectateur d'aujourd'hui, elles sont d'une intensité fascinante, à l'image d'un gros plan générateur de suspense dans un film[12]. Les types caravagesques (buveurs, musiciens, chanteurs, vêtus de costumes anachroniques et bigarrés) ont migré vers le nord par le biais de l'école caravagesque d'Utrecht, et vers la France par celui de Claude Vignon, de Nicolas Tournier et d'autres[13]. Ces artistes poussent même plus loin le procédé du Caravage en optant très souvent pour des figures individuelles, en tronquant encore davantage les corps et en omettant les détails narratifs.

De 1609 à 1620, à Anvers, Rubens réalisa une cinquantaine d'études de têtes, montrant principalement des vieillards barbus (fig. ci-dessus)[14]. Inspiré par l'expressivité des œuvres de Léonard de Vinci et de Raphaël qu'il avait vues en Italie, Rubens voulait faire de ces études des modèles pour ses élèves, de façon à accélérer la production par l'atelier de pièces historiques plus importantes et à exercer un contrôle plus poussé sur la qualité du processus. Après sa mort, ces œuvres se retrouvèrent sur le marché et les acheteurs se les arrachèrent, trop heureux d'acquérir un petit tableau du maître, synecdoque d'une œuvre plus imposante. L'habitude d'utiliser des têtes d'atelier a été perpétuée par les élèves de Rubens, parmi lesquels Van Dyck et d'autres artistes d'Anvers tels que Jacob Jordaens.

Au cours de la décennie suivante, à Leyde, Jan Lievens commença à peindre des sujets à partir de modèles vivants, habillés de costumes de fantaisie et baignés de lumière. Rembrandt

12. *Cf.* Pericolo, 2011. Pericolo étudie les analogies entre les débuts de la peinture et du cinéma in Pericolo, 2009, p. 1-29.
13. *Cf.* Toulouse/Montpellier, 2012 ; Baltimore/San Francisco, 1997-1998.
14. *Cf.* Gottwald, 2009 ; Black, 2014, p. 65-79.

lui emboîta le pas dans cette entreprise, et finit par le surpasser (fig. ci-contre)[15]. Leurs œuvres prirent le nom de « tronies » et gagnèrent rapidement en popularité auprès des collectionneurs. Bien que le *tronie* se rapproche du portrait dans sa volonté de saisir une physionomie particulière, il donnait à l'artiste davantage de latitude qu'un portrait de commande, l'occasion de travailler des points de vue inhabituels sur les visages ou une expression étrange, un coup de pinceau plus dynamique ou des jeux de lumière. Rembrandt était son propre modèle, jouant avec ses traits et portant des éléments de costume peu communs : chapeaux à plumes, médaillons ou tenues militaires. À Haarlem, l'intérêt de Frans Hals pour les expressions du visage, en particulier le sourire, s'étendit au-delà du cadre strict de l'art du portrait, comme en témoignent ses diverses représentations de gens du peuple au moyen d'une technique vibrante proche de l'esquisse. À Delft, Vermeer peignit des figures sensuelles et énigmatiques telles que *La Jeune Fille à la perle*[16]. Et, ensemble, les élèves et disciples de Rembrandt, parmi lesquels Gerrit Dou, Ferdinand Bol, Willem Drost, Jacob Adriaensz, Pieter Hermansz et Wallerant Vaillant, renforcèrent l'influence du *tronie* dans l'art hollandais du XVIIe siècle.

Rembrandt, *L'Homme au béret à plume*, La Haye, Mauritshuis

Les *Bamboccianti*, actifs à Rome au XVIIe siècle et dont la majorité venait du nord de l'Europe, réalisèrent des études sensibles et pleines d'esprit de gens du peuple. L'un des *Bamboccianti* les plus éminents dans la peinture des figures individuelles était Michael Sweerts (1618-1664), bruxellois d'origine : ses études d'enfants et de domestiques ainsi que d'autres types rustiques, à l'exécution très soignée, sont d'un naturalisme stupéfiant dû à l'influence de Vermeer, mais elles n'en affichent pas moins des traits caravagesques (Madrid, Museo Thyssen-Bornemisza, cat. 74). En Italie du Nord, un certain nombre d'artistes « misérabilistes » rendirent populaires le thème du paysan en haillons et autres scènes rustiques : Eberhard Keil (un élève danois de Rembrandt installé en Italie), Pietro Bellotti, Antonio Cifrondi et Giacomo Francesco Cipper, né en Allemagne et plus connu sous le nom de « Il Todeschini »[17]. Les vagabonds éponymes de Giacomo Ceruti, dit « Il Pitocchetto », sont, malgré leurs haillons, d'une dignité et d'un pathos frappants. L'Espagne possédait ses propres traditions de représentation de mendiants et d'indigents qui remontent à Jusepe de Ribera et son ténébrisme terre à terre ; dans un autre

15. *Cf.* Schwartz, 1989, p. 95.
16. *Cf.* New York/Londres, 2001, p. 386-393, n°s 74 et 75.
17. *Cf.* Brescia, 1998-1999.

Ubaldo Gandolfi, *Tête de jeune femme*, Oxford, Ashmolean Museum

Giambattista Tiepolo, *Jeune Femme au perroquet*, Oxford, Ashmolean Museum

style, les peintures de pauvres par Bartolomé Esteban Murillo se distinguent par leur beauté et l'émotion qui s'en dégage.

La figure de fantaisie a également pris une forme plus idéalisée dans l'art italien. Au tournant du XVIIIe siècle, Giuseppe Maria Crespi, de Bologne, réalisait des figures à mi-corps élégantes et énigmatiques s'inscrivant dans la catégorie de la peinture de genre. Celles-ci ont inspiré les générations suivantes, comme Donato Creti ou les frères Ubaldo et Gaetano Gandolfi, qui ont peint des figures très variées, Orientaux à barbe ou femmes à l'air morose (fig. ci-dessus à gauche). À Venise, les successeurs de Giorgione et de Titien ont fait renaître le type de la courtisane sensuelle : Rosalba Carriera a marié l'allégorie au portrait dans ses peintures de bustes au pastel (*Jeune Femme au perroquet*, Chicago, Art Institute). Giambattista Tiepolo a réalisé sa propre *Jeune Femme au perroquet* (fig. ci-dessus à droite), l'une des *teste a capriccio* dans lesquelles l'artiste joue sur les thèmes du déguisement et du désir. On peut observer des tendances plus réalistes dans les travaux de Giovanni Battista Piazzetta (1682-1754), qui représentait des sujets rustiques à l'air mystérieux et langoureux. Dans ses dessins, Piazzetta reproduisait la spontanéité des expressions du visage dans de saisissants formats recadrés qui rappellent le Caravage.

Jean-Siméon Chardin, *Portrait présumé du peintre Jean-Jacques Bachelier*, Cambridge (Mass), Fogg Art Museum

En France, au XVIIIe siècle, les figures de fantaisie de Jean-Baptiste Santerre, Jean Raoux, Alexis Grimou et Jacques Courtin étaient des pastiches délibérés, réalisés pour une nouvelle clientèle en pleine ascension sociale et avide d'aiguiser ses talents de connaisseur. Ces artistes s'inspiraient de la peinture européenne et surtout nord-européenne pour les types de sujets (musiciens, liseurs, femmes désirables), les formats (fenêtres, rebords), les expériences sur la lumière et le travail du pinceau. La tradition du costume fantaisiste — héritée du caravagisme, de Rembrandt et de son cercle, des Vénitiens — se reconnaît dans la mode de la tenue dite « espagnole ». Le mélange de traditions picturales et de costumes de théâtre de cette période devint une sorte de « code » ou de métaphore de la fantaisie elle-même : galanterie, désir érotique et évasion [18]. La série des figures de fantaisie exécutée librement par Fragonard (autour de 1767) est le produit de multiples influences, parmi lesquelles Rembrandt, Tiepolo et Grimou. Chardin ne s'essaya que rarement au costume (fig. ci-contre) mais ses études méticuleuses d'enfants et de domestiques s'inscrivent dans d'autres courants des figures de fantaisie que nous avons déjà rencontrés. De plus, la série de bustes au pastel, réalisée à la fin de sa vie, mêle librement les portraits aux sujets plus universels de la peinture de genre. Greuze, tout comme Piazzetta, retranscrivait de façon obsessionnelle les traits du visage dans ses croquis bruts d'un réalisme saisissant ; il retravailla ces derniers pour en faire dans ses tableaux des représentations à l'expression plus policée.

Plus à l'est, Antoine Pesne, artiste français vivant à la cour de Prusse (*Femme au turban*, Dresde, Staatliche Kunstsammlungen), et l'artiste hongrois Ján Kupetzký produisent des figures de fantaisie parallèlement à leurs portraits. L'Allemand Balthasar Denner et l'Autrichien Christian Seybold travaillent à la façon des *fijnschilders*, transcrivant avec un naturalisme extrême la peau parcheminée d'une personne âgée ou, un à un, les poils d'une fourrure [19]. Pietro Rotari, né à Vérone, évoluait à la cour de Vienne, de Dresde et de Saint-Pétersbourg : ses études de jeunes filles rougissantes, lisant, dormant ou pleurant, sont d'une intimité bouleversante.

Les peintres britanniques qui réalisaient des *fancy pictures* naviguaient également entre tradition et goût contemporain. Ils s'inspiraient directement des caravagesques, de Hals et de Murillo [20]. On estime que Philippe Mercier a contribué à la diffusion d'idées françaises

18. *Cf.* Percival, 2012, chap. 5.
19. *Cf.* Hirschfelder, *in* Hirschfelder, Krempel, 2013, p. 47-64.
20. *Cf.* Nottingham/Londres, 1998.

Thomas Gainsborough, *The Cottage Girl*, Dublin, National Gallery of Ireland

lorsqu'il s'est installé en Angleterre, réalisant lui-même de nombreux tableaux de groupes ou de figures dans lesquels on peut déceler un accent continental. Mais cette pratique s'est répandue tout autant par le biais de gravures inspirées de contemporains tels que Chardin. Des artistes britanniques comme Nathaniel Hone, Henry Morland et John Opie ont produit des versions plus sentimentales de servantes, d'enfants et de mendiants, qui eurent beaucoup de succès auprès des collectionneurs. Pour Joshua Reynolds, la *fancy picture* était une entreprise secondaire à laquelle il se consacrait en marge de son poste d'académicien et de la réalisation d'ambitieux portraits, mais il prenait cette occupation très au sérieux ; il semble en effet qu'elle lui ait permis d'intégrer certains cercles d'élite[21]. De même, Thomas Gainsborough s'intéressait à la représentation de figures dans un paysage (fig. ci-contre).

Cette exposition s'arrête à la fin du XVIIIe siècle, mais la figure humaine a continué d'intéresser l'art occidental bien au-delà de cette date. On peut distinguer certains changements autour de cette époque : les différences entre les genres deviennent plus marquées, conséquence des doctrines institutionnelles et de leur consécration ; à cela s'ajoute une vision du monde plus positiviste, qui cherche à comprendre l'individu dans sa relation à un milieu ou un environnement particulier et non comme une série de possibilités imaginaires. Le portrait de type « travesti » n'a pas joui d'une popularité durable auprès de la bourgeoisie, son parfum d'évasion et ses jeux sur l'identité devenant l'apanage de petits cercles d'artistes bohèmes. Ainsi le glissement créatif des portraits conventionnels vers les figures de fantaisie est-il devenu moins évident. Néanmoins, parmi les héritiers des figures de fantaisie de cette exposition, on compte (pour ne citer que des exemples français) les monomanes de Géricault, études consacrées à des sujets souffrant d'obsessions pathologiques, amalgames de types et d'individus, très largement influencées par le discours de l'époque sur les pauvres et les laissés-pour-compte ; les têtes d'expression de Delacroix, très abouties pour des études préparatoires à ses tableaux historiques, qui connaissaient un certain succès sur le marché (*Tête de vieille femme* pour les *Scènes des massacres de Scio*, Orléans, musée des Beaux-Arts) ; les autoportraits spectaculaires de Courbet, qui rappellent Rembrandt ; les philosophes et les toreros de Manet, plongés dans le silence et rendus intemporels par la neutralité du fond.

21. *Cf.* Londres, 2015 ; Postle, 1995.

Malgré l'attrait exercé par l'abstraction et l'art conceptuel, la figure humaine est représentée dans de nombreux courants artistiques du XXe siècle, du cubisme au surréalisme et au pop art. Plus récemment, Marlene Dumas, née en Afrique du Sud, a renoué avec les *tronies* du XVIIe siècle, bien que le point de vue soit différent, puisqu'elle travaille à partir de photos et non de modèles vivants[22]. Les « portraits de fantaisie » de Lynette Yiadom-Boakye (fig. ci-contre), finaliste du prix Turner, entretiennent des rapports multiples avec les figures de fantaisie, bien plus anciennes, qui sont exposées ici[23]. Ses sujets anonymes, tous des Noirs, installés dans des décors neutres, sont représentés dans des poses désinvoltes sur des surfaces volontairement peu travaillées. Ils incarnent la volonté de s'affranchir des normes qui régissent les comportements. Bien que les œuvres de Lynette Yiadom-Boakye soulignent implicitement l'absence de personnages noirs dans l'art européen, ses sujets transcendent les politiques de race, de genre et de classe, et s'adressent à l'humain universel. Ses figures libérées constituent une conclusion adéquate à notre tour d'horizon.

Lynette Yiadom-Boakye, *Uncle of The Garden*, 2014, collection particulière

Le visage dans tous ses états

Les artistes de cette exposition cherchaient à reproduire le visage humain dans toute sa complexité et peignaient souvent plusieurs versions du même visage pour en saisir les nuances ou travaillaient sur une palette de visages pour refléter la diversité de l'être humain (les pastels de Chardin, par exemple). De nombreux artistes créaient des séries : Rembrandt avait souvent recours au costume exotique ou à l'expression inhabituelle, non parce qu'il avait trouvé une recette qui faisait vendre mais parce qu'il voulait explorer en profondeur le tempérament humain. L'intérêt compulsif de Piazzetta et de Greuze pour les expressions du visage transparaît dans leurs nombreux dessins et tableaux. De plus, les collectionneurs appréciaient ces séries dédiées à la représentation du visage. Si les galeries de portraits de personnages célèbres remportaient un réel succès (ainsi de la célèbre collection d'autoportraits d'artistes à Florence), les collectionneurs affectionnaient tout autant les visages intéressants, à l'identité incertaine. Christian Ludwig von Hagedorn, critique et graveur de Dresde, est l'auteur d'écrits éloquents portant sur les figures de fantaisie de sa collection constituée de tableaux de Mányoki, Denner

22. Munich, 2010-2011.
23. *Cf.* Higgie, 2012.

et Rotari, ainsi que de six sujets à mi-corps de Nogari[24]. En Angleterre, en 1760, Thomas Frye réalisa une douzaine de têtes en mezzotinte ; elles furent commercialisées comme des équivalents des têtes de Piazzetta et comme un décor convenable pour une pièce unique. On peut les voir aujourd'hui dans le salon vert de Mompesson House, Salisbury[25]. Une série d'environ cinquante *teste de fantasia* vénitiennes et lombardes du XVIIIe siècle fut réunie en une sorte de concours d'académie par les membres de la famille Visconti di Modrone ou Visconti di San Vito. Comprenant des œuvres d'artistes importants comme Ricci, Tiepolo, Fontebasso et Ceruti, elles étaient conservées au château Visconti à Somma Lombardo, près de Milan[26]. L'impératrice de Russie commanda plus de trois cents têtes de femmes à Rotari pour remplir une salle de Peterhof à Saint-Pétersbourg[27]. Selon la rumeur, les séries de figures de fantaisie de Fragonard étaient destinées à un seul lieu, mais on manque d'informations précises à ce sujet[28]. Pour les amateurs qui n'avaient pas de galerie, on publiait des livres de gravures entièrement consacrés aux têtes. Les têtes de Piazzetta, Rotari, Tiepolo, Greuze et autres étaient reproduites dans de multiples séries réalisées par différents graveurs[29]. Ces pratiques artistiques et les habitudes des collectionneurs trahissent une quête perpétuelle : si une seule tête ne peut livrer tous les secrets de la condition humaine, une salle ou un livre entiers ne sauraient y parvenir non plus.

De nombreuses « têtes » étaient liées à un contexte d'enseignement, dans lequel les maîtres présentaient les rudiments des expressions du visage, ou différents types de visages, afin que leurs élèves les copient. On pense à l'atelier de Rubens, mais aussi à l'académie de dessin de Sweerts, ouverte à son retour à Bruxelles en 1656. Le livre *Diversae Facies in usum iuvenum et aliorum* de Sweerts (*cf.* fig. p. 146, cat. 25) contenait des têtes gravées d'après ses tableaux qui devaient servir de guide à ses élèves[30]. En 1667, la conférence de Charles Le Brun sur l'expression, destinée aux élèves de l'Académie de Paris, fut à l'origine d'une simplification et d'une codification radicales des traits du visage sous la forme d'une série de dessins au trait, chacun représentant une seule passion (cartésienne)[31]. Mais si le travail de Le Brun a, à juste titre, été envisagé comme pouvant servir de référence aux premières théories modernes de l'expression, il ne suffit pas à rendre compte de toutes les représentations du visage datant de cette époque. La publication de Sweerts, presque exactement au même moment, révèle une tout autre préoccupation qui concerne plutôt la personne que les passions : un vieillard barbu, un jeune homme enturbanné. Le souci de lisibilité de Le Brun servait l'ambition de la peinture historique, qui est de raconter une histoire, mais n'était pas nécessairement adapté aux tableaux non narratifs.

24. « Les autres figures à mi-corps, chacune avec deux mains, & des attributs ou ornemens convenables au sujet représentent St. Pierre et la Magdelaine ; un Philosophe avec son globe, & tenant la carte d'Italie ; une belle Espagnolette qui chante et joüe du luth ; un Garçon qui rit, & couvre de la main gauche un nid rempli de moineaux, pendant qu'il arrête de l'autre main un chat qui paroit leur en vouloir ; une jeune femme qui répose [*sic*], la tête appuyée sur la main gauche tenant de la droite une corbeille de fruits. » Hagedorn, 1755.

25. Chu, 2014, p. 66.

26. Venise, 2006, p. 37-41.

27. Guadalupi, 2000-2001, p. 113-128.

28. Pour les toutes dernières recherches sur ce sujet, *cf.* Blumenfeld, 2013, Dupuy-Vachey, 2015.

29. Sur les relations entre les figures de fantaisie peintes et gravées, *cf.* Adriano Mariuz, « "Questi xe visi... nu depensemo delle maschere", Giambattista Piazzetta e gli incisori delle sue "mezze figure" », *in* Venise, 2006, p. 53-61.

30. Amsterdam/San Francisco/Hartford, 2002.

31. *Cf.* Montagu, 1994.

De plus, son travail constituait un modèle théorique, un idéal qui, dans la pratique, se traduisait par une rigidité didactique, un manque de fraîcheur et de spontanéité[32]. Par opposition au « corps lisible »[33] de Le Brun, cette exposition explore des tendances physionomiques moins évidentes et moins manifestes de la peinture au début de la période moderne. Elle fait ressortir le paradoxe suivant : plus on scrute un visage, plus on cherche à en élucider le sens, moins on comprend la personnalité et l'état d'esprit du sujet. Mais cela n'est pas dû à un échec de la part des artistes, car ces derniers prenaient plaisir à relever le défi que représentaient les émotions contradictoires et le mystère de la personne humaine. Nombre des tableaux exposés ici ne sont pas faciles à déchiffrer, et pourtant, c'est précisément cette résistance qui est fascinante : la courtisane de Bordon (cat. 1), dédaigneuse et imperturbable, *L'Homme au stylet* de Lievens (cat. 61), perdu dans ses pensées, le vieil homme triste de Van Dyck (cat. 59). Au XVIIIe siècle, des théoriciens tentèrent de combler les lacunes du modèle des passions de Le Brun. L'exploration des passions conflictuelles et de leurs nuances par les artistes fut en fait à l'origine d'une perte de sens, parce que les différences entre les émotions finirent par devenir imperceptibles[34]. D'où une ambiguïté déroutante dans les visages de Greuze ou de Rotari, alors même qu'ils visent à l'éloquence. Nous considérerons plus tard le problème des « manques » et de l'illisibilité.

La fragilité de l'identité au début de l'époque moderne est ici le principal enjeu. La plupart des essais traitant du portrait à la Renaissance mettent l'accent sur les notions humanistes de transparence de l'âme et d'un ordre divin où intérieur et enveloppe extérieure sont perçus comme équivalents[35]. Le genre du portrait implique aussi la notion rassurante de *statu quo* : il atteste l'identité d'une personne et son rang dans une société donnée. Néanmoins, ce conservatisme inné peut également être attribué à l'anxiété. Comme l'a montré Ann Jensen Adams à propos de l'Âge d'or hollandais, l'art du portrait fournissait une image réconfortante de cohésion sociale et proposait de nouvelles identités à une période où la société connaissait un changement rapide[36]. C'est aussi de cette façon que l'on peut expliquer la récurrence de certains types dans les figures de fantaisie tels que les séductrices, les soldats, les musiciens, les liseurs, les vieillards, les enfants. En un sens, ils incarnent le concept aristotélicien de caractère, l'essence ou la quintessence de l'identité, la continuité de la vie[37]. Néanmoins, individuellement, ces sujets trahissent quelque chose de plus mystérieux quant à la nature humaine, qui tient de leur relation incertaine avec le spectateur. Un exemple tiré de l'art du portrait nous aidera à clarifier cette idée. On peut arguer que les portraits de Sweerts présentent une vision bien plus tourmentée de l'individu que les exemples choisis par Jensen Adams. Hanneke Grootenboer interprète le *Portrait d'un jeune homme* de Sweerts (Saint-Pétersbourg, Ermitage) sous l'angle de la subjectivité cartésienne et des théories modernes de la théâtralité[38]. Elle voit le jeune homme

32. Sur la contribution de Le Brun, *cf.* Kirchner, 1991.
33. Il s'agit de l'expression de Norman Bryson, *in* Bryson, 1981.
34. *Cf.* Percival, 1999.
35. *Cf.* Campbell, 1990.
36. Jensen Adams, 2009.
37. *Cf.* Bos, 2010, p. 11-23.
38. Grootenboer, 2010, p. 320-333.

comme étant à la fois double (à l'intérieur et à l'extérieur du corps) et écartelé, car il invite le regard du spectateur sans lui laisser la possibilité de répondre. De même, les figures de fantaisie sont en représentation devant le spectateur, mais elles sont incomplètes, car il manque des détails cruciaux quant à leur identité ou leur finalité. Ces détails sont fournis par l'imagination du spectateur, mais ne peuvent pas être restitués à la figure pour créer une entité holistique.

La même impression d'inachèvement et d'ambiguïté se dégage du message moral que les tableaux sont censés véhiculer. Si certaines figures de fantaisie se prêtent à une interprétation qui renforce les normes sociales (comme la paresse d'un serviteur endormi), l'insuffisance ou l'ambivalence des informations iconographiques, ou le déplacement de l'attention vers la pose ou encore vers les détails du costume viennent déstabiliser de telles lectures. De nombreuses figures de fantaisie sont issues des marges de la société respectable : *bravo*, hors-la-loi ou assassin, courtisane ou prostituée, musicien itinérant, toute une gamme de colporteurs, mendiants et petits vendeurs de rue. Malgré leurs beaux atours, les origines louches de ces sujets et leurs moyens présumés de subsistance jettent le doute sur la « transaction » qu'est la rencontre avec le spectateur. De plus, ils rappellent de manière ostensible que les modèles d'atelier eux-mêmes étaient souvent issus des milieux les plus modestes.

Toutefois, les tableaux n'invitent pas à une condamnation morale. Au contraire, les sujets appartiennent au domaine de la poésie et de la romance, et toute intimité avec eux n'est socialement admise que dans les limites de ce domaine. La présence de ces canailles dans les salons de riches collectionneurs, même si elles sont vêtues de costumes extravagants qu'elles n'auraient jamais pu s'offrir, et même si elles sont « policées » par le pinceau bienveillant du peintre, a quelque chose de piquant. Du point de vue de l'artiste, ces figures marginales offrent des possibilités d'exploration du corps humain que ne permet pas un portrait commandé par un aristocrate guindé ou un bourgeois sérieux. Bien loin des bonnes manières de la cour et de la bienséance de la bourgeoisie, il émane de ces sujets que personne ne regarde une grande fraîcheur et un sentiment de liberté, qu'ils soient dus à une franche naïveté ou à une profonde lassitude. Pour autant, ils sont empreints d'une certaine dignité car ils ont été choisis par l'artiste pour être représentés en gros plan. Dans leur propension à se défaire des contraintes sociales, à suggérer d'autres modèles et d'autres normes, en bref à imaginer la société autrement, les figures de fantaisie sont intrinsèquement radicales.

L'artiste prend pour modèles les personnes de son entourage : famille, amis, assistants, mais aussi sa propre personne, le but n'étant pas de saisir une ressemblance mais d'utiliser le visage comme point de départ. Ce glissement de la réalité à la fantaisie pose problème aux historiens de l'art, qui cherchent à remonter aux origines de l'œuvre et se heurtent à l'instabilité de la ressemblance. *Le Mangeur de haricots* de Carrache et *Le Jeune Bacchus malade* du Caravage (*cf.* fig. page 47) sont-ils ou non des autoportraits[39] ? En réalité, le mythe du modèle est même antérieur à cette époque. S'il est permis d'identifier Titus ou Saskia dans certains des tableaux

39. Sur le Caravage, *cf.* Fried 2010, chap. 1er, p. 9 ; sur Carrache, *cf.* McTighe, 2004, p. 301-323.

de Rembrandt (sans que ceux-ci soient nécessairement des « portraits »), qu'en est-il des multiples œuvres qui prétendent, à tort, représenter « la mère de Rembrandt » ? Cet étiquetage est la preuve d'un désir profondément humain de voir la personne réelle dans le visage peint, d'imaginer une relation entre l'artiste et le modèle là où il n'en existe peut-être pas. L'attribution d'une identité imaginaire était aussi répandue au XIXe siècle, époque à laquelle on disait de nombreux sujets en costume du XVIIIe siècle qu'il s'agissait « d'acteurs » en se fondant sur des faits peu fiables ; parmi eux, le Santerre offert en toute bonne foi à la Comédie-Française comme étant un portrait de Charlotte Desmares (cat. 76).

Dans son *Salon de 1767*, Diderot écrit : « Quelle différence y a-t-il entre une tête de fantaisie et une tête réelle ? »[40] D'après certains spécialistes, cette question a pour but de faire clairement la différence entre une œuvre d'imagination (« de fantaisie ») et une œuvre inspirée par la vie réelle (un portrait). Mais Diderot pourrait tout aussi bien opposer la représentation picturale d'une tête à son modèle vivant. Qu'il utilise la forme interrogative tend à suggérer qu'il a conscience de l'ambiguïté de la relation entre la personne qui pose et l'œuvre terminée. En outre, on est frappé de constater la vitesse à laquelle, après la mort du modèle, ou une fois sur le marché, une tête peut se retrouver séparée de ses origines et voir sa « signification » se métamorphoser.

Identité et théâtralité

Lorsqu'il est confronté à une figure de fantaisie, le spectateur fait l'expérience d'une rencontre à la fois intime et incertaine. C'est un plan rapproché, un tête-à-tête, et pourtant d'importants détails relatifs à l'identité de la figure restent inconnus. Le spectateur est impliqué dans l'acte de regarder et envahit ainsi « l'espace vital » de la figure. Peut-être l'examinera-t-il d'un peu trop près, peut-être avec un peu trop de désir et de nostalgie. Il peut se sentir à sa place ou mal à l'aise, amusé, intrigué ou embarrassé. La figure individuelle est d'un abord plus facile qu'une foule de personnes similaires ; sans doute invite-t-elle davantage le spectateur à se demander ce que le sujet représenté a de différent ou de particulier. Comme précisé plus haut, un certain nombre de ces figures sont associées à des marginaux socialement peu respectables, *desperados*, prostituées et autres. Par conséquent, le fait même de regarder l'une de ces personnes (en partant du principe qu'elles existent vraiment) est susceptible de mettre immédiatement en doute la respectabilité du spectateur lui-même. Mais la rencontre imaginaire a lieu dans un vide absolu, sans témoins ni sentiment d'appartenance, et personne n'assiste donc à l'illicite ni n'en prend note.

Parmi les figures de l'exposition, nombreuses sont celles qui incarnent la notion d'« absorbement » telle que la définit Michael Fried, lorsque la pose suggère une apparente indifférence vis-à-vis du spectateur. Les figures endormies en offrent un exemple extrême (Greuze, cat. 40, Piazzetta, cat. 38) et, de la même manière, les liseurs sont accaparés par leurs pensées

40. Diderot, 1983, III, p. 168.

(Gagneraux, cat. 34). Ce sont précisément ce détachement par rapport au spectateur ainsi que leur apparente impénétrabilité qui permettent la projection d'émotions et de désirs. Les premiers travaux, très novateurs, de Fried sur l'absorbement étaient axés sur la France du milieu du XVIIIe siècle, période au cours de laquelle la « fiction suprême » de l'absence du spectateur est devenue un principe théorique important[41]. Plus récemment, Fried est remonté dans le temps, situant « l'invention de l'absorbement » dans les années 1590, dans les œuvres du Caravage et de son cercle. Il soutient qu'à cette époque s'est manifesté « le besoin d'une projection empathique et relationnelle plus intense et plus centrée entre le spectateur et le tableau »[42]. Faire appel à l'absorbement en vue de captiver l'attention du spectateur correspond à ce qu'il appelle « l'adresse », situation où les personnages représentés montrent qu'ils ont conscience de l'existence d'un observateur (il ne faut pas confondre l'adresse avec le terme péjoratif de « théâtralité » employé par Fried dans le contexte du XVIIIe siècle français). Dans cette exposition, des séductrices ont recours à l'adresse pour exhiber leur semi-nudité ou leur crinière ensorcelante (Bordon, cat. 1). Attentives à leur environnement, elles sont parfois mises en valeur par un rideau ou une fenêtre qui font office de cadre (Schalcken, cat. 8). Des mendiants cherchent à capter un regard (Traversi, cat. 69, Opie, cat. 15). Le *Jeune Pêcheur* de Hals (cat. 46) fixe le spectateur d'un regard curieux et spontané, car personne ne lui a appris à contrôler son expression. Fried ne considère pas la figure individuelle comme formant une catégorie distincte, mais il est intéressant de noter que plusieurs de ses exemples les plus significatifs (la *Marie-Madeleine* du Caravage, *L'Ermite endormi* de Vien) sont des sujets solitaires. De plus, à partir de son étude de l'interaction entre l'absorbement et l'adresse dans les compositions de groupe comme *Les Tricheurs* du Caravage, nous pouvons déduire, en extrapolant quelque peu, que l'absorbement et l'adresse peuvent coexister dans une seule et même figure, qui redouble ainsi d'intensité pour subjuguer le spectateur. En effet, la tension entre ostentation et dissimulation de soi apparaît dans de nombreux tableaux, en particulier dans le domaine de la séduction.

Fried établit une distinction entre l'expression – au sens où l'entendent Alberti et, bien sûr, Le Brun, c'est-à-dire le fait de montrer une émotion – et une charge émotionnelle créée au moyen d'informations physionomiques minimales. Les tableaux du Caravage, leurs personnages inexpressifs, leurs profils perdus, leurs dos tournés et leur obscurité écrasante offrent de nombreux exemples de ce second registre. Fried suggère que, dans de tels cas, c'est le spectateur qui comble les manques, créant dans le même temps une relation intense avec la figure. Les figures de fantaisie sont aussi sémiotiquement pauvres, au sens où l'entend Fried, dans la mesure où elles obligent le spectateur à fournir les informations manquantes. Les artistes jouent fréquemment sur le vide physionomique : les traits s'effacent sur des visages inexpressifs, dans des poses « fermées » (figure vue de dos, par exemple), sous des vêtements qui dissimulent le

41. Fried, 1990 ; Fried décrit l'effondrement ultérieur du modèle anti-théâtral *in* Fried, 1996.
42. Fried, 2010, p. 117.

corps (un chapeau à large bord, un voile), dans la pénombre ou au milieu de détails superflus tels que des bijoux, des étoffes ou des fourrures, qui détournent l'attention du visage[43].

La figure de fantaisie comporte un niveau supplémentaire d'ambiguïté concernant cette fois l'identité du sujet. Si, dans son étude du Caravage, Fried s'intéresse pour l'essentiel à des personnages bibliques bien connus, les tableaux de cette exposition sont dénués de toute indication relative à leur rôle ou à leur fonction. De nombreuses figures sont vêtues de costumes, mais le statut de ces derniers est incertain. Dans le tableau de Nantes (cat. 79), la figure est-elle un soldat, une personne participant à un bal costumé ou un acteur[44] ? S'agit-il d'ailleurs d'un portrait, d'un tableau pour lequel un modèle a posé en atelier ou d'un sujet né de l'imagination de l'artiste ? La figure de fantaisie est à distinguer du « portrait d'apparat », portrait en costume en vogue aux XVIIe et XVIIIe siècles[45]. Dans le « portrait d'apparat », les modèles restent fondamentalement eux-mêmes, le costume servant à les magnifier ou à les mettre en valeur, habituellement sous les traits d'une divinité. Inversement, la figure de fantaisie opère un brouillage complexe, voire une dissolution de l'identité. C'est un contemporain de Santerre qui en décrit le mieux le processus au début du XVIIIe siècle :

> « [Santerre] quitta donc les portraits, c'est-à-dire il ne voulut plus s'engager à faire ressembler parfaitement. Il peignait des têtes de *fantaisie* où il mettait les traits les plus agréables de ceux pour qui il les faisait. Il eut le bonheur de trouver quantité de personnes qui se contentèrent d'avoir leur portrait avec cette condition. C'est dans ce temps-là qu'il imagina de peindre seulement une demi-figure dans chaque tableau qui représenta un art, une science, ou quelques actions naïves, auxquelles il sut donner une finesse de pensées et d'expressions qui lui était particulière. »[46]

Ce passage montre la bonne volonté avec laquelle les modèles collaborent à la fiction de l'artiste, lui permettant de transposer leurs traits en types ou de les adapter à la représentation d'un sentiment ou d'une anecdote. De la même manière, bien que le nom des modèles ait été retrouvé pour un grand nombre des figures de fantaisie de Fragonard, l'objectif de ces tableaux n'est pas pour autant de restituer la spécificité d'un individu. Les modèles se font plutôt complices d'un processus fictionnel qui les change en types universels d'une manière spirituelle et astucieuse. De plus, grâce à la technique expressive de Fragonard, le sujet individuel se dissout dans une démonstration de virtuosité picturale dans laquelle nous voyons plutôt triompher l'ego de l'artiste.

Fantaisie et imagination

Dans sa biographie de Reynolds, James Northcote décrit la façon dont son professeur travaillait sur les figures de fantaisie :

43. Sur le vide physionomique, *cf.* Percival, 2011.
44. Percival, 2012, chap. 5.
45. *Cf.* Hirschfelder, 2008.
46. « Éloge de feu Santerre », *Nouveau Mercure*, sept. 1718, p. 74-75.

« Sir Joshua désirait tant atteindre l'excellence que je l'ai vu travailler à ses sujets de fantaisie des jours et des semaines durant, se livrant à toutes sortes d'expériences pour le plaisir, tandis que nombre de ses portraits demeuraient inachevés [...] Le bonheur qu'il éprouvait à travailler sur ces sujets de fantaisie était tel qu'il n'hésitait pas à s'y laisser aller, même aux dépens de son intérêt immédiat. »[47]

Un certain nombre de tropes apparaissent dans ce passage : la *fancy picture* comme occasion pour les artistes de s'adonner à des expériences, comme source de plaisir mais aussi comme plaisir coupable qui éloigne d'obligations plus « sérieuses » (en l'occurrence, pour Reynolds, sa fonction de président de l'Académie royale et son activité aussi astreignante que lucrative de portraitiste). Ces éléments sont conformes à la signification de « fantaisie » (*fancy*) propre à cette période, celle de caprice, ou ce que Voltaire appelait « un désir singulier, un goût passager »[48]. Comme nous l'avons montré ailleurs, fantaisie et caprice, quasi synonymes, font partie d'un vaste réseau sémantique qui associe esprit, humour, spontanéité, improvisation, surprise, subversion de la norme, le banal et l'insignifiant, l'éphémère[49]. La fantaisie est l'antithèse des règles, de l'ordre, de la logique, de l'exactitude, du sérieux, du didactisme, de l'académisme. En bref, la figure de fantaisie comprend ce que le critique moderne Giuseppe Pavanello a appelé un « spazio d'evasione » (espace d'évasion)[50].

Nombre de sources font allusion au sentiment de libération ou de distraction qu'éprouvent les artistes, le plus souvent par opposition aux contraintes liées à l'art du portrait. Bartolomeo Nazzari évoque en ces termes son propre désir de travailler sur la figure de fantaisie : « se fosse per fare qualcosa di mio capriccio, o qualche mezza figura di vecchio o di giovane senza essere obbligato a copiare o star soggietto alla somiglianza, quello lo farei »[51]. Le biographe de Grimou, Lecarpentier, écrit : « Souvent pour se désennuyer de la gêne et de l'exactitude du portrait, il s'amusait à peindre de fantaisie de jolies têtes de femmes, qui sont aujourd'hui l'ornement des meilleures collections. »[52]

L'artiste est libre de dépeindre des postures et des expressions peu orthodoxes : personnage recroquevillé (Traversi, cat. 69), allongé (Keil, cat. 36), dos au spectateur (Giorgione), de profil (Van Dyck, cat. 59), arborant un large sourire (Ceruti, cat. 54). Il ou elle est libre d'animer la figure en jouant sur la taille des membres (Piazzetta, cat. 38, Traversi, cat. 69), en ayant recours à une plongée (Opie, cat. 15) ou en utilisant un spectaculaire jeu d'ombres et de lumières (Schalcken, cat. 8). Bien sûr, certains de ces éléments sont très courants dans la peinture d'histoire, et nous ne devons pas oublier que nombre de ces artistes travaillaient aussi sur des retables et des plafonds où les corps occupaient un espace important, quasi tridimensionnel. Mais, réduits à

47. Northcote, 1818, II, 28.
48. Diderot, le Rond d'Alembert, 1751-1772, VI, p. 403.
49. Percival, 2012, chap. 6.
50. Venise, 2006, p. 15.
51. « Si je pouvais céder à mes caprices, ou peindre quelques demi-figures de vieux ou de jeunes sans être obligé de copier ou d'être fidèle à la réalité, je le ferais volontiers », trad. L. Thyrion, F. Peracchione, S. Zaccaria. Lettre de Nazzari reproduite *in* Noris, 1982, p. 207.
52. Lecarpentier, 1821, II, p. 164.

un format de portrait, ces attitudes et ces points de vue créent une impression de simplicité, d'incongruité, de transgression des conventions artistiques. Libéré du devoir de magnifier le sujet, l'artiste construit une sorte de laboratoire du visage, s'attardant sur le détail d'un sourcil, d'une pommette, une barbe hirsute, une multitude de rides. Dans les travaux de Lievens et de Dou, de Denner et de Rotari, le réalisme tend vers l'hyperréalisme. Pour le spectateur, une proximité aussi poussée et le degré d'intimité qui sous-tendent la rencontre sont déconcertants. On trouve aussi toute une gamme d'expressions du visage en marge de ce qui est socialement admis : grimace ou rictus, sourire étrange (Carrache, cat. 45). La liberté et l'expérimentation apparaissent également dans la manière dont la peinture est appliquée. Les *tronies* de Rembrandt présentent un mélange d'empâtements et de sections inachevées qui crée un sentiment de spontanéité. Hals et Fragonard peignaient en superpositions de couches de peinture fraîche avec une touche très visible qui donne une impression de rapidité. À l'instar d'une nature morte, la figure de fantaisie offre à l'artiste la possibilité de faire montre de ses nombreux talents. « Exercices de style » dignes de virtuoses, ces pièces sont des hommages à la peinture, où l'art et la technique deviennent des fins en soi. Elles n'ont pas manqué d'attirer l'œil exercé des connaisseurs, car leur apparente immédiateté faisait naître un sentiment de complicité.

La diversité même des figures de fantaisie ainsi que ce que l'on pourrait prendre pour des contradictions font partie intégrante du terme de fantaisie. La fascination pour le futile et l'inconséquent se retrouve dans l'innocence d'un enfant, la joue rougissante d'une jeune femme, l'inclinaison d'une plume, le geste suspendu d'un serviteur. On ressent un désir aussi ardent qu'inexpliqué face à l'étrangeté d'un jeune berger arcadien ou d'un turban exotique. Ce désir peut devenir érotique à la vue d'une femme aguicheuse ou endormie. Ces peintures racontent bien peu ; il ne s'y passe pas grand-chose. Et pourtant, l'attrait et le charme des figures de fantaisie résident dans leur propension à exprimer désirs enfouis et aspirations secrètes, à valoriser le prosaïque, l'étrange et l'anodin.

Ces œuvres peuvent être difficiles à décrire en termes scientifiques. S'agissant de tableaux non narratifs dont les sujets sont indéterminés et comportent peu de détails contextuels ou iconographiques, il n'est guère surprenant qu'ils occupent au sein de l'histoire de l'art une place marginale. Néanmoins, à certains égards, ce qui est absent des figures de fantaisie est plus important que ce qui y est présent, car les vides sémiotiques mentionnés plus haut laissent libre cours à l'imagination. Et c'est pour cette raison que ces tableaux se prêtent volontiers à la poésie ou à la fiction. Dans son étude de deux figures individuelles de Nogari, Francesco Algarotti compare celles-ci à un madrigal ou à un sonnet[53]. Le sonnet est une forme poétique condensée et émotionnellement saturée, tout comme la figure de fantaisie, forme picturale très concise. Au XVIIIe siècle, en France et en Angleterre, les graveurs d'après les figures de fantaisie ont également recours à la poésie, intégrant des poèmes qui dépeignent la situation ou l'état d'esprit de la figure (Santerre, *La Jeune Femme au billet doux*, cat. 76). Les écrivains modernes ont, eux aussi,

53. Ces têtes étaient celles d'un philosophe et d'un avare. Cité *in* Venise, 2006, p. 15.

su tirer parti du potentiel que représente la figure de fantaisie dans les domaines de la fiction et du désir. Dans son roman *La Jeune Fille à la perle* (1999), Tracy Chevalier imagine une relation érotique entre Vermeer et la jeune servante qui posa pour son *tronie*. De même, des écrivains allemands se sont associés pour produire un volume de méditations sur les figures isolées « sans nom » de la Gemäldegalerie de Berlin[54].

Nous laisserons le mot de la fin à Francesco Maria Tassi. Ses propos font référence aux tableaux de Nazzari mais offrent surtout une définition concise de ce que sont, de manière plus générale, les figures de fantaisie, du point de vue tant des éléments qui les composent que de l'esprit dans lequel elles ont été réalisées :

> « Teste [...] prese dal naturale ornate poi a capriccio'[...] 'tanto varo [*sic ?*] que sembrano vive'[ ] Leggiadrissime teste fatte a capriccio di bellissime giovinette, con idee da Paradiso, altre vestite alla spagnola con collare a lattughe, altra da pastorelle con veli e pennacchi bizzarramente accomodati, ed in altre figure capricciose cosí si vive, pastose e delicate, che non può l'occhio qua giù in terra veder cosa più vaga, e dilettevole ! Con pari maestria seppe egle passare dal morbido e delicato al fiero e risoluto, come vedesi in altre capricciose deste di vecchi barbuti con turbanti e berrettoni in capo, tocchi con grandissima forza e finimento, riducendo egle in tali cose il più fino gusto della scuola fiamminga'. »[55]

Tassi décrit des types de figures divergents, des costumes insolites, de subtiles nuances dans l'expression des sentiments ou les techniques picturales, et souligne la reprise délibérée de modèles nordiques du XVIIe siècle. Ce sont autant d'hybrides mêlant nature et imagination de l'artiste, transformés en individus bien vivants par la magie du pinceau. À travers cette exposition, nous souhaitons susciter une admiration tout aussi grande pour la beauté et la singularité de ces figures de fantaisie.

Melissa Percival

54. Zischler, Schmitter, 2013.
55. « Les visages d'une extrême légèreté, ornés de fantaisies, des belles jeunes femmes, qui donnent des idées de Paradis, certaines vêtues à l'espagnole avec des cols en fraise, d'autres portent des capelines, avec des voiles et des plumes bizarrement arrangées, et d'autres formes de fantaisie si vives, douces et délicates, que l'œil ne peut observer ici-bas de chose plus gracieuse et agréable ! Avec une telle habileté, il a su passer du tendre et délicat au dur et résolu, comme on peut l'observer dans d'autres aspects fantaisistes de vieux barbus affublés de turbans et de grands chapeaux sur leur tête, peints avec force et délicatesse, résumant ainsi toute la finesse de l'école flamande. » Tassi, 1793, p. 84-85, 92-93.

SENSUALITÉ DES FIGURES À MI-CORPS ET THÉÂTRALITÉ DE LA PEINTURE

Une femme se présente à nous partiellement dénudée, son bras droit musculeux longe son buste langoureux et retient la cape vermillon qui drape son corps (cat. 1). Son regard se porte à notre droite, comme pour signifier la présence d'un amant ou d'un mécène, les doigts de sa main gauche entrelacés dans sa longue chevelure qui disparaît plus bas dans les plis de l'étoffe flamboyante. La fluidité de la pose, animée par le chatoiement nuancé de ses boucles ondulées et les plis sinueux de sa chemise, est accentuée par le décor de marbre derrière elle. Peinte par Paris Bordon à Venise dans les années 1540, aujourd'hui conservée à Lugano, la formule eut de toute évidence du succès : le modèle et la pose furent réutilisés par l'artiste pour la *Femme au manteau vert* autour de 1550, désormais dans les collections du Kunsthistorisches Museum à Vienne (fig. page 38). Bordon faisait partie des artistes vénitiens spécialisés dans ce type de représentations, où l'identité du modèle est inconnue et souvent secondaire.

Les peintures de femmes à moitié dévêtues, présentées en buste, étaient très répandues dans la Venise du XVIe siècle. La *Laura* de Giorgione, réalisée en 1506 et dont il est question ci-après, a donné de l'élan à ce nouveau genre développé par Titien et beaucoup d'autres, qui s'appropriaient les conventions du portrait pour mettre en avant leur virtuosité artistique. Prenons pour exemple la façon dont l'architecture révèle les possibilités de la peinture dans l'œuvre de Lugano (cat. 1). Sur la gauche, les lignes courbes du soubassement d'une colonnade font écho au corps de la femme et à sa chemise, dont les plis fluides évoquent les cannelures d'une colonne. La fenêtre, telle une image à l'intérieur du tableau, laisse voir un ciel dont les nuages diaphanes, rehaussés de touches de blanc, rappellent le vêtement et les perles qui ornent la chevelure de la femme. Le veinage rouge du marbre derrière elle reprend le tombé souple de la draperie vermillon qui l'enveloppe. La signature de l'artiste, « .O.PARIS.B », figure sur la moulure qui sépare ces deux éléments structuraux et nous rappelle qu'elle est l'image, et lui, son créateur.

Des stratégies similaires sollicitent le regard du spectateur devant des portraits d'hommes en buste mais les femmes étaient plus fréquemment représentées. Les collections actuelles

Paris Bordon, *Femme au manteau vert*, Vienne, Kunsthistorisches Museum

Sebastiano del Piombo, *Portrait d'une jeune fille*, Budapest, Szépmüvészeti Múseum

comptent plus de deux cents variations vénitiennes sur ce thème[1]. Dans un exemple, parmi les premiers du genre, conservé au musée de Budapest et peint par Sebastiano del Piombo (fig. ci-dessus à droite) aux alentours de 1508, l'artiste a préservé le caractère individuel des traits du visage du modèle plutôt que de les idéaliser, et sa tenue n'est pas des plus provocantes[2]. Cependant, seul un côté de son corps est drapé de rouge, sur lequel sa main droite attire l'attention tandis que, complice avec le spectateur, elle pointe du doigt quelque lieu ou personnage hors du cadre. L'inclinaison de sa tête nous permet d'admirer son long cou, et son regard suggestif brave les conventions qui voulaient qu'une femme baissât le regard[3]. Il est généralement vain de chercher à identifier ces personnages par leur nom, mais des traits particuliers, comme dans le tableau de Sebastiano, suggèrent que si le peintre s'attache à traduire la singularité du modèle, c'est qu'il y a un intérêt à reconnaître l'individu représenté.

La façon dont ces peintures sollicitent le regard du spectateur en brouillant les frontières entre catégories entrave toute tentative de classification. Des tableaux de mariées, déesses, dieux, courtisanes, musiciens et marchands comportant des références au portrait, à la mythologie

1. Junkerman, 1988.
2. À propos de cette peinture, on pourra se reporter aux ouvrages suivants : Hirst, 1981, p. 93-94 ; Frangi, 2013 ; David Ekserdjian éd., *in* Londres, 2010 ; Strinati, 2008 ; Minneapolis, 1995 ; Garas, 1973.
3. Berdini, 1998, p. 565-590 ; Simons, 1988, p. 4-30.

ainsi qu'à différentes catégories identitaires telles que l'occupation ou le statut marital, appellent l'interprétation. Modérément sensuel ou explicitement érotique, le concept a été repris et adapté à travers l'Europe. Le présent essai réexamine cette forme souple et bien connue en explorant les conditions sociales de son émergence à Venise, avant de s'attarder sur le potentiel du concept tel qu'il fut développé à Rome par le Caravage et renouvelé à Utrecht par les caravagesques.

Giorgione, *Laura*, Vienne, Kunsthistorisches Museum

L'inspiration qui a impulsé le tableau de Sebastiano mentionné plus haut se trouve dans la *Laura* de Giorgione, aujourd'hui conservée à Vienne (fig. ci-contre). Le regard tourné vers la gauche, la jeune femme révèle la fourrure du revers du grand manteau rouge qui l'enveloppe, doigts repliés sur le bord du vêtement, au niveau de sa poitrine. Le fait que le manteau appartienne à un homme contribue à la charge érotique et nourrit le doute qui pèse sur son geste : est-elle en train de s'en dévêtir ou de le fermer ? Le jeu des textures du voile, de la peau, de la fourrure et de la chevelure prolonge l'expérience sensuelle du spectateur. Le modèle de Giorgione a été identifié tour à tour comme étant une jeune mariée, une courtisane ou une poétesse, autant d'interprétations rendues plausibles par le recours au format du portrait et la présence du voile et des branches de laurier à l'arrière-plan[4]. Le voile, symbole de chasteté, sied à une jeune mariée, quoique la convention eût voulu que ses cheveux fussent dénoués plutôt qu'attachés. Le laurier et le sein nu sont des signes de chasteté et se prêtent donc bien au thème du mariage : le laurier est associé à Daphné qui, poursuivie par Apollon, fut métamorphosée en arbre, le sein rappelle les Amazones et leur légendaire indépendance vis-à-vis des hommes. Le laurier est peut-être une allusion aux poètes, une indication possible que le modèle est une courtisane, puisque la composition et la récitation de poésies étaient des talents cultivés par les femmes qui pouvaient vivre une vie indépendante et divertir leurs clients en usant de leur habileté à manier le langage et la musique. Veronica Franco fait partie des quelques poétesses vénitiennes renommées qui ont été représentées en buste vers la fin du XVIe siècle[5]. La présence du laurier pourrait encore s'expliquer par la volonté de susciter des interrogations quant au sujet de la peinture ou

4. Vienne, 2004, p. 197-198, cat. n° 8 ; Junkerman, 1993, p. 49-58 ; Dal Pozzolo, 1993, p. 257-292 ; Anderson, 1979, p. 153-158.
5. Land, 2003, p. 25-28 ; Rogers, 2000, p. 91-105.

simplement se rapporter au nom du modèle. La date inscrite au dos, le 1er juin 1506, étant plus précise que de coutume, laisse penser que le tableau pourrait avoir été un cadeau [6].

Quelle que soit la fonction de la *Laura* de Giorgione, son influence repose sur le rôle qu'elle a joué dans la reconnaissance des innovations artistiques qu'elle présente. Son potentiel naît de l'association de sa dimension érotique, qui s'exprime par le format du portrait et le rendu sensuel des détails vestimentaires, de la peau et des surfaces, sur lesquels le regard s'attarde, et de son caractère ouvert qui résiste à une interprétation unique. La formule, charmant à la fois le corps et l'esprit, est déclinable à l'infini et se prête au renouvellement. Les artistes pouvaient recourir à ce concept pour répondre à des intérêts existants, mais aussi en développer de nouveaux. Ces images de femmes et d'hommes à mi-corps font appel à la connaissance que le spectateur a des conventions artistiques, des styles et même des œuvres et artistes avec lesquels elles dialoguent et dont elles diffèrent. Elles constituaient un nouveau genre pictural, les peintures de cabinet, exposées dans les espaces de sociabilité et les collections, où elles engendraient discussions et débats [7].

De nombreux exemples de peintures de femmes à mi-corps associées à des figures mythologiques, en particulier Vénus et Flore, témoignent du potentiel innovant du genre. Flore était représentée avec des fleurs, emblèmes du printemps et de la jeunesse. Celles que la *Flore* de Titien (vers 1515, Florence, Galleria degli Uffizi) présente au spectateur évoquent à la fois les plaisirs érotiques recherchés auprès des courtisanes et la virtuosité du peintre grâce à la correspondance entre leurs couleurs et sa palette restreinte [8]. Beaucoup d'exemples s'avèrent cependant plus énigmatiques. Le modèle d'un panneau de Bartolomeo Veneto, peint vers 1520-1522 et conservé au Städelsches Kunstinstitut à Francfort, est orné de fleurs, que le personnage tient près de son visage, d'une couronne de myrte et d'un voile blanc, ses cheveux sont dénoués et l'un de ses seins est découvert. La peinture présente des éléments qu'on s'attendrait à trouver associés à la déesse Flore, à une courtisane, ou au portrait d'une jeune mariée, peut-être, ici, Lucrèce Borgia [9]. Ce va-et-vient entre des rôles féminins changeants et parfois conflictuels explique en partie le succès de cette peinture [10].

Bordon a fait de cette pluralité de personnages le sujet de *Vénus, Flore, Mars et Cupidon*, également connu sous le nom *Deux Femmes, un Cupidon et un Soldat* (1553-1355, page ci-contre), où l'entrecroisement des corps des deux femmes suggère qu'elles sont interchangeables. Au XVIIIe siècle, alors que le tableau se trouvait dans la collection du château de Houghton Hall, dans le comté de Norfolk, son sujet ambigu lui valut la description suivante : « Deux femmes, une Peinture allégorique par *Paris Bourdon*. » [11] Têtes inclinées l'une vers l'autre, les deux figures sont

6. « Le premier jour de juin, ce portrait fut réalisé de la main du maître Giorgio da Castelfranco, collègue du maître Vincenzo Catena, à la requête du sieur Giacomo », *in* Pagden, Scire, 2004, p. 197.
7. Wilson (Bronwen), Vanhaelen, 2012.
8. Emma Mellencamp avance que la *camicia* portée par Flore rappelle les costumes que les acteurs du XVIe siècle revêtaient lorsqu'ils interprétaient des nymphes. Mellencamp, 1969, p. 174-177. Pour une bibliographie, *cf.* Washington DC, 2006, p. 224-227.
9. Pagnotta, 1997, p. 39-47 ; Pagnotta, 2002 ; Aikema, Brown, 1999, p. 368-369 ; Tinagli, 1997, p. 98-104.
10. Simons, 1995, p. 263-311.
11. Walpole, 1767, p. 88. La première publication date de 1748.

Paris Bordon, *Vénus, Flore, Mars et Cupidon*, Saint-Pétersbourg, musée de l'Ermitage

poussées l'une contre l'autre par Cupidon, qui se penche au-dessus de la première pour coiffer la seconde d'une couronne de myrte. Ce geste, ajouté à une construction mythologique floue, pourrait indiquer que l'œuvre était un tableau de mariage[12]. Vénus, peut-être la femme couronnée à droite, cueille une fleur de la main de Flore ; la symétrie de leurs corps et l'entrelacement de leurs bras, bijoux, fourrures et nattes somptueuses alimentent le doute qui plane sur leur identité respective. Le regard des deux femmes se porte sur notre droite, au-delà de la scène, tandis qu'un homme, qu'on aperçoit en partie à droite, est représenté dans la tenue de Mars et muni d'une arme lustrée au galbe menaçant. La difficulté à cerner le sens iconographique engendre des discussions portant à la fois sur les plaisirs et les dangers de la contemplation.

Nous avons déjà noté que l'emplacement de la signature de Bordon était un moyen d'attirer l'attention sur l'acte de peindre. Cela relevait également de la stratégie commerciale, puisque le nom permettait d'identifier l'atelier[13]. La réutilisation délibérée de compositions servait aussi à des fins de promotion – un usage que Bordon avait appris aux côtés de Titien qui signait les œuvres destinées à des commanditaires hors de la ville et gardait dans son atelier, sur toile, des copies grandeur nature pour les commandes suivantes. La répétition d'une composition réussie répondait aussi à un besoin pratique, en particulier pour les artistes vénitiens, qui souvent concevaient leurs compositions directement sur toile plutôt que de passer par des esquisses préliminaires[14]. Peu d'artistes ont réutilisé le même modèle et la même pose aussi fréquemment que Bordon ; l'œuvre de Lugano et les Vénus et Flore du tableau de Saint-Pétersbourg sont des variantes de la *Flore* du Louvre, peinte dans les années 1540[15]. Le tableau de Lugano a été utilisé à son tour pour la *Femme au manteau vert* conservé à Vienne (fig. page 38). Le brocart vermillon flamboyant a été remplacé par un velours vert, les deux seins sont désormais à découvert, et les cheveux blonds sont un ton plus clair. Il n'y a plus de fenêtre, le modèle est intégré dans le décor architectural à la manière

12. *Ibid.*
13. Matthew, 1998, p. 616-648.
14. Sur les esquisses de Bordon, *cf.* Donati, 2014. Sur les peintures vénitiennes, *cf.* Rosand, 1997.
15. Canova, 1963, p. 85, fig. 89.

d'une sculpture dans une niche, une comparaison renforcée par les jambes du relief sculpté au-dessus de sa tête vers lesquelles ses cheveux tressés dirigent notre regard.

De telles variations contribuaient à un vocabulaire pictural de motifs et de gestes censés permettre aux collectionneurs et à leurs visiteurs d'exercer et de démontrer leurs talents de connaisseurs. Dans l'œuvre de Bordon de Lugano par exemple, les doigts de la femme, passés dans ses cheveux, rappellent le geste de la *Marie-Madeleine* de Titien, peinte vers 1533 et conservée au Palazzo Pitti. L'archétype de la beauté vénitienne représentée à mi-corps, seins nus en partie couverts par ses bras et ses longs cheveux blonds, était un sujet repris pour de nombreux commanditaires masculins. Bien qu'au XVIe siècle, et de plus en plus sous l'influence du concile de Trente (1545-1563), de tels exemples de nudité en peinture aient essuyé le feu de la critique pour leur caractère licencieux, l'érotisme contenu dans ces tableaux devait concourir à leur message pieux en impliquant le spectateur sur le terrain de la sensualité afin de l'y faire renoncer[16].

Cette opposition est frappante dans la *Marie-Madeleine* de Titien, dont le corps évoque la prostituée avant sa conversion religieuse et le visage, empreint de spiritualité, la figure pénitente qu'elle devient. Pour Vittoria Colonna, la poétesse renommée, ainsi que pour le mécène Frédéric Gonzague, duquel elle a manifestement reçu le tableau en cadeau, l'oscillation entre amour sacré et amour sensuel aura sans doute contribué à une méditation sur le renoncement perpétuel inhérent à la conversion religieuse. Nirit Ben-Aryeh Debby a mis en évidence les différentes traditions picturales dans lesquelles s'ancre la *Marie-Madeleine* de Titien : son corps était couvert quand il s'agissait de représenter la figure spirituelle et ascétique, tandis que le côté charnel de Madeleine pouvait être exprimé à travers Vénus et Flore, qui, du fait de leur identité mythologique, se prêtaient à l'évocation de sa vie de courtisane[17]. On retrouve ces allusions dans des descriptions littéraires, dont *Dell'humanità del Figliuolo di Dio* (« L'Humanité de Notre Sauveur Jésus-Christ ») de l'Arétin, publiée en 1535, peu après que son ami eut peint la *Marie-Madeleine* de Pitti. Sa description sensuelle des cheveux dorés et des seins de Marie-Madeleine est assortie de références à Citherea (Cythère ou Vénus) et aux joues vermillon d'Aurore[18]. Tout comme le texte de l'Arétin, et comme l'a affirmé Bernard Aikema, on a toujours cherché, avec les peintures de Marie-Madeleine, à encourager la résistance face au plaisir. Il est certain qu'à l'époque l'érotisme jouait un rôle crucial dans les images sacrées et la demande des sens aurait prolongé l'interaction avec l'œuvre. L'inverse était tout aussi vrai : bien que les images renvoyant à des courtisanes, telle celle de Bordon conservée à Lugano (cat. 1), nous apparaissent aujourd'hui purement sensuelles, pour les contemporains de l'époque la robe rouge et les cheveux de la femme pourraient avoir évoqué, quoique fugacement, ceux de Marie-Madeleine avant sa conversion.

16. Aikema, 1994, p. 48-59.
17. Ben-Aryeh Debby, 2003, p. 29-33.
18. Pietro Aretino, *Dell'humanità del Figliuolo di Dio*, Venise, 1628, p. 225-228. Cité par Bernard Aikema, *in* Aikema, 1994, p. 55, n. 42.

Ces glissements d'une identité féminine à l'autre prospéraient grâce au contexte social de la Venise du XVIe siècle. Marie-Madeleine était un objet de piété particulièrement prégnant, en partie du fait du contrôle de la prostitution exercé par le gouvernement mais aussi de l'existence d'institutions établies dans le but de détourner les jeunes filles de cette voie et de réformer les femmes qui l'avaient empruntée. Des voyageurs de passage à Venise ont régulièrement témoigné de la visibilité des prostituées, bien que le décompte incroyable d'« au moins vingt mille » fait par Thomas Coryat fût exagéré[19]. De nombreux contemporains ont relevé la confusion possible entre les corps richement parés des femmes de la haute société et ceux des courtisanes. La législation somptuaire était l'un des moyens par lesquels le gouvernement entendait faire la distinction entre prostituées et aristocrates. Une proclamation de 1543 remarque :

> « ... dans les rues et les églises, et partout ailleurs, tant et si bien vêtues et parées de bijoux, que bien souvent les dames de la noblesse et les femmes du peuple, parce que leurs atours ne diffèrent en rien de ceux des femmes dont il est ici question, leur ressemblent à s'y méprendre, non pas seulement aux yeux des étrangers, mais aussi des habitants de Venise, qui sont incapables de distinguer le bon du mauvais »[20].

Les femmes de la haute société tentèrent au moins une fois de réaffirmer la frontière entre elles et les courtisanes. Sir Henry Wotton, ambassadeur d'Angleterre à Venise, rapporte que la fête de l'Ascension de 1617 :

> « ... a cette année été célébrée par un spectacle de gondoles fort médiocre, en raison d'un décret du Sénat prononcé contre les courtisanes, stipulant qu'aucune d'entre elles ne saurait être transportée sur une gondole *con due remi* [à deux avirons] ; un décret décidé au bénéfice de toutes les femmes bien nées, qu'ici on ne savait distinguer de ces femmes de mauvaise vie »[21].

Le nombre même des prostituées leur a sûrement valu d'être confondues avec les aristocrates, y compris lorsqu'elles se déplaçaient en gondole à travers la ville. L'instabilité des catégories sociales alimentait la législation, les autorités s'efforçant de limiter la visibilité et la mobilité des prostituées par le biais de lois de recensement en les confinant au quartier du Rialto et en leur interdisant l'accès aux quartiers patriciens, aux églises et aux sites religieux de la ville[22].

La distinction entre identités sociales était combattue mais aussi alimentée par la législation somptuaire. Le déguisement et le travestissement, facilités par la circulation de costumes de seconde main, rendaient possible, dans la pratique sinon en théorie, la mobilité sociale[23]. Jusqu'au début du XVIIe siècle, avant que l'habillement des hommes ne connaisse une réglementation accrue, on prétendait que la préoccupation des femmes pour les modes, ces *dannate inventioni*, et les dépenses excessives qui en résultaient nuisaient à l'acquisition de liquidités

19. Coryat, 1611, p. 264.
20. Cité par Georgina Masson, *in* Masson, 1975, p. 152.
21. Cité par Edward Muir, *in* Muir, 1986, p. 133, n. 76.
22. ASV, *Provveditore alla Sanità 5*, p. 180-186 ; Bistort, 1912, p. 55-65, part. p. 65. *Cf.* Menetto, Zennaro, 1987, p. 45-64 ; Scarabello, 1980, p. 83.
23. Allerston, 1999, p. 4-56.

Titien, *Jeune Fille avec plateau de fruits*, Berlin, Staatliche Museen

Titien, *Salomé avec la tête de saint Jean-Baptiste*, Madrid, Museo Nacional del Prado

par le gouvernement, particulièrement en temps de troubles économiques et politiques[24]. Dans les archives des *Provveditori sopra le Pompe*, les magistrats chargés des lois somptuaires, figurent des prescriptions détaillées concernant les matières interdites, les tissus proscrits et les dépenses défendues. La défiance vis-à-vis du luxe ostentatoire se retrouve dans l'attention portée aux excès d'or, de plumes et, en tête des mentions les plus fréquentes, de perles[25].

Les femmes nobles, dont les apparitions publiques étaient, au XVIe siècle, de plus en plus limitées aux festivités, trouvaient là l'occasion de faire de leurs corps de véritables œuvres d'art. Le voyageur anglais Fynes Moryson, qui se rendit à Venise au tournant du siècle, s'exclama que les femmes « monstraient leur cou et leur gorge, de même que leurs tétins, bandés et gonflés de lin, d'une blancheur étudiée »[26]. La description de Moryson, qui pourrait être celle d'un tableau de Giorgione, Titien, Palma l'Ancien, Bordon ou de bien d'autres encore, révèle les moyens dont les femmes usaient pour enjoliver leur apparence en rembourrant leurs vêtements et en décolorant leurs cheveux.

Ce potentiel subversif de la matérialité est exploité dans de nombreuses demi-figures. Par exemple, dans la *Jeune Fille avec plateau de fruits* peinte par Titien vers 1555 et conservée aux Staatliche Museen à Berlin, les riches habits de la jeune femme, son collier de perles et son

24. Bistort, 1912, p. 141-184, part. p. 149-150, 180 et 184.
25. ASV, *Provveditore alla Sanità 5*, Capitolari 1-11 1488-1683 et Decreti 1334-1689. *Cf.* Bistort, *ibid.*, part. p. 197.
26. Moryson, 1908, p. 201 ; cité par Patricia H. Labalme, *in* Labalme, 1981, p. 106

diadème d'or contrastent avec sa fonction de servante (fig. page ci-contre). Le modèle, probablement la fille de Titien, Lavinia, se retourne avec un regard avenant, elle s'offre au spectateur en même temps que le fastueux plateau de fruits et de fleurs qu'elle soulève comme pour le porter à un banquet [27]. La figure a parfois été interprétée comme étant Pomone, la divinité des Fruits, et il est certain que la présence de symboles iconographiques dans ces œuvres permet de retenir l'attention du spectateur. La composition a été réutilisée par Titien et son atelier [28], ce qui témoigne de l'intérêt de l'artiste pour le potentiel de cette pose à susciter une analyse formelle, comme par la mise en relation de la forme de l'imposant citron avec ses yeux en amande, et de la fleur avec ses lèvres entrouvertes. Tout comme la fenêtre du tableau de Bordon à Lugano (cat. 1), le paysage de la peinture de Titien encadre le plateau comme s'il était une image indépendante et, ce faisant, attire l'attention sur l'intervention créatrice de l'artiste.

La composition a été utilisée pour une peinture de Salomé, aujourd'hui conservée au Prado, à Madrid, dans laquelle celle-ci tient sur un plat d'argent non plus des fruits, mais la tête de saint Jean-Baptiste (fig. page ci-contre). Le sujet se prête particulièrement bien à la pose, ce qui suggère que le tableau, peint vers 1550-1555, pourrait avoir été réalisé plus tôt que la *Jeune Fille avec plateau de fruits*. Curieusement, le costume et les cheveux parés de bijoux sont remarquablement similaires, à l'exception des manches et des perles autour du cou de la femme au plateau de fruits. Au lieu de tentures et, au loin, d'un paysage, Salomé et son plateau se détachent sur un fond monochrome qui souligne, avec un éclairage plus vif, la rotation de son buste et les parallèles entre son visage et celui de Jean-Baptiste. Cette juxtaposition démontre comment un changement de thème nous amène à percevoir sous un autre jour la même expression faciale, qui peut se révéler charmeuse mais aussi calculatrice et dangereuse.

Le passage de Salomé à une jeune fille élégamment vêtue portant des fruits rend compte des conceptions de l'époque s'agissant de la nature trompeuse des femmes. Bien qu'il n'existât pas de différenciation simple entre hommes et femmes sur la base du genre ou du sexe, on entretenait des idées sur la physiologie concourant à l'image qu'on se faisait des femmes, perçues comme changeantes. La virilité était une vertu fondée sur les humeurs chaudes et sèches attribuées aux hommes, auxquelles on imputait leur courage, leur corps ferme et leur esprit intransigeant. De leur côté, les femmes étaient sous l'emprise d'humeurs humides et froides, leur corps et leur esprit étaient donc délicats et malléables. Selon la pensée médicale contemporaine, les femmes étaient dépourvues d'organes génitaux mâles, car elles n'étaient pas pleinement formées. De ce fait, les femmes étaient à la fois instables et fausses [29].

À Venise, les croyances relatives à la physiologie recoupaient les diverses identités revêtues par la cité personnifiée sous les traits d'une femme. Alliant la Vierge Marie à Vénus, à la déesse de la Justice et à la déesse Roma, la personnification de Venise pouvait renvoyer à un idéal de

27. Goffen, 1997, p. 106 ; Contini, 2012, p. 32-40 ; Laurenze-Landsberg, 2012, p. 41-47.

28. Sur une copie d'atelier, la femme porte un coffret à la place du plateau. Wethey, 1971, p. 113-116.

29. La pensée théologique, défendue par Thomas d'Aquin et par d'autres, avançait que les femmes devaient être soumises aux hommes, chez qui prédominait la « discrétion de la raison ».

chasteté ou à la concupiscence. La Vierge en était la sainte patronne, par conséquent l'anniversaire de la fondation de la ville correspondait à la date de l'Annonciation. La contemplation des tableaux permettait de cultiver une faculté de discernement qui se développait dans la ville par l'observation des statues et peintures des différentes incarnations de Venise, des passantes et des femmes à leur fenêtre ou sur les gondoles.

La prostitution, l'homosociabilité et ce qui a peut-être été une sous-culture homosexuelle n'étaient pas rares en Italie, mais ces pratiques étaient plus facilement observables à Venise. L'enrichissement des *cittadini* menaçait le statut d'élite de l'aristocratie vénitienne, une classe déjà résolue à consolider l'organisation de la cité en castes en limitant les mariages et en faisant entrer dans les ordres un grand nombre de femmes patriciennes. Cette vision à court terme de la réalité démographique – qui occasionna une baisse du nombre des nobles – engendra une culture du célibat chargée d'érotisme[30]. On ne mariait qu'un fils et une fille, et, souvent, plusieurs frères cohabitaient avec une seule épouse. Des peintures et gravures concouraient à cette réputation, et les artistes profitaient par association de l'aura libérale et licencieuse de la ville. Prostitution et homoérotisme entretenaient l'intérêt porté aux représentations en buste de femmes et d'hommes séduisants[31]. Deux musiciens de la Galleria Borghese à Rome, peut-être peints par Giorgione, rendent compte de la malléabilité du concept quand il était étendu aux hommes. Dans *Le Chanteur passionné* (vers 1508-1510), un homme se tient face au spectateur mais baisse le regard, la main droite posée du bout des doigts sur la poitrine, dans un geste qui suggère qu'il parle, peut-être chante, entre ses lèvres écartées. Dans le *Joueur de flûte* (vers 1508-1510), l'homme est tourné vers la gauche mais nous regarde, bouche entrouverte.

Le caractère théâtral de ces femmes et hommes habillés en musiciens, courtisanes et déesses, où le corps est porteur de sens, fut pour le Caravage un moyen de renforcer sa position auprès des mécènes à la fin du XVIe siècle[32]. D'après son biographe Giovan Pietro Bellori, sa renommée auprès des collectionneurs grandit lorsqu'il adopta le style de Giorgione, après un passage à Venise, pour l'adapter aux figures en buste du *Jeu de cartes*. Grâce à quoi Bellori rapporte que le tableau fut acheté par le cardinal del Monte, qui devint le mécène du Caravage[33]. L'une de ses peintures en buste représente une femme qui porte des fleurs à sa poitrine. Le modèle, probablement dans le rôle de Flore, a été identifié par les spécialistes comme étant Fillide Melandroni, une prostituée et l'un des modèles de l'artiste. Le tableau, détruit dans un incendie à Berlin en 1945, réalisé autour de 1597, était exposé dans la collection du marquis Vincenzo Giustiniani aux côtés d'une autre œuvre attribuée au Caravage, *Portrait d'une courtisane célèbre*. Ces deux courtisanes comptaient parmi quinze tableaux attribués à l'artiste dans une collection de cinq cents œuvres[34].

30. Herlihy, 1980, p. 73 ; Ruggiero, 1989.
31. Simons, 1997, p. 29-51.
32. Del Re, 2013, p. 168-173 ; Pericolo, 2011.
33. Sur les représentations en buste et l'influence de Giorgione, *cf.* Bellori, 2005, p. 179-181.
34. Les tableaux étaient répertoriés sous le nom de *Portrait d'une courtisane célèbre* (no 11), *Portrait d'une courtisane* (aussi connu sous le nom de *Portrait de Fillide*) (no 12). Salerno, 1960, p. 135-149 ; Del Re, 2013, p. 88, n. 161.

Le Caravage, *Le Jeune Bacchus malade*, Rome, Galleria Borghese

Le Caravage se prit lui-même pour modèle dans *Le Jeune Bacchus malade* (fig. ci-contre), réalisé quelques années plus tôt vers 1593, peu après son arrivée à Rome. Une toge blanche jetée en travers de son corps, une couronne de feuilles de vigne sur la tête, une grappe de raisin entre les mains, il regarde dans notre direction, assis derrière un parapet en pierre où une nature morte et le nœud de sa ceinture se disputent notre attention. Comme dans les exemples vénitiens, le format en buste rappelle les codes du portrait et des figures mythologiques, mais le caractère théâtral explicite subvertit ces faux-semblants : ses ongles sont sales, sa toge est faite d'un drap de lit et le nœud de sa ceinture est disposé avec un négligé étudié. Il nous offre et nous refuse son corps tout à la fois, bras et raisin tenus près du torse ; sa pose et son regard attentif impliquent le spectateur dans la transaction. Le Caravage use d'une stratégie similaire dans *Garçon à la corbeille de fruits*, de la même époque, également conservé à la Galleria Borghese. L'expression et la pose du jeune androgyne oscillent sans cesse entre séduction langoureuse et repli mélancolique. L'ambiguïté de ce type d'image, dont on ne sait si le sujet rajuste ou enlève son vêtement, s'il s'agit d'une prostituée ou d'une dame de la noblesse, d'une déesse ou d'une courtisane, se trouve déplacée sur le jeu avec le spectateur.

Francesco Porzio a relevé différentes façons dont les traditions populaires du carnaval et des images comiques ont ouvert la voie à des catégories intermédiaires, de nouveaux genres d'images qui ont ébranlé les hiérarchies des représentations existantes[35]. Il évoque *Le Jeune Bacchus malade*, qu'il décrit comme étant un portrait transgressif qui prend le contre-pied des préoccupations d'usage concernant le statut et la profession. Les quelques fruits sur la table au premier plan, par exemple, témoignent de l'entrée du quotidien et du jeu de rôle dans des images qui à leur tour pouvaient engendrer plus d'échanges sociaux horizontaux. Pour Porzio, la tradition populaire assure en quelque sorte un rôle d'intermédiaire, auquel on doit l'émergence de quelque chose de nouveau dans l'imagerie picturale, comme en philosophie, au théâtre et dans la littérature. La licence et le naturalisme sont essentiels à ce procédé « anti-rhétorique et anti-dogmatique » qui était « un instrument de recherche de la spontanéité et de la sincérité »[36]. Il identifie trois caractéristiques majeures des images comiques : la sphère érotique, le langage domestique et la gestuelle du quotidien.

35. Porzio, 2008, p. 11.
36. *Ibid.*, p. 13.

Gerrit van Honthorst, *Jeune Homme souriant écrasant des raisins*, Worcester Art Museum

Ces caractéristiques figurent au nombre de celles reprises par les caravagesques, des peintres des Pays-Bas qui voyagèrent à Rome au XVIIe siècle mais qui poursuivirent les innovations du Caravage dans des directions différentes. Gerrit van Honthorst et Dirck van Baburen, qui étaient logés par les Giustinani, avaient personnellement accès à la collection d'œuvres du Caravage du marquis et à celles d'importants collectionneurs[37]. De retour à Utrecht en 1620, Honthorst peignit deux ans plus tard le *Jeune Homme souriant écrasant des raisins* (fig. ci-contre)[38]. Honthorst combine des éléments du *Jeune Bacchus malade* et du *Bacchus* du Caravage de la Galleria degli Uffizi et transforme le jeu de la séduction homoérotique en scène burlesque. Il parodie en même temps qu'il imite le contenu et le style des peintures du Caravage, le contraste saisissant de la luminosité de sa chair contre le fond presque noir projette le sujet vers le spectateur. Le désordre de son costume, de son couvre-chef et la houppe de plumes maintenue par un lacet violet encadrent sa grimace éméchée et canaille. Au lieu de l'élégant verre de vin offert par le *Bacchus* du Caravage dans la collection de la Galleria degli Uffizi, le modèle de Honthorst presse du raisin dont le jus, pareil à du sang, ruisselle goutte à goutte dans une simple tasse en terre cuite. À la place de la toge improvisée, la chemise de l'homme a glissé de son épaule gauche et dévoile une partie de son torse à la manière des portraits de courtisanes d'élite, telle la *Flore* de Titien mais transposée en prostituée de rue. Le *Garçon au turban tenant un bouquet de fleurs* de Michael Sweerts (cat. 74) en est une variation surprenante, réalisée vers 1661 (Madrid, Museo Thyssen-Bornemisza). Sweerts joue avec le thème homoérotique de l'androgynie : le garçon tient des fleurs comme le ferait une courtisane ou une mariée, une écharpe nouée en turban soulignant ses traits charmants. La coiffe saugrenue, dont les franges bordent ses yeux telles des touffes de cheveux, sans parler de l'apparente réticence révélée par son attitude distante face au spectateur, témoigne de la théâtralité intentionnelle de la pose.

À l'instar de Giorgione un siècle plus tôt et du Caravage, la portée de l'œuvre de Honthorst repose sur le renouvellement du rapport au spectateur. Comme leurs prédécesseurs, les caravagesques cultivaient aux Pays-Bas un marché de mécènes éclairés. Bien que la question

37. Del Re, 2013, part. p. 89.
38. *Ibid.*, p. 221-224.

de la moralité se posât, un aspect important de l'intérêt revêtu par ces peintures résidait dans leur caractère théâtral. Sonia Del Re a insisté sur le fait que les figures « évoquent l'idée d'une distribution de rôles » par laquelle elles s'inscrivaient dans les pratiques sociales et le théâtre de rue, aux Pays-Bas et à Utrecht en particulier[39]. En portant son attention, non plus sur la façon dont ces artistes ont imité le Caravage, mais sur la théâtralité de la peinture, Del Re repense les pratiques des caravagesques et leur traitement caractéristique du corps humain. Comme pour les artistes de rue, l'attrait du *Jeune Homme souriant* de Honthorst et du *Garçon au turban tenant un bouquet de fleurs* de Sweerts s'explique en partie par l'hésitation de l'intellect entre plaisirs grivois et libertins et un rendu sensuel remarquable.

Le tableau de Honthorst servit à son tour d'inspiration, en 1628, pour la *Bergère au plat de raisins* d'Abraham Bloemaert (Karlsruhe, Staatliche Kunsthalle) (cat. 2)[40]. Bloemaert n'a jamais visité Rome, mais il a exploité le format en buste en même temps que ses élèves, dont Honthorst. La figure en habits de bergère est déshabillée d'une manière rigoureusement identique à celle du *Jeune Homme souriant*, de façon à révéler entre le bras et le sein une ombre qui ressemble à un orifice corporel. De telles associations sont encouragées par la présence de la chèvre sur la colline, près du chapeau, qui affiche son arrière-train tout en broutant de la vigne, comme celle au-dessus de la tête de la femme. Les plaisirs charnels ne se veulent pas subtils étant donnés les rapprochements établis entre la croupe et la chemise, le raisin et le bout du sein, les vrilles et les cheveux.

De façon significative, Bloemaert a combiné le format en buste à l'italienne aux scènes de marché des peintres flamands et hollandais, qui introduisaient régulièrement des comparaisons entre les corps de femmes et les étals de nourriture. La combinaison provocatrice de la séduction et des activités commerciales qui se manifeste dans les marchés, cuisines, maisons closes et tavernes était un sujet idéalement propice à la mise en valeur des charmes de la peinture, comme l'a montré Elizabeth Honig pour les scènes de genre flamandes et hollandaises[41]. Le *Marché* de Joachim Beuckelaer, peint en 1565, et *La Cuisinière*, peinte en 1559 par son oncle Pieter Aertsen, tous deux acquis par Girolamo Balbi à Anvers entre 1595 et 1617 et désormais conservés au Palazzo Bianco à Gênes, en sont deux exemples[42]. La chair des femmes est comparée à celle des volailles qu'elles manipulent, mais leur sollicitation du spectateur, bien que directe, écarte toute promesse de séduction, ce en dépit de la thématique résolument charnelle. Contrairement aux scènes de marchés et cuisines du XVIe siècle, où la tension entre désir et retenue exhorte à l'introspection morale, les tableaux de Bloemaert et Honthorst présentent un caractère délibérément théâtral. La *Bergère* de Bloemaert (cat. 2) au regard langoureux et suggestif laisse peu de place aux tergiversations morales, pas plus que la sexualité saturnienne du *Jeune Homme souriant* de Honthorst. Ces personnages opèrent une rupture entre classes sociales élevées et classes

39. *Ibid.*, p. 44.
40. Roethlisberger, Bok, 1993 ; Nogrady, 2009 ; Helmus, Seelig, 2011, p. 46-54.
41. Honig, 1998, p. 170-212.
42. Boccardo, 2004. Sur *La Cuisinière* d'Aertsen, p. 168-169 ; sur le *Marché* de Beuckelaer, p. 170-171.

Godfried Schalcken, *Jeune Fille au citron*, Amsterdam, Rijksmuseum

défavorisées, et permettent aux spectateurs de se distinguer des artistes de rue grâce à « la représentation dans l'art noble de personnages grossiers », selon Del Re[43].

Dernier exemple, Godfried Schalcken, qui travaillait à Dordrecht et dont l'œuvre illustre le caractère évolutif et autoréférentiel du format en buste dont l'historique a été retracé ici. Dans sa *Jeune Fille à la fenêtre*, des collections du National Museum of Wales, à Cardiff (cat. 8), la figure de la femme se donne déjà comme une image, et le volet de bois, le cadre, le loquet, les gonds et le rideau derrière elle s'ajoutent aux couches et aux agrafes de sa tenue spectaculaire. Schalcken lie la performance plus intimement à son modèle dans la *Jeune Fille au citron*, conservée au Rijksmuseum, à Amsterdam, et peinte entre 1585 et 1590 (fig. ci-contre). Un parapet nous sépare de la femme et sert aussi de table pour l'élégante nature morte dont elle fait partie. L'écorce du citron déroule une spirale voluptueuse du bord du plateau en argent, un repère couramment utilisé pour marquer les limites de la table et du plan de la peinture, ainsi qu'une démonstration de virtuosité artistique, comme on peut en voir dans les natures mortes du peintre haarlémois Willem Claeszoon Heda. Schalcken tire profit de ce langage pictural tout en le parodiant, substituant au drapé de la robe sur le coussin rouge, la pelure du citron. La femme nous prie de poursuivre le jeu et de la pointe de son petit couteau nous offre une tranche de citron qui fait écho au dessin et aux détails chatoyants de ses manches. Il ne fait pas de doute que le couteau qui a pelé le fruit doit être vu comme un substitut du pinceau de l'artiste si l'on s'en réfère à la représentation traditionnelle des écorces de citron ainsi qu'au positionnement stratégique du couteau, à l'endroit précis où une fenêtre perce le mur. Il suffit de se souvenir des portraits et autres images, notamment érotiques, qui étaient parfois dissimulés derrière une tenture pour que le rideau de velours vert tiré sur le côté et son énorme gland de passementerie nous rappellent que nous ne sommes pas séduits par une jeune femme avec un citron, mais par la théâtralité de la peinture.

Bronwen Wilson

43. Del Re, 2013, p. 45.

PATHOS ET MYSTÈRE : LA FIGURE DE FANTAISIE ENDORMIE

Au sein de la vaste typologie des figures de fantaisie établie par Melissa Percival dans son essai (pages 17 à 36), celle des dormeurs occupe une place à la fois singulière et fascinante. En effet, les figures endormies sont très répandues dans les tableaux du XVIIe et du XVIIIe siècle. Mais alors que nombre d'entre elles appartiennent clairement à la peinture d'histoire et de genre, certaines pouvant même être qualifiées de figures allégoriques ou de portraits [1], une quantité non négligeable de ces représentations résiste à la classification et mériterait d'être considérée comme des figures libres. Les figures de fantaisie endormies telles celles que l'on rencontre dans cette exposition, dans les tableaux de Tomás Hiepes, Eberhard Keil, Jean-Baptiste Santerre (à la manière de), Giambattista Piazzetta, Jean-Baptiste Deshays et Jean-Baptiste Greuze, semblent souvent physiquement proches, les corps étant généralement cadrés de près, mais ne communiquent pas ou peu avec le spectateur. Plus que toute autre figure de fantaisie, ces figures « sont dans l'être plutôt que dans l'action », pour reprendre la formule de Melissa Percival [2]. En ce sens, elles s'apparentent à un genre pictural qui semble *a priori* fort éloigné d'elles : la nature morte.

Mis à part le dieu gréco-romain du Sommeil Hypnos (Somnus), la majorité des figures de fantaisie endormies du début de l'art moderne représente des femmes. Il existe à ce jour peu d'études répertoriant le nombre de dormeurs par rapport au nombre de dormeuses dans l'art entre le XVIIe siècle et le début du XXe siècle [3]. Cependant, en l'absence de données plus fiables et en s'appuyant sur un outil actuel relativement utile pour relever une tendance, on constate

1. Quelques exemples de figures endormies dans la peinture d'histoire des XVIIe et XVIIIe siècles : eau-forte de Rembrandt, *Le Songe de Jacob* (Bartsch 36), Ferdinand Bol, *Vénus et Mars endormi* (Brunswick, Herzog Anton Ulrich Museum), Le Guerchin, *Renaud et Armide* (Rome, plafond du palais Costaguti), et Anne-Louis Girodet-Trioson, *Le Sommeil d'Endymion* (Paris, musée du Louvre) ; dans la peinture de genre : Adriaen Brouwer, *Beuverie paysanne* (La Haye, Mauritshuis), Nicolaes Maes, *Dame âgée assoupie* (Bruxelles, Musées royaux des beaux-arts), Johannes Vermeer, *Une jeune fille assoupie* (New York, Metropolitan Museum), et Pietro Antonio Rotari, *Jeune Fille endormie* (Munich, Alte Pinakothek) ; dans l'allégorie : Francisco Goya, *Le sommeil de la raison engendre des monstres* (eau-forte), et Heinrich Füssli, *Le Cauchemar* (Detroit Institute of Art et autres) ; dans les portraits : Bernardo Strozzi, *Enfant endormi* (Salzbourg, Residenzgalerie), et (probablement) Domenico Fetti, *Une jeune fille endormie* (Budapest, Szépmûvészeti Múzeum). Pour plus d'exemples, *cf.* Pigler, 1974. Cet ouvrage d'A. Pigler, *Barockthemen*, est un dictionnaire des thèmes de l'art des XVIIe et XVIIIe siècles, où l'on peut par exemple trouver « Jahel und Sisera » ou « Luna (Diana) besucht den Schlafenden Endymion » et de nombreux exemples de figures endormies dans des peintures d'histoire, allégoriques ou même de genre (comme « Schlafendes Mädchen »).
2. Percival, 2012.
3. *Cf.* McNelly, 1985. Entre autres références, Kulterman, 1990, p. 129-191.

que Wikimedia Commons possède une rubrique consacrée aux femmes endormies dans les arts, alors qu'il n'en existe aucune pour les hommes endormis[4]. Cela est sans doute lié à l'apparence de vulnérabilité propre au dormeur, une qualité traditionnellement jugée indésirable chez les sujets masculins. En effet, les dormeurs que l'on rencontre dans la peinture d'histoire (Argus, Holopherne, Samson ou Siséra, notamment) connaissent souvent une fin tragique ou sont tournés en ridicule (Noé).

Les figures de fantaisie se prêtent à des types d'analyse variés, mais les démarches sémiotiques et iconographiques paraissent ici particulièrement fructueuses. D'un point de vue sémiotique, ces tableaux invitent le spectateur ou la spectatrice à réfléchir sur le type de relation, physique ou mentale, qu'il ou qu'elle entretient avec la figure endormie. D'un point de vue iconographique, un certain nombre d'entre eux peut être rapproché d'un ou de plusieurs modèles traditionnels du sommeil. Dans la suite de cet article, je m'attacherai aux aspects sémiotiques des figures de fantaisie endormies, puis je proposerai quelques lectures iconographiques auxquelles se prêtent certains tableaux.

Les dormeurs et l'absorbement

Plus que toute autre figure de fantaisie, les dormeurs invitent à une vision rapprochée. En effet, ces figures sont ignorantes du regard porté sur elles et laissent tout loisir au spectateur de les observer aussi longuement et intensément qu'il le désire puisqu'elles ne le regardent pas. Bien entendu, aucune figure peinte ne regarde réellement son spectateur, mais si l'on suppose que toute image conserve une part de l'aura de son modèle, on peut affirmer qu'un tableau représentant une figure endormie permet à celui qui l'observe de se sentir plus libre que s'il y avait échange de regards.

Dans son ouvrage de référence *La Place du spectateur* (1990), l'historien d'art américain Michael Fried se concentre principalement sur les figures de fantaisie dans les tableaux du XVIIIe siècle pour distinguer deux relations possibles entre le sujet et le spectateur : l'« absorbement » et la « théâtralité ». Les figures absorbées sont tellement accaparées par leur activité ou plongées dans leurs pensées qu'elles semblent en oublier la présence du spectateur. Les figures théâtrales, quant à elles, sont conscientes de la présence du spectateur et prennent délibérément une pose afin d'établir une forme de communication avec lui[5]. Dans un ouvrage plus récent, *The Moment of Caravaggio* (2010), c'est au peintre du XVIIe siècle Michelangelo Merisi da Caravaggio, dit le Caravage, que Fried attribue l'invention de l'absorbement, pour l'opposer non plus à la théâtralité, mais à ce qu'il nomme désormais l'« adresse ». En d'autres termes, il établit une distinction entre les figures peintes ou sculptées qui, par l'expression de leur visage ou leur langage corporel, semblent avoir été conçues pour communiquer avec le

4. *Cf.* http://commons.wikimedia.org/wiki/Category:Sleeping_women_in_art. Il existe des rubriques pour *sleeping in art*, « le sommeil dans l'art », et *sleeping people in art*, « personnages endormis dans l'art ». Elles montrent des hommes, des femmes, des enfants et même, pour la première rubrique, des animaux. Elles comprennent moins d'éléments que celle consacrée aux *sleeping women in art*, « femmes endormies dans l'art », qui contenait 135 images lors de la dernière consultation de la page (10/02/2015).

5. Fried, 1990.

spectateur (*adresse*), et celles qui sont représentées comme étant « si captivées par ce qu'elles font, ce qu'elles ressentent ou pensent, qu'elles frappent le spectateur par leur oubli de ce qui les entoure et leur ignorance de la présence du spectateur devant le tableau » (*absorbement*)[6]. Fried insiste sur le fait que, bien que les figures absorbées ne s'« adressent » pas au spectateur, ou du moins ne communiquent pas avec lui au sens où nous entendons généralement la communication entre deux personnes (paroles, contact visuel, mouvements), elles parviennent toutefois à transmettre l'intensité d'une émotion ou d'une humeur. Il prend pour exemple la *Madeleine repentante* du Caravage, dans la galerie Doria Pamphilj à Rome[7]. Assise voûtée sur une chaise basse, la tête baissée sur la poitrine, les yeux fermés ou presque, elle semble comme retirée du monde qui l'entoure. Bien qu'elle ne s'adresse en aucune façon au spectateur, elle parvient néanmoins à lui communiquer l'ampleur de sa peine et de son remords.

Les figures endormies semblent ainsi incarner parfaitement cette notion d'absorbement ou plutôt, comme le précise Fried, représenter « une modalité extrême de l'absorbement »[8]. Bien qu'elles ressemblent à d'autres figures absorbées inconscientes de la présence du spectateur, elles s'en distinguent en ne communiquant ni émotion ni humeur (contrairement à la *Madeleine repentante* du Caravage). L'inspection voyeuriste à laquelle le spectateur est convié se heurte alors à l'insondabilité radicale de ces figures. En effet, selon James F. A. Pyre, spécialiste de littérature anglaise, le sommeil se caractérise à la fois par son pathos et par son mystère[9]. Bien que physiquement accessible jusqu'à en être vulnérable, le dormeur reste mentalement absent et inexpressif, tel un cadavre. Toutefois, à la différence du cadavre, la personne endormie continue d'être animée d'une vie intérieure secrète. J. F. A. Pyre conclut son analyse en expliquant que le sommeil « ôte du récit des actions du dormeur, de la confession ou de l'analyse de sa vie psychique, tout le caractère artificiel d'une narration calculée ou d'un savant monologue pour envelopper ces révélations d'une aura merveilleuse empreinte de surnaturel »[10]. Autrement dit, les dormeurs sont déroutants et énigmatiques.

Dans *Fragonard and the Fantasy Figure*, Melissa Percival étudie la représentation emblématique de l'« Imagination » telle qu'elle est présentée dans l'ouvrage de Jean-Baptiste Boudard, *Iconologie tirée de divers auteurs* (1759)[11]. Dans son analyse de cet emblème qui représente une femme tranquillement assise, les mains jointes, les jambes croisées, le regard dirigé vers le haut, Boudard note : « Quoique l'imagination se représente assise tranquillement, & dans une attitude pensive ; elle ne laisse pas de tenir l'esprit continuellement en mouvement, même pendant le sommeil. » Boudard fait ici référence à une croyance ancienne selon laquelle, durant le sommeil, notre imagination opérerait toujours, peut-être même plus intensément, donnant ainsi naissance à nos rêves et à nos cauchemars. Dans la mythologie grecque, Hypnos,

6. Fried, 2010, p. 69.
7. Pour en voir une reproduction : http://www.doriapamphilj.it/maddalena.asp. Consulté le 10/02/2015.
8. Fried, 2010, p. 70.
9. Pyre, 1916. Shakespeare Online, 20 août 2011, http://www.shakespeare-online.com/biography/shakespearepathos5.html. Consulté le 11/02/2014.
10. *Ibid.*
11. Percival, 2012, p. 5-6.

dieu du Sommeil, avait trois fils (Morphée, Phobétor et Phantasos) chargés de créer les rêves (*oneiroi*). Selon Ovide, Morphée avait le pouvoir de prendre une apparence humaine, Phobétor imitait les « quadrupèdes, les oiseaux ou le serpent aux vastes replis », tandis que Phantasos « prend tour à tour la forme de terre, d'une pierre, de l'eau, d'un arbre et des objets inanimés » (*Les Métamorphoses*, XI, 633ff)[12]. C'est donc à double titre qu'un lien peut être établi entre la figure de fantaisie endormie et la fantaisie en soi. En effet, la figure est le produit de la fantaisie de l'artiste mais elle est également elle-même productrice de fantaisies, aussi mystérieuses et inaccessibles soient-elles pour le spectateur.

Le sommeil et la mort

Outre leur relation singulière avec le spectateur, les dormeurs dans l'art participent d'une tradition iconographique riche et variée[13]. Dans l'Antiquité classique, le sommeil était étroitement lié à la mort. Les dieux grecs du Sommeil et de la Mort, Hypnos et Thanatos, étaient frères jumeaux. Selon le poète grec Hésiode, ils étaient fils de Nyx, la Nuit, et d'Érèbe, les Ténèbres (*Théogonie*, vers 700 av. J.-C.). Les deux frères se ressemblaient beaucoup[14], mais alors qu'Hypnos, selon Hésiode, « va parcourant la terre et le vaste dos de la mer, tranquille et doux pour les hommes », Thanatos « a un cœur de fer, une âme d'airain, implacable dans sa poitrine ; il tient à jamais l'homme qu'il a pris ; il est en haine même aux dieux immortels »[15].

La proximité avec la mort reste à ce jour une partie importante de l'iconographie du sommeil. En effet, il existe une longue tradition euphémique, que ce soit en art, en littérature ou dans la culture populaire, consistant à substituer le sommeil à la mort. On retrouve cette euphémisation dans l'expression courante « *Requiescat in pace* », R.I.P, « Repose en paix »[16]. Le succès des portraits d'Endymion sur les sarcophages de la fin de l'Empire romain (près de soixante-dix exemples datant des IIe et IIIe siècles de notre ère sont répertoriés)[17] marque le début de cette tradition dans l'art occidental[18]. Plongé par Zeus dans un sommeil éternel à la demande de Séléné, déesse de la Lune éprise du beau chasseur[19], le jeune Endymion semble adoucir, par sa présence sur les sarcophages, la frontière nous séparant de la mort en la présentant comme un sommeil juvénile. L'association du sommeil et de la mort devient particulièrement explicite au XIXe siècle, au cours duquel se répand la mode des sculptures funéraires figurant les défunts endormis, particulièrement lorsqu'il s'agit d'enfants. Parmi les exemples les plus célèbres, la tombe d'Ellen-Jane et de sa sœur Marianne Robinson (1817) réalisée par Francis Chantrey, dans la cathédrale de

12. Ovide, 2008, p. 235.
13. Sur ce même sujet, *cf.* Ten-Doesschate Chu, *in* Lausanne 2000, p. 5-17, et Ten-Doesschate Chu, 1998, vol. II, p. 843-849.
14. Comme nous pouvons le remarquer sur le célèbre Cratère d'Euphronios (auparavant exposé au Metropolitan Museum of Art de New York ; désormais à la Villa Giulia, Rome), qui les représente soulevant le corps du héros grec Sarpédon du champ de bataille.
15. Hésiode, 2008, p. 81.
16. À propos de l'utilisation de cette formule comme épitaphe, *cf.* Rieckenberg, 1966. Cette locution est également employée dans le requiem tridentin.
17. Morford, Lenardon, Shamm, 1999, p. 43.
18. Pour une réflexion sur le thème d'Endymion sur les sarcophages romains, *cf.* Koortbojian, 1995 ; e-book sur http://ark.cdlib.org/ark:/13030/ft4199n900), chap. 4 et 5.
19. Endymion, très souvent mentionné dans de nombreuses sources classiques, est considéré par certains comme un chasseur (princier) et par d'autres, comme un berger.

Lichfield, représente deux petites filles mortes très jeunes comme endormies dans les bras l'une de l'autre[20]. Plus tard, au cours du XIXe siècle, le motif de l'enfant endormi devient particulièrement courant sur les tombes victoriennes[21].

Certaines figures de fantaisie endormies évoquent clairement cette association entre le sommeil et la mort, soit à travers leurs attributs, soit au moyen d'allusions aux modèles iconographiques traditionnels, ou les deux à la fois. C'est notamment le cas du *Cazador dormido*, le « Chasseur endormi », de Tomás Hiepes (1595-1674), au Museu de Belles Arts à Valence, en Espagne (cat. 35). Ce tableau oblong représente un jeune chasseur endormi qui se repose après une chasse aux oiseaux. Sa position semble inconfortable : il est allongé, accoudé à une pierre, le flanc appuyé contre sa gibecière et son fusil. Seule sa jambe droite repliée contre son torse est visible, tandis que son autre jambe est cachée par une pierre. Face à lui, posés au sol ou suspendus à une souche d'arbre, on aperçoit ses trophées de chasse – un colvert, deux chevaliers gambettes, un guêpier et un rollier – autant d'oiseaux caractéristiques, de nos jours comme à l'époque, de la région de Valence où Hiepes passa sa vie[22]. Le corps allongé du chasseur tient à peine dans ce plan pictural rectangulaire, donnant l'impression que le personnage est si proche du spectateur que celui-ci pourrait être tenté de toucher son bras pour le réveiller. Hiepes s'était spécialisé dans la peinture de natures mortes de fleurs. Les tableaux représentant des sujets humains, tels que *Cazador dormido* ou son pendant, *Cazador bebiendo*, qui nous montre un autre chasseur buvant à la source (*cf.* fig. page 168, pendant cat. 35), sont donc rares dans son œuvre[23]. Le chasseur se désaltérant est placé près du plan pictural, tout comme son équivalent endormi. Cependant, la tête du premier est à gauche, alors que celle du second est à droite. De plus, le chasseur endormi est allongé sur le côté, tandis que le chasseur qui boit se tient à quatre pattes, penché en avant pour atteindre la source. Faire de ces deux tableaux des pendants apparaît comme une évidence, non seulement du fait de leurs dimensions et de leur composition similaires, mais aussi parce que les mêmes oiseaux y sont présents, quoique disposés différemment. Dans ces deux œuvres, Hiepes semble avoir fait de la figure humaine un sujet de nature morte, et même une série de sujets de nature morte : la position crispée des corps détruit leur cohérence, les présentant comme un assemblage aléatoire de têtes, de bras et de jambes, un peu à la manière dont Théodore Géricault, environ un siècle et demi plus tard, représentera dans ses natures mortes des restes humains. Leur disposition désordonnée rappelle et renvoie à la désinvolture avec laquelle les oiseaux morts, clairement visibles dans le *Cazador bebiendo*, ont été jetés à terre. Ces deux tableaux peuvent ainsi être considérés comme d'extraordinaires vanités, dans lesquelles le spectacle confus des corps et des membres suggère l'insignifiance du corps, simple enveloppe charnelle, après la mort.

Si l'on considère au contraire ces deux jeunes hommes en tant que personnages, et non en tant que sujets de nature morte, il paraît évident que, malgré leurs costumes, ces jeunes paysans

20. Pour en voir une reproduction : http://en.wikipedia.org/wiki/The_Sleeping_Children#mediaviewer/File:Chantreys_Sleeping_Children.jpg.
21. À ce même sujet, *cf.*, entre autres, Snyder, 1992.
22. Je tiens à remercier Ruud Foppen et Roelof ten Doesschate pour l'identification de ces oiseaux.
23. Ces deux tableaux, mesurant chacun 68,2 × 113,2 cm, se trouvent au Museu de Belles Arts de Valence, Espagne.

espagnols vêtus comme au XVIIe siècle ne sont pas sans évoquer la mythologie classique. Le chasseur endormi renvoie à Endymion, tandis que le buveur rappelle Narcisse tombant amoureux de sa propre image alors qu'il s'abreuve à la source. Ces deux chasseurs mythologiques étaient déjà associés dans l'Antiquité et furent notamment appairés dans deux fresques disparues de Pompéi ayant figuré dans la Casa dei Dioscuri et dans la Casa dell' Argenteria. Selon Michael Koortbojian, leur juxtaposition invite à comparer deux types de mort : l'une pour l'amour de soi, l'autre pour l'amour d'autrui[24].

Le sommeil et l'amour

Comme le suggère le mythe d'Endymion, le sommeil n'est pas uniquement associé à la mort, il l'est également à l'amour. En effet, le lien iconographique qui existe entre le sommeil et l'amour est aussi étroit, sinon plus étroit encore, que celui unissant le sommeil et la mort, particulièrement pendant la Renaissance et jusqu'à l'époque moderne. Rappelons qu'Éros, divinité de l'Amour, était fils de Nyx, déesse de la Nuit, tout comme Hypnos et Thanatos. Endymion, amant de la déesse de la Lune qui le plonge dans un sommeil éternel semblable à la mort, peut être considéré comme l'incarnation de ce triangle fraternel.

L'association du sommeil et de l'amour est notamment présente, à l'époque hellénistique, dans les sculptures d'Hermaphrodite endormi(e)[25] (lui/elle-même étant le fruit d'un amour passionnel) ou d'Éros endormi. Ces deux types de sculptures étaient très connus à l'époque romaine, de nombreuses répliques ayant été créées afin de décorer maisons et jardins[26]. Souvent représentés au beau milieu d'un paysage et toujours chargés d'érotisme, les nus féminins endormis devinrent courants dans les peintures du début du XVIe siècle[27]. D'abord à Venise, ils s'inspirent souvent de déesses classiques (comme Vénus), de nymphes ou de mythes classiques présentant des jeunes vierges endormies (Ariane, Callisto, Danaé) sur le point d'être surprises ou violées par les dieux. Ils devinrent fréquents partout en Europe et perdurèrent au XVIIe siècle (Rembrandt van Rijn, Pierre Paul Rubens), au XVIIIe siècle (François Boucher, Jean Honoré Fragonard), au XIXe (Gustave Courbet, Achille Devéria) et même au XXe siècle (Henri Matisse, Pablo Picasso).

C'est à partir du XVIIe et surtout au cours du XVIIIe siècle que la plupart de ces nus endormis cessèrent d'être considérés comme des sujets mythologiques pour devenir des figures de fantaisie, vaguement liées à la peinture mythologique d'une part et à la peinture de genre d'autre part. *Une femme qui dort* de Jean-Baptiste Deshays (cat. 41), peinte à Rome en 1757-1758, en est un exemple. Le tableau représente une jeune femme endormie, en position assise, cadrée au niveau

24. Koortbojian, 1995, ch. 5, partie « Endymion Awake » (s.l., s.n.).

25. La sculpture originale (perdue) en bronze d'Hermaphrodite est mentionnée dans l'*Histoire naturelle* de Pline l'Ancien comme étant l'œuvre du sculpteur hellénistique Polyclès (connu vers 155 avant J.-C.). Parmi les répliques romaines en marbre, la plus célèbre se trouve au musée du Louvre, à Paris. Elle repose sur un matelas de marbre exécuté par Le Bernin en 1619 à la demande de son propriétaire, Scipion Borghèse.

26. À propos des sculptures d'*Hermaphrodite endormi*, *cf.* l'excellent document en ligne du musée du Louvre : http://www.louvre.fr/oeuvre-notices/hermaphrodite-endormi ; à propos d'*Éros endormi*, *cf.* Söldner, 1986, et les documents en ligne à propos d'une exposition de 2013, portant essentiellement sur l'*Éros endormi*, au Metropolitan Museum of Art de New York, sur http://www.metmuseum.org/exhibitions/listings/2013/sleeping-eros. Consulté le 12/02/2015.

27. *Cf.* l'article de référence de Meiss, 1966, p. 348-362.

des genoux. Sa nudité partielle, ses jambes écartées, le placement de ses mains sur son sexe, ses joues rougies ainsi que le décor nocturne sont autant d'éléments évoquant le thème de l'amour. Bien que l'érotisme du tableau ne fasse aucun doute, une ambivalence délibérée subsiste toutefois quant à son exposition (ce terme étant employé dans son sens rhétorique). Il y a, tout d'abord, l'ambiguïté du décor : une grande draperie jaune doré retombe en cascade depuis le haut du tableau et paraît envelopper un ou plusieurs meubles, à moins qu'il ne s'agisse de l'affleurement d'une roche. D'autre part, la femme elle-même est énigmatique. Jeune, belle, elle est vêtue d'une ample chemise diaphane dont l'ouverture laisse entrevoir un sein. Est-ce une figure mythique ou une femme réelle ? Appartient-elle au passé ou au présent ? Elle rappelle les images classiques d'Ariane, de Danaé ou de nymphes endormies[28]. Pourtant, tandis que sa chemise semble intemporelle, sa coiffure tressée avec un ruban et enroulée au-dessus de sa tête est typique du début du XVIIIe siècle, comme on peut le voir dans les tableaux et les dessins de Jean-Antoine Watteau. Mais c'est sans doute la position des mains de la jeune femme qui reste l'élément le plus ambigu. À première vue, elle les tient croisées contre elle, comme pour éviter de laisser échapper l'extrémité d'un ruban bleu auquel est attaché un petit épagneul noir et blanc bien éveillé, assis tranquillement à côté d'elle. Leur position peut être perçue comme pudique et protectrice comme chez la *Venus pudica* de Praxitèle[29], une interprétation qui semble confirmée par la présence du chien qui paraît « garder » la jeune femme (et sa virginité) pendant son sommeil. Mais si l'on observe plus attentivement le placement de ses mains sur son sexe et la façon dont les doigts sont entrecroisés, l'index droit pénétrant la fente étroite entre le majeur et l'index de la main gauche, le geste peut être considéré comme obscène. Une description contemporaine de l'une des deux gravures d'Antoine-François Hémery d'après ce tableau intitulée « La Fidélité surveillante » confirme cette ambiguïté[30] :

> « une femme à demi-nue, endormie dans l'attitude la plus naturelle et la plus voluptueuse sous la garde de son épagneul, qu'elle tient à son bras par un ruban. Cet animal, symbole de la Fidélité, paraît prêt à éloigner les indiscrets qui ne respecteroient pas le sommeil paisible de la maîtresse »[31].

Cette description démontre que la fascination suscitée par le tableau chez les spectateurs contemporains était précisément due au mélange d'allégorie et de réalité, d'expérience et d'innocence, de volupté et de domesticité, ici incarnée par l'épagneul au ruban bleu. La taille minuscule de ce chien de garde symbolise le peu de résistance à laquelle « les indiscrets » se verront confrontés s'ils essayent d'interrompre « le sommeil paisible de la maîtresse ».

---

28. Sandoz, 1977, p. 66. M. Sandoz y voit également un lien avec la Bible, en particulier avec les représentations traditionnelles de Bethsabée.

29. L'original de l'*Aphrodite de Cnide* de Praxitèle, surnommée *Venus pudica* (Vénus pudique), a disparu, mais de nombreuses répliques et variantes existent.

30. Je n'ai pas trouvé la véritable gravure d'A. F. Hémery, seulement sa description (*cf.* note 31) ; une autre gravure d'après le tableau de J.-B. Deshays par Per Fustaf Floding ne comporte pas de titre mais seulement l'inscription « I.I., Peint à Rome par J.B. Deshays et I.r., Gravée à Paris par Floding, 1759 ». *Cf.* von Heinecken, 1790, vol. IV, p. 612.

31. Anonyme, 1780, p. 431-432. Le journal nous informe également qu'au moment où la publication a été rédigée, le tableau appartenait à la collection de l'architecte Charles de Wailly. De Wailly a probablement acquis le tableau de J.-B. Deshays à l'époque où les deux artistes étudiaient à Rome, à la fin des années 1750. Selon le catalogue en ligne de la Kunsthalle de Brême, l'œuvre a par la suite intégré la collection du comte de Lonsdale, au château de Lowther.

Philip Galle, *La Paresse*, San Francisco, Fine Arts Museums of San Francisco, Achenbach Foundation for Graphic Arts

Le sommeil et la paresse

Au-delà de l'évocation de la mort et de l'amour, le sommeil est également associé à la paresse et à la négligence du devoir. Dans *Acedia* ou *La Paresse* (fig. ci-contre), l'une des gravures faisant partie d'une série de Philip Galle représentant les péchés capitaux[32], on voit une femme assoupie, la tête contre sa main. L'encadrement somptueux de cette gravure nous montre aussi quatre *putti* dans différentes postures de sommeil. Dans l'art du XVIIe siècle (Nicolaes Maes, Jan Vermeer) et jusqu'au XIXe siècle (Gustave Courbet), il existe beaucoup de dormeurs, et surtout de dormeuses, délaissant leurs tâches. Alors qu'au XVIIe siècle les dormeurs paresseux sont généralement représentés dans des contextes précis et détaillés (souvent des cuisines ou d'autres cadres de travail) qui les situent clairement dans la tradition de la peinture de genre, au XVIIIe siècle en revanche, la tâche qu'ils abandonnent n'est que suggérée. On trouve plusieurs exemples de dormeurs paresseux dans cette exposition, notamment *Jeune Paysanne endormie* de Giovanni Battista Piazzetta (1682/1683-1754) (cat. 38), *Jeune Fille endormie à la chandelle*, anonyme, à la manière de Jean-Baptiste Santerre (1658-1717) (cat. 37) et *Le Petit Paresseux* de Jean-Baptiste Greuze (1725-1805) datant de 1755 (cat. 40). Notons que les deux tableaux de paresseuses sont teintés d'érotisme, car oisiveté et disponibilité sexuelle sont chez elles associées, alors que dans la peinture représentant le garçon, c'est l'abandon du devoir qui est mis en avant.

La *Jeune Paysanne endormie* de Giovanni Battista Piazzetta, conservée à la Residenzgalerie de Salzbourg (cat. 38), dépeint, avec un effet de raccourci saisissant, une jeune paysanne endormie à même le sol. Sa tête repose sur son bras droit, lui-même placé sur un vêtement négligemment plié. Son bras gauche retient un panier contenant les fruits et légumes qu'elle a peut-être tenté de vendre, en vain, au marché. Le creux de sa paume gauche est peint avec un effet de raccourci en trompe-l'œil tel que la main semble dépasser du cadre ovale du tableau, comme pour inviter le spectateur à y déposer quelques pièces en échange d'une pomme de son panier. Ou peut-être de quelque autre service ? Comme la plupart des dormeuses évoquées jusqu'à présent, cette

32. Cette série de gravures des sept péchés capitaux fut conçue par Philip Galle et gravée par Hieronymus Wierix. La série entière est, entre autres, détenue par les Fine Arts Museums de San Francisco (Achenbach Foundation). Pour en voir des reproductions : http://art.famsf.org/philip-galle. Consulté le 13/02/2015. La paresse est également représentée par une figure endormie, en l'occurrence un moine, dans *Les Sept Péchés capitaux et les Quatre Dernières Étapes humaines* de Jérôme Bosch (v. 1450, Madrid, Prado).

représentation est clairement empreinte d'érotisme puisqu'elle dévoile, en plein milieu du tableau, une poitrine ferme et engageante, dont la taille et la forme rappellent celles des pommes. Le *Jeune Berger* (*cf.* fig. page 174, pendant cat. 38) sert de pendant à la *Jeune Paysanne endormie*. Il s'agit d'une autre figure de fantaisie, masculine cette fois, également placée tout près du plan pictural. Bien qu'elle ne soit pas endormie, cette figure n'en semble pas moins insondable dans la mesure où son profil échappe au spectateur, les yeux cachés par un chapeau à large bord.

À première vue, la figure délicate de la *Jeune Fille endormie à la chandelle*, à la manière de Santerre (cat. 37), semble très différente de celle de la paysanne de Piazzetta. En y regardant de plus près, on voit toutefois qu'elle appartient également à la classe laborieuse, comme l'attestent sa robe simple, l'absence d'apparat et, plus important encore, le fait qu'elle semble s'être endormie sur ses travaux d'aiguille. Sa tête repose sur une surface inclinée recouverte d'un mouchoir, ou peut-être d'un vêtement. Au coin de la table sont posés une paire de ciseaux et du fil à coudre. La chandelle placée près d'elle indique qu'elle a passé une partie de la nuit à son ouvrage. Bien sûr, cet éclairage est également l'occasion pour le peintre de créer un effet de clair-obscur, technique introduite par le Caravage et popularisée par ses successeurs, en particulier en France avec Georges de La Tour et aux Pays-Bas avec des artistes tels que Gerrit van Honthorst d'Utrecht, Gérard Dou de Leyde et son élève Godfried Schalcken, à qui ce tableau fut un temps attribué. Tous ces artistes ont peint des figures de fantaisie, souvent rendues plus énigmatiques par la lueur de la chandelle éclairant le décor. En réalité, la *Jeune Fille endormie à la chandelle* est probablement davantage porteuse de significations variées qu'énigmatique. C'est à la fois l'image voluptueuse d'une jeune fille rendue vulnérable par son sommeil et une image de paresse. En même temps, le tableau suscite la compassion par son évocation de la vie difficile de cette jeune fille à peine sortie de l'enfance forcée à travailler de longues heures durant.

Le Petit Paresseux, de Jean-Baptiste Greuze (cat. 40) appartient à une longue tradition iconographique d'élèves, de savants et de moines assoupis sur leur livre. Ces peintures représentent généralement l'acédie, péché capital de paresse, plus particulièrement lorsqu'elle se manifeste par le délaissement d'une tâche intellectuelle ou spirituelle. Toutefois dans le tableau de Greuze, même si cette interprétation n'est pas complètement mise de côté, elle semble plus nuancée du fait que le « coupable » est un jeune enfant, un garçonnet adorable de surcroît, auquel nous pardonnons volontiers l'ennui dans lequel l'ont plongé ses leçons. Peinte à une époque où l'on considérait de plus en plus les enfants comme des individus à part entière, aux intérêts et aux modes d'apprentissage différents de ceux des adultes, cette œuvre peut même être vue comme une critique à peine voilée des mornes manuels scolaires traditionnels. La devise d'Horace « *Delectando monemus* » (« Instruisons-les tout en les amusant ») fut peu à peu adoptée par les éducateurs éclairés de l'époque de Greuze. L'éditeur britannique John Newbery choisit même d'imprimer la devise « L'instruction par l'amusement » sur son abécédaire moderne, *A Little Pretty Pocket-Book, intended for the Amusement of Little Master Tommy and Pretty Miss Polly* (1744). Non content d'enseigner l'alphabet de façon divertissante grâce à des images et des poèmes inspirés de jeux d'enfants, ce livre était vendu avec, en supplément, une balle ou un pique-aiguilles, selon le sexe de l'enfant[33]. On peut se demander si le petit garçon de Greuze avait accès à ce nouveau genre de littérature ou s'il étudiait encore dans de vieux manuels scolaires soporifiques.

Le Petit Paresseux trouve son équivalent dans un autre tableau de Greuze, datant de 1759 : *La Tricoteuse endormie* (*cf.* fig. page 178, cat. 40). Ces deux tableaux figuraient, à une certaine époque, dans la collection d'Ange Laurent Lalive de Jully, un financier français grand collectionneur d'art. Il n'est pas exclu que ces deux tableaux aient été réalisés en pendants, dans la mesure où ils représentent deux enfants endormis, un garçon et une fille, qui négligent tous deux les activités propres à leur genre. Toutefois, ces tableaux sont de dimensions différentes et ils n'ont probablement pas été peints à la même époque[34]. Il est fort possible, cependant, qu'ils aient été accrochés tels des pendants dans la collection de Lalive.

Le sommeil de l'innocence

Comme nous l'avons vu précédemment, l'état de sommeil peut être propice à l'activité de l'imagination, produisant des rêves et des cauchemars extraordinaires. À partir du début de la Renaissance et jusqu'au XXe siècle, les dormeurs apparaissent entourés de leurs visions oniriques. *Le Rêve* de Raphaël, *Le sommeil de la raison engendre des monstres* de Goya (aquatinte), *Le Cauchemar* de Füssli, *L'esprit des morts veille* de Gauguin, *La Nuit* de Hodler : dans tous ces tableaux figurent des dormeurs et leurs visions. Ces représentations du sommeil mettant en scène des dormeurs tout sauf paisibles peuvent être comparées à celles dépeignant le sommeil comme un état de repos bien mérité, de paix intérieure et même d'innocence, cet état que Macbeth décrit comme « l'innocent sommeil,/ Le sommeil qui démêle les fils enchevêtrés du souci,/ Lui, le bain qui lave le dur labeur, la mort de chaque jour de vie,/ Baume des esprits blessés, seconde offrande de la grande Nature/ Chef nourricier du festin de la vie » (acte II, scène 2)[35]. Un tel sommeil est la récompense du dur labeur (comme dans *Les Moissonneurs* de Pieter Bruegel l'Ancien, conservé au Metropolitan Museum of Art de New York), ou de la bonne conscience et de la foi. Le Christ endormi à bord d'un bateau en pleine tempête sur le lac de Tibériade, qui est représenté dans plusieurs tableaux d'Eugène Delacroix[36], constitue un exemple du sommeil comme paix intérieure, résultant de la confiance en la providence divine. Les enfants endormis, fréquemment présents dans l'art à partir du XVIIe siècle, incarnent le sommeil innocent et « confiant », comme dans les œuvres de Rembrandt, de Jean-François Millet, de Vincent van Gogh et de Bernhard Keil.

Bien que la *Fillette dormant* de Keil, présente dans cette exposition (cat. 36), offre des similarités de sujet avec les deux tableaux de Greuze précédemment cités, elle s'en distingue de plusieurs

33. Ce « petit livre de poche » devint très populaire et fut également publié aux États-Unis. Pour consulter une édition complète en ligne de la version américaine : http://lcweb2.loc.gov/cgi-bin/ampage. Consulté le 07/11/2014.

34. Dans son catalogue raisonné de l'œuvre de Greuze (Paris, 1908), Jean Martin précise que *Le Petit Paresseux* (cat. 40) était exposé au Salon de 1755, il aurait donc été peint en 1754 ou 1755. *La Tricoteuse endormie* date de 1759.

35. Shakespeare, 2014, p. 40.

36. Plusieurs d'entre eux figuraient dans l'exposition *Delacroix, les dernières années*, aux Galeries nationales du Grand Palais (Paris, 1998). Pour voir des reproductions et pour plus d'explications, consulter le catalogue de l'exposition en question.

manières. En effet, peinte près d'un siècle plus tôt, cette œuvre est de style baroque et non rococo et, surtout, son sujet et son message semblent également différents. Contrairement aux deux enfants bourgeois de Greuze, bien à l'abri à l'école ou chez eux, la petite fille de Keil se trouve dans un espace indéfini. La tête sur un coussin, elle dort sur un matelas grossier, mais ses vêtements ne sont pas ceux d'une vagabonde. Il pourrait s'agir d'une jeune fille de cuisine, dormant dans l'arrière-cuisine ou dans le garde-manger. Au creux de ses jambes repliées se trouve un panier contenant ses affaires, parmi lesquelles, détail intéressant, on distingue un livre, probablement un missel ou un almanach. De toutes les figures endormies présentes visibles dans cette exposition, c'est celle qui ressemble le moins à une figure de « fantaisie ». En effet, le sujet frappe par son apparente « authenticité », par le naturel de ce portrait d'une jeune fille dormant paisiblement dans un coin sombre. Le tableau de Keil suggère une relation personnelle entre son sujet, la petite fille endormie, et l'artiste ou peut-être le commanditaire de l'œuvre.

Les figures endormies constituent une sous-catégorie singulière parmi les figures de fantaisie. Alors que les autres figures de fantaisie communiquent une émotion ou une humeur par l'expression de leur visage, un geste de la main et/ou le langage corporel en général, les figures endormies emploient des moyens plus détournés. Leurs vêtements, leur gestuelle (comme dans le tableau de Jean-Baptiste Deshays) et, plus rarement, une position ou un mouvement de la main apparemment involontaire (comme dans la *Jeune Paysanne endormie* de Piazzetta), peuvent guider notre lecture des figures de fantaisie endormies. Pourtant, cette lecture est le plus souvent conditionnée par ce que l'on connaît des modèles iconographiques célèbres, voire populaires, du sommeil. Il suffit de regarder *Blanche-Neige et les Sept Nains* vus par Walt Disney pour trouver des modèles iconographiques comparables à ceux qui ont été abordés dans cet essai. Telle Endymion, Blanche-Neige endormie dans son cercueil de verre est le symbole de la mort et de l'amour, tandis que Dormeur, son équivalent comique, représente la paresse. À l'évidence, ces modèles iconographiques du sommeil trouvent leur origine dans des perceptions et des associations profondément ancrées dans la culture occidentale.

Petra ten-Doesschate Chu

LA TÊTE DE VIEILLARD DANS L'ART EUROPÉEN: SACRÉE ET PROFANE

En janvier 2015, lors d'un séjour à New York, j'ai assisté à une vente aux enchères de tableaux de maîtres anciens par Sotheby's. Comme je préparais cet article, mon attention a été attirée par le nombre étonnant de têtes de vieillards exposées, dont un saint Joseph du Greco, le saint Jacques et le saint André de José de Ribera, un saint Antoine Abbé attribué à Vélasquez, la tête d'un vieillard attribuée à Jan Lievens, un Démocrite joyeux et un Héraclite triste de Charles Antoine Coypel, une étude d'homme barbu attribuée à un disciple d'Augustin Carrache et un saint Pierre en prière de Matthias Stom[1]. L'ensemble de ces images témoigne de l'essor du genre qui fait l'objet du présent article : le portrait en buste d'un homme barbu âgé ou vieillissant. Dans chaque cas, l'artiste s'est appliqué à dépeindre les traits ridés et expressifs de l'individu qui était vraisemblablement un mendiant posant comme modèle afin de gagner quelques sous (même si la représentation de mendiants et clochards en tant que tels est un sujet à part). Un certain nombre des « vieillards » que j'ai observés chez Sotheby's prennent l'apparence de saints répertoriés bien que ni la tenue ni les accessoires (si ce n'est un livre, un pommeau d'épée ou un bâton) ne détournent vraiment l'attention de l'expression du visage, tour à tour mélancolique, songeuse, narquoise ou même joyeuse, comme dans le cas de Démocrite. Toutes ces peintures présentaient dans l'ensemble un intérêt scientifique, mais l'une d'entre elles dépassait d'une bonne tête, si j'ose dire, les autres. Il s'agissait de l'*Étude pour le portrait d'un homme barbu* par Van Dyck (fig. page suivante).

L'Homme barbu de Van Dyck appartient au genre de la tête de vieillard, le visage tourné vers le côté et légèrement vers le haut, les yeux levés vers le ciel comme en adoration, les longs cheveux bouclés tombant en cascade sur les épaules et la barbe éparse grisonnante. Les traits du modèle sont distingués et nous paraissent quelque peu familiers, même si son identité demeure inconnue[2]. La nature inachevée de la peinture et son exécution sommaire et rapide suggèrent

1. Sotheby's, New York, 29 janvier 2015, *I*, lots 41, 46, 48, 49, 55, 88 ; *II*, lots 314, 315, 330.
2. Bien que l'attribution à Van Dyck soit acceptée depuis au moins les années 1960, la peinture était attribuée, au XIXe siècle, à l'artiste anglais William Dobson et fut vendue en 1911 en tant qu'étude de l'éminent architecte Inigo Jones. Christie's, Londres, 7 juillet 1911, lot 42, « W. Dobson – Head of Inigo Jones ».

Sir Antoon Van Dyck, *Étude pour le portrait d'un homme barbu*, Sotheby's New York, 29 janvier 2015

qu'elle a été réalisée, comme beaucoup d'autres, dans l'atelier de Van Dyck et de son maître Pierre Paul Rubens, et qu'il s'agit vraisemblablement d'une étude, peut-être destinée à être intégrée dans une composition historique plus vaste. Toutefois, comme beaucoup d'autres images de la sorte, elle a depuis acquis le statut d'œuvre d'art à part entière. Bien qu'on ne connaisse pas son histoire antérieure, on sait qu'elle faisait partie, au XIXe siècle, de la collection d'Andrew Fountaine à Narford Hall dans le Norfolk, remarquable collection particulière de tableaux de maîtres anciens qui comptait des œuvres célèbres de maîtres italiens, français, hollandais et flamands[3]. Comme nous le verrons, l'acquisition de telles œuvres par des collectionneurs aussi prestigieux et éminents joua un rôle important dans la vogue que connut ce genre au cours des XVIIe et XVIIIe siècles.

Avant d'examiner la façon dont la tête de vieillard a évolué durant la période, il nous faut prendre en considération un certain nombre de questions fondamentales liées à la vieillesse qui dépassent de loin les paramètres de l'histoire de l'art. Dans l'un de ses derniers livres, *The Long History of Old Age*, l'historienne Pat Thane, qui fait autorité en la matière, remet en cause un certain nombre de perceptions profondément ancrées dans les esprits ; tout d'abord, la vieillesse est, depuis des siècles et même des millénaires, beaucoup plus courante que ce que l'on croit généralement. Au XVIIIe siècle, par exemple, au moins dix pour cent de la population française, espagnole et anglaise était âgée de plus de soixante ans[4]. Le deuxième point, tout aussi pertinent, concerne l'âge à partir duquel un individu était considéré comme vieux. Thane constate une « remarquable continuité » au cours des siècles, puisque la vieillesse commence vers soixante ou soixante-dix ans, de l'Antiquité grecque jusqu'à aujourd'hui. Cependant, fait-elle remarquer, c'est la condition physique et mentale qui définit l'âge, autrefois comme de nos jours, et pas seulement le passage des années. La vieillesse peut évoquer la faiblesse mais aussi la *force* de l'âge ou la noblesse vénérable de

3. *Cf.* « Catalogue of Pictures from the Celebrated Fountaine Collection, Removed from Narford Hall, Norfolk, chiefly formed by Sir Andrew Fountaine, in the early part of the last century », Christie's, Londres, 7 juillet 1894. Le tableau en question correspondait au lot 9, « W. Dobson. Head of a Gentleman », et s'est vendu £50 8s.

4. Thane, 2005, p. 9.

l'esprit, trope qui sous-tend les représentations de vieillards étudiées dans le présent article puisque ces individus incarnent des prophètes, des guerriers ou encore des apôtres. Il convient également d'envisager la vieillesse au regard des autres âges ou de ce que l'on appelle les « âges de l'homme », dont le nombre varie de seulement trois (jeunesse, maturité et vieillesse) à sept selon Shakespeare. Ainsi que l'écrit Thane, on admet généralement deux types de vieillesse : le « jeune vieil âge » et le « vieux vieil âge » ou, comme les Français les appellent, le « troisième âge » puis le « quatrième âge ». Bien qu'il empiète parfois sur le quatrième âge, l'aspect souvent héroïque de la tête de vieillard, avec des attributs de force, de sagesse et de perspicacité, évoque généralement le troisième âge. Que ce soit sous une apparence sacrée ou profane, le vieillard fut un emblème important dans l'Europe entière tout au long des XVIIe et XVIIIe siècles, même si, nous le verrons, ses diverses manifestations dans différents pays de l'Ancien Continent étaient inextricablement liées à des circonstances et conditions particulières, qu'elles soient religieuses, sociales ou culturelles.

Il est évident que la représentation de la tête de vieillard s'est transformée au XVIIe siècle, mais par où commencer ? *Saint Jérôme écrivant* (Rome, Galleria Borghese), apparemment offert par le Caravage à son mécène, le cardinal Scipione Caffarelli-Borghese, à Rome en 1605, constitue un bon point de départ. L'image est réduite au strict minimum : un vieillard à demi nu associé à une tête de mort. Avec cette figure et son compagnon à la composition plus resserrée, *Saint Jérôme en méditation* (musée de Montserrat), le Caravage créa un mode de représentation qui exerça une forte influence sur ses disciples, les peintres dits caravagesques, en Italie et dans certaines parties du nord de l'Europe. L'image de saint Jérôme, en particulier, contribua fortement à la diffusion de l'œuvre du Caravage et de sa méthode picturale. Figure clé de l'Église paléochrétienne, saint Jérôme était un personnage important en tant que commentateur des Évangiles et traducteur de la Bible en latin. Son choix d'une vie érémitique et ascétique et la réclusion qu'il s'imposait pour mener à bien ses recherches faisaient aussi de lui le sujet idéal pour l'étude d'un personnage isolé. D'innombrables représentations de saint Jérôme écrivant ou en méditation ont été réalisées à la suite de l'exemple pionnier du Caravage. Les tableaux des artistes italiens Lionello Spada (1610, Rome, Galleria Nazionale d'Arte Antica) et Orazio Gentileschi (vers 1609-1611, Turin, Museo Civico d'Arte Antica e Palazzo Madama) en sont des illustrations caractéristiques et précoces. Plus tard dans le siècle, le sujet fut traité de façon similaire par, entre autres, José de Ribera, Simon Vouet, Georges de La Tour et Hendrick Van Somer, peintres respectivement espagnol, français et hollandais.

Dans le cadre du présent article et du brouillage du fictif et du réel, le *Saint Jérôme* d'Orazio Gentileschi (fig. page suivante) est d'un intérêt particulier car, exceptionnellement, nous disposons d'un témoignage de première main du vieillard ayant posé comme modèle, un pèlerin âgé de soixante-treize ans du nom de Giovanni Pietro Molli. Ce dernier, alors qu'il témoignait lors du procès du viol d'Artemisia, la fille de Gentileschi, déclara que l'artiste « [le] fit [se] déshabiller jusqu'à la taille pour faire un St Jérôme qui [lui] ressemblât ». Selon le barbier de Gentileschi,

Orazio Gentileschi, *Saint Jérôme*, Turin, Museo Civico d'Arte Antica

Molli était « de belle apparence, avec un visage comme celui de saint Paul, le crâne dégarni, des cheveux blancs et une belle barbe fournie, aussi bien sur les joues que sur le menton »[5]. En effet, Gentileschi était tellement captivé par le modèle qu'était Molli qu'il l'employa trois ou quatre jours par semaine pendant les quarante jours du Carême, en vue d'une série d'études d'autres figures bibliques[6].

Que saint Jérôme ait attiré les disciples plus tardifs du Caravage comme personnification de la vieillesse sanctifiée est particulièrement manifeste dans les diverses représentations du saint par José de Ribera, notamment les versions de la Galleria Doria Pamphilj à Rome, de la Pinacoteca di Brera à Milan, du musée Thyssen-Bornemisza à Madrid et les deux versions du musée du Prado à Madrid. Bien qu'espagnol de naissance et de formation, Ribera (également connu sous le nom de « lo Spagnoletto ») exerça son activité de peintre en Italie, à Parme et à Rome, avant de s'installer en 1616 à Naples, où sa carrière progressa sous le mécénat des vice-rois espagnols et de l'Église catholique. À Naples, les modes d'expression artistique et le choix des sujets étaient de plus en plus déterminés par les contraintes imposées par la Contre-Réforme qui, à petite échelle, eut un effet décisif sur le genre artistique examiné ici. L'art sacré napolitain jouissait d'une hégémonie culturelle qui étouffait tout désir d'innovation artistique dans le cadre d'une économie de marché. Les occasions qui se présentaient de produire des images d'ascètes éprouvés par l'âge tels que saint Jérôme étaient sans fin et, en effet, le fait qu'on encourageait la représentation naturaliste du corps humain entraîna une fascination morbide pour le flétrissement de la chair reproduite avec une attention méticuleuse et une volonté d'exactitude anatomique. Il était primordial, après tout, que celui qui regarde le tableau soit non seulement témoin de la douleur et de l'abnégation du personnage souffrant mais éprouve également de l'empathie envers ce dernier. Il a été noté que « les thèmes les plus importants étaient les sacrements, le péché originel tel qu'il est présenté dans l'épisode biblique de la chute de l'Homme et le culte des saints et des vertus. L'obéissance était la qualité

5. Christiansen, Mann, 2001, p. 94, cat. 16.
6. *Idem*, p. 96.

suprême »[7]. Afin de suivre l'évolution du portrait de vieillard comme genre à part entière et cette fois-ci profane, il nous faut donc élargir notre horizon en nous tournant vers ces artistes qui, bien que profondément influencés par les tendances artistiques du sud de l'Europe, échappèrent aux contraintes de leurs mécènes et de leur milieu culturel et religieux.

C'est grâce à l'influence du Caravage que le portrait de vieillard devint un genre à part entière dans le sud de l'Europe, dans le cadre d'une tradition d'art sacré où prédominait le mécénat de l'Église. Dans le nord de l'Europe, si le genre conserva une teneur sacrée, une tendance profane se développa avec l'émergence d'un mécénat séculier et d'un véritable marché de l'art. Parmi les artistes ayant traité du sujet, Pierre Paul Rubens fut un intermédiaire notoire entre le Nord et le Sud pendant les premières décennies du XVIIe siècle.

Élevé à Anvers dans la religion catholique, Rubens arriva en Italie en 1600. Il y étudia de près l'art des maîtres de la Renaissance et du Caravage, son contemporain. C'est en Italie qu'il commença à produire des études de têtes, les plus célèbres étant les *tronies* de vieillards aux longues barbes flottantes et aux visages expressifs. À son retour à Anvers en 1609 et jusqu'au début des années 1620, ces études de tête devinrent une partie essentielle de son travail en atelier, alors en pleine croissance. C'est dans cet atelier qu'elles furent exploitées par ses assistants au sein de grandes compositions historiques. Bien qu'elles en vinssent à être appréciées comme œuvres d'art à part entière, prisées comme telles par les collectionneurs, les têtes étaient, comme il a été dit, « essentiellement un outil pour contrôler les images peintes par ses collaborateurs les moins expérimentés »[8]. La plupart du temps, Rubens peignait ses études de tête sur des panneaux de bois, supports plus durables que les autres, et il réalisait parfois la même tête sous différents angles sur un même panneau. Cette pratique fut également adoptée par ses contemporains plus jeunes, Antoon Van Dyck et Jacob Jordaens. Alors que ces têtes avaient un rôle pratique en atelier, leur valeur commerciale augmenta de manière régulière quand elles pénétrèrent le marché de l'art et se retrouvèrent dans des collections particulières dans toute l'Europe. Leur popularité, ajoutée au fait qu'elles avaient été conçues pour être répliquées, incita aussi par la suite, comme nous le verrons, des artistes à les copier et à en produire des variations, parfois dans un but frauduleux.

Alors que le rôle pédagogique de Rubens, par son travail considérable en atelier, permit de promouvoir de façon significative l'étude de la tête de vieillard, l'évolution du sujet comme « figure de fantaisie », ou de ce que l'on désigne en Grande-Bretagne sous le terme de *fancy picture*, fut plus intimement liée à la pratique des peintres des Pays-Bas, notamment dans les cercles artistiques d'Utrecht et d'Amsterdam. Bien que centre économique modeste, Utrecht était reconnu, dès les années 1620, comme le foyer international de la production artistique

7. De Maio, 1982, p. 33.
8. Black, 2014, p. 65.

dans la République des Provinces-Unies. Ses principaux artistes, dont Hendrick ter Brugghen, Gerard Van Honthorst et Dirck van Baburen, se formèrent à Rome, où ils s'imprégnèrent des procédés du Caravage en matière de lumière, de représentation naturaliste du corps humain et d'accentuation de l'expressivité des figures au sein de mises en scène spectaculaires. Et pourtant, tout en continuant à produire à Utrecht des peintures narratives religieuses influencées par le dogme de la Contre-Réforme catholique, ces artistes se lancèrent dans le filon des têtes profanes de personnages isolés. En 1628, Ter Brugghen réalisa deux pendants, des portraits des philosophes Héraclite et Démocrite (Amsterdam, Rijksmuseum), l'un se désolant de la folie humaine et l'autre, s'en riant[9]. À cette époque, des compositions similaires avec un ou deux personnages en plan resserré gagnaient en popularité : les personnages illustraient des proverbes ou des adages, ou servaient d'emblèmes des sens, des mois ou des saisons. Par exemple, les vieillards faisaient partie intégrante de représentations allégoriques de l'Hiver, comme dans le tableau d'Hendrick Bloemaert datant de 1631 où est assis un personnage à la barbe fournie, élégamment vêtu et coiffé d'un chapeau de fourrure, qui se réchauffe les mains au-dessus d'un petit brasero, observé par une vieille dame au visage parcheminé[10].

L'une des figures fondamentales dans l'évolution et la multiplication des études de personnage isolé n'est autre qu'Abraham Bloemaert, le père d'Hendrick Bloemaert. Bien qu'il ne fût jamais allé en l'Italie, Abraham Bloemaert était sensible au style naturaliste qui faisait florès à Rome et Naples chez les disciples du Caravage. Dans le cadre de son enseignement et de son travail en atelier, Bloemaert avait pour habitude de faire des études détaillées de parties du corps, de têtes, et des compositions entières, à des fins didactiques, pour que ses élèves puissent ensuite les copier. Un recueil imprimé de dessins gravés, réalisé par Frederick, le fils de Bloemaert, indique que les études physionomiques de vieillards jouaient un rôle important[11]. En outre, Bloemaert réalisa aussi des têtes peintes, ou *tronies*, souvent tout à fait abouties. Comme il a été dit, ses *tronies* « doivent être considérés comme des peintures à part entière », notamment parce qu'un seul d'entre eux a été intégré de manière identifiable dans une composition plus vaste[12]. Bloemaert réalisa plus de vingt portraits achevés de personnes âgées, parfois à partir d'un même modèle et dont certains sont des pendants. À la différence d'autres *tronies* peints par des artistes d'Utrecht, les têtes de Bloemaert sont plus petites que nature et se détachent sur des fonds unis. La plupart des portraits sont également datés. S'échelonnant entre 1632 et 1641, ces dates correspondent à l'époque à laquelle Bloemaert (né en 1566) était lui-même un vieil homme et se sentait peut-être personnellement concerné par les effets de l'âge. Parmi les têtes de vieillards de Bloemaert les plus remarquables, on peut citer une petite huile sur bois de la National Gallery of Art à Washington. Une fois n'est pas coutume, l'homme

9. Spicer, Orr, 1997, cat. nos 23, 24, p. 201-203.
10. Christie's, Londres, 2 décembre 2014, lot 25. *Cf.* Roethlisberger, Bok, 1993, I, p. 269 et 456, no H27 ; II, fig. H33.
11. Bloemaert, 1740. Le livre a d'abord été publié entre 1650 et 1656 en plusieurs parties sous le titre *Artis Apellae liber*, les planches sont gravées par Frederick Bloemaert d'après les dessins de son père.
12. Gero Seelig *in* Spicer, Orr, 1997, p. 232.

est glabre, sa chemise ouverte sur sa poitrine permettant à l'artiste de s'appliquer à rendre l'ossature du modèle. Les cheveux sont relativement courts mais hirsutes, l'expression, éplorée et mélancolique. Bien qu'on puisse l'assimiler à un saint ou à un philosophe fictif, l'image ne se prête pas à des associations allégoriques mais se suffit à elle-même comme représentation d'un homme âgé, ni en saint ni en pécheur.

À Utrecht, les têtes de vieillards d'Abraham Bloemaert faisaient figure d'anomalies. Cependant, s'il l'on considère le cercle artistique d'Amsterdam à la même période, on s'aperçoit que de telles représentations y étaient de plus en plus courantes, notamment dans l'œuvre de ses deux principaux peintres, Rembrandt et Jan Lievens. De tous les artistes mentionnés jusqu'ici, aucun n'est aussi étroitement associé à la représentation de la vieillesse que Rembrandt. Né à Leyde en 1606, Rembrandt grandit dans un monde qui vit se réaliser l'indépendance politique et culturelle de la Hollande. Fils d'un père protestant et d'une mère catholique, il fut élevé dans une atmosphère de tolérance religieuse. Il prenait pour modèles des personnes qu'il connaissait : entourage familial, voisins et membres de sa communauté, des personnes qu'il admirait et respectait. Dans son art, la frontière entre les genres est généralement floue ; ainsi, le portrait et l'étude de caractère sont toujours intimement liés. L'exemple le plus remarquable est sans doute la célèbre représentation d'une vieille femme, qui a fait école, peinte à Leyde par Rembrandt à la fin des années 1620 et offerte peu après au roi d'Angleterre Charles Ier[13]. On pense que l'image, qui recouvre un portrait de vieillard, est peut-être celle de la mère de l'artiste, Neeltgen Willemsdochter, même si l'identité de cette femme en particulier n'a aucune importance au regard du véritable sujet, celui du grand âge vénérable.

Pendant ses années de formation à Leyde, Rembrandt ne fut pas seul dans sa quête : il collabora étroitement avec Jan Lievens avec lequel il partagea cet intérêt ainsi qu'un atelier (et parfois des modèles) de 1626 à 1631. Parmi les *tronies* réalisés par Lievens à cette époque, on compte le *Portrait d'un homme barbu portant un béret* : le couvre-chef et la tenue confèrent au sujet un air contemporain qui le démarque des représentations traditionnelles du vieil âge idéalisé et sanctifié. Lievens a été, jusque récemment, sous-estimé par rapport à Rembrandt. Or ses têtes attiraient déjà, au début des années 1630, l'attention de collectionneurs de premier plan, dont Frédéric-Henri de Nassau, prince d'Orange, et son secrétaire Constantin Huygens. C'est peut-être ce succès qui l'encouragea à s'installer en Angleterre, vers 1632, pour y travailler à la cour de Charles Ier. Ce fut également le succès qu'il connut à la cour anglaise qui le détourna probablement de ce genre dans lequel il avait excellé et avait été pionnier.

À Amsterdam, Rembrandt rechercha pour ses peintures de vieillards des membres de la communauté juive, notamment les ashkénazes réprouvés, pauvres et âgés, communauté qui

13. Une vieille femme, appelée « La mère de l'artiste », huile sur panneau, 61,3 × 47,4 cm, vers 1627-1629, Royal Collection Trust, RCIN, 405000. Tableau offert à Charles Ier par sir Robert Kerr, devenu ensuite comte d'Ancram.

« était une source inépuisable de modèles du vieil âge chenu et de la sagesse acquise par acceptation silencieuse du destin qui était le leur »[14]. Rembrandt illustrait parfois l'appartenance ethnique de ses personnages en intégrant des tenues et coiffes exotiques, par exemple dans l'*Homme en costume oriental* (Amsterdam, Rijksmuseum). Il utilisa aussi toute une gamme de costumes pour conférer un air aristocratique ou militaire à ses figures, sans doute pour satisfaire les demandes de clients et du marché local. Un des modèles les plus facilement reconnaissables est le vieillard ayant posé à la fois pour un *Vieil Homme à la chaîne d'or* (Chicago, Art Institute), un *Vieil Homme en costume militaire* (Los Angeles, Getty Center) et le portrait connu sous le nom de *Noble slave* (New York, The Metropolitan Museum of Art). Dans chaque cas, bien que la tenue suggère un personnage différent et souvent haut en couleur, c'est la physionomie du modèle qui attire l'œil, car le véritable sujet est bel et bien le visage de ce vieillard anonyme au regard énigmatique et impénétrable.

Jusqu'à présent, nous avons envisagé le portrait du vieillard par rapport à un artiste, un pays ou une ville. Cependant, ce genre ne se réduisait pas à certains artistes, certaines cultures ou même certains modèles. Au XVIIe siècle, la carrière du médailliste Abraham Simon, à la fois comme artiste et comme modèle, peut faire l'objet d'une étude de cas fascinante qui témoigne de la fluidité du genre et de sa place en Europe. Simon, fils d'un commerçant français naturalisé anglais, est né à Londres en 1617. Une fois diplômé de l'université d'Oxford, il suivit une formation d'avocat, mais, pendant les années 1640, il travailla comme fabricant de modèles et de médailles en cire aux côtés de son frère aîné, Thomas Simon. Après un voyage aux Pays-Bas, Abraham Simon se rendit au début des années 1650 en Suède, où il s'attira les bonnes grâces de la reine Christine, qui lui remit une médaille qu'il portait avec fierté sur une double chaîne[15]. Par la suite, Simon se joignit au cortège de la reine lors d'une visite à la cour française, après son abdication. Comme Christine, Simon avait un comportement et une apparence pour le moins excentriques, « un homme de petite taille, qui faisait penser à quelque antique philosophe et qui portait toujours ses cheveux et sa barbe à la mode de ses ancêtres »[16]. En 1660, lorsque Charles II accéda au trône d'Angleterre, Simon fut employé à la Cour mais il tomba rapidement en disgrâce à la suite d'un acte irrespectueux envers le duc d'York[17]. « Ainsi ignoré et méprisé, il sombra dans l'obscurité et le besoin, mais conserva ses anciennes habitudes et apparence... » Et c'est précisément cette allure qui « faisait fureur auprès de plusieurs peintres éminents, lesquels entreprirent de le dessiner de son vivant »[18].

14. White, 1984, p. 75. *Cf* aussi Baskind, février 2007, sur http://sephardic.fiu.edu/journal/SamanthaBaskind.pdf. Consulté le 19/02/2015.
15. Le British Museum possède une médaille en argent par Stuart, datée de 1650 environ, représentant Simon avec barbe et cheveux longs, de profil, portant la médaille de la reine Christine autour du cou, suspendue à une double chaîne, inv. M.7554. Dans la même collection, on trouve un médaillon avec un portrait d'Abraham Simon en cire rose sur ardoise noire, provenant de la collection d'Hans Sloane et représentant un vieillard de profil tourné vers la droite, avec une barbe et des cheveux longs et hirsutes, lequel semble être son autoportrait, SLPictures.292.
16. Vertue, 1780, p. 58.
17. *Idem*, p. 59-60.
18. *Idem*, p. 60.

Sir Godfrey Kneller, *Étude de tête de vieil homme (Abraham Simon)*, collection particulière

Peter Lely, Peintre principal en ordinaire de Charles II, est l'un de ces artistes qui s'intéressèrent à Simon en tant que modèle. Son portrait en buste ayant appartenu au célèbre sculpteur Grinling Gibbons, aujourd'hui perdu, est attesté par une gravure du Néerlandais Abraham Blooteling datant de 1680 environ[19]. Parmi les autres artistes, le peintre de cour danois Heinrich Dittmers exécuta une figure de saint Jérôme sous les traits de Simon (Copenhague, Statens Museum for Kunst). Puisqu'il n'y a, pour autant que je sache, aucune preuve de voyage de Dittmers en Angleterre, le tableau, signé et daté de 1665, a peut-être été peint lors d'un voyage de Simon au Danemark. Cependant, c'est Godfrey Kneller qui s'intéressa le plus à Simon. Né allemand et formé par Ferdinand Bol aux Pays-Bas, il travailla à Rome, Venise et Hambourg, avant de s'installer en Angleterre en 1676 et de succéder à Lely comme Peintre principal du roi en 1680. Dans un premier portrait à mi-corps, connu seulement grâce à un dessin à la sanguine du graveur et « connoisseur » George Vertue, Simon est assis, tenant ce qui est probablement une de ses œuvres : un profil en cire sur une tablette en ardoise[20]. Le deuxième portrait est une peinture grandeur nature de Simon vêtu d'un long manteau brun, un grand livre dans les mains, peinture qui a souvent été qualifiée de « saint Jérôme », de « saint ermite » ou même d'« Élisée dans le désert »[21]. Le troisième est une esquisse ovale à l'huile représentant la tête de Simon (fig. ci-dessus). Bien qu'inachevé, comme les *tronies* évoqués plus haut, ce tableau fut sûrement conçu comme œuvre d'art à part entière plutôt que comme étude dans la mesure où Kneller devait être un habitué du genre depuis sa formation aux Pays-Bas. Curieusement, une étude de tête similaire, ovale et de taille identique, inclinée de la même manière, avec Simon comme modèle, a récemment été vendue par Christie's, à Londres, sous le simple titre *Tête d'un homme barbu* ; elle a été attribuée à un artiste anonyme de l'école

19. Pour l'impression de la gravure, avec les lettres « ABRAHAMUS SYMONDS / P. Lely Pinxit / I Smith exced: / A; Blooteling fecit », *cf.* The British Museum, inv. 1902,1011.249. Au British Museum sont conservées deux autres gravures représentant Simon. La première gravure, probablement réalisée par Simon lui-même, représente sa tête à trois âges différents : jeune, adulte et vieux ; ce triple portrait est juché sur les ailes d'un aigle surmontant un globe, où il est inscrit : « Abr Symonds the Medalist / very rare etched by him », inv. 1858,0417.268. La seconde est une gravure de pèlerin avec un bâton, par un graveur inconnu, inv. 1849, 0315.70, qui, bien qu'aujourd'hui identifiée comme étant le dramaturge Thomas Killigrew, pourrait être Abraham Simon, comme le suggère une comparaison avec le modèle représenté sur la gravure exécutée par Booteling d'après Lely.
20. Inscrit au crayon par Vertue sur un vieux montage : « ABRAHAM SYMONDS modeler in wax & embosser of medals. Kneller p. G.Vertue del. » The British Museum, inv. 1852,0124.377.
21. Stewart, 1993, p. 250.

française du XVIIIe siècle[22]. Cependant, il est possible qu'elle soit de la main du jeune artiste suédois Michael Dahl en raison de similitudes stylistiques et du fait qu'il travaillait dans l'atelier de Kneller au début des années 1680. Tout cela ne peut manquer d'intriguer étant donné les liens de Simon avec la Suède. Selon George Vertue, qui écrivit une série de notes biographiques posthumes sur Simon, ses longs cheveux, sa barbe, sa conversation et son apparence négligée étaient calculés pour mettre en valeur son allure de « parfait cynique »[23]. Comme la remarque en a été faite, Kneller avait le mérite « de ne pas s'arrêter aux apparences de l'artiste bourru, sale, excentrique… et d'y déceler l'artiste intelligent et sensible »[24].

Au début du XVIIIe siècle, la tête de vieillard était bel et bien devenue un genre identifiable à part entière, indépendant de toute narration mythologique ou historique de plus grande ampleur. Alors que les anciennes têtes de Rubens avaient été essentiellement réalisées comme modèles pour l'atelier, leur nouveau statut en tant qu'œuvres d'art leur fit gagner en prestige et elles devinrent de plus en plus recherchées par les collectionneurs. L'une d'elles fut achetée en 1758 par un aristocrate irlandais, lord Charlemont, qui la montra à son ami, l'artiste William Hogarth. Dans un premier temps, elle plut à Hogarth, mais ce dernier émit ensuite des réserves quant à son authenticité :

> « Prenez un vieux morceau de toile grossière et représentez un vieux mendiant barbu en cachant ses traits dans des zones d'ombre, faites les yeux rougis et jetez librement quelques coups de crayon dans la barbe, flanquez une large tache de lumière sur le front que vous modulerez par du cirage, vernissez bien le tout, et la chose pourra sans problème être vendue aux enchères. J'ai rarement croisé un poissonnier qui ne réussît point l'un de ces chefs-d'œuvre ; ce vieux Peters, connu pour imiter d'anciens tableaux, avait l'habitude de dire, et même avec mépris, au sujet de cette production un peu facile de Rubens, qu'il lui était très aisé de ch..r des têtes, puisqu'après tout, ma foi, c'était un Néerlandais. »[25]

Jan Pieters III, né à Anvers, était arrivé à Londres en 1685 à l'âge de dix-huit ans, un « homme plein d'énergie, d'un tempérament libre et ouvert, un amateur de bonne compagnie et de boisson ». D'abord élève de Kneller, il devint ensuite son principal assistant d'atelier chargé des drapés. Cependant, il se forgea par la suite une réputation de restaurateur de tableaux et passa maître aussi, semble-t-il, dans l'art du pastiche de têtes de vieillards, qui pouvaient passer pour des originaux dans les maisons de vente aux enchères londoniennes[26].

22. « French School, 18th century, Head of a bearded man », huile sur toile, ovale, 55,3 × 45,7 cm, Christie's, South Kensington, 29 octobre 2010, lot 130.
23. Vertue, « Notebooks », Walpole Society, 18 (1929-1930), p. 123, cité *in* Stewart, 1993, p. 250.
24. Stewart, 1993, p. 251.
25. Lettre de William Hogarth à William Caulfeild, premier comte de Charlemont, 26 novembre 1758. British Library, Add. MS, 40, 015, fol. 20. Cité par Paulson, 1971, II, p. 268 et 451. Bien qu'Hogarth doutât de l'authenticité de son acquisition, Charlemont conserva le tableau, notant : « The Head in question is the uppermost Picture over the Fire Place in the Green Drawing Room » (*ibid.*, f° 19).
26. National Portrait Gallery, Londres, British Picture restorers, 1660-1950 – P, John Peeters, Antwerp to 17685, Londres 1685-1727. http://www.npg.org.uk/research/programmes/directory-of-british-picture-restorers/british-picture-restorers-1600-1950-p.php. Consulté le 26/02/2015.

Le marché des têtes de vieillards, issues des traditions de l'art sacré, demeura florissant au XVIIIe siècle dans toute l'Europe. Pour ne prendre qu'un exemple, le portraitiste et peintre d'histoire romain Pompeo Batoni peignit, dans les années 1740, une série d'apôtres avec Dieu le Père pour le comte Cesare Merenda de Forlì, qui les exposa non pas dans une église ou une chapelle mais dans sa nouvelle galerie de peintures. De petites dimensions et centrées sur l'expression des personnages, ces œuvres épurées sont en réalité des « têtes de caractère » sacrées, à savoir Dieu le Père, saint Pierre et saint Paul, figures exécutées à partir de modèles choisis pour leur parfaite allure de patriarches. Comme cela a été observé, les « apôtres [de Batoni] sont convaincants et naturels, et couvrent un large spectre d'expressions, depuis la vigueur énergique jusqu'à la contemplation introspective »[27]. Ailleurs, à Paris, l'artiste français Nicolas de Largillière réalisa une série d'apôtres pour sa propre demeure rue Geoffrey-l'Angevin, série décrite dans un inventaire comme huit « têtes d'apôtres » et sans doute exécutée pour montrer que son talent s'étendait au-delà du genre du portrait mondain[28]. En Angleterre, Joshua Reynolds réalisa dans un registre sacré une tête de vieillard connue sous le nom de « Joab », inspirée d'un ermite, et son ami Henry Temple, deuxième vicomte Palmerston, en fit l'acquisition[29]. Cette œuvre fut par la suite attribuée à Domenico Fetti. Malgré ces exemples, les sujets profanes étaient de plus en plus convoités par rapport aux sujets sacrés, le mécénat laïc gagnant en importance.

Que ce soit au nord ou au sud des Alpes, les artistes étaient conscients que les têtes de personnages profanes constituaient un marché lucratif. En Allemagne, le portraitiste Balthasar Denner se spécialisa dans les têtes de caractère peintes dans un style naturaliste très détaillé, notamment celle d'une vieille femme qu'il emmenait partout avec lui comme morceau de bravoure (cat. 66). Cette huile fut achetée à l'artiste pour une somme considérable par l'empereur Charles VI, lequel commanda également une tête de vieil homme comme pendant au tableau[30]. Dans le nord de l'Italie, dès les années 1730, les « figures de fantaisie » d'un homologue de Denner, le Vénitien Giuseppe Nogari, trouvèrent facilement preneur dans la haute société, par exemple le comte Charles-Gustave de Tessin, homme d'État suédois, le maréchal allemand Johann Matthias de Schulembourg et Joseph Smith, consul britannique à Venise. Également dans le nord de l'Italie, un artiste un peu plus âgé se révéla particulièrement important dans la diffusion des personnages profanes et influença grandement Nogari ; il s'agit du peintre vénitien Giovanni Battista Piazzetta. Ses dessins à la craie de toute une série de personnages de rue rencontrèrent un grand succès commercial. Parmi ceux qui collectionnèrent les œuvres de Piazzetta, Joseph Smith, le consul britannique à Venise mentionné ci-dessus, acheta un ensemble de trente-six « têtes de caractères », dont plusieurs vieillards, ensemble qui passa ensuite dans la collection de George III. Ces têtes furent imitées et copiées entre autres par les filles du roi[31].

27. *Cf.* Bowron, 2007, p. 8-11.
28. Lastic (de), 1981, p. 24-25.
29. Mannings, Postle, 2000, I, cat. 2133, p. 554-555 ; II, fig. 1675.
30. Pilkington, 1805, p. 153.
31. *Cf.*, par exemple, les bustes d'une paysanne et d'un paysan copiés par la princesse Augusta Sophia (1768-1840), Royal Collection Trust, RCIN 980315.

Ces dessins de Piazzetta inspirèrent une des séries les plus remarquables de ce genre au milieu du XVIIIe siècle, à savoir dix-sept têtes à la craie grandeur nature par Thomas Frye, exécutées entre 1760 et 1762. Il en imprima douze dans un recueil de gravures publié par souscription. À la différence des personnages de Piazzetta, les sujets de Frye étaient résolument bourgeois et d'apparence respectable, inspirés de la famille et des amis de l'artiste. Son vieil homme, par exemple, est très éloigné des mendiants ridés qui servaient habituellement de modèles pour ce genre d'œuvres. Vu de profil avec son visage glabre, son couvre-chef en velours et ses bésicles, il ressemble plutôt à un maître d'école à la retraite. Finalement, les dessins à la craie de Frye servirent de base à des gravures de reproduction, qu'il fit paraître sous forme d'un recueil publié par souscription en 1760 sous le titre *Twelve Mezzotinto Prints from Designs in the Manner of Piazzetta, Drawn from Nature and as Large as Life* (« Douze gravures en mezzotinte à partir de dessins à la manière de Piazzetta, inspirées par la nature et grandeur nature »). Non seulement les séries de gravures de ce type firent florès mais elles attirèrent également les membres des plus hautes sphères du mécénat artistique. Un exemple fascinant en est les têtes de « fantaisie » réalisées par Giandomenico Tiepolo au cours des années 1760, alors qu'il travaillait avec son père et son frère pour le compte de Charles III au palais royal de Madrid. À l'instar de la série de dessins de Frye, les têtes de Tiepolo comprenaient une gamme de personnages variés, dont des jeunes femmes et des hommes orientaux barbus et plus âgés[32].

Au XVIIIe siècle, l'Angleterre faisait partie des plus importants foyers commerciaux de création et d'évolution de la « figure de fantaisie », genre qui y était connu sous le nom de « *fancy picture* ». Non seulement les peintures connaissaient un certain succès, mais aussi et surtout les gravures, qui s'adressaient à un vaste public. En effet, les pionniers de la *fancy picture* en Angleterre, notamment l'artiste d'origine française Philip Mercier, dépendaient en grande partie de l'expertise de graveurs éminents pour promouvoir, reproduire et vendre leurs œuvres. Les artistes choisissaient fréquemment leurs sujets dans l'optique des gravures à venir et du potentiel marchand de l'image. Dans ce climat commercial, les plus populaires d'entre eux représentaient des enfants et des jeunes femmes séduisantes, caressant souvent de petits animaux. Des images de vieillards étaient produites à l'occasion, non pas comme saints ou prophètes mais en tant que curiosités. Dans le catalogue de portraits britanniques gravés d'Henry Bromley publié en 1793, la dernière catégorie était réservée aux « Phénomènes, prisonniers et personnes autrement remarquables ». Parfois, ces vieillards étaient non seulement représentatifs d'un type, mais aussi bel et bien identifiables comme personnalités à part entière. James Turner, par exemple, était « un vil mendiant, à qui les boucles argentées et la barbe flottante donnaient une apparence de patriarche ». Il arrondissait ses fins de mois en servant de modèle à des artistes, leur réclamant un shilling de l'heure en partant du principe qu'il pouvait gagner autant

32. Úbeda de los Cobos, *in* Bilbao, 2014.

s'il passait l'heure à mendier[33]. Apparemment, Turner, « bien qu'âgé, avait tant d'expérience dans sa profession qu'il considérait le fait d'apparaître plus vieux encore qu'il ne l'était comme un avantage significatif »[34].

Sir Joshua Reynolds, *Denys l'Aréopagite*, collection particulière

Joshua Reynolds commença à exécuter des études de caractère en prenant des vieillards comme modèles pendant les années 1760. L'une des premières est un portrait en buste d'une silhouette échevelée à la barbe et aux cheveux longs et blancs. Ici, aucune ambiguïté en ce qui concerne le sujet : il s'agit du roi Lear, de Shakespeare[35]. Même si le tableau fut copié et gravé, il resta en la possession de Reynolds ; manifestement, il l'avait peint pour son propre plaisir et non dans un but lucratif. Au début des années 1770, peu après avoir pris la présidence de la Royal Academy et avoir été fait chevalier par le roi, Reynolds rencontra un vieil homme nommé George White, qui lui servit de modèle pour plusieurs figures de fantaisie et peintures historiques au cours des années qui suivirent. White, qui travaillait alors comme paveur, était un personnage imposant aux traits anguleux et saillants, aux longs cheveux et à la barbe grisonnante. Comme l'artiste David Allen le fit remarquer quelques années plus tard, il était relativement difficile de tomber sur de tels modèles en Grande-Bretagne, car il était rare de trouver « un visage pareil à celui d'un Franciscain ou d'un mendiant italien, si plein de caractère, si expressif et si utile dans l'étude de la peinture d'histoire »[36]. Reynolds profita au mieux de cette occasion qui se présentait à lui en lui faisant endosser l'apparence de personnages historiques et littéraires variés, notamment celle du comte Ugolin della Gherardesca de *L'Enfer* de Dante, de la figure allégorique représentant la « Résignation » d'après les vers du *Village abandonné* d'Oliver Goldsmith, de Denys l'Aréopagite, un disciple de saint Paul (fig. ci-dessus), et même de « Pope Pavarius », vêtu d'hermine et d'une chape cramoisie, le titre, parodique, faisant référence au métier de paveur exercé par White[37]. Sur ces tableaux, bien que le modèle fût reconnaissable,

33. Pour une gravure de William Baillie représentant Turner, datée de 1774, d'après une miniature de Nathaniel Hone, *cf.* la National Portrait Gallery, Londres, NPG D3826. Il y est inscrit : « Ja^{s}. Turner a Beggar ^ $^{aged\ 93}$ valued his Time at a Shill^{g} an hour in the year 1750 ».
34. Caulfield, 1819, p. 223.
35. Mannings, Postle, 2000, I, cat. 2100, p. 542-543 ; II, fig. 1649.
36. Dédicace de David Allen à Gavin Hamilton de ses illustrations pour Allan Ramsay, *The Gentle Shepherd, a Pastoral Comedy*, Glasgow, A. Foulis, 1788, p. i.
37. Postle, 1988, p. 735-744. *Cf.* aussi Mannings, Postle, 2000, I, cat. 2172, 2139, 2166 et 2136.

l'artiste « améliora » délibérément son apparence pour se conformer à un type, remplaçant parfois sa barbe et ses cheveux grisonnants par de longues et gracieuses boucles argentées [38]. Au sujet de ces modèles masculins âgés, James Northcote, élève de Reynolds, nota : « peut-être est-il maintenant nécessaire de peindre de vieux bonshommes, mais il convient de les garder hors de vue. Sir Joshua peignit, bien sûr, de vieux bonshommes, mais il réussit à les rendre plaisants d'une façon ou d'une autre » [39].

Reynolds exposa ses peintures de « vieux bonshommes » à la Royal Academy et dans sa propre galerie, aux côtés de sa collection de maîtres anciens. On rapporte qu'un visiteur fut particulièrement séduit par une étude de tête du « vieux George », comme on l'appelait :

> « Il examina le portrait avec sa loupe, s'éloigna, s'avança, puis, avec beaucoup de solennité et d'importance, s'exclama auprès du chevalier : "Excellent! Vraiment ! Ce personnage, quelle dignité ! N'être qu'un paveur, et avoir pareille tête ! Singulier, vraiment singulier ! Eh bien je pense, sir Joshua, qu'une tête joue un rôle tout à fait capital dans un tableau." » [40]

Dans ces études de personnages utilisant White, Reynolds mena un dialogue visuel avec les maîtres anciens et revisita délibérément les diverses expressions historiques du genre dans l'art européen, tout en y combinant l'attrait contemporain pour la grande littérature et les arts nobles. En raison de la position prééminente de Reynolds à la Royal Academy et de son rôle très en vue d'arbitre du goût, le modèle lui-même connut une popularité sans précédent. Au milieu des années 1770, White avait déjà figuré dans tout un éventail d'études de caractère et de peintures d'histoire, dont *Saint Pierre* du pastelliste John Russell, *Charité romaine* de Johan Zoffany, et *Le Pèlerin faisant le deuil de son âne* de Benjamin West, d'après le roman de Laurence Sterne publié peu auparavant, *Voyage sentimental à travers la France et l'Italie* [41]. Même si ces œuvres ne comprenaient qu'un ou deux personnages, elles avaient généralement une forte composante narrative.

On peut affirmer qu'à la fin du XVIIIe siècle, le trope du portrait du vieil homme s'était transformé et l'idéal du patriarche fictif était alors en passe d'être supplanté par l'identité visible et spécifique du modèle vivant. Si ces vieillards avaient diversement incarné des philosophes, des personnages dans de grandes compositions historiques ou des figures vénérables, ils faisaient désormais partie intégrante du répertoire d'un artiste ; leurs images étaient même considérées comme une sorte de cliché artistique. Commençaient à apparaître, signe des temps, des scènes de genre satiriques inspirées des portraits de vieillards, où l'artiste est assis dans son atelier, près de son chevalet, parfois même en compagnie de son modèle vieillissant. L'une de ces représentations, probablement inspirée de la pratique de Joshua Reynolds, nous vient

38. *Cf.* « Old Man as an Apostle », Mannings, Postle, 2000, I, cat. 2135, p. 555 ; II, fig. 1677.
39. Fletcher, 1901, p. 191.
40. Moser, 1803, p. 12.
41. John Russell, *St Peter*, coll. part. ; Benjamin West, *The Pilgrim Mourning his Dead Ass*, Houston, Museum of Fine Arts ; Johan Zoffany, *Carita Romana*, Melbourne, National Gallery of Victoria.

de Thomas Rowlandson. On y voit un vieil homme barbu en pardessus, passif, assis tandis que l'artiste est en train de le transformer sans doute en figure de patriarche, en présence d'un connaisseur à monocle[42]. Dans une gravure un peu plus tardive intitulée *La Chambre du génie*, Rowlandson représente un artiste raté dans une mansarde sordide, peignant le visage tourmenté de ce qui a été qualifié de « prophète hébreu brandissant des menaces » sorti de son imagination, tandis qu'un chat s'agrippe à sa jambe et que sa femme débauchée sommeille à côté, négligeant les jeunes enfants qui jouent avec une bouteille de vin et attisent un feu[43].

Jean-Jacques de Boissieu, *Portrait du centenaire de Lyon*, Bibliothèque municipale de Lyon

S'il me fallait choisir une image pour résumer la situation à la fin de la période étudiée, ce serait une gravure de l'artiste français Jean-Jacques de Boissieu (fig. ci-dessus). Dessinateur et graveur accompli, largement autodidacte, Boissieu réalisa de nombreuses études expressives de têtes et de personnages, dont un certain nombre de remarquables eaux-fortes de vieillards[44]. Intitulée *Portrait du centenaire de Lyon*, cette eau-forte représente un artiste vieillissant en train de peindre le portrait d'un vieillard barbu assis et las, les paupières lourdes comme s'il luttait contre le sommeil. Ainsi que le suggère le titre de la gravure, il est probablement là en raison de son âge extrêmement avancé plutôt que comme modèle potentiel de patriarche ou de prophète charismatique. L'artiste est observé à son tour par un troisième vieillard penché en avant : trois représentations distinctes de la vieillesse, ou quatre si l'on inclut la tête esquissée sur le chevalet. Cette gravure moderne aux multiples facettes révèle ainsi le processus artistique qui sous-tend la tradition vénérable de la tête de vieillard, tout en explorant de façon plus générale la représentation et le concept de la vieillesse elle-même – la manière dont on en garde trace, dont on en est témoin et dont on en fait l'expérience.

Martin Postle

42. *Cf.* Postle, 1988, p. 738, fig. 6. Marché d'art de Londres, 1986, non localisée.
43. Pour une impression de la gravure, datée de 1812, *cf.* Department of Prints and Drawings, British Museum, inv. 1935,0522.5.217. *Cf.* aussi George, 1949. Pour l'aquarelle originale de Rowlandson, *cf.* Royal Collection Trust, RCIN 913706 ; cette aquarelle fut achetée en 1811 par le prince régent, futur George IV.
44. *Cf.*, par exemple, « Study of thirteen heads », New York, The Metropolitan Museum of Art, The Elisha Whittelsey Fund, 1967 (67.793.25). Pour une exposition récente de l'œuvre de Boissieu, *cf.* Francfort, 2015.

LES FENÊTRES DU POSSIBLE : LA FIGURE DE FANTAISIE ET L'ESPRIT D'ENTREPRISE AU DÉBUT DU XVIIIe SIÈCLE

Au début du XVIIIe siècle, un engouement pour une nouvelle forme séduisante de figures de fantaisie s'empara des capitales européennes qui donnaient le ton en matière de haute culture. Ces tableaux, destinés à l'origine aux élites parisiennes durant les dernières années du règne de Louis XIV, se caractérisaient par la représentation grandeur nature de femmes jeunes et belles, le plus souvent seules, et présentaient un niveau de finition élevé. Ces images intégraient le plus souvent une action mineure ou un accessoire significatif ayant pour but d'animer la figure ou de raconter quelque chose au-delà du sujet relativement limité de l'œuvre. Les lettres d'amour, par exemple, revenaient de manière très régulière (cat. 76), mais on pouvait tout aussi bien surprendre les personnages en train de se regarder dans un miroir, assoupis sur leurs travaux d'aiguille (*cf*. fig. page 178), ou simplement en train de soulever un voile pour adresser au spectateur un sourire impénétrable (cat. 10). En raison de ces effets piquants et indéterminés, on ne s'étonnera pas qu'aucune terminologie précise n'ait pu être établie pour caractériser ce genre de tableaux au moment de leur création. On a ainsi préféré avoir recours à une phraséologie nébuleuse, du terme général et sans relief de « demi-figure » jusqu'aux expressions plus évocatrices comme « figures de fantaisie » ou « sujets de caprice », qui soulignaient à la fois l'inventivité frivole de leur production et les variations sérieuses, mais pas trop, de l'imagination badine qu'elles ont inspirées [1].

Cet essai propose une analyse détaillée de cinq figures de fantaisie, regroupées autour de l'un des motifs favoris de cette forme artistique : la femme à la fenêtre (fig. pages suivantes). Cet ensemble de tableaux composés entre 1715 et 1739 permet de mieux comprendre l'attrait exercé par ce type d'images, ainsi que les circonstances de leur production. Leurs auteurs, Jean Raoux, Antoine Pesne, Jean-Baptiste Van Loo et Philippe Mercier, figuraient parmi les peintres les plus importants et les plus prolifiques de la figure de fantaisie de cette époque. Bien qu'étant français

1. Par exemple, Dézallier d'Argenville, 1745, p. 263, 264, 385.

de souche ou d'origine française, ils eurent tous une activité remarquable dans les réseaux artistiques européens de plus en plus internationaux du début du XVIIIe siècle. En effet, la figure de fantaisie féminine, et la femme à la fenêtre en particulier, semble avoir joué un rôle distinctif dans les échanges commerciaux transfrontaliers de ce nouveau siècle, réapparaissant dans le répertoire de tous ces artistes tandis qu'ils s'imposaient dans chacun des trois pôles principaux de mécénat – Paris, Londres et, dans une moindre mesure, Berlin. Nous allons nous interroger dans les pages qui suivent sur le plaisir particulier que procurent ces figures de fantaisie féminines, ainsi que sur leur contribution unique au commerce international d'œuvres d'art.

Galanterie et illusion

La figure de la femme à la fenêtre fut sans doute au cœur même de l'intense intérêt pour la peinture de genre néerlandaise qui se développa parmi les artistes et amateurs parisiens au début du XVIIIe siècle. Ayant acquis dans la précipitation la *Fille à la fenêtre* de Rembrandt aux Pays-Bas (Londres, Dulwich Picture Gallery) (*cf.* fig. page 148), le très influent théoricien Roger de Piles lui attribua « une place considérable dans [son] cabinet »[2] et ne tarit pas d'éloges à son propos auprès de l'Académie royale. À la suite d'un tel soutien, la renommée du tableau eut tôt fait de s'étendre grâce à la circulation de reproductions gravées, ainsi que par la production de copies et de variantes par divers artistes de l'époque[3]. Il était bien connu que ce motif était très répandu dans l'art hollandais du XVIIe siècle, comme l'illustre, dans cette exposition, le tableau *Jeune Fille à la fenêtre* de Godfried Schalcken (cat. 8)[4]. Les peintres français du siècle débutant ont néanmoins apporté une touche de nouveauté manifeste dans la manière dont ils ont revisité le sujet. L'utilisation d'un ton galant, d'effets de trompe-l'œil ainsi que l'exécution picturale raffinée renouvellent l'interprétation de la femme à la fenêtre, qui s'adressait résolument aux plaisirs d'un âge nouveau.

La figure d'une belle jeune femme à la fenêtre était un motif artistique récurrent parmi tous les arts en vogue, notamment au théâtre et dans la littérature, ayant été spécifiquement créé pour le divertissement des élites fortunées du Paris de l'époque. À la Comédie-Italienne, par exemple, la fenêtre supérieure du décor offrait le cadre habituel des improvisations comiques, un emplacement fort pratique qui permettait de donner libre cours à l'action entre les descriptions scéniques du tumulte des *piazze* vénitiennes ou napolitaines et les manigances hors scène, dans des intérieurs invisibles du public[5]. Depuis ces ouvertures dans le décor, les actrices interprétaient toute la gamme des rôles malicieux de la *commedia dell'arte* tels que Colombine, Zélie ou Léonore, parmi tant d'autres, sortant brusquement la tête, interrompant de diverses façons l'action se déroulant au-dessous et influençant celle-ci par leurs commentaires piquants, leurs éclats de rire et leurs commérages volubiles. Ces figures étaient aussi une caractéristique nouvelle

2. Piles (de), 1990, p. 11.
3. Percival, 2012, p. 138-143.
4. Olivier Zeder, « Raoux, peintre inégal, mais quand il a réussi, il a égalé Rembrandt », *in* Montpellier, 2009-2010, p. 45-52.
5. Tylus, 1997, no 3, p. 323-342 ; Crow, 2000, p. 48-52.

John Faber II d'après Philippe Mercier, *Courtisane vénitienne*, Londres, The British Museum

des opéras-ballets novateurs. Ainsi, dans le deuxième acte du ballet d'André Campra, *Les Fêtes vénitiennes* (1710), qui remporta un vif succès, le parieur français Léandre chante sous la fenêtre d'une jeune Vénitienne, Irène, mais il est repoussé par une *aria da capo* italienne aux trilles volubiles[6]. Au même moment, dans les œuvres littéraires à la mode, la fenêtre n'en était pas moins associée à l'espace féminin et mettait l'accent avec insistance sur des thèmes liés à la séduction. On retrouve la figure de la dame à la fenêtre de manière extrêmement fréquente dans les récits espagnols, que ce soit sous la forme de traductions et d'adaptations théâtrales populaires du *Don Quichotte* de Cervantès ou dans des pastiches modernes des récits picaresques par des auteurs tels qu' Alain-René Lesage. Dans le système de récits enchâssés de l'*Histoire de Gil Blas de Santellane* (1715-1735), de multiples histoires d'amour – ou du moins supposées telles – s'amorcent à partir de telles figures[7]. Tandis qu'elles contemplent les rues de Tolède ou de Madrid depuis la fenêtre de leur chambre, des veuves élégantes, des héritières recluses et des épouses négligées sont à l'affût de leurs amants, attendent l'hommage de sérénades, et laissent tomber leurs billets doux dans une représentation sans fin de ce qui était considéré comme un rituel typiquement ibérique de badinage amoureux. En effet, comme l'a observé Montesquieu tandis qu'il jouait de ce stéréotype, les Espagnols « sont les premiers hommes du monde pour mourir de langueur sous la fenêtre de leurs maîtresses, et tout Espagnol qui n'est pas enrhumé ne saurait passer pour galant »[8].

Tout comme les Séraphine et Violante de Lesage, pour qui la fenêtre du boudoir constitue l'antichambre du récit, les créations de Raoux, Pesne, Van Loo et Mercier mettent en scène un sas entre l'alcôve féminine privée et la jungle de la rue. Même si les intérieurs qu'occupent ces femmes sont typiquement sombres, le tableau n'en offre pas moins au spectateur un aperçu extrêmement tentant d'une vie de luxe et d'oisiveté où les pièces sont parées de soie, où l'on élève des animaux de compagnie, et où les rubans et lacets tombent dans un désordre désinvolte. Dans la *Courtisane vénitienne* de Mercier (fig. ci-dessus), la femme fait signe au spectateur de s'approcher, comme elle appellerait n'importe lequel des nombreux personnages comiques vénitiens (un habile gondolier, peut-être, ou un *senatore* lubrique) pour un rendez-vous galant à

6. *Recueil général des opéra représentez par l'Académie Royale de Musique*, Paris, Christophe Ballard, 1714, X, p. 159-161.
7. Lesage, 1942, I, p. 260-272, 277-333 ; II, p. 151-165.
8. Montesquieu, 1964, p. 135. Cité *in* Barker, 2007, p. 587-615.

Jean Raoux, *Dame à la fenêtre*, New York, Sotheby's, 9 juin 2010

Jean-Baptiste Van Loo, *Jeune Femme à l'oiseau*, Londres, Victoria & Albert Museum

sa fenêtre, ou dans sa chambre. La *Dame à la fenêtre* de Raoux (fig. ci-dessus à gauche) est montrée couvrant nonchalamment son corps d'un drap de soie comme si, ayant été interrompue durant sa toilette, elle s'arrêtait pour assister à l'aubade d'un don Alphonse ou d'un don Gaston qui se tiendrait au pied de sa fenêtre. Dans un décor épuré, les costumes et la gestuelle jouent un rôle prépondérant dans l'établissement de l'atmosphère voluptueuse du jeu amoureux. Des vitres repoussant l'humidité et le froid ne semblent donc en rien nécessaires. Robes décolletées, cous dénudés et une certaine langueur dans le port de bras sont les signes de la chaleur ambiante. Seule la jeune femme de Van Loo (fig. ci-dessus à droite) est parée d'atours au sommet de la mode vestimentaire de l'époque. Le plus souvent, la robe dépeinte correspond à une version simplifiée des représentations théâtrales des *figures à l'espagnole*, des *innamorate* de la *commedia dell'arte* : les rangées de rubans et les gerbes de fleurs sont plus fréquemment représentées que les bijoux, en écho aux charmes naturels, et les cheveux lustrés attachés en chignon sont préférés aux boucles poudrées en vogue à la cour. Dans ces contrées méridionales imaginaires, l'improvisation était présentée comme l'un des principaux délices de ces images. Tout comme les actrices comiques improvisaient des farces et des histoires sentimentales depuis leurs fausses fenêtres et tout comme les romanciers inventaient des dénouements originaux sur la base de scénarios du répertoire, le spectateur pouvait donner libre cours à son imagination quant au personnage que la figure peinte – ou lui-même – montrait dans ces rencontres scéniques. En effet, si la scène comique et le récit espagnol enseignaient une chose au public des divertissements à la mode au XVIIIe siècle, c'était bien qu'il ne fallait pas se fier aux apparences de ces demi-figures élégantes et souriantes : ainsi, une voisine charmeuse pouvait se métamorphoser en une mère disparue depuis longtemps, et une riche héritière, se révéler n'être qu'une servante sous la toilette de sa maîtresse.

Si les thèmes de cette vogue artistique eurent le pouvoir de transporter l'imagination dans un monde suave de galanteries méditerranéennes, l'insistance tout aussi marquée sur le jeu visuel – sur l'illusion et la manipulation de la perspective – trahit les origines de cette mode, née dans les hôtels particuliers du Paris du XVIIIe siècle où les intérieurs arrangés de manière théâtrale mettaient en scène la « dimension de représentation qui est la quintessence du loisir des nobles »[9]. Bien qu'aucun plan décoratif incluant des figures de fantaisie n'ait survécu de cette période, nous savons qu'à la fin des années 1720, le chevalier d'Orléans, principal mécène de Raoux, conçut un intérieur remarquable dans son hôtel particulier du faubourg Saint-Germain en intégrant dans les panneaux de ses appartements plusieurs exemples des demi-figures réalisées par l'artiste[10]. Dans de tels lieux, l'interaction imaginée entre le public et la femme à la fenêtre non seulement faisait intervenir un personnage adressant un signe au spectateur ou le regardant, mais suscitait aussi, grâce à la composition, une certaine friction entre l'espace inventé du tableau et l'espace réel du spectateur. À chaque fois, la grandeur nature de la figure et l'ombre profonde de laquelle elle émerge suggèrent un espace pictural situé quelque part derrière le mur sur lequel (ou dans lequel) le tableau était exposé. En d'autres termes, tout se passe comme si le tableau lui-même s'était transformé en fenêtre donnant sur une pièce dérobée, et comme si la pièce intérieure était devenue la rue.

Les critiques français ne manquaient jamais de rappeler l'anecdote concernant la *Fille à la fenêtre* de Rembrandt (*cf.* fig. page 148), selon laquelle le grand maître s'amusa un jour à placer l'œuvre devant sa fenêtre, amenant ainsi les naïfs passants hollandais à croire que son sujet était réel, voire à engager la conversation avec elle[11]. Cette histoire a été racontée afin de vanter la virtuosité de l'artiste, mais ces versions modernes du thème, nettement plus raffinées, semblent flatter tout autant la maîtrise du jeu des représentations du spectateur que celle du peintre. On a pu dire des angles droits brisés que comportaient les vues de jardin décoratives des années 1720 réalisées par Jacques de Lajoue qu'ils font de la « perspective une fin en soi, à l'intérieur d'une illusion contrôlée et perçue d'un point de vue privilégié ». De la même façon, les petites ruptures dans l'espace fictif occupé par ces figures de fantaisie peuvent être perçues comme des offrandes morcelées attendant d'être « unifiées et stabilisées par un regard aristocratique »[12]. D'une part, le rebord de la fenêtre longeant le bas de l'encadrement de chacun de ces tableaux contredit

10. Dézallier d'Argenville, 1752, p. 264 ; Montpellier, 2009-2010, p. 28, 180-181.
11. Piles (de), 1990, p. 11 ; Piles (de), 1699 (repr. 1969), p. 423 ; Dubos, 1770 (repr. Genève, Slatkine, 1993), p. 432.
12. *Ibid.*

Jean Raoux, *Jeune Fille donnant à manger à des oiseaux*, Christie's, New York, 6 juin 2012

immédiatement l'idée selon laquelle le cadre du tableau réel (ou l'ouverture dans les panneaux) pourrait être interprété comme l'embrasure d'une fenêtre fictive. Ce procédé de repoussoir qui, dans la composition classique de la perspective, devrait établir l'illusion d'un espace pictural brise ici l'illusion. Évidemment, l'introduction de ces rebords peut facilement s'expliquer par la surface pratique qu'ils fournissent pour les détails anecdotiques – un oiseau dans sa cage, un vase en équilibre précaire –, tandis que le positionnement quelque peu illogique du cadre de la fenêtre peinte, souvent placé à l'oblique, semble résolument viser un effet de dissonance spatiale saisissant. De fait, dans l'œuvre de Van Loo, le rebord indique à l'œil que le mur s'éloigne légèrement du spectateur de la droite vers la gauche ; la profondeur de l'embrasure interne construit un point de vue qui longe le mur à un angle bien plus abrupt. La verticale de pierre ébréchée de l'architrave extérieure, par contraste, apparaît exactement ajustée au plan de l'image, comme pour réaffirmer la continuité entre l'espace réel et l'espace fictif.

La figure de fantaisie en itinérance

Bien que le tableau *Dame à la fenêtre* de Raoux fût très vraisemblablement peint à Paris, les autres œuvres examinées ici sont de provenance plus cosmopolite. La *Jeune Fille donnant à manger à des oiseaux* de Raoux (fig. ci-dessus), par exemple, est étroitement liée au voyage du peintre à Londres (septembre 1720 – mai 1721) [13], puisque le tableau – ou du moins l'une de ses versions – se trouvait certainement dans la capitale anglaise lorsque Jacques Chéreau II grava cette œuvre [14]. Il semblerait donc que l'artiste ait transporté le tableau avec lui, voire l'ait peint durant son séjour. De même, la *Jeune Femme à l'oiseau* de Van Loo (fig. page 82) date de 1738 environ, début de la période londonienne du peintre, qui dura jusqu'en 1742 [15]. Mercier, de son côté, travaillait en Angleterre depuis plus de vingt ans lorsqu'il exposa le tableau original de la *Courtisane vénitienne* (fig. page 81) dans son nouvel atelier à Covent Garden, en 1739 [16]. Antoine Pesne fit également un voyage à Londres en 1724 [17], bien qu'il y ait tout lieu de croire que la *Femme regardant par la fenêtre* (Pommersfelden, Schloss Galerie) date d'une période légèrement plus

13. Dézallier d'Argenville, 1752, p. 261-262.
14. Sur cette planche, publiée à la fois à Londres et Paris, est inscrit « Chéreau le Jeune Sculpsit London ». *Cf.* Royal Academy of Arts, Londres (04/1995), et Bibliothèque nationale de France (Ed-90 in-fol. [p. 52]).
15. *Nouvelles Archives de l'art français*, 1878, p. 26-27.
16. *The York Courant*, 1er mai 1739.
17. Hattori, 2004, p. 30.

avancée, alors qu'il se produisait dans plusieurs cours allemandes (principalement à Berlin, mais aussi à Dessau et Dresde) [18]. Qu'y avait-il donc dans ce genre de figure de fantaisie qui se prêtait si bien à cette pratique itinérante ? Et pourquoi ce thème de la femme à la fenêtre en particulier était-il le plus prisé à l'international ? Après tout, Mercier fut prolifique et fit preuve d'une inspiration variée dans les choix de ses sujets lorsqu'il peignit la *Courtisane vénitienne*, même si la *Jeune Fille donnant à manger à des oiseaux* (fig. page ci-contre) est la seule œuvre associée au séjour de Raoux à Londres. Comparé à Mercier et Raoux, le répertoire des figures de fantaisie de Pesne était assez restreint, mais il n'en réalisa pas moins trois versions différentes de la femme à la fenêtre au début de la période itinérante de sa carrière [19]. Quant à Van Loo, il s'agit de sa seule figure de fantaisie connue.

Le marché de l'art dans lequel cette nouvelle forme raffinée de figure de fantaisie fit son apparition fut alimenté de façon significative par les rivalités éclatant au sein du mécénat parisien au début du XVIIIe siècle. Alors que les classes supérieures de l'aristocratie commençaient à passer plus de temps dans leurs hôtels particuliers parisiens aménagés à la dernière mode – notamment pendant la Régence du duc d'Orléans –, une classe montante de grands financiers consacrait beaucoup d'énergie à afficher sa culture, notamment en décorant ses propres résidences dans le style qui était en vogue dans la noblesse [20]. En effet, même lorsque le mécénat monarchique se mit à retrouver sa puissance, au début du règne de Louis XV, la demande d'œuvres d'art séduisantes et surtout ornementales, telle la demi-figure féminine, demeura un important moteur de production. Ainsi, le projet de décor constitué de figures de fantaisie que Raoux réalisa pour le chevalier d'Orléans (le fils légitimé du Régent) semble avoir très rapidement inspiré à François-Christophe de Lalive, un financier du gouvernement, la décoration de sa propre demeure avec une commande encore plus considérable de tableaux similaires passée à Jean-François de Troy [21]. Raoux lui-même tira considérablement parti de cette vague soudaine d'imitations au sein de ce milieu attentif aux modes en fournissant des copies de ses sujets les plus appréciés et, semble-t-il, en conservant une réserve de demi-figures inachevées qui pouvaient lui servir de référence pour travailler [22]. Cependant, en dépit de son inventivité et de son dynamisme, ce marché s'est révélé bâti sur une base assez instable pour l'établissement d'une carrière prospère, notamment lorsque le mécénat d'État connut un déclin progressif après le pic de la fin du XVIIe siècle. Le mécénat était inconstant et souvent de courte durée et les sources privées de richesse qui finançaient l'essentiel de la production artistique de l'époque n'étaient pas moins capricieuses. En effet, la fortune de Van Loo fut menacée lors de la faillite de la Compagnie du Mississippi en 1720, tout comme celle de nombreux grands mécènes de cette époque, situation que son voyage à Londres avait pour but de corriger [23]. Étant donné

18. Rey, 1931, p. 39-40.
19. Berckenhagen (von Ekhart), Poensgen (von), 1958, p. 204, nos 489, 490.
20. Ziskin, 2012.
21. Leribault, 2002, p. 48-50, 292-293.
22. Wildenstein, 1958, p. 311-312, 317-318.
23. Dézallier d'Argenville, 1762, p. 394.

l'instabilité de la conjoncture, on ne peut s'étonner qu'un grand nombre d'artistes français aient tenté leur chance sur les marchés éloignés de leur capitale d'origine.

De même, les autres villes européennes où se concentraient la fortune et le pouvoir possédaient leurs propres et puissants attraits. Alors qu'il avait été invité à peindre des portraits à la cour de Prusse à Berlin, Pesne découvrit qu'on pouvait bâtir des carrières (et des fortunes) entières dans les demeures royales, qui accordaient une place prépondérante aux signes extérieurs du raffinement français. À cet égard, Londres était une ville particulièrement prometteuse puisqu'elle abritait à la fois la cour de la nouvelle dynastie hanovrienne et une population urbaine mêlée manifestant un goût grandissant pour les ornements domestiques cosmopolites. Ainsi Mercier arriva-t-il d'abord à Londres avec le projet d'entrer au service de la nouvelle cour georgienne, avant de s'orienter vers le marché libre et en pleine expansion des portraits et des gravures décoratives en mezzotinte une fois qu'il eut perdu les faveurs de la cour[24]. De même Pesne, qui avait été envoyé en 1724 de Berlin à la cour de Saint James à Londres pour une mission artistique et diplomatique, s'installa dans la capitale anglaise avec femme et enfants dans l'espoir de tirer profit du fameux marché local du portrait, particulièrement lucratif[25]. Van Loo rencontra un vif succès à cet égard, produisant un grand nombre de portraits pour la cour et l'aristocratie grâce au vaste atelier qu'il dirigeait[26]. Raoux, quant à lui, arriva dans la capitale anglaise avec un « desir [*sic*] de voir, & peut-être l'appas [*sic*] du gain » et réalisa par la suite des portraits pour la noblesse, apportant ainsi une contribution innovante au marché spéculatif des œuvres imprimées[27].

Il apparaît que rapidement, à travers le monde itinérant de l'art européen qui se concentrait principalement dans les capitales, on eut vent des opportunités offertes par le marché florissant de Londres ainsi que des genres de tableaux qui s'y vendaient bien. Le cercle très fermé de Pierre Crozat, financier et amateur d'art, semble avoir joué un rôle particulièrement important à cet égard. On pouvait y trouver, par exemple, Antoine Watteau, qui possédait une excellente connaissance du marché des tableaux de genre français modernes dans les cercles de la cour hanovrienne, étant donné qu'il y avait tenté sa chance en 1719[28]. Auprès de la noblesse, des connaisseurs également marchands tels que Jean de Julienne et Jean-Pierre Mariette étaient en même temps étroitement impliqués dans les spéculations de part et d'autre de la Manche du commerce des œuvres imprimées[29]. Tout cela n'a guère échappé à des artistes comme Pesne et Raoux, qui tous deux entretenaient des liens d'amitié avec Nicolas Vleughels, peintre éminent proche de Crozat[30]. Qui plus est, Pesne, Raoux, Van Loo et Mercier étaient liés entre eux par un réseau dense de relations. Ainsi Mercier, né et élevé dans la vaste communauté de Prussiens

24. Vertue, 1933, p. 40, 84.
25. *Ibid.*, p. 20 ; Hattori, 2004, p. 30.
26. Vertue, 1933, p. 82-84.
27. Dezallier d'Argenville, 1752, p. 261-262 ; Raines, Sharpe, 1973, p. 38-46.
28. Hanson, 2003, p. 265-272.
29. Lippincott, 1983, p. 24-25, 133.
30. Vogtherr, 2013, p. 304-308.

huguenots fabricants de produits de luxe, fut formé dans l'atelier berlinois de Pesne[31] ; et tous deux, comme nous l'avons vu, travaillaient à la cour d'Angleterre. Pesne et Raoux s'étaient en outre liés d'amitié dans leur jeunesse, à Venise, pendant leurs années d'études dans la péninsule italienne[32] et tous ces peintres, à l'exception de Mercier, étaient membres de l'Académie royale. Tout comme l'avait fait Watteau, Van Loo rejoignit le convivial Rose and Crown Club, qui avait été fondé dans le but d'organiser des rencontres informelles entre collègues où ces derniers pouvaient échanger les potins[33]. Mercier, au même moment, fut admis dans la Society of the Virtuosi of Saint Luke, plus formelle et plus exclusive, qui mettait en commun des fonds destinés à des projets artistiques et des banquets réguliers[34]. Pour sa part, Raoux – qui ne fut jamais très actif au sein de l'Académie royale – semble avoir été un membre assez enthousiaste de la Saint Martin's Lane Academy, comptant parmi l'un de ses trente-cinq membres fondateurs[35].

Avec ces figures de fantaisie galantes et illusionnistes, ces peintres abordaient de nouveaux marchés avec un produit inédit, testé et approuvé par les milieux arbitres du goût en France. Il est vrai qu'il s'agit d'une période durant laquelle les acheteurs internationaux étaient prêts à tout pour s'offrir des tableaux éminemment emblématiques du luxe français, quitte à se les procurer de façon parfois illégale[36]. En effet, il est important de noter que la plupart des références de la figure de fantaisie parisienne étaient elles-mêmes largement connues. En 1717, par exemple, George Ier demanda personnellement au duc d'Orléans d'envoyer une troupe française de *commedia dell'arte* pour jouer sur la scène londonienne, requête qui conduisit plusieurs compagnies du genre à tourner régulièrement dans la capitale anglaise jusqu'à la fin des années 1720[37]. Les versions françaises des récits narratifs espagnols étaient à la même époque tout aussi populaires en Angleterre, avec les volumes successifs de *Gil Blas* dont chaque épisode était aussitôt traduit en anglais dès sa publication[38]. De plus, le caractère typiquement français de cette imagerie aux yeux du public londonien est évident du fait de l'adoption, en traduction partielle, de sa terminologie originale : ainsi, « demi-figures » et « figures de fantaisie » devinrent à Londres « demy figures » et « plaisant fancies »[39].

Ouvertures commerciales

Le déplacement de cette forme d'art raffiné ne fut-il que la réponse du peintre aux modes aristocratiques françaises et une nouvelle tendance en provenance directe de Paris à proposer sur le marché international du luxe ? Ou bien y avait-il quelque chose de particulier dans la figure de fantaisie – et surtout dans la femme à la fenêtre – qui servait les intérêts de ces

31. Ingamells, Raines, 1976-1978, p. 8.
32. Dézallier d'Argenville, 1752, p. 260.
33. Bignamini, 1988, p. 55.
34. *Ibid.*, p. 36.
35. *Ibid.*, p. 84.
36. Miller, 2014.
37. Simon, 2007, p. 13.
38. Par exemple, Lesage, 1716.
39. Vertue, 1933, p. 135.

Jacques Chéreau d'après Jean Raoux, *Jeune Fille donnant à manger à des oiseaux*, Londres, Royal Academy of Arts

pérégrinations commerciales et artistiques ? Une réponse à ces questions réside peut-être dans la correspondance parfaite entre la capacité particulière de ces images à susciter des dérives fantasques et leur potentiel commercial infini. Malgré toutes ses subtilités, il s'agissait après tout d'une forme d'art largement accessible et son adéquation avec le marché international en pleine expansion des œuvres imprimées peut avoir été, entre autres, particulièrement propice à la spéculation. En Angleterre, le commerce des gravures de reproduction encourageait la production de nouveaux styles d'images, ce que ne permettait pas le mécénat pour les tableaux contemporains. Contrairement aux tableaux, les nouveautés imprimées de ce genre ne nécessitaient ni un lourd investissement financier ni un espace mural conséquent. Le plus important était de s'intéresser à la demande croissante d'un public plus modeste qui souhaitait consacrer une petite partie de son argent à l'acquisition de produits domestiques de luxe. Pendant son séjour à Londres, par exemple, Raoux participa avec une œuvre à la série innovante de gravures consacrée à la vie de Charles Ier, qui fut vendue en masse par une grande maison d'édition. Et si ce peintre a introduit la *Jeune Fille donnant à manger à des oiseaux* (fig. page 84) dans les milieux anglais en gardant un œil vigilant sur le marché des œuvres imprimées, son intuition fut sans doute la bonne. Cette œuvre fut gravée au moins à deux reprises pour mise en vente sur le marché : une fois par Chéreau (fig. ci-dessus), comme nous l'avons vu, puis plus tard par un éditeur anglais[40]. La figure de Raoux *Dame à la fenêtre* (fig. page 82) était également disponible sur le marché des œuvres imprimées sous la forme d'un mezzotinte qui semble être un plagiat réalisé par Jean-Baptiste Poilly à partir d'une gravure de Raoux par Bernard Lens II (fig. page ci-contre). La *Courtisane vénitienne* de Mercier, qui fut publiée après souscription en même temps que huit autres mezzotintes de figures de fantaisie de grande qualité, joua également un rôle dans l'industrie anglaise de l'impression. Notons en effet que les souscriptions pour la série furent versées par plusieurs détaillants dans tous les quartiers marchands de la ville, dont une boutique de dentelle dans Ludgate Hill[41]. Ainsi, dans cet exemple, la figure de fantaisie était promue au rang d'article, au même titre que les produits de luxe que de tels tableaux prenaient pour sujets.

40. The British Museum, Londres, 1988, inv. 0514.62.
41. *The York Courant*, 1er mai 1739.

À Berlin comme à Londres, le portrait était à certains égards le genre de tableau le plus demandé. Ce n'est donc pas une coïncidence si les artistes présents sur ces marchés choisissaient de pratiquer un art qui, sans nécessiter de commande, mettait en évidence le talent du portraitiste[42]. Tout en offrant une source de divertissement et une certaine forme d'ornement, ces images vantaient l'aptitude du portraitiste à mettre en scène des figures grandeur nature avec aisance et élégance, et à magnifier son sujet au moyen de tissus et accessoires opulents. Ainsi la *Courtisane vénitienne* de Mercier fut peinte et exposée dans son atelier de Covent Garden immédiatement après le séjour du peintre à la cour, époque à laquelle il sollicita des souscripteurs pour ses projets imprimés tout en essayant d'inciter tout un ensemble de mécènes à s'offrir ses services de portraitiste[43]. De même, le tableau *Jeune Femme à l'oiseau* de Van Loo date de la période de son arrivée à Londres, tandis qu'il s'établissait à proximité de Henrietta Street. Arrivé dans la ville sans la protection d'« aucun noble ou grand de la Cour », Van Loo choisit de peindre à cette époque des acteurs en vue et importants de l'élite, dans le but de susciter l'intérêt des plus grands mais également, et c'était tout aussi crucial, pour « montrer ses talents »[44]. Comme les modèles masculins, qui se précipitèrent rapidement dans son atelier dans le but de faire réaliser leur portrait sur la base de ces premiers tableaux, les dames de haute naissance telles que la duchesse de Queensbury (Collection Clarendon) ou lady Frances Coningsby (coll. part.) se mirent à commander des portraits d'elles-mêmes faisant clairement écho à sa *Jeune Femme à l'oiseau* (fig. page 82), posant dans des tenues quasiment identiques voire apparaissant à une fenêtre[45].

Bernard Lens II d'après Jean Raoux, *Femme à sa fenêtre*, Londres, National Portrait Gallery

Tout comme ces artistes itinérants français cherchaient à susciter l'intérêt de nouveaux cercles de mécénat, la manière avec laquelle leurs figures de fantaisie attirèrent et captivèrent le regard peut s'apparenter à la façon dont un commerçant met sa marchandise en valeur. Il convient de souligner que les ateliers londoniens de Mercier et Van Loo, comme l'académie de Saint Martin's Lane fréquentée par Raoux, se trouvaient à quelques pas du Strand, l'une des plus longues rues commerciales de Londres dont les vitrines étaient réputées à travers l'Europe pour leur variété, leur nombre et leur splendeur. Une telle renommée était en partie due à l'utilisation

42. Börsch-Supan, 1977, p. 112-117.
43. Vertue, 1933, p. 84.
44. *Ibid.*, p. 82.
45. Wilson, 1993, n°s 11, 31.

tout à fait récente des vitrines, mais aussi de l'usage inventif de l'étal, qui incite à acheter[46]. Dans de tels lieux, les marchands pouvaient vendre leurs produits directement auprès des passants et attirer l'attention de ceux-ci sur la qualité des articles qui y étaient présentés. L'œuvre de Van Loo, en particulier, pourrait presque être confondue avec une telle scène, surtout par la façon dont le tableau place la figure au niveau du regard, et par la manière ingénieuse dont l'artiste arrange la gaze brodée de dentelles sur le rebord de la fenêtre afin de montrer sa douceur, sa complexité et sa transparence – voire d'en faire la publicité. Un tel lien entre les stratégies de vente dans la rue et les morceaux de choix de la peinture française de genre n'est pas si « fantaisiste » qu'il y paraît. Après tout, à la même époque, Watteau reçut d'Edme-François Gersaint la commande de réaliser l'enseigne (Berlin, Schloss Charlottenburg) de sa boutique représentant des figures modernes et raffinées afin d'attirer les consommateurs de luxe dans ses locaux sur le pont Notre-Dame. Au même moment, le jeune Chardin faisait la joie d'une foule de passants avec une enseigne de barbier (aujourd'hui perdue) affichant une scène tumultueuse de la vie quotidienne[47]. Des peintres tels que Raoux, Pesne, Mercier et Van Loo, qui jetèrent leur dévolu sur le marché de l'art le plus prestigieux, n'auraient pas compromis le raffinement de leur pratique en ayant recours à une stratégie de vente aussi évidente qu'une enseigne – encore moins une vitrine –, mais cela n'empêcha pas la figure de fantaisie d'incarner l'esprit attrayant de la nouveauté du commerce de luxe sur la scène urbaine du début du XVIIIe siècle, ni d'empêcher la fièvre acheteuse bienvenue que cela pouvait susciter chez le client potentiel. Si l'on s'accorde à concevoir la figure de fantaisie comme une invitation ouverte aux interprétations inventives, ces femmes à la fenêtre évoquent non seulement les fantasmes relatifs aux rues de Madrid et canaux de Venise mais aussi les artères principales du commerce moderne, non moins étincelantes mais plus réelles.

Bien que la femme à la fenêtre soit caractérisée par sa position entre deux espaces (entre le va-et-vient de la rue et les activités de la chambre à l'abri des regards), elle représente néanmoins une figure statique bien curieuse. Même lorsqu'elle est représentée dans un monde en mouvement, ses propres gestes sont réduits à un buste qui se penche, se tourne ou s'étire. C'est le monde qui doit venir à elle, aussi a-t-elle a recours à tout un attirail de charmes pour parvenir à ses fins. Il est de ce fait d'autant plus remarquable que, de tous les motifs à la mode de la figure de fantaisie récurrents dans la peinture du début du XVIIIe siècle, ce soit la femme à la fenêtre que l'on associe si étroitement au déplacement, à la fois par l'imagination qui s'envole vers des cieux méridionaux et par la circulation des objets en vogue sur le

46. Walsh, 2014, p. 37-56.
47. Dussieux, Soulié *et al.*, 1854, II, p. 431-432.

marché international. Le présent essai entend démontrer que, même si cette imagerie hautement raffinée a été inventée pour le divertissement et le souci ornemental d'un milieu parisien spécifique, les effets d'ouverture au monde qui permettaient de rêver à de lointains horizons méditerranéens aux parfums de galanterie l'ont rendue particulièrement adaptable aux aspirations nouvelles et aux contextes inédits dans lesquels celles-ci s'inscrivent. Sur les marchés du luxe berlinois et londonien, loin de l'environnement trié sur le volet des hôtels particuliers de la capitale française, ces coquettes fictives représentées avec minutie se voyaient assigner une mission commerciale bien particulière : piéger le regard de l'acquéreur, étaler le talent de leur créateur, et se proposer elles-mêmes comme modèles pour des gravures et des portraits. Ne se pliant plus seulement aux caprices des *honnêtes hommes* parisiens qui affluaient en masse dans les nouveaux centres urbains de pouvoir, ces figures de fantaisie alimentèrent aussi désormais les spéculations d'un nombre croissant de producteurs et de consommateurs de produits de luxe cosmopolites, transportés et animés par l'esprit d'entreprise.

John Chu

Jeux de regards

1

Paris Bordon

(Trévise, 1500 – Venise, 1571)

Portrait d'une jeune femme

H.s.t. : H. 1,07 ; L. 0,82
S. fond d. .*O.Paris.B*
Galleria Canesso Lugano

Historique : Collection Watney puis Vernon Watney ; acheté par J. Paul Getty chez Christie's, Londres, 23 juin 1967, no 51 ; légué au Getty Museum en 1978 ; vendu par le musée chez Christie's, New York, 21 mai 1992, no 37 ; New York, collection particulière.
Expositions : Naples/Paris, 2006-2007, p. 190-191/p. 204-205.
Bibliographie : Damian, 2011, p. 8-13.

Formé dans l'atelier de Titien à Venise selon le grand biographe des peintres de la Renaissance, Vasari, Bordon s'inspira d'abord largement de son maître et de Giorgione avant de définir son style avec des compositions à l'érotisme subtil où l'architecture joue un rôle important. Il séjourna en France, à Augsbourg et à Milan, signe du succès recueilli par ses œuvres.

La prostitution a une longue histoire à Venise mais il n'est guère aisé de définir le genre du portrait de courtisane. Le terme est d'usage ambivalent. Le sens que l'on peut donner au concept et à l'activité des courtisanes à Venise au XVIe siècle et aujourd'hui n'est pas le même. Le tableau de Carpaccio, *Deux Dames vénitiennes* (Venise, Museo Correr), a longtemps été considéré comme la première représentation de courtisanes. Si le débat n'est pas totalement tranché, la majorité de la critique y voit aujourd'hui une allégorie de la fidélité conjugale.

L'archétype du portrait de femme à mi-corps légèrement dénudée est la *Flore* de Titien (Florence, Galleria degli Uffizi), modèle que l'artiste a développé en de nombreuses variantes. Palma le Vieux a également largement diffusé ce type de modèle. Paris Bordon va toutefois renouveler le genre en choisissant de couper les corps bien en dessous de la taille, en enrichissant le fond par un décor architectural et, comme c'est le cas ici, en ouvrant une fenêtre pour évoquer un paysage. Le caractère sculptural de ses femmes est renforcé par leur attitude relativement fermée, le regard fuyant. Le contraste entre la sensualité de la nudité, l'opulence de la chevelure aux boucles couleur blond vénitien, la richesse des atours, d'une part, et la solennité du cadre et la froideur de la pose, d'autre part, ne saurait être plus marqué.

Bordon a réalisé, entre 1540 et 1550, toute une série de tableaux aux caractéristiques similaires incitant à penser qu'il a utilisé le même modèle. C'est le cas du *Portrait de jeune femme avec un miroir* (États-Unis, coll. part., *cf.* Damian, 2011, p. 10), dans lequel le personnage est habillé. Ce modèle est néanmoins réinterprété et idéalisé sans qu'on puisse y voir toutefois une recherche systématique de perfection : le sein est généreux, l'avant-bras, viril, le visage, empâté. Certaines de ces particularités se retrouvent dans d'autres compositions, comme s'il y avait un type propre à l'artiste. Est-il d'ailleurs légitime de parler de portrait ? C'est ici l'iconographie qui prime. La *Flore* de Bordon du Louvre, dont la posture, la poitrine dénudée et le fond architectural sont très proches de notre tableau, exhibe clairement les fleurs qui constituent son attribut. En revanche, aucun élément d'identification ne permet de déterminer la nature de la représentation pour notre tableau. Si l'on s'autorise à employer le vocable « portrait », il ne peut s'agir que de la commande d'un homme amoureux désireux d'obtenir du peintre une image idéale de sa bien-aimée. Ridolfi, biographe des peintres vénitiens, évoque les figures *fatte a capriccio* qui peuvent tout à fait définir la nature fantaisiste de tableaux comme celui-ci. Le décor constitué d'un entablement avec trois colonnes jumelées et une échappée sur le ciel, à la manière de la grande tradition de Moroni ou Lotto voire de certains Titien, rappelle la dignité et le *decorum* du genre du portrait.

Quel que ce soit le contexte de sa création, cette œuvre nous charme par la brillance du rendu des tissus, l'intensité des couleurs et la grâce propre à cette grande époque de l'art vénitien.

AH

2

Abraham Bloemaert

(Gorinchem, 1566 – Utrecht, 1651)

Bergère au plat de raisins, 1628

H.s.t. ; H. 1,04 ; L. 0,83
S.d. *Abloemaert fe 1628*
Karlsruhe, Staatliche Kunsthalle, inv. 222

Historique : Acquis par la margrave Caroline Louise vers 1761 de la collection du peintre Jean-Étienne Liotard à Genève.
Expositions : Utrecht/Schwerin, 2011-2012, no 60.
Bibliographie : Roethlisberger, Bok, 1993, I, no 452, p. 293-294.

Abraham Bloemaert fut au cours de sa longue carrière la personnalité artistique la plus en vue d'Utrecht. Fils du sculpteur et architecte Cornelis Bloemaert, il se forma entre Utrecht, Paris et Amsterdam. Définitivement installé dans cette première ville en 1593, il fut l'un des fondateurs de la guilde de Saint-Luc locale en 1611, dont il devint le doyen en 1618. Il est également à l'initiative d'une académie de dessin en 1612. Il forma la plupart des peintres d'Utrecht mais n'entreprit jamais le voyage en Italie. De formation maniériste, il fut brièvement tenté par le caravagisme avant de s'orienter vers un certain classicisme.

Le genre pastoral à Utrecht s'inscrit au croisement du paysage et de la scène de genre. En revanche, il ne se confond jamais avec le portrait. Ni Bloemaert ni Moreelse, les deux principaux tenants du genre, ne pratiquent par ailleurs le portrait allégorique où des aristocrates et bourgeois se travestissent en bergers. L'apparition de ces pastorales se situe au cœur de leurs longues carrières marquées par une évolution du maniérisme vers un classicisme « courtois », non sans avoir lorgné brièvement vers le caravagisme. Sous l'influence de textes littéraires, dont le plus célèbre est *Granida et Daiphilo* de Hooft, les deux chefs de file de l'École d'Utrecht élaborent un archétype de femme élégante, légèrement dénudée, arborant un chapeau à fleurs. Les modèles à la carnation pâle sont dotés d'une expression modeste dénotant une personnalité peu affirmée et dégagent un érotisme froid et désincarné. Une prairie où paissent quelques chèvres suffit à situer le sujet. Les notes naturalistes comme le bâton et la gourde caractéristique du berger contrastent avec la robe somptueuse et le couvre-chef raffiné. La présence exotique du raisin détonne dans ces idylles paysannes qui exaltent les valeurs locales d'une vie simple et saine. On sait aussi que Bloemaert ne fit jamais le voyage en Italie que la plupart de ses élèves devaient entreprendre.

De même que pour les natures mortes hollandaises, des débats agitent la communauté des historiens de l'art quant à la signification de ces compositions. Roethlisberger décèle dans cette représentation du raisin associé à la nudité une allusion érotique et bachique. En accord avec Liesbeth Helmus, nous préférons voir dans ce tableau une représentation ostentatoire de la générosité de la nature où l'abondance des fruits s'allie à la fécondité du sein nourricier. Cela n'empêchait sans doute pas un œil lettré d'associer immédiatement à ces notions naturalistes des images mythologiques et érotiques qui nous paraissent toutefois secondaires.

Le succès de ces sujets tient à la capacité de l'artiste à recréer artificiellement une Arcadie en sélectionnant des éléments naturels caractérisés par une plus ou moins grande apparence de réalité. Cela explique le choix d'une lumière égale, d'une peinture claire dénuée de contrastes, du rappel d'un paysage familier mais ne se référant à aucun lieu précis et d'une figure dépourvue de personnalité. L'adoption d'un format relativement imposant pour une représentation à mi-corps d'un personnage occupant l'espace entier du tableau et qui attire toute la lumière indique l'ambition humaniste de l'artiste. C'est bien une paysanne de composition que Bloemaert représente, pour le plus grand plaisir d'un public cultivé, mais il le fait dans le style clair et lisible qui sera celui de la tendance classicisante de la peinture néerlandaise et avec les outils conceptuels de la peinture de cour contemporaine de son élève Honthorst, revenu du caravagisme. Contrairement aux nombreuses variantes d'atelier et à certaines productions de son fils Hendrick, le tableau de Karlsruhe témoigne de la justesse de la nature morte et de la qualité de dessin d'un maître au sommet de sa force.

AH

3

Jan Van Bijlert

(Utrecht, 1597/1598-1671)

Bergère

H.s.t. ; H. 0,83 ; L. 0,65
S.b.g. *Jv bijlert*
Dunkerque, musée des Beaux-Arts, inv. BA.1976.008.1

Historique : Vente Paris Drouot, 13 juin 1976.
Expositions : Calais/Tourcoing/Douai/Maubeuge, 1978-1979, n° 4.
Bibliographie : Huys Jansen, 1998, n° 85, p. 132.

Formé dans l'atelier de Bloemaert à Utrecht, Bijlert voyagea en France et en Italie. Il fut l'un des fondateurs de la Schildersbent, confrérie de peintres nordiques de Rome. De retour à Utrecht en 1624, il ne quitta plus sa ville natale, où il connut un grand succès. Son adhésion au style caravagesque évolua vers une démarche plus classique et des tonalités plus claires. Il apparaît comme l'un des meilleurs représentants de ce classicisme caravagesque de troisième génération.

Bijlert a peint plus d'une vingtaine de pastorales, généralement des représentations d'une figure isolée. Les bergères sont systématiquement dévêtues, portent le chapeau et tiennent le bâton. Rien ne permet de les identifier aux personnages littéraires les plus souvent représentés dans la peinture du Nord, Granida, Silvia ou Laura. La plupart de ces tableaux figurant des bergères s'assemblaient en pendants avec des bergers à l'épaule découverte et arborant des bérets à plumes. Dans ces œuvres en regard, l'homme et la femme, tournés l'un vers l'autre, semblent communiquer. La *Bergère* de Dunkerque n'a pas de pendant officiel. Le musée a acquis un *Berger* quelques années plus tard mais de format plus petit et d'une expression fort différente, sans aucun lien avec notre tableau. Parmi les œuvres connues, une seule ferait office de pendant possible, le *Berger avec un bâton* autrefois dans une collection particulière anglaise (Huys Jansen, 1998, cat. 77, pl. 40). Non seulement le format et la signature sont très proches, mais la gestuelle et l'élégance des personnages s'accordent. Ce n'est bien sûr qu'une hypothèse, la seule certitude étant l'existence ancienne d'un pendant.

La typologie des bergers de Bijlert s'étend à d'autres représentations de genre dans sa production. On peut citer les musiciens (qui sont parfois des bergers musiciens), les paysans ainsi que plusieurs personnages à l'activité difficile à interpréter. Ces mêmes types se retrouvent sans variation dans ses scènes de groupe plus ambitieuses, banquets, concerts ou assemblées dans les bordels, que l'on qualifiera de caravagesques à défaut de définition plus précise.

Il est vraisemblable que Bijlert ait utilisé un modèle pour le visage de la *Bergère* de Dunkerque. Néanmoins, les traits de la femme définissent bien moins son identité que son chapeau ou sa poitrine dénudée. Bijlert s'inscrit dans un genre créé par la génération de son maître Abraham Bloemaert (cat. 2) et de Paulus Moreelse, représentations dont tout le vocabulaire formel plonge ses racines dans le maniérisme, celui de l'École de Fontainebleau comme celui de la Prague de Rodolphe II. La femme de Bijlert répond donc à un idéal féminin caractérisé par une peau très blanche, des seins menus et un contrôle de l'expression, ici humble et légèrement ironique. Par rapport aux Bergères de Bloemaert, celles de Bijlert sont moins monumentales, moins figées. Le cadre s'est resserré sur le modèle, privant ainsi le peintre des possibilités narratives du paysage et du sens du détail attaché à la flore et à la faune. C'est dans cette modeste mesure que l'on peut lire ici une influence caravagesque superficielle. D'une certaine manière, la représentation se focalise sur l'humanité. C'est une humanité proprette, bien nourrie et sans mystère. Heureusement, la maîtrise impressionnante de l'artiste lui permet d'animer cette représentation très conventionnelle et codifiée, et de séduire le spectateur. Le drapé se développe ainsi avec une fluidité brillante et naturelle. L'éclairage vient rehausser et accentuer les points forts de la composition en dépit du choix résolu d'une ambiance diurne. En un seul tableau, on comprend l'ampleur du registre de Bijlert, aussi à l'aise en tant que portraitiste que peintre de cour et détenteur de qualités éminemment classiques. **AH**

Anonyme XVIIe siècle

Gitane au tambourin

H.s.t. ; H. 0,61 ; L. 0,47
Varèse, Sacro Monte,
Museo Baroffo dall'Oglio, inv. 48

Historique : Don du baron Baroffo dall'Oglio en 1929.
Expositions : Milan, 1951, nº 63 ; Rotterdam/Rome, 1958, nº 42, 1996.
Bibliographie : Bloch, 1968, fig. 15 ; Kultzen, 1996, nº R 18, p. 138 ; Jansen, Meijer, Squellati Brizio, 2002, nº 772, p. 199.

La merveilleuse *Zingarella* de Varèse constitue un exemple probant de la façon dont certains tableaux peuvent accéder à la célébrité – une participation à l'exposition mythique de Roberto Longhi de 1951 à Milan sur Caravage, ce n'est pas rien – avant de retomber dans un relatif anonymat.

Bien qu'elle présente des traits originaux, le jeune modèle du tableau anonyme de Varèse obéit à une typologie que l'on trouve dès le XVIe siècle avec les pythies, les magiciennes (l'inoubliable *Circé* de Dosso Dossi) ou les *zingarelle* (*cf.* celle du Parmesan à Naples où l'iconographie mariale croise le thème de la bohémienne). Ces femmes ambivalentes, à la fois gracieuses et inquiétantes, occupent une grande partie de l'espace réservé à celles qui ne sont ni des saintes ni des mères.

Sur un fond neutre, le peintre a ménagé un plan serré à mi-corps qui produit une sensation de vie et de réalité poignante. Armée d'un tambourin aussi volumineux qu'elle est menue, une jeune femme à la beauté rebelle toise le spectateur avec un mélange de dédain et de raillerie non sans une distance qui confine à l'absence et à la lassitude. Le turban qui anoblit et donne une tournure exotique à ceux qui l'arborent voit son effet annulé par la simplicité de sa tenue et par ses traits de femme du peuple. La splendide tunique bleue nous éloigne des représentations des figures populaires qui baignent en général dans des tonalités plus brunes et monochromes. L'emploi d'un lapis ou d'un azurite laisserait entendre qu'il s'agit là d'une commande relativement prestigieuse.

Le peintre est fort habile dans la maîtrise des drapés, incisifs et dotés d'une vie presque autonome. Il ménage également avec bonheur des zones plus ou moins éclairées avec une science consommée du clair-obscur. Il excelle, plus généralement, à capter la vie et à rendre le détail avec vérité (les fossettes, le menton, les cernes, la moue). Parvenu à ce point, on pourrait penser à une main très prestigieuse.

Toutefois, une analyse plus approfondie permet de percevoir les limites de l'œuvre. L'anatomie est pour le moins approximative. La ligne des épaules est asymétrique et le décolleté, traité d'une manière plus que sommaire, ne révèle pas les formes promises par les typologies habituelles de bohémiennes. Le raccourci du tambourin est difficilement compréhensible et sa taille même est aberrante, sans parler de l'ébauche de main qui le tient.

On comprend aisément que le nom de Sweerts ait été rapproché de ce tableau qui présente quelques-unes de ses qualités, la sensibilité aux émotions humaines, la lumière mystérieuse, l'originalité du type physique de la gitane. Par ailleurs, l'exécution reste en dessous du génie du peintre flamand. Il reste à savoir s'il faut continuer à envisager une attribution nordique ou s'il est préférable de penser à un peintre italien autour de Cerquozzi. Nous pencherions pour la seconde hypothèse mais une enquête approfondie sur la technique du tableau permettrait peut-être d'avancer des arguments plus probants. **AH**

5

Adriaen Brouwer

(Audenarde, 1605/1606 – Anvers, 1638)

Un joyeux buveur

H.s. bois ; H. 0,25 ; L. 0,19
S.d. *A. Brouwer*
Nantes, musée des Beaux-Arts, inv. 381

Historique : Vente Destouches, 21 mars 1794, nº 83 ; don Urvoy de Saint-Bedan, 1854.
Exposition : Paris, 1977-1978, nº 25.
Bibliographie : De Clippel, 2006, I, nº D 5, p. 301-302.

Originaire des Flandres mais sans doute formé à Haarlem dans l'entourage de Frans Hals, Brouwer est le premier spécialiste de scènes de vie paysanne et d'auberges de la peinture hollandaise. Sa mort précoce à Anvers, où il vécut à partir de 1631, serait due aux excès qu'il semblait partager avec les modèles de ces tableaux. Peintre d'une expression forte et âpre, il fut très admiré par Rubens et Rembrandt, qui collectionnaient ses œuvres.

Brouwer s'est rendu immensément populaire par ses scènes d'auberge traitées dans un style apparemment rustique mais en fait très virtuose. Spécialiste des groupes d'ivrognes, il a parfois concentré son attention sur une seule figure, comme dans la célèbre *Potion amère* (Francfort, Städel Museum). Le choix du cadrage de son personnage se détachant sur un paysage de dunes au vaste ciel est caractéristique de cet artiste. Le tableau est même signé mais selon Jacques Foucart, qui devait attribuer le tableau à Craesbeeck en 1977, cette signature est apocryphe. Karolien De Clippel présentait le tableau dans les œuvres rejetées de sa monographie sur Craesbeeck de 2006 et proposait de revenir à l'attribution traditionnelle en raison de l'authenticité, à ses yeux, de la signature, du petit format caractéristique, de la souplesse du pinceau, du traitement du paysage et des rehauts de lumière sur les yeux et le nez. La comparaison qu'elle opère avec la *Potion amère* de Francfort, le chef-d'œuvre évoqué plus haut de Brouwer, ne nous paraît pas très convaincante. En revanche, l'autre tableau qu'elle cite, *Luxuria* (La Haye, Mauritshuis), représente, à nos yeux, le même modèle dans une attitude assez similaire. Il convient cependant de noter que Craesbeeck a copié ce tableau de Brouwer de manière assez fidèle avec toutefois un traitement un peu plus sommaire (localisation inconnue). L'hésitation sur l'attribution, entre le maître et l'imitateur partageant les mêmes sujets, est donc tout à fait compréhensible.

Il arrive parfois que les tableaux nordiques fonctionnent au premier degré comme des représentations simples de la vie quotidienne et il est opportun dans ces cas d'oublier les approches strictement iconographiques qui tendent à surinterpréter systématiquement les images. Néanmoins, le plus souvent, un sujet se prête à des exégèses multiples. Dans l'exemple qui nous intéresse, l'attitude du protagoniste est trop manifeste pour que cela résulte du hasard. Tenant une bourse serrée contre lui, il tend sa coupe comme pour une libation. Il porte l'habit noir des portraits officiels avec un couvre-chef plus fantaisiste et regarde dans la direction opposée à la coupe de vin. L'appartenance du tableau à une série des cinq sens a été suggérée. Toutefois, le goût est en général signifié de manière plus explicite. L'hypothèse d'une allégorie de l'Automne est un peu plus convaincante en raison de la présence du vin, de l'âge du personnage et de la bourse que l'on peut interpréter comme un gage d'abondance ou un symbole d'avarice. Cependant, le paysage n'est nullement automnal et l'homme paraît d'une bonhomie pétillante à peine voilée par un soupçon de mélancolie.

Nous préférons avancer une autre piste qui rejoint quelque peu celle formulée lors de la vente Destouches de 1794, celle d'un portrait d'artiste ou d'un autoportrait. Ce n'est d'ailleurs pas forcément d'un peintre qu'il s'agit mais peut-être d'un *rederijker*, un homme de lettres appartenant à une des nombreuses confréries néerlandaises du XVIIe siècle. Si le toast est bien porté à Bacchus, il l'est par une personne de condition. Rien dans le tableau ne dénote une volonté critique ou satirique. Brouwer n'hésitait jamais à souligner les effets de la boisson. Nous sommes donc

vraisemblablement en présence du portrait détourné d'un ami du peintre ou d'un client bienveillant.

La technique de Brouwer dans ce tableau est extrêmement fluide. Son traitement quasiment monochrome du paysage et du ciel exploite la couche de préparation fine du panneau. La grande masse noire du manteau ressort avec un effet de contraste puissant. L'intensité surprenante du regard du modèle lui confère un magnétisme insoupçonné qui tranche avec son expression de bon vivant.

AH

Anonyme
XVIIe siècle
L'Odorat

H.s.t. : H. 0,79 : L. 0,61
Vienne, Gemäldegalerie der Akademie der bildenden Künste, inv. GG-A 16

Historique : Collection Johanna et August von Albrecht-Hönigschmied, donné à l'Académie entre 1936 et 1938.
Bibliographie : Trnek, 1992, nº 177.

Ce tableau est parfois désigné comme *Le Toucher* mais il semble que l'encensoir fumant ait évoqué davantage une odeur qu'une sensation pour les rédacteurs des catalogues du musée. Il a toujours été rapproché de deux tableaux dans une collection particulière de Cologne représentant *La Vue* et *Le Goût*, faisant partie d'une série des cinq sens. Rolf Kultzen considérait dans sa thèse sur Michael Sweerts en 1954 que le cycle devait être attribué à ce peintre.

Dans son catalogue des tableaux hollandais de la collection viennoise, Renate Trnek distingue les deux œuvres de Cologne comme nettement supérieures à celle de Vienne. Elle juge *L'Odorat* relativement faible avec des erreurs de raccourci et une difficulté à traiter les drapés. Elle estime qu'il s'agit au mieux d'une imitation du grand peintre flamand et peut-être d'une copie postérieure au XVIIe siècle.

Nous la suivons aisément dans son rejet de la production autographe de Sweerts, surtout quand on se place au niveau stratosphérique du *Garçon au turban tenant un bouquet* (cat. 74), qui est aussi une allégorie d'un sens. Surtout, l'intuition géométrique de la forme, que le maître flamand possède au plus haut point, paraît ici absente.

Toutefois, Trnek nous paraît excessivement sévère dans son jugement et ce tableau démontre de véritables qualités. La composition est séduisante et astucieuse. Grâce à la torsion du buste, l'artiste parvient à capter l'intérêt du spectateur et à souligner le geste du modèle. Il saisit ainsi l'ironie du regard fuyant du personnage. Le cadrage serré offre l'avantage d'entrer de plain-pied dans la scène. Les deux mains sont loin d'être parfaitement dessinées et elles sont assez différentes l'une de l'autre mais elles ont le mérite de l'expressivité et de la vivacité. Le raccourci anatomique produit l'effet d'une déformation et d'un volume ramassé, et permet aussi à l'artiste de rendre les détails vestimentaires avec une exubérance assez heureuse.

Avec son turban et ses plumes ainsi que son élégant justaucorps, le personnage incarne l'un de ces dandys orientaux de la peinture nordique. Au carrefour de l'allégorie et du *tronie*, le petit tableau constitue une étude de type. Autrefois attribué au peintre de nature morte flamand Jan Fyt en raison de sa matière généreuse, on peut se demander à bon droit s'il ne faudrait pas sortir ce tableau de l'école flamande pour le rapprocher du foyer rembranesque, avec lequel il nous semble partager plus de points communs. Bien que ce ne soit pas un chef-d'œuvre, cette image bienveillante et pittoresque mérite de rester dans les mémoires. **AH**

Bartolomé Esteban Murillo

(Séville, 1617-1682)

La Jeune Marchande de fleurs

H.s.t. ; H. 1,21 ; L. 0,99
Londres, The Governors of Dulwich Picture Gallery, inv. DPG 199

Historique : Collection Justino de Neve, Séville ; collection Omasur, Séville ; comtesse de Verrue, Paris, 1773 ; vente Lassay, Paris, 1776 ; vente Blondel de Gagny ; collections Bassan et Randon de Boisset ; vente Calonne, Londres, 1795 ; collection Desenfans, Londres, 1804 ; sir Francis Bourgeois le donne à Dulwich College.
Expositions : Madrid/Londres, 1982-1983, n° 69 ; Londres/Munich/Madrid, 2001, n° 6 (puis 16 et 14).
Bibliographie : Valdivieso, 2010, p. 236, 548, n° 399, p. 549.

Murillo, *Allégorie de l'Été*, Édimbourg, National Galleries of Scotland

Toute la carrière de Murillo s'est déroulée dans sa ville natale de Séville sans événement marquant hormis un voyage à Madrid en 1658. Au départ de Zurbarán pour la capitale en 1659, Murillo resta sans rival à Séville, où il figura parmi les fondateurs de l'école de dessin. Le peintre a répondu à d'innombrables commandes des ordres religieux de la ville andalouse tout en peignant des tableaux de genre pour les collectionneurs. Sa manière douce et alanguie et son inspiration baroque lui ont valu une célébrité incomparable de son vivant qui ne s'est jamais démentie par la suite.

La célèbre *Flower Girl* de Dulwich est l'une des plus populaires visions de l'enfance par Murillo. Elle a longtemps passé pour une représentation idéalisée d'une jeune fille de type gitan à laquelle on prêtait une dimension érotique. Valdivieso a justement souligné la chasteté de l'image, rebaptisant le tableau *Allégorie du Printemps*. Il considère qu'il ne peut s'agir d'une marchande de fleurs. En effet, les fleurs fraîchement coupées constituent un résumé de la nature et non une marchandise de rue. Il a donc rapproché la jeune fille de Dulwich du jeune homme d'Édimbourg du même peintre qui présente une corbeille de fruits (fig. ci-contre), les interprétant comme deux éléments d'une série des quatre saisons, le printemps et l'été. Bien que les pendants n'aient pas le même format, les figures se caractérisent toutes deux par la présence d'un turban et la même façon de présenter les fleurs ou les fruits. Nous pouvons avancer une autre comparaison qui renforce la théorie de Valdivieso. Il existe au musée Pouchkine de Moscou une *Jeune Fille avec fruits et fleurs* de Murillo antérieure de près d'une dizaine d'années. Le tableau russe est incontestablement une figure de genre naturaliste par sa recherche d'émotion immédiate alors que le tableau de Dulwich appartient à un registre plus noble.

L'intérêt de Murillo pour l'enfance et les scènes de vie populaire qui y sont associées se développe sur toute la durée de son activité. Au fil du temps, on ne constate pas d'évolution marquée dans ses choix de thèmes alors que son style s'épanouit. Les historiens de l'art espagnols ont insisté sur l'originalité du naturalisme de Murillo, relativisant l'influence des nordiques et des *Bamboccianti* présents dans les collections de Séville. Sans nier que les sujets illustrant la vie du peuple sont dans l'air du temps en Europe, la constance de Murillo dans ce domaine est remarquable. D'une part, il traduit les destinées humaines telles qu'elles sont narrées par la littérature picaresque du Siècle d'or mais, en même temps, il s'élève au-dessus des problèmes sociaux et refuse la laideur habituellement associée à la misère. Sa vision embellie et sentimentale de la pauvreté explique son succès posthume dans les grandes collections européennes du XVIIIe siècle et son influence sur la peinture de Reynolds. Au-delà de la peinture de genre et de la figure de fantaisie, les images de dévotion représentant Jésus enfant ou le petit saint Jean-Baptiste s'abreuvent à la même source enfantine.

Au seuil des années 1670, Murillo n'a pas tourné le dos à sa manière brune monochrome. Cette harmonie domine entre le châle, le paysage et l'architecture. Le peintre introduit des blancs, des jaunes et des roses qui confèrent fraîcheur à l'ensemble et se combinent avec la douceur de la carnation. Le paysage joue un rôle essentiel avec sa vaste étendue de ciel. Le pinceau est totalement assuré et la matière, moins marquée que dans la production de jeunesse. Le cadrage centré sur la jeune fille entourée du paysage et du pilier confère une évidence sculpturale à la composition. L'attitude spontanée du modèle, son sourire franc et la complexité des drapés contribuent à l'animation de l'ensemble. La réputation de cette œuvre délicate et solennelle à la fois n'est nullement usurpée et en fait un archétype de la figure de fantaisie.

AH

8

Godfried Schalcken

(Made, 1643 – La Haye, 1706)

Jeune Fille à la fenêtre

H.s. bois ; H. 0,32 ; L. 0,27
Cardiff, National Museum of Wales, inv. NMWA 35

Historique : Transféré en 1921 de Turner House.
Bibliographie : Wedmore, 1900, no 141 ; Cardiff, 1955, no 259.

D'abord élève de Hoogstraten, lui-même élève de Rembrandt, Schalcken se forma ensuite auprès de Gérard Dou, dont il devint un temps le meilleur imitateur. Suivant l'évolution du goût des élites néerlandaises, il se tourna vers des sujets d'histoire d'esprit classique. Il est connu comme le meilleur spécialiste des éclairages à la chandelle qui confèrent un véritable mystère à ses délicats tableaux de petit format au fini irréprochable. Il est réputé comme l'exemple même des *fijnschilders*, ces peintres « fins » si populaires à la fin du XVIIe siècle et au XVIIIe siècle.

La création du type d'image avec un personnage rêveur et désœuvré à la fenêtre est due à Rembrandt. Gérard Dou a popularisé encore davantage ce genre en plongeant dans le tourbillon de la vie ses modèles à la fenêtre. Qu'ils soient fumeur de pipe, tambour, violoniste ou le peintre lui-même, ils s'exhibent à la vue de tous et interagissent avec le spectateur. Schalcken reprend, comme à son habitude, les compositions de son maître en y apportant une note de préciosité toute personnelle. De plus, il y ajoute l'ingrédient supplémentaire de l'éclairage à la chandelle, également pratiqué par Dou mais moins régulièrement associé à la fenêtre par ce dernier.

La jeune fille de Schalcken ne se contente pas d'occuper sa place dans l'embrasure de la fenêtre. Elle agit véritablement dans l'espace. Elle ouvre cette fenêtre et semble accueillir un visiteur. Son physique avenant, souligné par l'éclairage artificiel, s'inscrit de manière frontale dans l'encadrement de la fenêtre. Cet élément architectural ne remplit donc pas la fonction de pur dispositif scénique déconnecté de toute narration mais joue plutôt un rôle de vitrine à l'effet démultiplicateur et de sas de communication entre intérieur et extérieur également invisibles. Loin d'être un simple cadre, le peintre nous le montre dans sa totalité, jusqu'à l'extrémité du volet.

Le modèle est jeune et accorte. La jeune fille n'est pas en tenue de nuit mais sa mise, pour soignée qu'elle soit, est réservée à l'intimité de la demeure. Son attitude accueillante, la bouche entrouverte, ses cheveux décoiffés retenus par un ruban, son décolleté, tous ces détails comportementaux laissent peu de doutes sur son métier de courtisane. La flamme en position horizontale en raison de l'appel d'air consécutif à l'ouverture de la fenêtre est aussi un symbole érotique bien connu.

À la manière du *Couple éclairé par une bougie* du Louvre, le cadrage familier sur ce seuil domestique qu'est la fenêtre et l'effet d'éclairage révèlent une scène interlope que la morale aurait souhaité cacher. Cela n'empêchait nullement les collectionneurs au goût raffiné de s'arracher la production du peintre. Ce métier lisse où toute trace de labeur pictural, toute scorie de matière avaient été patiemment expurgées parvenait à donner respectabilité et dignité même à ces sujets. Contrairement à l'usage caravagesque de la chandelle, le précédent historique des *fijnschilders* dans l'exploitation de cet effet, qui vise à découvrir et à masquer alternativement la vérité de l'homme et les mouvements de l'âme, la bougie agit ici plutôt comme un accessoire pittoresque qui souligne le charme vénéneux de la scène.

Les visages délicats et souriants de Schalcken ne constituent pas des portraits, genre qu'il a par ailleurs pratiqué. Ce sont les acteurs d'une comédie humaine à laquelle on croit un peu parce que le peintre est doué. À la vue d'un exemple aussi remarquable que le tableau de Cardiff, on comprend mieux la fascination que Schalcken, à l'image de Ter Borch, Dou ou Mieris, a exercée sur les artistes et collectionneurs français du XVIIIe siècle. **AH**

9

Hyacinthe Rigaud

(Perpignan, 1659 – Paris, 1743)

Portrait d'une femme inconnue,
dite *La Menaceuse*, 1708

H.s.t. ; H. 0,68 ; L. 0,56
Signé au revers de la toile
Fait par Hyacinthe Rigaud, 1708.
Aix-en-Provence, musée Granet, inv. 880-1-20

Historique : Legs de Françoise-Joséphine Sebillot (veuve de Louis-Joseph-Alphonse, dernier marquis de Gueidan), 1880.
Expositions : Nantes/Toulouse, 1997, p. 72, no 90, p. 243 ; Paris, 2001-2002, no 72, p. 236-237.
Bibliographie : Perreau, 2004, p. 174-176 ; Perreau, 2014, no P1054, p. 216.
Œuvres en rapport : Suiveurs de Rigaud : 1) h.s.t., 0,73 × 0,59 m, Versailles, Palais des Congrès, 7 avril 1974, no 29, localisation actuelle inconnue ; 2) h.s.t. (réplique), 0,50 × 0,41 m, Phillips, Londres, 27 février 1990, no 37, localisation actuelle inconnue ; 3) h.s.t. (variante), 0,63 × 0,51 m, Drouot Beaussant Lefèvre, 6 juillet 2012, sans numéro, collection particulière.

Jean-Baptiste Santerre, *La Menaceuse*, collection particulière

D'origine catalane, Rigaud étudia à Montpellier et à Lyon avant de s'établir à Paris en 1681. Il y établit un commerce de portraits florissant et rejoignit l'Académie royale. Inspiré par Van Dyck, l'artiste développa une manière unique de peindre les portraits d'apparat, à la française, avec des formes et des drapés dynamiques. Les modèles de Rigaud étaient issus des plus hautes sphères de la société française ; ce peintre est d'ailleurs surtout connu pour son portrait emblématique de *Louis XIV en costume de sacre* (1701, musée du Louvre).

Longtemps considéré comme une exception dans l'œuvre de Rigaud, ce tableau très apprécié est replacé, grâce à cette exposition, dans un contexte européen de figures féminines de fantaisie séductrices et espiègles. Rigaud peignit beaucoup plus d'hommes que de femmes, prétendument parce qu'il n'aimait pas avoir à flatter ses modèles féminins (Dézallier d'Argenville, 1745, II, p. 412). Il réalisa beaucoup moins de portraits « travestis » que ses rivaux, Largillierre et Nattier. Ce tableau fut commandé par un certain M. Boucher, receveur des tailles du Mans. Un livre de raison appartenant à Rigaud mentionne en 1709 : « la menasseuse pour M. Boucher, 1 400 livres ». Il s'agissait d'une somme importante pour un format aussi modeste, et le prix élevé de la toile a donné lieu à bien des conjectures quant à une possible affaire illicite. Quelle que soit la véritable identité du modèle, Rigaud travailla dans le même esprit que ses contemporains Santerre, Raoux et Grimou pour créer une figure à la croisée du réel et de l'imaginaire. Le langage corporel ambigu de la jeune femme, qui se montre tout à la fois avenante et distante, partage des similitudes flagrantes avec la *Jeune Femme au corsage bleu* de Courtin (cat. 77) et le *Portrait de femme au collier de perles* de, ou d'après, Raoux (cat. 10). Rigaud fut clairement influencé par *La Menaceuse* de Santerre (fig. ci-contre), toile exposée au Salon en 1704, dans laquelle le doigt levé de la femme peut être interprété comme une invite ou un avertissement à l'égard du spectateur. Ces œuvres sont le miroir de traditions plus lointaines : celle des courtisanes vénitiennes de Giorgione, de Titien et de Bordon, qui revinrent à la mode au début du XVIIIe siècle grâce à Rosalba Carriera, mais aussi celle des peintres nordiques, y compris ceux de l'école caravagesque, qui utilisaient le format en buste afin d'accentuer les décolletés (De Bray, *Jeune Femme vue en buste, se peignant*, Paris, musée du Louvre ; Van Everdingen, *Joueuse de cistre*, Rouen, musée des Beaux-Arts). La posture de la figure de Rigaud a quelque chose d'érotique : son torse est présenté dans un écrin voluptueux de soie satinée mauve, la poitrine à peine couverte par des sous-vêtements en lin plissés. Le costume de la jeune femme est couronné d'un béret mauve assorti, orné de plumes orange, de perles et d'un chignon, rappelant vaguement l'univers de Rembrandt et celui du théâtre. Sa peau baignée de lumière est aussi douce et parfaite que les tissus, la ligne de son épaule et de son cou formant une courbe sinueuse. Et pourtant, il ne s'agit pas d'une déesse classique, car le réalisme de Rigaud y est bien visible. Ses traits ont un air contemporain : nez pointu et double menton à la mode ; joues et lèvres maquillées. Sa tête inclinée vers l'arrière, sa paupière à demi baissée et son doigt pointé vers le haut suggèrent une certaine résistance. Le côté droit de son visage est plongé dans l'obscurité et le fond noir évoque une absence de contexte, indiquant que la figure restera à jamais une énigme. **MP**

10

D'après Jean Raoux

(Montpellier, 1677 – Paris, 1734)

Portrait de femme au collier de perles

H.s.t. ; H. 0,93 ; L. 0,74
Marseille, musée des Beaux-Arts, inv. BA 729

Historique : Collection de Paul ; legs Suriar en 1891.
Expositions : Paris, 2001-2002, no 74, p. 240-241 ; Montpellier, 2009-2010, fig. 21 et catalogue 68, p. 67, 190.
Bibliographie : *Parcours. Catalogue guide du musée des Beaux-Arts de Marseille*, s.d., p. 100.
Œuvre en rapport : *Portrait de femme aux mains croisées*, Marseille, musée des Beaux-Arts, h.s.t., 0,93 × 0,74 m, inv. BA 730.

D'après Jean Raoux, *Portrait de femme aux mains croisées*, Marseille, musée des Beaux-Arts

Voltaire considérait Raoux comme l'égal de Rembrandt et, bien que cette allégation puisse paraître quelque peu exagérée, elle démontre l'importance des peintres nordiques pour Raoux et sa génération. Après avoir étudié avec Antoine Ranc à Montpellier, Raoux rejoignit l'atelier de Bon Boullogne. Il remporta le premier prix de l'Académie en 1704 et se rendit à Rome, à Venise, puis à Florence, avant de revenir en France en 1714. Raoux fut principalement inspiré par Schalcken et Netscher, retravaillant leurs sujets de prédilection et leurs effets de lumière pour un public français.

La tension entre dévoilement et dissimulation est au cœur de cette figure de fantaisie. Une jeune femme séduisante regarde le spectateur dans les yeux en esquissant un sourire avenant. Elle a la tête inclinée, comme si elle tendait l'oreille ou, plutôt, comme si elle exhibait la perle qui pend à son oreille. Ses mains levées attirent l'attention sur son voile bordé d'or : est-elle en train de l'ôter ou de le mettre ? Cet habit connu sous le nom de « pèlerine » était généralement accompagné d'un masque de façon à se protéger du soleil, mais il évoque également les rencontres secrètes lors de bals masqués ou de carnavals. Le contraste entre le vêtement noir et le collier de perles accentue la blancheur de porcelaine de la peau de la jeune femme. Cela, ajouté au corsage décolleté qui semble sur le point de se délacer, exerce un attrait supplémentaire sur le spectateur.

Raoux et son cercle peignirent de nombreuses demi-figures féminines séduisantes relevant de traditions nordiques (*cf.* Schalcken, cat. 8) : lisant, se regardant dans un miroir, jouant avec des oiseaux, apparaissant au rebord d'une fenêtre, ou esquissant des gestes derrière un rideau (*Le Silence* ou *L'Indiscrète*, Avignon, musée Calvet). D'inspiration vénitienne, les diagonales formées par la posture de la femme apportent légèreté et fluidité à la composition. Cet artifice est encore plus flagrant dans d'autres œuvres de Raoux telles que la *Jeune Fille faisant voler un oiseau* (Sarasota, Ringling Museum) ou *La Liseuse* (Paris, musée du Louvre). Le tableau de Marseille possède un pendant de dimensions comparables représentant un sujet féminin plus placide, également couvert d'un voile. Non seulement le *Portrait de femme au collier de perles* partage des similitudes avec les nombreux tableaux de vestales de Raoux (le voile étant un signe présumé de vertu dans ce contexte), mais il est également comparable à celui d'autres femmes voilées de la même période : la coquette *Beauté dangereuse* de Jean-Baptiste Santerre (gravée par S. Chevillet) est ainsi proche de l'esprit de l'œuvre de Raoux, tandis qu'une autre femme voilée, également de Santerre (*Femme voilée*, Saint-Pétersbourg, Ermitage), est d'une humeur différente, car le visage et les yeux de la jeune femme sont plongés dans l'obscurité, ce qui suggère le désir troublant de garder l'incognito. Bien que distant de plusieurs décennies, le chef-d'œuvre d'Alexander Roslin *La Dame au voile* (1768, Stockholm, Nationalmuseum) possède la même franchise et la même volupté que le tableau de Marseille. Dans le tableau de Raoux, on peut distinguer, presque oubliée dans le sombre arrière-plan rembranesque, une vieille femme à l'air hagard juste au-dessus de l'épaule de la jeune femme. En forçant un peu le thème des apparences, on peut se demander s'il s'agit d'une duègne réprobatrice ou bien d'un amant déguisé. À cette époque, le mythe de Vertumne et Pomone était populaire. Il fut remarquablement traité par le maître de Raoux, Jean Ranc (Montpellier, musée Fabre), et représenté également par Largillierre, Gobert et Tournières. **MP**

Pietro Longhi [Pietro Falca]

(Venise, 1700/1702-1785)

Berger en pied, vers 1740

H.s.t. ; H. 0,60 ; L. 0,45
Rovigo, Pinacoteca del Seminario Vescovile, inv. 78

Historique : Legs Silvestri, 1878.
Bibliographie : Pignatti, 1969 ; John T. Spike *in* Fort Worth, 1986 ; Pallucchini, 1996, p. 365-401 ; Romagnolo, Fantelli, 2001, nº 125, p. 134-135.

Longhi s'est formé auprès d'Antonio Balestra, puis à Bologne avec Giuseppe Maria Crespi. De retour à Venise en 1730, il se consacre à la peinture de genre, d'abord dans le style de Crespi. Il développe ensuite une veine unique de réalisme social, captant des personnes et des événements dans les rues de Venise d'un regard intelligent, avec un sens du détail et de l'humour. Il rejoint l'Académie de Venise en 1756, dont il est directeur de 1763 à 1766 .

Les premières peintures de genre de Longhi étaient des visions de la vie paysanne influencées par Crespi et par des artistes du Nord. Dans cette scène pastorale, Longhi crée une atmosphère de mystère et de charme qu'il doit à son professeur bolonais. L'œuvre est très différente des scènes cosmopolites de vie urbaine avec lesquelles l'artiste s'est fait connaître : dans celles-ci, les couleurs sont vives, les intérieurs, détaillés, et les femmes vénitiennes portent des voiles et des masques noirs. En revanche, le berger de Rovigo peut être comparé à plusieurs autres figures simples et rustiques peintes par Longhi tôt dans sa carrière, et surtout avec le *Berger s'appuyant sur un bâton* (Bassano, Museo Civico) dans la même position. Un écrit de Bartoli au sujet d'un « pastorello ritto in piedi in mezzo ad un paese » indique que le tableau de Rovigo était dans la collection Silvestri vers 1793. Ce jeune berger séduisant se détache sur un fond sombre et indéterminé selon la technique du clair-obscur à la manière de Piazzetta. Il a un visage rond, sa pose est décontractée et son expression, joyeuse. Son apparence agréable mais bourrue s'harmonise avec la couleur et le paysage rocheux. La formation minérale à la droite du personnage est une création fantaisiste, puisque exagérément verticale. La peinture fait écho aux Jean-Baptiste dans le désert, jeune homme avec un bâton pour Raphaël, le Caravage, Reni et Ribera, et enfant pour Murillo et Reynolds. Mais cette iconographie est en fait implicite et le regard droit et direct du personnage nous rappelle qu'il concentre toute l'attention. Contrairement à de nombreux personnages dans cette exposition qui cherchent activement une réponse à travers le flirt, la mendicité ou la vente, le jeune berger ne demande rien, n'attend rien du spectateur. Son regard est simple, serein. Quelque chose de ce traitement lyrique d'un sujet rural, mais avec une technique différente, se retrouvera plusieurs décennies plus tard dans les tableaux de fantaisie de Gainsborough. **MP**

D'après François Boucher

(Paris, 1703-1770)

Tête de jeune femme,
dite *La Voluptueuse*

H.s.t., H. 0,41 ; L. 0,33
Toulouse, Fondation Bemberg, inv. 1042

Historique : Collection Matthew Schutz, New York, vente Sotheby's 12 janvier 1995, n° 60 ; acquis à cette vente.
Expositions : Londres, 1993, n° 17, p. 56 ; Lyon/Lille, 2000-2001, n° 49, p. 148-149.
Bibliographie : Jean-Richard, 1978 ; Polazzo, 1990 ; Mann, 1999, n° 13, p. 80-86 ; Cros, 2000, p. 54-55 ; Jeffares, http://www.pastellists.com
Œuvres en rapport : Cinquante-trois répliques, copies et autres versions au pastel, à l'huile, au crayon, gravées et en miniature. Pour une liste exhaustive, *cf.* Jeffares.

J. F. Poletnich, *La Voluptueuse*, gravure d'après Boucher, Paris, musée du Louvre

Peintre et dessinateur prolifique, Boucher fut le grand pourvoyeur du goût pour l'art décoratif et érotique du XVIIIe siècle à Paris. Son atelier, rempli d'élèves, était la salle des machines du mouvement rococo français. Il produisit des scènes mythologiques, des pastorales et des scènes de genre ainsi que des dessins pour des tapisseries et de la porcelaine. Boucher était le protégé de Madame de Pompadour, dont il peignit le portrait à plusieurs reprises. Il gravit les échelons de l'Académie pour devenir Premier Peintre du roi, en 1765.

Nous profitons de cette exposition pour désigner François Boucher comme l'auteur de la composition à l'origine de la peinture de la Fondation Bemberg, excluant ainsi Pietro Rotari. Boucher a peint deux études de femmes en buste, probablement au pastel, autour de 1740. Elles sont aujourd'hui connues comme *La Voluptueuse* et *La Dormeuse*. Les originaux ont été perdus, mais ils semblent avoir enflammé de nombreuses imaginations car ils ont donné lieu à de multiples copies et variantes aux XVIIIe et XIXe siècles. La gravure de J. F. Poletnich vers 1758-1763 (fig. ci-contre) apporte une preuve concluante que l'auteur de *La Voluptueuse* est François Boucher puisqu'elle le nomme directement (Jean-Richard, 1978, n° 1476). D'autres documents de la période (*cf.* Jeffares) relient le sujet encore plus directement à ce peintre. Par exemple, les versions de la collection de Bergeret de Grandcourt sont susceptibles d'avoir été peintes par Boucher lui-même, étant donné les liens étroits de l'artiste avec l'amateur.

À un moment, probablement à Saint-Pétersbourg, Rotari a pris connaissance de la composition de Boucher. Il a calqué son propre style sur la conception de Boucher et modifié certains détails. Il en produisit plusieurs versions à l'huile avec un fini caractéristique et un éclairage puissant. L'une d'entre elles se trouve dans la salle dite Rotari au palais de Peterhof (Polazzo, 1990, n° 177). Il a peint aussi une *Jeune Femme avec un brin de jasmin* (Columbia, musée d'Art et d'Archéologie, université de Missouri, *cf.* Mann, 1999) et un autre tableau dont le pendant est une femme assoupie aujourd'hui dans une collection privée en Espagne (*cf.* Londres, 1993). Ces exemples représentent une femme avec un col de dentelle et des boucles d'oreilles en perles, dans la même pose que l'original de Boucher. Cependant, dans la peinture de Peterhof, elle porte un chapeau de fourrure et d'autres différences apparaissent telles que la chaise sur laquelle elle est assise (absence de coussin) ainsi que le placement de la branche de jasmin. L'œuvre de Toulouse n'a pas les contours nets et le naturalisme désarmant de Rotari. Elle est peinte délicatement, comme d'après un pastel. Nous sommes d'avis que le tableau n'est pas de Boucher lui-même mais qu'il s'agit d'une des nombreuses répliques documentées du XVIIIe siècle.

Bien que les faits discutés ici le soient publiquement depuis un certain temps, ils n'ont pas été envisagés du point de vue de la figure de fantaisie. Dans l'optique d'une attribution à Boucher, la femme de Bemberg prend une pose plus raide que ce que l'on pourrait normalement attendre de la part de l'artiste, sa façon de représenter les femmes – y compris les études de tête et en buste – étant habituellement chaleureuse et suave. On voit ainsi qu'elle est peinte dans la même veine que Santerre, Rigaud et Courtin (cat. 76, 9, 77), combinant la maladresse et l'incertitude avec la séduction.

Pour Rotari, qui s'était déjà fait un nom en tant que peintre de jeunes femmes en gros plan passant par toute une gamme d'émotions, ce prototype d'un autre artiste lui offrait l'opportunité d'explorer et de développer son propre répertoire. Ainsi, les

dents, signe de sensualité, sont plus visibles dans le travail de Rotari que dans l'original de Boucher. Enfin, c'est un cas d'étude fascinant sur la propagation et la diffusion de la figure de fantaisie à travers l'Europe. Il est très probable que Rotari ait découvert l'image en reproduction car il n'a jamais rencontré Boucher ni séjourné en France. Mais nous savons que les notables russes observaient d'un œil attentif le marché de l'art à Paris et Boucher était une denrée prisée. En somme, la formule de Boucher s'est avérée captivante, facilement reproductible mais également adaptable. C'est la durabilité et la polyvalence de cette figure de fantaisie, plutôt que les incertitudes à propos de sa paternité, qui importent le plus dans ce contexte. **MP**

13

Louis Aubert

(actif 1740-1780)

Enfant en pénitence ou *Boudeur*

H.s. bois ; H. 0,41 ; L. 0,31
Lyon, musée des Beaux-Arts, inv. H 675

Historique : Don de Jacques Bernard, 1877.
Bibliographie : Gaston-Dreyfus, 1923, n° 231, p. 91 ; Barker, 2009, p. 426-445.

Il reste peu de traces de ce peintre et dessinateur. Heineken, dans son *Dictionnaire des artistes* (1778), affirme qu'il était le fils d'un violoniste de l'orchestre de l'Opéra de Paris et qu'il était toujours actif au moment de sa rédaction. Principalement peintre de genre, Aubert est également l'auteur de portraits, de paysages et d'animaux. Il a remporté de prestigieuses commandes pour les châteaux de Fontainebleau, Versailles, Choisy et Compiègne.

Cette peinture fut longtemps considérée de la main de Nicolas-Bernard Lépicié, mais est maintenant attribuée à Louis Aubert, un peintre obscur actif à la même période. Elle a été produite au cours de la vague de « peinture morale » (expression de Diderot) dont Greuze fut le fer de lance au milieu du XVIIIe siècle. Les enfants furent souvent placés sous le feu des projecteurs dans ce type d'œuvre, les artistes cherchant à dépeindre les nuances des émotions vécues par leurs jeunes sujets à travers les leçons de la vie. Le petit garçon dans la peinture d'Aubert vient de toute évidence de se faire gronder. Il a été mis au coin dans la cuisine, un repas frugal de pain et d'eau en guise de punition. La tête basse, il porte un mouchoir à son visage pour essuyer ses larmes. Mais il n'est pas accablé de douleur au point de n'avoir pas conscience du spectateur. Avec un seul œil visible, il transmet plus d'émotions qu'il ne pourrait le faire des deux yeux. Il y a ambiguïté dans le contact qu'il cherche à établir : est-il un enfant gâté puni à juste titre ou a-t-il été traité injustement ? Est-il vraiment désolé et donc digne de pardon ? Ou est-ce un semblant de chagrin enfantin conçu pour contourner les prérogatives des adultes ? Le double titre de la peinture suggère des lectures différentes de la situation. Le concept de pénitence a des connotations religieuses associées principalement à Marie-Madeleine. Les images de Madeleine dans la tradition catholique sont généralement saturées d'émotion, un poids que de si frêles épaules ne seraient pas en mesure de porter. La peinture de Louis Aubert a coïncidé avec une valorisation de l'enfance par Jean-Jacques Rousseau et d'autres penseurs qui considéraient l'enfant comme un être fondamentalement innocent. Ce nouveau cadre moral entraîna une redéfinition de ce qui constituait le bien et le mal. La pose du boudeur est devenue un thème populaire dans les arts visuels. On la retrouve dans plusieurs des compositions de groupe de Greuze, par exemple *Silence !* (Royaume-Uni, Royal Collection). Greuze a également traité le sujet magistralement dans son tableau à figure unique, *Le Petit Boudeur* (Christie's, Paris, 23 juin 2010, n° 64). Comme son *Petit Paresseux* (cat. 40), cette peinture était autrefois dans la prestigieuse collection de La Live de Jully. Face à la peinture à l'eau de rose d'Aubert, le spectateur a le choix de la meilleure réaction émotionnelle. **MP**

Ubaldo Gandolfi

(Bologne, 1728 – Ravenne, 1781)

Buste de garcon avec une pièce, vers 1777

H.s.t. ; H. 0,47 ; L. 0,38
Bologne, Pinacoteca Nazionale, inv. 420.

Historique : Don des héritiers de Vittoria Modena, 1917.
Expositions : Ottawa, Little Rock, 1993, fig. 187.
Bibliographie : Roli, 1977, p. 175, ill. 332d ; Bernardini 1987, nº 319 ; Biagi Maino, 1990, nº 128, p. 272.

Né dans une importante famille d'artistes bolonais, Gandolfi était peintre, dessinateur et sculpteur. Il remporta le prix de dessin de l'Accademia Clementina en 1745 puis en 1759. Entre ces deux dates, il a probablement voyagé à Florence et à Venise. Dans les années 1760 et 1770, il a exécuté de nombreuses commandes, des compositions religieuses à plusieurs personnages et des études de figures isolées. Il est réputé pour ses études du corps humain et sa capacité à capter les nuances de l'émotion.

L'œuvre d'Ubaldo Gandolfi témoigne d'une maîtrise impressionnante de la figure humaine, en partie grâce à sa formation en anatomie. Ses nombreuses « teste di carattere », produites dans les années 1760 et 1770, illustrent les passages entre peinture religieuse et peinture profane : saints réalistes et études sensibles d'hommes, de femmes et d'enfants (fig. page 24), les personnages profanes prenant des poses d'inspiration religieuse – yeux levés en extase ou regard baissé et plein de tristesse –, ce qui donne des compositions dynamiques, chargées d'émotion. Comme celles de son frère Gaetano, les « teste » peintes par Ubaldo se vendaient bien et ont peut-être été utilisées en tant que répertoire d'images d'atelier. Ce garçon aux cheveux bouclés de la Pinacothèque de Bologne a été peint pour le marquis Gregorio Casali, ardent partisan et ami de l'artiste. Casali avait précédemment commandé à Gandolfi une série de petites peintures de saints pour un orphelinat, le Conservatoire de Santa Maria del Barraccano. Probablement était-il impressionné par la façon dont Gandolfi peignait les êtres humains, en plan rapproché, puisqu'en 1777 il commanda une série de « mezze figure », principalement des enfants. Comme c'est le cas avec d'autres figures de fantaisie, les œuvres de Gandolfi résultaient d'une forme de complicité avec un mécène désireux de mieux appréhender le processus artistique. Le jeune garçon angélique est serein face au regard du spectateur. Il tient précieusement une pièce de monnaie dont la signification reste ouverte. Rappelant la notion biblique selon laquelle il faut rendre à César ce qui appartient à César et à Dieu ce qui appartient à Dieu, l'œuvre pourrait symboliser une tension entre le matériel et le spirituel. Les représentations de l'argent dans les arts visuels tendent généralement à traiter de l'avarice ou de la vanité. Les vieillards sont montrés comptant des pièces de monnaie, signe de la dernière étape de la vie. Cependant, le jeune personnage apparaît ici insensible à ces préoccupations ; une leçon de morale paraît donc inappropriée. Il n'est pas non plus vêtu de haillons et ne semble pas malheureux. Si c'est un mendiant, c'en est un bien plus chanceux que celui d'Opie (cat. 15) : il a déjà obtenu son obole. Comme pour nombre de figures de fantaisie, le « sens » en est finalement assez ténu, réduit à la force de l'instant et aux qualités pittoresques de l'œuvre d'art. La pièce est un petit bijou, tout comme le garçon, et ses éclats dorés projettent une lumière vers le haut, illuminant le visage. Le même modèle peut être vu peint en berger dans un autre tableau de Gandolfi, également propriété de Casali (Bologne, Pinacoteca Nazionale). **MP**

15

John Opie

(Saint Agnes, Cornouailles, 1761 – Londres, 1807)

Jeune Mendiant

H.s.t. ; H. 0,91 ; L. 0,71
Falmouth Art Gallery,
inv. FAMAG 2004.16

Historique : Collection des ducs de Sutherland ; acheté en 2004 avec l'aide de la subvention de l'Heritage Lottery Fund, du MLA/V&A Museum Achat Fonds, du Fonds d'art Beecroft Legs, de la Cornwall Fiducie du patrimoine et des Canterbury Auction Galleries.
Exposition : Royaume-Uni, 1962-1963.
Bibliographie : Hendra, 2007 ; Chu, 2014, p. 136-137, 213 ; Mould, online archive.

John Opie a entamé une modeste carrière en Cornouailles comme peintre de portraits et de tableaux de fantaisie. Arrivé à Londres en 1781, il fut salué comme « la merveille de Cornouailles », artiste autodidacte avec une telle compréhension instinctive du clair-obscur qu'il fut comparé au Caravage et à Rembrandt. Exploitant ses origines rustiques, il a dépeint mendiants et campagnards, personnages populaires parmi l'élite urbaine. Il est devenu un membre à part entière de l'Académie royale en 1786.

Ce plan rapproché d'un jeune mendiant qui nous fixe attire l'attention sur l'acte de regarder. Le visage grave, les pieds nus, le gamin tend son chapeau vide et lève les yeux. Ses cheveux en boucle sur le front accentuent son innocence. C'est un détail charmant qui peut attendrir le spectateur, fût-il le plus endurci. L'enfant est vu en plongée et, par conséquent, semble encore plus vulnérable, tandis que le spectateur est implicitement adulte, riche, dans une position d'influence. Mais cette hiérarchie entre les points de vue des protagonistes est contrariée par la sensation que c'est l'enfant qui domine. La présence du spectateur est évoquée par une ombre distincte sur la manche et la main gauche du garçon. C'est ce genre d'effets de clair-obscur qui a forgé la réputation de l'artiste. Il crée ainsi une relation aussi bien physique qu'émotionnelle et implique plus encore le spectateur dans la scène : en bougeant, il briserait l'illusion.

Les premiers sujets peints par Opie étaient des campagnards de ses Cornouailles natales. Par chance, il est arrivé dans la capitale au moment où la mode des tableaux de fantaisie représentant les pauvres gens était à son apogée. Reynolds a connu le succès avec son *Jeune Mendiant et sa sœur* (1775, Buscot Park, The Faringdon Coll.), tandis que *Un berger* de Gainsborough (détruit ; connu grâce au mezzotinte de Richard Earlom [1743-1822]) a fait sensation à l'exposition de la Royal Academy en 1781. Ces trois artistes avaient une dette envers Murillo (cat. 7) et ses charmants enfants mendiants, ainsi qu'envers Ribera. Selon toute vraisemblance, le *Jeune Mendiant* du Falmouth est le « mendiant » qu'Opie a présenté à la Royal Academy en 1782 et qui a été très bien reçu. Exploitant sa solide authenticité et son talent d'assimilation des maîtres anciens, il a continué à peindre d'humbles sujets dont le regard fixe arrête le spectateur, par exemple *Portrait d'un garçon dans un chapeau haut-de-forme* (Londres, Victoria & Albert Museum). Son très grand tableau *La Famille du paysan* (Londres, Tate Britain) confère aux gens simples une sorte de dignité monumentale. Émouvant bien que déterminé, plus encore que le vagabond couché de Traversi (cat. 69), le *Jeune Mendiant* d'Opie nous incite à regarder le monde à travers ses yeux. **MP**

Musiciens

16

Antiveduto Gramatica

(Rome, vers 1571-1626)

Joueur de théorbe

H.s.t. ; H. 1,19 ; L. 0,85

Turin, Galleria Sabauda, inv. 93

Historique : Collection Del Monte ? ; marquis Falletti di Barolo, Turin.
Expositions : Londres/Rome, 2001, no 33.
Bibliographie : Papi, 1995, p. 89.

La carrière de Gramatica, romain mais issu d'une famille originaire de Sienne, croisa à plusieurs reprises celle du Caravage, qui pourrait avoir travaillé dans son atelier. Ils furent soutenus par les mêmes mécènes, le cardinal Del Monte et le marquis Giustiniani. Le parcours de Gramatica est assez prestigieux puisqu'il entra à l'académie de Saint-Luc en 1593 pour en devenir prince en 1624, position dont il fut rapidement chassé à la suite d'une cabale. Sa production reste mal documentée et se caractérise par des formes géométriques et un clair-obscur violent. Il fait partie des artistes plus âgés ou contemporains du Caravage qui ont été totalement influencés par le génie de ce dernier.

L'attitude de cet élégant musicien ne s'explique que par notre connaissance de l'histoire matérielle du tableau. Il n'est pas rare de voir des représentations d'instrumentistes totalement absorbés dans leur jeu au point de tourner leur regard vers un point intérieur, visible d'eux seuls. Ici, le joueur de théorbe fixe un point hors champ. Une copie aujourd'hui perdue de la composition originelle nous le montre faisant face à une femme qui joue de la flûte. D'ailleurs, la zone gauche du tableau de Turin présente des traces de reprise à l'emplacement où apparaissaient une épaule et un bras de la femme. L'inventaire de 1627 de la collection Del Monte comporte la mention d'un concert de la main de Gramatica et ses dimensions semblent correspondre à la composition complète.

On peut donc légitimement se demander si ce personnage isolé se définit comme une figure de fantaisie ou comme le fragment d'une scène de genre à deux personnages. Selon nous, certains concerts caravagesques agrémentés d'éléments narratifs (des regards de séduction appuyés, une complicité active entre les protagonistes) doivent être rangés dans la catégorie des scènes de genre tandis que ceux où chaque musicien s'isole dans une célébration inspirée nous paraissent plus conformes à notre définition ouverte d'une figure de fantaisie en quête de sujets universels.

La source de ce tableau comme d'autres représentations de musiciens du mouvement caravagesque est le *Joueur de luth* du Caravage peint pour Del Monte (New York, The Metropolitan Museum of Art) plus que celui destiné à Giustiniani (Saint-Pétersbourg, musée de l'Ermitage). Les modèles du musicien ne sont pas comparables : l'adolescent androgyne du Caravage ne ressemble en rien au courtisan accompli de Gramatica. Le second a emprunté au premier le dispositif de la table recouverte d'un tapis rouge, à la nature morte instrumentale modelée par la lumière, ainsi que les doigts effilés véritablement ciselés. Le clair-obscur est d'une intensité rarement atteinte, l'ombre de la main droite du musicien sur la caisse du théorbe offrant le morceau de bravoure d'une composition qui n'en manque pas. La virtuosité de l'artiste se manifeste dans le rendu des vêtements et des objets mais l'expression du personnage est totalement intériorisée, sans aucune recherche de pittoresque. L'atmosphère de raffinement et de contrôle n'est pas sans évoquer Orazio Gentileschi, peut-être un effet du tropisme toscan de ces deux peintres.

Le tableau a longtemps été attribué au Caravage lui-même et il passait pour l'un de ses chefs-d'œuvre, ce qui est un bon indice de sa qualité. On comprend aisément les difficultés de datation des œuvres de Gramatica en constatant que le style du tableau correspondrait à une exécution vers 1605. Néanmoins, l'association du théorbe et de la guitare espagnole, qui avaient supplanté le luth, n'est courante qu'après 1615.

Même mutilé, le tableau reste l'un des plus beaux exemples dans le milieu caravagesque de ces représentations de musiciens inspirés. **AH**

17

Bernardo Strozzi

(Gênes, 1581/1582 – Venise, 1644)

Le Joueur de piffero (Il Pifferaio), vers 1624-1625

H.s.t. ; H. 0,73 ; L. 0,61
Gênes, Musei di Strada Nuova
Palazzo Rosso, inv. PR 56

Historique : Collection Brignole-Sale à partir de 1684 au moins ; donné à la Ville de Gênes en 1874.
Exposition : Gênes, 1995, no 38.
Bibliographie : Mortari, 1966, p. 28, 47, 116.

Strozzi fut l'élève du peintre siennois Pietro Sorri avant d'entrer dans l'ordre des Capucins à Gênes en 1597, d'où ses surnoms de Cappuccino ou Prete Genovese. Il s'illustra dans tous les genres de la peinture jusqu'à ce qu'il décide de rompre ses vœux. Emprisonné, il s'évada pour s'installer à Venise en 1630. Narrateur à l'imagination débordante, son style se prête au grand décor et à la peinture religieuse, dont il laissa de beaux témoignages dans ces deux villes. Une inspiration naturaliste est présente dans toute sa production qui se caractérise par des dons exceptionnels de coloriste.

L*e Joueur de piffero* du Palazzo Rosso de Gênes constitue la plus célèbre version d'une composition traitée à de nombreuses reprises par Strozzi. La collection Brignole-Sale, dont il constituait une pièce de choix, était l'une de celles que l'on montrait aux visiteurs de passage. Ainsi, le président de Brosses (qui le désigne comme « le *Flûteur* du Capuccino »), Cochin ou Flaubert ont mentionné ce tableau. Le *pifferaio* est parfois représenté seul comme dans les tableaux autrefois dans les collections Ferrari de Gênes ou Mazzucchelli de Milan. Le peintre a aussi développé la composition en un véritable concert de trois à cinq musiciens (entre autres, San Francisco, Legion of Honor, ou Pommersfelden, collection Schönborn). Aux côtés d'un flûtiste et d'un joueur de cornemuse, le *pifferaio* s'impose toujours comme le personnage le plus savoureux. Tantôt il offre le visage chenu du soliste de Gênes, tantôt il arbore un chapeau à plumes, mais il ne s'agit pas systématiquement du même modèle.

Les représentations de musiciens des Pays-Bas du XVIe siècle ou des caravagesques insistaient sur l'enthousiasme presque mystique lié à la pratique musicale et sur la faculté d'absorbement de ces praticiens dans leur art. Dans ces œuvres, seul le visage du chanteur est déformé. Dans ses versions des *pifferai*, Strozzi souligne les joues gonflées dans l'effort, la rougeur du visage, le froncement des rides et le regard concentré de l'interprète. Le cadrage serré sur l'instrumentiste permet au spectateur d'appréhender d'un seul coup d'œil la totalité de la figure et d'en percevoir tous les détails. Une prise de vue en réflectographie infrarouge effectuée en 1995 a révélé un repentir du peintre. Initialement, le *piffero* était légèrement plus court et Strozzi s'est contenté d'élargir de manière spectaculaire le pavillon de l'instrument, ce qui augmente la profondeur de la composition.

Si Strozzi s'est plu à reprendre des compositions caravagesques en les adaptant (*Les Pèlerins d'Emmaüs*, *David*), *Il Pifferaio* est sans doute l'une de ses œuvres les plus naturalistes. Plus qu'au caravagisme, c'est à la confrontation avec la peinture nordique ancienne et aux artistes flamands actifs à Gênes que Strozzi doit le choix du sujet et son interprétation.

Les joueurs de *piffero* ou de cornemuse, encore présents dans les villes italiennes au moment de Noël, sont souvent des bergers des montagnes. Néanmoins, ici, le statut de berger du protagoniste est secondaire. Ni d'une pastorale ni d'une allégorie, il s'agit d'une figure pittoresque mise en scène pour le plaisir d'un amateur.

Les délicates harmonies mettent en lumière les talents exceptionnels de Strozzi comme coloriste, reconnus en son temps et célébrés de nos jours. Le pourpre du gilet se détachant sur la chemise blanche constitue une véritable signature de l'artiste. Ce blanc lui-même vibre d'infinies nuances sur un fond de mur clair également varié. La carnation du vieil homme se présente en passages raffinés d'un gris verdâtre jusqu'à un rouge homard. Quelques touches de lumière habilement dispensées donnent une qualité extrêmement sensuelle et vivante à cet être qui s'anime.

Une datation vers 1624-1625 semble aujourd'hui réunir la majorité des suffrages autour de ce malicieux chef-d'œuvre. **AH**

18

Pietro Bellotti

(Volciano, 1625 – Gargnano del Garda, 1700)

Un vieux chanteur

H.s.t. ; H. 0,72 ; L. 0,54
Courtesy galerie Canesso, Paris

Historique : Paris, collection particulière ; Milan, collection particulière ; Paris, galerie Canesso.
Exposition : Paris, 2009, p. 42-47.
Bibliographie : Anelli, 1996, p. 83, R 70.

Pietro Bellotti se forma dans l'atelier de Forabosco à partir de l'âge de douze ans. Sa notoriété de son vivant contraste avec l'oubli dans lequel il tomba par la suite. Si son séjour à Paris n'est pas avéré, il fut peintre à Munich à la cour de l'Électeur de Bavière en 1668-1669 et à Milan auprès du gouverneur, le duc d'Ucedo, entre 1670 et 1674. Il fut nommé en 1681 surintendant des Galeries ducales de Mantoue. Son talent s'exerça essentiellement dans le domaine du portrait et dans les représentations en buste de mendiants et de vieillards.

Longtemps oublié, Pietro Bellotti est aujourd'hui considéré comme l'un des meilleurs représentants des peintres de la vie quotidienne du XVIIe siècle lombard. Au sein d'une production inégale et mal datée, ce tableau partage des caractéristiques avec le *Vieux Mendiant avec la bouteille du pèlerin sur le globe* (Londres, The National Gallery) et le *Vieux Pèlerin avec un bâton* (Dallas, Museum of Art). Francesco Frangi a proposé de dater ces tableaux de la période de maturité de l'artiste, après 1664. Il s'agit de représentations à mi-corps de mendiants en haillons figurés dans une activité noble qui contraste avec leur apparence misérable. Rien ne permet d'affirmer que les trois tableaux constituaient une série mais la qualité d'exécution très élevée et la forte présence des personnages permettent d'imaginer que la formule a rencontré un grand succès auprès des amateurs. On sait que la carrière de Bellotti fut véritablement européenne avec des séjours attestés à Venise, Milan, Munich, Mantoue et hypothétique à Paris.

Face aux peintres originaires d'Europe du Nord comme Monsù Bernardo qui traitaient leurs sujets populaires dans un style rustique appuyé, Bellotti incarne une tendance opposée qui consiste à affirmer la noblesse des sentiments et la science du pinceau. Aucun attribut ne permet de sortir ce vieillard de l'anonymat des mendiants des rues. Toutefois, l'artiste lui confère la dignité que Ribera, son modèle à bien des égards par l'insistance sur les rides et l'intensité de la lumière, prêtait aux ermites chrétiens et aux philosophes antiques. L'abandon total du personnage dans le chant, les yeux baissés vers la partition, constitue une reprise du thème caravagesque du musicien absorbé et inspiré.

L'éclairage généreux et égal fait ressortir toutes les aspérités des surfaces, le tissu rapiécé du manteau, les rides profondes du visage et des mains, les poils chenus de la barbe bien fournie, les ongles sales. Le peintre affiche ostensiblement le travail du pinceau aussi bien dans les effets de surépaisseur que dans les transparences. Néanmoins, la lumière uniforme donne un aspect fini qui contraste avec la spontanéité de la touche. Bellotti accomplit ainsi la transformation de la peinture d'exécution en art libéral, rendant le sujet acceptable pour un connaisseur raffiné.

S'il ne faut pas surinterpréter ces scènes de la vie quotidienne, les figures de vieux sages qui parcourent le monde ont une valeur universelle. Ils incarnent la dignité humaine et une aspiration artistique d'ordre spirituel. Le *Vieux Chanteur* de Bellotti est un caractère de la comédie humaine qui ne s'oublie pas. **AH**

19

Luca Giordano

(Naples, 1634-1705)

Musicien accordant son luth

H.s.t. ; H. 1,28 ; L. 1,02
Amiens, musée de Picardie,
inv. M.P. Lav. 1894-246

Historique : Collection du peintre Guillon-Lethière ; donation Lavalard, 1890.
Exposition : Amiens, 1998-1999, p. 5-8.
Bibliographie : Brejon, Volle, 1988, p. 170 ; Ferrari, Scavizzi, 1992, I, n° A 24, p. 254, II, p. 291.

Luca Giordano fut le plus grand peintre napolitain de la seconde moitié du XVIIe siècle ainsi qu'un acteur majeur de la culture européenne. Formé dans l'entourage de Ribera, il voyagea à Rome, Venise et Florence en 1652. Il réalisa des commandes importantes pour les Médicis à Florence en 1665 puis à partir de 1682. De 1692 à 1702, il sera actif pour la cour d'Espagne, à l'Escurial ou au Buen Retiro à Madrid. À Naples et en Italie du Sud, ses réalisations les plus importantes sont destinées à l'abbaye du Mont-Cassin, l'église de Santa Brigida et la cathédrale de Naples. Son œuvre est considérable et sa rapidité d'exécution, proverbiale, d'où son surnom *Luca fa presto*. Son talent protéiforme en fait l'un des plus grands peintres baroques.

Ribera fut le premier à développer le portrait de philosophe antique figuré en haillons et à mi-corps, avec une forte présence physique. Giordano reprit cette thématique au début de sa carrière avec la volonté évidente d'imiter son modèle. Ses philosophes débraillés sont systématiquement représentés devant une table où sont posés des écrits. Leurs expressions truculentes et excessives évoquent davantage le cynisme et l'épicurisme que la sagesse antique « bien-pensante ».

Si le *Musicien* d'Amiens s'intègre aisément dans cette galerie de personnages hauts en couleur, il a gêné les commentateurs, qui l'interprètent soit comme un philosophe soit comme un musicien, le titre adopté ici étant celui qui lui était donné dans la collection Guillon-Lethière. De toute évidence, la typologie du musicien correspond à celle de l'allégorie de l'Ouïe dans les cycles des cinq sens. L'attention portée à l'instrument par le personnage et sa place dans la composition en témoignent avec éloquence. Toutefois, il ne s'agit pas d'un musicien des rues, d'un loqueteux contemporain auquel on jette quelques pièces, mais bien d'un luthiste dans la tenue intemporelle du philosophe antique.

Quelques-uns des philosophes de Giordano sont des autoportraits ou des portraits de membres de son entourage. On ne peut rien affirmer quant au modèle du *Musicien* d'Amiens. Le regard sournois et gourmand à la fois du personnage ainsi que sa force animale font penser aux représentations de bourreaux inquiétants et de vieux philosophes dégénérés de la main de notre artiste. Néanmoins, son visage joufflu et son expression finalement sympathique laissent entrevoir l'utilisation d'un membre de l'entourage du peintre comme modèle de cette figure de fantaisie.

Avant de devenir l'un des grands metteurs en scène de la clarté surnaturelle du baroque méridional grâce à son étude assidue de Titien, Rubens et Pierre de Cortone, Giordano a exploré longuement au début des années 1650 les effets du clair-obscur en se replongeant dans la tradition napolitaine du Caravage et de Ribera. Ici, sur le fond de mur nu, délimitation bien connue des scénographies caravagesques, Giordano dirige son éclairage sur sa figure habillée de noir et à la sombre pilosité. Seuls la carnation, le feuillet et le reflet sur l'âme luisante du luth ressortent de cette obscurité envahissante, avec un effet d'une puissance spectaculaire. On comprend pourquoi on a parlé de l'art des ténébristes.

Giordano est l'un des plus grands virtuoses de l'histoire de la peinture. Il s'astreint, certes, à une relative sobriété dans ses hommages juvéniles à Ribera mais il sait mieux que quiconque porter à ses plus radicales conséquences le clair-obscur dans son chant du cygne. Les touches nerveuses qui animent les carnations du musicien, donnant l'illusion de la vie, sont des modèles du genre. L'efficacité du traitement pictural persuade aisément le public de la vérité de la représentation. C'est ce qui lui permet de brouiller les frontières des genres entre portrait, histoire et fantaisie, et de nous présenter un musicien qui est aussi un philosophe et une allégorie de l'Ouïe. **AH**

20

Alexis Grimou

(Argenteuil, 1678 – Paris, 1733)

Portrait d'un joueur de vielle à roue, 1732 ?

H.s.t. ; H. 1,30 ; L. 1,00
Montluçon, musée des Musiques populaires, inv. 1973.2.1

Historique : Acquis par la Ville de Montluçon en 1973.
Exposition : Bourg-en-Bresse, 2008, no 22, p. 108.
Bibliographie : Réau, 1930, II, p. 195-215 ; Dufour, 1984 ; Jacquot, 1994 ; Gétreau, 1996, p. 90-103.

Élève de François de Troy et de Bon Boullogne, Grimou obtint son agrément à l'Académie royale en 1705, mais n'acheva jamais son morceau de réception. Il préféra rejoindre l'académie de Saint-Luc. Spécialisé dans l'exécution de demi-figures, Grimou introduisit en France les types de figures nordiques (musiciens, soldats), tout en composant ses propres variations de pèlerins et d'« Espagnolettes ». Il peignit aussi plusieurs autoportraits le représentant en train de boire. Sa réputation posthume d'ivrogne fut nettement exagérée et il était fort apprécié de ses contemporains, qui le surnommaient le « Rembrandt français ».

La figure de fantaisie de Grimou fusionne deux royaumes de fantaisie qui étaient à la mode à son époque : le mode pastoral et le mode « espagnol ». Au Moyen-Âge, la vielle à roue était perçue comme un instrument noble mais, au cours de la Renaissance, elle était plus courante chez les bergers et les mendiants pauvres, souvent aveugles. On peut en voir dans les scènes de kermesse de Breughel et de Teniers, chez les sujets humbles de Jacques Callot et de Georges de La Tour, ainsi que dans les diverses séries gravées de « Cris de Paris » représentant les vendeurs des rues de la ville. Dans la seconde partie du XVIIe siècle, jouer de la vielle à roue avec d'autres instruments « populaires » telle la cornemuse redevint à la mode à la cour et parmi les aristocrates, dans un esprit de nostalgie d'un passé arcadien. S'habiller à la savoyarde en se munissant des accessoires associés, c'est-à-dire de la vielle à roue et des marmottes savantes, était en vogue auprès des élites, surtout féminines, du XVIIIe siècle, comme en témoignent les portraits de Loir, de Nonnotte, de Drouais et de Carmontelle. Avec ce portrait et ceux d'autres musiciens (joueurs de pipeau, de tambourin et de mandoline), Grimou représente le croisement entre formes de musique populaire et élitiste, comme le faisait également son contemporain Watteau. Le musicien joue d'un instrument de forme trapézoïdale. Représenté dans un format relativement grand, le musicien a l'air d'une « personne de qualité ». Vêtu élégamment, il porte la fraise, les manches à crevés, la cape et les rosettes typiques du costume dit « espagnol », mélange anachronique de références picturales et théâtrales évoquant l'imaginaire et l'exotisme. Tout comme les pèlerins et les soldats de Grimou, ce joueur de vielle à roue semble plus à sa place dans un bal masqué que dans la rue. Cependant, les ombres rembranesques ne dévoilent rien sur le lieu et instaurent une atmosphère mystérieuse. Cette toile est probablement le *Joueur de vielle* que Grimou présenta lors de l'Exposition de la Jeunesse de 1732, place Dauphine, où elle suscita une vive admiration. Il avait déjà peint en 1728 une joueuse de vielle à roue (localisation actuelle inconnue, ill. Gétreau, 1996, p. 90). Il ne fait aucun doute qu'il s'agit là d'une œuvre peinte pendant la période de maturité de Grimou. En totale harmonie de forme et de ton avec son instrument, le joueur de vielle à roue semble alerte et pourtant détendu, absorbé par sa musique, mais conscient de la présence du spectateur.

MP

21

Philippe [Philip] Mercier

(Berlin, 1689 – Londres, 1760)

Joueur de cornemuse, vers 1740

H.s.t. ; H. 0,91 ; L. 0,71
S.g. *P. M.*
Strasbourg, musée des Beaux-Arts, inv. 1866

Historique : Dépôt des Musées nationaux (MNR 67), 1951 ; œuvre récupérée en 1945 par les Alliés ; attribuée au musée du Louvre par l'Office des biens et intérêts privés en 1950 ; déposée au musée des Beaux-Arts de Strasbourg en 1951.
Expositions : York/Londres, 1969, nº 54, p. 48.
Bibliographie : Haug, 1955, nº 335 bis, p. 6-7 ; Ingamells, Raines, 1976-1978, p. 1-70, nº 178, p. 46 ; Chu, 2014.
Œuvre en rapport : Mezzotinte de John Faber II, vers 1745-1750, 0,29 × 0,22 m, gravure extraite d'une série de six œuvres intitulée *The Rural Life* (« Scènes pastorales »). *Cf.* Smith, 1878-1883, nº 405.

John Faber II d'après Philippe Mercier, mezzotinte de la série *The Rural Life*, Londres, The British Museum

Mercier naquit à Berlin dans une famille d'émigrés huguenots et se forma aux côtés d'Antoine Pesne. Après avoir séjourné en France et en Italie, il s'installa à Londres en 1716 où il se fit connaître comme peintre et graveur de scènes inspirées de Watteau. Peintre principal de Frédéric, prince de Galles, entre 1736 et 1739, il réalisa des portraits de membres de la famille de Hanovre. Il s'attira également une clientèle bourgeoise, à Londres comme en province. Mercier est considéré comme le créateur de la « fancy picture » en Angleterre et son travail s'inscrit dans une démarche novatrice mêlant le style français en vogue à l'époque à la représentation des vertus de la vie domestique ainsi qu'à celle des sentiments.

L'artiste a saisi toute l'expressivité de ce jeune musicien profondément absorbé dans ses pensées. Sa cornemuse est bien en place et ses doigts sont en position, prêts à jouer ou jouant déjà peut-être. L'instrument fonctionne par le jeu des soufflets coincés sous son bras, aussi les traits du personnage ne sont-ils pas déformés, comme ils le seraient avec d'autres types de cornemuse. Bien que le garçon soit vêtu simplement, dans des tons sourds, son habit comporte quelques détails ornementaux : une veste aux reflets légèrement satinés, une rosette bleue sur le chapeau et, touche éloquente, un ruban rose noué au-dessus du coude. En outre, un examen attentif de son instrument laisse à penser que nous ne sommes pas là en présence d'un musicien des rues ordinaire. Dans cette œuvre pastorale, le joueur est confortablement assis au pied d'un arbre dont les hautes branches font saillie à l'horizontale, à l'instar des tuyaux de la cornemuse, formant ainsi une discrète canopée. Mercier se forgea une solide réputation en Angleterre grâce à ses « fantaisies plaisantes », selon l'expression utilisée par l'éditeur George Vertue dans ses carnets (Vertue, 1933, p. 84). Cette peinture appartient à cette catégorie d'œuvres où sont représentés des personnages seuls ou en groupes qui se consacrent à la musique, au jeu ou à la conversation : accortes servantes tout absorbées par des tâches domestiques ou commerçants en plein négoce. L'artiste reste aujourd'hui relativement inconnu en France, et le tableau exposé à Strasbourg appartient à la petite poignée d'œuvres conservées dans les collections françaises. Pourtant, Mercier sut traduire l'esprit de Watteau, de De Troy et de Chardin, et cette touche française avait une très forte valeur marchande outre-Manche.

Dans des tableaux plus anciens, de Brueghel et Teniers, cet instrument est associé à des festivités champêtres, de même que chez Ter Brugghen, où il s'impose au centre, en gros plan (*cf.* le tableau exposé à l'Ashmolean Museum d'Oxford, par exemple). Comme la vielle à roue (cat. 20), la cornemuse gagna ses lettres de noblesse aux XVIIe et XVIIIe siècles en France. On en trouve une variante, la « musette de cour », chez Watteau, et dans les portraits « savoyards » d'aristocrates qui posèrent pour Rigaud et Drouais. En revanche, cet instrument n'était pas répandu dans les arts visuels anglais (sauf dans les scènes paysannes truculentes revisitées par Hogarth). Il se peut donc que les peintures de Mercier aient eu un attrait quelque peu exotique. Dans la série de huit gravures à la manière noire réalisées par John Faber le Jeune d'après les tableaux de Mercier, le thème pastoral du joueur de cornemuse trouve son plein épanouissement. Ces gravures, sous le nom de *The Rural Life* (« La Vie champêtre »), dépeignent, par exemple, un jeune paysan jouant de la flûte et du tambourin, une servante barattant de la crème et une jeune fille munie d'un râteau. Faber collabora avec Mercier dans les années 1730 et 1740 sur différents projets (fig. page 81) ; on peut supposer que le commerce des gravures permit à Mercier de financer son activité picturale. **MP**

22

Il Maggiotto, Domenico Fedeli, *dit*

(Venise, 1712-1794)

Jeune Flûtiste

H.s.t. ; H. 0,72 ; L. 0,57
Venise, Ca'Rezzonico, Museo del Settecento Veneziano, inv. Cl. I n. 1393

Historique : Collection Manfrin (1872) ; Richetti (1901).
Exposition : Merkel, *in* Venise, 1983, nº 63, p. 157-158.
Bibliographie : Bulgarelli, 1973, p. 220-235 ; Pallucchini, 1996, II, p. 172-178.

Maggiotto fut l'élève et l'assistant de Giambattista Piazzetta à partir de l'âge de dix ans et ses premières peintures furent fortement influencées par son maître. Après la mort de Piazzetta, en 1754, Maggiotto eut du mal à trouver sa voie, peignant des œuvres religieuses plutôt froides. Élu à l'Accademia delle Belle Arti en 1756, il développa un nouveau style narratif tendant vers le classicisme, produisant des peintures d'histoire moralisatrices, ainsi que des sujets de genre. Il vécut également de la restauration de peintures.

Considérée comme l'un de ses meilleurs tableaux, cette étude d'un jeune musicien est un bel exemple de la façon dont Maggiotto s'exerça brillamment dans le genre créé par son maître Piazzetta. Il est daté de la période féconde pendant laquelle Maggiotto, jeune homme, travaillait dans l'atelier de Piazzetta aux côtés d'artistes tels que Giuseppe Angeli et fournissait des figures de fantaisie fortement demandées dans la Venise du XVIIIe siècle. Piazzetta avait lui-même mis au point un type unique de peinture à partir de diverses influences telles que celles du Caravage et de Crespi : un format d'image hautement ramassé, des personnages dans des poses suggestives ou énigmatiques, une gamme chromatique réduite comprenant principalement des bruns et des rouges, des ombres profondes et un éclairage lumineux de certains détails (*cf. Jeune Paysanne endormie*, cat. 38). Toutes ces caractéristiques peuvent être vues dans la peinture de Maggiotto. Comme dans d'autres tableaux traitant de musique dans cette exposition, le *Jeune Flûtiste* évite la représentation littérale de la création musicale et offre une interprétation plus spirituelle. Le garçon ne joue pas de sa flûte à bec, mais tourne la tête pour répondre au regard du spectateur. Il saisit son instrument dans un geste quelque peu protecteur. L'embout de la flûte pointant vers sa poitrine peut être lu comme un signe d'introspection. Pourtant, son regard ne montre pas de surprise et n'a rien d'agressif : il semble inoffensif, curieux, sans craindre la personne qui l'a interrompu. Par un emploi habile des expressions du visage, Maggiotto fournit plusieurs récits et plusieurs points de relation possible avec le jeune flûtiste. L'effet vaporeux est créé par une combinaison de techniques : une peinture appliquée avec allant, un *sfumato* sur le contour du visage et une ombre profonde. Ces procédés rendent la figure mystérieuse, à la fois présente et insaisissable. Le garçon porte une chemise blanche et une cape lâche, finement mises en place pour créer de riches harmonies de couleurs. Le gland retenant le drapé sur son épaule est une synecdoque du musicien lui-même : une petite chose sans conséquence à laquelle l'on donne de l'importance et de la valeur. Maggiotto a peint un grand nombre de musiciens, hommes et femmes, joueurs de flûte, de tambourin, ou chanteurs. Il a aussi représenté divers personnages ou petits groupes en buste : bergers, tricheurs aux cartes, fumeurs, artistes au travail, enfants portant des fruits, jeune femme versant du café, vieillards et vieilles femmes. Comme celles de Piazzetta, ses peintures étaient populaires également dans leur version gravée. Maggiotto apporte à ces personnages ordinaires, enveloppés dans l'ombre, pressés contre la surface picturale, du comique ou de l'étrangeté, de l'excentricité ou de la beauté.

MP

Vies intérieures

Jacob Backer

(Harlingen, 1608/1609 – Amsterdam, 1651)

Jeune Garçon au béret

H.s. bois ; H. 0,54 ; L. 0,47
Monogrammé d. *JAB*
Rotterdam, Museum Boijmans Van Beuningen, inv. 2483

Historique : Colin Agnew, Londres, 1913 ; Stephan Auspitz von Artenegg, Vienne ; commerce d'art K. W. Bnachstitz, La Haye ; D. G. van Beuningen ; acquis par le musée en 1958.
Expositions : Amsterdam/Aix-la-Chapelle, 2008-2009, n° 22, A 80.
Bibliographie : Sumowski, 1983-1995, I, p. 138, 199, 251, et VI, p. 3591 ; Hirschfelder, 2008, p. 150, 196.

Descendant d'une famille de boulangers (d'où son nom de famille) d'origine frisonne, Jacob Backer est élevé entre Harlingen et Amsterdam. Il est l'apprenti à Leeuwarden du peintre d'histoire Lambert Jacobsz entre 1626 et 1632. Il s'installe ensuite à Amsterdam, où il réalise une belle carrière, se consacrant à la peinture d'histoire et au portrait. Tout au long de sa vie, il peint aussi des *tronies*. Il fut considéré de son temps comme l'un des plus importants peintres d'Amsterdam. Selon une lecture erronée des sources, il aurait été l'élève de Rembrandt mais il n'en est rien.

L'existence à la documentation du RKD à La Haye de la photographie d'une variante ou d'une copie du tableau de Rotterdam rappelle, si besoin en était, la fragilité de l'usage du terme « tronie ». En effet, cette tête d'enfant non localisée porte une inscription « Fl. Aetat suae 14 », ce qui nous apprend deux choses : une attribution non vérifiable à Flinck, compagnon d'apprentissage de Backer chez Lambert Jacobsz, et surtout l'âge du jeune modèle, quatorze ans. Or les *tronies* n'étant pas des portraits, il est hautement inusuel de trouver mention de l'âge ou de l'identité du modèle. Toutefois, cet effet de surprise passé, il est possible de réconcilier ces deux notions et de considérer que nous sommes en présence de l'effigie réelle d'un garçon traitée sur le mode du *tronie*.

Ce que Backer a réussi à rendre à merveille et qui transcende l'idée de ressemblance, c'est l'indétermination même des traits des très jeunes personnes. Les yeux flottent dans le vide au fond de larges orbites, les lèvres vermillonnes paraissent à peine posées sur le visage et semblent à deux doigts de s'effondrer sur la fossette. Un accent lumineux vient souligner ce que la carnation du jeune homme peut avoir de fraîcheur presque humide. Ce préadolescent, comme on dirait aujourd'hui, appartient encore de plein droit au monde de la petite enfance. Son expression évoque plutôt la rêverie créative que l'action et l'énergie vitale. À la manière d'autres têtes d'enfants, garçons et filles, qu'il peignit au cours de sa carrière, Backer choisit de mettre en valeur un détail saillant de l'habillement de ses modèles, ici le bonnet en fourrure à plumes, dérivé de Rembrandt. Le col blanc se détache également sur le manteau brun. À part ces éléments, aucun décor ne vient troubler la contemplation de cette représentation en buste, de trois quarts sur un fond monochrome brunâtre. La technique picturale est à la fois brillante et extrêmement simple. L'exécution frappe par sa rapidité. Le pinceau ne semble s'être arrêté qu'à de rares reprises pour renforcer sur une boucle l'épaisseur de la chevelure ou pour accentuer les lignes de force du drapé. La couche de préparation est perceptible sur une grande partie du mur de fond mais également sur le manteau. Cette vitesse correspond certes aux pratiques d'atelier pour ce type de tête d'étude mais il y a chez Backer, et c'est en cela qu'il se distingue de Rembrandt, une volonté de conférer un fini et une délicatesse à toutes les productions de son atelier. Comme dans la *Petite Fille au collier de perles* (coll. part.), il y a dans le *Jeune Garçon au béret* une forme de compromis entre la manière des *fijnschilders* et l'informel rembranesque.

Le but premier de Backer est la recherche de l'émotion grâce au contraste entre le déguisement d'adulte et l'innocence de l'enfance. Dans ce but, il entreprend au début des années 1640 de recycler les recettes antérieures de l'atelier de Rembrandt datant du début des années 1630 dans le costume, la facture et l'harmonie monochrome. En y ajoutant une touche finale de joliesse, il parvient à créer une image sentimentale. La langue allemande aurait un adjectif parfait pour décrire ce jeune garçon : *Bildhübsch*, soit joli comme une image. **AH**

Francesco Giovani, ou Juvanis

(Rome, 1611-1669)

La Lecture avec des bésicles

H.s. bois ; H. 0,51 ; L. 0,41
S.b.d. *Giovanj*
Lecce, collection Luciano Treggiari

Exposition : Conversano, 2014, n° 9.

Élève d'Andrea Sacchi et de Pier Francesco Mola, deux des peintres majeurs de la Rome classique du XVIIe siècle, Francesco Giovani est surtout connu comme graveur. Bien qu'il ait gravé l'un de ses tableaux, il ne semble pas s'être formé dans l'atelier de Maratta, comme on le lit parfois. Parmi ses quelques peintures répertoriées, on trouve des tableaux d'histoire et des figures de fantaisie.

Le principe des représentations de lecteurs réside dans la difficulté à déterminer le statut et la condition sociale des modèles. La lecture même devient ainsi une condition de leur être bien plus qu'un simple passe-temps. Le vieil homme étant enveloppé dans l'obscurité, seuls son visage, ses mains et le petit *in-octavo* sont détaillés par la lumière, ce qui empêche d'examiner son costume, unique élément à même de nous renseigner sur son identité. Raffaele De Giorgi, auteur de la notice (*cf.* Conversano, 2014), parle d'un ecclésiastique car il interprète le livre comme un bréviaire. C'est tout à fait possible mais nous en resterons au terme de lettré, plus neutre et juste sociologiquement parlant.

Le visage du vieillard est bien détaillé et on peut y déceler la présence d'une balafre sur la joue droite, la seule visible. Cette notation, apparemment non signifiante du point de vue du sujet, souligne une volonté certaine de naturalisme. En effet sont montrés les rides, le front dégarni et les fins cheveux blancs. Toutefois, l'esprit de l'artiste est à mille lieux de celui des *Pitocchetti* qui ne nous font grâce d'aucun détail dermatologique et développent une véritable esthétique de la décrépitude, comme dans cette exposition le Maître de l'Annonce aux bergers, Bellotti ou Keil (cat. 60, 64, 63). L'usage de l'éclairage est chez Juvanis particulièrement bienveillant. Il ne vise pas à faire ressortir les aspérités mais adoucit une surface usée fondamentalement harmonieuse. La tonalité dominante des carnations se résume en une teinte miel très chaleureuse que l'on retrouve sur la tranche du livre.

Chez les peintres nordiques, qui ont de toute évidence inspiré Giovani, les figures à bésicles sont traitées avec humour voire ironie. Dans *Le Christ et la femme adultère* de Stom (Montréal, musée des Beaux-Arts), un représentant de l'ancienne foi obscurantiste porte des bésicles qui ne l'aident pas à être visionnaire. Chez Rembrandt, qui semble avoir influencé Juvanis, elles soulignent la quasi-cécité des vieillards. Dans le tableau de Lecce, le vieux lettré jouit apparemment d'une vue satisfaisante.

La production de Giovani est trop méconnue pour que l'on se hasarde à une évaluation de son art. Nous avons cependant affaire à une œuvre de très haute qualité. La présence d'une signature, rare sur ce type de têtes d'étude, témoigne à tout le moins de la satisfaction et de l'ambition de l'artiste. Il atteste la pénétration des modèles de Rembrandt en Italie, connue depuis les recherches de Francis Haskell, et montre qu'il existe un naturalisme baroquisant moins radical que les recherches lombardes ou napolitaines. **AH**

25

Michael Sweerts

(Bruxelles, 1618 – Goa, 1664)

Fileuse

H.s.t. ; H. 0,52 ; L. 0,43
Gouda, Museum Het Catharina-Gasthuis, inv. 55250

Historique : Galerie Goudstikker, en Allemagne durant la Deuxième Guerre mondiale, Stichting Nederlandisch Kunstbezit en 1946.
Expositions : Rotterdam/Rome, 1958, n° 35 (n° 36) ; Amsterdam/San Francisco/Hartford, 2002, p. 177
Bibliographie : Kultzen, 1996, p. 44-45, n° 65, p. 107-108.
Œuvre en rapport : Estampe publiée dans *Diversae Facies*, Bruxelles, 1656.

Michael Sweerts, *Tête de femme* (gravure extraite de *Diversae Facies*), Vienne, Graphische Sammlung Albertina

La vie de Sweerts est un roman, ce qui a contribué à teinter sa production remarquable d'une aura singulière. Les débuts de ce Bruxellois sont inconnus et la première trace de sa présence à Rome date de 1646, où il est signalé jusqu'en 1651 et travaille pour de puissants mécènes romains, comme Camillo Pamphilj, ou hollandais, comme les frères Deutz. En 1655, il se trouve à Bruxelles, où il fonde une académie de dessin. Il y est mentionné pour la dernière fois en 1661, où il semble s'être rapproché de la Société des missions étrangères. Embarquant la même année à Marseille pour l'Orient, il meurt en 1664 à Goa. Sa peinture oscille en permanence entre ambition classique et goût nordique pour la scène de genre.

Le thème de la fileuse a fasciné Sweerts au cours de sa carrière. On connaît de sa main plusieurs femmes filant (The Fitzwilliam Museum, Cambridge, Musei Capitolini, Rome, et collections particulières en Allemagne et en Californie). Chez ce peintre brillant, la description de la vie du peuple n'est jamais détachée d'ambitions allégoriques ou de significations multiples. La fileuse, même affublée de la tenue traditionnelle de la campagne romaine, peut assumer les traits d'une Parque inquiétante.
On doit se contenter de conjectures quant à l'usage et au statut de la série d'estampes des *Diversae Facies* dans laquelle la jeune fileuse du tableau de Gouda est reprise (fig. ci-contre). Le but premier de cet album datant de 1656, époque de la fondation éphémère de l'école de dessin de Sweerts à Bruxelles, consiste à servir de support d'enseignement. Néanmoins, la volonté de l'artiste de montrer l'étendue de son talent est également présente. Rien ne relie véritablement ces figures entre elles, si ce n'est qu'il s'agit d'un répertoire de figures imaginaires dotées pour la plupart de couvre-chefs pittoresques.
Les autres Fileuses de Sweerts sont des études naturalistes de l'époque romaine de l'artiste qui peuvent être rattachées au genre de la bambochade. Celle du musée de Gouda est la seule connue qui soit postérieure au séjour italien. La composition ne diffère pas fondamentalement de celle des tableaux romains. Le principe est toujours celui de la représentation intégrale d'une figure assise en position légèrement surélevée (seule celle de Cambridge est coupée à hauteur des genoux). La profondeur de la pièce peut être indiquée par une fenêtre.
En revanche, la composition de Gouda se détache par le choix d'un éclairage uniforme qui cisèle les formes. On devine derrière la chaise la présence du foyer d'une cheminée. L'expression de la femme est tout intériorisée. Elle semble s'être interrompue dans sa tâche pour méditer. L'artiste ne fait preuve d'aucune empathie pour son personnage, l'exposant à la lumière avec une stupéfiante objectivité.
L'ambition classique de Sweerts lui permet de réinterpréter les sujets anciens avec une absolue rigueur géométrique. En dépit de l'exactitude avec laquelle le métier, la quenouille et le costume de la fileuse sont reproduits, il est difficile d'envisager le sujet comme purement naturaliste. Les tendances mystiques connues de Sweerts laissent supposer une signification allégorique plus profonde.
Rolf Kultzen a envisagé un rapport de Sweerts avec la culture française, en particulier les Le Nain. La carrière du peintre bruxellois fut en effet européenne. Toutefois, il nous paraît que le milieu des *Bamboccianti* à Rome et de tous les peintres séduits à un moment par leurs thèmes (comme des artistes fort différents ont pu être attirés superficiellement vers le caravagisme) est animé d'une ambition humaniste classique puissante. Des artistes comme Rosa, Mola, Bourdon ont commis des bambochades par goût ou par concession à la mode, ce qui ne les a pas empêchés de produire un art d'une haute exigence intellectuelle, à la construction mathématique. C'est le cas de Sweerts lors

de ses dernières années. Une influence directe des frères Le Nain ne nous paraît pas nécessaire pour comprendre l'évolution de Sweerts. On pourrait plutôt envisager des ressemblances fortuites avec l'univers de Georges de La Tour.

L'impassible *Fileuse* de Gouda est l'un des plus hauts témoignages de cet art de la construction par la lumière, dont témoigne si éloquemment Vermeer. **AH**

26

Willem Drost

(Amsterdam, 1633 –
Venise, 1659)

Femme âgée à sa fenêtre,
1654

H.s.t. ; H. 0,74 ; L. 0,61
Lille, palais des Beaux-Arts, inv. P2047

Historique : Collection John Hope, Amsterdam, avant 1785 puis de très nombreuses transactions (*cf.* Bikker) ; acheté par le musée chez Tajan, 25 juin 2002, lot 46.
Bibliographie : Bikker, 2005, p. 15-19, nº 11, p. 75-78.
Œuvres en rapport : Une copie sur bois au musée des Beaux-Arts de Caen ; une autre passée en vente à Genève en 1972 ; un dessin d'Abraham Delfos au cabinet des Estampes de l'université de Leyde.

Rembrandt, *Fille à la fenêtre*,
Londres, Dulwich Picture Gallery

Drost fut l'un des meilleurs élèves de Rembrandt. Après une formation à Amsterdam, il se rendit en Italie, où il a été documenté à Rome et à Venise. En raison de sa mort à l'âge de vingt-six ans, sa production restreinte annonce le talent précoce d'un amoureux des effets de matière, l'un des disciples ayant compris en profondeur l'humanité de Rembrandt.

Pendant tout le XIXe siècle, le tableau a été considéré comme une œuvre importante de Rembrandt alors même que les premiers propriétaires de l'œuvre, parmi lesquels le célèbre marchand Le Brun, l'attribuaient à Drost. Il faut dire que la confusion entre le maître et l'élève portait sur des tableaux exécutés avec des empâtements spectaculaires. La toile avait même été rapprochée de la *Fille à la fenêtre* (le tableau du maître à la Dulwich Collection de Londres, fig. ci-contre), objet d'une anecdote célèbre de Roger de Piles qui racontait que Rembrandt l'avait mise à la fenêtre pour tromper le voisinage. Le retour à l'attribution traditionnelle a été favorisé par l'apparition de la copie dessinée de Delfos qui porte la signature de Drost et la date de 1654 sur le rebord de la fenêtre. Le premier à défendre cette attribution fut Falck à partir de 1924. Des grands historiens de l'art hollandais, seul Hofstede de Groot maintenait l'attribution à Rembrandt mais aujourd'hui, tout le monde accepte le nom de Drost.

La force singulière de l'image tient à son cadrage si particulier très resserré sur le modèle. Les représentations de personnages à la fenêtre sont fréquentes dans la peinture néerlandaise mais, habituellement, les peintres traitent cet élément de décor en détail. Ici, le rebord de la fenêtre n'est qu'un fin liseré se développant sur trois côtés, une simple baguette plutôt qu'un cadre structurant. L'effet de trompe-l'œil est renforcé par cette volonté de masquer le plus possible le cadre. La cuisinière paraît avoir été appelée soudainement et elle se penche en tenant encore le couteau avec lequel elle vaquait à ses tâches ménagères. Cette spontanéité apparente doit beaucoup à Rembrandt, le créateur du genre des femmes à la fenêtre, et à ses tableaux de la Dulwich Collection et du Nationalmuseum de Stockholm.

Un autre aspect significatif de la représentation est l'absence d'attrait immédiat du personnage. Il s'agit d'une personne assez banale, relativement âgée sans être une « belle vieillarde ». Son expression n'est ni rêveuse ni activement curieuse mais simplement concentrée. Pourtant, l'image est forte et produit une véritable émotion. L'absorbement de la cuisinière permet au spectateur d'entrer dans son monde. Le corps du modèle déborde dans l'espace, baigné dans une lumière chaude et généreuse. Le fichu blanc procure une sensation enveloppante et matelassée et une explosion de lumière qui rappelle la célèbre *Bethsabée* de Rembrandt du Louvre, datée elle aussi de 1654. Il n'est pas inutile à ce propos de rappeler que Drost est son seul élève à avoir peint une *Bethsabée*, également au Louvre.

Drost oscille régulièrement entre rusticité et raffinement, et ce tableau en est l'un des exemples les plus éloquents. La cuisinière est indubitablement une personne de basse condition aux traits grossiers avec un nez en patate à la Rembrandt et des mains de travailleuse. Néanmoins, ce poing fermé tient un couteau dont la lame est traitée en un raccourci d'une grande subtilité. La touche épaisse correspond au style le plus radical de Rembrandt, celui qu'il a pratiqué toute sa vie en alternance avec une manière plus fine, et l'élève en développe tout le potentiel à la fois de fluidité et de construction par empâtements superposés. L'harmonie chromatique est simple et d'une remarquable efficacité.

Le tableau de Lille est l'interprétation la moins enjôleuse ou anecdotique du riche motif du personnage à la fenêtre. Le choix du cadrage résulte d'une nécessité narrative

impérieuse et de la volonté chez le jeune peintre talentueux d'égaler le maître. **AH**

27

Antonio Carneo

(Concordia Sagittaria, 1637 – Portogruaro, 1692)

Le Vagabond (Il Giramondo)

H.s.t. ; H. 1,77 ; L. 1,21
Udine, Civici Musei e Gallerie di Storia e Arte, inv. n.452

Historique : Collection Caiselli ; collection Colombatti, Castellerio ; antiquaire Marchetti, Udine ; acquis par le musée en 1952.
Exposition : Brescia, 1998-1999, n° 83.
Bibliographie : Bergamini, 1983, p. 487 ; Rizzi, 1995, p. 98-99 ; Bergamini, Goi, 1995.

Antonio Carneo, *Vieille Femme en méditation*, Udine, Civici Musei e Gallerie di Storia e Arte

On ignore à peu près tout de l'existence de Carneo qui s'est déroulée entièrement dans le Frioul, loin des grands centres artistiques. L'apogée de sa carrière se situe lors de son long séjour à Udine de 1667 à 1687. Il reçoit alors gîte et couvert chez les comtes Caiselli. Il peut ainsi peindre sans se soucier de sa subsistance. Si ses tableaux les plus connus aujourd'hui sont des représentations de pauvres, sa production est constituée essentiellement de tableaux religieux, mythologiques, et de portraits.

Ce tableau et son pendant, la *Vieille Femme en méditation* (fig. ci-contre), furent désignés à l'origine sous le terme « d'un pithoco e d'una pithoca ». Les *pitocchi* sont littéralement les pouilleux, ce prolétariat italien des XVIIe et XVIIIe siècles immortalisé par les spécialistes du genre appelés *Pitocchetti*. Le genre est proche de celui des *Bamboccianti* mais ses représentants s'en distinguent par une focalisation sur la misère et ses stigmates les plus spectaculaires. Le terme « giramondo », vagabond errant par le monde, a été inventé par Rizzi pour ce tableau en 1960. Nous l'avons conservé car l'œuvre a acquis une véritable célébrité sous ce nom, qui paraît par ailleurs tout à fait pertinent pour évoquer ce personnage inoubliable.

Il s'agit d'un grand format correspondant à celui des portraits en pied. Toutefois, ici le modèle est figuré assis au pied d'un talus. Cette masse de végétation qui bouche le panorama oblige le regard à se fixer sur le *giramondo*. Les chaussures en lambeaux, la gourde et le caractère protecteur de ce coin de campagne rappellent que l'homme est en mouvement et qu'il jouit d'une halte momentanée. Capté dans une attitude naturelle mais l'esprit aux aguets, le vieillard ne s'abandonne pas aux joies du repos. Son regard franc oppose une relative méfiance aux imprévus du chemin.

Les *Pitocchetti* d'Italie du Nord s'expriment le plus souvent dans des harmonies d'une palette fort réduite, proche du monochrome. Si Carneo sacrifie en partie à cette tradition incarnée par Monsù Bernardo ou Bellotti pour le manteau de sa figure, il propose également une gamme plus ouverte. Ses blancs, tantôt intenses sur la chemise, tantôt crémeux pour les chausses, rappellent la note dominante de la *Vieille Femme en méditation*. La végétation du talus est traitée en gradations savantes de verts et de bleus soulignées par le jour laiteux donné par le ciel nuageux. La transparence de la lumière révèle de manière équilibrée tous les détails de la composition, excepté quelques recoins.

On connaît l'histoire du tableau et de son pendant grâce à des documents publiés par Geiger en 1940. Entre 1667 et 1676, Carneo avait offert un ensemble de tableaux à la famille noble des Caiselli en échange du logis et d'un prêt d'argent. Ceux-ci étaient présentés dans le salon de la maison familiale. L'intérêt porté par une clientèle aristocratique à des sujets populaires voire misérabilistes à condition qu'ils soient bien peints est ici prouvé. Ce type de tableaux en arrive à remplacer à la place d'honneur de la galerie familiale les sujets d'histoire et les portraits d'apparat. Ils en partagent en tout cas le format et le cadre.

Carneo n'a jamais atteint ailleurs dans sa production désormais assez bien connue le niveau exceptionnel des deux pendants du musée d'Udine. Même si le peintre a vécu à l'écart des plus grands centres artistiques, il a su associer à l'observation du réel et des maîtres du genre l'étude de peintres plus raffinés actifs en Vénétie comme Domenico Fetti, Jan Lyss ou Pietro Ricchi. La rencontre d'une émotion humaine sincère et d'une technique élaborée a produit cette œuvre poignante et forte. **AH**

Paul Ponce Antoine Robert, *dit* Robert de Séry

(Séry-en-Porcien, 1686 – Paris, 1733)

Étude de femme

H.s.t. ; H. 0,71 ; L. 0,58
S.d.b.g. *P. P. Robert 1722*
Lille, palais des Beaux-Arts, inv. 347

Historique : Don de Paul Leroi (pseudonyme du marchand Léon Gauchez), 1883.
Expositions : New York, 1992, n° 22, p. 125-127.
Bibliographie : Oursel, 1984, p. 48-49 ; Lille, 1997, p. 108-109 ; Brejon, de Wambrechies, 2001, p. 168.
Œuvre en rapport : Gravure de l'artiste, avec inscription dans la marge à gauche *P.P.A. Robert de Seri fec. Rom. 1723*. *Cf.* Robert-Dumesnil, 1835, I, p. 280, n° 5.

Paul Ponce Robert, *dit* Robert de Séry, étudia la peinture auprès de Jean Jouvenet à Paris. En 1706, il partit pour Rome : il y gagna sa vie grâce à la peinture, la gravure et la vente d'œuvres d'art, et visita également Venise et Parme. De retour à Paris en 1724, entré au service du cardinal de Rohan, il produisit un certain nombre de peintures religieuses. Refusé à deux reprises au concours de l'Académie royale, il fonda sa propre école de dessin pour jeunes femmes. Il collabora aussi, pour le compte de l'amateur d'art Pierre Crozat, à la publication d'un catalogue de tableaux et dessins remarquables présents dans les collections françaises, ouvrage connu sous le nom de « Cabinet Crozat ».

Cette remarquable étude de femme en contemplation a captivé l'imagination de bien des spectateurs. Elle a été comparée aux travaux d'artistes tels que Rubens et Rembrandt et, plus tard, Manet et Renoir. Ce que nous savons de son auteur vient essentiellement de la biographie rédigée par son ami, le collectionneur et marchand de gravures Pierre-Jean Mariette (*Abecedario* IV, p. 411-413). Le tableau fut achevé lors du séjour de Robert à Rome, comme l'attestent la date et la signature de la gravure. Celle-ci, réalisée par un artiste pleinement au fait de ce marché, prouve qu'il existait, à l'époque, une vraie demande pour les gravures de femmes énigmatiques et séduisantes (*cf.* l'essai de John Chu, pages 79 à 91, et notre notice sur Courtin, cat. 77). Le modèle, une inconnue, nous apparaît dans un moment d'abandon, accoudée à une balustrade. Par bien des aspects, sa pose et son vêtement suggèrent un certain laisser-aller : le corps massif nettement penché en avant, gorge débordante ; les cheveux négligemment tirés en arrière et les mèches indisciplinées qui lui encadrent le visage ; l'écharpe jetée sur les épaules avec désinvolture et la manche, dénouée, de la chemise. Elle a la peau marbrée, le visage luisant de sueur, deux signes indéniables de son épaisseur charnelle. Il est clair qu'il ne s'agit pas d'un portrait à proprement parler, car une telle sensualité dans l'abandon chez une femme respectable aurait déclenché la censure. Rien ne nous dit non plus qui est cette femme. Elle est trop bien habillée pour être une servante, et les détails du premier plan, la fleur blanche comme l'étoffe rouge drapée sur la balustrade, évoquent davantage l'oisiveté que le labeur. Par analogie avec la figure traditionnelle de la courtisane (*cf.* l'essai de Bronwen Wilson, pages 37 à 50), elle pourrait facilement passer pour une prostituée, à cela près qu'elle porte une bague à la main gauche et que la fleur de jasmin symbolise l'amour et le mariage. En tant que Français séjournant en Italie, Robert se montre ici sensible à ce qui relève pour lui de l'« exotisme », saisissant l'atmosphère nonchalante et le charme rustique de la campagne romaine à travers la pose du personnage et certains détails de son costume (l'écharpe). Des décennies plus tard, Greuze allait développer plus explicitement encore le trope de l'indolence féminine avec un autre personnage bien en chair portant également une écharpe, *La Paresseuse italienne* (Hartford, Wadsworth Atheneum). Dans *Étude de femme*, la figure principale se situe à mi-chemin entre réalisme et idéalisme. Alors qu'émane du premier plan une impression de solidité et de présence (avec, cependant, quelques touches de raffinement), la toile de fond, d'une délicatesse digne de Watteau avec ses détails architecturaux et ses silhouettes discernables au loin, semble la figuration visuelle de la rêverie à laquelle s'abandonne cette femme. Le jeu sur les genres et les registres a été jugé à la fois étrange et moderne mais en fait, plus qu'à toute autre chose, il tient à la diversité des influences picturales dont se nourissait le travail de Robert. La séduction y est moins directe que chez Bordon (cat. 1) ou Rigaud (cat. 9), mais il n'en reste pas moins évident que l'image de cette femme a été conçue pour être regardée et désirée. **MP**

 *

Giacomo Ceruti, *dit* Il Pitocchetto

(Milan, 1698-1767)

Fileuse

H.s.t. ; H. 1,21 ; L. 1,53
Brescia, Civici Musei, Pinacoteca Tosio Martinengo

Historique : Brescia, famille Salvegado ; acquis en 2003 par Hopa SpA et déposé à la Pinacoteca Tosio Martinengo ; donné en 2010 à la Ville de Brescia.
Expositions : Brescia, 1987, n° 27, p. 176 ; Brescia, 1998-1999, n° 112, p. 437-438 ; Crémone/New York, 2004.
Bibliographie : Gregori, 1982, n° 67, p. 437.

Ceruti fut l'un des acteurs du naturalisme lombard. Peintre de sujets religieux, de portraits, de scènes de genre et de natures mortes, il est plus célèbre pour ses études émouvantes de *pitocchi* (pouilleux). Ceux-ci lui ont valu son surnom et justifié les comparaisons avec le Caravage. Ceruti a voyagé en Lombardie, Vénétie et Émilie tout en jonglant entre deux familles et deux épouses. À Venise, il bénéficia de la protection du maréchal Johann Matthias von der Schulenburg et fut influencé par Piazzetta.

Considérée comme l'une des œuvres majeures de Ceruti, *La Fileuse* est l'un des éléments du « cycle de Padernello ». Cette série de quinze tableaux représentant des mendiants et des pauvres fut exécutée par Ceruti dans les années 1720 à 1730 pour une famille noble de Brescia, les Avogadro. La redécouverte, en 1931, par Giuseppe Delogu de nombreuses toiles de ce cycle dans le Palazzo Salvegado à Padernello a entraîné une réévaluation et une nouvelle appréciation du travail de l'artiste. De nombreuses hypothèses ont été émises sur ce qui a pu pousser les riches mécènes de Ceruti à se lancer dans cette collection hétéroclite de petites gens figurées sur de grands formats – toujours traitées avec justesse et tendresse. Le cycle inclut d'autres sujets comme un nain, un mendiant au repos, une rencontre dans les bois entre un homme et une femme ainsi qu'une jeune mendiante accompagnée d'une fileuse plus âgée. Le travail des femmes est un thème récurrent de l'ensemble avec des représentations de lavandières et d'une école de couture. Mina Gregori a soutenu que cette *Fileuse* était probablement l'une des dernières peintures de la série à avoir été réalisée du fait de son raffinement dans le traitement de la lumière.

La *Fileuse* est le reflet de diverses influences, le naturalisme lombard faisant écho au caravagisme, à la pureté nordique de Vermeer et de Sweerts, le sujet lui-même, proche des *Bamboccianti* et autres peintres de *pitocchi* (Keil, Bellotti, Cifrondi, Cipper), le tout retravaillé avec une grandeur imposante. Nous pouvons comparer la *Fileuse* de Ceruti à celle de Sweerts (cat. 25), que Ceruti a peut-être connue à travers la gravure et qui présente de nombreuses similarités d'ambiance et d'exécution avec notre œuvre. Chardin, contemporain de Ceruti, peut aussi venir à l'esprit bien qu'il n'y ait jamais eu de contacts connus entre eux et que Chardin préférait de loin les formats plus petits. Les deux artistes ont cherché à rendre la vie silencieuse et la dignité des gens du peuple ; ils décrivaient la communion permanente des êtres avec les objets et leur environnement. Ils utilisaient aussi tous deux le blanc pour donner vie, comme par magie, à leurs palettes couleur terre.

Le filage a souvent été dépeint dans l'art occidental. Les Moires grecques et leurs héritières les Parques romaines avaient le pouvoir de tisser les fils de toutes les destinées humaines. De ce fait, le filage fut associé à la vie et à la mort et devint le symbole d'une forme mystérieuse du pouvoir féminin. Il était également parfois utilisé pour représenter les sens du toucher et de la vue. En dépit de ces références, la jeune fileuse de Ceruti ne semble pas présenter de sens allégorique évident. Elle existe par elle-même, tandis que le format horizontal et l'arrière-plan nu procurent un espace vierge à ses pensées. Elle n'interagit pas avec le spectateur, bien que son regard soit tourné vers lui, mais semble au contraire enfermée dans sa mélancolie. Son caractère grave est éclairé et accentué par sa coiffe blanche. La maîtrise des couleurs de Ceruti est manifeste dans l'alternance subtile des tons de rouge et de gris de la robe de la jeune femme. Le rendu des plis complexes et du fil tissé est une autre forme de respect de l'artiste envers son sujet, une démonstration que, dans le moindre détail, il est digne de lui inspirer de l'intérêt. **MP**

* Œuvre non exposée

Noël Hallé

(Paris, 1711-1781)

L'Hiver. Vieillard se chauffant les mains à un brasero, vers 1747

H.s.t ; H 0,60 ; L 0,48
Dijon, musée des Beaux-Arts, inv. 1461

Historique : Acquis en janvier 1901 de M. Paul Devaux, antiquaire, au prix de 280 francs ; vente Baudot avec attribution Le Nain.
Bibliographie : Guillaume, 1980, A. 2, n° 3, p. 131-322 ; Willk-Brocard, 1995, n° 23, p. 368.
Œuvre en rapport : Réplique (version d'atelier), chez Éric Turquin, Paris, octobre 2000.

Influencé par le style rococo, Hallé fut formé par son père, Claude, et par Jean Restout. Lauréat du prix de Rome en 1736, il étudia à l'Académie de France à Rome de 1737 à 1744. De retour à Paris, il fut agréé en 1746 puis reçu en 1748. Connu principalement comme peintre de sujets mythologiques et religieux, il fit aussi des portraits et des scènes de genre et fut un prodigieux dessinateur, graveur et illustrateur de livres. Hallé produisit de grandes tapisseries pour les Gobelins, y compris la très admirée *Course d'Hippomène et Atalante* (1765, Paris, musée du Louvre). Il occupa divers rôles au sein du monde de l'art, notamment en tant que directeur de l'Académie de France à Rome en 1775.

Ce vieil homme contemplatif se chauffant au-dessus d'un poêle est traité de façon fruste par Hallé bien qu'avec une grande attention aux détails. Au Salon de 1747, la peinture attire l'œil de l'abbé Le Blanc, qui remarque « de la vigueur et de la beauté » dans toutes les œuvres de l'artiste, mais « surtout celuy Qui Représente l'Hyver » (*Lettre de l'exposition des ouvrages de peinture*, p. 96). C'est un des vieillards peints par Hallé à son retour de Rome, à la fois étude de visage et portrait en pied. Un portrait comparable à ce tableau est *Le Pauvre dans son réduit* (Willk-Brocard, n° 26), connu grâce à la gravure de Jean-Augustin Patour. Ces œuvres partagent des tonalités sombres rehaussées de blanc et une forte présence de la matière. Plus tard dans sa carrière, Hallé continuera à représenter la pauvreté pittoresque et les Savoyards (Willk-Brocard, n° 44, n° 69) mais plus joyeusement, avec une palette plus légère et une surface plus lisse.

Hallé puise dans une longue tradition allégorique assimilant l'hiver et la vieillesse, avec des personnages réchauffant leurs mains sur un brasier. Ainsi Artus Wolffort (Dessau, Schloss Georgium), Hendrick Bloemaert (Christie's, Londres, 2-3 décembre 2014, n° 25) et Michael Sweerts, *Allégorie de l'Hiver* (coll. part.). Exceptionnellement, une jeune femme a incarné l'hiver dans un tableau de Cesar Van Everdingen (vers 1644-1648, Amsterdam, Rijksmuseum). Il existe aussi un portrait de vieille femme se réchauffant les mains par l'artiste vénitien Giuseppe Nogari, presque contemporain du tableau de vieil homme de Hallé (vers 1745, Londres, Royal Collection).

Dans la peinture de Hallé, l'allégorie évolue en anecdote. Un effet de halo est créé par le rétroéclairage et par la coloration blanche de la barbe sur les longueurs : le pauvre vieillard est alors investi de la dignité d'un sage ou d'un apôtre (un rappel du talent de Hallé en tant que peintre religieux). Dans le tableau, l'accent mis sur son état mental crée un espace imaginaire, loin du monde environnant. Mais le doute subsiste : est-il un philosophe ou simplement un homme usé par le travail physique ? Sa pauvreté et ses préoccupations sont évidentes à en juger par son genou nu : en fait, son bas a glissé mais, de loin, ce pourrait être une plaie. Ses grandes chaussures improbables signent une vie passée à s'accommoder de peu. Dans la cuisine, faiblement éclairée, les tomettes craquelées sont éloquentes, faisant écho à l'état d'esprit soucieux de l'homme. L'œuvre présente une accumulation subtile de nuances et de textures de peinture, en particulier sur les mains noueuses et la barbe. Les tons rouges sur le visage et les mains du vieillard suggèrent la lente montée en puissance de la chaleur émanant du feu, ses braises incandescentes apportant le réconfort attendu. **MP**

31

Henry Robert Morland

(Londres, vers 1716-1797)

La Jolie Chanteuse de ballades

H.s.t. ; H. 0,76 ; L. 0,63
The National Trust, Saltram,
The Morley Collection, inv. 872273

Historique : Don recueilli dans le cadre du legs effectué par le 6e comte de Morley, 1957.
Expositions : Nottingham/Londres, 1998, no 64.
Bibliographie : National Trust, 2013, p. 135, 181, 397 ; Chu, 2014.
Œuvres en rapport :
Peintures, *Jeune Fille chantant des ballades à la lumière d'une lanterne en papier*, vers 1765-1782, 0,76 × 0,62 m, Londres, Tate Gallery ; *The Ballad Singer/La Chanteuse de ballades*, vers 1764, 0,63 × 0,76 m, New Haven, Yale Centre for British Art ; *The Ballad Singer/La Chanteuse de ballades*, vers 1764, huile sur toile, 0,66 × 0,55 m, tableau photographié en juin 1927 lors d'une vente à Londres (Frick Art Reference Library Photoarchive).
Pastel, (Morland), *Chanteuse de ballades*, craie grasse, exposition de la Society of Artists of Great Britain, 1764, no 73 (lieu de conservation inconnu).
Mezzotinte, (Philip Dawe), *La Jolie Chanteuse de ballades*, 1769, 0,35 × 0,25 m ; (Thomas Watson), *Jeune Fille chantant des ballades à la lumière d'une lanterne en papier*, 1767-1782, 0,32 × 0,23 m.

Morland naquit dans une famille d'artistes. À partir de 1760, il présenta ses toiles, une centaine en tout, lors d'expositions organisées par la Society of Artists, la Free Society of Artists et la Royal Academy. Ses tableaux, essentiellement des portraits et des *fancy pictures* qui s'inspirent de Dou, de Schalcken et de Chardin, furent souvent reproduits sous forme de gravures. Son succès populaire n'empêchant pas sa situation financière d'être précaire, il complétait ses revenus en travaillant comme restaurateur et marchand de tableaux et comme vendeur de matériel pour artistes.

La multiplication des expositions à Londres au cours des années 1760 stimula le goût du public pour les *fancy pictures* et une nouvelle génération de peintres fit son entrée sur la scène artistique, parmi lesquels Henry Robert Morland, Nathaniel Hone et Joseph Wright of Derby. Avec leurs surfaces finement travaillées et leurs scènes nocturnes, ces peintres de fantaisies renouvelèrent le travail de leurs prédécesseurs néerlandais – caravagesques et représentants de la manière dite « fine » ou « précieuse » (*fijnschilder*) – et l'adaptèrent à un public moderne. Morland peignit fréquemment de nombreuses versions du même tableau, lesquelles étaient à leur tour reproduites sous forme de gravures. Cette production en multiples exemplaires est également une caractéristique des figures de fantaisie réalisées ailleurs (par Santerre et Grimou, par exemple). En 1764, lors du Salon de la Society of Artists de Grande-Bretagne, l'artiste exposa *La Chanteuse de ballades* à la craie grasse avec une version au pastel de son tableau intitulé *Femme au voile*. Il est probable que ces pastels, dont la trace s'est perdue, aient été les prototypes, respectivement, du tableau conservé au manoir de Saltram et de l'une des œuvres les plus célèbres de Morland, *La Belle Religieuse démasquée* (Leeds, Temple Newsham House). Différentes versions de *La Jolie Chanteuse de ballades* firent régulièrement leur apparition lors d'expositions qui se tinrent entre 1760 et 1770. Aujourd'hui, celles qui furent réalisées à l'huile se trouvent dans les collections de la Tate Gallery et à Yale. Ce fascinant travail sur la lumière artificielle fait songer à un autre tableau de Morland, portrait d'un personnage à l'air plus aristocratique : *Femme lisant près d'un abat-jour de papier* (New Haven, Yale Center for British Art). La jeune femme représentée dans cette *Jolie Chanteuse de ballades*, une marchande de partitions, tient près de la lanterne une liasse de feuilles qu'elle regarde avec force attention. Sa bouche est un simple trait qui excite la curiosité : l'on ne saurait dire avec certitude si elle chante ou non. La composition s'ordonne autour d'un thème, le déploiement de plis auparavant serrés, emblématique des désirs que cette jeune femme éveille chez le spectateur. La lumière, dirigée vers le haut, illumine le visage ; la paupière exagérément oblique et la ligne d'ombre qui barre à angle vif la pommette dessinent un V dont la pointe plonge vers le bas. Voici là une banale fille des rues, que son teint clair et son air grave différencient néanmoins du gros des mendiants et des prostituées. Son métier évoque la disponibilité sexuelle : des ballades comme celles qu'elle vend, au contenu paillard, étaient alors affichées dans les tavernes. Elle semble se retenir de chanter leurs paroles crues et ne pas être disposée à offrir des plaisirs faciles. Le désir qu'elle suscite est plus délicat, plus raffiné, et l'arrière-plan, tout en tonalités denses et sombres, ouvre un espace propice à des rêveries plus subtiles. **MP**

32

Jean-Baptiste Greuze

(Tournus, 1725 – Paris, 1805)

Jeune Berger tenant une fleur, 1760-1761

H.s.t. ; H. 0,72 ; L. 0,59
Paris, musée du Petit Palais, inv. PDUT 1192

Historique : Achat sur les arrérages du legs Dutuit, 1975.
Expositions : Ottawa/Washington DC/Berlin, 2003-2004.
Bibliographie : Ledbury, 2000 ; Conisbee, 2007.
Œuvre en rapport : pendant : Jean-Baptiste Greuze, *La Simplicité*, 1759, 0,71 × 0,60 m, Fort Worth, Kimbell Art Museum, inv. AP 1985.03.

Jean-Baptiste Greuze, *La Simplicité*, Fort Worth, Kimbell Art Museum

Originaire de la province, Greuze fit sensation lorsqu'il arriva sur la scène artistique parisienne en 1755 en introduisant sa marque de fabrique : la peinture de genre sentimentale et moralisante. Sa déception fut amère lorsqu'en 1769 il ne fut pas reçu à l'Académie royale en tant que peintre d'histoire, mais il rencontra un succès certain auprès de l'élite des amateurs et du grand public, qui achetaient ses gravures.

Dans ce tableau, Greuze exploite le genre de la figure de fantaisie sur le mode de la pastorale et à travers l'exploration d'états psychologiques. Un jeune garçon en tenue de paysan se tient debout, perdu dans ses pensées, un pissenlit à la main qu'il ne regarde pas : le tableau saisit l'instant juste avant qu'il ne souffle sur la fleur. Ce tableau fut exposé au Salon de 1761 (n° 101) sous le titre *Un berger qui tente le sort pour savoir s'il est aimé de sa bergère*. Son pendant, *La Simplicité*, exposé deux ans plus tôt, représente une jeune femme qui effeuille la marguerite et sonde les sentiments de son bien-aimé : « Il m'aime, un peu, beaucoup… » Ensemble, ces deux tableaux symbolisent l'innocence de la jeunesse avec, cependant, de subtiles nuances selon le sexe du personnage : tandis que *La Simplicité* évoque sans ambiguïté l'existence d'un amoureux, le *Berger*, en revanche, considéré sans son pendant et sans le titre sous lequel il fut exposé au Salon, pourrait se lire comme une simple méditation sur le temps qui passe. Réalisés dans l'esprit des pastorales de Boucher, les deux tableaux se répondent harmonieusement : le panier de fleurs du jeune garçon est assorti au chapeau de paille de la jeune fille, l'un et l'autre tiennent leur fleur d'un air grave et un cadre ovale les entoure avec douceur. L'apparente simplicité des blancs et des pastels délicats n'exclut pas le raffinement des détails : les drapés, les fleurs et le panier d'osier sont très finement travaillés, le ciel et le feuillage, en toile de fond, rendus avec un soin extrême.

Ces deux tableaux étaient destinés aux appartements de Mme de Pompadour à Versailles, dont la décoration venait d'être refaite. Le contrat avait été négocié en 1756 par le marquis de Marigny, frère de Mme de Pompadour et directeur général des Bâtiments du roi : il appréciait fort l'artiste prometteur qu'était alors Greuze et lui avait laissé le choix de son sujet. Cependant, malgré cette liberté et l'occasion qui lui était donnée de se faire un nom, le jeune peintre mit du temps à réaliser cette commande. Il est possible que ces deux tableaux n'aient pas plu : l'apparence asexuée du berger – son corps tronqué juste au-dessus des parties génitales, son air presque abattu – pouvait être perçue comme un commentaire ironique sur la relation qu'entretenait le roi avec sa maîtresse. Le tableau n'avait certainement rien de cette « mâle » vigueur prônée par Marigny, qui s'était donné pour mission de réformer la représentation de l'histoire dans la peinture française. Tout cela valut à Greuze une étiquette d'anticonformiste, au projet esthétique très personnel. Le message d'innocence manifeste dans ce portrait est affaibli par l'ambiguïté de l'ensemble. Diderot jugea le regard du berger vide et inexpressif, et le thème du tableau, difficile à identifier (*Salon de 1761*). C'est cette incertitude qui crée un sentiment de malaise chez le spectateur. L'effacement de la sexualité la rend paradoxalement présente et il convient de voir dans le jeune couple représenté sur ces pendants un double prélude à l'exploration minutieuse par Greuze de thèmes tels que l'amour, la perte, la culpabilité et le ressentiment. Le plus souvent, ce sont des personnages féminins qui incarnent cette thématique, à tel point que la jeune fille greuzienne a fini par devenir un lieu commun de la figure de fantaisie. Le garçon que l'on voit ici fait écho à un autre thème cher à l'artiste : l'accession à l'âge d'homme. C'est pourquoi ce ravissant tableau a un contenu implicite à la fois troublant et novateur. **MP**

33

François-André Vincent

(Paris, 1746-1816)

Vieillard lisant,
vers 1772-1773

H.s.t. ; H. 0,71 ; L. 0,55
Agrandi de 5,5 cm en haut et à gauche, de 2,5 cm en bas
Étiquette au dos : *Etude d'une tête/ de Vieillard. Par/ Vincent, peintre du/ Roi. – no 149*
Besançon, musée des Beaux-Arts et d'Archéologie, inv. D. 843.1.36

Historique : Collection de l'architecte Pierre-Adrien Pâris (1745-1819), catalogue manuscrit de sa collection, 1806, nº 98 ; légué par ce dernier à la bibliothèque municipale de Besançon en 1819 ; déposé au musée des Beaux-Arts en 1919.
Exposition : Besançon, 1992, p. 57, nº 24.
Bibliographie : Cuzin, 2013, nº 67P, p. 355 ; Mansfield, 2011.

Peintre et dessinateur prolifique, Vincent est associé au mouvement néoclassique naissant en France bien que son travail ne se cantonne pas à un seul style. Il étudia auprès de Joseph-Marie Vien puis, de 1771 à 1775, à l'Académie française de Rome. Brillant peintre d'histoire, il peignit aussi des portraits officiels et informels. Il fut d'abord académicien puis, après la Révolution, devint membre de jeunes organisations artistiques. Vincent fut l'époux de l'artiste Adélaïde Labille-Guiard (1749-1803).

Un intérêt multiple pour les expressions du visage est au cœur de l'œuvre de Vincent. Lauréat du prix Caylus 1767 (prix de l'Académie pour l'expression) avec son étude de « l'Abattement », Vincent continua à esquisser de nombreuses caricatures animées de ses condisciples à l'École française de Rome. Les têtes de vieillards furent des sujets récurrents dans son œuvre. Une peinture exprime remarquablement la maturité de Vincent, *Le Prêtre grec* (vers 1782, Galerie d'État, château de Johannisburg, Bayerische Staatsgemäldesammlungen). Le vieil homme de Besançon est une œuvre plus ancienne, datant probablement du début du séjour de l'artiste à Rome. Le naturalisme de la peinture et son éclairage contrasté reflètent l'influence d'artistes bolonais, en particulier le Guerchin et Reni. Le thème est issu de représentations d'apôtres et de saints, sans être ouvertement religieux ; c'est plutôt une étude digne et soigneusement travaillée sur la vieillesse. L'homme a les traits fins quoique burinés et un regard studieux : son front est profondément ridé et la lumière tombe sur son crâne chauve, suggérant la vie intérieure. Ses cheveux grisonnants et sa barbe sont peints dans divers tons de noir, gris et blanc : épais et laineux par endroits et ondulés dans d'autres. L'humeur est à la contemplation tranquille, contrairement à la version beaucoup plus fougueuse de Fragonard d'un vieil homme lisant, à la même période (Hambourg, Kunsthalle). Ici, le livre est fermé et les paupières de l'homme, profondément closes. Peut-être n'est-ce pas l'acte de lire lui-même qui est représenté mais plutôt un moment de réflexion avant ou après la lecture. Cette ambiguïté donne au tableau une subtilité fascinante.

Vieillard lisant de Vincent a appartenu à l'architecte et *connoisseur* Pierre-Adrien Pâris, qui se trouvait en Italie en même temps que Vincent. Ils s'y côtoyaient avec un autre collectionneur, Bergeret de Grandcourt, qui possédait deux têtes de vieillards à sa mort, en 1785. L'une d'elles était peut-être le *Vieillard buvant* de Vincent, aujourd'hui à Fécamp (*cf.* Cuzin, 2013, nº 69P). La présence des têtes de vieillards de Vincent dans ces prestigieuses collections du XVIIIe siècle montre à quel point elles étaient recherchées. **MP**

Bénigne Gagneraux

(Dijon, 1756 – Florence, 1795)

Jeune Homme lisant Homère, 1786

H.s.t. ; H. 0,46 ; L. 0,38
D.s. *B. Gagneraux 1786*
Dijon, musée des Beaux-Arts, inv. 2000-1-1

Historique : Pierre-Dominique-Francois Bertholet, chevalier de Campan ; don de la Société des amis des Musées de Dijon, avec la participation du FRAM, 2000.
Exposition : Rome, 1983.
Bibliographie : Sandström, 1981 ; Starcky, 2000a, p. 75-76 ; Starcky, 2000b, p. 94-95.

Gagneraux fut absent de la scène artistique parisienne ; c'est pourquoi son nom, injustement, ne figure pas dans les histoires de l'art français. Cet artiste talentueux, originaire de Dijon, séjourna à Rome de 1776 à 1780 aux frais de la province de Bourgogne. Il se forgea une solide réputation au sein de la Rome cosmopolite, principalement en tant que peintre d'histoire néoclassique, et compta la famille royale de Suède parmi ses clients. Poussé au suicide en raison d'une déception amoureuse, selon la rumeur, il mourut prématurément comme tant d'autres Werther de son temps.

Il s'agit d'une œuvre de Gagneraux inhabituellement intimiste dans laquelle le thème traditionnel du lecteur absorbé par sa tâche est traité dans le style néoclassique de la Rome du XVIIIe siècle. Le tableau était une commande du chevalier de Campan, gentilhomme amateur d'art résidant à Rome, dont l'épouse devint la Première Femme de chambre de la reine Marie-Antoinette la même année. Le jeune homme de la peinture fut d'abord identifié comme un parent, peut-être le fils du couple, mais les dates de naissance des enfants excluent cette possibilité. Il s'agit plutôt d'un hybride anonyme de modèles classiques, tel Antinoüs, et de figures d'artistes baroques italiens, comme le *Saint Jean-Baptiste* de Reni. Les traits du sujet s'apparentent à ceux des figures de Gagneraux dans *Bacchus et Ariane* et l'*Éducation d'Achille* (1785 et 1787, Suède, château de Löfstad). Ce jeune homme idéalisé et quelque peu efféminé incarne le mode anacréontique, variante plus douce et plus lyrique du néoclassicisme qui s'oppose à la virilité vigoureuse de Jacques-Louis David et qui s'inspire davantage du style grec que du style romain. Calme, plasticité et clair-obscur soulignent la concentration du sujet sur sa lecture. Ses traits sont modelés avec soin et la peinture est appliquée minutieusement – ainsi de la teinte des sourcils et des ombres des narines rehaussées par du rouge. Ce soin apporté aux détails rappelle la popularité des *fijnschilders* au sein des cercles français de l'époque. Les vêtements du jeune homme sont modernes, mais drapés de façon à imiter une tenue classique. Le rebord en pierre, évocateur de ruines anciennes, érige une barrière physique, ajoutant encore à la distance qui sépare spectateur et sujet. Dans cette peinture riche de sens, l'épique est ramené à l'échelle humaine et la trame temporelle qui relie Homère au présent s'efface devant les espoirs et les rêves de jeunesse. **MP**

Dormeurs

Tomás Hiepes ou Yepes

(Valence ?, entre 1595 et 1610 – Valence, 1674)

Chasseur endormi dans un paysage

H.s.t. ; H. 0,68 ; L. 1,13
S.b. *Tomás Hiepes*
Valence, Museu de Belles Arts, inv. 13195

Historique : Acquis avec son pendant chez Caylus Anticuario en 1995.
Bibliographie : Benito Doménech, 2003, n° 126, p. 254 ; Saure, 2012, p. 119.

Tomás Hiepes, *Chasseur s'abreuvant à un ruisseau*, Valence, Museu de Belles Arts

Tomás Hiepes (ou Yepes) fut le peintre le plus important de natures mortes à Valence au XVIIe siècle. Sa vie est fort mal connue. On sait que sa famille était d'origine tolédane. À ses débuts, il se consacra essentiellement aux tableaux de dévotion avant de devenir un spécialiste quasi exclusif du *bodegón* (ou nature morte). Il privilégia les mises en scène sobres avec peu d'objets, dont des céramiques de sa région, comme celle de Manises, ou des vases en métal de style mauresque.

Avec son pendant, *Chasseur s'abreuvant à un ruisseau* (fig. ci-contre), la paire semble, selon Benito Doménech, avoir fait office de dessus-de-porte ou de fenêtre en raison de ses formats et du raccourci. Il s'agit d'un rare exemple chez le peintre de scène avec figure dans un contexte non religieux. Néanmoins, nous pouvons nous interroger avec Petra ten-Doesschate Chu (*cf.* son essai, pages 51 à 61) sur ce type d'image et sa source. En effet, les chasseurs endormis au milieu de la nature évoquent irrésistiblement les figures tragiques et poétiques d'Adonis et d'Endymion. Le repos paisible associé au gibier et à la force vitale du paysage constitue une forme de prémonition de la mort. Il est toutefois difficile de rapprocher ce chasseur rustique de la grâce des héros mythologiques aimés des déesses. Les oreilles décollées et le nez épais du personnage sont les attributs d'un homme du peuple guère idéalisé. L'inconfort de la pose ne permet pas de regagner en prestance corporelle le terrain perdu. L'arme, un fusil contemporain, ne rappelle en rien les nobles chasses traditionnelles. La faune est constituée d'oiseaux aquatiques, comme c'est le cas également dans le pendant.

La sensation de vérité et de naturel de la scène est cependant notable. Un tronc d'arbre décharné et un rocher imposent la vision d'une nature sauvage et inquiétante. L'écorce éclatée de l'arbre et les aspérités de la roche sont traitées avec précision et acuité. Le gibier exposé est envisagé comme un fragment de nature morte indépendant, à la manière de spécialistes italiens tels que Paolo Anesi.

La composition caractérisée par l'horreur du vide emplit parfaitement l'espace disponible, le tronc et les bras du chasseur contrastant par leurs verticales avec l'horizontalité dominante.

Les deux pendants représentent des attitudes inversées où les repères visuels, comme le rocher, sont diamétralement opposés. Ainsi, le *Chasseur s'abreuvant à un ruisseau* présente des tonalités plus chaudes et l'action se déroule en plein jour. En toute logique, le *Chasseur endormi dans un paysage* est une scène nocturne baignant dans une clarté lunaire plus égale.

Les chasseurs constituent, au même titre que le gibier et l'échantillon de nature environnant, un trophée de chasse et une allégorie vivante et humanisée de cette activité ancestrale, entre économie de subsistance et passion. On peut qualifier ce tableau de vanité en raison de l'exhibition des oiseaux morts doublée de l'abandon au sommeil du jeune homme. Il s'agit toutefois d'un abandon relatif puisque le chasseur reste dans une attitude de vigilance, prêt à saisir son arme à tout moment. Contrairement à la plupart des dormeurs de la peinture, il n'offre pas au peintre et par là même au spectateur une face paisiblement assoupie mais plutôt un profil rigide. Tout le charme de l'œuvre de Hiepes réside dans cette contradiction et dans le goût de la superposition qui prime sur la recherche d'une harmonie d'ensemble. La force rustique de l'expression, la sensibilité pour le paysage, le goût du clair-obscur, ici atténué par rapport au pendant, font penser à l'art d'un grand peintre valencien contemporain, Pedro Orrente.

AH

Eberhard Keil ou Bernardo Keilhau, *dit* Monsù Bernardo

(Elseneur, 1624 – Rome, 1687)

Fillette dormant

H.s.t. ; H. 0,62 ; L. 0,96
Munich, Bayerische Staatsgemäldesammlungen, en dépôt au château de Schleissheim, inv. Nr. 2357

Historique : Collection de l'électeur Jean-Guillaume de Palatinat (1658-1716), galerie de Düsseldorf.
Bibliographie : Longhi, 1938, p. 122 ; Heimbürger, 1988, no 107, p. 207.
Œuvre en rapport : *Garçon endormi avec un chat*, vente Sotheby's, Londres, 12 décembre 1979, no 98.

La carrière d'Eberhard Keil fut véritablement européenne. De nationalité danoise, il se forma à Amsterdam dans l'atelier de Rembrandt. Il partit ensuite pour l'Italie en 1651, visitant Venise et la Lombardie avant de s'installer définitivement à Rome en 1656. L'artiste connut un grand succès grâce à ses sujets de genre picaresques qui mettent en scène des petites gens avec un traitement pictural rustique.

La figure endormie est un véritable *topos* de la vaste production de Keil. À toutes les époques, le peintre représente des jeunes chasseurs, des dentellières, des vieillards ou des enfants des deux sexes endormis, le plus souvent assis, la tête dans les mains. Heimbürger a pu regrouper un groupe de six tableaux de format oblong figurant des enfants allongés. Elle explique les dimensions inhabituelles de ces œuvres par leur fonction de dessus-de-porte, peut-être pour une chambre d'enfant, et situe cet ensemble après 1656, au début du séjour romain de l'artiste danois.

Le tableau de Munich fait partie de cette série, dont il se distingue par une disproportion moins marquée entre longueur et hauteur. Il partage un certain nombre d'éléments figuratifs avec les autres tableaux tels un oreiller, un matelas, un panier en osier. C'est avec la *Jeune Fille endormie à l'éventail* du Statens Museum for Kunst de Copenhague, le seul où ne figure pas un animal domestique, que les similitudes sont les plus frappantes. Le choix d'un plan serré sur l'enfant, le placement de sa tête à gauche ne se retrouvent que dans le tableau passé chez Sotheby's, Londres, en 1979.

Les représentations d'enfants saisis au moment où ils s'abandonnent au sommeil sont nombreuses dans l'histoire de la peinture occidentale (*cf.* l'essai de Petra ten-Doesschate Chu, pages 51 à 61). Elles témoignent d'une profonde ambivalence entre attendrissement innocent et érotisme coupable de la part de l'adulte. Le tableau autrefois dans la collection C. et B. Goodstein, *Jeune Fille allongée à l'éventail*, nous offre peut-être une clé quant à la signification du sujet pour Keil. L'éventail porte une inscription dont le premier mot est *AMORE*. Heimbürger y voit une allégorie de l'amour où la jeune fille jouerait le rôle de Cupidon.

En dépit du changement de genre, il nous semble que l'iconographie la plus proche de notre sujet, très populaire pendant la Contre-Réforme, est celle de l'Enfant Jésus endormi sur la croix. Évidemment, il ne s'agit pas d'une représentation directe de ce sujet mais à tout le moins d'une allégorie de l'amour sacré plutôt que de l'amour profane et surtout de l'image pittoresque d'une jolie enfant en train de dormir.

Dans le contexte de la production abondante et inégale de Keil, ce tableau est d'une qualité supérieure. Le sens de la couleur de l'artiste, dont témoignent les rouges intenses, est bien présent. En revanche, le traitement pictural du visage et des drapés des vêtements de la petite fille est très fluide. Keil s'amuse parfois, pour le plus grand bonheur de ses commanditaires, à adopter un style rustique qui peut être à la limite de la vulgarité. Il dispose également d'un registre plus savant, moins heurté, qu'il adopte pour ses sujets plus délicats. C'est celui qu'il a retenu pour le tableau de Munich. Il fait aussi preuve d'une grande rigueur dans sa composition, centrée sur l'enfant. L'artiste parvient à animer par un jeu de drapés la masse géométrique constituée par la jeune fille pelotonnée sur son lit. Ce type de sujet, plus émouvant que misérabiliste, qui transforme un enfant des rues en paradigme universel connaîtra une descendance au XVIIIe siècle dans la peinture d'un Giacomo Ceruti avec, cette fois, une qualité picturale encore plus élevée que celle du meilleur Monsù Bernardo. **AH**

37

D'après Jean-Baptiste Santerre

(Magny-en-Vexin, 1658 – Paris, 1717)

Jeune Fille endormie à la chandelle

H.s.t. ; H. 0,60 ; L. 0,64
Nantes, musée des Beaux-Arts, inv. 779

Historique : Collection Cacault ; achat par la Ville de Nantes en 1810.
Bibliographie : Lesné, 1988, p. 75-118 ; Gerin-Pierre, 2005, p. 183, no 208 ; Lesné, Waro, 2011, p. 74-76.
Œuvre en rapport : Santerre, *Jeune Fille endormie sur son ouvrage* [disparue]. Citée par Pahin de La Blancherie, 1783, IV, p. 113.

Biographie : *cf.* cat. 51.

Le tableau de Nantes est une copie séduisante réalisée par un artiste inconnu d'après un original de Jean-Baptiste Santerre. S'inspirant, au niveau à la fois du thème et de l'exécution, des peintres nordiques tels que Dou, Mieris ou Metsu, cette œuvre fut attribuée à Schalcken au cours du XIXe siècle. Cette étude d'une jeune fille endormie à la lueur d'une chandelle partage de nombreuses similitudes avec l'un des tableaux de Schalcken ou peut-être de son apprenti, A. Boonen. Santerre aurait pu en avoir connaissance grâce à une gravure de J. Smith (reprod. Lesné, 1988, p. 76, ill. 2). La genèse de cette œuvre peut s'expliquer par le fort attrait qu'exerçaient les pastiches et les copies de maîtres nordiques sur les collectionneurs d'art français du XVIIIe siècle, œuvres qui furent à leur tour largement copiées et diffusées par d'autres artistes français.

La jeune fille s'est endormie sur son ouvrage : le tissu forme une sorte d'oreiller où repose sa tête inclinée et dont la blancheur immaculée reflète la lumière, illuminant ainsi son visage et ses mains. La chandelle ajoute aux jeux de lumière, faisant ressortir les détails : un front pur, des cheveux ramenés en arrière révélant de jeunes mèches, une chemise d'une blancheur délicate, et des ongles polis qu'affectionnaient tant les *fijnschilders*. Le thème de la jeune fille endormie est traditionnellement associé à l'oisiveté. Cependant, dans ce tableau, de telles préoccupations morales le cèdent à la beauté et à la sérénité du sujet. Le carmin de ses joues évoque le pouvoir de rêves auxquels le spectateur n'a pas accès. Si la composition trahit par sa perspective et sa légère gaucherie anatomique la main d'un imitateur, cette maladresse sert à accentuer la compression due au format, car le tableau n'est que visage, mains et décolleté sensuels. Santerre est l'auteur de nombreuses demi-figures féminines prenant part à des « actions naïves » (*Nouveau Mercure*, 1718, p. 75) : aides-cuisinières, femmes lisant des lettres, jeunes filles à la fenêtre, « Espagnolettes », Vénitiennes. Le tableau de Nantes peut être comparé aux autres tableaux de Santerre de femmes éclairées à la chandelle, parmi lesquels *La Brodeuse à la bougie* (Libourne, musée des Beaux-Arts et d'Archéologie) et la *Jeune Femme lisant une lettre à la lumière d'une chandelle* (Chaumont, musée d'Art et d'Histoire), mais aussi à d'autres figures endormies (Barcelone, MNAC). Cette étude intimiste d'une douce jeune fille contribue à tourmenter le spectateur : elle est rendue doublement inaccessible par la combinaison de l'obscurité et du sommeil.

MP

38

Giovanni Battista Piazzetta

(Venise, 1682-1754)

Jeune Paysanne endormie

H.s.t. ; H. 0,66 ; L. 0,82
Salzbourg, Residenzgalerie, inv. 475

Historique : Acquisition Galerie Sanct Lucas, Vienne, 1978.
Exposition : John T. Spike, « Giuseppe Maria Crespi and the Emergence of Genre Painting in Italy », *in* Fort Worth, 1986, n° 34, p. 182-184 ;
Bibliographie : Jones, 1981 ; Knox, 1992, p. 68-74 ; Groschner, Habersatter, Mayr-Oehring, 2002, p. 68 ; Juffinger, 2010, p. 173.
Œuvres en rapport : Pendant : *Jeune Berger*, Salzbourg, Residenzgalerie, inv. 476 ; esquisse, localisation inconnue (ill. *Piazzetta*, Washington, 1983, fig. 4).

Giovanni Battista Piazzetta, *Jeune Berger*, Salzbourg, Residenzgalerie

Piazzetta fut d'abord formé à Venise avant d'étudier à Bologne sous la direction de Crespi. Influencée par le Guerchin et le Caravage, sa palette était plus sombre que celle de ses rivaux vénitiens, Ricci et Tiepolo. Artiste polyvalent, il réalisa des peintures religieuses et des scènes de genre énigmatiques. Les nombreuses têtes et demi-figures de Piazzetta, exécutées au fusain et à la craie blanche, étaient prisées des collectionneurs et fréquemment gravées. Vers la fin de sa vie, il devint directeur de l'Académie des beaux-arts de Venise.

Le regard du spectateur est placé à hauteur du décolleté de la jeune paysanne endormie, dans une intention explicitement sexuelle. L'inclinaison du personnage, ses membres raccourcis et la lumière crue qui expose sa chair nue rendent sa poitrine encore plus accessible. Il s'agit là de la représentation d'un stéréotype, celui de la servante négligente, incarnation de la paresse qui, dans sa version féminine, était souvent liée à la sexualité. L'incapacité de la jeune fille à préserver sa chasteté suscite un mélange hypocrite de désir et de désapprobation chez ceux qui l'observent. Bien que le tableau ne montre qu'une simple servante, sa composition est élaborée. Le format oblong laisse transparaître la fatigue du personnage. En imitant et en accentuant la rondeur de ses formes, l'ovale devient l'expression physique de son laisser-aller. Le panier, entremêlé au corps de la femme, esquisse la forme tridimensionnelle et complexe d'un huit. Les navets rondelets qui s'en échappent complètent cette dialectique de l'aspect plantureux de la classe paysanne. Traditionnellement, les navets étaient considérés comme des symboles de l'amour en raison de leur forme en cœur, mais, dans un contexte paysan, leur signification était plus ouvertement sexuelle. De plus, comme le souligne Leslie Jones dans son livre, le mot italien « rapa » (navet) signifie « imbécile » dans son acception la plus courante. Le tableau, qui, selon les estimations, remonte au début des années 1720, s'inspire en partie de l'art bolonais, et de Crespi notamment. Par ailleurs, l'influence du Caravage est perceptible dans les effets de clair-obscur et la tonalité terreuse du sujet, qui est dépeint avec sensibilité en dépit de sa rusticité. Piazzetta est l'auteur d'autres œuvres de genre, qui furent plus tard appelées « capricci fiamminghi », ou caprices flamands (Knox, 1992, p. 74). Le pendant à cette peinture représente un jeune berger : il a le regard perdu au loin, son profil s'efface et ses yeux, ainsi qu'une grande partie de son visage, sont dissimulés derrière un chapeau sombre. Ces tableaux jumeaux jouent sur la notion d'accessibilité et de distance, le détachement du garçon contrastant avec la proximité très marquée de la jeune femme. Les deux tableaux de Salzbourg peuvent être comparés à des œuvres complémentaires de la même période : *Jeune Paysanne attrapant une puce* et *Jeune Paysan au marché*, conservés au Museum of Fine Arts de Boston. Une esquisse associée représente une jeune fille endormie avec un panier de navets. Sous-tendue par une dialectique complexe du concave et du convexe, du confinement et de l'ouverture, ce tableau exsude un sentiment de chaleur et la femme dégage douceur et vulnérabilité en dépit de ses traits grossiers.

MP

39

École de Pietro Antonio Rotari

(Vérone, 1707 – Saint-Pétersbourg, 1762)

Dormeuse

H.s.t. ; H. 0,38 ; L. 0,32
Rovigo, Pinacoteca del Seminario Vescovile, inv. 111

Historique : Inconnu.
Expositions : Gregor J. M. Weber *in* Dresde, 1999-2000 ; Vérone, 2011-2012.
Bibliographie : Donzelli, 1957, p. 201, fig. 293 ; Polazzo, 1990 ; Romagnolo, Fantelli, 2001, no 111, p. 119.

Rotari se forma auprès de Balestra avant de partir à Rome étudier avec Trevisani et à Naples dans l'atelier de Solimena. De retour à Vérone, il connut le succès comme peintre d'histoire et de sujets religieux. De 1750 jusqu'à sa mort, Rotari se fit une place dans les cours de Vienne, de Dresde et de Saint-Pétersbourg où il peignit des portraits et mit au point un genre fort apprécié de bustes de femmes jeunes et moins jeunes aux prises avec toutes sortes d'émotions.

Cette peinture fut attribuée à Rotari par Carlo Donzelli en 1957 mais cette analyse ne résiste pas à un examen approfondi. La conception et la réalisation de ce gros plan très élaboré d'une petite fille innocente sont évidemment proches de l'œuvre de Rotari. Parmi sa vaste production, Rotari a peint plusieurs filles endormies, notamment les tableaux se trouvant à Dresde, Gemäldegalerie (Polazzo, no 100), à Peterhof, près de Saint-Pétersbourg (Polazzo, no 189), au musée de Petrodvorets (Polazzo, nos 227, 232). À l'Alte Pinakothek de Munich se trouve une plus grande peinture de Rotari représentant un jeune homme chatouillant la joue d'une jeune fille endormie avec un épi de blé (Polazzo, no 104). Rotari a aussi exploré l'état de somnolence dans un dérivé du pendant de *La Voluptueuse* de François Boucher (Espagne, coll. part., *cf.* cat. 12). Cette fillette de Rovigo est détaillée en un plan serré vertical qu'affectionnait Rotari, le corps comprimé à la surface de l'image et éclairé de biais. La tension dramatique tient dans le fait que le spectateur est comme penché au-dessus d'elle, au risque de la réveiller. L'innocence et la douceur de l'enfance sont suggérées par la mèche de cheveux sur le front, les taches de rousseur sur le nez et les mains sagement jointes. La tête tombe doucement sur le côté, créant une légère fossette sur la joue arrondie. Selon Romagnolo, ce tableau paraît être une libre interprétation d'une œuvre de Rotari. Bien que représentant un sujet plus rond et plus jeune qu'habituellement, le modèle ressemble ici à celui de sa *Jeune Fille en train de coudre* (Vérone, Collezione della Fondazione Cariverona, *Il Settecento a Verona*, no 68F, p. 208, ill. p. 210). Comme chez les enfants endormis de Greuze, le charme de cette scène tient dans le fait que la fillette est tout à fait relâchée et oublieuse de l'attention qu'on lui porte. **MP**

Jean-Baptiste Greuze

(Tournus, 1725 – Paris, 1805)

Le Petit Paresseux, 1755

H.s.t. ; H. 0,65 ; L. 0,54
Montpellier, musée Fabre,
inv. 837-1-35

Historique : Legs François-Xavier Fabre, 1837.
Expositions : Ottawa/Washington DC/Berlin, 2003-2004, n° 63, p. 246-247.
Bibliographie : Barker, 2005 ; Hilaire, 2007, n° A4527, p. 67 ; Barker, 2009, p. 426-445.
Œuvre en rapport : pendant : Jean-Baptiste Greuze, *La Tricoteuse endormie*, vers 1758, 0,60 × 0,50 m, San Marino, Californie, The Huntington Art Collection, inv. 78.20.8.

Biographie : *cf.* cat. 32, *Jeune berger tenant une fleur.*

Jean-Baptiste Greuze, *La Tricoteuse endormie*, San Marino, Californie, The Huntington Library, Art Collections

Le jeune garçon s'est endormi sur son livre et il n'a pas conscience d'être regardé, ce qui laisse au spectateur tout loisir pour contempler ses traits gracieux et admirer le charme rustique avec lequel l'artiste a traité son sujet. Ce tableau est l'un des trois qui valurent à Greuze d'obtenir l'agrément de l'Académie royale en 1755. Il appartint à l'amateur d'art Ange-Laurent de La Live de Jully, collectionneur de peinture nordique qui apporta son soutien à Greuze. Greuze réalisa de nombreuses compositions hybrides représentant un personnage unique et mêlant des éléments du portrait, de la peinture de genre et de l'allégorie. Ainsi, son portrait de La Live jouant de la harpe (1759, Washington DC, National Gallery of Art) partage avec les figures de musiciens de cette exposition une certaine dimension narrative. Par son thème ainsi que par son exécution, *Le Petit Paresseux* puise dans la tradition des pays du Nord, en particulier chez Rembrandt ; il reflète également l'influence d'artistes qui mirent à la mode les thèmes et le style nordiques, tel Santerre (cat. 37). Exposé au Salon de 1755, ce tableau fut jugé par certains critiques d'une facture trop peu soignée, inappropriée pour une peinture de cabinet. Pourtant, l'audace du coup de pinceau témoigne du talent remarquable de Greuze ; les effets qu'il obtient ici n'ont rien à voir avec son très rococo *Berger* (cat. 32), ce qui constitue une preuve supplémentaire de la flexibilité de son art. Ce tableau nous rappelle également que le fini voulu par l'artiste, qu'il fût heurté ou léché, était un élément d'appréciation important pour les consommateurs de figures de fantaisie. Le pendant de ce tableau, le portrait d'une petite fille assoupie sur son tricot, est d'une facture plus élaborée, qui évoque Dou et Netscher. Traditionnellement, comme l'a montré Petra ten-Doesschate Chu, il était courant d'interpréter les figures endormies comme des représentations de la paresse, mais les enfants de ces deux portraits ont un air délicieusement innocent, à l'instar des quelques autres enfants endormis dans l'œuvre de Greuze. L'arrondi du visage du jeune garçon, la grâce de ses traits pleins de douceur, que soulignent ses boucles enfantines, et le diminutif du titre – « petit paresseux » – font de sa distraction une faute vénielle. De délicats cils roux de la couleur de ses cheveux ourlent la courbe de ses paupières et ses cheveux sont mis en valeur par des rehauts de blanc et de brun orangé. Les nuances de la carnation ont été obtenues par la superposition visible de couches de peinture crème, blanche et grise, appliquées sans trop de soin ; de larges touches de rouge sur les joues rendent fidèlement cette roseur que l'on observe sur le visage des enfants endormis. Des ombres marquées, sur les tempes et derrière l'oreille, rappellent la vulnérabilité de l'enfant. Les tons bruns du reste du tableau contrastent avec la pâleur de son visage, où se concentre la lumière. Sa posture forme un léger angle qui se retrouve dans le livre et d'autres éléments du décor. Plusieurs lignes horizontales accentuent l'impression de fatigue : la tête de l'enfant repose sur sa main et celle-ci sur le livre, lui-même posé sur la table. Le livre a beau n'être qu'un modeste volume, le contenu s'en est avéré trop lourd pour ce jeune esprit. Le tableau de Greuze fut réalisé à un moment où émergeaient de nouvelles théories sociales qui mettaient en avant l'innocence et la liberté de l'enfance. Pour des penseurs tels que Jean-Jacques Rousseau, acquérir un savoir livresque n'était pas nécessairement souhaitable pour de jeunes êtres aussi impressionnables. Au premier plan du tableau, un rebord en bois, emprunt à la peinture de genre d'Europe du Nord, crée subtilement une distance supplémentaire entre le personnage et le spectateur qui le contemple. Il n'en reste pas moins impossible de ne pas être charmé par cette gracieuse figure de fantaisie. **MP**

41

Jean-Baptiste Deshays ou Deshayes

(Colleville, près de Rouen, 1729 – Paris, 1765)

Une femme qui dort ou *La Fidélité surveillante*, vers 1757-1758

H.s.t. ; H. 1,01 ; L. 0,76
Inscription au verso, en haut à droite : *Antoine Watteau/A Lady Sleeping/-/ The Earl of Lonsdale/Lowther Castle* (« Antoine Watteau/Femme endormie/-/comte de Lonsdale/ Lowther Castle »)
Brême, Kunsthalle, inv. 832-1960/24

Historique : Acquis en 1960 par autorisation spéciale de la Ville de Brême à l'occasion de la réouverture de son musée, la Kunsthalle.
Bibliographie : Sandoz, 1977, no 13, p. 40, 66-68 ; Höper, 1998, I, p. 74-75 ; Bancel, 2008, no P26, p. 100-102.
Œuvres en rapport : esquisse peinte préparatoire, perdue (Bancel, 2008, no P25) ; dessin à la sanguine d'après le tableau et préparant sans doute la gravure, musée de Chalon-sur-Saône (Bancel, 2008, DE 8) ; gravures : Pierre-Gustave Flöding, *La Fidélité surveillante*, Paris, 1759, Antoine-François Hémery, 1780 ; il existe non moins de sept copies du tableau, ainsi que deux adaptations (*cf.* Bancel, 2008).

Salué comme « le soleil levant de l'Ecole françoise » par l'abbé de La Porte, Deshays incarna au milieu du XVIIIe siècle les espoirs de sa génération de voir s'épanouir un renouveau de la peinture d'histoire française. Il reçut à Paris une formation des plus rigoureuses, couronnée par d'insignes honneurs. Après quatre années passées à Rome, il regagna la France où il épousa la fille de son maître, François Boucher. Deshays connut le succès dans tous les genres picturaux qu'il embrassa, mais plus particulièrement dans la peinture religieuse. Il était réputé pour le caractère spectaculaire de ses compositions, la puissance de ses couleurs et son excellent rendu des sentiments. Sa mort prématurée mit fin à une carrière prometteuse.

Tableau sans doute le plus explicitement érotique de cette exposition, la femme endormie de Deshays explore le thème fascinant de la sexualité féminine. Conçue dans la tradition française de la peinture galante de style rococo portée par Watteau, Boucher et Fragonard, la *Femme qui dort* nous stupéfie par son décor naturaliste autant que par l'étroite proximité du spectateur avec cet être désirable, à demi-nu. Réalisé au cours du séjour de l'artiste à Rome, le tableau fut présenté lors de la première exposition parisienne de Deshays, au Salon de 1759. La scène artistique publique était alors davantage plurielle et tolérante qu'on ne le pense : c'est en tout cas ce que suggèrent le choix du sujet, son acceptation implicite par l'Académie et le fait que le tableau ne suscita pas plus les passions que les foudres des critiques d'art (pas même celles du réformiste qu'était Diderot). Du fait de sa position influente à l'épicentre de la production artistique française, Deshays pouvait, sans difficulté aucune, passer de la peinture religieuse à la peinture extrêmement profane. La jeune femme est vêtue d'une chemise vaporeuse et transparente. Plongée dans l'inconscience, elle ne fait aucun effort pour se couvrir. Un mamelon rosé s'expose sans voile au regard, et l'on aperçoit le haut d'une cuisse. Une étoffe drapée, d'un jaune éclatant, l'enveloppe dans un espace que l'on ne saurait définir et la projette subtilement vers la surface du tableau. La diagonale dessinée par son corps ainsi que son visage en pointe rappellent fortement Watteau, et l'inscription portée au dos de la toile indique que le tableau fut d'abord attribué à tort à ce dernier. Le sous-titre de l'œuvre est une référence au chien de salon, symbole classique de la fidélité, qui monte la garde tandis que dort sa maîtresse. Que cette femme porte au doigt un anneau suggère qu'elle est mariée, bien que pléthore de procédés visuels vienne en réalité saper l'idée même de fidélité. Peut-être la dormeuse a-t-elle les mains sur les cuisses, doigts enlacés, parce qu'elle veut se protéger. Pourtant, le V que ces mains forment semble plutôt attirer l'attention vers ses parties génitales, et l'index droit, semblable à un phallus, est un signe sexuel éloquent. Il existe également un contraste entre, d'un côté, la petite taille du chien et son air sans prétention et, de l'autre, l'abandon de sa maîtresse : le calembour visuel exprime l'idée qu'il n'a de toute évidence pas les qualités requises pour faire face si jamais la vertu de sa maîtresse venait à faillir. Ce tableau propose plusieurs récits possibles. Le scénario qui nous parlerait de fidélité semble le moins plausible étant donné les ambiguïtés évoquées précédemment. Dans son sommeil, elle imagine peut-être une rencontre avec un amant, et sa semi-nudité serait alors la transposition visuelle de ses rêveries. Il se peut également qu'il n'y ait pas d'amant, et que la jouissance sexuelle ait été le fruit d'un plaisir solitaire (l'onanisme féminin implicite était un thème relativement courant du style rococo). Le dernier scénario impliquerait l'idée d'une infidélité commise avec le spectateur, ce dernier jouant le rôle de l'amant putatif, placé dans une position stratégique pour profiter de cette femme dévêtue et inconsciente. Ce tableau de Deshays accéda

à la notoriété grâce à la gravure de Flöding, *La Fidélité surveillante*, dédiée au comte de Tessin. Dans une lettre adressée à Tessin et datée du 1er juin 1759, Flöding note qu'il est possible que son mécène juge le sujet « peu décent », mais que le fini du tableau ainsi que le traitement des étoffes sont extrêmement beaux. La popularité de l'œuvre ne laisse pas de doute quand on sait qu'il existe une seconde gravure de Flöding réalisée une vingtaine d'années plus tard, ainsi que plusieurs copies, dont certaines en miroir, d'après les gravures (par exemple, à l'Institut Tessin, inv. P 324). Deshays peignit plusieurs autres figures de fantaisie féminines représentant des coquettes (*cf.* Bancel, p. 139-140), mais aucune avec autant de liberté et de puissance d'évocation que celle exposée ici.

MP

Rires et sarcasmes

42

Giovanni Francesco de Luteri, *dit* Dosso Dossi

(Mirandola, 1486/1487 – Ferrare, 1542)

Bouffon

H.s.t. ; H. 0,60 ; L. 0,53
Inscr. b.d. *Sic Gi...ius*
Modène, Galleria Estense, inv. G.E. 474

Historique : Cardinal d'Este, Rome en 1624 ou collection Roberto Canonici, Ferrare, avant 1631 ; peut-être Camillo Pamphilj, Rome, 1648 ; Galerie ducale, Modène, entre 1663 et 1720 ; Académie des beaux-arts, Modène, en 1797 ; Galleria Estense à partir de 1854.
Expositions : Ferrare/New York/Los Angeles, 1998-1999, no 2.
Bibliographie : Longhi, 1934 (1975), p. 114, 117 ; Mezzetti, 1965, p. 56, 97-98 ; Gibbons, 1968, p. 121, 189-190 ; Ballarin, 1994-1995, I, p. 28, 293.

La formation de Giovanni Francesco de Luteri est mal connue mais il semble avoir séjourné à Venise au cours de sa jeunesse. Dès 1513, il entrait au service des Este de Ferrare, dont il fut le peintre de cour durant toute sa carrière. Il voyagea à de nombreuses reprises à Venise et en Italie du Nord. Il a régulièrement travaillé avec son frère Battista et on a parfois du mal à identifier les œuvres des deux frères. Doté d'une sensibilité particulière pour le paysage, Dosso Dossi s'est spécialisé dans des sujets raffinés d'esprit onirique. Il fut influencé par les nouveautés venues de Venise, de Giorgione puis de Titien.

L'art de la vallée du Pô au tournant du XVIe siècle se situe au croisement de courants naturalistes d'influence nordique et des nouveautés de la culture vénitienne, singulièrement celles suscitées par les créations de Giorgione. Les premières œuvres du peintre ferrarais Dosso Dossi témoignent de son intérêt pour les têtes d'expression de Giorgione comme la *Vecchia* (Venise, Gallerie dell'Accademia). D'autres tableaux intéressants pour notre propos sont d'attribution plus disputée comme les *Musiciens* (Rome, Galleria Borghese) qui rejoignent la cohorte des productions dites giorgionesques, adjectif qui recouvre des figures de fantaisie d'un nouveau genre. Il est en effet difficile de situer précisément le genre de ce type de sujet entre l'allégorie, le portrait ou le caprice artistique. Ce sont en tout cas des représentations pleines d'empathie envers les modèles, chargées parfois de mélancolie, qui connaîtront une grande postérité jusqu'à l'avènement du caravagisme.

À la manière de Giorgione, Dosso Dossi isole son personnage sur un fond de paysage d'un vert profond. Il introduit des détails *a priori* signifiants tel le mouton, les fabriques se détachant sur la forêt, la médaille en boucle d'oreille et le cartel portant une inscription. En fait, cette inscription incomplète *Sic Gi... ius* n'a jamais suscité l'unanimité chez les historiens de l'art. Longhi pensait qu'il s'agissait du bouffon Giullare mais cette identification paraît avoir été abandonnée. Aucune explication convaincante n'a pu être donnée des autres éléments iconographiques.

Le *Bouffon* est à rapprocher de sujets mythologiques du début de la carrière de l'artiste comme *Nymphe et Satyre* (Florence, Galleria Palatina) et d'allégories tels les sept panneaux en losange peints pour le *studiolo* du duc Alfonso d'Este à Ferrare. Il est généralement daté du séjour du peintre à Venise, au cours de la deuxième décennie du XVIe siècle. Si Dosso est un peintre de cour travaillant dans un milieu humaniste d'un grand raffinement, ses figures s'imposent avec une assurance qui confine à la brutalité. Ici, le personnage habillé en gentilhomme détourne les règles du portrait aristocratique par son air railleur. Curieusement, le mouton qu'il tient ostensiblement, en soi une magnifique étude naturaliste, est totalement dénué d'expression. Ce contraste et l'absurdité même de la situation constituent le comique de la représentation. Les bouffons sont régulièrement représentés à côté d'animaux, comme un rappel de leur humanité.

En dépit de l'usure de la couche picturale, particulièrement sensible dans le paysage, la vision de ce personnage haut en couleur ne s'oublie pas. Il est probable que le tableau ait été découpé car une copie apparue en vente publique à Londres en 1967 présente plus de surface à droite et en hauteur.

Le *Bouffon* est avant tout une tête d'expression, un *scherzo* à destination d'un public cultivé, peut-être du duc lui-même, et il représente sans doute un personnage de la cour. Toutefois, il nous manque de toute évidence des clés de lecture qui permettraient sans doute de tirer ce tableau vers l'allégorie. Il s'inscrit dans le vaste répertoire des représentations de bouffons qui apparaissent avec le *Portrait du bouffon Gonella* de Fouquet et se développent avec Antonio Moro puis Vélasquez à la cour d'Espagne. **AH**

Giovan Paolo Lomazzo

(Milan, 1538-1592)

Autoportrait en abbé de l'académie de la Val di Blenio, 1568

H.s.t. ; H. 0,56 ; L. 0,44
Inscr. en bas *ZAVARGNA.NABAS. VALLIS. BREGNI.ET.IPL.PI(C)T(O)R*
Milan, Pinacoteca di Brera, inv. Reg. Cron. 112

Historique : Acquis en 1821 à Milan auprès du peintre et scénographe Pasquale Canna.
Expositions : Naples/New York, 1985, n° 5 ; Lugano, 1998, n° 27.
Bibliographie : Porzio, 1989, p. 254-256.

Formé à Milan dans l'admiration de Gaudenzio Ferrari et dans la tradition léonardesque, Lomazzo voyagea à Rome afin d'étudier les œuvres de Michel-Ange. Il connut un succès très précoce comme portraitiste et auteur de fresques et de tableaux religieux destinés aux églises de Milan. Frappé de cécité à trente-trois ans, il se tourna vers la rédaction de traités théoriques (*Trattato della Pittura, Idea del Tempio della Pittura*) et de poésies. Il fut de loin la personnalité artistique la plus influente à Milan au cours de la seconde moitié du XVIe siècle.

Cette œuvre singulière est un exemple de maniérisme lettré et de primitivisme en même temps qu'un manifeste de l'art et de la pensée de Lomazzo, l'un des théoriciens de l'art les plus influents de la Renaissance. Si une analyse iconographique est nécessaire pour comprendre la subtile construction de ce rébus, un simple regard permet d'en mesurer l'originalité et la force expressive. Il s'agit ici véritablement d'un autoportrait intellectuel de l'artiste. *L'arte è cosa mentale* disait le grand modèle lombard de Lomazzo, Léonard de Vinci.

Les circonstances de la réalisation du tableau ont été éclaircies par Porzio en 1989. En 1568, Lomazzo fut nommé abbé de l'académie de la Val di Blenio et il est probable que l'œuvre a été peinte à l'occasion de cette élection. Fondée en 1560 et placée sous la protection de Bacchus, cette académie tire son nom d'une vallée alpine située entre la Lombardie et la Suisse. Le rude dialecte qui y était parlé, adopté par les académiciens comme un langage secret, devint le symbole d'une recherche de réalisme grotesque d'essence populaire partagée par les hommes de lettres et les artistes membres.

Zavargna (Moqueur) est le nom d'académicien de Lomazzo tandis que *nabas* est une variante dialectale d'*abate*, abbé en français. Le peintre arbore le costume des porteurs de vin originaires de cette vallée. Le médaillon doré représente un récipient plein de vin et orné de feuilles de vigne. Cette plante est omniprésente avec la couronne de laurier, symbole de la fureur poétique. Le chapeau de paille et la peau de chèvre signifient l'humilité. Par ailleurs, Lomazzo se représente avec un compas pour le calcul et le dessin, et sa main s'appuie sur une toile dont on voit le revers percé de pitons d'accrochage pour montrer l'aspect matériel du travail. La bague bien en évidence à son majeur pourrait suggérer, selon Porzio, l'union de la théorie et de la pratique chère à l'artiste théoricien et empruntée à Léonard de Vinci et Dürer, deux de ses sources privilégiées.

La composition résulte de la reprise et de la transformation par Lomazzo d'un modèle issu de l'entourage de Giorgione, *Portrait de berger à la flûte*, dont la version de Bowood Castle (Wilshire) est attribuée à Sebastiano del Piombo et où le cadrage, la position du buste et le couvre-chef sont très similaires.

Derrière la surcharge de symboles et d'allusions savantes se cache un homme au regard détaché et subtilement ironique. Le soin accordé au traitement de la barbe et de la moustache, le délicat incarnat des lèvres indiquent une volonté de rendu mimétique et de personnalisation d'une image destinée à la postérité. L'emprunt d'un motif giorgionesque et d'une technique de *sfumato* léonardesque marque une forte revendication d'insertion dans une tradition lombarde où l'Idéal se nourrit de naturalisme.

Au sein d'une production un peu oubliée de nos jours et qui pâtit face à l'importance de ses écrits théoriques, l'*Autoportrait* reste le tableau le plus attachant de Lomazzo et celui qui incarne le mieux à nos yeux son talent de peintre.

AH

44

Hans von Aachen

(Cologne, 1552 – Prague, 1615)

Deux Hommes riant (Double Autoportrait)

H.s. bois ; H. 0,48 ; L. 0,38
Kromeriz, Arcibiskupstvi olomoucke, Arcibiskupsky zamek a zahrady v Kromerizi, inv. KE 3177 O 288

Historique : Collection Imstenraedt, Cologne, avant 1667 ; évêque d'Olomouc Karl von Liechtenstein-Castelnuovo en 1673 ; donné par ce dernier à l'évêché d'Olomouc en 1691.
Expositions : Prague, 1997, nº I, 1 ; Aix-la-Chapelle/Prague/Vienne, 2010-2011, nº 2.
Bibliographie : Jacoby, 2000, nº 74, p. 221-223.

Hans von Aachen, *Autoportrait*, Cologne, Wallraff-Richartz-Museum

La carrière de Hans von Aachen est représentative de l'intensité des échanges artistiques dans les terres d'Empire. Formé à Cologne dans l'atelier du peintre flamand Jorrigh, il partit en 1574 pour Venise puis Rome. Après avoir travaillé pour le duc de Bavière à son retour en Allemagne en 1588, il se fixa à Prague à partir de 1596, nommé peintre de chambre de l'empereur Rodolphe II. Il est avec Spranger le plus grand représentant du foyer maniériste étincelant de la cour de Rodolphe II. Ses inventions iconographiques sophistiquées et sa richesse de coloris en font un artiste brillant et attachant.

Cette image fascinante de deux hommes qui se ressemblent comme deux gouttes d'eau a été comprise très tôt comme un double autoportrait du jeune peintre. Hans von Aachen s'est en effet représenté à plusieurs reprises au cours de sa carrière. Il l'a fait tout d'abord dans l'*Autoportrait* sensiblement contemporain du Wallraff-Richartz-Museum de Cologne (fig. ci-contre) puis dans celui bien plus tardif de la Galleria Palatina de Florence. De plus, le peintre a également associé son effigie à des figures féminines dans des scènes de genre à deux personnages comme en témoignent la *Donna venusta* (coll. part.), la *Jeune Femme avec un homme et un miroir* ou le *Couple riant avec une bourse* (tous deux à Vienne, Kunsthistorisches Museum).

Si l'autoportrait burlesque jouit d'une tradition solidement ancrée dans la peinture de l'Europe du Nord, la double effigie de l'artiste est plus rare et troublante. Hans von Aachen prend bien soin de conférer aux deux visages la même énergie vitale. La figure au deuxième plan saisit ainsi le lobe de l'oreille du personnage de devant qui, de son côté, désigne son partenaire de l'index. Devant ce contact physique direct, force est d'accepter le fait que le deuxième Hans von Aachen n'est ni la réflexion dans un miroir ni la représentation sur un tableau du premier.

Les spécialistes s'accordent à situer ce tableau au tout début de la carrière de l'artiste, avant 1574, alors qu'il se trouvait encore à Cologne. Il n'était pas encore le peintre cultivé vivant dans le milieu humaniste de la cour de Rodolphe II à Prague. Néanmoins, l'œuvre offre une multitude de pistes d'interprétation à un public capable de les comprendre. Les personnages hilares évoquent immédiatement le philosophe cynique Démocrite qui se gaussait des malheurs du monde et qui était si populaire dans l'art néerlandais au tournant des XVIᵉ et XVIIᵉ siècles (cat. 48). On ne peut manquer de se remémorer l'anecdote selon laquelle Zeuxis serait littéralement mort de rire devant le portrait d'une vieille femme qu'il avait peint. Franz von Imstenraedt, propriétaire du tableau au XVIIᵉ siècle, avait comparé l'artiste à Mopsus, génie antique du Rire, ou à Démocrite.

La force immédiate de l'image réside dans sa franchise et sa simplicité. Le futur artiste de cour au raffinement exacerbé s'exprime ici avec une vraie rusticité. Le coup de pinceau est rapide et allusif. Le second visage, à la carnation terreuse, peine à sortir de l'obscurité. À la manière des paysans de Pieter Brueghel l'Ancien, l'efficacité sans affectation de la technique sert à divertir les milieux cultivés au spectacle d'un monde grossier et laid, ce monde qu'on préfère contempler en peinture. Le maniérisme nordique, dont Hans von Aachen fut l'un des plus purs représentants, ne se cantonne pas aux sphères précieuses mais éprouve le besoin de se ressourcer en réinterprétant les stéréotypes populaires. En exhibant deux études de son propre visage en état d'hilarité, Hans von Aachen avance masqué sur la scène du théâtre du monde. **AH**

45

Annibale Carracci, *dit* Annibal Carrache

(Bologne, 1560 – Rome, 1609)

Tête d'homme qui rit

H.s. papier marouflé sur toile ;
H. 0,42 ; L. 0,28
Rome, Galleria Borghese, inv. 83

Historique : Première description dans l'inventaire Borghèse de 1693 sans indication d'auteur. Peut-être collection Harpur à Rome en 1677.
Expositions : Bologne, 1956, no 54 ; Bologne, 1984, no 80 ; Bologne/Rome, 2006-2007, no 9
Bibliographie : Longhi, 1928 (1967, p. 317, 337, fig. 275) ; Della Pergola, 1955, p. 21, no 16 ; Posner, 1971, II, p. 6, no 10.

Annibale Carracci fonda avec son frère Agostino et son cousin Ludovico une académie du dessin à Bologne en 1582 où se formèrent tous les grands peintres de cette ville au XVIIe siècle. Après avoir voyagé en Italie du Nord et avoir travaillé dans plusieurs palais de Bologne, il fut appelé à Rome en 1594 pour décorer le palais Farnèse, qui constituera sa plus grande réalisation. Les premiers tableaux bolonais du peintre, marqués par une influence nordique, représentent des sujets populaires et réalistes. Son art évolue ensuite vers une idéalisation classique, dont témoignent les représentations des amours des dieux au palais Farnèse. Son art influencera tout un pan de la peinture classique en Italie et en France au XVIIe siècle.

Cette œuvre séduisante et informelle s'affiche au croisement de plusieurs genres et expériences artistiques. Elle se situe au cœur des expérimentations du jeune Annibale à partir des types et des distractions populaires. Elle s'inscrit dans la tradition lombarde et émilienne des portraits de bouffons à la fin du XVIe siècle. Elle appartient enfin au corpus des huiles sur papier si nombreuses à cette période, d'abord résidus d'atelier à valeur documentaire, dont les collectionneurs s'empareront rapidement pour leur conférer le statut d'œuvre d'art à part entière et de témoignage de première main du talent d'un artiste.

L'attribution de l'esquisse n'a pas toujours été universellement acceptée. D'abord anonyme dans le premier inventaire Borghèse puis attribuée au Caravage et enfin à Annibale Carracci, c'est Roberto Longhi qui la rattachait définitivement à la production du maître bolonais. Encore récemment, dans le catalogue de la grande exposition monographique de Bologne et Rome en 2006-2007, Daniele Benati paraissait exprimer un doute quant à l'attribution. Il nous semble néanmoins que le rapprochement avec le *Mangiafagioli* (Rome, Galleria Colonna) est tout à fait probant. La fluidité virtuose du trait, la capacité à capter une expression quasi magnétique, le soulignement des carnations par des rehauts de blanc nous paraissent similaires dans ces deux œuvres. L'état d'inachèvement de la tête de la Galleria Borghese en renforce le sentiment d'immédiateté. Les traits à la pierre noire débordent les contours avec une rusticité qui ne contredit pas la science de la couleur dont témoigne le jeune artiste. Dans ses nombreuses études de têtes contemporaines, Annibale joue sur tous les modes de représentation, de face, de profil, de trois quarts, adoptant un cadrage serré et recherchant toujours une empathie avec ses modèles. Ici, la légère torsion du cou et le rictus déformant le bas du visage ne permettent pas au spectateur d'échapper à l'emprise du jeune homme. S'agit-il d'un acteur, du portrait d'un familier dans une attitude moqueuse, d'un personnage de saynète populaire ? Il est difficile de privilégier une piste plutôt qu'une autre.

Depuis l'Antiquité, les humanistes ont glosé sur la sagesse de ceux qui sont fous en apparence et sur la fonction salutaire et subversive de l'humour. On connaît l'atelier des Carrache comme un lieu de création collective en contact avec les milieux lettrés de Bologne. Cette esquisse rapide et brillante s'apparente probablement à un jeu de rôle littéraire. Annibale travaille ici à la fois sur son rapport au naturel et au quotidien dans une perspective naturaliste et sur l'expression des *affetti* (affects) sur un mode plus intellectuel et artificiel. L'association de ces deux registres est précisément ce qui fait d'Annibale Carracci un artiste aussi essentiel dans l'art du *Seicento* et aussi irréductible à une classification qui privilégierait une tendance au détriment de l'autre. **AH**

46

Frans Hals

(Haarlem, 1582-1666)

Jeune Pêcheur

H.s.t. ; H. 0,74 ; L. 0,61
S.b.d. *FH*
Anvers, Koninklijk Museum voor Schone Kunsten, inv. 188

Historique : Vente Alphonse Oudry, Paris, 16 avril 1869, n° 35 ; acheté par le musée à J. C. Mertz, Paris, en 1871.
Expositions : Haarlem, 1962, n° 27 ; Londres, 1989, n° 34.
Bibliographie : Slive, 1970-1974, I, p. 141-143 ; Grimm, 1972, p. 214 ; Koslow, 1975, p. 429-432.

La vie de Frans Hals nous est fort peu connue en dépit de sa célébrité qui ne le cède qu'à Rembrandt et Vermeer. Toute sa carrière se déroula à Haarlem où il fut l'élève de Van Mander, peintre et théoricien imprégné d'influences italiennes. Il est membre de la guilde de Saint-Luc à Haarlem en 1610 et sa première commande d'un portrait de groupe est datée de 1616. Les dernières années de l'artiste se déroulent dans un grand dénuement. La profondeur psychologique de ses portraits et le brio vertigineux de sa touche ô combien ! moderne lui assurent une place de premier rang au panthéon de la peinture.

Sur un fond de paysage de dunes, devant la mer, un jeune pêcheur nous observe les bras croisés. Le paysage surmonté d'un ciel menaçant est proche du monochrome. La seule note colorée est constituée par le béret et la chemise rouges du garçon. Il est représenté à mi-corps, détaché sur le fond de ciel.

Hals a réalisé dans les années 1630 une série de jeunes pêcheurs aujourd'hui à Burgsteinfurt, à Dublin, et dans une collection particulière à New York. L'unanimité quant à l'attribution de ces tableaux est assez récente. Trivas les rejetait en bloc et Grimm avait créé un « Maître des enfants pêcheurs » auquel il attribuait cet ensemble. La *Petite Pêcheuse* d'une collection particulière new-yorkaise a pu être considérée comme le pendant du tableau d'Anvers mais il ne semble pas que ce soit le cas en dépit de dimensions proches et de sa présence à la même vente à Bruxelles en 1746 et à Paris en 1869.

Avec ce tableau, Hals s'inscrit dans une veine naturaliste. Si les vêtements et l'attitude du garçon nous renseignent immédiatement sur son appartenance à un milieu populaire, le panier et la présence de la mer nous apprennent son métier. Plus qu'à un portrait, genre reposant sur la commande, nous avons ici affaire à la représentation d'un type universel. Ce personnage est autant un pêcheur exemplaire que Malle Babbe est une sorcière modèle dans son célèbre portrait.

Hals choisit de traiter la simplicité et la franchise du garçon par un rendu fluide qui souligne son caractère rustique. La rapidité de la touche restitue à merveille son bonheur de vivre. Ses traits marqués, sa peau sale, son œil figé font comprendre la dureté de son existence. Le choix de la frontalité de la représentation favorise l'empathie avec le modèle. Les bras croisés n'ont sans doute pas d'autre fonction que la nécessité pratique d'optimiser la force requise pour porter un panier rempli de poissons.

On ne décèle pas chez Hals la moindre trace de critique sociale bien que ses jeunes pêcheurs soient indiscutablement pauvres et confrontés trop tôt, à nos yeux d'hommes du XXIe siècle, au monde du travail. Seymour Slive, à la suite d'une communication orale de Julius Held, rapproche ces représentations d'un poème de Jacob Cats exaltant les vertus de la vie au grand air contre l'existence à la ville. Cela expliquerait la joie de vivre manifestée par les enfants et leurs paniers qui semblent refléter une certaine abondance.

Van Gogh mentionnait ce tableau en premier parmi les œuvres dont il se souvenait au musée d'Anvers. Sa modernité est tout à fait évidente à la fois par le traitement synthétique du paysage, la force expressive du visage, l'énergie du corps et la ductilité de la touche. Loin de se réduire aux portraits de groupe de Haarlem, comme Fromentin, ennemi de la « vulgarité » du peintre, le fit croire au public français, l'art de Hals présente une diversité digne des plus grands peintres. Dans ce tableau, il montre une compréhension des valeurs tonales des paysages de Van Goyen. Sa capacité de synthèse et sa virtuosité en font le prédécesseur immédiat de *La Marchande de crevettes* de Hogarth (Tate Gallery).

AH

47

Adriaen Brouwer

(Audenarde, 1605/1606 – Anvers, 1638)

Le Flûtiste

H.s. cuivre ; H. 0,16 ; L. 0,13
Bruxelles, Musées royaux des beaux-arts de Belgique, inv. 3464

Historique : Acquis à la vente Valentin-Roussel (Roubaix), Bruxelles, Maison d'art, 14 juin 1899, no 2.

Biographie : *cf.* cat. 5.

En dépit de son titre et de la présence d'un musicien parmi les deux personnages, le tableau est à ranger dans le vaste corpus des scènes de taverne, la spécialité absolue de Brouwer. Ce n'est pas la musique qui semble motiver l'hilarité des deux compères mais l'ivrognerie et l'atmosphère des auberges propice à la moquerie. La raillerie s'exerce vraisemblablement à l'égard d'une tierce personne hors cadre, ce qu'indique sans ambages le geste de l'homme en arrière-plan. Le visage déformé par le rire du flûtiste est offert au public selon une formule propre à l'artiste, mi-complice de ses créatures, mi-moralisateur.
L'adoption d'un format miniature et d'un support précieux comme le cuivre contraste avec la grossièreté du sujet. Le personnage secondaire est traité de manière assez cursive et laissé dans l'ombre. En revanche, le flûtiste et toutes les parties éclairées de la scène sont peints avec une grande maestria. Les dominantes verticales et horizontales sont inscrites avec force, comme l'arête du mur, le dossier de la chaise ou le plan de la table. La composition se détache avec bonheur sur ce qu'il faut bien appeler sans sacrilège « un petit pan de mur jaune ».
Ce type de scène à deux personnages appartient au début de la carrière de Brouwer. On peut le rapprocher des petits panneaux de Munich, *Deux Paysans fumant près d'une cheminée* et *Rixe de deux paysans à côté d'un tonneau*. En dépit de l'absence de date, on pourrait les situer vers 1633, au début de la période anversoise. La littérature artistique a attribué à Brouwer le mode de vie de ses personnages sans doute au prix d'exagérations. Il serait tentant de voir dans le flûtiste un autoportrait, ce qui conviendrait à l'âge du peintre, autour de vingt-cinq ans. Rien ne permet toutefois d'étayer cette hypothèse.
Le tableau n'a curieusement pas été étudié dans les ouvrages sur Brouwer en dépit de son caractère indiscutablement autographe. On comprend aisément son succès commercial et l'estime que lui accordaient ses confrères au vu de son efficacité narrative, de son sens de l'humour et de la sympathie déclenchée par ses personnages. Dans un format miniature et un registre moins universel, il est le véritable héritier de la veine paysanne de Pieter Brueghel l'Ancien. Il sait à merveille faire de personnages affreux, sales et méchants, le sujet même d'une peinture brillante et inventive.

AH

48

Johannes Pauwelsz Moreelse

(Utrecht, après 1602-1634)

Démocrite

H.s. bois ; H. 0,60 ; L. 0,69
S.h.g. *Joann' Moreelse*
Utrecht, Centraal Museum,
inv. nr. 13824

Historique : Collection du prince Frédéric-Henri de Prusse, Erbach ; vente Christie's, Londres, 23 novembre 1962, n° 38 ; acquis par le musée.
Expositions : Utrecht/Brunswick, 1986-1987, n° 71 ; Lille, 2011, n° 22.
Bibliographie : Blankert, 1967, p. 52, 55, 56 ; Nicolson, 1974, p. 620-623.

J. P. Moreelse, *Héraclite*, Utrecht, Centraal Museum

Fils du célèbre Paulus Moreelse qui dirigea l'un des plus grands ateliers de l'école d'Utrecht, entre maniérisme et classicisme, Johannes Pauwelsz Moreelse est assez peu connu. Vraisemblablement formé dans l'atelier paternel, il était en Italie en 1627. Sa mort précoce à Utrecht en 1634 est sans doute due à la peste. J. P. Moreelse penche très nettement vers le caravagisme, dont il adopte quelques formules tout en restant fidèle à une expressivité toute nordique. Il semble avoir abandonné le maniérisme tardif caractéristique de la production paternelle.

Les figures de Démocrite et Héraclite appartiennent à des personnages historiques de l'Antiquité. On pourrait donc considérer les tableaux les représentant comme des peintures d'histoire. Toutefois, leurs codes iconographiques sont incontestablement ceux du *tronie*, du moins pour les exemples néerlandais connus. Les artistes visaient à la plus grande efficacité par un cadrage sur le protagoniste et une insistance sur son expression. Démocrite, le philosophe qui rit devant les malheurs du monde, et Héraclite, le philosophe qui en pleure, deviennent par la grâce des peintres les archétypes de l'homme hilare et du dépressif.

Il existe des représentations dans une composition unique des deux philosophes qui, il faut le rappeler, n'ont pas vécu à la même époque et n'ont pu se connaître. Néanmoins, dans la plupart des cas, les collectionneurs néerlandais ont plébiscité la formule des pendants. Moreelse junior a retenu l'idée d'une continuité entre les deux tableaux : les philosophes se font face, Démocrite à gauche et Héraclite à droite, et le globe terrestre semble se prolonger de part et d'autre de ces tableaux. Conformément aux canons de l'époque, Démocrite est un jeune homme extraverti tandis que Héraclite est un vieillard frileux tourné sur lui-même (fig. ci-contre).

L'expression de Démocrite n'est pas seulement celle d'une gaieté profonde mais elle témoigne d'une joie débridée et potentiellement destructrice. Ce rire est celui de la raillerie et de l'excès. Il n'y a pas loin de la bonhomie du bon vivant à la cruauté de la moquerie qui déforme les traits. Cette hilarité s'exerce sur la savante construction intellectuelle du monde, d'où le globe. Elle démontre la vanité des connaissances. C'est ce que vient illustrer la merveilleuse nature morte sur l'étagère, composée d'une bougie éteinte, signe d'épuisement des facultés vitales, et d'une pile de livres inutilisés.

L'exécution du tableau est rapide et aisée, ce qui en renforce le sentiment de vérité. Son étude radiographique a démontré qu'il n'y avait pas eu de reprises ou d'hésitations de la part du peintre. Le drapé laissant l'épaule découverte est tracé d'un geste fluide. La figure se détache nettement sur le fond quasiment monochrome. Il s'agit de la seule œuvre, avec son pendant, signée de l'artiste. Il devait, à bon droit, la considérer comme un chef-d'œuvre.

J.P. Moreelse n'est pas le seul caravagesque d'Utrecht qui ait traité ce sujet. On en connaît des versions par Bijlert et surtout par ter Brugghen dans les sublimes tableaux au Rijksmuseum. Dans une autre belle version par Moreelse de *Démocrite* au Mauritshuis de La Haye, le philosophe se penche sur le globe qu'il semble terrasser de son rire communicatif. Deux autres pendants à Chicago ont été donnés autrefois à Moreelse mais il faut renoncer à cette attribution. On comprend tout l'intérêt du sujet chez des artistes fascinés par l'étude des types humains et de leurs passions contrastées. La tête d'un homme qui rit a pour fonction de montrer le caractère universel d'une attitude devant la vie. La force de la représentation et la qualité du métier du peintre se réunissent pour nous offrir une image éloquente et inoubliable.

AH

49

Jan Miense Molenaer

(Haarlem, 1610-1668)

Jeune Garçon griffé par un chat

H.s. panneau ; H. 0,40 ; L. 0,31
Monogramme au fond d *JM*
Épinal, Musée départemental d'art ancien et contemporain, inv. L I 30

Historique : Saisie révolutionnaire : collection du prince de Salm.
Expositions : Paris, 1970-1971, p. 273 (Jacques Foucart, répertoire) ; Épinal, 1993-1994, no 25.

Vraisemblablement élève des frères Frans et Dirck Hals, Molenaer s'imposa très jeune sur la scène artistique de sa ville natale, Haarlem. Connu pour des scènes de genre paysannes, il pratiqua tous les genres de la peinture, privilégiant une technique précise et les petits formats sur panneau. Marié avec la célèbre femme peintre Judith Leyster, il connut une existence difficile écrasée par les dettes et l'exercice de plusieurs professions.

Les représentations d'enfants jouant avec des animaux, c'est-à-dire les maltraitant et recevant la monnaie de la pièce sous la forme d'une griffure ou d'une morsure, sont légion dans la peinture hollandaise. On pourrait à bon droit classer ce type de saynète moralisante dans la peinture de genre. Il n'est toutefois pas illégitime de considérer l'étude de la physionomie et des affects de ce jeune garçon comme la figuration d'un type universel, le chat faisant ici fonction d'attribut plutôt que de protagoniste de la narration.

Molenaer a fréquemment représenté des animaux dans son œuvre, essentiellement des chiens, des chats et des singes. Parfois, ils sont à peine visibles au milieu d'une assemblée. Parfois, en revanche, leur présence est indispensable et acquiert une véritable signification.

Son choix de cadrer ses compositions sur une ou deux têtes d'enfants aux traits déformés par le plan rapproché date des premières années de sa carrière, avant 1630. La grossièreté des physionomies est renforcée par le rictus arboré par les enfants. Ces derniers apparaissent comme des petits monstres cruels et incontrôlables. Molenaer a ainsi réalisé un cycle des cinq sens constitué de représentations de figures isolées d'enfants (Phoenix Art Museum, collections particulières). Si ces modèles sont engagés dans des occupations enfantines, ils portent des couvre-chefs excentriques et archaïques destinés aux adultes. Les deux tableaux les plus proches de celui d'Épinal sont les *Deux Enfants avec un chat* (localisation inconnue, *cf. Jan Miense Molenaer. Painter of the Dutch Golden Age*, cat. exp. Raleigh, Columbus, Manchester, 2003, fig. 8, p. 34) et *Enfants jouant avec un chat* (musée de Dunkerque, *op. cit.*, fig. 12, p. 36). Ce deuxième exemple montre un garçon au chapeau déchiqueté. Faut-il comprendre que le chat en est responsable ?

Le tableau d'Épinal s'en distingue par son effet d'instantané et par son étonnante frontalité. Le chat est vu de dos. Il se débat et ses griffes laissent une trace visible sur la poitrine du garçon. Ce dernier ouvre largement la bouche, s'esclaffant et exprimant sa douleur tout à la fois. Comme sa tête bascule vers l'arrière, son grand chapeau caractéristique revêt une apparence quelque peu informe au point de ne pas être immédiatement identifiable. Son costume est en tout point similaire à celui de ses représentations d'enfants contemporaines.

Molenaer se limite à une gamme réduite de couleurs, proche du monochrome, palette répandue aussi bien dans la scène de genre que dans la nature morte et le paysage de l'époque. En dépit de la vulgarité des expressions, du prosaïsme des occupations et de l'aspect populaire des types, la peinture de Molenaer est habile voire brillante. Sans parvenir à transfigurer ses sujets à la manière de son maître putatif Frans Hals, notre peintre a la capacité d'intéresser et d'émouvoir dans chacune de ses tranches de vie. Dans les œuvres de sa maturité, il montrera un registre plus étendu mais il ne parviendra plus à retrouver la force radicale de sa vision sans concession du monde de l'enfance.

AH

50

Godfried Schalcken

(Made, 1643 – La Haye, 1706)

Jeune Homme mangeant de la bouillie

H.s.t ; H. 0,76 ; L. 0,63
S.b.g. *G. Schalcken*
Bruxelles, Musées royaux des beaux-arts de Belgique, inv. 177

Historique : Vente baron Schönborn, Amsterdam, 1738 ; vente Van der Lande, Amsterdam, 1776 ; vente Servad, Amsterdam, 1778 ; vente comte de Vaudreuil, Paris, 1784 ; collection Thijs, Bruxelles ; acquis par le musée en 1834.
Bibliographie : Beherman, 1988, no 202, p. 297-298.

Biographie : *cf.* cat. 8.

Schalcken fut un peintre à l'ambition classique qui privilégia le genre de l'histoire ou de l'allégorie dans ses scènes à la lumière de la bougie. Une partie non négligeable de sa production est toutefois constituée de variations sur les standards de la peinture de genre nordique, femmes dans l'encadrement d'une fenêtre (cat. 8), couples d'amoureux, enfants en train de jouer. Le plus souvent, l'atmosphère sereine et policée de ses saynètes trouve une correspondance naturelle dans la qualité finie, dite porcelainée, du traitement pictural.
Parfois, comme ici, le peintre choisit un sujet d'esprit plus populaire. À la manière de son spectaculaire tableautin représentant un garçon se faisant un masque à partir d'une crêpe (Hambourg, Kunsthalle) ou de la *Jeune Fille mangeant une pomme* (Schwerin, Staatliches Museum), la nourriture devient ainsi prétexte à une fête des sens quelque peu grotesque. La présence de la jeune fille désignant son compagnon d'un air malicieux indique bien la critique sociale. Si certains éléments formels font penser à une allégorie de la gloutonnerie ou du goût, la composition s'inscrit plutôt dans la tradition moralisatrice des scènes de cuisine de Beuckelaer et Aertsen qui ont influencé des générations de peintres. À la manière de la ricotta du célèbre tableau d'Annibal Carrache, la bouillie est un aliment vulgaire, informe et enfantin. La grosse cuillère en bois contient une masse gluante et peu ragoûtante.
La flamme de la bougie qui semble agitée par un brusque courant d'air confère au visage du jeune homme, figé en un rictus bête, une immobilité de masque. Seule la partie inférieure est éclairée et il faut faire appel à l'imagination pour reconstituer son regard. La virtuosité des effets d'éclairage des scènes nocturnes amène à soulever la question de l'importance secondaire réservée aux figures dans ces représentations. Toutefois, au-delà du jeu sur l'alternance de la disparition et de la révélation des formes, Schalcken pose un regard détaché, un point de vue des Lumières avant la lettre, sur les visions héritées des siècles précédents quant au sens accordé au corps et aux humeurs. Son succès considérable auprès des amateurs de tableaux nordiques truculents tout comme auprès des tenants d'une peinture plus raffinée s'explique alors aisément.
Le tableau de Bruxelles est l'un de ceux qui poussent le plus loin le jeu des contrastes entre les bas instincts et la noblesse de la peinture, entre l'informe et la pensée structurée, entre le quotidien et la solennité spectaculaire du nocturne. **AH**

51

Jean-Baptiste Santerre

(Magny-en-Vexin, 1658 – Paris, 1717)

La Curiosité, dit aussi *Les Curieuses*

H.s.t. ; H. 0,73 ; L. 0,92
Orléans, musée des Beaux-Arts, inv. 788

Historique : Acquis par le musée entre 1837 et 1843.
Bibliographie : O'Neill, 1981, I, p. 128-129, et II, p. 123 ; Lesné, 1988, p. 100, n° 40 ; Benedict, 2002 ; Lesné, Waro, 2011, p. 71-72.
Œuvres en rapport : gravures *Les Curieuses*, Bernart Picart, 1701 ; Claude Duflos, avant 1727.

Santerre étudia auprès de François Lemaire et de Bon Boullogne avant d'être reçu à l'Académie royale en 1704 avec *Suzanne au bain* (Paris, musée du Louvre). Ses portraits et ses figures de fantaisie, remarquables par la manière dont ils entremêlent allégorie, habits somptueux et thèmes de genre nordiques, constituent l'essentiel de sa production. Au centre de sa pratique se trouve un traitement méticuleux et sensuel du corps de la femme. Protégé de Louis XIV, l'artiste recevait une pension et était logé au Louvre. Il devint par la suite Peintre ordinaire du Régent, Philippe d'Orléans.

Cette peinture est probablement celle exposée au Salon de 1704 sous le titre *Deux figures de filles dans un même tableau, qui représente la curiosité*. Cette étude de deux figures de fantaisie est une exception dans l'œuvre de Santerre ainsi que dans cette exposition. Et pourtant, la même logique de la figure de fantaisie unique règne ici, à savoir une attention soutenue sur les émotions des sujets, mais aussi sur l'ambiguïté de la scène. La plus jeune fille a une expression spontanée, ce qui rend la peinture inhabituelle et frappante car Santerre y sonde un type d'expression qui serait inacceptable dans ses portraits officiels. La tête est tendue vers l'avant, le regard est fixe, les sourcils sont levés d'un air interrogateur et la bouche est entrouverte. Peut-être a-t-elle momentanément oublié les règles du manuel de savoir-vivre selon lequel les filles bien élevées doivent maîtriser leurs émotions. Manifestant également sa curiosité, l'aînée à ses côtés se comporte beaucoup plus coquettement, la tête inclinée, le sourire soigneusement dessiné et le regard de biais. Elle joue de manière calculée de son voile, le soulevant pour révéler son joli visage et ses cheveux tout en faisant barrière de son bras gauche, se protégeant de ce que l'on suppose être un admirateur se tenant à l'extérieur du cadre. Elle est conforme à un type de femmes désirables peintes par d'autres à la même période tels que Raoux (cat. 10), Courtin (cat. 77) et Rigaud (cat. 9). Et pourtant, en juxtaposant les deux visages, Santerre semble déjouer les rouages de la femme coquette ou plus généralement de la psyché féminine. La jeune fille symbolise ce qui se cache sous le masque de son amie plus âgée : les désirs incontrôlés tapis à l'intérieur de soi, mais contenus par la maturité et le conformisme social. Les deux visages se confondent finalement en un seul être, le passage du temps (de la jeunesse à la maîtrise des codes de la mondanité) est éludé. Le lien ne fonctionne pas, cependant, car la jeune fille est repoussée par son amie plus âgée. Telles des sœurs en compétition, la plus jeune ricane-t-elle dans l'intention d'embarrasser l'aînée en présence d'un nouvel amant ? Ou bien l'aînée est-elle protectrice et non pas dédaigneuse ? Comme dans les *Deux Actrices* (Saint-Pétersbourg, musée de l'Ermitage), Santerre ne donne pas facilement de réponse à ses énigmes psychologiques. Chaque visage ayant un point de fuite différent, le jeu des regards traduit un désaccord. La curiosité féminine était un sujet très prisé dans les débuts de la culture moderne, sans aucun doute liée à l'exploration sexuelle et à ses dangers potentiels. Les traitements traditionnels tels qu'en témoigne *La Curiosité* de Gerard ter Borch (New York, The Metropolitan Museum of Art) ont tendance à tenir des récits plus simples. En outre, la gravure d'après la peinture de Santerre par Claude Duflos tente d'imposer une lecture morale conventionnelle avec son verset : « Claudine l'autre jour demandait à sa mère / Quel mérite il falloit versez pour se faire aymer / Sa mère en souriant luy répondit ma chère / l'Eclat de la vertu peut Nous faire aymer. » Santerre, quant à lui, dépeint la curiosité féminine de manière bien plus subversive et résolument plus nuancée. **MP**

52

Giuseppe Maria Crespi, *dit* Lo Spagnuolo

(Bologne, 1665-1747)

Fillette jouant avec un chat et une souris morte

H.s.t. ; 0,44 ; L. 0,35
Cambridge, The Fitzwilliam Museum, inv. 221

Historique : Legs de Daniel Mesman au musée en 1834.
Expositions : Spike, *in* Fort Worth, 1986 ; Bologne/Stuttgart/Moscou, 1990-1991, nº 11, p. 272-273.
Bibliographie : Zanotti, 1739 ; Roli, 1977, p. 186, ill. 339 ; Pajes Merriman, 1980, nº 215, p. 296.

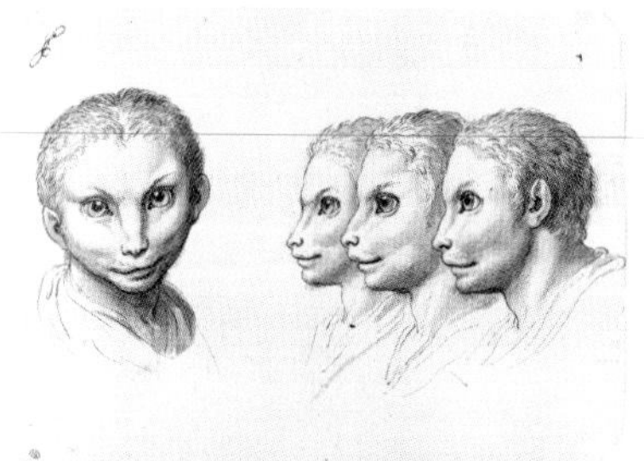

Charles Le Brun, *Quatre têtes d'hommes en relation avec le chat*, Paris, musée du Louvre

Connu pour sa technique picturale libre, Crespi fut influencé par les Carrache, Véronèse et Corrège. Membre respecté de la communauté artistique de Bologne, il dirigea une école de dessin pendant plus de vingt ans. Peintre d'histoire accompli, il réalisa de nombreuses commandes religieuses et mythologiques. Comme peintre de genre, il fut audacieux et novateur avec des scènes et des personnages tantôt comiques et satiriques, tantôt beaux et étranges.

Crespi, selon son principal biographe, Zanotti, était « pieno di capricci e di fantasie » (« plein de caprices et de fantaisie », 1739, II, p. 52), et son imagination fougueuse s'exerce dans cette peinture d'une fillette jouant avec un chat et une souris morte. Les chercheurs sont très divisés sur la date d'exécution de la peinture. Merriman proposait les dernières années du XVIIe siècle. Lors de l'exposition Crespi en 1990-1991, Giorlano Viroli eut l'occasion de confirmer la suggestion de Renato Roli qui, par comparaison avec d'autres œuvres, penchait pour une datation beaucoup plus tardive (vers 1740). C'est cette date que nous retiendrions nous aussi.

Cette image tronquée dévoile une scène dramatique : une jeune fille à turban blanc vêtue d'un manteau bleu et d'une robe blanche agite une souris morte qu'elle tient par la queue face à son chat, lequel exprime son désir viscéral de nourriture par ses griffes sorties, mais la jeune fille le retient par le cou, l'empêchant d'atteindre sa proie. La tension dramatique est intensifiée par les traits félins du personnage et par ses doigts raides, telles des griffes. Crespi a peut-être fait sciemment allusion à une ancienne tradition physionomiste qui mettait en correspondance les traits physiques et moraux entre hommes et animaux. Cette pratique s'était répandue en Italie grâce à Giambattista della Porta et son ouvrage *De humana physiognomonia* (1586), réimprimé plusieurs fois au XVIIe siècle. Les illustrations de Charles Le Brun à sa conférence sur la physionomie (1671) comprennent un dessin d'une personne féline étonnamment similaire à la jeune fille de Crespi : long nez pointu, bouche large placée beaucoup plus bas qu'une bouche humaine, pommettes obliques prononcées et un drôle de sourire (fig. ci-contre). Le Brun avait annoté son dessin avec les adjectifs « opiniâtre », « méfiant », « farouche », « craintif ». Il est peu probable que Crespi ait connu les dessins de Le Brun, qui ne furent publiés qu'en 1806. Il est pourtant possible que le public de Crespi ait envisagé ces traits de caractère chez la jeune fille : à la fois douce, enjouée, distante et menaçante. Elle porte les couleurs de l'innocence et de la pureté mais des ombres profondes créent un sentiment d'incertitude. Crespi était un maître de l'humeur et de l'atmosphère et utilisait le format simple du portrait pour exprimer, grâce à son talent pictural, toute une gamme émotionnelle. Une relation entre l'homme et l'animal très différente est explorée dans le tableau aux couleurs pêche *Dame avec un chien* (Miami, Lowe Art Gallery) dans lequel un épagneul charme avec coquetterie sa maîtresse. On retrouve des caractéristiques félines similaires à celles de la peinture du Fitzwilliam Museum dans la *Femme avec une rose et un chat* de Crespi (Bologne, Pinacoteca Nazionale). **MP**

Cosmas Damian Asam

(Benediktbeuern, 1686 – Munich, 1739)

Autoportrait avec ses frères

H.s.t. ; H. 1,16 ; L. 0,89
Freising, Diözesanmuseum, inv. L8004

Historique : Prêt de la fondation paroissiale St. Johann Nepomuk, Munich.
Expositions : Vienne, 2004a, p. 148 ; Munich, 2005-2006, p. 150-151 ; Freising, 2007-2008, n° I.1, p. 119-120.
Bibliographie : Hanfstaengl, 1939 ; Bushart, Rupprecht, 1986, G15, p. 304, ill. p. 10 ; Trottmann, 1986, p. 151.
Œuvre en rapport : Dessus-de-porte ovale en grisaille à droite de l'autel, Munich, Asamkirche.

La dynastie bavaroise des Asam est synonyme d'un art et d'une architecture baroques stupéfiants. Cosmas Damian, peintre et architecte, apprit auprès de son père. Après un séjour de formation à Rome, il dessina nombre d'églises et de palais en Allemagne du Sud et dans les pays avoisinants. Il excellait dans les structures dynamiques comme les coupoles, les fresques éclatantes de lumière et les effets illusionnistes. D'une profonde dévotion, les frères Asam construisirent pour leur usage propre l'église Saint-Jean Népomucène, plus connue à Munich sous le nom d'« Asamkirche ».

Dans cet autoportrait merveilleusement excentrique, Cosmas Damian Asam se dépeint comme la figure centrale d'une dynastie artistique importante. On pense généralement que le personnage de droite est son frère aîné Philipp Emanuel (1683-1752), musicien talentueux, également connu sous son nom de frère cistercien comme Pater Engelbert. L'homme à gauche a été identifié comme leur frère cadet, le sculpteur et plâtrier Egid Quirin (1692-1750). Cosmas Damian et Egid Quirin travaillèrent ensemble sur de nombreux projets et cette peinture traite le thème de la collaboration artistique avec une bonne humeur fraternelle. Cosmas Damian étant la personnalité dominante, il confine son jeune frère dans un espace exigu derrière son dos. Néanmoins, le talent de sculpteur d'Egid Quirin est symbolisé par le masque en plâtre sur le mur et la gouge qu'il brandit d'un air quelque peu menaçant. En dépit du sentiment d'horreur du vide, l'attirail d'atelier assure une forme d'égalité entre la peinture et la sculpture. La raison n'en réside pas dans une sorte d'injonction théorique (*cf.* les débats autour du *Paragone* ou *Parallèle des arts*) mais plutôt dans les affaires familiales qui impliquaient de produire en étroite collaboration des œuvres d'art total.

En dehors de ses aspects biographiques, le tableau est étourdissant d'excentricité. Cosmas Damian porte un costume inhabituel, cape en fourrure brune et longue plume blanche. Ses boucles d'oreille en perles lui donnent un air androgyne et les plis creusés du drapé rouge rappellent vaguement une toge. Il est possible d'établir un parallèle avec d'autres autoportraits en costume, de Lomazzo (cat. 43) à Zoffany (cat. 83) en passant par Rembrandt, mais l'accoutrement d'Asam a une logique propre passablement compliquée. Son visage tend vers la caricature avec ses yeux enflés, ses sourcils sombres, sa ligne de rides frontales et la moue de ses lèvres vermeilles. S'agit-il d'une parade d'artiste, des affres de l'inspiration ou d'un semblant de consternation ? Ce visage offre un double en la personne de son frère Philip Emanuel. En dehors de l'air de famille, les deux figures aux sourcils froncés regardent dans la même direction. Les pinceaux dans la main gauche de Cosmas Damian sont à deux doigts de chatouiller le menton de son frère. Mais cette proximité singulière révèle son secret car il s'agit bien du portrait du frère auquel Cosmas Damian travaillait et non de la personne réelle. C'est ce type d'illusion que le peintre utilisait dans ses grands décors. L'absence d'un cadre autour du portrait rappelle sa pratique consistant en d'autres cas à dépasser la bi- et la tridimensionnalité et à brouiller les limites entre réalité et représentation.

Cosmas Damian se représenta à plusieurs reprises dans ses fresques. Au plafond du Schloss Alteglofsheim, une joyeuse célébration de la lumière et de la nature, il apparaît sous l'aspect d'un chasseur jovial tenant une chope de bière. De manière plus sensible, sur un plafond à la fresque de l'église conventuelle d'Osterhofen, il joue le rôle du collecteur d'impôts repenti de la parabole du pharisien et du publicain. L'autoportrait de fantaisie à la spatialité complexe qui figure dans notre exposition doit moins au genre du portrait qu'à l'expression dynamique et animée de ses œuvres décoratives. **MP**

Giacomo Ceruti, *dit* Il Pitocchetto

(Milan, 1698-1767)

Garçon avec un panier de poissons, vers 1734-1736

H.s.t. ; H. 0,56 ; L. 0,73
Florence, Galleria Palatina,
Polo Museale Fiorentino,
inv. OdA n. 301

Historique : Parme, collections royales.
Expositions : Brescia, 1987, n° 42, p. 181-182 ; Crémone/New York, 2004.
Bibliographie : Chiarini, 1984, p. 537-538 ; Chiarini, Padovani, 2003, n° 175, p. 120.

Biographie : *Cf.* cat. 29.

Un jeune vendeur de rue présente son panier de marchandises au spectateur : plusieurs grands poissons et un crabe, mis en valeur par un citron adroitement placé. Il étreint son panier fermement, penchant la tête comme pour attirer l'attention sur la qualité de ses biens. Cette posture apparemment négligée, mais soigneusement mise en scène, est évidemment une incitation à acheter. Ceruti, toujours soucieux de la situation des pauvres, met en lumière l'importance de la prise pour l'enfant, l'urgence pour lui de finaliser une vente. Le paradoxe tient dans le fait qu'il ne peut pas se permettre de manger ces aliments de choix, aussi ce qui est physiquement proche est-il en réalité très lointain. Le jeune garçon affiche un certain sourire, peut-être narquois. Comme Hals (cat. 46), Ceruti cherche à dépeindre le côté rustre du personnage sans pour autant s'en moquer, manifestant de l'empathie pour sa vie dans la réalité, au-delà du tableau. Malgré le côté ostentatoire des poissons au premier plan, c'est le sourire de l'enfant qui est au centre de la toile ; la poignée du panier et l'arrondi de ce dernier faisant écho à ce large sourire. Les représentations de marchands de victuailles sont apparues dans le nord de l'Italie à la fin du XVIe siècle dans l'œuvre de Campi, Passarotti et Annibale Carracci. Dans le sillon de ces artistes, Ceruti peignit plusieurs serviteurs et pourvoyeurs de nourriture et leurs paniers, notamment le fameux « Portarolo » vendant des poulets et un panier d'œufs conservé à la Pinacoteca di Brera de Milan. Dans ces œuvres, il mit l'accent sur la plus-value économique liée au transport à dos d'homme qui assurait le train de vie des riches. Ceruti dépeint les travailleurs faisant une pause dans un labeur physiquement exigeant, en train de jauger le spectateur et de tirer leurs propres conclusions. Dans le *Garçon avec un panier de poissons*, à la fois figure de fantaisie et nature morte, le peintre s'assigne un double objectif : dépeindre la vie quotidienne mais sous une lumière nouvelle. Ceruti utilise les natures mortes dans d'autres représentations de personnages (les légumes dans le pendant du *Garçon avec un chien*, cat. 55) mais aussi dans des peintures indépendantes telles que la *Nature morte avec oiseaux, homard et lièvre*, appartenant autrefois à Schulenburg (Kassel, Gemäldegalerie Alte Meister), ou la *Nature morte avec plat d'étain, écrevisses, citron et objets* conservée à la Pinacoteca di Brera. **MP**

55

Giacomo Ceruti, *dit* Il Pitocchetto

(Milan, 1698-1767)

Garçon avec un chien

H.s.t. ; H. 0,70 ; L. 0,95
Belfast, Ulster Museum, National Museums, Northern Ireland, inv. BELUM.U20

Historique : Paris, G. Duseigneur ; acheté par le musée en 1893.
Expositions : Brescia, 1987, no 63, p. 188-189 ; Crémone/New York, 2004 ; Milan, 2013.
Bibliographie : Gregori, 1982, no 169, p. 459.
Œuvre en rapport : pendant : *Garçon avec des légumes,* h.s.t., 0,70 × 0,95 m, Belfast, Ulster Museum, National Museums, Northern Ireland, inv. BELUM.U19.

Biographie : *cf.* cat. 29.

Ceruti présente ici un chien et son maître posant ensemble, affectueusement. Leur complicité se lit dans l'étreinte de l'enfant mais aussi dans la façon dont il serre la patte de l'animal pour jouer et par l'harmonie de leurs visages, les deux ayant un nez rond et souriant à pleines dents. On note de même un parallèle entre la pièce de tissu en forme de losange sur la manche du garçon et la tache de fourrure blanche sur la poitrine du chien. La corne dans la gueule de l'animal a été interprétée comme une allusion à la chasse. Mais il ne s'agit pas du monde éthéré de Diane ou de l'affirmation du statut social d'aristocrates à cheval : c'est un garçon qui travaille et un chien de chasse dont la collaboration est essentielle à leur gagne-pain partagé. Au cours de sa carrière, Ceruti a peint un grand nombre de personnes pauvres : marchands des rues, pèlerins, fonctionnaires, nains, vieillards, lavandières. Le point culminant de cette inspiration est le cycle de Padernello comprenant une quinzaine de personnages, probablement exécutés pour la famille noble Avogadro, de Brescia. Avant lui, des artistes actifs dans le nord de l'Italie tels que Keilhau (Monsù Bernardo, cat. 36), Bellotti (cat. 18), Cifrondi (1655-1730) et Cipper (Il Todeschini, 1664-1736) avaient eux aussi mis en lumière ces scènes de la vie du peuple. Ici, Ceruti recourt au format oblong également utilisé par le Caravage et Piazzetta afin d'intensifier l'aspect psychologique du point de vue porté sur le sujet. Cependant, cette peinture, en raison de sa taille et de l'attitude détendue de l'enfant, est empreinte d'une sorte de grandeur digne d'un portrait. Le socle en pierre sur lequel est assis le chien et l'arrière-plan nuageux donnent aux sujets une monumentalité qui les élève au-dessus de leur humble condition. On remarque de nettes similitudes entre cette peinture et le *Garçon avec un panier de poissons* de Ceruti (cat. 54), notamment le chapeau rouge et le sourire, si particulier. Le pendant du *Garçon avec un chien*, également à Belfast et représentant un garçon avec un panier de légumes (fig. ci-contre), est encore plus proche en termes de sujet. **MP**

Giacomo Ceruti, *Garçon avec des légumes*, Belfast, Ulster Museum

Le laboratoire du visage

56

Jacob Jordaens

(Anvers, 1593-1678)

Figure d'apôtre (Saint Pierre), vers 1620-1621

H.s. panneau (chêne) ; H. 0,64 ; L. 0,50
Caen, musée des Beaux-Arts, inv. 115

Historique : Envoi de l'État en 1813.
Expositions : Caen/Gand, 2012, p. 9-10, 20 et 31 ; Paris, 2013-2014, nº I-13.
Bibliographie : Debaisieux, 1994, p. 249-251.

Élève de Van Noordt, Jordaens fut reçu franc-maître à la maîtrise d'Anvers en 1615. Il devient le collaborateur de Rubens à partir de 1620, alors qu'il est déjà un peintre confirmé, tout en poursuivant une carrière personnelle. À la disparition de Rubens et après le départ de Van Dyck pour l'Angleterre, il reste le maître incontesté de la peinture à Anvers après 1640. Momentanément séduit par le caravagisme, il développe une variante originale de l'art de Rubens, excellant dans la même multitude de genres. Peintre d'histoire, portraitiste, adepte des scènes de genre truculentes, il cultive un goût pour le paysage et devient un grand spécialiste des cartons de tapisserie.

La question de l'inclusion de ce tableau dans une exposition sur le thème de la figure de fantaisie était légitime. Les commissaires avaient posé comme principe l'idée de sélectionner des œuvres déconnectées de toute narration au sens de la peinture d'histoire ou même de la scène de genre. Néanmoins, Jordaens joue sciemment sur plusieurs registres, ce qui confère à ce chef-d'œuvre modernité et puissance expressive. La fonction ultime de l'œuvre était sans doute de dévotion privée, comme un élément isolé d'un *apostolado*. Le peintre opte pour une forme très ébauchée, proche de l'esquisse, mais le contraste entre le personnage et le fond indique l'achèvement du tableau.

Le modèle de l'apôtre est connu. Il s'agit d'Abraham Grapheus, une personnalité familière du monde de l'art anversois, peintre de second rang et commis de la guilde des peintres, des années 1580 à sa mort en 1624. Jordaens et Van Dyck, après d'autres artistes tels Pourbus l'Ancien, Maerten ou Cornelis de Vos, ont exploité ses traits caractéristiques pour réaliser des têtes d'étude ou des figures de leurs tableaux d'histoire. Le tableau de Caen, bien que représentant un personnage réel sous l'aspect d'un apôtre plus ou moins identifiable (les mains jointes en prière et les yeux contrits baignés de larmes évoquent la figure de saint Pierre), ne dépare pas au côté des *tronies*. En effet, Jordaens s'y livre à un jeu virtuose sur les stigmates de la vieillesse et invite le spectateur à entrer en empathie avec ce vieillard débonnaire.

Rarement un peintre n'avait figuré avec une telle acuité les muscles distendus du cou, les plis adipeux du double menton, le teint couperosé, les fossettes creusées et le regard perdu. Jordaens ne force toutefois pas le trait et représente uniquement ce qu'il voit, en grand portraitiste qu'il est. Il ne faut pas déceler dans ce tableau une prémonition du futur peintre des proverbes et scènes de genre à la veine affirmée de caricaturiste. L'œuvre de Caen est très représentative de la première phase de la production de Jordaens, qui se termine au début des années 1620, marquée par les esquisses de Rubens et un naturalisme d'inspiration caravagesque. C'est le moment où l'artiste s'enivre du potentiel expressif du clair-obscur, faisant de chaque tableau un manifeste de ce talent spécifique.

On admirera la fluidité du pinceau, qui parcourt avec une sensibilité extrême les accidents du visage du saint, ménageant des petites touches de lumière sur le nez, les yeux, le menton ou les pommettes, offrant à ce vieillard magnifique la sensualité de traitement habituellement réservée aux femmes. À la tension des muscles du cou fait écho le deuxième point focal de l'énergie liée au personnage, les magnifiques mains jointes qui disparaissent totalement l'une dans l'autre, image de piété forte et inoubliable.

Un détail a rarement été évoqué. Il oriente pourtant la signification du tableau et nous entraîne bien loin de saint Pierre *a priori*. Il s'agit du dessin d'une tête sur le mur à la droite de l'apôtre. Elle est peu discernable et très rudimentaire, comme un dessin d'enfant, n'offrant aucune indication de

sexe, de pilosité ou d'âge. Appartient-elle à une première pensée pour le tableau ou a-t-elle une signification propre ? Nous ne le saurons sans doute jamais.

Parmi les nombreuses têtes de Jordaens, isolées ou couplées, réalisées à fin d'étude ou en tant que portraits, peintures d'histoire ou de genre, celle de Caen est sans conteste la plus émouvante et la plus parfaite.

AH

57

Jacob Jordaens

(Anvers, 1593-1678)

Tête d'étude

H.s. bois ; H. 0,41 ; L. 0,29
Douai, musée de la Chartreuse, inv. 198

Historique : Probablement saisie révolutionnaire. Attesté dans les collections du musée en 1809.
Expositions : Lille/Calais/Arras, 1977 ; Paris, 1977-1978 ; Anvers, 1993, nº A23.
Bibliographie : Van Puyvelde, 1953, p. 80, 84, 209, fig. 57 ; D'Hulst, 1982, p. 103, 110-111, 114, fig. 69.

Biographie : *cf.* cat. 56.

Parmi les nombreuses études de tête pour lesquelles Abraham Grapheus a servi de modèle, celle de Douai est la plus éloignée de son modèle, dont on reconnaît immédiatement les traits saillants comme les yeux chassieux, les fossettes creusées et le nez déformé. Il s'agit d'une étude de mouvement et d'attitude, d'un document brut proche du croquis dessiné et apte à être réutilisé pour des figures tournant la tête vers le haut. Le cadrage est fort original car la figure est coupée en haut de la poitrine, à la manière d'un buste, mais les épaules ne sont qu'évoquées. De cet effet de *sotto in su* acrobatique découle un élan vertical impressionnant qui souligne un cou proéminent. La tête renversée en arrière ne laisse un peu d'espace que sur la droite. Jordaens n'a fait que suggérer un ciel sur la couche de préparation.

La technique de Jordaens est ici rapide, légère et informelle. Les riches empâtements du visage contrastent avec la finesse du fond. Les contours sont renforcés d'un halo clair. Des coups de pinceau marqués créent le paysage tourmenté et noueux du cou, des joues et du front de Grapheus. Des touches de blanc éclairent des zones de son nez et de sa tempe. Les pilosités sont rendues à la hampe du pinceau selon une pratique d'atelier courante. La carnation rouge brique semble cuite par les vicissitudes de l'existence.

Cette tête d'expression se prête à toutes les transformations. L'attitude est tout indiquée pour la représentation d'un saint mais elle siérait également à un philosophe cynique. Pourquoi ne serait-ce pas aussi une évocation symbolique de l'hiver ? La seule certitude est l'identification de Grapheus, le modèle-caméléon. Ce personnage aux faux airs de Michel Simon a indiscutablement une gueule, ou une trogne si on veut revenir à l'étymologie du *tronie*.

À la manière de Rubens et de Van Dyck, Jordaens fait de l'atelier un terrain d'expérimentation ouvert à toutes les audaces. Il établit une différence entre divers types de commandes, plus ou moins parfaites ou achevées, mais le geste rapide et brillant est à la racine de tout ce qu'il entreprend. Ce geste atteint ici une radicalité rarement égalée dans sa production mais aussi dans l'histoire de la peinture. Si l'on veut rester dans des pratiques contemporaines, seul Rembrandt est allé aussi loin dans l'abandon des traits reconnaissables du portrait. On sait aujourd'hui que Jordaens, comme Rembrandt, pouvait laisser coexister au sein de son travail d'atelier des manières diamétralement opposées au même moment. Le choix d'une œuvre achevée ou d'une esquisse informelle s'opérait en fonction du commanditaire mais aussi selon l'humeur du moment, aucun grand artiste ne pouvant être enfermé dans une pratique unique. **AH**

58

Giovanni Serodine

(Ascona, 1594, ou Rome, 1600 – Rome, 1630)

Portrait de jeune dessinateur

H.s.t. : H. 0,66 ; L. 0,49
Rancate, Pinacoteca Cantonale Giovanni Züst, inv. PZ 393

Historique : Collection Greenville, Londres ; vente Christie's, Londres, 31 mars 1810 ; marquis d'Aberdeen ; vente Christie's, Londres, 7 mai 1943 ; vente Christie's, Londres, 11 juillet 1980 ; prêt d'un particulier new-yorkais au Metropolitan Museum of Art ; acquis par la Pinacoteca Cantonale Giovanni Züst en 1996.
Expositions : Milan, 1998-1999, p. 235 ; Varèse, 2002, no 58 ; Rancate, 2012-2013, no 8.
Bibliographie : Giovanni Testori *in* Chiappini, 1987, p. 23.

Descendant d'une famille de maîtres-maçons et sculpteurs originaires du Tessin, Serodine se forma dans la Rome caravagesque. Il se forgea un style très original qu'il développa dans de rares tableaux religieux, dont le maître-autel de l'église d'Ascona, des fresques pour l'église de Spolète et quelques rares portraits. Redécouvert par Roberto Longhi, il reste l'une des personnalités artistiques les plus mystérieuses du début du XVIIe siècle.

Un très jeune garçon a levé le nez de son étude pour nous fixer d'un air intense et boudeur. Cadré au niveau du buste, il est environné de feuilles de dessin roulées. Les traits fortement individualisés du modèle renvoient à l'idée d'un portrait voire d'un autoportrait. En même temps, l'omniprésence des dessins de l'artiste laisse également envisager une allégorie des arts ou tout au moins la représentation archétypale d'un artiste. L'absence de référence à un milieu, à un type de commande ou à un style vestimentaire marqué permet à Serodine de se libérer de la notion de portrait au sens premier du terme.

Cette œuvre apparue récemment dans le corpus de Serodine a connu une histoire d'attributions complexe. Le prestige des noms avancés au fil du temps confirme que l'on se trouve en présence d'une œuvre de premier plan. À son apparition en 1810, le tableau fut associé au nom d'Annibal Carrache. Lors de sa deuxième vente aux enchères, il passa pour un Guido Reni. Enfin, Nicolson le rapprochait du Bernin jeune. Il fallut attendre 1987 pour que Testori et Marini l'attribuassent au peintre du Tessin. Les historiens de l'art se sont aussi divisés sur la nature de l'œuvre. C'est Contini qui devait exclure de manière convaincante l'hypothèse de l'autoportrait. En effet, le tableau doit être situé dans les dernières années de sa brève carrière et le jeune modèle ne peut avoir plus de seize ans et non entre vingt-cinq et trente ans, comme Serodine à cette époque. Plutôt que d'un artiste établi, il doit s'agir ici d'un élève ou d'un assistant d'atelier qui répète ses gammes inlassablement.

La production connue de Serodine se compose d'un nombre fort réduit d'œuvres, parmi lesquelles l'un des portraits les plus émouvants du XVIIe siècle, celui de son père (Lugano, Museo Civico). L'artiste se frotte aux jeux de matière, élaborant une pâte dense et épaisse. Il travaille une lumière généreuse et sensuelle presque irréelle. Parmi les représentants du naturalisme du début du XVIIe siècle aux inflexions caravagesques, il est l'un de ceux qui renoncent à tout effet et cachent leur virtuosité pour parvenir à la vérité. Le fond clair permet de mettre en place une harmonie délicate et chaude et de faire ressortir la souplesse de la touche. Cette vibration lumineuse entre le blond et l'orange apparaît comme la réponse originale de Serodine aux fonds noirs du Caravage, une véritable marque de fabrique.

Les spécialistes ont tenté de retrouver le même modèle dans un personnage de *Jésus parmi les docteurs* du Louvre. La comparaison nous paraît superficielle mais on peut affirmer l'intérêt du peintre pour les figures d'adolescents, manifeste dans le saint Jean-Baptiste du *Couronnement de la Vierge* d'Ascona ou les juvéniles Adam et Ève de la fresque de l'église de la Concezione di Maria à Spolète.

L'atmosphère de cette étude d'atelier très élaborée est caractéristique de Serodine par son intensité expressive et son empathie pour le modèle. Nous sommes bien là en présence d'un des tableaux les plus modernes du XVIIe siècle, entre force mystique et évidence plastique. **AH**

59

Antoon Van Dyck

(Anvers, 1599 – Londres, 1641)

Étude de tête de vieillard : profil gauche

H.s. panneau ; H. 0,49 ; L. 0,38
Grenoble, musée de Grenoble, inv. MG 98

Historique : Acquis par Louis-Joseph Jay à Paris en 1799 avec les fonds d'une souscription des habitants de Grenoble.
Bibliographie : Destot, 1994, p. 79.

L'un des peintres les plus doués de l'histoire de la peinture, Van Dyck, fut un talent précoce. Son maître Rubens lui accorda très jeune un rôle autonome dans son atelier. Il séjourna en Italie, particulièrement à Gênes, avant d'effectuer un premier séjour à Londres puis de s'établir à Anvers. Il finit par s'installer définitivement en Angleterre, devenant le portraitiste de la cour et des grandes familles aristocratiques. Cet immense portraitiste était également un grand peintre d'histoires mythologiques. La charge des commandes de portraits entraîna sa spécialisation dans ce genre. Disparu prématurément, Van Dyck fut le véritable fondateur de l'école moderne de peinture en Angleterre.

Ce tableau relativement mais injustement méconnu a traditionnellement été attribué à Rubens ou à son école. L'hypothèse Jordaens a également été émise. Jacques Foucart, suivi par Marcel Destot, optait finalement pour Van Dyck. La question de la pratique des têtes d'étude dans les ateliers anversois autour de Rubens est effectivement fort complexe. La comparaison avec les têtes de Grapheus de Jordaens (cat. 56 et cat. 57) présentes dans l'exposition met en évidence un même filon rustique mais une conception moins visionnaire et une exécution plus délicate, sans les empâtements caractéristiques de Jordaens, chez Van Dyck. Il s'agit toutefois là de nuances et la virtuosité des deux plus grands disciples de Rubens ne permet pas d'exclure la pratique du pastiche. L'œuvre connue de Van Dyck la plus proche du tableau de Grenoble est le *Saint Barthélemy* (collection particulière) d'une série d'apôtres datée vers 1619-1620. Certes, ce dernier présente une facture plus achevée mais il partage avec le panneau de Grenoble une représentation de profil (dans le sens opposé par rapport à l'esquisse) et un traitement raffiné des pilosités. Dans les deux cas, le personnage baisse les yeux. Ce n'est donc pas le regard qui porte son énergie mais plutôt une sombre intériorité. Le cadrage de l'étude de Grenoble est encore plus original avec le point de vue de l'artiste légèrement en surplomb et l'espace libéré entre le visage penché du modèle et le bas de la composition.

Le statut du tableau est vraisemblablement celui d'une étude mais pas forcément pour un tableau déterminé. La production de ces œuvres au sein des ateliers anversois permettait d'effectuer des exercices picturaux pratiques pour entraîner les élèves tout en constituant un répertoire de figures réutilisable dans les tableaux d'histoire. Constatant le goût manifesté par les amateurs devant ce nouveau genre artistique, les artistes se mirent à les conserver et à en faire commerce.

Le charme de cette étude tient dans sa légèreté et ses effets de transparence. Le peintre laisse apparaître le ton de préparation sur lequel la carnation du vieillard semble à peine plus marquée. Il joue sur des tonalités presque monochromes avec une grande économie de moyens. Le manteau et le col sont davantage évoqués que dépeints. Les cheveux bouclés et clairsemés font l'objet d'un traitement virtuose et raffiné.

Le *tronie* est étroitement lié à l'expérimentation artistique. Or les ateliers d'Anvers ont constitué l'un des grands pôles de créativité européens du début du XVIIe siècle. Point de départ d'un travail collectif, la pratique libre et solitaire de ces têtes d'expression a permis aux jeunes génies qu'étaient Jordaens et Van Dyck de tester leurs inventions et de bénéficier d'un répertoire d'images pour toute leur carrière.

AH

Maître de l'Annonce aux bergers

(actif à Naples au milieu du XVIIe siècle)

Prophète en buste lisant

H.s.t. ; H. 0,73 ; L. 0,56
Bordeaux, musée des Beaux-Arts, inv. Bx E 486

Historique : Collection Grateloup, Bordeaux ; collection Oldekop, Bordeaux ; légué en 1858.
Exposition : Lille, 2011, nº 16.
Bibliographie : Habert, 1987, nº 53, p. 97.

De nombreuses hypothèses ont été échafaudées autour de l'identité du Maître de l'Annonce aux bergers. Elles tournent toutes autour d'une origine espagnole (Juan Do) ou napolitaine (Bartolomeo Passante ou Nunzio Rossi) mais aucune n'est entièrement convaincante. Un corpus a été constitué à partir de plusieurs compositions monumentales représentant *L'Annonce aux bergers*. Sa manière faisant la part belle aux empâtements est tout à fait reconnaissable.

Cette représentation saisissante d'un vieux juif lisant la Bible, enveloppé d'un châle de prière, appartient *stricto sensu* au genre de la peinture d'histoire puisque la référence au Livre et la digne gravité du personnage incitent à y voir un prophète. Toutefois, de la même manière que certaines figurations d'apôtres comme le *Saint Pierre* de Jordaens dans cette exposition (cat. 56), elle partage bien des traits thématiques et stylistiques avec les têtes d'étude. Si un modèle vivant a pu poser à l'origine, le peintre a puisé dans un répertoire ancestral d'images de prophètes et d'anachorètes décharnés, dont Donatello offrait déjà de prestigieux exemples.

Comme toujours chez le Maître de l'Annonce aux bergers, la peinture devient un exercice de rendu du caractère granuleux des matières et des surfaces. Le prophète a les yeux rivés sur le livre, l'ensemble des crêtes et des ravines qui constituent le visage sont modelées par la lumière tandis que les orbites sont envahies par les ténèbres. Si la chair est la pâte préférée du peintre, il réserve à chaque élément un traitement pictural qui en souligne la matérialité, du lourd châle rituel à la fruste chemise jusqu'au livre où la reliure en peau contraste avec le papier d'impression.

Le Maître de l'Annonce aux bergers tient cette radicalité absolue du travail pictural, à la limite de la violence expressive, du premier Ribera des années romaines. Le large mouvement du châle, solide comme une construction, est un rappel direct des apôtres de la collection Cusida du maître espagnol. Son étude impitoyable des ravages du temps sur les visages va encore plus loin. Cette accentuation à la limite de la caricature rend l'artiste immédiatement reconnaissable, en dépit de son statut d'anonyme. Ce serait toutefois une erreur que de le considérer comme rustique et grossier. Quelques maladresses ci et là dans ses grandes compositions avec des Annonciations aux bergers, dont il tire son nom provisoire, pourraient le laisser croire. Il suffit d'examiner attentivement la subtilité des nuances de la carnation du vieil homme avec ses pointes de vermillon pour comprendre sa maîtrise et le succès qu'il recueillait auprès d'authentiques connaisseurs.

Notre tableau n'a été rapproché du peintre qu'en 1983 grâce à une intuition d'Arnauld Brejon. Auparavant, il avait été attribué à Valentin de Boulogne puis, plus logiquement, à des naturalistes napolitains, Ribera, Francesco Fracanzano ou Bassante.

Le Maître a peint une autre représentation similaire, la *Tête de vieux lisant* (Lecce, Museo Provinciale), avec une même attitude et les mêmes lèvres rouges mais avec une moindre radicalité. S'il a parfois tendance à surpeupler de personnages et d'animaux ses compositions religieuses (ses moutons sont proverbiaux), il parvient dans ses représentations de figures isolées en buste à une parfaite insertion dans l'espace.

Un tableau tel celui de Bordeaux s'impose comme un modèle d'économie de moyens et d'efficacité expressive. La tonalité dominante est presque monochrome avec des gradations qui vont d'un jaune éteint à des verts, des bruns et des noirs mais l'extraordinaire vivacité de coloris du visage apporte une touche de fraîcheur fort inattendue. Le plan très rapproché permet à l'observateur d'entrer dans le tableau dans un silence respectueux qui reflète l'absorbement du

personnage dans la lecture ou la prière. Chef-d'œuvre intemporel d'un grand artiste, ce tableau inoubliable rend l'anonymat de son auteur encore plus irritant. **AH**

Jan Lievens

(Leyde, 1607 – Amsterdam, 1674)

L'Homme au stylet

H.s. bois ; H. 0,60 ; L. 0,45
Pau, musée des Beaux-Arts (dépôt du musée du Louvre), inv. D 872.5.32 (M.I. 1285)

Historique : Collection La Caze, déposé par le musée du Louvre à Pau en 1872.

Lievens a été formé dans l'atelier de Lastman, à Amsterdam, en compagnie de Rembrandt. C'est avec ce dernier qu'il retourne à Leyde et développe une association artistique sur un pied d'égalité. Leurs chemins se séparent lorsque Lievens part pour l'Angleterre, au début des années 1630. Puis, de 1635 à 1644, il travaille à Anvers avant de s'installer à Amsterdam, jusqu'à sa mort. Ce peintre virtuose, adepte des expérimentations artistiques dans sa jeunesse, va adopter les modes d'une peinture de cour de type flamand dans ses portraits et ses commandes de décors à l'hôtel de ville d'Amsterdam. Oublié aujourd'hui, il fut à ses débuts aussi célèbre que Rembrandt.

En dépit de la simplicité de sa composition, ce panneau a présenté de réelles difficultés d'interprétation. Il est traditionnellement connu sous le titre de *L'Homme à la pipe*. Toutefois, le fin objet qu'il tient dans sa main n'est que partiellement visible et ne fait pas immédiatement penser à une pipe. De plus, l'attitude du personnage ne paraît pas particulièrement liée à l'habitude ou au plaisir de fumer. La forme effilée évoque davantage un stylet. Néanmoins, le geste de l'homme qui serre son poignet droit de sa main gauche n'est pas très compréhensible. La première interprétation qui vient à l'esprit serait un acte d'automédication, comme une prise de pouls avant une saignée. Il reste encore difficile aujourd'hui de trancher définitivement la question.

La qualification du genre artistique auquel appartient ce tableau est plus aisée. On y retrouve, en effet, les caractéristiques du *tronie* tel que développé par Lievens et Rembrandt dans leurs jeunes années leydoises d'après des figures isolées des scènes de genre du XVIe siècle. Le cadrage serré révèle un vieil homme vigoureux. Son apparence entière se place sous le signe d'une force tranquille et d'une nature généreuse, du visage large aux mains de lutteur jusqu'au nez épaté. Sa tenue vestimentaire, une sorte de robe d'intérieur, ne dévoile rien de son statut social ou de sa profession. Son expression concentrée est celle de l'absorbement chère à Michael Fried. Sa présence nous semble aussi familière qu'énigmatique. Le travail sur le cuir tanné de sa peau et les rides ne fait pas de cette étude de tête un pur exercice de naturalisme mais bien une variation poétique sur la vieillesse à la manière de Jordaens, à qui le tableau fut attribué. Il nous manque toutefois une clé pour comprendre pleinement l'intention de l'artiste.

Lievens avait au début de sa carrière une approche directe de ses sujets. On ne décèle aucune trace d'artifice dans sa présentation. Le modèle est livré au public sans prise de distance. Seul le clair-obscur vient perturber la quasi-frontalité de la mise en place. Les mains monumentales produisent une saisissante impression de vérité, plus forte encore que le visage. Le vêtement, avec son drapé rudimentaire, se présente avec la même simplicité. Cela ne l'empêche pas de démontrer l'étendue de sa science picturale par les vibrations de la touche et de la lumière sur les veines et l'épiderme.

Ce tableau est très représentatif de la peinture de Lievens avant 1630. Il est contemporain de ses cycles d'apôtres ainsi que des scènes de genre de son ami et rival Rembrandt. À cette époque, le plus doué des deux était sans nul doute celui qui allait être le plus oublié. Chez le Rembrandt de ces années, l'invention déjà prodigieuse suppléait parfois la qualité sommaire de l'exécution. Dans la production de jeunesse de Lievens, le sentiment de vie et de vérité se conjugue à une maîtrise impressionnante. L'absence d'affectation, le naturel et l'exactitude psychologique sont exceptionnels chez un artiste âgé alors d'une vingtaine d'années. Point n'est besoin d'avoir vécu pour peindre avec justesse un vieillard. La mise au point du *tronie* est donc à la fois un terrain d'expérimentation artistique au sein de l'atelier et une approche d'une typologie humaine universelle. **AH**

62

Pieter Hermansz Verelst

(Dordrecht ?, vers 1618 ? – Hulst, après 1678 ?)

Tête de vieillard

H.s. panneau de chêne ; H. 0,72 ; L. 0,55
S.d.b.g. *P VERELST 1648*
Toulouse, musée des Augustins,
inv. 2004 1 200

Historique : Galerie du duc de Brunswick-Wolfenbütel, saisi par les armées napoléoniennes en 1807, envoi de l'État en 1812.
Exposition : Paris, 1970-1971, répertoire, p. 277.
Bibliographie : Fiozzi, 2004, no 37.

P. H. Verelst, *Vieillard barbu dans son cabinet,* Porto Rico, Museo de Arte de Ponce

Pieter Verelst reste relativement peu connu. Élève de Gérard Dou, il était inscrit en 1638 à la guilde de Saint-Luc de Dordrecht. Il vécut durant l'essentiel de sa carrière à La Haye. Ses portraits et *tronies* témoignent de l'influence de Rembrandt. Ses fils Herman et Simon, également peintres, s'établirent en Angleterre.

Isolé sur un fond de mur neutre, le vieillard positionné de trois quarts nous observe d'un air attentif et sévère. Aucun élément de décor, aucun attribut, aucun détail vestimentaire ne peuvent faire penser à la peinture d'histoire ou au portrait. Le tableau appartient donc sans conteste au genre du *tronie*. Pour autant, nous ne sommes pas en présence d'une tête d'étude à usage d'atelier, exécutée de manière hâtive sur un support rudimentaire. Bien au contraire, Verelst a employé un panneau soigneusement préparé, dans la plus pure tradition du beau métier nordique. Pour bien marquer la qualité et l'achèvement du travail, il a signé son tableau, ce qui est loin d'être toujours le cas pour ce type de production.

La *Tête de vieillard* présente tous les traits reconnus du *tronie* : une tête pittoresque et attachante, pleine de noblesse, une indétermination spatiale, une absence d'indication sur le moment de la journée, un clair-obscur prononcé, une insistance sur des points saillants de la physionomie (un nez proéminent, des rides profondes, une barbe fournie).

Verelst exploite en virtuose les possibilités du support. Il crée des effets de transparence en jouant sur la finesse des glacis jusqu'à la couche de préparation. C'est ainsi qu'il délimite une sorte de halo lumineux autour du visage du vieillard. Il construit les carnations en empâtements, parsemant le front et l'arête nasale de touches plus claires afin d'indiquer les points de lumière. Le visage du vieillard ressort avec un effet de relief saisissant, tel un parchemin buriné par le passage des années. L'ampleur de la barbe est renforcée par l'emploi, habituel depuis le XVIe siècle, de la hampe du pinceau qui permet d'isoler chaque poil pour accentuer le sentiment de vérité.

Le tableau de Toulouse est un bon exemple de l'art de Verelst, qui est à la fois proche du style informel de Rembrandt par ses épaisseurs de matière et ses effets d'éclairage mais aussi de la manière plus finie de Gérard Dou par le rendu lisse de la surface. On ne distingue chez lui ni tendance à la caricature ni critique sociale mais la volonté de s'inspirer des études d'atelier pour créer un produit fini et raffiné.

Le modèle du tableau de Toulouse apparaît dans un *tronie* du même peintre antérieur d'une année, le *Vieillard barbu dans son cabinet* du Museo de Arte de Ponce (Porto Rico, fig. ci-contre) ainsi que sur un tableau passé en vente publique (Londres, Christie's, 15 décembre 1989, no 173). À la manière des peintres caravagesques avec leurs soldats, les peintres de *tronies* faisaient poser les mêmes modèles de manière récurrente sans pour autant faire des portraits. D'ailleurs, lors de ses incursions dans ce dernier genre, Verelst adoptera un style de peinture plus lumineux. **AH**

Eberhard Keil ou Bernardo Keilhau, *dit* Monsù Bernardo

(Elseneur, 1624 – Rome, 1687)

Vieille Paysanne

H.s.t. ; H. 0,75 ; L. 0,63
Besançon, musée des Beaux-Arts
et d'Archéologie, inv. 945.10

Historique : Date et mode d'acquisition inconnus.
Bibliographie : Brejon, Volle, 1988, p. 198 ; Heimbürger, 1988, p. 241 ; Pinette, Soulier-François, 1992, p. 90.

Biographie : *cf.* cat.36.

Minna Heimbürger a rapproché le tableau de Besançon de la *Dentellière*, dite aussi *Allégorie de la Vue*, du peintre danois à l'Ashmolean Museum d'Oxford. Elle considère la tête de Besançon comme un fragment d'un tableau plus important et donne des dimensions bien plus petites (32 × 27 cm). En fait, elle confond le tableau de Besançon avec une œuvre conservée au musée des Beaux-Arts de Nantes qui semble, elle, bien en relation avec celle d'Oxford.

La typologie du cadre dans le cadre indique qu'il s'agit non pas d'un fragment mais bien d'une œuvre autonome. Ce dispositif est en général employé pour des portraits officiels en raison de son rapport avec les effigies en gravure des frontispices de livre. C'est celui qu'avait choisi Murillo dans son célèbre *Autoportrait* de la National Gallery de Londres. L'épaisseur du cadre permet toutefois d'affirmer qu'il s'agit ici d'un élément architectural plus que d'une mise à distance symbolique. L'encadrement ovale joue le même rôle que dans les représentations de fenêtres à la mode de Rembrandt (*cf.* fig. dans l'essai de John Chu, pages 79 à 91).

L'effet d'étrangeté produit par la composition réside dans le manque total d'apprêt du modèle. Le costume et la coiffure de la vieille femme sont ceux de tous les jours. Aucun signe distinctif ne permet de deviner son métier. Son attitude et sa pose sont vivantes et naturelles, son expression, bienveillante et tout en retenue. De toute évidence, le personnage est de basse condition. Néanmoins, l'image n'est pas misérabiliste. La robe présente une blancheur immaculée et un regard exercé ne saurait y détecter de rapiéçage. La femme est relativement âgée mais son visage n'affiche pas les surfaces parcheminées de rides si appréciées par les collectionneurs contemporains. Son sourire ne se mue pas en un rictus inconvenant qui risquerait de démasquer la comédie sociale.

À l'intérieur de son cadre synonyme de peinture solide et bien exécutée, Keilhau a rendu son modèle dans un style très esquissé. Il a monté ses couleurs sur un fond de préparation brun qui ressort sous la carnation ou les drapés de la robe blanche. Il a souligné ses contours de traits insistants avec des repentirs visibles. Il a su s'astreindre à une simplicité et à une sobriété exemplaires. Les marques de vieillesse sont évoquées et sublimées par un éclairage qui tourne autour du cadre ovale en accentuant les incertitudes de la perspective.

Monsù Bernardo est parfois hâtivement considéré comme un peintre simpliste, abonné aux sujets grossiers, qu'il traite dans un style rustique. Une meilleure connaissance de sa production permet d'appréhender l'étendue de son registre. S'il se prive rarement de se moquer ou de s'attendrir sur la pauvreté pittoresque de ses modèles, dont il sait mieux que quiconque dépeindre les haillons ou les cicatrices intérieures, il est également un observateur de premier rang. Dans le tableau de Besançon, le peintre adopte la posture du témoin qui s'abstient de juger. Cette neutralité bienveillante l'aide à restituer l'existence de cette femme dans toute sa dignité. Le cadre architectural n'agit pas comme un repoussoir exotique mais bien comme un écrin à la beauté sereine et intemporelle de la vieille femme. **AH**

64

Pietro Bellotti

(Volciano, 1625 – Gargnano del Garda, 1700)

Vieille ou *Lachesis*

H.s.t. ; H. 0,51 ; L. 0,43
Rovigo, Pinacoteca dell'Accademia dei Concordi, inv. 344

Historique : Legs Casilini, 1833.
Exposition : Rovigo, 2006, n° 93.
Bibliographie : Anelli, 1996, p. 154.

Biographie : *cf.* cat. 18.

Ce visage de vieille femme est l'un des plus souvent représentés par Bellotti. Anelli en a recensé neuf versions distinctes. Il convient tout d'abord de comprendre quel est le rapport entre cette figure en buste et les compositions élargies et plus ambitieuses de Stuttgart, datée de 1654 (fig. ci-dessous), et de Feltre. L'iconographie de ces deux derniers tableaux est dénuée de toute ambiguïté puisque le sujet en est la Parque Lachesis tenant une quenouille. Assise à une table, la vieille Parque est coupée à hauteur des genoux. Le rendu des carnations et des tissus s'impose avec une netteté quasiment hyperréaliste. Connaissant la diffusion de la tête, Cinzia Tedeschi (Rovigo, 2006) considère, après Anelli, la version de Rovigo comme une réplique tardive. La répétition du motif brodé du foulard rend cette hypothèse hautement vraisemblable et permet d'écarter l'idée de l'esquisse. Pour autant, Bellotti n'a pas cherché à rééditer l'effet de précision du tableau d'histoire. Il marque ainsi moins d'acharnement dans la restitution de la moindre ride. L'expression de la vieille femme est également plus débonnaire. C'est comme s'il avait souhaité rappeler à un collectionneur peu exigeant des traits familiers grâce à une composition fameuse mais au prix d'un petit format. Ce processus consiste à recycler le motif de l'histoire en une tête de fantaisie.

Pietro Bellotti, *Lachesis*, Stuttgart, Staatsgalerie

Dans la production de Bellotti, cette vieille femme fonctionne, toutes proportions gardées, comme « la mère » de Rembrandt, qui devint un sujet d'atelier et n'était pas la mère de l'artiste. L'hypothèse formulée par Gerhard Ewald (Ewald *et alii*, 1992, p. 46) selon laquelle la vieille paysanne ayant servi de modèle serait la mère de l'artiste n'a pas été reprise.

La toile a souffert et son usure semble répondre aux atteintes de l'âge qui affligent la vieille dame. Cette effigie toute simple sur fond noir produit une véritable émotion, peut-être davantage encore que les grandes versions d'un métier plus parfait. Si cette femme n'est qu'une paysanne et non plus une Parque, elle n'en évoque pas moins un passé ancestral et mystérieux, à mi-chemin entre la vie et la mort. **AH**

65

Christoph Paudiss

(Basse-Saxe, 1625/1630 – Freising, 1666)

Jeune Homme au béret à plume

H.s. bois ; H. 0,64 ; L. 0,51
Vienne, Kunsthistorisches Museum, Gemäldegalerie, inv. 770

Historique : Collections impériales au Belvédère supérieur, Vienne, depuis 1783.
Exposition : Freising, 2007, no 14.
Bibliographie : Sumowski, 1983-1995, p. 2322, cat. 1577.

La vie nomade de Paudiss est fort mal connue. Né en Allemagne du Nord, il se forme dans l'atelier de Rembrandt, à Amsterdam, de 1645 à 1650 approximativement. Entre des pérégrinations en Slovaquie et dans différentes villes d'Allemagne du Sud et d'Autriche, il est peintre de cour à Dresde et ensuite à Freising, à la cour du comte-évêque Albert Sigismond, où il passe les dernières années de sa vie, de 1662 à 1666. Auteur d'une production variée, Paudiss fut un élève libre de Rembrandt, dont il reprit le goût pour l'expérimentation.

Paudiss a peint une série de représentations de jeunes hommes coiffés de bérets à plume parmi lesquels les spécialistes tentent d'identifier des autoportraits. Le tableau de Munich figurant un homme d'une quarantaine d'années évoque véritablement un autoportrait par sa pose et sa recherche d'intériorité. Les autres œuvres présentent des visages fort différents et suggèrent davantage des exercices virtuoses. C'est le cas du tableau de Vienne, un bel exemple de *tronie* rembranesque.

La grande puissance expressive des effigies peintes par Paudiss vient de sa prédilection pour les représentations frontales. Le visage est ainsi livré au public dans une nudité pleine de franchise en dépit de la masse de cheveux et du couvre-chef complexe. La bouche légèrement entrouverte est soulignée par une fine moustache tandis que les yeux contemplent placidement le peintre. La pose et l'expression du modèle traduisent stabilité et fixité alors que le traitement pictural reflète mobilité et explosivité. La mise en place des carnations et des traits du visage est à rapprocher de la tradition de la peinture achevée, contrairement aux cheveux et aux plumes qui appartiennent à une pratique plus expérimentale et informelle. C'est précisément ce contraste assumé qui produit l'impression d'étrangeté irréductible de cette image.

En bon élève de Rembrandt, Paudiss se nourrit de la matière collective d'un atelier au sein duquel le maître confie à tous un répertoire pourtant très personnel où l'on croise les représentations de la famille élargie, y compris des autoportraits. Le tableau de Paudiss a été rapproché de l'*Autoportrait* de Rembrandt jeune conservé à Nuremberg, ce qui est vrai pour les longs cheveux. Toutefois, les effigies du grand maître en béret à plume sont nombreuses et elles constituent des modèles encore plus directs comme l'*Autoportrait en fils prodigue dans l'auberge* de Dresde ou l'*Autoportrait au béret à plume* de Boston. Si Paudiss reprend la production de jeunesse du peintre hollandais, c'est pourtant au cours de la seconde moitié des années 1640 qu'il semble avoir fréquenté l'atelier de ce dernier. Dans un exercice d'hommage plutôt que de pastiche, le peintre allemand capte l'expression bravache d'éternelle jeunesse qui avait valu un tel succès au jeune Rembrandt. Il emploie les mêmes recettes d'atelier en laissant le bois respirer sous une couche de préparation extrêmement légère, en jouant sur des tonalités quasiment monochromes où ne ressortent que le blanc et le rouge, et en esquissant à peine les boucles de la chevelure.

Paudiss est l'un de ces artistes européens qui ont diffusé sous d'autres horizons, à Vienne, Munich et Freising, le genre du *tronie* et le style de Rembrandt. Cette mise en scène spectaculaire de personnages hauts en couleur a facilité l'avènement des figures de fantaisie baroques et rococo de l'Europe centrale de Seybold ou de Kupezky.

AH

66

Balthasar Denner

(Altona, 1685 – Rostock, 1749)

Vieille Femme

H.s.t. ; H. 0,37 ; L. 0,31
Vienne, Kunsthistorisches Museum, Gemäldegalerie, inv. 675

Historique : Acquis en 1721 par Charles VI.
Bibliographie : Feigenbaum, 1976-1977, p. 66-68 ; Wellmann, 2008, p. 167-183 ; Schroeder, 2013 ; Hirschfelder, Krempel, 2013, p. 47-53.
Œuvre en rapport : Pendant : *Vieil Homme*, 1726, h.s.t., s.d., 0,37 × 0,31 m, Vienne, Kunsthistorisches Museum, Gemäldegalerie, inv GG 676.

Balthasar Denner, *Vieil Homme*, Vienne, Gemäldegalerie

Membre de l'Académie d'art de Berlin à partir de 1707, Balthasar Denner fut employé comme portraitiste de la cour dans le nord de l'Allemagne et au Danemark. À Londres entre 1721 et 1728, il peignit la cour de la maison de Hanovre et d'autres personnalités influentes, dont George Friedrich Haendel (Londres, National Portrait Gallery), qui était aussi un collectionneur de Denner. Il connut un grand succès commercial avec ses têtes de vieillards et de femmes dont les qualités réalistes étonnantes lui valurent le surnom de « Porenmaler » (« peintre des pores »).

Lorsque Denner se rendit à Londres en 1721, il emporta cette étude remarquablement pénétrante d'une vieille femme et s'en servit pour faire sa publicité. L'œuvre suscita un grand intérêt et Denner se trouva en position de rejeter une offre de cinq cents guinées : il choisit plutôt d'envoyer le tableau à Vienne où il fut acheté par Charles VI pour un montant encore plus élevé. L'empereur avait également commandé un pendant, la tête de vieil homme achevée en 1726 (fig. ci-contre). L'histoire raconte que Charles était tellement attaché à cette vieille femme qu'il gardait sur lui la clé de la boîte qui la contenait. Ces anecdotes, rapportées par le biographe de Denner, Van Gool, et par Horace Walpole dans ses carnets, sont la preuve des sommes parfois improbables payées pour des figures de fantaisie au XVIIIe siècle (quelques décennies plus tard, Reynolds égala l'exploit de Denner). Elles révèlent aussi comment des collectionneurs privés ont pu chérir ces peintures comme des objets intimes. La vieille femme dans la peinture de Denner capte immédiatement l'attention en raison de son regard direct et des réseaux complexes de rides profondes qui accentuent le front, les yeux et la bouche. La couleur est subtilement appliquée pour suggérer un teint vieillissant : les ombres de gris et de jaune, le rouge vif des rides qui semblent autant de blessures, contrastent avec la pâleur de papier mâché du modèle. Le visage est fortement éclairé et l'expression, indomptable. Avec ses lèvres pincées, exprime-t-elle la désapprobation, peut-être à l'encontre d'un spectateur plus jeune et plus chanceux qui ne sait rien des affres de la vieillesse ? En tout cas, le regard et le niveau de détail créent un sentiment de proximité troublant. Le tissu fait écho au visage ridé : volutes animées de la fourrure, foulard et ses plis entrecroisés. Le statut social de la femme est incertain, ses vêtements sont fantaisistes. Cette combinaison d'un réalisme sans faille et d'une figure imaginaire à l'identité indéterminée laisse le spectateur perplexe. Avec son sens de la physionomie des personnes âgées, Denner imite Rembrandt et Lievens. Avec des surfaces finement travaillées et une attention scrupuleuse au détail, il peint consciemment, à la manière de Gérard Dou et autres *fijnschilders*, mais pousse la précision de la perception à un degré supérieur. Denner a produit beaucoup de variantes de sa formule – homme et femme –, souvent en utilisant le même modèle. Les sujets présentent toute une gamme d'humeurs ou d'états psychologiques : un sourire bienveillant (Saint-Pétersbourg, Ermitage), l'introspection (Brunswick, Herzog Anton Ulrich Museum), un regard en biais un peu particulier – ou est-ce un ricanement ? – (Gotha, Schloss Friedenstein). Ces explorations brutes des émotions peuvent être comparées à celles de Pietro Rotari (*cf.* cat. 39) et Jean-Étienne Liotard. Bien que Winckelmann et sa génération aient trouvé le réalisme de Denner prosaïque, il a, tout au long de sa vie, attiré un public fidèle et des imitateurs inspirés tels que Christian Seybold (*cf.* cat. 67).

MP

67

Christian Seybold

(Neuenhain, 1695 – Vienne, 1768)

Petite Fille blonde

H.s.t. ; H. 0,50 ; L. 0,40
Vienne, Gemäldegalerie
der Akademie der bildenden Künste,
Schloss Belvedere, inv. GG.333

Historique : Comte Anton Lamberg-Sprinzenstein ; depuis 1821, Gemäldegalerie der Akademie der bildenden Künste, Vienne.
Bibliographie : Baum, 1980, p. 463 ; Garas, 1981, p. 13, n°s 56-57 ; Trnek, 2002, p. 256 ; Ruhe, 2008, p. 16-29 ; Hirschfelder, Krempel, 2013, p. 47-53.
Œuvre en rapport : Gravure par Joseph Fischer (1769-1822), Vienne, Graphische Sammlung Albertina, Ö.k. Fischer J., II, fol. 22.284.

Né près de Mayence, Seybold fut principalement actif à Vienne. Il travailla pour Auguste III de Pologne puis devint en 1749 le peintre officiel de la cour de François Ier et Marie-Thérèse à Vienne. Autodidacte, il peignit des portraits, souvent en plan rapproché sur fond neutre, ainsi que des autoportraits d'invention. Influencé par Balthasar Denner, il produisit aussi des têtes naturalistes de vieillards, de vieilles femmes et un grand nombre de portraits d'enfants.

Dans cette étude aiguisée de petite fille, Seybold restitue les caractéristiques de la prime jeunesse. L'innocence transparaît dans la pâleur de sa peau, ses cheveux blonds, son épaule découverte et son sein nu. Le tissu qui couvre son corps, lâche, presque transparent, donne à penser qu'elle n'a rien à cacher. Ce n'est pas une beauté classique : un nez rond, de grands yeux noirs, et des paupières éclatantes. Elle se mord la joue droite, faisant remonter le côté de sa bouche et accentuant sa fossette. Elle regarde droit devant elle avec un air de malice, ou peut-être de menace. L'arrière-plan sombre ajoute au sentiment que son innocence est insaisissable et menacée.

Seybold s'ancre dans la tradition hollandaise et les *tronies* de Lievens constituent là une influence évidente. L'intérêt porté aux humeurs et à la candeur d'une fillette rapproche la peinture de l'œuvre de Rotari et de Greuze. Ce travail a probablement été exécuté assez tôt, avant la période (1740-1745) pendant laquelle le style de l'artiste est devenu plus raffiné, à la manière du rococo français. Le même jeune modèle a servi pour *Gouvernante et jeune fille avec un livre de chant* (Winterthur, Museum Briner und Kern Rathaus, Stiftung Jakob Briner), qui date probablement de la même période. Lilian Ruhe a émis l'hypothèse que le sujet et modèle des deux peintures pourrait être un garçon. Bien que peu convaincante dans ce cas précis, sa proposition est valable pour la figure de fantaisie en général, où les sujets peuvent avoir une apparence androgyne. Cela s'explique en partie par la subversion intrinsèque à la figure de fantaisie et sa tendance à transcender les catégories et les limites. Mais, de façon plus pragmatique, les modèles, garçons ou filles, étaient utilisés en fonction de leur disponibilité dans l'atelier. Le visage de la fille de Seybold se retrouve dans deux sujets, masculin et féminin (*cf.* le *Portrait de garçon*, également au Schloss Belvedere). Le *Garçon avec un manuel scolaire* de Greuze (Édimbourg, National Galleries of Scotland) est un autre exemple de cette ambivalence. La *Petite Fille blonde* appartenait au diplomate et collectionneur influent, le comte Anton Lamberg-Sprinzenstein (1740-1822). La gravure par Joseph Fischer d'après la peinture de Seybold est révélatrice de la popularité de cette jeune fille énigmatique dans les décennies qui suivirent la mort de l'artiste.

MP

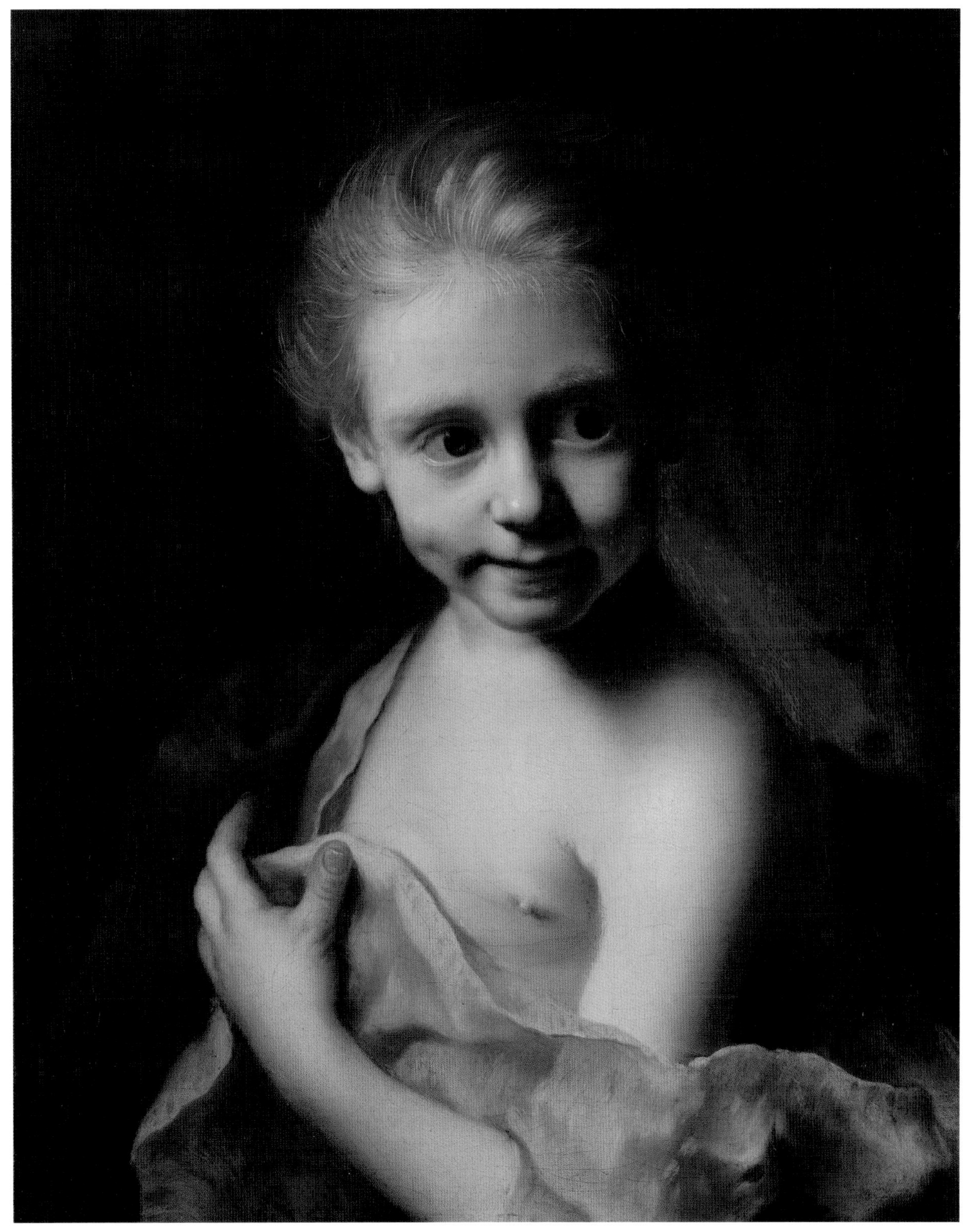

68

Giuseppe Nogari

(Venise, 1699-1766)

Vieille Femme en prière

H.s.t. ; H. 0,60 ; L. 0,47
Rovigo, Pinacoteca dell'Accademia dei Concordi, inv. 271

Historique : Legs Silvestri, 1878.
Bibliographie : Honour, 1957, p. 154-159 ; Romagnolo, Fantelli, 1981, nº 71, p. 158 ; Pallucchini, 1996, p. 570-578.
Œuvre en rapport : Pendant : *Vieil Usurier*, Rovigo, Pinacoteca dell'Accademia dei Concordi, inv. 72.

Mieux connu pour ses « têtes » dans l'esprit de Rembrandt et de Rosalba Carriera, Nogari peignit aussi des sujets religieux. Vivant à Venise, il fut probablement formé par Giambattista Piazzetta et gagna le parrainage d'amateurs influents tels que le comte Tessin, le consul Smith, von der Schulenburg et Francesco Algarotti. Grâce à ces connaissances, il gagna en visibilité internationale et devint particulièrement prisé en Allemagne. En 1756, il fut élu membre de l'Accademia di Pittura e Scultura de Venise.

Un grand nombre de « teste di carattere » de Nogari représentent la vieillesse, mais celle-ci est une étude particulièrement frappante par ses effets sur la peau et les os. Tout comme dans la peinture de Jordaens visible dans cette exposition (cat. 56), le cou de la vieille femme en est le morceau le plus marquant avec ses plis profonds de la peau qui se relâche, rendus plus dramatiques encore par un jeu d'ombres. La peinture est traitée librement, avec des effets d'empâtement, donnant rugosité et relief à la chair. D'autres rides sont concentrées autour de la bouche et l'on peut voir des ombres foncées sur les tempes qui contrastent avec les cheveux blancs vaporeux du sujet. Un autre détail finement observé est la main aux doigts déformés par l'arthrite. La femme a un air quelque peu pincé, serrant sa mâchoire comme si la vie avait été difficile et que la vieillesse l'était encore plus. Au bas de l'image, une miniature représente un homme, peut-être un mari mort qui lui manque cruellement. Les titres de cette œuvre et de son pendant, le *Vieil Usurier* (fig. ci-dessous), impliqueraient un contraste, outre le genre, dans les traitements terrestres et spirituels de la vieillesse. Mais la différence n'est pas si marquée. Bien que la femme se penche sur ce qui peut être un livre de prières, elle n'est pas représentée en prière et son regard intense semble évoquer des préoccupations plus laïques.

Giuseppe Nogari, *Vieil Usurier*, Rovigo, Pinacoteca dell'Accademia dei Concordi

Le travail de Nogari atteste la convergence des influences nordiques et italiennes : la noirceur, le réalisme et l'acuité psychologique de Rembrandt et de Piazzetta. Autour des ateliers de Piazzetta et Tiepolo, Venise au XVIIIe siècle était un lieu de production important de personnages posant en plan large, dans un décor minimal et souvent déguisés. La création régulière par Nogari de figures d'hommes, de femmes et d'enfants de même que son activité pour les plus éminents collectionneurs témoignent de la réussite de son art. Le même modèle a été peint par Nogari dans une pose similaire, tenant un bol (Venise, Galleria dell'Accademia). Parmi les autres œuvres de Nogari représentant des vieilles femmes, on trouve la très admirée *Femme âgée dans un châle rayé* (Washington DC, National Gallery of Art) ainsi qu'une autre œuvre montrant la même femme se réchauffant les mains sur un brasero (Dresde, Gemäldegalerie Alte Meister).

MP

69

Gaspare Traversi

(Naples, vers 1722 – Rome, 1770)

Vieux Mendiant

H.s.t ; H. 0,55 ; L. 0,68
Narbonne, musée d'Art et d'Histoire, inv. 859.3.74

Historique : Collection Maurice Peyre ; musée de Narbonne, 1859.
Expositions : Brescia, 1998-1999, no 54, p. 353 ; Stuttgart, 2003, no 6, p. 76 et 158 ; Naples, 2003-2004, no 20, p. 114-115 ; Parme, 2004.
Œuvre en rapport : *Vieux Mendiant*, h.s.t., 0,55 × 0,68 m, vers 1750, collection particulière, Florence (ill. *in* Fornari Schianchi, Spinosa, 2004, p. 224, R 29).

L'artiste napolitain Traversi était un disciple de Solimena et fut aussi bien influencé par le classicisme romain que par les peintres naturalistes du XVIIe siècle. Peintre religieux, il se créa en outre un style unique de peinture de genre rendant compte de la vie quotidienne de ses contemporains. Ayant recours à la compression caravagesque et accentuant les expressions faciales de ses sujets, il décrivait la difficulté des rapports humains. La justesse de sa description des travers de l'homme lui valut d'être comparé à Steen, à Hogarth ou encore à Longhi.

Un mendiant émerge de la pénombre, la main tendue, implorant le spectateur de le prendre en pitié. Il est allongé, comme s'il était souffrant ou accablé par son infortune, les genoux repliés en un geste défensif, dernier vestige de sa dignité. Le format horizontal du tableau accentue sa détresse. Le cadrage resserré fait de l'espace un lieu exigu et inconfortable ; il piège le spectateur en n'offrant aucune échappatoire à son regard. Dans l'esprit du Caravage, il s'agit d'un dialogue de chair et d'os. La semi-nudité du sujet est mise en relief par la lumière crue : le creux de sa clavicule, les rides de son cou et de ses pieds, ses ongles sales. Cette œuvre, qui compte parmi les premiers tableaux de Traversi, s'inspire peut-être de ses compositions pour l'église Santa Maria dell'Aiuto, à Naples. L'artiste a également peint d'autres figures allongées, notamment la *Vieille Mendiante avec un gamin des rues* (Milan, Pinacoteca di Brera) et la *Vieille Gitane* (Florence, coll. part., ill. *in* Fornari Schianchi, Spinosa, 2004, p. 224, R 28). Il a su capter la spontanéité de la vie napolitaine avec ses portraits authentiques des classes moyennes et populaires. Si son réalisme se teinte fréquemment d'une connotation satirique poussée à l'extrême, avec des grimaces gênées et des corps comprimés dans des espaces étroits, ses représentations des plus démunis sont touchantes et dénuées de préjugés. À la manière de Ribera, à qui cette œuvre était précédemment attribuée, Traversi met en lumière un individu abandonné par la société. De façon inhabituelle dans une composition au sujet unique, le visage est relégué à l'arrière-plan, et cette distance physique instaurée avec la bonne société ajoute une touche de pathos à son regard implorant. **MP**

L'atelier du costume

70

Nicolas Tournier

(Montbéliard, 1590 – Toulouse, 1639)

Soldat

H.s.t. ; H. 0,96 ; L. 0,71
Toulouse, musée des Augustins, inv. 91 1 2

Historique : Achat en 1991 auprès d'une famille toulousaine.
Exposition : Toulouse, 2001, no 22.
Bibliographie : Hémery, 2010, II, p. 731.

Nicolas Tournier, *Saint Paul*, Toulouse, musée des Augustins

La formation de Nicolas Tournier, protestant né à Montbéliard, en terre de l'Empire romain germanique, n'est pas connue. Sa présence est attestée de 1619 à 1626 à Rome mais il est possible qu'il se soit fixé en Italie quelques années plus tôt. Il est l'un des peintres caravagesques les plus importants, auteur de grandes compositions pour les familles aristocratiques, concerts, scènes de jeu, musiciens. Son sujet de prédilection est le reniement de saint Pierre. Proche de Bertrand de Reich, trésorier du Languedoc, il réside de 1627 à sa mort en 1639 entre Narbonne, Carcassonne et Toulouse. Au cours de ses dernières années, il abandonne le caravagisme au profit d'un style austère et géométrique d'une belle simplicité qui n'aura pas de descendance.

Le *Soldat* de Tournier est un bel exemple de figure à mi-corps représentant un spadassin ou un *bravo* romain. Aucun élément de décor ou d'anecdote n'ajoute de dimension narrative ou de sens moral au sujet. On connaît un autre tableau du peintre sur ce thème, conservé dans une collection particulière, dans lequel l'artiste a figuré le personnage arborant une épée à l'épaule. Les figures de fantaisie les plus typiques de Tournier sont les deux pendants de la Galleria Estense de Modène, le *Buveur à la fiasque* et le *Buveur levant son verre*. L'œuvre toulousaine présente toutefois un caractère original car elle constitue le pendant d'un *Saint Paul* (fig. ci-contre) avec lequel elle partage les mêmes dimensions et une même histoire. On a d'ailleurs détecté grâce à une radiographie une composition sous-jacente et déchiffrée au revers du *Saint Paul* l'inscription *3 quadri per il Sr Pennautier* qui permet d'associer les deux pendants et le *Portrait de Bertrand de Reich, seigneur de Pennautier* (château de Pennautier). On comprend ainsi l'installation de Tournier au service du trésorier du Languedoc après son départ de Rome. La paire constituée d'un tableau sacré et d'un autre, profane, est inédite. Rien ne pourrait d'ailleurs différer davantage que l'auréole de l'apôtre et l'élégant chapeau à plumes du soldat. Toutefois, ce dernier effectue une action significative. En effet, il s'apprête à dégainer l'épée de son fourreau. On peut y voir l'attitude habituelle de ces hommes de main qui vagabondaient dans Rome en quête d'aventures. On peut aussi imaginer un rappel subtil de Paul représenté avec son épée en gladiateur du Christ ou une évocation de Pierre blessant les assaillants du Christ au mont des Oliviers. Tournier, protestant ayant abjuré sa foi, est coutumier des sujets ambivalents qui peuvent parler aux protestants comme aux catholiques (« Laissez venir à moi les petits enfants », saint Paul, le reniement de saint Pierre, la parabole de la poutre et de la paille). Le peintre utilise un modèle qui apparaît de manière récurrente dans sa production romaine. Il lui confère l'expression d'attention intense soulignée par un plissement du front presque archétypale chez les peintres caravagesques. On connaît la présence d'accessoires dans les ateliers. La cuirasse, le chapeau à plumes, l'épée sont des éléments qui permettent de peindre un soldat « pour rire ». Toutefois, les chroniques de la vie turbulente de cette ruche picturale concentrée dans quelques rues de cette bourgade qu'était Rome au début du XVIIe siècle nous apprennent que les peintres se muaient parfois en hommes de main capables d'intimidation et d'agression. On ne sait pratiquement rien sur la vie de Tournier mais sa peinture parle d'une existence austère et silencieuse, sans pathos ni éclat. Ses personnages du quotidien, joueurs, courtisanes, soldats, manquent de bonhomie et de gouaille. Ils sont graves, introvertis et expriment des émotions intenses. Cet homme travesti en soldat ne diffère pas des figures sacrées de saints et apôtres. Il incarne une époque chargée d'énergie et lourde de mélancolie. Le tableau et son pendant peuvent être datés de la fin du séjour romain du peintre, vers 1625-1626. **AH**

Salomon de Bray

(Amsterdam, 1597 – Haarlem, 1664)

Femme en costume de fantaisie ou *Sémiramis*, 1652

H.s. bois ; H. 0,99 ; L. 0,83
S.d. *SD Bray 1652*
Haarlem, Frans Hals Museum, inv. Os I-687

Historique : Peut-être vente P. Boetens, Londres, 1763, n° 35 ; Christie's, Londres, 6 mai 1927, n° 108 ; marchand Buttery, 1927-1938 ; acheté par la Société des amis et donné au Frans Hals Museum en 1939.
Expositions : Rotterdam/Francfort, 1999-2000, n° 9 ; Haarlem/Londres, 2008, n° 8.

Fondateur d'une dynastie de peintres attachée à Haarlem, Salomon de Bray naquit à Amsterdam. Également architecte et poète, ce fut un peintre d'histoire proche de Lastman incarnant cette génération qui ne fut totalement séduite ni par le caravagisme ni par Rembrandt. Son influence fut décisive pour l'apparition du classicisme du milieu du XVIIe siècle, dont son fils Jan fut un important représentant.

La production de Salomon de Bray se répartit entre tableaux d'histoire, pastorales et études d'après le modèle vivant. Le tableau de Haarlem a été interprété de diverses manières. Pour certains observateurs, il s'agit d'un portrait idéalisé, pour d'autres, d'une représentation historique, celle de Sémiramis, reine de Babylone.

Fait étonnant pour un sujet historique, le peintre se prive de tout détail narratif. Le traitement traditionnel de la scène s'assimile à une scène de cour où la reine interrompt sa toilette pour aller réprimer l'émeute qui se trame. De plus, aucun attribut clair n'est discernable. L'héroïne est figurée dans une attitude de sérénité absolue et rien n'indique un brusque changement d'humeur ou une résolution nouvelle. Pieter Biesboer (Haarlem/Londres, 2008) reconnaît cette absence d'attribut mais considère que la reine a cessé sa toilette, s'est drapée rapidement dans une cape et s'est posé un béret sur la tête. Il nous semble plutôt que la femme paraît dans la tenue caractéristique des figures de fantaisie hollandaises. L'aspect informel ne constitue qu'un *topos* de cette peinture. La sublime cape de velours, le délicat chapeau à plumes posé de guingois, la boucle d'oreille et le coussin vermeil sont autant d'accessoires intemporels. Cela n'exclut toutefois absolument pas que l'on ait affaire à un portrait allégorique d'une Hollandaise contemporaine déguisée en Sémiramis ou en quelque autre héroïne mythologique ou biblique. Rembrandt nous a habitués à représenter Saskia ou Hendrickje sous bien des traits.

Le tableau de Salomon de Bray est un merveilleux morceau de peinture. Le visage de la femme s'offre dans une frontalité parfaite, à peine perturbée par un effet de clair-obscur. Son expression est absolument impénétrable et énigmatique, à la manière d'autres créateurs contemporains de peintures de fantaisie comme Vermeer ou Paulus Bor. L'équilibre pyramidal de la silhouette de la jeune femme est contrarié par le jeté de la cape soulignée par les plis profonds du drapé et le retour de la main posée sur le coussin. À la manière de Rembrandt, Salomon de Bray a travaillé dans ce tableau sur une gamme limitée de rouges et de bruns. La lumière joue un rôle unificateur dans la composition, révélant les formes avec une intensité solaire.

Friso Lammertse (Rotterdam/Francfort, 1999-2000) a évoqué l'influence des courtisanes vénitiennes du XVIe siècle, dont on connaît l'importance pour Rembrandt ; cette comparaison est plutôt convaincante bien que la femme de De Bray soit bien moins déshabillée que les courtisanes. D'ailleurs, dans la peinture hollandaise du Siècle d'or, seules les bergères arborent des décolletés plongeants (cat. 2 et cat. 3).

Quelle que soit l'identité de ce personnage remarquable, le peintre sait créer une émotion singulière et conférer aux traits du visage une noblesse qui donne envie d'y voir une reine. On ne peut pas parler ici de *tronie* mais bien plutôt de portrait historique, allégorique ou de genre selon l'interprétation que l'on en donne. Ce tableau exceptionnel incarne une certaine plénitude de l'art hollandais dans ce moment de transition entre rembranisme et classicisme. **AH**

72

Jan Van den Hoecke

(Anvers, 1611-1651)

La Sibylle agrippine

H.s.t. ; H. 1,06 ; L. 0,80
Düsseldorf, Museum Kunst Palast, inv. M 125

Historique : Acquis en 1939.
Exposition : Amsterdam, 2008, nº 22.
Bibliographie : Vlieghe, 1990, p. 166-170 ; McGrath, 2005, p. 359-361, fig. 8.

Élève et collaborateur de Rubens à Anvers, Van den Hoecke effectua le traditionnel voyage en Italie puis fut nommé peintre de cour de l'archiduc Léopold Guillaume à Vienne. Il revint s'installer à Anvers en 1647. Sa production est aujourd'hui fort peu connue.

Le tableau représente une sibylle. L'apparence massive et junonienne de cette femme et son turban sont caractéristiques de ces représentations. Il faut y ajouter les instruments de la Passion du Christ et le phylactère portant l'inscription *Siccabitur ut folium* (« Il séchera comme une feuille », allusion au sort du Christ). Cette prophétie est associée à la seule sibylle noire, tantôt considérée comme libyenne, tantôt appelée Agrippa ou sibylle agrippine, ce qui serait, selon certains spécialistes, une déformation d'égyptienne. En principe, les représentations de personnages mythologiques, de prophètes ou de saints sortent du champ de cette exposition. Nous nous sommes autorisé deux exceptions et voici l'une d'elles. Les sibylles ont une longue histoire dans la peinture européenne, dont le sommet est constitué par celles de Michel-Ange à la chapelle Sixtine. Il a paru aux commissaires de l'exposition que le peintre s'aventurait dans sa recherche d'exotisme et d'étrangeté vers des territoires foulés par les auteurs de figures de fantaisie : le travestissement et une introspection non dénuée de coquetterie, le tout traduit dans un style brillant et informel.
Le tableau était traditionnellement attribué à Abraham Janssens (vers 1573-1632) avant que Hans Vlieghe ne découvre une série de douze sibylles peinte par Van den Hoecke, cycle qui semble avoir connu un certain succès car il a été copié. Les rares exemples connus passés sur le marché de l'art, la *Sibylle cimmérienne* ou la *Sibylle de Cumes*, sont de bien moindre qualité que le tableau de Düsseldorf. En règle générale, Jan Van den Hoecke ne s'impose pas comme l'un des élèves les plus talentueux de Rubens. Il est donc compréhensible qu'on ait pensé à des noms plus prestigieux comme Abraham Janssens, voire plus récemment Theodoor Van Loon. Toutefois, outre le sérieux de l'étude de Vlieghe qui emporte l'adhésion, on peut aussi souligner des traits de style qui laissent peu de doutes quant à l'attribution à Van den Hoecke. En particulier, les drapés se caractérisent par un relatif schématisme. Néanmoins, la robe rouge produit un effet de somptuosité fort spectaculaire grâce à l'usage presque obsessionnel des *cangianti*. Le foulard bigarré et la partie inférieure du turban sont plus heureux encore tandis que le sommet du couvre-chef pourrait avoir été ajouté postérieurement car il n'est pas présent sur les copies peintes ou gravées. Le visage constitue l'un des plus beaux exemples d'approche empathique des Noirs, dont la peinture nordique n'est pourtant pas avare. Les grands ports comme Anvers ou Amsterdam rassemblaient des populations venues des quatre coins de la planète, que Rubens et Rembrandt ont représentées avec respect et sensibilité. Contrastant avec la fantaisie de la tenue, le visage semble être le fruit d'une étude précise d'après modèle. L'expression charmeuse et réservée, doublée d'une distance ironique, apparaît d'un naturel parfait. Le travail de la carnation est poussé afin de capter la chair dans toute sa vérité.
À la croisée de plusieurs genres picturaux, ce chef-d'œuvre unique d'un petit maître exploite tous les ressorts d'une théâtralité exotique tout en nous renvoyant une image d'humanité et de simplicité. **AH**

Siccabitur ut folium

École de Rembrandt

Portrait d'homme en costume polonais

H.s.t. ; H. 0,68 ; L. 0,55
Bordeaux, musée des Beaux-Arts, inv. Bx E 10

Historique : Collection de Louis XIV à Versailles ; collection du duc d'Antin à Paris en 1715 ; Louvre en 1785 ; envoi de l'État à Bordeaux en 1803.
Bibliographie : Le Bihan, 1990, nº 72.

En dépit de son illustre provenance, ce tableau fascinant a connu une histoire complexe et ne peut à ce jour être attribué de manière convaincante. Longtemps considéré de la main du Mantouan Domenico Fetti puis de l'élève de Vouet François Tortebat, il a été un temps rapproché de l'école de Guido Reni. Jacques Foucart a envisagé le Bavarois Christoph Paudiss. L'école hollandaise est celle qui réunit le plus de suffrages mais il est significatif que des peintres de quatre écoles aient été cités, deux de type plutôt classique et deux plus fantasques.

Il est plus aisé de déterminer le genre de peinture auquel appartient ce tableau, celui du *tronie*. Nous sommes en effet en présence d'un exercice de style sur le thème de l'étude de tête en costume de fantaisie. L'association de la cuirasse et de la toque de fourrure indique un costume polonais, comme dans le célèbre *Cavalier polonais* de Rembrandt (New York, The Frick Collection). Sous son volumineux couvre-chef, le jeune homme présente une expression de grande intensité et fixe le spectateur. Son visage large et pâle est identifiable et fait penser à un portrait. Toutefois, la présence dominante du costume folklorique justifie qu'on décrive l'œuvre comme une figure de fantaisie.

Si l'on a pu parler de l'influence de Rembrandt, c'est de manière générique pour l'emprunt d'un type. Stylistiquement, la manière est plus appliquée, plus laborieuse que celle du maître. Si Rembrandt sait adapter sa technique au contexte de la commande tout au long de sa carrière, il est presque toujours informel et virtuose pour les *tronies*. Nous sommes toutefois en terres rembranesques familières dans le choix d'une gamme de bruns, d'un clair-obscur marqué, d'un fond légèrement moins soutenu que la note dominante du costume. L'anonymat gêne en raison de la grande maîtrise manifestée par le peintre, qui excelle à souligner les points saillants de la tenue, le bandeau de tissu, le col de la cuirasse, le col en fourrure.

Si le costume est indubitablement exotique, l'artiste ne recherche pas l'invention d'une figure pittoresque. Son intention consiste à étonner et émouvoir par sa présentation d'un visage énigmatique et intériorisé. Le style du peintre n'évoque aucun rembranesque notoire, une école où les artistes présentent des caractéristiques assez marquées. S'il fallait avancer un nom prudemment, nous opterions pour Barent Fabritius en raison de la matière picturale et de la force expressive. **AH**

74

Michael Sweerts

(Bruxelles, 1618 – Goa, 1664)

Garçon au turban tenant un bouquet de fleurs

H.s.t. ; H. 0,76 ; L. 0,62
Madrid, Museo Thyssen-Bornemisza, inv. 1981.19 (385)

Historique : Collection Andrea Busiri Vici, Rome, 1955 ; sa vente, Londres, Sotheby's, 10 juillet 1968, lot 32 ; collection J. Hargreaves, Allemagne ; sa vente, Londres, Christie's, 10 avril 1981, lot 81 ; baron H. H. Thyssen-Bornemisza, Lugano ; museo Thyssen-Bornemisza, 1988.
Expositions : Rotterdam/ Rome, 1958, nº 38 (nº 37) ; Amsterdam/San Francisco/Hartford, 2002, nº XXIII.
Bibliographie : Gaskell, 1990, p. 116-129, nº 49 ; Kultzen, 1996, nº 122.

Biographie : *cf.* cat. 25.

La signification du tableau du musée Thyssen a suscité plusieurs hypothèses. Celle d'une représentation de l'Odorat et de son appartenance à un cycle des cinq sens est évoquée par Kultzen mais rejetée par Guido Jansen (Amsterdam/San Francisco/ Hartford, 2002) en raison de l'absence d'autres tableaux connus du cycle. Il faut bien avouer que le jeune homme tient son bouquet de manière plutôt passive et ne semble pas réagir à son parfum. De plus, les paraboles et allégories de Sweerts répondent habituellement à un mode plus narratif.

Toutefois, l'artiste aime à brouiller les pistes et ses représentations sont rarement exemptes d'intentions moralisatrices. Il nous semble, pour l'essentiel, que le modèle, dont bien des observateurs ont souligné l'ambivalence de genre voire l'androgynie, répond au type des mignons caravagesques. L'accoutrement excentrique du jeune homme et le bouquet délicat qu'il arbore comme un attribut ajoutent au déguisement le travestissement au sens premier du terme. Cet adolescent habillé en femme pose dans une attitude féminine, entouré de symboles féminins. Le chaînon manquant pour une compréhension complète de l'œuvre est sans doute le regard fuyant du jeune homme, qui ne peut être gratuit.

Le turban constitue l'un des plus extravagants couvre-chefs du peintre, pourtant véritable fétichiste des chevelures et des chapeaux. Ce n'est pas un turban ordinaire mais plutôt un châle enroulé autour de la tête, dont on voit les franges se répandre sur le front du modèle. Il n'y a pas de véritable équivalent à cette représentation dans l'œuvre du peintre. Les turbans portés par les *Deux Hommes en costume oriental* du Getty Museum présentent une surface bien plus plane. Sweerts a tendance à accentuer l'effet des coiffes traditionnelles qu'il emploie dans ses compositions, que ce soit les foulards de la *campagna romana* ou les bérets des hommes du peuple. Néanmoins, c'est vers les planches gravées des *Diversae Facies* (fig. page 146) qu'il faut se tourner pour trouver des turbans similaires. Les deux jeunes hommes avec turban présentent le même type de visage imberbe et inexpressif. Leurs turbans se caractérisent par des plis tout aussi marqués. Cependant, ils ne se prolongent pas par des franges débordant sur le front.

Le cadrage sur le jeune homme est très resserré sur un fond sombre uniforme. Les drapés larges et creusés de la chemise et de la cape répondent à ceux du turban, créant la principale animation d'une composition statique. Le personnage est coupé à mi-corps, légèrement courbé, sans que l'on puisse comprendre s'il est assis ou debout. La palette est fort économe, constituée de la juxtaposition de larges bandes de bleu, blanc et jaune. Seuls la carnation et le bouquet résultent de mélanges de tons. Une analyse de la technique picturale a été menée sur le tableau. On a pu démontrer que l'outremer de la cape a été appliqué sur une couche de blanc de plomb. Ce bleu très pur a perdu de sa puissance, qui devait être éclatante au contact du blanc des manches de chemise. La double préparation, blanc de plomb et carbone sur de la craie et de l'ocre, correspond à une technique employée par Sweerts à son retour dans les Pays-Bas, justifiant ainsi une datation vers 1655-1656.

Dans cette œuvre fulgurante, le peintre parvient à combiner étude psychologique, recherche d'expression au moyen des empâtements et du travail graphique sur les drapés, et un travail sur la perfection formelle. Ce tableau est ainsi l'un des plus surprenants d'un corpus qui ne manque pas d'œuvres inoubliables. **AH**

75

Francesco Solimena

(Canale di Serino, 1657 – Barra, 1747)

Portrait de femme

H.s.t. ; H. 1,29 ; L. 1,00
Toulouse, musée des Augustins, inv. 2004 1 50

Historique : Envoi du gouvernement consulaire en 1805.
Expositions : Lyon/Lille, 2000-2001, no 115, p. 272-273.
Bibliographie : Bologna, 1958, p. 91, 275, fig. 139 ; Spinosa, 1986, no 22, p. 107 ; Hémery, 2003, no 39, p. 102-103.

Solimena se forma auprès de son père et tira son inspiration des artistes baroques romains tels Giordano, Lanfranco et Preti. Son atelier napolitain domina la vie artistique de la ville pendant près d'un demi-siècle. Connu pour ses retables de grande envergure et ses compositions mythologiques, Solimena excella dans tous les genres, y compris l'architecture et le décor. Il remporta un large succès international grâce à des commandes provenant de France, d'Autriche et de Bavière. Ses talents artistiques lui valurent de faire fortune.

Cette exposition est l'occasion de revenir sur une peinture longtemps admirée par les Toulousains mais qui reste une énigme pour les chercheurs et le public, une exception dans l'œuvre de Solimena, qui produisit plutôt des compositions à plusieurs personnages mais peu de portraits. Cette peinture se classe difficilement dans les catégories habituelles de sujets. Les tentatives visant à identifier le modèle (la chanteuse Flaminia Scarlatti, fille du compositeur ?) ou à y voir une allégorie de la Modestie (Spinosa) sont restées peu convaincantes. De nouveaux éléments provenant d'un catalogue de vente de Paris de 1767 indiquent que cette figure était autrefois reconnue comme celle de Cléopâtre. La description du lot 38 dans le *Catalogue des tableaux qui composent le coffret du feu monsieur le maréchal de Noailles* (1767) correspond indéniablement à la peinture de Toulouse : « Cléopâtre, figure de proportion naturelle, vue jusqu'aux genoux, le fond est un paysage, & de l'architecture : ce tableau dont on fait cas, est peint sur toile de quatre pieds de haut, sur trois pieds de large. » Nous savons que l'œuvre fut saisie par les autorités révolutionnaires à la veuve du quatrième duc de Noailles en 1794. Il semblerait donc qu'elle ne fût pas vendue en 1767 après la mort du troisième duc mais serait restée dans la famille. Selon un récit de Pline l'Ancien, Cléopâtre et Marc-Antoine parient à qui donnera la fête la plus onéreuse. Cléopâtre est la gagnante qui dissout une boucle d'oreille en perle dans une tasse de vinaigre avant de la boire. Si l'on examine à nouveau la peinture, la perle est visible, posée dans un plateau sur la table. À côté se trouve un récipient en métal pouvant contenir le vinaigre. D'autres détails antiques ou exotiques tels que le vase à tête de bélier ou la coiffure en turban de la femme appuieraient la thèse accréditant l'idée que nous nous trouvons face à la reine d'Égypte (vue à travers le prisme de Naples au XVIIIe siècle). Mais le symbolisme reste très discret. D'autres représentations de Cléopâtre privilégient la dissolution de la perle, comme le montrent le tableau de Carlo Maratta (1695, Rome, Palazzo Venezia) ou la scène de banquet, grandeur nature, de Tiepolo (1744, Melbourne, National Gallery of Victoria). Ici, le personnage de Solimena regarde pensivement devant elle et son humeur semble en contradiction avec le pari aux enjeux sexuels et politiques de l'histoire telle que rapportée traditionnellement. L'artiste semble choisir un thème pour explorer d'autres possibilités narratives. Il est impossible d'ignorer l'église au second plan ainsi que les vêtements qui rappellent les représentations de saints napolitains autant que d'héroïnes classiques. Face à de tels messages contradictoires, loin de toute notion de temps, de lieu ou de contexte, nous ne pouvons qu'admirer la beauté et la peinture pour elles-mêmes : l'éclat magnifique des tissus, le jeu des drapés, une jeune femme épanouie à la peau si blanche. Entourée par d'autres figures de fantaisie dont les costumes, l'identité et le but sont tout aussi obscurs, la jeune femme de Solimena apparaît moins insolite, telle une véritable célébration de tout ce qu'il y a de mystérieux. **MP**

Jean-Baptiste Santerre

(Magny-en-Vexin, 1658 – Paris, 1717)

La Jeune Femme au billet doux, anciennement *Mlle Desmares*

H.s.t. ; H. 0,82 ; L. 0,63
Paris, bibliothèque-musée de la Comédie-Française, inv. I 0204

Historique : Acheté 60 francs à M. Vigny, 15, rue Neuve-Saint-Augustin, en août 1832.
Bibliographie : Monval, 1897, no 99 ; Lesné, 1988, p. 75-118 ; Lesné, Waro, 2011, p. 79-81.
Œuvres en rapport : *Jeune Fille au billet doux*, h.s.t., 0,84 × 0,74 m, de la collection du Conseiller Tronchin, Bessinge (à côté de Genève), au XVIIIe siècle ; localisation actuelle inconnue. *Portrait d'une jeune femme avec une lettre présumée Mademoiselle Christine-Antoinette-Charlotte Desmares*, h.s.t., 0,91 × 0,73 m, New York, Sotheby's, 31 janvier-1er février 2013, no 102. *Jeune Femme avec une lettre d'amour*, h.s.t., 0,87 × 0,63 m, Boston, Museum of Fine Arts, inv. 47.245. Gravure, N. Château, 1708. Miniature, K. G. Klingstedt, vers 1720, Stockholm, Nationalmuseum, inv. NMB 682. Suiveur d'Alexis Grimou, École française du XVIIIe siècle, *Portrait d'une jeune femme et de son esclave*, 0,125 × 0,94 m, Drouot, 28 oct. 2005, no 37 ; *idem*, Drouot, 10 nov. 2005, no 8.

Biographie : *cf.* cat. 51.

Lorsque la Comédie-Française fit l'acquisition de ce tableau en 1832, elle pensait qu'il s'agissait du portrait de l'actrice Christine-Antoinette-Charlotte Desmares (1682-1752). Cependant, cette hypothèse fut réfutée en 1897 par George Monval, qui compara la toile avec le portrait de Charlotte Desmares tenant une dague et un masque (*Charlotte Desmares : en costume tragique*) réalisé par Charles-Antoine Coypel dans la même collection. Les formes généreuses de la comédienne telles que les dépeint Coypel ne sont pas reconnaissables chez le sujet mince et imaginaire, à la cambrure prononcée, du tableau de Santerre. Cette confusion tient probablement au costume « espagnol » du sujet : corsage de velours noir orné de broderies d'or, manches à bourrelets rouges et blancs, toque de velours arborant deux plumes bleues. À l'époque de Santerre, on associait ces atours aux jeunes femmes incarnant un personnage principal au théâtre, mais on leur attribuait aussi des connotations plus libres d'imagination et de désir. La jeune « Espagnolette » représentée ici tient une lettre hermétiquement pliée et cachetée à la cire, correspondance implicite avec son amant. La gravure, réalisée par Château en 1708 d'après cette peinture, était accompagnée d'un quatrain dans lequel elle met de potentiels prétendants au défi d'égaler son intelligence : « A me voir j'ai les traits d'une beauté divine / Les yeux noirs et brillants, un teint vif et charmant / Mais j'ai l'esprit d'une étoffe si fine / Que j'en donne à garder au plus subtil amant. » La version originale du tableau de Santerre était la propriété du grand collectionneur d'art suisse François Tronchin (1704-1798) et il en existe au moins trois répliques connues d'excellente qualité, dont celle en question ici. La pose et la tenue vestimentaire de son sujet ne sont pas sans rappeler les portraits clairement identifiés réalisés par Santerre, notamment celui de madame Le Pelletier des Forts, 0,91 × 0,74 m (coll. part., ill. Lesné, 2011, p. 80 ; copie, Le Mans, musée de Tessé) et de lady Thales (coll. part., Lesné, no 21). Cela illustre la perméabilité dans la production de Santerre entre figures de fantaisie et portraits réalisés sur commande.

MP

77

Jacques-François Courtin

(Sens, 1672 – Paris, 1752)

Jeune Femme au corsage bleu

H.s.t. ; H. 0, 84 ; L. 0,66
Dijon, musée des Beaux-Arts, inv. 4732

Historique : Don de la Société des amis des Musées de Dijon, 1967.
Bibliographie : Faré, 1966, p. 293-320 ; Starcky, Meyer, Gras, 1992, p. 80.
Œuvre en rapport : Gravure « Espagnolette » par Nicolas Château, 1715.

Courtin fut l'élève de Louis de Boullogne. Outre des sujets mythologiques et religieux comme *Saint Paul ressuscitant Eutyque* (Toulouse, cathédrale Saint-Étienne), il peignit des sujets de fantaisie et de genre. Avec Santerre, Raoux et Watteau, il établit une nouvelle mode, les thèmes galants, au début du XVIIIe siècle. Il devint membre de l'Académie royale en 1710 et exposa régulièrement au Salon entre 1737 et 1751.

Le traitement du sujet de l'« Espagnolette » par Courtin se démarque des versions de Grimou et de Santerre par sa sensualité audacieuse. Le personnage est représenté en *contrapposto* et semble s'avancer tout en regardant par-dessus son épaule. Dans la continuité de cette torsion, la plume de sa toque s'élance de manière provocante dans la pénombre prolongeant son regard. La lumière éclaire crûment son décolleté plongeant, son cou et ses pommettes. Ce mouvement est atténué par la douceur du profil de la jeune femme, les volutes blondes de ses cheveux et le carmin tendre de sa joue. L'épure de son visage rappelle l'idéal féminin de la Renaissance italienne. Son état d'esprit est extrêmement ambigu (modestie ? mélancolie ? dédain ?). C'est la conséquence directe de sa représentation de profil, la moitié du visage plongée dans l'obscurité, le regard baissé. Le costume « espagnol », anachronique, est composé de manches à crevés et d'un corsage taillé en V d'un bleu vibrant et ostentatoire, tant et si bien que l'identité du sujet passe au second plan par rapport à cet étalage de vêtements et de chair. Au cours de sa carrière, Courtin peignit de nombreuses figures de fantaisie féminines empreintes d'érotisme. Sa *Jeune Femme devant un miroir* (1713), propriété de l'éminent collectionneur d'art Pierre Crozat (Saint-Pétersbourg, musée de l'Ermitage), représente une autre femme en décolleté, la tête inclinée, en train de s'admirer, soucieuse de son apparence. Parmi ses autres portraits de femmes se trouvent *Porcie* (propriété du duc de Conti ; gravée par Claude Duclos), une *Vestale* (Saint-Pétersbourg, musée de l'Ermitage) et une *Femme astronome avec un globe et un compas* (Londres, Sotheby's, 02/05/2015, n° 160). Lors du Salon de 1737, Courtin exposa une *Jeune Femme badinant avec un écureuil* et, en 1740, un tableau de fantaisie d'une jeune *Prêtresse de Vénus tenant une colombe* (gravée par Michel Aubert). Occasionnellement, Courtin s'aventurait dans un domaine plus ouvertement sexuel, à l'instar du bachique et phallique *Jeu de bilboquet* (coll. part.). Les gravures réalisées d'après les portraits de fantaisie de Courtin étaient très populaires : les frères François et Jean-Baptiste de Poilly gravèrent au moins vingt-six de ses tableaux avant leur décès, survenus respectivement en 1723 et 1728. Ces gravures connurent une seconde vague de popularité lorsque le *Mercure de France* annonça en septembre 1735 la publication de « quatre Estampes en demi Figures, nommées vulgairement Fantaisies, gravées par le sieur Michel Aubert » et promit de nouvelles gravures. Par son exploration de la sémiotique du désir, Courtin préfigure la sensualité de Boucher et l'intensité psychologique de Greuze. **MP**

78

Alexis Grimou

(Argenteuil, 1678 – Paris, 1733)

Étude de jeune fille

H.s.t. ; H. 0,72 ; L. 0,59
Toulouse, musée des Augustins,
inv. Ro 691

Historique : Acquisition en 1892, legs Maury.
Bibliographie : Réau, 1930, t. II, p. 195-215 ; Lespinasse, 1937, p. 286-292 ; Marcus, 1976 ; Dufour, 1984.
Œuvres en rapport : *Jeune Femme en costume espagnol*, h.s.t., 0,80 × 0,64 m, Karlsruhe, Staatliche Kunsthalle, inv. 477 ; *Espagnolette*, h.s.t., 0,71 x 0,57 m, Prague, Narodni Galerie ; *Espagnolette*, h.s.t., 0,72 × 0,58 m, Avignon, musée Calvet, no 183, inv. 204 ; *Jeune Femme en costume de théâtre*, h.s.t., 0,73 × 0,59 m, Saint-Pétersbourg, musée de l'Ermitage, inv. 125 ; *La Marquise de la Salle*, h.s.t., 0,73 × 0,58 m, Auxerre, musée Leblanc-Duvernoy, inv. 24-I-22 ; *La Marquise de La Salle* dite *L'Espagnolette*, sanguine (trois crayons sur papier bleu, 0,35 × 0,29 m), galerie Éric Coatalem, *Œuvres sur papier et esquisses*, mars-avril 2005. Pendant : *Liseuse*, Toulouse, musée des Augustins, inv. Ro 690.

Biographie : *cf.* cat.20.

Alexis Grimou, *La Liseuse*, Toulouse, musée des Augustins

Il s'agit ici d'un exemple typique d'Espagnolette, genre de figure de fantaisie que Grimou a rendu populaire. Le terme « Espagnolette » vient du costume espagnol : toque en velours à plumes, col montant plissé, corsage émeraude et or et manches à crevés parées de bourrelets aux épaules, le tout complété d'une ample cape enveloppant le sujet. Le costume « espagnol » consistait en une sorte d'idéal esthétique situé entre peinture nordique, costumes de théâtre et traditions de romance chevaleresque telles qu'elles furent parodiées avec éloquence par Cervantes. Grimou commença à peindre des sujets « espagnols » – des figures féminines essentiellement – dans les années 1720. Le tableau conservé à Toulouse est une copie de l'Espagnolette de Karlsruhe, légèrement plus grande, signée et datée de 1731. Plusieurs autres répliques (Avignon, Prague, Saint-Pétersbourg, Auxerre) remontent à la même période. Grimou s'inspira probablement d'un modèle vivant (« il avoit soin de ne rien peindre, qu'il n'eût devant les yeux », vente Galloys, 15 mars 1764). Bien que la légende familiale suggère qu'il existe un lien entre le tableau d'Auxerre et la marquise de La Salle, les traits du sujet sont génériques comme dans ses autres tableaux et, par conséquent, n'évoquent pas un portrait traditionnel. La lumière dans la peinture de Toulouse a une teinte plus dorée que celle des tableaux en rapport, ce qui confère à l'œuvre un charme unique. La pose de la jeune femme est caractéristique de l'œuvre de Grimou : celle-ci adresse un regard au spectateur par-dessus son épaule. Le léger *contrapposto* évoque la danse ou bien un mouvement leste, effet renforcé par la ligne serpentine esquissée par la toque et le col, ainsi que par la position délicate de sa main gauche. La moitié du visage de la jeune femme est plongée dans la pénombre, ce qui donne à ses traits un caractère énigmatique à la manière de Rembrandt mais aussi des *Tenebrosi* de Rome et de Bologne. Fragonard était fasciné par les Espagnolettes de Grimou et réalisa le pastiche d'une jeune femme qu'il signa d'un autre nom (Dulwich Picture Gallery). De même, sa série de « figures de fantaisie » (vers 1767) s'est fortement inspirée des figures « espagnoles » de Grimou. À Toulouse comme à Karlsruhe, la fille « espagnole » va de pair avec une lectrice vêtue d'une robe d'époque (fig. ci-contre). Avec son mélange subtil de simplicité et de sophistication, l'Espagnolette de Toulouse dégage un air de mystère et de possibilités inexplorées. **MP**

Anonyme français du XVIIIe siècle

Portrait d'un acteur, ou d'un homme en costume de fantaisie, vers 1785

H.s.t. ; H. 0,91 ; L. 0,74
Nantes, musée des Beaux-Arts, inv. 725

Historique : Collection Cacault ; achat par la Ville de Nantes, 1810.
Bibliographie : Gerin-Pierre, 2005, nº 236, p. 208-209 ; Percival, 2012, p. 81.

Ce tableau représentant un homme en costume de fantaisie dont la stature imposante contraste avec son air songeur fut tout d'abord attribué à Carle Van Loo, dont les « espagnoleries » étaient en vogue en France au milieu du XVIIIe siècle. De légères faiblesses d'exécution (la main droite du personnage, par exemple, trop petite) font cependant pencher pour un artiste moins accompli, quelqu'un qui, probablement, appartenait au cercle du maître. La facture soignée de l'œuvre tout comme ses tonalités audacieuses suggèrent que la toile fut exécutée au plus tôt dans les années 1780, si ce n'est par Van Loo, du moins par quelqu'un de l'entourage de François-André Vincent, ou même d'Élisabeth Louise Vigée Le Brun. L'épée que porte le personnage rappelle la riche tradition des portraits de fantaisie mettant en scène des figures militaires : les *bravi* de la Renaissance vénitienne, les toiles des caravagesques, celles de Rembrandt et de ses disciples ainsi que les énigmatiques cuirassiers d'Alexis Grimou et les flamboyantes figures de fantaisie de Fragonard (*cf. Cavalier assis près d'une fontaine*, cat. 82). L'homme est vêtu avec élégance, dans un style espagnol aisément reconnaissable de ses contemporains. Il porte en outre une longue perruque flottante qui eût été à la mode au siècle précédent : l'anachronisme délibéré est le signe qu'il s'agit bien là d'une œuvre de fantaisie. Il est possible d'y voir une allusion à l'univers du théâtre à travers le caractère hybride du costume. Dans une étude inédite conservée au musée de Nantes, Maria Ines Aliverti établit un lien entre l'homme du tableau et Crispin, le valet intelligent et sans scrupules du théâtre français : mêmes chapeau, cape et pourpoint noirs, même fraise blanche amidonnée, mêmes gants et même épée. Certes, il arriva que Crispin fût représenté sous les traits d'un personnage à la fois sombre et corpulent : il suffit pour s'en convaincre de regarder *Comédiens français* de Watteau (1720, New York, The Metropolitan Museum of Art) ainsi que des portraits de Raymond Poisson et de Préville peints à la même époque. Cependant, dans le tableau conservé à Nantes, la représentation qui est faite du personnage est par trop elliptique et composite pour renvoyer avec certitude à un acteur ayant existé ou à un contexte spécifique. À l'image de son épée, l'homme se tient grand et droit. Tel le *Joueur de vielle* de Grimou (cat. 20), il donne le sentiment d'être une « personne de qualité ». Son embonpoint et son triple menton font de lui quelqu'un de trop gros pour être soldat et de trop indolent pour songer à brandir son épée ou à salir ses gants gris et élégants. De nombreux éléments de sa parure sont en métal ouvragé : la broche sur le chapeau, les boutons, la poignée de l'épée et la chaîne quelque peu insolite qui s'étale sur sa poitrine. Tout se passe comme si l'armure protectrice avait été transformée en un ensemble purement ornemental, emblème d'une vie consacrée aux plaisirs plutôt qu'à la guerre. Les étoffes sont riches et soyeuses, et des touches de rouge distribuées çà et là viennent éclabousser les contrastes de blanc et de noir. En dépit de la beauté de l'œuvre et de sa puissance d'évocation, il est bien difficile de ne pas y voir la représentation d'une aristocratie trop gâtée et désormais inutile, que la Révolution viendra bientôt balayer. **MP**

Giambattista Tiepolo

(Venise, 1696 – Madrid, 1770)

Tête de vieillard, vers 1752

H.s.t. ; H. 0,65 ; L. 0,51
Wurzbourg, Martin von Wagner Museum der Universität, inv. F80(K136)

Historique : Ancien fonds du musée.
Expositions : Venise, 1983 ; Diane De Grazia *in* New York, 1996-1997, p. 255-261 ; Paris, 1998-1999, p. 187-193 ; Barcelone, 2006, nº 51, p. 107.
Bibliographie : Gernin, Pedrocco, 2002, nº 72, p. 515.

Tiepolo incarne la quintessence du peintre de fantaisie de la Venise du XVIIIᵉ siècle, célèbre pour une maîtrise de l'espace à couper le souffle et sa recherche de l'effet produit par la lumière naturelle. Il a travaillé à la fresque et sur toile, exécutant des commandes mythologiques et religieuses pour le doge et autres notables vénitiens. Parmi ses plus belles œuvres, on compte les plafonds de la résidence de Wurzbourg, peints entre 1750 et 1753. On considère que son imagination a trouvé son expression la plus libre dans ses eaux-fortes, les *Capricci* (vers 1740-1742) et *Scherzi di fantasia* (1743-1757).

L'attribution de ce portrait divise les experts car il est peut-être de la main du fils de Giambattista, Giandomenico. Pedrocco et Gernin le classent dans leur catalogue raisonné de Tiepolo père dans la rubrique des « œuvres attribuées », de quoi semer le doute. Mais aucun argument ne l'emporte et cela reste sans conséquence sur cette exposition. Nous avons ici un exemple exceptionnel d'une tête d'Oriental, très prisée par les collectionneurs vénitiens, comme en produisaient, entre autres, les fils de Giambattista, Giandomenico et Lorenzo, mais aussi Pittoni, Nogari et Fontebasso. De telles œuvres ont également inspiré Fragonard lors de sa visite à la Sérénissime (*cf.* cat. 81).

Tiepolo a peut-être commencé à peindre des têtes de vieillards dès le milieu des années 1740. Elles faisaient partie d'une production plus large de figures de fantaisie comprenant des femmes sensuelles (par exemple, *Jeune Femme au perroquet*, fig. page 24) et des jeunes garçons (ainsi *Garçon tenant un livre*, New Orleans Museum of Art). Inspirées par Giorgione, Titien et les exemples plus récents de Piazzetta et Rosalba Carriera, les figures de fantaisie de Tiepolo ont été mentionnées dans les écrits contemporains comme « teste a capriccio ». Leur but était de capter les traits généraux d'une personne au moyen d'une pose et d'un visage expressifs, de vêtements exotiques et d'un attribut occasionnel. Certaines têtes de vieillards de Tiepolo ont peut-être été peintes pour une série, mais il semblerait que la demande du marché ait dépassé rapidement toute commande unique. En 1757, Giandomenico commençait à travailler sur deux livres d'eaux-fortes de têtes de vieillards intitulés *Raccolta di teste* et basés sur une vingtaine de peintures de son père. Les deux fils peignirent de nombreuses têtes de vieillards, soit des copies des œuvres paternelles, soit leurs propres compositions. En outre, près de quatre cents dessins de vieillards à l'encre, au lavis et à la pierre noire peuvent également être attribués à l'atelier des Tiepolo.

Comme Fragonard, Tiepolo s'inspire dans ce tableau des représentations traditionnelles des philosophes classiques, des prophètes de l'Ancien Testament et des apôtres. Il travaille dans la même veine que Rembrandt et Castiglione mais de façon à faire ressortir le thème de la fantaisie. Le sujet est hybride, une sorte de sage idéal, traité avec sincérité, mais aussi avec une touche d'humour. Ses traits sont exagérés : les yeux sont enfoncés, le regard est intense, le froncement de sourcils, soucieux. La barbe est épaisse et touffue, le poil, hirsute et rebelle, suggérant les détours de la pensée elle-même. Le costume de fantaisie est également un peu caricatural : large turban, plein de mouvement et d'effets, col raide bien qu'ondulé, riche en détails d'or et de rouge, toutes ces caractéristiques relevant autant de l'imagination de l'artiste que de celle du personnage. **MP**

81

Jean-Honoré Fragonard

(Grasse, 1732 – Paris, 1806)

Tête de vieillard

H.s.t. ; H. 0,53 ; L. 0,42
Tableau ovale à l'origine
Paris, Institut de France,
musée Jacquemart-André,
inv. MJAP-P 1232

Historique : Collection F. de Villars jusqu'en 1867 ; collection E. André ; legs Mme André à l'Institut de France, 1912.
Expositions : Paris/New York, 1987-1988, n° 98, p. 203-204 ; Barcelone, 2006, n° 46, p. 102-103.
Bibliographie : Cuzin, 1988, n° 106 ; S. Join Lambert *in* Strasbourg/Tours, 2003, n° D.

Jean-Honoré Fragonard, *Portrait d'un homme*, Chicago, Chicago Art Institute

Incarnant l'éclat du rococo français, l'œuvre de Fragonard est une exploration de la fantaisie et de l'imaginaire. Élève de François Boucher et lauréat du prix de Rome, Fragonard étudia à l'École royale des élèves protégés avant de sillonner l'Italie. Son tableau *Le grand prêtre Corésus se sacrifie pour sauver Callirhoé* (1765, Paris, musée du Louvre) lui valut d'être admis à l'Académie royale, mais il abandonna par la suite la peinture historique pour se consacrer à des commandes privées de moindre envergure. Artiste prolifique et polyvalent, Fragonard est connu pour ses scènes de genre érotiques et sa touche impétueuse, proche de celle de l'esquisse.

Ce tableau est généralement considéré comme étant la tête de vieillard la plus vénitienne de toutes celles peintes par Fragonard ; dans l'esprit, elle est proche de la superbe tête de Giambattista Tiepolo présentée dans cette exposition (cat. 80). Sa composition remonte probablement au début des années 1760 et non à 1769. Fragonard se rendit à Venise en 1761, et certains indices visuels suggèrent qu'il était au fait de la véritable ligne de production en série de « teste di fantasia » qui vit le jour dans l'atelier de Tiepolo au milieu des années 1750, et fut perpétuée à travers la peinture et la gravure par ses fils Giandomenico et Lorenzo. Sur la toile de Fragonard, on peut observer de petites touches de peinture rouge sur le nez, des rehauts blancs et une barbe peinte par empâtement rappelant quelque peu la *Tête de philosophe* attribuée à Giandomenico Tiepolo (1758-1764, Chicago Art Institute). Outre les comparaisons directes, ce qui est frappant dans l'œuvre de Fragonard, c'est qu'il se soit consacré avec ferveur à un type et un idiome que d'autres artistes tels que Nogari, Fontebassso et Pittoni ont également embrassés. Il s'agissait là d'un mélange entre philosophes classiques et prophètes de l'Ancien Testament, dans lequel l'influence de Rembrandt et de Castiglione est palpable. Ces patriarches barbus symbolisaient la sagesse antique, mais d'une manière plus fantasque que didactique. Le vieillard de Fragonard porte un costume « oriental » orné de broderies et de galons d'or ; le médaillon sur sa poitrine arbore un « F », signature de l'artiste. Fragonard peignit et dessina de nombreuses autres têtes de vieillards, principalement dans les années 1760 (à voir par exemple à Hambourg, Kunsthalle, et Nice, musée Chéret). Elles furent identifiées de diverses manières dans des documents contemporains comme des têtes de philosophes ou de saints (saint Jérôme, saint Pierre) et considérées comme peintes à la manière de Rembrandt. L'influence de peintres bolonais tels que le Guerchin et Guido Reni est, elle aussi, flagrante (ainsi à Amiens, musée de la Picardie). La capacité de Fragonard à pasticher avec talent non seulement d'autres artistes mais aussi ses propres toiles est manifeste dans son *Portrait d'un homme* (fig. ci-contre), qui fait partie d'une de ses célèbres séries de « figures de fantaisie » et qui semble être une version caricaturale du même modèle que le *Cavalier assis près d'une fontaine* (cat. 82), arborant une cape et un col haut similaires.

MP

82

Jean-Honoré Fragonard

(Grasse, 1732 – Paris, 1806)

Cavalier assis près d'une fontaine, traditionnellement *Jean-Claude Richard, l'abbé de Saint-Non, habillé à l'espagnole*, vers 1769

H.s.t. ; H. 0,94 ; L 0,74
Barcelone, MNAC, Museu Nacional d'Art de Catalunya, inv. 65010

Historique : Vente [*dit* Varanchan de Saint Geniès], 29-31 décembre 1777, n° 16, « Un cavalier vêtu à l'Espagnol. Il est assis près d'une fontaine, et tient la bride de son cheval qui se désaltère ; ébauche librement touchée [...] » ; vente De Ghendt, 15 novembre 1779, n° 599 [...] Legs Francesc Cambó, 1949.
Expositions : Barcelone, 2006, n° 53, p. 110-111 ; Paris, 2007-2008, n° 53.
Bibliographie : Percival, 2012 ; Blumenfeld, 2013 ; Dupuy-Vachey, 2015, p. 241-247.
Œuvre en rapport : *Esquisses de portraits*, encre bistre et pierre noire sur papier vergé, 0,23 × 0,35 m, Drouot, 1er juin 2012, salle 14, n° 145, collection particulière.

Biographie : *cf.* cat. 81.

Il s'agit de l'un des portraits de l'éblouissante série de quelque seize « figures de fantaisie » de Fragonard, représentant des sujets masculins et féminins en costumes « espagnols », exécutée aux environs de 1769. Au début du XXe siècle, Pierre de Nolhac estima qu'il s'agissait d'un portrait du mécène de Fragonard, l'abbé de Saint-Non, figurant dans l'un des autres tableaux de la série (Paris, musée du Louvre). En 2012, un dessin constitué de plusieurs croquis de Fragonard fit son apparition sur le marché de l'art parisien. Sous chacun des croquis des figures de fantaisie connues de l'auteur se trouvent des noms qui remettent en question nos certitudes sur de nombreux points. Interprétant la légende à peine lisible du croquis du *Cavalier assis près d'une fontaine*,

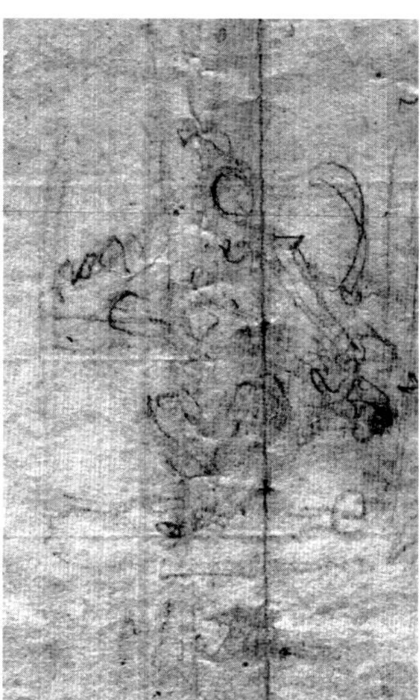

Jean-Honoré Fragonard, *Esquisses de portraits* (détail), collection particulière

Carole Blumenfeld a émis l'hypothèse qu'il s'agissait du portrait du peintre et architecte Michel-Ange Challe. Ces identifications restent toutefois de l'ordre de la spéculation et, quelle que soit l'identité du modèle, l'exactitude de la ressemblance ne figure guère au rang des préoccupations de Fragonard. Contrairement à ses autres figures de fantaisie, le cavalier est représenté devant un parapet. Comme le suggère la description de la vente de 1777, il s'agit d'un personnage traité sur le mode de la fiction, peut-être peint lors d'une halte au cours d'un voyage, mais le traitement en est léger et audacieux. Appuyé sur son épée, il arbore la fraise, les plumes, les gants et le médaillon caractéristiques du costume « espagnol », qui renforcent la dimension imaginaire du tableau. La figure occupe un espace tridimensionnel dynamique où se croisent des arcs. Une impression de déséquilibre naît du point de vue *da sotto in sù*, de l'inclinaison exagérée de son corps ainsi que de ses atours. Sa tunique vermeille et son écharpe jaune contrastent avec les bruns ocre de la partie inférieure de son corps et de l'arrière-plan à peine esquissé. Les énergiques coups de pinceau renforcent une impression de mouvement et témoignent d'une exécution rapide. Le dessin récemment découvert a permis une nouvelle révélation : l'existence de trois autres portraits en pied réalisés par Fragonard, de taille et de composition similaires au *Cavalier assis près d'une fontaine*, qui un jour pourraient être retrouvés. **MP**

83

Johan Zoffany

(Francfort-sur-le-Main, 1733 – Londres, 1810)

Autoportrait à la palette, vers 1778

H.s.t. ; H. 0, 70 ; L. 0,56
Inscription au verso : *Imago Eqvitis Ioannis Zofani ab eodem picta et Academiae Etruscor Cortonen. D.D. Anno Pvbl. Salvtis M DCC LXXVIII Mense Aprili*
Cortone, Museo dell'Accademia Etrusca (MAEC), inv. 002707

Historique : Don de l'artiste en avril 1778.
Expositions : New Haven/Londres, 2011-2012.
Bibliographie : Pressly, 1987, p. 88-101 ; Treadwell, 2009, p. 268, 281-282 ; Webster, 2011.

Johan Zoffany, *Autoportrait*, Florence, Galleria degli Uffizi

Originaire de Bohême, Zoffany partit pour l'Angleterre en 1760 et fit une brillante carrière en peignant des portraits d'individus ou de grands groupes, des *conversation pieces*, ainsi que des figures de fantaisie. Immortalisant des scènes dramatiques allant du milieu londonien à la Révolution française, sa peinture est saisissante, pleine d'humour tout en étant empreinte d'émotion. Ayant ses entrées en Angleterre et sur le continent, il fut nommé par le roi George III à la Royal Academy of Arts en 1769. Il séjourna ultérieurement à Florence et en Inde.

Cet autoportrait excentrique fut présenté à l'Académie étrusque en 1778 lorsque Zoffany en devint membre. Il fut probablement peint à Florence, où il avait passé les six années précédentes. James Northcote qualifia ce tableau de « fort médiocre » (lettre du 5 juillet 1779), mais ce jugement péremptoire ne rend pas justice au caractère inventif et audacieux de cette toile ou à la riche exploration du genre de l'autoportrait que fit Zoffany tout au long de sa carrière. Ses œuvres de jeunesse telles que son *Autoportrait en David avec la tête de Goliath* (vers 1756, Melbourne, National Gallery of Victoria) illustrent comment Zoffany superposait par jeu ses propres traits à ceux d'un personnage de peinture d'histoire, dans l'esprit du Caravage et de Rembrandt. Le visage de Zoffany apparaît dans certains de ses portraits de groupe, comme *Les Académiciens de l'Académie royale* et *La Tribune des Offices* (respectivement 1772 et 1772-1777, Windsor, Royal Collection), où il détonne particulièrement parmi les autres artistes et dignitaires. La personnalité excentrique de Zoffany est plus marquée dans son autoportrait de 1776 (fig. ci-contre), où il apparaît sous les traits d'un Démocrite grimaçant entouré des symboles de la mortalité, de l'art et de la mondanité. L'autoportrait de Cortone suit de près le tableau de Florence, bien que la figure soit plus narquoise. Zoffany porte son habituelle blouse d'artiste ornée de fourrure et tient une palette et des pinceaux, attributs que l'on retrouve typiquement dans ses autoportraits. Son chapeau est une création imposante et improbable toute de fourrure et de plumes, perché de guingois sur sa tête et orné de ce qui pourrait être l'insigne de l'Académie. Ses cheveux longs et négligés lui tombent dans le dos. Les sourcils fournis et les plis du cou constituent un étalage de chair peu flatteur qui peut être interprété comme une subversion des autoportraits de Dürer, dans lesquels la nudité est virile et sensuelle. Sur le fermoir de sa blouse, on peut lire la maxime suivante : « Col tempo / Si spera » (« Avec le temps / On espère »), peut-être une référence au désir de tout artiste de finir par atteindre la grandeur. Alors que le regard de Zoffany se porte à mi-distance, la toile exsude le pathos, mais demande à ne pas être prise trop au sérieux. Zoffany a poussé la moquerie personnelle à un tout autre niveau dans un autoportrait ultérieur (1779, Parme) en se représentant affublé d'un habit de moine et tiraillé entre poursuites spirituelles et terrestres. Ce type d'autoportrait expérimental peut aussi être replacé dans le contexte des académies et des sociétés informelles des artistes italiens, comme on peut le voir dans l'autoportrait de Lomazzo en Bacchus (cat. 43). **MP**

Annexes

INDEX DES ARTISTES EXPOSÉS

BIBLIOGRAPHIE

Aikema, 1994
Bernard Aikema, « Titian's Mary Magdalen in the Palazzo Pitti: An Ambiguous Painting and Its Critics », *Journal of the Warburg and Courtauld Institutes*, vol. 57, 1994.

Aikema, Brown, 1999
Bernard Aikema, Beverly Louise Brown, *Renaissance Venice and the North: Crosscurrents in the Time of Durer, Bellini and Titian*, Londres, 1999.

Allerston, 1999
Patricia Allerston, « Reconstructing the Second-Hand Clothes Trade in Sixteenth and Seventeenth Century Venice », *Costume*, vol. 33, 1999.

Anderson, 1979
Jaynie Anderson, « The Giorgionesque Portrait: From Likeness to Allegory », *Giorgione: atti del Convegno internazionale di studio per il 5° centenario della nascita, 29-31 maggio 1978*, Venise, 1979.

Anelli, 1996
Luciano Anelli, *Pietro Bellotti, 1625-1700*, Brescia, 1996.

Anonyme, 1780
Anonyme [Jean-Baptiste Gabriel Alexandre Grosier ?], « Gravure », *Journal de littérature, des sciences et des arts*, n° 3, 1780.

Ballarin, 1994-1995
Alessandro Ballarin, *Dosso Dossi : La Pittura a Ferrara negli anni del ducato di Alfonso I*, 2 vol., Padoue, 1994-1995.

Bancel, 2008
André Bancel, *Jean-Baptiste Deshays, 1729-1765*, Paris, 2008.

Barker, 2005
Emma Barker, *Greuze and the Painting of Sentiment*, Cambridge, 2005.

Barker, 2007
Emma Barker, « Mme Geoffrin, Painting and Galanterie: Carle Van Loo's "Conversation Espagnole" and "Lecture Espagnole" », *Eighteenth-Century Studies* 40, n° 4, 2007.

Barker, 2009
Emma Barker, « Imaging Childhood in Eighteenth-Century France: Greuze's *Little Girl with a Dog* », *The Art Bulletin*, 91/4, décembre 2009.

Baskind, 2007
Samantha Baskind, « Distinguishing the Distinction: Picturing Ashkenazi and Sephardic Jews in Seventeenth- and Eighteenth-Century Amsterdam », *The Journal for the Study of Sephardic and Mizrahi Jewry*, février 2007.

Baum, 1980
Elfriede Baum, *Katalog des österreichischen Barockmuseums im Unteren Belvedere in Wien* – II, Vienne, 1980.

Beherman, 1988
Thierry Beherman, *Godfried Schalcken*, Paris, 1988.

Bellori, 2005
Giovan Pietro Bellori, *The Lives of the Modern Painters, Sculptors and Architects*, traduit et édité par Alice Sedgewick Wohl, Hellmut Wohl et Tomaso Montanari, [Rome, 1672], New York, 2005.

Belting, 2007
Hans Belting, *Image et culte*, Paris, 2007.

Ben-Aryeh Debby, 2003
Nirit Ben-Aryeh Debby, « Titian's Pitti Magdalen », *Woman's Art Journal*, vol. 24, n° 1, printemps-été 2003.

Benedict, 2002
Barbara Benedict, *Curiosity: A Cultural History of Early Modern Inquiry*, Chicago, 2002.

Benito Doménech, 2003
Fernando Benito Doménech, *Museu de Belles Arts de València. Obra selecta*, Valence, 2003.

Berckenhagen, Poensgen, 1958
Ekhart Berckenhagen, Georg Poensgen, *Antoine Pesne*, Berlin, 1958.

Berdini, 1998
Paolo Berdini, « Women Under the Gaze: a Renaissance Genealogy », *Art History*, vol. 21, n° 4, décembre 1998.

Bergamini, 1983
Giuseppe Bergamini, « Antonio Carneo », *Allgemeines Künstlerlexikon*, Leipzig, 1983.

Bergamini, Goi, 1995
Giuseppe Bergamini, Paolo Goi, éd., *Antonio Carneo e il suo tempo. Atti della giornata di studio, 26 marzo 1993*, Portogruaro, 1995.

Bernardini, 1987
Carla Bernardini, *La Pinacoteca Nazionale di Bologna. Catalogo generale delle opere esposte*, Bologne, 1987.

Biagi Maino, 1990
Donatalla Biagi Maino, *Ubaldo Gandolfi*, Turin, 1990.

Bignamini, 1988
Ilaria Bignamini, « Art Institutions in London, 1689-1768: A Study of Clubs and Academies », *The Walpole Society*, LIV, 1988.

Bikker, 2005
Jonathan Bikker, *Willem Drost (1633-1659). A Rembrandt Pupil in Amsterdam and in Venice*, New Haven/Londres, 2005.

Bistort, 1912
Giulio Bistort, *Il magistrato alle pompe nella repubblica di Venezia*, Venise, 1912.

Black, 2014
Peter Black, « A Rubens Tronie of an "Old Man with Curly Beard" in Glasgow. The Life and Afterlife of a Head Study Painting », *in* Dagmar Hirschfelder, León Krempel, éd., *Tronies. Das Gesicht in der Frühen Neuzeit*, Berlin, 2014.

Blankert, 1967
Albert Blankert, « Heraclitus en Democritus in het bijzonder in de Nederlandse kunst van de zeventiende eeuw », *Nederlands Kunsthistorisch Jaarboek*, n° 18, 1967.

Bloch, 1968
Vitale Bloch, *Michiel Sweerts*, La Haye, 1968.

Bloemaert, 1740
Abraham Bloemaert, *Oorspronkelyk -en vermaard konstryk tekenboek*, Amsterdam, 1740.

Blumenfeld, 2013
Carole Blumenfeld, *Une facétie de Fragonard. Les révélations d'un dessin retrouvé*, Paris, 2013.

Boccardo, 2004
Piero Boccardo, *L'Età di Rubens*, Milan, 2004.

Bologna, 1958
Ferdinando Bologna, *Francesco Solimena*, Naples, 1958.

Börsch-Supan, 1977
Helmut Börsch-Supan, « Antoine Pesne and His School », *Apollo*, CVI, n° 186, 1977.

Bos, 2010
Jacques Bos, « Between Physiognomy and Pathognomy: Theoretical Perspectives on the Representation of Characters and Emotions in the Seventeenth Century », *in* K. Van der Stighelen, B. Watteeuw, éd., *Pokerfaced? Flemish and Dutch Baroque Faces Revealed*, Turnhout, 2010.

Bowron, 2007
Edgar Peters Bowron, *Pompeo Batoni: Prince of Painters in Eighteenth-Century Rome*, New Haven/Londres, 2007.

Brejon, Volle, 1988
Arnauld Brejon de Lavergnée, Nathalie Volle, *Musées de France. Répertoire des peintures italiennes du XVIIᵉ siècle*, Paris, 1988.

Brejon, de Wambrechies, 2001
Arnauld Brejon de Lavergnée, Annie Scottez de Wambrechies, *Catalogue du musée des Beaux-Arts de Lille, sommaire illustré des peintures – II École française*, Paris, 2001.

Bulgarelli, 1973
Maria Angela Bulgarelli, « Profilo di Domenico Maggiotto », *Arte Veneta*, XXVII, 1973.

Bushart, Rupprecht, 1986
Bruno Bushart, Bernhard Rupprecht, éd., *Cosmas Damian Asam, 1686-1739. Leben und Werk*, Munich, 1986.

Bryson, 1981
Norman Bryson, *Word and Image: French Painting in the Ancien Régime*, Cambridge, 1981.

Campbell, 1990
Lorne Campbell, *Renaissance Portraits: European Portrait Painting in the Fourteenth, Fifteenth and Sixteenth Centuries*, New Haven/Londres, 1990.

Canova, 1963
Giordana Canova, *Paris Bordon*, Venise, 1963.

Cardiff, 1955
Cardiff, *National Museum of Wales. Catalogue of Oil Paintings*, 1955.

Caulfield, 1819
James Caulfield, *Portraits, memoirs, and characters, of remarkable persons: from the revolution in 1688 to the end of the reign of George II: collected from the most authentic accounts extant*, Londres, 1819.

Chiappini, 1987
Rudy Chiappini, *Serodine. L'Opera completa*, Milan, 1987.

Chiarini, 1984
Marco Chiarini, « Un attribuzione al Ceruti », *Scritte di storia dell'arte in onore di Roberto Salvini*, Florence, 1984.

Chiarini, Padovani, 2003
Marco Chiarini, Serena Padovani, *La Galleria Palatina e gli Appartamenti Reali di Palazzo Pitti. Catalogo dei dipinti – II*, Florence, 2003.

Christiansen, Mann, 2001
Keith Christiansen, Judith W. Mann, *Orazio and Artemisia Gentileschi*, New York/New Haven, 2001.

Chu, 2014
John Chu, *The Fortunes of Fancy Painting in Eighteenth-Century England*, thèse de doctorat, Courtauld Institute, université de Londres, 2014.

Conisbee, 2007
Philip Conisbee, éd., *French Genre Painting in the Eighteenth Century*, New Haven/Londres, 2007.

Contini, 2012
Roberto Contini, « Un modello dall'antico per la "Ragazza col vassoio di frutta" », *Studi tizianeschi*, VIII, 2012.

Coryat, 1611
Thomas Coryat, *Coryats Crudities*, Londres, 1611.

Cros, 2000
Philippe Cros, *Fondation Bemberg. Peintures anciennes, de Cranach à Tiepolo*, Paris, 2000.

Crow, 2000
Thomas E. Crow, *La peinture et son public à Paris au XVIIIᵉ siècle*, Paris, 2000.

Cuzin, 1988
Jean-Pierre Cuzin, *Jean-Honoré Fragonard. Vie et œuvre. Catalogue complet des peintures*, Fribourg, 1988.

Cuzin, 2013
Jean-Pierre Cuzin, *François-André Vincent (1746-1816). Entre Fragonard et David*, Paris, 2013.

Dal Pozzolo, 1993
Enrico Maria Dal Pozzolo, « Il lauro di Laura e delle "maritate venetian" », *Mitteilungen des Kunsthistorischen Institutes in Florenz*, vol. 37, nᵒ 2-3, 1993.

Damian, 2011
Véronique Damian, *De Paris Bordon à Pompeo Batoni. Un parcours dans la peinture italienne*, Paris, 2011.

D'Hulst, 1982
R.-A. D'Hulst, *Jacob Jordaens*, Anvers, 1982.

De Clippel, 2006
Karolien De Clippel, *Joos van Craesbeeck (1605/06-ca. 1660). Een Brabants Genreschilder*, Turnhout, 2006.

De Maio, 1982
Romeo De Maio, « The Counter-Reformation and Painting in Naples », *in* Clovis Whitfield, Jane Martineau, éd., *Painting in Naples from Caravaggio to Giordano*, Londres, 1982.

De Pauw de Veen, 1969
Lydia De Pauw de Veen, *De begrippen « schilder », « schilderij » en « schilderen » in de zeventiende eeuw*, Bruxelles, palais des Académies, 1969.

Debaisieux, 1994
Françoise Debaisieux, *Caen, musée des Beaux-Arts*, Paris, 1994.

Del Re, 2013
Sonia Del Re, *Re-forming Images: Utrecht, Caravaggio, and the Body*, thèse, université McGill, 2013.

Della Pergola, 1955
P. Della Pergola, *Galleria Borghese. I dipinti*, Rome, 1955.

Destot, 1994
Marcel Destot, *Peintures des écoles du Nord. La Collection du musée de Grenoble*, Paris, 1994.

Dézallier d'Argenville, 1745
Antoine-Joseph Dézallier d'Argenville, *Abrégé de la vie des plus fameux peintres... Deuxième partie*, Paris, 1745.

Dézallier d'Argenville, 1752
Antoine-Joseph Dézallier d'Argenville, *Abrégé de la vie des plus fameux Peintres : troisième partie*, Paris, 1752.

Dézallier d'Argenville, 1762
Antoine-Joseph Dézallier d'Argenville, *Abrégé de La Vie Des plus Fameux Peintres : Tome Quatrième*, Paris, 1762.

Diderot, le Rond d'Alembert, 1751-1772
Denis Diderot, Jean le Rond d'Alembert, éd., *Encyclopédie* ou *Dictionnaire raisonné des sciences, des arts et des métiers, par une société de gens de lettres*, 28 vol., Paris, 1751-1772.

Diderot, 1983
Denis Diderot, *Salons*, 3 vol., Oxford, 1983.

Donati, 2014
Andrea Donati, *Paris Bordone. Catalogo ragionato*, Soncino, 2014.

Donzelli, 1957
Carlo Donzelli, *I pittore veneti del Settecento*, Florence, 1957.

Dubos, 1770
Jean-Baptiste Dubos, *Réflexions critiques sur la poésie et sur la peinture*, 1719, 7e éd., Paris, 1770.

Dufour, 1984
Philippe Dufour, *Alexis Grimou, 1678-1733*, mémoire de maîtrise, université de Toulouse Le Mirail, 1984.

Dupuy-Vachey, 2015
Marie-Anne Dupuy-Vachey, « Fragonard's Fantasy Figures: Prelude to a New Understanding », *The Burlington Magazine*, CLVII, avril 2015.

Dussieux, Sulié *et al.*, 1854
Louis-Étienne Dussieux, Eudore Sulié *et al.*, *Mémoires inédites sur la vie et les ouvrages des membres de l'Académie Royale*, Paris, 1854.

Ewald *et alii*, 1992
Gerhard Ewald, Edeltraud Rettich, Rüdiger Klapproth, *Staatsgalerie Stuttgart Alte Meister*, 1992.

Faré, 1966
Michel Faré, « Un peintre indépendant : Jacques Courtin de l'Académie royale, 1672-1752 », *Gazette des beaux-arts*, mai-juin 1966.

Feigenbaum, 1976-1977
Gail Feigenbaum, « Head Studies by Balthasar Denner », *Allen Memorial Art Museum Bulletin, Oberlin College*, vol. 34, 1976-1977.

Ferrari, Scavizzi, 1992
Oreste Ferrari, Giuseppe Scavizzi, *Luca Giordano*, Naples, 1992.

Fiozzi, 2004
David Fiozzi, *Les Tableaux hollandais des XVIIe et XVIIIe siècles du musée des Augustins. Catalogue raisonné*, Toulouse, 2004.

Fletcher, 1901
Ernest Fletcher, *Conversations of James Northcote R. A. with James Ward on Art and Artists*, Londres, 1901.

Fornari Schianchi, Spinosa, 2004
Lucia Fornari Schianchi, Nicola Sponosa, *Luce sul Settecento. Gaspare Traversi e l'arte del suo tempo in Emilia*, Naples, 2004.

Frangi, 2013
Francesco Frangi, *Di pinti in Valpadanatra Medioevo e Rinascimento Studi al Museo di Belle Arti di Budapest in ricordo di Miklós Boskovits*, avril 2013.

Fried, 1990
Michael Fried, *La Place du spectateur. Esthétique et origines de la peinture moderne*, Paris, 1990.

Fried, 1996
Michael Fried, *Le Modernisme de Manet*, Paris, 1996.

Fried, 2010
Michael Fried, *The Moment of Caravaggio*, Princeton, 2010.

Garas, 1973
Klára Garas, *The Budapest Gallery: Paintings in the Museum of Fine Arts*, Budapest, 1973.

Garas, 1981
Klára Garas, « Christian Seybold und das Malerbildnis in Österreich im 18. Jahrhundert », *Bulletin des musées hongrois des Beaux-Arts*, Budapest, nº 50, 1980.

Gaskell, 1990
Ivan Gaskell, *The Thyssen-Bornemisza Collection. Seventeenth Century Dutch and Flemish Painting*, Londres, 1990.

Gaston-Dreyfus, 1923
Philippe Gaston-Dreyfus, *Catalogue raisonné de l'œuvre peint et dessiné de Nicolas-Bernard Lépicié, 1735-1784*, Paris, 1923.

George, 1949
M. Dorothy George, *Catalogue of Political and Personal Satires in the British Museum* – IX, Londres, 1949.

Gerin-Pierre, 2005
Claire Gerin-Pierre, *Musée des Beaux-Arts de Nantes. Catalogue des peintures françaises XVIe-XVIIIe siècles*, Paris, 2005.

Gernin, Pedrocco, 2002
Massimo Gernin, Filippo Pedrocco, *Giambattista Tiepolo: Dipinti, opera completa*, New York, 2002.

Gétreau, 1996
Florence Gétreau, « Les belles vielleuses au siècle de Louis XV. Peinture d'une mode triomphante », *in* Pierre Imbert, éd., *Vielle à roue : territoires illimités*, Nantes, 1996.

Gibbons, 1968
Felton Gibbons, *Dosso and Battista Dossi: Court Painters at Ferrara*, Princeton, 1968.

Goffen, 1997
Rona Goffen, *Titian's Women*, New Haven/Londres, 1997.

Gottwald, 2009
Franziska Gottwald, *Das Tronie. Muster – Studie – Meisterwerk: Die Genese einer Gattung der Malerei vom 15. Jahrhundert bis zu Rembrandt*, Munich, 2009.

Gregori, 1982
Mina Gregori, *Giacomo Ceruti, 1698-1767*, Milan, 1982.

Grimm, 1972
Claus Grimm, *Frans Hals: Entwicklung, Werkanalyse, Gesamtkatalog*, Berlin, 1972.

Grootenboer, 2010
Hanneke Grootenboer, « How to Become a Picture: Theatricality as Strategy in Seventeenth-Century Dutch Portraits », *Art History*, Londres, nº 33/2, avril 2010.

Groschner, Habersatter, Mayr-Oehring, 2002
Gabriele Groschner, Thomas Habersatter, Erika Mayr-Oehring, éd., *Masterworks. Residenzgalerie Salzburg*, Salzbourg, 2002.

Guadalupi, 2000-2001
Gianni Guadalupi, « Les Demoiselles de Peterhof : Pietro Rotari à St Petersburg », *FMR* (Franco Maria Ricci), nº 89, déc. 2000-janv. 2001.

Guillaume, 1980
Marguerite Guillaume, *Catalogue raisonné du musée des Beaux-Arts de Dijon. Peintures italiennes*, Dijon, 1980.

Habert, 1987
Jean Habert, *Bordeaux, musée des Beaux-Arts. Peinture italienne, XVe-XIXe siècles*, Paris, 1987.

Hagedorn (von), 1755
Christian Ludwig von Hagedorn, *Lettre à un amateur de la peinture avec des éclaircissemenns historiques sur un cabinet et les auteurs des tableaux qui les composent*, Dresde, 1755.

Hanfstaengl, 1939
Erika Hanfstaengl, *Cosmas Damian Asam*, Munich, 1939.

Hanson, 2003
Craig Hanson, « Dr Richard Mead and Watteau's "Comédiens italiens" », *The Burlington Magazine*, vol. 145, n° 1201, 2003.

Hattori, 2004
Cordélia Hattori, « Passeports délivrés à des artistes au XVIIIe siècle », *Les Cahiers d'histoire de l'art* 2, 2004.

Haug, 1955
Hans Haug, *La Peinture française au musée des Beaux-Arts de Strasbourg*, Strasbourg, 1955.

Heimbürger, 1988
Minna Heimbürger, *Bernardo Keilhau, detto Monsù Bernardo*, Rome, 1988.

Heinecken (von), 1790
Karl Heinrich von Heinecken, *Dictionnaire des artistes dont nous avons des Estampes : avec une notice détaillée de leurs ouvrages gravés*, Leipzig, 1790.

Helmus, Seelig, 2011
Liesbeth M. Helmus, Gero Seelig, « Artistic Series: an Utrecht Specialty », *The Bloemaert Effect: Color and Composition in the Golden Age*, Petersberg, 2011.

Hémery, 2003
Axel Hémery, *La peinture italienne au musée des Augustins*, Toulouse, 2003.

Hémery, 2010
Axel Hémery, « Nicolas Tournier », *Strinati/Zuccari*, II, 2010.

Hendra, 2007
Viv Hendra, *The Cornish Wonder: A Portrait of John Opie*, Truro, 2007.

Herlihy, 1980
David Herlihy, « Popolazione e Strutture Sociali dal XV al XVI Secolo », *Tiziano e Venezia: Convegno Internazionale di Studi, Venezia, 1976*, Vicence, 1980.

Hésiode, 2008
Hésiode, *Théogonie*, tr. P. Mazon, Paris, 2008.

Higgie, 2012
Jennifer Higgie, « A Life in a Day: The Fictitious Portraits of Lynette Yiadom-Boakye », *Frieze*, n° 46, avril 2012.

Hilaire, 2007
Michel Hilaire, *Le Musée Fabre*, Paris, 2007.

Hirschfelder, 2008
Dagmar Hirschfelder, *Tronie und Porträt in der niederländischen Malerei des 17. Jahrhunderts*, Berlin, 2008.

Hirschfelder, Krempel, 2013
Dagmar Hirshfelder, León Krempel, éd., *Tronies: Das Gesicht in der frühen Neuzeit*, Berlin, 2013.

Hirst, 1981
Michael Hirst, *Sebastiano del Piombo*, Oxford, 1981.

Honig, 1998
Elizabeth Honig, « Value in Display and the Aesthetic of Judgment », *Painting and the Market in Early Modern Antwerp*, New Haven, 1998.

Honour, 1957
Hugh Honour, « Giuseppe Nogari », *Connoisseur*, CXL, 1957.

Höper, 1998
Corinna Höper, *Meisterwerke der Kunsthalle Bremen – I Meiserwerke, Gemälde, Skulpturen und Neue Medien*, Brême, 1998.

Huys Jansen, 1998
Paul Huys Jansen, *Jan Van Bijlert. Catalogue raisonné*, Amsterdam/Philadelphie, 1998.

Ingamells, Raines, 1976-1978
John Ingamells, Robert Raines, « A Catalogue of the Paintings, Drawings and Etchings of Philip Mercier», *The Volume of the Walpole Society*, vol. 46, 1976-1978.

Jacoby, 2000
Joachim Jacoby, *Hans von Aachen 1552-1615*, Munich/Berlin, 2000.

Jacquot, 1994
Dominique Jacquot, *Alexis Grimou (1678-1733)*, mémoire de maîtrise, université Paris-Sorbonne, 1994.

Jansen, Meijer, Squellati Brizio, 2002
Guido Jansen, Bert W. Meijer, Paola Squellati Brizio, *Repertory of Dutch and Flemish Paintings in Italian Public Collections – II Lombardy 2 (MZ)*, Florence, 2002.

Jean-Richard, 1978
Pierrette Jean-Richard, *L'Œuvre gravé de François Boucher dans la collection Edmond de Rothschild du Louvre*, Paris, 1978.

Jeffares
Neil Jeffares, *Dictionary of Pastellists before 1800*, édition online : http://www.pastellists.com

Jensen Adams, 2009
Ann Jensen Adams, *Public Faces and Private Identities in Seventeenth-Century Holland: Portraiture and the Production of Community*, Cambridge, 2009.

Jones, 1981
Leslie Jones, *The Paintings of Giovanni Battista Piazzetta*, Ann Arbor, 1981.

Juffinger, 2010
Roswitha Juffinger, *Residenzgalerie Salzburg. Gesamtverzeichnis der Gemälde*, Salzbourg, 2010.

Junkerman, 1988
Anne Christine Junkerman, *Bellissima Donna: An Interdisciplinary Study of Venetian Sensuous Half-Length Images of the Early Sixteenth-Century*, thèse, université de Californie, Berkeley, 1988.

Junkerman, 1993
Anne Christine Junkerman, « The Lady and the Laurel », *Oxford Art Journal*, 16, n° 1, 1993.

Kirchner, 1991
Thomas Kirchner, *L'Expression des passions: Ausdruck als Darstellungsproblem in der französischen Kunst und Kunsttheorie des 17. und 18. Jahrhunderts*, Mayence, 1991.

Knox, 1992
George Knox, *Giambattista Piazzetta, 1682-1754*, Oxford, 1992.

Koortbojian, 1995
Michael Koortbojian, *Myth, Meaning, and Memory on Roman Sarcophagi*, Berkeley, 1995.

Koslow, 1975
Susan Koslow, « Frans Hals *Fisherboys*: Exemplars of Idleness », *The Art Bulletin*, LVII, 1975.

Kulterman, 1990
Udo Kulterman, « Woman Asleep and the Artist », *Artibus et Historiae*, vol. XI, n° 22, 1990.

Kultzen, 1996
Rolf Kultzen, *Michael Sweerts*, Doornspijk, 1996.

Labalme, 1981
Patricia H. Labalme, « Venetian Women on Women: Three Early Modern Feminists », *Archivio Veneto*, 117, 1981.

Land, 2003
Norman Land, « Veronica Franco, Tintoretto, and Narcissus », *Notes in the History of Art* 22, n° 2, hiver 2003.

Lastic (de), 1981
Georges de Lastic, « Nicolas de Largillière, documents notariés inédits », *Gazette des beaux-arts*, vol. XCVII, juillet-août 1981.

Laurenze-Landsberg, 2012
Claudia Laurenze-Landsberg, « La *Ragazza col vassoio di frutta*: indagini radiografiche e autoradiografiche al neutrone per un dipinto berlinese di Tiziano », *Studi tizianeschi*, 8, 2012.

Le Bihan, 1990
Olivier Le Bihan, *L'Or et l'Ombre. La Peinture hollandaise du XVII*e *et du XVIII*e *siècle au musée des Beaux-Arts de Bordeaux*, Bordeaux, 1990.

Lecarpentier, 1821
Charles-Jacques-François Lecarpentier, *Galerie des peintres célèbres*, 2 vol., Paris, 1821.

Ledbury, 2000
Mark Ledbury, *Greuze, Sedaine and Hybrid Genre*, Oxford, 2000.

Leribault, 2002
Christophe Leribault, *Jean-François de Troy (1679-1752)*, Paris, 2002.

Lesage, 1716
Alain-René Lesage, *The History and Adventures of Gil Blas of Santillane in two volumes*, Londres, 1716.

Lesage, 1942
Alain-René Lesage, *Gil Blas de Santillane*, Paris, 1942.

Lesné, 1988
Claude Lesné, « Jean-Baptiste Santerre, 1651-1717 », *Bulletin de la Société de l'histoire de l'art français*, 1988.

Lesné, Waro, 2011
Claude Lesné, Françoise Waro, *Jean-Baptiste Santerre (1651-1717)*, Cergy-Pontoise, 2011.

Lespinasse, 1937
M. P. Lespinasse, « Deux œuvres de Grimou », *Mémoires de l'Académie des sciences, inscriptions et belles-lettres de Toulouse*, douzième série, t. XV, 1937.

Lille, 1997
Lille, *Palais des Beaux-Arts, guide des collections*, Paris, 1997.

Lippincott, 1983
Louise Lippincott, *Selling Art in Georgian London: The Rise of Arthur Pond*, New Haven/Londres, 1983.

Longhi, 1928 (1967)
Roberto Longhi, *Precisioni nelle gallerie italiane. La Galleria Borghese*, Rome, 1928 (éd. 1967).

Longhi, 1934 (1975)
Roberto Longhi, *Officina ferrarese*, Rome, 1934 (éd. Florence, 1975).

Longhi, 1938
Roberto Longhi, « Monsù Bernardo », *Critica d'arte*, 1938.

Mann, 1999
Judith Mann, « Pietro Rotari's *Young Woman with a Sprig of Jasmine* », *in* Norman E. Land, éd., *The Samuel H. Kress Study Collection at the University of Missouri*, Columbia, 1999.

Mannings, Postle, 2000
David Mannings, Martin Postle, *Sir Joshua Reynolds. A Complete Catalogue of his Paintings*, New Haven/Londres, 2000.

Mansfield, 2011
Elizabeth Mansfield, *The Perfect Foil: François-André Vincent and the Revolution in French Painting*, Minneapolis, 2011.

Marcus, 1976
Claude-Gérard Marcus, « Alexis Grimou (1678-1733) : peintre de portraits », *Art et curiosité*, 1976.

Marseille, 1990
Parcours. Catalogue guide du musée des Beaux-Arts de Marseille, Marseille, 1990.

Masson, 1975
Georgina Masson, *Courtesans of the Italian Renaissance*, Londres, 1975.

Matthew, 1998
Louisa C. Matthew, « The Painter's Presence: Signatures in Venetian Renaissance Pictures », *The Art Bulletin*, 80, n° 4, décembre 1998.

McGrath, 2005
E. McGrath, « Sibyls, Sheba and Jan Boeckhorst's *Parts of the World* », *Florissant. Bijdragen tot de kunstgeschiedenis der Nederlanden (15de-17de eeuw). Liber Amicorum Carl Van de Velde*, Bruxelles, 2005.

McNelly, 1985
Sheila McNelly, « Ariadne and Others: Images of Sleep in Greek and Early Roman and Art », *Classical Antiquity*, vol. IV, n° 2, oct. 1985.

McTighe, 2004
Sheila McTighe, « Foods and the Body in Italian Genre Painting about 1580: Campi, Passarotti, Carracci », *The Art Bulletin*, 86/2, juin 2004.

Meiss, 1966
Millard Meiss, « Sleep in Venice: Ancient Myths and Renaissance Proclivities », *Proceedings of the American Philosophical Society*, 110. 5, oct. 1966.

Mellencamp, 1969
Emma Mellencamp, « A note on the Costume of Titian's Flora », *The Art Bulletin*, 51, 1969.

Menetto, Zennaro, 1987
Luciano Menetto, Gianni Zennaro, éd., *Storia del Malcostume a Venezia nei Secoli XVI-XVII*, Abano Terme, 1987.

Merriman, 1980
Mira Pajes Merriman, *Giuseppe Maria Crespi*, Milan, 1980.

Mezzetti, 1965
Amalia Mezzetti, *Il Dosso e Battista ferraresi*, Ferrare, 1965.

Miller, 2014
Lesley Ellis Miller, *Soieries. Le Livre d'échantillons d'un marchand français au siècle des Lumières*, Lausanne, 2014.

Montagu, 1994
Jennifer Montagu, *The Expression of the Passions: The Origin and Influence of Charles Le Brun's « Conférence sur l'expression générale et particulière »*, New Haven/Londres, 1994.

Montesquieu, 1964
Montesquieu, *Lettres persanes*, Jacques Roger, éd., Paris, 1964.

Monval, 1897
Georges Monval, *Les Collections de la Comédie-Française. Catalogue historique et raisonné*, Paris, 1897.

Morford, Lenardon, Shamm, 1999
Mark P. O. Morford, Robert J. Lenardon, Michael Shamm, *Classical Mythology*, New York, 1999.

Mortari, 1966
Luisa Mortari, *Bernardo Strozzi*, Rome, 1966.

Moryson, 1908
Fynes Moryson, *An Itinerary Containing His Ten Yeeres Travell*, [1617], Glasgow, 1908.

Moser, 1803
Joseph Moser, « Vestiges, Collected and Recollected, by Joseph Moser Esq. », *The European Magazine*, XIII, juillet-décembre 1803.

Mould
Philip Mould, *Historical Portraits Image Library* (online archive): http://www.historicalportraits.com/

Muir, 1986
Edward Muir, *Civic Ritual in Renaissance Venice*, Princeton, 1986.

National Trust, 2013
Oil Paintings in National Trust Properties in National Trust, Londres, The Public Catalogue Foundation, 2013.

Nicolson, 1974
Benedict Nicolson, « Additions to Johan Moreelse », *The Burlington Magazine*, vol. 116, 1974.

Nogrady, 2009
Elizabeth Ann Nogrady, *Abraham Bloemaert: « Netherlandish Academy » and Artistic Collaboration in Seventeenth Century Utrecht*, thèse, université de New York, 2009.

Noris, 1982
Fernando Noris, Bartolomeo Nazzari, in I Pittori Bergamaschi dal XIII al XIX secolo – I *Il settecento*, Bergame, 1982.

Northcote, 1818
James Northcote, *Memoirs of sir Joshua Reynolds*, 2e éd., Londres, 1818.

Nouvelles Archives de l'art français, 1878
Nouvelles Archives de l'art français, Paris, 1878.

O'Neill, 1981
Mary O'Neill, *Musée des Beaux-Arts d'Orléans. Les peintures de l'École française des XVIIe et XVIIIe siècles*, catalogue critique, 2 tomes, Orléans, 1981.

Oursel, 1984
Hervé Oursel, *Le Musée des Beaux-Arts de Lille*, Paris, 1984.

Ovide, 2008
Ovide, *Les Métamorphoses*, tr. E. Gros, Clermont-Ferrand, 2008.

Pagden, Scire, 2004
Silvia Pagden, Giovanna Nepi Scire, *Giorgione*, Milan, 2004.

Pagnotta, 1997
Laura Pagnotta, *Bartolomeo Veneto. L'Opera completa*, Florence, Centro Di, 1997.

Pagnotta, 2002
Pagnotta, *The Portraits of Bartolomeo Veneto*, Seattle, 2002.

Pahin de La Blancherie, 1783
Pahin de La Blancherie, *Essai d'un tableau historique des peintres de l'école française*, Paris, 1783.

Pajes Merriman, 1980
Mira Pajes Merriman, *Giuseppe Maria Crespi*, Milan, 1980.

Pallucchini, 1996
Rodolfo Pallucchini, *La Pittura nel Veneto – II Il Settecento*, Milan, 1996.

Papi, 1995
Gianni Papi, *Antiveduto Gramatica*, Soncino, 1995.

Paulson, 1971
Ronald Paulson, *Hogarth: His Life, Art, and Times*, 2 vol., New Haven/Londres, 1971.

Percival, 1999
Melissa Percival, *The Appearance of Character: Physiognomy and Facial Expression in Eighteenth-Century France*, Leeds, 1999.

Percival, 2011
Melissa Percival, « Weniger ist mehr: Das Imaginieren des Gesichts im 18. Jahrhundert », *in* Tobias Klein, Erik Porath, éd., *Figuren des Ausdrucks: Formation einer Wissenskategorie zwischen 1700 und 1850*, Berlin, 2011.

Percival, 2012
Melissa Percival, *Fragonard and the Fantasy Figure: Painting the Imagination*, Farnham, Surrey, 2012.

Pericolo, 2009
Lorenzo Pericolo, « The Invisible Presence: Cut-In, Close-Up and Off-Scene in Antonello da Messina's Palermo "Annunciate" », *Representations*, 107/1, été 2009.

Pericolo, 2011
Lorenzo Pericolo, *Caravaggio and Pictorial Narrative: Dislocating the Istoria in Early Modern Painting*, Turnhout, 2011.

Perreau, 2004
Stéphan Perreau, *Hyacinthe Rigaud (1659-1743). le peintre des rois*, Montpellier, 2004.

Perreau, 2014
Stéphan Perreau, *Hyacinthe Rigaud. Catalogue concis de l'œuvre*, Sète, 2014.

Pigler, 1974
Andor Pigler, *Barockthemen*, Budapest, 1974.

Pignatti, 1969
Terisio Pignatti, *Pietro Longhi: Paintings and Drawings*, Londres, 1969.

Piles (de), 1699 (repr. 1969)
Roger de Piles, *Abrégé de la vie des peintres avec des réflexions sur leurs ouvrages*, Paris, 1699, reprint Hildesheim, 1969.

Piles (de), 1990
Roger de Piles, *Cours de peinture par principes*, [1708], Nîmes, 1990.

Pilkington, 1805
Matthew Pilkington, *A Dictionary of Painters: from the revival of the art to the present period*, Londres, 1805.

Pinette, Soulier-François, 1992
Matthieu Pinette, Françoise Soulier-François, *De Bellini à Bonnard. Chefs-d'œuvre de la peinture du musée des Beaux-Arts et d'Archéologie de Besançon*, Paris, 1992.

Polazzo, 1990
Marco Polazzo, *Pietro Rotari: Pittore veronese del settecento, 1707-1762*, Vérone, 1990.

Porzio, 1989
Francesco Porzio, « G. P. Lomazzo, "Autoritratto in veste di abate" dell'Accademia della Valle di Blenio », *Pinacoteca di Brera. Scuole lombarda, ligure e piemontese, 1535-1796*, Milan, 1989.

Porzio, 2008
Francesco Porzio, *Pitture ridicole: scene di genere e tradizione popolare*, Milan, 2008.

Posner, 1971
Donald Posner, *Annibale Carracci. A Study in the Reform of Italian Painting around 1590*, Londres, 1971.

Postle, 1988
Martin Postle, « Patriarchs, prophets and paviours: Reynolds's images of old age », *The Burlington Magazine*, vol. CXXX, 1988.

Postle, 1995
Martin Postle, *Joshua Reynolds: The Subject Pictures*, Cambridge, 1995.

Pressly, 1987
William L. Pressly, « Genius Unveiled: The Self Portraits of Johan Zoffany », *The Art Bulletin*, 69/1, mars 1987.

Pyre, 1916
J. F. A. Pyre, « Shakespeare's Pathos », *Shakespeare Studies*, Madison, université du Wisconsin, 1916.

Raines, Sharpe, 1973
Robert Raines, Kenneth Sharpe, « The Story of Charles the First: Part I », *The Connoisseur*, n° 184, 1973.

Réau, 1930
Louis Réau, « Grimou », *in* Louis Dimier, *Les Peintres du XVIIIe siècle*, Paris/Bruxelles, 1930.

Rey, 1931
Robert Rey, *Quelques satellites de Watteau*, Paris, 1931.

Rieckenberg, 1966
Hans Jürgen Rieckenberg, *Über die Formel « Requiescat in pace » in Grabinschriften*, Göttingen, 1966.

Ringbom, 1997
Sixten Ringbom, *De l'icône à la scène narrative*, Paris, 1997.

Rizzi, 1995
Aldo Rizzi, « Profilo di Antonio Carneo », *in* Bergamini, Goi, 1995.

Robert-Dumesnil, 1835
A. P. F. Robert-Dumesnil, *Le Peintre-graveur français*, Paris, 1835.

Roethlisberger, Bok, 1993
Marcel G. Roethlisberger, Marten Jan Bok, *Abraham Bloemaert and His Sons. Paintings and Prints*, 2 vol., Doornspijk, 1993.

Rogers, 2000
Mary Rogers, « Fashioning Identities for the Renaissance Courtesan », *in* Mary Rogers, éd., *Fashioning Identities in Renaissance Art*, Farnham, Surrey, 2000.

Roli, 1977
Renato Roli, *Pittura Bolognese 1650-1850: Dal Cignani ai Gandolfi*, Bologne, 1977.

Romagnolo, Fantelli, 1981
Antonio Romagnolo, Pier Luigi Fantelli, *La Pinacoteca dell'Accademi dei Concordi*, Rovigo, 1981.

Romagnolo, Fantelli, 2001
Antonio Romagnolo, Pier Luigi Fantelli, *La Pinacoteca del Seminario Vescovile di Rovigo*, Rovigo, 2001.

Rosand, 1997
David Rosand, *Painting in Sixteenth-Century Venice: Titian, Veronese, and Tintoretto*, Cambridge UK, 1997.

Ruggiero, 1989
Guido Ruggiero, *The Boundaries of Eros: Sex Crime and Sexuality in Renaissance Venice*, Oxford, 1989.

Ruhe, 2008
Lilian Ruhe « Christian Seybold (Neuenhain 1695-Wenen 1768) en zijn Bildnis eines blonden kleinen Mädchens. Nieuwe inzichten omtrent leven en werk », *Desipientia* 15/2, novembre 2008.

Salerno, 1960
Luigi Salerno, « The Picture Gallery of Vincenzo Giustiniani III: The Inventory, Part II, » *The Burlington Magazine*, 102, n° 685, avril 1960.

Sandoz, 1977
Marc Sandoz, *Jean-Baptiste Deshays, 1729-1765*, Paris, 1977.

Sandström, 1981
Birgitta Sandström, *Bénigne Gagneraux, 1756-1795 : éducation, inspiration, œuvre*, thèse de doctorat, université de Stockholm, 1981.

Saure, 2012
Gabriele Saure, « Tomás Hiepes », *Allgemeines Künstlerlexikon*, Berlin/Boston, 2012.

Scarabello, 1980
Giovanni Scarabello, « Devianza sessuale ed interventi di giustizia a Venezia nella prima metà del XVI secolo », *Tiziano e Venezia: Convegno Internazionale di Studi, Venezia, 1976*, Vicence, 1980.

Schroeder, 2013
Helena Schroeder, *Painting the Face: Likeness and Lifelikeness in the Work of Balthasar Denner*, mémoire de maîtrise, université d'Oxford, 2013.

Schwartz, 1989
Frederick Schwartz, « The Motions of the Countenance: Rembrandt's Early Portraits and the Tronie », *Res: Anthropology and Aesthetics*, Harvard Peabody Museum of Archeology and Ethnology, n° 17/18, printemps/automne 1989.

Scott, 1996
Katie Scott, *The Rococo Interior: Decoration and Social Spaces in Early Eighteenth-Century Paris*, New Haven, 1996.

Shakespeare, 2014
William Shakespeare, *Macbeth*, tr. Ariane Mnouchkine, Paris, 2014.

Simon, 2007
Robin Simon, *Hogath, France and British Art*, Londres, 2007.

Simons, 1988
Patricia Simons, « Women in Frames: The Gaze, the Eye, the Profile in Renaissance Portraiture », *History Workshop Journal*, n° 25, printemps 1988.

Simons, 1995
Patricia Simons, « Portraiture, Portrayal, and Idealization: Ambiguous Individualism in Representation of Renaissance Women », *in* Alison Brown, éd., *Language and Images of Renaissance Italy*, Oxford, 1995.

Simons, 1997
Patricia Simons, « Homosociality and Erotics in Italian Renaissance Portraiture », *in* Joanna Woodall, éd., *Portraiture: Facing the Subject*, Manchester, 1997.

Slive, 1970-1974
Seymour Slive, *Frans Hals*, 3 vol., New York/Londres, 1970-1974.

Smith, 1878-1883
John Chaloner Smith, *British Mezzotinto Portraits*, 4 vol., 1878-1883.

Snyder, 1992
Ellen Marie Snyder, « Innocents in a Worldly World: Victorian Children's Gravemarkers », *in* Richard E. Meyer, éd., *Cemeteries & Gravemarkers: Voices of American Culture*, Logan, Utah, 1992.

Söldner, 1986
Magdalene Söldner, *Untersuchungen zu liegenden Eroten in der hellenistischen und romischen Kunst*, New York, 1986.

Spicer, Orr, 1997
Joaneath A. Spicer, Lynn Federle Orr, *Masters of Light. Dutch Painters in Utrecht during the Golden Age*, New Haven/Londres, 1997.

Spinosa, 1986
Nicola Spinosa, *Pittura napoletana del Settecento dal Barocco al Rococò*, Naples, 1986.

Starcky, 2000a
Emmanuel Starcky, « *Un portrait d'un jeune homme lisant* de Bénigne Gagneraux », *Bulletin des musées de Dijon*, nº 6, 2000.

Starcky, 2000b
« Acquisitions du musée des beaux-arts de Dijon », *La Revue du Louvre*, nº 4, octobre 2000.

Starcky, Meyer, Gras, 1992
Emmanuel Starcky, Hélène Meyer, Catherine Gras, *Le Musée des Beaux-Arts de Dijon*, Paris/Dijon, 1992.

Stewart, 1993
J. Douglas Stewart, « Sir Godfrey Kneller as Painter of 'histories' and *Portraits Historiés* », *in* David Howarth, éd., *Art and Patronage in the Caroline Courts. Essays in honour of sir Oliver Millar*, Cambridge, 1993.

Strinati, 2008
Claudio Strinati, *Sebastiano del Piombo 1485-1547*, Rome, 2008.

Sumowski, 1983-1995
Werner Sumowski, *Gemälde der Rembandt-Schule*, 6 vol., Landau, 1983-1995.

Tassi, 1793
Francesco Maria Tassi, *Vite de' pittori, scultori, architetti bergamaschi*, trad. L. Thyrion, F. Peracchione et S. Zaccaria, Bergame, 1793.

Ten-Doesschate Chu, 1998
Petra ten-Doesschate Chu, « Sleep/Sleeping », Helen Roberts, éd., *Encyclopedia of Comparative Iconography*, Chicago/Londres, 1998.

Thane, 2005
Pat Thane, éd., *The Long History of Old Age*, Londres, 2005.

Tinagli, 1997
Paola Tinagli, « Images of Beautiful Women in Venetian Painting », *Women in Italian Renaissance Art: Gender, Representation, and Identity*, Manchester, 1997.

Treadwell, 2009
Penelope Treadwell, *Johan Zoffany, Artist and Adventurer*, Londres, 2009.

Trnek, 1992
Renate Trnek, *Die Holländischen Gemälde des 17. Jahrhunderts in der Gemäldegalerie der Akademie der bildenden Künste in Wien*, Vienne, 1992.

Trnek, 2002
Renate Trnek, *The Picture Gallery of the Academy of Fine Arts in Vienna: An Overview of the Collection*, Cologne, 2008.

Trottmann, 1986
Helene Trottmann, *Cosmas Damian Asam (1686-1739). Tradition und Invention im malerischen Werk*, Nuremberg, 1986.

Tylus, 1997
Jane Tylus, « Women at the Windows: Commedia Dell'arte and Theatrical Practice in Early Modern Italy », *Theatre Journal*, nº 49, 1997.

Valdivieso, 2010
Enrique Valdivieso, *Murillo. Catálogo razonado de pinturas*, Madrid, 2010.

Van Puyvelde, 1953
Leo Van Puyvelde, *Jordaens*, Paris/Bruxelles, 1953.

Vertue, 1780
George Vertue, *Medals, Coins, Great Seals, and Other Works of Thomas Simon, Engraved as Described by George Vertue*, 2e édition, Londres, 1780.

Vertue, 1933
George Vertue, « Vertue – III. Note-Books », *Walpole Society Annual*, XXII, 1933.

Vlieghe, 1990
Hans Vlieghe, « Nicht Jan Boeckhorst, sondern Jan van der Hoecke », *Westfalen*, LXVIII, 1990.

Vogtherr, 2013
Christoph Martin Vogtherr, « Antoine Pesne's "Samson and Delilah" », *The Burlington Magazine*, nº 1222, vol. 155, mai 2013.

Walpole, 1767
Horace Walpole, *Aedes Walpolianae: Or, A Description of the Collection of Pictures at Houghton-Hall in Norfolk*, Londres, 1767.

Walsh, 2014
Claire Walsh, « Stalls, Bulks, Shops and Long-Term Change in Seventeeth- and Eighteenth-Century England », *in* Jan Hein Furnée, Clé Lesger, éd., *The Landscape of Consumption: Shopping Streets and Cultures in Western Europe, 1600-1900*, Basingstoke, 2014.

Webster, 2011
Mary Webster, *Johan Zoffany 1733-1810*, New Haven, 2011.

Wedmore, 1900
F. Wedmore, *Turner House Catalogue*, 1900.

Wellmann, 2008
Marc Wellmann, « Die Studienköpfe Balthasar Denners (1685-1749): Natur- und Selbstwahrnehmung im Medium extremster Feinmalerei », *in* Werner Busch, éd., *Verfeinertes Sehen: Optik und Farbe im 18. und frühen 19. Jahrhundert*, Oldenbourg, 2008.

Wethey, 1971
Harold Wethey, *The Paintings of Titian – II The Portraits*, Londres, 1971.

White, 1984
Christopher White, *Rembrandt*, Londres, 1984.

Wildenstein, 1958
Georges Wildenstein, « Inventaire après décès de Jean Raoux, 1734 », *Gazette des beaux-arts*, LI, n° 6, 1958.

Willk-Brocard, 1995
Nicole Willk-Brocard, *Une dynastie, les Hallé*, Paris, 1995.

Wilson, 1993
Fiona Wilson, *Jean-Baptiste van Loo in England 1737-1742*, mémoire de maîtrise, Courtauld Institute of Art, université de Londres, 1993.

Wilson (Bronwen), Vanhaelen, 2012
Bronwen Wilson, Angela Vanhaelen, éd., « The Erotics of Looking: Materiality and Solicitation in Netherlandish Visual Culture », *Art History*, édition spéciale, 2012.

Zanotti, 1739
G. P. Zanotti, *Storia dell'Accad. Clementina*, Bologne, 1739

Zischler, Schmitter, 2013
Hanns Zischler, Elke Schmitter, éd., *Galerie der Namenslosen: Porträts von Unbekannten aus der Sammlung der Berliner Gemäldegalerie*, Berlin, 2013.

Ziskin, 2012
Rochelle Ziskin, *Sheltering Art: Collecting and Social Identity in Early Eighteenth-Century Paris*, University Park, Pennsylvanie, 2012.

EXPOSITIONS

Aix-la-Chapelle/Prague/Vienne, 2010-2011
Aix-la-Chapelle, Suermondt-Ludwig-Museum/Prague, Cisarska konirna/Vienne, Kunsthistorisches Museum, 2010-2011, *Hans von Aachen (1552-1615). Court Artist in Europe*.

Amiens, 1998-1999
Amiens, musée de Picardie, 1998-1999, *Couleurs d'Italie*.

Amsterdam/San Francisco/Hartford, 2002
Amsterdam, Rijksmuseum/San Francisco, Fine Arts Museum/Hartford, Wadsworth Atheneum Museum of Art, 2002, *Michael Sweerts (1618-1664)*.

Amsterdam, 2008
Amsterdam, De Nieuwe Kerk, 2008, *Black is beautiful. Rubens to Dumas*.

Amsterdam/Aix-la-Chapelle, 2008-2009
Amsterdam, Museum Het Rembrandthuis/Aix-la-Chapelle, Suermondt-Ludwig-Museum, 2008-2009, *Jacob Backer (1608/9-1651)*.

Anvers, 1993
Anvers, Koninklijk Museum voor Schone Kunsten, 1993, *Jacob Jordaens (1593-1678). Tableaux et tapisseries*.

Baltimore/San Francisco, 1997-1998
Baltimore, Walters Art Gallery/San Francisco, Fine Arts Museums, 1997-1998, *Masters of Light: Dutch Painters in Utrecht during the Golden Age*.

Barcelone, 2006
Barcelone, CaixaForum, Centro Social y Cultural, 2006, *Jean-Honoré Fragonard (1732-1806). Orígines e influencias. De Rembrandt al siglo XXI*.

Besançon, 1992
Besançon, musée des Beaux-Arts et d'Archéologie, 1992, *La Levrette et le Financier : à propos de l'acquisition d'un tableau de François-André Vincent (1746-1816)*.

Bilbao, 2014
Bilbao, Museo de Bellas Artes, 2014, *El artista en la Corte. Giandomenico Tiepolo y sus retratos de fantasia*.

Bologne, 1956
Bologne, Museo Archeologico, 1956, *Mostra dei Carracci*.

Bologne, 1984
Bologne, Museo Archeologico, 1984, *Bologna 1584. Gli esordi dei Carracci e gli affreschi di Palazzo Fava*.

Bologne/Stuttgart/Moscou, 1990-1991
Pinacoteca Nazionale di Bologna/ Stuttgart, Staatsgalerie /Moscou, musée Pouchkine, 1990-1991, *Giuseppe Maria Crespi (1665-1747)*.

Bologne/Rome, 2006-2007
Bologne, Museo Archeologico/Rome, Chiostro del Bramante, 2006-2007, *Annibale Carracci*.

Bourg-en-Bresse, 2008
Bourg-en-Bresse, monastère royal de Brou, 2008, *Le Vielleux : métamorphoses d'une figure d'artiste du XVIIe au XIXe siècle*.

Brescia, 1987
Brescia, Monastero di S. Guilia, 1987, *Giacomo Ceruti*.

Brescia, 1998-1999
Brescia, Museo di Santa Giulia, 1998-1999, *Da Caravaggio a Ceruti. La scena di genere e l'immagine dei pitocchi nella pittura italiana*.

Caen/Gand, 2012
Caen, musée des Beaux-Arts/Gand, Museum voor Schone Kunsten, 2012, *Jacob Jordaens et son modèle Abraham Grapheus. L'œuvre en question*.

Calais/Tourcoing/Douai/Maubeuge, 1978-1979
Calais, musée des Beaux-Arts et de la Dentelle/Tourcoing, musée des Beaux-Arts/Douai, musée de la Chartreuse/Maubeuge, musée des Beaux-Arts, 1978-1979, *Trésors des musées du nord de la France. La peinture hollandaise au XVIIe siècle*.

Conversano, 2014
Conversano, Castello degli Acquaviva, 2014, *L'Eredità di Caravaggio in Europa. Uno sguardo privato*.

Crémone/New York, 2004
Crémone, Museo Civico/New York, Metropolitan Museum of Art, 2004, *Painters of Reality: The Legacy of Leonardo and Caravaggio in Lombardy*.

Dozza, 2001
Dozza, Castello Malvezzi-Campeggi, 2001, *Figure come il naturale: Il ritratto a Bologna dai Carracci al Crespi*.

Dresde, 1999-2000
Dresde, Semperbau, 1999-2000, *Pietro Graf Rotari in Dresden. Ein italienischer Maler am Hof König Augusts III*.

Épinal, 1993-1994
Épinal, Musée départemental d'art ancien et contemporain, 1993-1994, *La Collection des princes de Salm*.

Ferrare/New York/Los Angeles, 1998-1999
Ferrare, Galleria d'Arte moderna e contemporanea/New York, The Metropolitan Museum of Art/Los Angeles, The J. Paul Getty Museum, 1998-1999, *Dosso Dossi*.

Fort Worth, 1986
Fort Worth, Kimbell Art Museum, 1986, *Giuseppe Maria Crespi and the Emergence of Genre Painting in Italy*.

Francfort, 2015
Städel Museum, Francfort, février-mai 2015, *Jean-Jacques de Boissieu. A contemporary of Städel's*.

Freising, 2007
Freising, Diözesanmuseum, 2007, *Christopher Paudiss. Der bayerische Rembrandt ?*

Freising, 2007-2008
Freising, Diözesanmuseum, 2007-2008, *Asam in Freising*.

Gênes, 1995
Gênes, Palazzo ducale, 1995, *Bernardo Strozzi. Genova 1581/82-Venezia 1644*.

Haarlem, 1962
Haarlem, Frans Hals Museum, 1962, *Frans Hals. Exhibition on the Occasion of the Centenary of the Municipal Museum at Haarlem*.

Haarlem/Londres, 2008
Haarlem, Frans Hals Museum/Londres, Dulwich Picture Gallery, 2008, *Painting Family: The De Brays. Master Painters of 17th Century Holland*.

Lausanne, 2000
Lausanne, Musée cantonal des beaux-arts, 2000, *Le Sommeil ou Quand la raison s'absente*.

Lille, 2011
Lille, palais des Beaux-Arts, 2011, *Portraits de la pensée*.

Lille/Calais/Arras, 1977
Lille, palais des Beaux-Arts/Calais, musée des Beaux-Arts et de la Dentelle/Arras, musée des Beaux-Arts, 1977, *Trésors des musées du nord de la France. III. La Peinture flamande au temps de Rubens*.

Londres, 1989
Londres, Royal Academy of Art, 1989, *Frans Hals*.

Londres, 1993
Londres, Colnaghi, 1993, *Master Paintings 1400-1800*.

Londres/Munich/Madrid, 2001
Londres, Dulwich Gallery of Art/Munich, Alte Pinakothek/Madrid, Museo del Prado, 2001, *Murillo. Scenes of Childhood (Murillo. Kinderleben in Sevilla ; Niños de Murillo)*.

Londres/Rome, 2001
Londres, Royal Academy of Arts/Rome, Palazzo Venezia, 2001, *Il Genio di Roma 1592-1623*.

Londres, 2010
Londres, Royal Academy of Arts, 2010, *Treasures from Budapest: European Masterpieces from Leonardo to Schiele*.

Londres, 2015
Londres, Wallace Collection, 2015, *Sir Joshua Reynolds: Experiments in Paint*.

Lyon/Lille, 2000-2001
Lyon, musée des Beaux-Arts/Lille, palais des Beaux-Arts, 2000-2001, *Settecento. Le Siècle de Tiepolo. Peintures italiennes du XVIIIe siècle dans les collections publiques françaises*.

Lugano, 1998
Lugano, Museo Cantonale d'Arte, 1998, *Rabisch. Il Grottesco nell'arte del Cinquecento*.

Madrid/Londres, 1982-1983
Madrid, Museo del Prado/Londres, Royal Academy of Arts, 1982-1983, *Bartolomé Esteban Murillo (1617-1682)*.

Milan, 1951
Milan, Palazzo Reale, 1951, *Mostra del Caravaggio*.

Milan, 1998-1999
Milan, Palazzo Reale, 1998-1999, *L'Anima e il Volto. Ritratto e Fisiognomica da Leonardo a Bacon*.

Milan, 2013
Milan, Robilant + Voena, 2013, *Popolo e Nobiltà alla vigilia dell'età de Lumi*.

Minneapolis, 1995
The Minneapolis Institute of Arts, 1995, *Treasures of Venice: Paintings from the Museum of Fine Arts Budapest*, 1995.

Montpellier, 2009-2010
Montpellier, musée Fabre, 2009-2010, *Jean Raoux (1677-1734). Un peintre sous la Régence*

Munich, 2005-2006
Munich, Haus der Kunst, 2005-2006, *Kunstlerbrüder, von den Dürers zu den Duchamps*.

Munich, 2010-2011
Munich, Haus der Kunst, 2010-2011, *Tronies: Marlene Dumas and the Old Masters*

Nantes/Toulouse, 1997
Nantes, musée des Beaux-Arts/Toulouse, musée des Augustins, 1997, *Visages du Grand Siècle. Le portrait français sous le règne de Louis XIV*.

Naples/New York, 1985
Naples, Museo di Capodimonte/New York, The Metropolitan Museum of Art, 1985, *L'Età di Caravaggio/The Age of Caravaggio*.

Naples, 2003-2004
Naples, Castel Sant'Elmo, 2003-2004, *Gaspare Traversi, napoletani del '700 tra miseria et nobiltà*.

Naples/Paris, 2006-2007
Naples, Museo di Capodimonte/Paris, musée du Luxembourg, 2006-2007, *Tiziano e il ritratto di corte da Raffaello ai Carracci/Titien. Le pouvoir en face*.

New Haven/Londres, 2011-2012
New Haven, Yale Centre for British Art/Londres, Royal Academy of Arts, 2011-2012, *Johan Zoffany RA: Society Observed*.

New York, 1992
New York, The Metropolitan Museum of Art, 1992, *Masterworks from the Musée des Beaux-Arts, Lille*.

New York, 1996-1997
New York, The Metropolitan Museum of Art, 1996-1997, *Giambattista Tiepolo (1696-1770)*

New York/Londres, 2001
New York, The Metropolitan Museum of Art/Londres, National Gallery, 2001, *Vermeer and the Delft School*.

Nottingham/Londres, 1998
Nottingham, University of Nottingham, Djanogly Art Gallery/Londres, Kenwood House, 1998, *Angels and Urchins: The Fancy Picture in Eighteenth-Century British Art*.

Ottawa/Little Rock, 1993
Ottawa, National Gallery of Canada/Little Rock, Arkansas Arts Center, 1993, *Bella Pittura. The Art of the Gandolfi*.

Ottawa/Washington DC/Berlin, 2003-2004
Ottawa, National Gallery of Canada / Washington DC, National Gallery of Art/Berlin, Staatliche Museen, Gemäldeagalerie, 2003-2004, *The Age of Watteau, Chardin and Fragonard: Masterpieces of French Genre Painting*.

Paris, 1970-1971
Paris, musée du Petit Palais, 1970-1971, *Le Siècle de Rembrandt. Tableaux hollandais des collections publiques françaises*.

Paris, 1977-1978
Paris, Galeries nationales du Grand Palais, 1977-1978, *Le Siècle de Rubens dans les collections publiques françaises*.

Paris/New York, 1987-1988
Paris, Galeries nationales du Grand Palais/New York, The Metropolitan Museum of Art, 1987-1988, *Fragonard*.

Paris, 1998-1999
Paris, Petit Palais, 1998-1999, *Tiepolo*.

Paris, 2001-2002
Paris, musée de la Musique, 2001-2002, *Figures de la Passion*.

Paris, 2007-2008
Paris, musée Jacquemart-André, 2007-2008, *Fragonard. Les plaisirs d'un siècle*.

Paris, 2009
Paris, galerie Canesso, 2009, *Sweerts, Tanzio, Magnasco et autres protagonistes du Seicento italien*.

Paris, 2013-2014
Paris, Petit Palais, 2013-2014, *Jordaens (1593-1678)*.

Parme, 2004
Parme, Galleria Nazionale, 2004, *Luce sul Settecento: Gaspare Traversi e l'arte de suo tempo in Emilia*.

Prague, 1997
Prague, palais Wallenstein, 1997, *Rudolf II and Prague, the Court and the City*.

Rancate, 2012-2013
Rancate, Pinacoteca Cantonale Giovanni Züst, 2012-2013, *Serodine e brezza caravaggesca sulla « Regione dei laghi »*.

Rome, 1983
Rome, Galleria Borghese, 1983, *Bénigne Gagneraux (1756-1795), un pittore francese nella Roma di Pio VI*.

Rotterdam/Rome, 1958
Rotterdam, museum Boijmans-Van Beuningen/Rome, Palazzo Venezia, 1958, *Michael Sweerts en tijdgenoten (Michael Sweerts e i Bamboccianti)*.

Rotterdam/Francfort, 1999-2000
Rotterdam, Museum Boijmans-Van Beuningen/Francfort, Städelsches Kunstinstitut, 1999-2000, *Hollands Classicisme in de zeventiende-eeuwse schilderkunst*.

Rovigo, 2006
Rovigo, Palazzo Roverella, 2006, *Le Meraviglie della pittura tra Venezia e Ferrara dal Quattrocento al Settecento*.

Rovigo, 2010
Rovigo, Pinacoteca di Palazzo Roverella, 2010, *Bortoloni, Piazzetta, Tiepolo: il '700 veneto*.

Royaume-Uni, 1962-1963
[Touring exhibition], Arts Council, 1962-1963, *John Opie*.

Strasbourg/Tours, 2003
Strasbourg, musée des Beaux-Arts/Tours, musée des Beaux-Arts, 2003, *L'Apothéose du geste. L'esquisse peinte au siècle de Boucher et de Fragonard*.

Stuttgart, 2003
Stuttgart, Staatsgalerie, 2003, *Gaspare Traversi (1722-1770) Heiterkeit im Schatten*.

Toulouse, 2001
Toulouse, musée des Augustins, 2001, *Nicolas Tournier (1590-1639). Un peintre caravagesque*.

Toulouse/Montpellier, 2012
Toulouse, musée des Augustins/Montpellier, musée Fabre, 2012, *Corps et ombres : Caravage et le caravagisme européen*.

Utrecht/Brunswick, 1986-1987
Utrecht, Centraal Museum/Brunswick, Herzog Anton Ulrich Museum, 1986-1987, *Holländische Malerei in neuem Licht. Hendrick ter Brugghen und seine Zeitgenossen*.

Utrecht/Schwerin, 2011-2012
Utrecht, Centraal Museum/Schwerin, Staatliches Museum, 2011-2012, *The Bloemaert Effect. Colour and Composition in the Golden Age*.

Varèse, 2002
Varèse, Castello Masnago, 2002, *Il Ritratto in Lombardia da Moroni a Ceruti*.

Venise, 1983
Venise, Palazzo Vendramin-Calergi, 1983, *Giambattista Tiepolo. Il suo tempo, la sua scuola*.

Venise, 2006
Venise, Palazzo Cini, 2006, *Teste di fantasia del settecento veneziano*.

Vérone, 2011-2012
Vérone, Palazzo della Gran Guardia, 2011-2012, *Il Settecento a Verona, Tiepolo, Cignaroli, Rotari. La nobilità della pittura*.

Vienne, 2004
Vienne, Kunsthistorisches Museum, 2004, *Giorgione, Myth and Enigma*.

Vienne, 2004a
Vienne, Gemäldegalerie der Akademie der Bildenden Künste, 2004, *Selbstbildnis. Der Kunstler und sein Bildnis*.

Washington DC, 1983
Washington DC, National Gallery of Art, 1983, *Piazzetta: A Tercentenary Exhibition of Drawings, Prints, and Illustrated Books*.

Washington DC, 2006
Washington DC, National Gallery of Art, 2006, *Bellini, Giorgione, Titian, and the Renaissance of Venetian Painting*.

York/Londres, 1969
York, City Art Gallery/Londres, Iveagh Bequest, 1969, *Philip Mercier*.

CRÉDITS PHOTOGRAPHIQUES

Cet ouvrage a été composé en Filosofia, Roboto et Crique Grotesk, imprimé sur papier GardaMatt, intérieur, 150 g et couverture, 400 g.
La photogravure a été réalisée par Quat'Coul (Toulouse).
Cet ouvrage a été achevé d'imprimer sous les presses de PBTisk (République tchèque) en octobre 2015.